Meggs' History of Graphic Design

Fourth Edition

Meggs' History of Graphic Design

Fourth Edition

Philip B. Meggs

Alston W. Purvis

WILEY

John Wiley & Sons, Inc.

This book is printed on acid-free paper. ∞

Copyright © 2006 by John Wiley & Sons, Inc. All rights reserved

Published by John Wiley & Sons, Inc., Hoboken, New Jersey

Published simultaneously in Canada

No part of this publication may be reproduced, stored in a retrieval system, or transmitted in any form or by any means, electronic, mechanical, photocopying, recording, scanning, or otherwise, except as permitted under Section 107 or 108 of the 1976 United States Copyright Act, without either the prior written permission of the Publisher, or authorization through payment of the appropriate per-copy fee to the Copyright Clearance Center, 222 Rosewood Drive, Danvers, MA 01923, (978) 750-8400, fax (978) 646-8600, or on the web at www.copyright.com. Requests to the Publisher for permission should be addressed to the Permissions Department, John Wiley & Sons, Inc., 111 River Street, Hoboken, NJ 07030, (201) 748-6011, fax (201) 748-6008.

Limit of Liability/Disclaimer of Warranty: While the publisher and the author have used their best efforts in preparing this book, they make no representations or warranties with respect to the accuracy or completeness of the contents of this book and specifically disclaim any implied warranties of merchantability or fitness for a particular purpose. No warranty may be created or extended by sales representatives or written sales materials. The advice and strategies contained herein may not be suitable for your situation. You should consult with a professional where appropriate. Neither the publisher nor the author shall be liable for any loss of profit or any other commercial damages, including but not limited to special, incidental, consequential, or other damages.

For general information about our other products and services, please contact our Customer Care Department within the United States at (800) 762-2974, outside the United States at (317) 572-3993 or fax (317) 572-4002.

Wiley also publishes its books in a variety of electronic formats. Some content that appears in print may not be available in electronic books. For more information about Wiley products, visit our web site at www.wiley.com.

Interior design, layout, and production: Jeff Baker at BookMechanics

Library of Congress Cataloging-in-Publication Data:

Meggs, Philip B.
   Meggs' history of graphic design / Philip B. Meggs, Alston W. Purvis.—
4th ed.
       p. cm.
     Rev. ed. of: A history of graphic design. c1998.
     Includes bibliographical references and index.
     ISBN-13: 978-0-471-69902-6 (cloth : alk. paper)
     ISBN-10: 0-471-69902-0 (cloth : alk. paper)
     1. Graphic design (Typography)—History. 2. Book design—History. I.
Purvis, Alston W., 1943– II. Meggs, Philip B. History of graphic design.
III. Title.
     Z246.M43 2005
     686.2'2--dc22
                                    2005008604

Printed in the United States of America

10 9 8 7 6 5 4 3 2

Contents

Preface

The first edition of *A History of Graphic Design* was described by Philip B. Meggs as an attempt "to chronicle the evolution of graphic design" and as "the author's personal diary of discovery, compiled over a decade of research." In subsequent editions the research would span more than thirty years and become increasingly comprehensive and refined.

Various approaches can be used to explore the development of graphic design: examining the visual characteristics of design, considering its economic ramifications, analyzing the connections it makes with its audiences, and finally tracing the impact of technology. Although the visual aspects of graphic design are obviously important, we should also address the designers' philosophies, the effect their work has on audiences, and the signification of forms and their syntactic relationships. Conventional art history research methods are usually inadequate for approaching the relatively fresh and intricate history of graphic design. Concentrating solely on individual designers and their major works or placing them methodically into schools or movements does not fully serve our purposes. New developments have often been spurred by changes in technology, such as the invention of movable type or of lithography. Creative exchange among designers has also played a role, and this is especially true today, with the World Wide Web as a medium of communication.

My personal tastes and those of Philip Meggs inevitably played a role in the selection of images, but great effort was made to defer to grounds beyond our own aesthetic predilec-

tions. Ideally, selections were based on how clearly they present ideas, design concepts, or particular graphic forms, even when other examples might be considered of superior quality. Obstacles in obtaining publication rights or appropriate photographic reproductions were also factors, and some work simply arrived too late to fit into the book's production schedule.

Although in the history of design there are moments when a collective vision has emerged that defies attribution to any one designer, there have also been individual designers who clearly forged a new direction, with fresh typographic and expressive forms and original methods for presenting information. An objective of *A History of Graphic Design* has been to document graphic design innovation and those designers who have influenced its continuing evolution. Attempting to single out particularly consequential designers, especially from the past two decades, has proved to be a challenging and intriguing task. By "consequential" I mean those who have not only produced magnificent work but also made a significant contribution to the evolution of the field. The question of what distinguishes a master from his or her talented colleagues is both perplexing and difficult. One must have a distinctive aesthetic vision, an instantly recognizable visual vocabulary, and a unique approach that transcends the problem-solving process. No doubt some have been overlooked, but there has been an unwavering attempt to avoid such omissions. History has judged for us the great masters of bygone eras. The innovative ideas and achievements of these designers have stood the test of time and continue to inform and inspire us today. The graphic design of the past decade, however, is a more complex arena, with a far more level playing field. The perimeters between various visual disciplines have also become increasingly blurred. Attribution, too, has become more complex. Especially during the last century, most designers will have produced hundreds and even thousands of publications in firms with a revolving staff of colleagues and interns. Such designs are the products of a number of individuals, and crediting everyone who was involved in a piece is not always feasible.

The visual feast that is graphic design becomes more abundant as time passes. Offering a definitive account of contemporary graphic design will always be a vexing task, as this chapter inevitably has no ending. As philosopher R. G. Collingwood wrote in 1924, "Contemporary history embarrasses a writer not only because he knows too much, but also because what he knows is too undigested, too unconnected, too atomic. It is only after close and prolonged reflection that we begin to see what was essential and what was important, to see why things happened as they did, and to write history instead of newspapers."

Most works included in *Meggs' History of Graphic Design* represent only a minute fraction of what was produced in any particular era. Most of the images in this book represent either schools, movements, styles, or individual approaches, and there are seldom pieces that show the crowning achievement of any designer. In such a survey one can present the work of designers only at a particular stage in their careers, and not their overall development. Readers in pursuit of a fuller account of any aspect of the history presented here should refer to the bibliography for further research.

A History of Graphic Design was never intended to be an all-encompassing historical encyclopedia, as that would require far more than a single volume. Instead, we have attempted to provide a broad survey of notable stages and accomplishments in the evolution of graphic design. In deciding what to include, a guiding consideration was how, through the centuries, particular cultures, movements, works, and individuals affected what graphic design has become today. The contemporary graphic design field is much broader than in the past, and encompasses emerging disciplines such as motion graphics, environmental communications, and new media. Limitations of space prevented a thorough exploration of these exciting new areas. Although graphic design is closely tied to illustration, photography, printing, and computer technology, it was not possible to include an extensive examination of these related fields within a single volume.

As with any work of this magnitude, some pivotal figures and topics were omitted in previous editions. Clearly the most pressing matter, however, was to document developments since 1996, the date of the most recent images included in the third edition. Although the structure of *Meggs' History of Graphic Design* is essentially chronological, there are instances where periods intermingle and overlap. The order of chapter 2, "Alphabets," and chapter 3, "The Asian Contribution," is reversed, relative to the previous edition, to better facilitate the historical flow of the text. The closely related chapters 9, 10, and 11 of the previous edition have here been condensed and combined into a single chapter to make room for additional material at the end of the book.

For the fourth edition, we have added many illustrations, and some text and illustrations have been removed to make room for additional content. Many designers who deserve to be in this book could not be included because of space limitations, and to these I extend my apologies. Although we have become more of a global culture since research for *A History of Graphic Design* began over thirty years ago, many regions and countries were excluded for similar reasons.

William Addison Dwiggins coined the term *graphic design* as early as 1922, but it was seldom used until after World War II—before then graphic designers were referred to as commercial artists. The profession has grown extensively during the latter half of the twentieth century, with technology playing an increasingly important role. As we move deeper into the digital age, graphic design is undergoing dramatic changes. It is only natural that the new generation of graphic designers with provocative ideas should question existing modes of perception and established notions of aesthetics. Each time we think we are at the forefront, we find that we are only at the outset, and the future is an open vista.

We are constantly surrounded by visual messages, and those that endure must be visually arresting, intellectually challenging, and distinctively genuine. Although contemporary graphic design is largely defined by technology, there are still strong threads binding it to past crafts and aesthetics. The computer, though, has increased the speed with which graphic design problems are solved and allows designers to work more efficiently. Projects that in the past would have taken weeks are now solved in a matter of days. The new technology has even made the process of manufacturing books and posters more fluid. The Internet has engendered an unprecedented exchange of ideas among designers. The profession is no longer confined to books, posters, and advertisements but now includes movement and interactive media. Despite the exciting developments in electronic media, printed works remains as vital as ever. One has only to walk through a bookstore to see the vast number of well-designed books lining the shelves.

Graphic design is built firmly upon historical foundations, and history now occupies a central role in graphic design education. During this transition period, when traditional notions of graphic design are being challenged, it is vital that graphic designers have a historical understanding of their profession. The responsibility is to ourselves: to avoid reinvention and unintentional plagiarism, we need to be literate in the history of our profession. And it is to the field as a whole: in deriving inspiration from the work that came before, designers acknowledge and honor the evolution that, in the words of Philip Meggs, has "enabled designers to achieve a gradual transition from Renaissance design to the modern epoch."

Since it was first published in 1983, *A History of Graphic Design* has remained the most thorough book in its field. With its balanced insight and comprehensive historical background, it is widely accepted as the most authoritative and enlightened book of its kind. No other work on the subject approaches the range of its coverage. It is my objective that it maintain its position while being updated and refined. Having used *A History of Graphic Design* as a text for my own classes, I found it a distinct honor to be asked to serve as reviser for this new edition. I hope that this fourth edition, with its expanded content and fresh images, will, like those previous, enlighten and nourish both students and professionals as a foundation and continuing resource for this exciting and ever-evolving field.

Alston W. Purvis

Preface to the First Edition

There is a German word, *Zeitgeist,* that does not have an English equivalent. It means the spirit of the time, and refers to the cultural trends and tastes that are characteristic of a given era. The immediacy and ephemeral nature of graphic design, combined with its link with the social, political, and economic life of its culture, enable it to more closely express the Zeitgeist of an epoch than many other forms of human expression. Ivan Chermayeff, a noted designer, has said: the design of history is the history of design.

Since prehistoric times, people have searched for ways to give visual form to ideas and concepts, to store knowledge in graphic form, and to bring order and clarity to information. Over the course of history, these needs have been filled by various people, including scribes, printers, and artists. It was not until 1922, when the outstanding book designer William Addison Dwiggins coined the term *graphic design* to describe his activities as an individual who brought structural order and visual form to printed communications, that an emerging profession received an appropriate name. However, the contemporary graphic designer is heir to a distinguished ancestry. Sumerian scribes who invented writing, Egyptian artisans who combined words and images on papyrus manuscripts, Chinese block printers, medieval illuminators, and fifteenth-century printers and compositors who designed early European printed books all became part of the rich heritage and history of graphic design. By and large, this is an anonymous tradition, for the social value and aesthetic accomplishments of graphic designers, many of whom have been creative artists of extraordinary intelligence and vision, have not been sufficiently recognized.

History is in large measure a myth, because the historian looks back over the great sprawling network of human struggle and attempts to construct a web of meaning. Oversimplification, ignorance of causes and their effects, and the lack of an objective vantage point are grave risks for the historian. When we attempt to record the accomplishments of the past, we do so from the vantage point of our own time. History becomes a reflection of the needs sensibilities, and attitudes of the chronicler's time as surely as it represents the accomplishments of bygone eras. As much as one might strive for objectivity, the limitations of individual knowledge and insights ultimately intrude.

The concept of art for art's sake, a beautiful object that exists solely for its aesthetic value, did not develop until the nineteenth century. Before the Industrial Revolution, the beauty of the forms and images that people made were linked to their function in human society. The aesthetic qualities of Greek pottery, Egyptian hieroglyphics, and medieval manuscripts were totally integrated with useful values; art and life were unified into a cohesive whole. The din and thunder of the Industrial Revolution turned the world upside down in a process of upheaval and technological progress that continues to accelerate at an ever-quickening pace. By jolting the arts and crafts from their social and economic roles, the machine age created a gulf between people's material life and their sensory and spiritual needs. Just as voices call for a restoration of humanity's unity with the natural environment, there is a growing awareness of the need to restore human and aesthetic values to the man-made environment and mass communications. The design arts—architecture and product, fashion, interior, and graphic design—offer one means for this restoration. Once more a society's shelter, artifacts, and communications might bind a people together. The endangered aesthetic and spiritual values might be restored. A wholeness of need and spirit, reunited through the process of design, can contribute in great measure to the quality and raison d'être of life in urban societies.

This chronicle of graphic design is written in the belief that if we understand the past, we will be better able to continue a culture legacy of beautiful form and effective communication. If we ignore this legacy, we run the risk of becoming buried in a mindless morass of a commercialism whose mole-like vision ignores human values and needs as it burrows forward into darkness.

Philip B. Meggs

Acknowledgments

During the course of this project many scholars, collectors, friends, colleagues, and designers generously offered their advice and expertise, and it would be impossible to adequately express my gratitude to all of them. I am especially grateful to Elizabeth Meggs for her encouragement, confidence, friendship and painstaking cataloguing of images from the previous edition.

Among my collaborators I first want to express my thanks and indebtedness to Robert and June Leibowits for their generosity, assistance, and intellectual support for this and all of my writing endeavors. In addition, they provided access to their extensive collection of twentieth century graphic design, and this has greatly enriched *Meggs' History of Graphic Design,* fourth edition.

For many years the loyal support of Wilma Schuhmacher has been especially gratifying. She continues to generously share her unparalleled knowledge and understanding of Dutch graphic design, and has also provided incalculable editorial advice.

I am grateful to the staff at the Wolfsonian at Miami Beach for their consistent support and hospitality. Special thanks are extended to Cathy Leff, director; Marianne Lamonaca, assistant director; Frank Luca, associate librarian; Nicholas Blaga, associate librarian; Anthony DiVivo, art director; Jonathan Mogul, fellowship program coordinator; Sarah Schleuning, assistant curator; and Lisa Li, curatorial assistant.

To the staff at the Gotlieb Archival Research Center at Boston University I extend my appreciation: these include Howard B. Gotlieb, the founding director; Vita Paladino; managing director; Sean Noel, associate director; Katherine Kominis, assistant director, rare books; and Perry Barton, exhibition and publication coordinator.

I am especially indebted to Lance Hidy for his insightful observations regarding Egyptian design and medieval manuscripts, to Roger Remington for sharing his ideas and for providing valuable reproduction material for this edition, and to Michael Hearn for his sagacious advice on Russian graphic design. By making available his extensive archives on H.N. Werkman, the late Jan Martinet was my principal mentor on this subject.

Special thanks are extended to my colleagues at Boston University. Jeannette Guillemin, our assistant director, has constantly provided me with encouragement and help when needed. Others include Judith Simpson, director ad interim; Walt Meissner, dean ad interim; Jessica Day, fiscal coordinator; and Logen Zimmerman, student affairs coordinator and collections manager.

My colleague Richard Doubleday was an active collaborator in locating graphic designers for the final chapter, and his research and counsel on contemporary British and Mexican graphic design was illuminative and invaluable. Robert Burns' insight regarding the graphic design of Paul Rand was discerning and invaluable.

Alvin Eisenman, John T. Hill, and Bonnie Scranton were especially helpful in providing information about the legacy of graphic design program at Yale University.

Karin Carpenter's unstinting assistance in cataloguing the large amount of incoming work during the summer of 2004 was of inestimable value. Also, her organization of my schedules helped to keep me focused on goals along the way.

Kathryn Noyes and Berk Veral, my graduate assistants at Boston University, approached their tasks with unwavering dedication. Their loyal, professional, and tireless support were essential in bringing this project to a successful ending. Among other tasks, their contributions included the following: contacting designers chosen for the book; ensuring that all files are in the required format; researching designers' biographies and information about their work; drafting letters to designers requesting reprint permissions for all new work appearing in the book; tracking status and following up on receipt of all permission forms; working with publishers' licensing departments to secure permissions for selected works; making editorial contributions to the text; scanning original art; and preparing slides, art files, and original art for delivery to publisher.

Margaret Cummins, my editor at John Wiley, was a source of patience, encouragement and consistent help throughout.

Cees de Jong, my publisher in The Netherlands, was instrumental making available numerous images from his extensive archives.

Martijn Le Coultre, with whom I have collaborated on three previous publications, provided information, incisive advice, and many fresh images for this edition.

Stephen Goldstein was always available to help conduct the large amount of research needed for this edition. A thorough researcher, he often unearthed material that would otherwise have remained undiscovered.

In addition, grateful acknowledgement is made to the following people whose contributions have greatly enriched this edition. These include Al Gowan, Bryce Ambo, Claudia Baeza, Anthon Beeke, James Lapides, Samir Chorbachi, Murray Forbes, Stephen Frank, Laura Giannitrapani, Steven Heller, John Kristensen, Michael Lance, Pieter and Jolanda van Voorst van Beest, Ernst H. von Metzsch, Stephen Pekich, Pim Reinders, and Erik Voorrips.

James M. Storey's consistent counseling about writing was invaluable.

And most importantly I want to thank my wife Susan and my son Alston for their patience and understanding during the long periods when I was away while working on this project.

Part I

The Prologue to Graphic Design

The visual message from prehistory through the medieval era

The Invention of Writing

1

c 3500 BC *Sumerians settle in Mesopotamia*
Sledges with wheels in use by Sumerians

c 1930-1880 BC **Law Code of Hammurabi**

c 2750 BC **Formal land-sale contracts written in cuneiform**

c 3100 BC **Early Sumerian pictographic scripts on clay tablets**

c 15,000–10,000 BC **Cave paintings at Lascaux**

c 1792–1750 BC *Hammurabi, Babylonian king, rules Mesopotamia*

c 2500 BC **Wedge-shaped cuneiform**

c 1100 BC *Iron is widely used for weapons and tools*

c 3600 BC **Blau Monument combines images and early writing**

c 2600 BC **Early surviving papyrus manuscripts**

c 600 BC *Nebuchadnezzar II builds the "Tower of Babel"*

c 1500 BC **Hieratic scripts**

c 3000 BC *Copper tools and weapons*

c 1600 BC *bronze in general use*   332–330 BC *Alexander the Great conquers Egypt*

c 2900 BC **Early cylinder seals**

538 BC *Babylon falls*

c 1730 BC **Scarab of Ikhnaton and Nefertiti**

c 2345 BC **Pyramid Texts in tomb of Unas**

c 1300 BC *Temple of Ramses II at Thebes*

c 3100 BC **King Zet's ivory tablet, earliest Egyptian pictographic writing**   c 1300 BC ***Early Book of the Dead*** **papyrus scrolls**

c 2500 BC *Great Pyramids and Sphinx at Gizeh*   c 1420 BC **Papyrus of Ani**   c 197 BC **Rosetta Stone**

c 3200 BC *Menes, first Pharoah, unites Egypt*   525–404 BC *Persians conquer and rule Egypt*

c 400 BC ***Demotic*** **script**

Alphabets

2

c 2000 BC **Early Cretan pictographs**
Phaistos Disk

146 BC *Rome destroys Carthage*

300 BC *Euclid's geometry*

c 1130 BC *Iron weapons and tools*

323 BC *Alexander the Great dies in Babylon*

753 BC *Legendary Romulus establishes Rome*   44 BC *Julius Caesar assassinated*

c 1000 BC **Early Greek alphabet**   c 190 BC **Parchment used for manuscripts**

c 776 BC *1st Olympic games*   c 29 BC *Vergil's* Georgics

c 1500 BC **Ras Shamra script**   399 BC *Execution of Socrates*

683 BC *Aristocratic democracy established in Athens*

c 850 BC **Aramaic alphabet**   516 BC *Israelites return from Babylonian exile*

c 750–700 BC *Homer's* Odyssey   429 BC *Sophocles' tragedy* Oedipus Rex

447–432 BC *Parthenon built in Athens*

The Asian Contribution

3

c 528 BC *Siddhartha Gautama becomes the supreme Buddha*
551 BC *Confucius is born*

c 1800 BC **Legendary Tsang Chieh invents writing**

c 250 BC **Small-seal calligraphy**

c 1500 BC **Oracle bone writing**

221 BC *Shih Huang-ti unites China*
The Great Wall of China is underway

NOTE: Many dates on these timelines are approximate because exact dates are difficult to establish in early history, and some dates are in dispute.

World events / **Chapter events**

c 394 AD **Last hieroglyphic inscription**

79 AD *Roman Colosseum*

410 AD *Visigoths sack Rome*

330 AD *Constantine moves Roman capital to Constantinople*

c 114 AD **Trajan's Column**

1000 AD **Nashki becomes dominant Arabic alphabet**

476 AD *Fall of the Western Roman Empire*

1446 AD **Hangul, Korean alphabet**

c 1 AD *Birth of Christ*   c 500 AD **Early Arabic alphabet**

c 250 **AD Greek unicals**

c 100 AD **Pompeiian wall writing**

c 200-500 AD **Roman square capitals and rustic capitals**

c 770 AD **Early datable Chinese relief printing**
Printed Buddhist charms

c 165 A **Confucian classics carved in stone**

1150 AD *Compass is invented*

c 300 AD **Chops are used as identifying seals; Chops used in Han Dynasty**

c 1000 AD *Gunpowder in use in China*

c 200 AD **Regular-style calligraphy**

868 AD *Diamond Sutra*

105 AD **Ts'ai Lun invents paper**

c 1000 AD **Chinese calligraphy printed with perfection**

c 1040 AD **Pi Sheng invents movable type in Korea**

Illuminated Manuscripts

330 AD *Constantine moves Roman capital to Constantinople*

c 781 AD **Alcuin establishes school at Aachen;**
Caroline minuscules are developed

1209 AD *Cambridge University founded*

4

c 1450 AD **Printing with movable type in Germany**

c 600 AD **Insular script**

c 1265 AD *Marco Polo travels to China*

c 698 AD **Lindisfarne Gospels**

1095–99 AD *First Crusade*

1431 AD *Joan of Arc burned at Rouen*

c 1320 *Firearms used in Europe*

660 AD *Organ used in church services*

1170 AD *Thomas à Becket murdered*

c 1387 AD *Chaucer begins* The Canterbury Tales

771 AD *Moors defeat Spanish army*

c 500 AD **Uncial lettering flourishes**

c 800 AD **Book of Kells, Coronation Gospels**

1348 AD *The Black Death*

1163 AD *Notre Dame Cathedral begun in Paris*

c 1413–16 AD **Les Tres Riches Heures du Duc de Berry**

c 680 AD **Book of Durrow**

c 1265 AD **Douce Apocalypse**

570 AD *Birth of Mohammad*

751 AD **Arabs learn papermaking from Chinese prisoners**

c 1478 AD **Washington Haggadah**

800 AD *Charlemagne crowned Emperor*

c 1300 AD **Ormesby Psalter**

c 425 AD **Vatican Vergil**

1215 AD *King John signs* Magna Carta

The Invention of Writing

1

It is not known precisely when or where the biological species of conscious, thinking people, *Homo sapiens,* emerged. The search for our prehistoric origins continues to push back into time the early innovations of our ancestors. It is believed that we evolved from a species that lived in the southern part of Africa. These early hominids ventured out onto the grassy plains and into caves as the forests slowly disappeared in that part of the world. In the tall grass, they began to stand erect. Perhaps this adaptation was a result of the need to watch for predators, to help discourage enemies by increasing the hominids' apparent size, or to hold branches as weapons. In any event, the hand developed an ability to carry food and hold objects. Found near Lake Turkana in Kenya, a nearly three-million-year-old stone that had been sharpened into an implement proves the thoughtful and deliberate development of a technology—a tool. Early shaped stones may have been used to dig for roots or to cut away flesh from dead animals for food. While we can only speculate about the use of early tools, we know that they mark a major step in the human species' immense journey from primitive origins toward a civilized state. A number of quantum leaps provided the capacity to organize a community and gain some measure of control over human destiny. Speech—the ability to make sounds in order to communicate—was an early skill developed by the species on the long evolutionary trail from its archaic beginnings. Writing is the visual counterpart of speech. Marks, symbols, pictures, or letters drawn or written upon a surface or substrate became a graphic counterpart of the spoken word or unspoken thought. The limitations of speech are the fallibility of human memory and an immediacy of expression that cannot transcend time and place. Until the electronic age, spoken words vanished without a trace, while written words remained. The invention of writing brought people the luster of civilization and made it possible to preserve hard-won knowledge, experiences, and thoughts.

The development of writing and visible language had its earliest origins in simple pictures, for a close connection exists between the drawing of pictures and the marking of writing. Both are natural ways of communicating ideas, and early people used pictures as an elementary way to record and transmit information.

Prehistoric visual communications

Early human markings found in Africa are over 200,000 years old. From the early Paleolithic to the Neolithic period (35,000 B.C. to 4000 B.C.), early Africans and Europeans left paintings in caves, including the Lascaux caves in southern France (Fig. 1–1) and Altamira in Spain. A black was made from charcoal, and a range of warm tones, from light yellows through red-browns, were made from red and yellow iron oxides. This palette of pigments was mixed with fat as a medium. Images of animals were drawn and painted upon the walls of these former subterranean water channels occupied as a refuge by prehistoric men and women. Perhaps the pigment was smeared onto the walls with a finger, or a brush was fabricated from bristles or reeds. This was not the beginning of art as we know it. Rather, it was the dawning of visual communications, because these early pictures were made for survival, and for utilitarian and ritualistic purposes. The presence of what appear to be spear marks in the sides of some of these animal images indicates that they were used in magical rites designed to gain power over animals and success in the hunt.

Abstract geometric signs, including dots, squares, and other configurations, are intermingled with the animals in many cave paintings. Whether they represent man-made objects or are protowriting is not known, and will never be, because they were made before the beginning of recorded history (the 5,000-year period during which people have recorded in writing a chronicle of their knowledge of facts and events). The animals painted on the caves are pictographs—elementary pictures or sketches to represent the things depicted.

Throughout the world, from Africa to North America to the islands of New Zealand, prehistoric people left numerous *petroglyphs* (Fig. 1–2), which are carved or scratched signs or simple figures on rock. Many of the petroglyphs are pictographs, and some may be *ideographs*, or symbols to represent ideas or concepts. (Fig. 1–3) A high level of observation and memory is evidenced in many prehistoric drawings. In an engraved reindeer antler found in the cave of Lorthet in southern France (Fig. 1–4),

1–1. Cave painting from Lascaux, c. 15,000–10,000 B.C. Random placement and shifting scale signify prehistoric people's lack of structure and sequence in recording their experiences.

1–2. Found carved and sometimes painted on rocks in the western United States, these petroglyphic figures, animals, and signs are similar to those found all over the world.

1–3. Fremont rock painting from San Raphael Swell, c. 2000–1000 B.C. The Fremont people lived in southern Utah.

1–4. Engraved drawing on a deer antler, c. 15,000 B.C. This prehistoric image is shown in a cast made by rolling the antler onto clay.

1–1

1–2

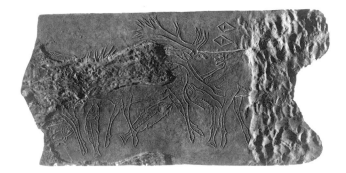

1–4

1–3

the scratched drawings of deer and salmon are remarkably accurate. Even more important, however, are two diamond-shaped forms with interior marks, which imply an early symbol-making ability. The early pictographs evolved in two ways: First, they were the beginning of pictorial art—the objects and events of the world were recorded with increasing fidelity and exactitude as the centuries passed; second, they formed the basis of writing. The images, whether the original pictorial form was retained or not, ultimately became symbols for spoken-language sounds.

The Paleolithic artist developed a tendency toward simplification and stylization. Figures became increasingly abbreviated and were expressed with a minimum number of lines. By the late Paleolithic period, some petroglyphs and pictographs had been reduced to the point of almost resembling letters.

The cradle of civilization

Until recent discoveries indicated that early peoples in Thailand may have practiced agriculture and manufactured pottery at an even earlier date, archaeologists had long believed that the ancient land of Mesopotamia, "the land between rivers," was the cradle of civilization. Between the Tigris and Euphrates rivers, which flow from the mountains of eastern Turkey across the land that is now Iraq and into the Persian Gulf, there lies a flat, once-fertile plain whose wet winters and hot, dry summers proved very attractive to early human culture. Here, early humans ceased their restless nomadic wanderings and established a village society. Around 8000 B.C., wild grain was planted, animals were domesticated, and agriculture began. By the year 6000 B.C., objects were being hammered from copper; the Bronze Age was ushered in about 3000 B.C., when copper was alloyed with tin to make durable tools and weapons, followed by the invention of the wheel.

The leap from village culture to high civilization occurred after the Sumerian people arrived in Mesopotamia near the end of the fourth millennium B.C. The origin of the Sumerians—who settled in the lower part of the Fertile Crescent before 3000 B.C.—remains a great mystery. As vital as the technologies developed in Mesopotamia were for the future of the human race, the Sumerians' contribution to social and intellectual progress had even more impact upon the future. The Sumerians invented a system of gods headed by a supreme deity named Anu, who was the god of the heavens. An intricate system of god-man relationships was developed. The city emerged, with the necessary social order for large numbers of people to live together. But of the numerous inventions in Sumer that launched people onto the path of civilization, the invention of writing brought about an intellectual revolution that had a vast impact upon social

order, economic progress, and technological and future cultural developments.

The history of Mesopotamia records waves of invaders who conquered the peoples living there. The culture established by the Sumerians conquered the invaders in turn, and the sequence of ruling peoples who dominated Mesopotamia during its long history include Akkadians, Assyrians, Babylonians, and Chaldeans. Persians from the west and Hittites from the north also conquered the area and spread Mesopotamian civilization beyond the Fertile Crescent.

The earliest writing

Religion dominated life in the Mesopotamian city-state, just as the massive ziggurat, a stepped temple compound, dominated the city. Its vast, multistory brick temples were constructed as a series of recessed levels, becoming smaller toward the top of the shrine. Inside, priests and scribes wielded enormous power, as they controlled the inventories of the gods and the king and ministered to the magical and religious needs of the people. Writing may have evolved because this temple economy had an increasing need for record keeping. The temple chiefs consciously sought a system for recording information.

In human memory, time can become a blur, and important facts are often forgotten. In Mesopotamian terms, such important facts might include the answers to questions like: Who delivered their taxes in the form of crops? How much food was stored, and was it adequate to meet community needs before the next harvest? As even these relatively simple questions show, an accurate continuum of knowledge became imperative if the temple priests were to be able to maintain the order and stability necessary in the city-state. One theory holds that the origin of visible language evolved from the need to identify the contents of sacks and pottery containers used to store food. Small clay tags were made that identified the contents with a pictograph and the amount through an elementary decimal numbering system, based on the ten human fingers.

The earliest written records are tablets from the city of Uruk (Fig. **1–5**). They apparently list commodities by pictographic drawings of objects accompanied by numerals and personal names inscribed in orderly columns. An abundance of clay in Sumer made it the logical material for record keeping, and a reed stylus sharpened to a point was used to draw the fine, curved lines of the early pictographs. The clay mud tablet was held in the left hand, and pictographs were scratched in the surface with the wooden stylus. Beginning in the top right corner of the tablet, the lines were written in careful vertical columns. The inscribed tablet was then dried in the hot sun or baked rock-hard in a kiln.

1–5

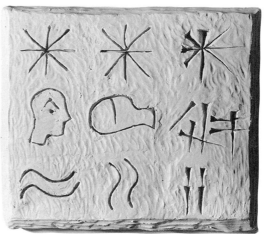

1–6

1–7

1–5. Early Sumerian pictographic tablet, c. 3100 B.C. This archaic pictographic script contained the seeds for the development of writing. Information is structured into grid zones by horizontal and vertical division.

1–6. This clay tablet demonstrates how the Sumerian symbols for "star" (which also meant "heaven" or "god"), "head," and "water" evolved from early pictographs (3100 B.C.). The latter were turned on their side by 2800 B.C. and evolved into the early cuneiform writing by 2500 B.C.

1–7. Cuneiform tablet, c. 2100 B.C. This clay tablet lists expenditures of grain and animals.

This writing system underwent an evolution over several centuries. Writing was structured on a grid of horizontal and vertical spatial divisions. Sometimes the scribe would smear the writing as his hand moved across the tablet. Around 2800 B.C. scribes turned the pictographs on their sides and began to write in horizontal rows, from left to right and top to bottom (Fig. **1–6**). This made writing easier, and it made the pictographs less literal. About three hundred years later, writing speed was increased by replacing the sharp-pointed stylus with a triangular-tipped one. This stylus was pushed into the clay instead of being dragged through it. The characters were now composed of a series of wedge-shaped strokes rather than a continuous line drawing (Fig. **1–7**). This innovation radically altered the nature of the writing; pictographs evolved into an abstract sign writing called cuneiform (from the Latin for "wedge-shaped").

While the graphic form of Sumerian writing was evolving, its ability to record information was expanding. From the first stage, when picture-symbols represented animate and inanimate objects, signs became ideographs and began to represent abstract ideas. The symbol for sun, for example, began to represent ideas such as "day" and "light." As early scribes developed their written language to function in the same way as their speech, the need to represent spoken sounds not easily depicted arose. Adverbs, prepositions, and personal names often could not be adapted to pictographic representation. Picture symbols began to represent the sounds of the objects depicted instead of the objects themselves. Cuneiform became rebus writing, which is pictures and/or pictographs representing words and syllables with the same or similar sound as the object depicted. Pictures were used as phonograms, or graphic symbols for sounds. The highest development of cuneiform was its use of abstract signs to represent syllables, which are sounds made by combining more elementary sounds.

1–8

1–9

1–11

1–10

1–8. The Blau monument, early Sumerian, third quarter, fourth millennium B.C. Etched writing and carved relief figures are combined on this early shale artifact.

1–9. Black stone duck weight, c. 3000 B.C. The cuneiform inscription dedicates this weight to the god Nanna by the King of Ur, and confirms a weight of five minas. A mina weighed about 0.559 kilograms, or 18 ounces.

1–10. Stele bearing the Code of Hammurabi, which was initially written between 1792 and 1750 B.C. Above the densely textured law code, King Hammurabi is shown on a mountaintop with the seated sun god Shamash, who orders the king to write down the laws for the people of Babylon. A graphic image of divine authority as the source for the code becomes powerful visual persuasion.

1–11. Detail of the Code of Hammurabi, c. 1800 B.C. Whether pressed into clay or carved into stone as shown here, Mesopotamian scribes achieved a masterful control and delicacy in their writing and arrangement of the strokes in the partitioned space.

Cuneiform was a difficult writing system to master, even after the Assyrians simplified it into only 560 signs. Youngsters selected to become scribes began their schooling at the *edubba*, the writing school or "tablet house," before the age of ten and worked from sunrise to sunset every day, with only six days off per month. Professional opportunities in the priesthood, estate management, accounting, medicine, and government were reserved for these select few. Writing took on important magical and ceremonial qualities. The general public held those who could write in awe, and it was believed that death occurred when a divine scribe etched one's name in a mythical Book of Fate.

Early Sumerian artisans mixed writing with relief images. The Blau monument (Fig. **1–8**) may be the oldest extant arti-fact combining words and pictures on the same surface.

The knowledge explosion made possible by writing was remarkable. Libraries were organized and contained thousands of tablets about religion, mathematics, history, law, medicine, and astronomy. There was a beginning of literature as poetry, myths, epics, and legends were recorded on the clay tablets. Writing also fostered a sense of history; tablets chronicled with meticulous exactitude the events that occurred during the reign of each monarch. Thousands of commercial contracts and records still remain.

Writing enabled society to stabilize itself under the rule of law. Measurements and weights were standardized and guaranteed by written inscription (Fig. **1–9**). Law codes, such as the Code of Hammurabi, who reigned 1792–1750 B.C., spelled out crimes and their punishments, thus establishing social order and justice. The Code of Hammurabi is written in careful cuneiform on a 2.44-meter (8-foot) tall stele, an inscribed or carved stone or slab used for commemorative purposes (Figs. **1–10** and **1–11**). The stele contains 282 laws gridded in twenty-one columns. Steles with Hammurabi's reformed law code were erected in the main temple of Marduk at Babylon and in other cities. Written in a precise style, harsh penalties were expressed with clarity and brevity. Some of these commandments include: "a thief stealing from a child is to be put to death"; "a physician operating on a slightly wounded man with a bronze scalpel shall have his hands cut off"; and "a builder who builds a house that falls and kills the owner shall be put to death."

Mesopotamian visual identification

Two natural by-products of the rise of village culture were the ownership of property and the specialization of trades or crafts. Both made visual identification necessary. Cattle brands and proprietary marks were developed so that ownership could be established and the maker of pottery or other objects identified in case problems developed or superior quality inspired repeat purchases. A means of identifying the author of a clay cuneiform tablet certifying commercial documents and contracts and proving the authority of religious and royal proclamations was needed. Mesopotamian cylinder seals provided a forgery-proof method for sealing documents and proving their authenticity (Fig. **1–12**). In use for over three thousand years, these small cylinders had images and writing etched into their surfaces. When they were rolled across a damp clay tablet, a raised impression of the depressed design, which became a "trademark" for the owner, was formed. Because the image carved into the round stone appeared on the tablet as a raised flat design, it was virtually impossible to duplicate or counterfeit. Many such stones had a hollow perforation running through them so that they could be worn on a string around the neck or wrist. Since the images could be reproduced, this can be seen as an initial form of printing.

The widely traveled Greek historian Herodotus (c. 500 B.C.) wrote that the Babylonians each wore a cylinder seal on a cord around their wrists like a bracelet. Prized as ornaments, status symbols, and unique personal signatures, cylinder seals were even used to mark a damp clay seal on the house door when the occupants were away, to indicate whether burglars

1–12. Hittite cylinder seal, undated. Thought to portray a ritual, possibly with a sacrificial offering on the right, this seal combines decorative ornamentation with figurative images. It has both an image on the side, for rolling, and an image on the bottom, for stamping. Because it allows images to be reproduced, the cylinder seal can be seen as a precursor to printing.

1–12

1–13

1–14

1–13 and 1–14. Persian stamp seal, c. 500 B.C. Incised into a precious pale blue quartz called chalcedony in a gold mount, this seal, with its symmetrical design of a pair of heraldic beasts locked in combat, probably belonged to a member of the royal family or the high priesthood.

had entered the premises. Cutters of cylinder and stamp seals developed great skill and a refined sense of design. The earliest seals were engraved with simple pictures of kings, a line of cattle, or mythic creatures. Later, more narrative images developed; for instance, one god would present a man (probably the seal's owner) to another god, or a man would figure prominently in fighting a battle or killing a wild animal. In the later Assyrian period, north of Mesopotamia a more stylized and heraldic design approach developed. Stories of the gods were illustrated and animals were shown engaged in battle (Figs. **1–13** and **1–14**).

The last glory of Mesopotamian civilization occurred during the long reign of King Nebuchadnezzar (d. 562 B.C.) in the city-state of Babylon. But in 538 B.C., after less than a century of great power during which Babylon became the richest city in the world, with a population reaching close to a million inhabitants, Babylon and Mesopotamia fell to the Persians. The Mesopotamian culture began to perish as the region became a province of Persia, then of Greece and Rome. By the time of the birth of Christ, great cities such as Babylon were abandoned, and the ziggurats had fallen into ruins. The dawning of visible language, the magnificent gift to the future of mankind that was writing, passed forward to Egypt and Phoenicia. The Egyptians evolved a complex writing based on pictographs, and the Phoenicians replaced the formidable complexity of cuneiform with simple phonetic signs.

Egyptian hieroglyphs

By the time King Menes unified the land of Egypt and formed the First Dynasty around 3100 B.C., a number of inventions from the Sumerians had reached Egypt, including the cylinder seal, architectural designs of brick, decorative design motifs, and the fundamentals of writing. Unlike the Sumerians, who evolved their pictographic writing into the abstract cuneiform, the Egyptians retained their picture-writing system, called hieroglyphics (Greek for "sacred carving," after the Egyptian for "the god's words"), for almost three-and-a-half millennia. The earliest known hieroglyphs (Fig. **1–15**) date from about 3100 B.C., and the last known written hieroglyphic inscription was carved in A.D. 394, many decades after Egypt had become a Roman colony.

For nearly fifteen centuries, people looked with fascination upon Egyptian hieroglyphs without understanding their meaning. The last people to use this language system were fourth-century Egyptian temple priests. They were so secretive that Greek and Roman scholars of the era believed hieroglyphs were nothing more than magical symbols for sacred rites. In August 1799, Napoleon's troops were digging a foundation for an addition to the fortification in the Egyptian town of Rosetta, which they were occupying. A black slab was unearthed bearing an inscription in two languages and three scripts: Egyptian hieroglyphics, Egyptian demotic script, and Greek (Fig. **1–16**). This decree had been written in 197 or 196 B.C. after a great council of Egyptian priests met to commemorate the ascension of Pharaoh Ptolemy V (born c. 210 B.C.) to the throne of Egypt nine years earlier. It was realized that the inscription was probably the same in the three languages, and translation efforts began. In 1819 Dr. Thomas Young (1773–1829) proved that the direction in which the glyphs of animals and people faced was the direction from which hieroglyphics should be read and that the cartouche for Ptolemy occurred several times (Fig. **1–17**).

The major deciphering of the Rosetta Stone hieroglyphs was done by Jean-François Champollion (1790–1832). He realized that some of the signs were alphabetic, some were syllabic, and some were determinatives (signs that determined how the preceding glyphs should be interpreted). Realizing that the hieroglyphs often functioned as phonograms and not simply pictographs, Champollion was able to sound out the names Ptolemy and Cleopatra. This breakthrough happened in 1822, after Champollion was given a copy of an inscription on an obelisk, a tall, geometric totemlike Egyptian monument. As Champollion studied its hieroglyphs, he was surprised to see the cartouches—bracketlike plaques containing the glyphs of important names—of both Ptolemy and Cleopatra, which he had recognized earlier. Champollion assigned sounds to the three glyphs found in both words: *p*, *o*, and *l*. Then he

1–15

1–17

1–16

1–15. Ivory tablet of King Zet, First Dynasty. This five-thousand-year-old tablet is perhaps the earliest known example of the Egyptian pictographic writing that evolved into hieroglyphics.

1–16. The Rosetta Stone, c. 197–196 B.C. From top to bottom, the concurrent hieroglyphic, demotic, and Greek inscriptions provided the key to the secrets of ancient Egypt.

1–17. Details of the Rosetta Stone showing the name *Ptolemy* in hieroglyphics (top) and as the Greek word *Ptolemaios* (bottom).

patiently sounded out the others until he had a dozen hiero-glyphic translations (Fig. **1–18**). Armed with this new knowl-edge, he proceeded to decipher the cartouche for Alexander.

Champollion gathered all the cartouches he could find from the Greco-Roman era and quickly translated eighty, building a large vocabulary of glyphs in the process. After his death at age forty-two, Champollion's *Egyptian Dictionary* and *Egyptian Grammar* were both published. His progress toward translating hieroglyphics enabled other nineteenth-century Egyptologists to unlock the mysteries of Egyptian history and culture silently preserved in hieroglyphics.

Hieroglyphics consisted of pictograms that depicted objects or beings. These were combined to designate actual ideas, phonograms denoting sounds and determinatives identifying categories. When the early Egyptian scribes were confronted with words difficult to express in visual form, they devised a rebus, using pictures for sounds, to write the desired word (Fig. **1–19**). The American designer Paul Rand (1914–96) cleverly utilized the rebus system in his 1981 IBM poster (Fig. 20–17). At the same time they designated a pictorial symbol for every consonant sound and combination of consonants in their speech. Even though they never developed signs for the connecting sounds, combining the various glyphs produced a skeletal form for every word. By the time of the New Kingdom (1570–1085 B.C.) this remarkably efficient writing system had over seven hundred hieroglyphs, over one hun-dred of which remained strictly visual pictographs or word-pic-tures. The remainder had become phonograms. Because the Egyptian language contained so many homonyms (such as, for example, a pool of water and the game of pool), determi-natives were used after these words to ensure that the reader correctly interpreted them. Hinew, for example, could refer to a liquid measure or to neighbors. In the former case it was followed by the glyph for beer pot; in the latter by glyphs for a man and a woman. Presenting far more possibilities than cuneiform, hieroglyphics were used for historical and commer-cial documents, poetry, myths, and epics, and, among other topics, addressed geography, science, astronomy, medicine, pharmacy, and the concept of time.

Ancient Egypt clearly represents the early phases of Western civilization as we know it today. Greek culture received much of its knowledge from the Egyptians. Our use of visual symbols originated with the Egyptians; from them we inherited the zodiac, the scales of justice, and the use of ani-mals to represent concepts, cities, and people. In Greece, the owl symbolized Athena, and the image of an owl on a Greek coin indicates that it was minted in Athens. Today we have the American eagle, the Atlanta Falcons, the Carolina Gamecocks, and the dove symbolizing peace. Graphic designer and historian Lance Hidy writes, "Our cultural debt

to the idolatry of pagan Egypt was largely expunged from his-tory by Christian revisionists."

The ancient Egyptians had an extraordinary sense of design and were sensitive to the decorative and textural qualities of their hieroglyphs. This monumental visible language system was ubiquitous. Hieroglyphs were carved into stone as raised images or incised relief (Fig. **1–20**), and color was often applied. These covered the interior and exterior of temples and tombs. Furniture, coffins, clothing, utensils, buildings, and jewelry all bore hieroglyphs with both decorative and inscrip-tional purposes. Frequently, magical and religious values were ascribed to certain hieroglyphs. The hieroglyph *ankh*, a cross surmounted by a loop (see Fig. 1–26), had modest origins as the symbol for a sandal strap. Due to phonetic similarity it gained meaning as a symbol for life and immortality and was widely used as a sacred emblem throughout the land.

The design flexibility of hieroglyphics was greatly increased by the choice of writing direction. One started from the direc-tion in which the living creatures were facing. The lines could be written horizontally or vertically, so the designer of an arti-fact or manuscript had four choices: left to right horizontally; left to right in vertical columns; right to left horizontally; and right to left in vertical columns. Sometimes, as demonstrated in the schematic of the sarcophagus of Aspalta (Fig. **1–21**), these design possibilities were combined in one work.

Papyrus and writing

The development of papyrus, a paperlike substrate for manu-scripts, was a major step forward in Egyptian visual communi-cations. In ancient times the *Cyperus papyrus* plant grew along the Nile in shallow marshes and pools. Egyptians made extensive use of this plant, whose 4.6-meter (about 15-foot) stems grew up above the water. Papyrus flowers were used for garlands at the temples; roots were used for fuel and utensils; and stems were the raw material for sails, mats, cloth, rope, sandals, and, most importantly, papyrus.

In his *Natural History*, Roman historian Pliny the Elder (A.D. 23–79) tells how papyrus was made. After the rind was peeled away, the inner pith of the stems was cut into longitu-dinal strips, laid side by side. A second layer of strips was then laid on top of the first layer, at right angles to it. These two layers were soaked in the Nile River and then pressed or ham-mered until they were a single sheet—apparently, the gluti-nous sap of the papyrus stem acted as an adhesive. After dry-ing in the sun, sheets were smoothed with an ivory or stone polisher. If such flaws as spots, stains, or spongy areas appeared, the faulty sheet would be peeled apart and remade. Eight different papyrus grades were made for uses ranging from royal proclamations to daily accounting. The fin-ished sheets had an upper surface of horizontal fibers called

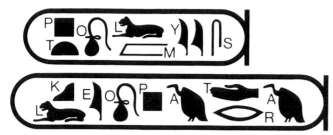

1–18

1–19

1–20

1–18. Alphabet characters placed beside each hieroglyph in the cartouches of Ptolemy and Cleopatra demonstrate the approximate phonetic sounds deciphered by Champollion.

1–19. These Egyptian hieroglyphs illustrate the rebus principle. Words and syllables are represented by pictures of objects and by symbols whose names are similar to the word or syllable to be communicated. These hieroglyphs mean bee, leaf, sea, and sun. As rebuses (using the English language) they could also mean belief and season.

1–20. Offering niche of the Lady Sat-tety-lyn, Sixth Dynasty. In contrast to the raised images in the lower registers, these hiero-glyphs are carved into the surface and are contained in a mathematical grid of carved lines.

1–21. Sarcophagus of Aspalta, King of Ethiopia, c. 593–568 B.C. The inscriptions carved into this granite sarcophagus demon-strate the flexibility of hieroglyphics.

1–21

the recto and a bottom surface of vertical fibers called the verso. The tallest papyrus sheets measured 49 centimeters (19 inches), and up to twenty sheets would be pasted together and rolled into a scroll, with the recto side facing inward.

As in Sumer, knowledge was power, and the scribes gained significant authority in Egyptian society. Learning to read and write the complex language took many years, and the profession of scribe was highly respected and brought many privileges, not the least of which was exemption from taxation.

The wooden palette used by the scribe was a trademark identifying the carrier as being able to read and write (Fig. **1–22**). The example shown is 32.5 centimeters (12 inches) long. One end has at least two depressions, to hold black, red, and sometimes other ink cakes. With a gum solution as a binder, carbon was used to make black ink and ground red ocher to make red ink. These were dried into cakes similar to contemporary watercolor blocks, and a wet brush would then be rubbed onto the cake to return the ink to a liquid state for writing. A slot in the middle of the palette held the brushes, which were made from rush stems. The stem tips were cut on an angle and chewed by the scribe to separate the fibers into a brush.

Holding the scroll with his left hand, the scribe would begin at the outer right edge and write a column of hieroglyphs from top to bottom, writing column after column as shown in the detail of the Book of the Dead of Tuthmosis III (Fig. **1–23**). This hieroglyphic book handwriting evolved from the monumental form—the scribes simplified the inscriptional hieroglyphs from a carefully constructed picture to a quickly drawn gesture.

By 1500 B.C. a cursory *hieratic* (from the Greek for "priestly") script, a penstroke simplification of the hieroglyphic book hand, was developed by the priests for religious writings. The earliest hieratic script differed from the hieroglyphs only in that the use of a rush pen, instead of a pointed brush, produced more abstract characters with a terse, angular quality. An even more abstract script called *demotic* (from the Greek word for "popular") came into secular use for commercial and legal writing by the year 400 B.C. The hieroglyph for *scribe* was a pictorial image of the very early brush-holder, palette, and sack of ink. The characters accompanying the photograph of these artifacts show this evolution (Fig. **1–24**). Hieratic and demotic scripts supplemented rather than supplanted hieroglyphs, which continued in use for religious and inscriptional purposes.

The first illustrated manuscripts

The Egyptians were the first people to produce illustrated manuscripts in which words and pictures were combined to communicate information. A preoccupation with death and a strong belief in the afterlife compelled the Egyptians to evolve a complex mythology about the journey into the afterlife. Through inventive myth and legend, the inexplicable was explained and faced. A final judgment would ultimately allow the deceased either to be admitted into the company of the gods or to suffer eternal damnation. The prayer of every Egyptian was to be cleansed of sin and found worthy at the final judgment. Scribes and artists were commissioned to prepare funerary papyri, called the Chapters of Coming Forth by Day. A nineteenth-century scholar named them the Book of the Dead, and this name is generally used today.

The Book of the Dead was a third phase in the evolution of funerary texts. Beginning with the pyramid of Unas (c. 2345 B.C.), the walls and passages of the pyramids were covered with the *pyramid texts* of hieroglyphic writings, including myths, hymns, and prayers relating to the godlike pharaoh's life in the afterworld. This practice was followed by the *coffin texts*. All surfaces of the wooden coffin and/or stone sarcophagus were covered with writings and often illustrated with pictures of possessions for use in the afterlife. Thus, high officials and noblemen could now enjoy the benefits of funerary texts even though the cost of a pyramid was beyond their means.

The dawning of the New Kingdom, around 1580 B.C., saw papyrus manuscripts come into use for funerary texts. Even citizens of fairly limited means could afford to have at least simple papyri to accompany them on the journey into the afterlife. From pyramid to coffin to papyri—this evolution toward cheaper and more widespread use of funerary texts paralleled the increasingly democratic and secular aspects of Egyptian life.

The Book of the Dead was written in a first-person narrative by the deceased and placed in the tomb to help triumph over the dangers of the underworld. The artists who illustrated the Book of the Dead papyri were called upon to foretell what would occur after each subject died and entered the afterlife (Fig. **1–25**). Magical spells could enable the deceased to turn into powerful creatures, passwords to enter various states of the underworld were provided, and the protection of the gods was sought. Wonderful futures were illustrated. One might dwell in the Fields of Peace, ascend into the heavens to live as a star, travel the sky with the sun god Ra in his solar boat, or help Osiris rule the underworld.

The journey into the underworld is depicted as a chronological narrative. The final judgment is shown in the Papyrus of Ani (Fig. **1–26**). The jackal-headed god Anubis, keeper of the dead, prepares to weigh Ani's heart against a feather symbolizing truth to see if he is "true of voice" and free from sin. Thoth, the ibis-headed scribe of the gods and keeper of the magical arts, is poised with a scribe's palette to write the verdict. To the right, the monster Ammit, the devourer of the dead, stands poised for action should Ani fail to pass the moment of judgment. An

1–22

1–24

1–23

1–22. Egyptian scribe's palette with an inscription in hieratic script.

1–23. Detail from the Book of the Dead of Tuthmosis III, c. 1450 B.C. Written hieroglyphics were simplified, but they maintained their pictographic origin.

1–24. The hieroglyph for *scribe* depicted the Old Kingdom palette, the drawstring sack for dried ink cakes, and a reed brush holder. The changes in this glyph demonstrate the evolutionary process (from left to right): hieroglyph, 2700 B.C.; hieroglyphic manuscript hand, c. 1500 B.C.; hieratic script, c. 1300 B.C.; and demotic script, c. 400 B.C.

1–25

1–26

1–25. Detail from the Papyrus of Hunefer, c. 1370 B.C. Hunefer and his wife are worshipping the gods of Amenta. The sun god Ra bears an ankh symbol on his knee, and Thoth holds the udjat, the magical protective "sound eye" of the god Horus.

1–26. Vignette from the Papyrus of Ani, c. 1420 B.C. Ani, a royal scribe, temple accountant, and granary manager from Thebes, and his wife, Thuthu, arrive for his final judgment.

imaginative visual symbol, Ammit has the head of a crocodile, the torso of a lion, and the hindquarters of a hippopotamus. A register across the top shows twelve of the forty-two gods who sit in judgment. Addressing each god in turn, a "negative confession" denies a host of sins: "I have not done evil; I have not stolen; I have not killed people; I have not stolen food." Then, Ani speaks to his heart: "Set not thyself to bear witness against me. Speak not against me in the presence of the judges, cast not your weight against me before the Lord of the Scales." Upon being found virtuous, his soul spends the night after death traveling into the underworld and arrives at his "coming forth by day" on the following morning.

A consistent design format evolved for the illustrated Egyptian papyri. One or two horizontal bands, usually colored, ran across the top and bottom of the manuscript. Vertical columns of writing separated by ruled lines were written from right to left. Images were inserted adjacent to the text they illustrated. Images often stood on the lower horizontal band, the columns of text hanging down from the top horizontal band. Frequently, a horizontal friezelike register ran along the top of a sheet. A sheet was sometimes divided into rectangular zones to separate text and images. The functional integration of text and image was aesthetically pleasing, for the dense texture of the brushdrawn hieroglyphs contrasted handsomely with the illustration's open spaces and flat planes of color.

In the earlier versions of the Book of the Dead, the scribe designed the manuscript. If it was to be illustrated, blank areas were left that the artist would fill in as best he could.

1–27

1–28

1–27 and 1–28. Scarab of Ikhnaton and Nefertiti, c. 1370 B.C. This 6-centimeter (2.4-inch) scarab bears the cartouche of Ikhnaton on the side shown. The engraved hieroglyphs of the flat bottom were etched with a bronze needle.

The vignettes gradually became more important and dominated the design. The artist would draw these illustrations first. Then the scribe would write the manuscript, trying to avoid awkward blank spaces and sometimes writing in the margins if the illustrator did not leave adequate room for the text. Skilled artists were retained to create the images, but the scribes who did this work were not scholars. Often, passages were omitted for purposes of layout or through poor workmanship. The manuscript illustrations were drawn in simplified contour lines using black or brown ink, then flat color was applied using white, black, brown, blue, green, and sometimes yellow pigments. Perhaps the extensive use of luminous blue and green was a response to the intense blue of the Nile and the rich green of the foliage along its banks, a cool streak of life winding through vast reaches of desert.

Wall paintings and papyri used similar design conventions. Men were shown with darker skin color than women, and important persons were in larger scale than less important persons. The human body was drawn as a two-dimensional schematic. The frontal body had arms, legs, and head in profile. The stylized eye reads simultaneously as both profile and frontal image. Even though flatness was maintained, Egyptian artists were capable of sensitive observation and recording of details.

One could commission a funerary papyrus or purchase a stock copy and have one's name written in appropriate places. The buyer could select the number and choice of chapters, the number and quality of illustrations, and the length. Excepting the 57-meter (185-foot) great Turin Papyrus, the Book of the Dead scrolls ranged from 4.6 meters (15 feet) to 27.7 meters (90 feet) long and were from 30 centimeters (about 12 inches) to 45 centimeters (about 18 inches) tall. Toward the final collapse of Egyptian culture, the Book of the Dead often consisted merely of sheets of papyrus, some of which were only a few inches square.

Egyptian visual identification

The Egyptians used cylinder seals and proprietary marks on such items as pottery very early in their history. Both forms of identification certainly were inherited from the Sumerians. From prehistoric times the scarab beetle was considered sacred or magical. In the Twelfth Dynasty, carved scarab emblems (Figs. 1–27 and 1–28) were commonly used as identification seals. These oval stones, usually of a glazed steatite, were sculpted likenesses of the scarab beetle. The flat underside, engraved with a hieroglyphic inscription, was used as a seal. Sometimes the scarab was mounted as a signet ring. Although every Egyptian of any standing had a personal seal, very little evidence of scarabs actually being used for sealing has survived. Possibly the communicative function was secondary to the scarab's value as talisman, ornament, and symbol of resurrection. The creator sun god, Kheper, linked to the scarab beetle, was sometimes depicted rolling the sun across the sky, just as the living scarab or dung beetle was seen forming a ball of dung and rolling it across the sand to its burrow to be eaten over the following days. Ancient Egyptians apparently believed that the scarab beetle laid its eggs in this ball and related the scarab's life cycle to the cyclical processes of nature, especially the daily rebirth of the sun. A scarab called a "heart-scarab" was placed over the heart of a mummy with its wrappings. Its engraved undersurface had a brief plea to the heart not to act as a hostile witness in the Hall of Justice of Osiris.

The majestic Egyptian culture survived for over three thousand years. Hieroglyphics, papyri, and illustrated manuscripts are its visual communications legacy. Along with the accomplishments of Mesopotamia, these innovations triggered the development of the alphabet and graphic communications in Phoenicia and the Greco-Roman world.

Alphabets

Early visual language systems, including cuneiform, hieroglyphs, and written Chinese (see chapter 3), contained a built-in complexity. In each, pictographs had become rebus writing, ideographs, logograms, or even a syllabary. But these early writing systems remained unwieldy and required long, hard study to master. For centuries, the number of individuals who gained literacy was small. Their access to knowledge enabled them to acquire great power in the early cultures. The subsequent invention of the *alphabet* (a word derived from the first two letters of the Greek alphabet, *alpha* and *beta*) was a major step forward in human communications.

An alphabet is a set of visual symbols or characters used to represent the elementary sounds of a spoken language. They can be connected and combined to make visual configurations signifying sounds, syllables, and words uttered by the human mouth. The hundreds of signs and symbols required by cuneiform and hieroglyphs were replaced by twenty or thirty easily learned elementary signs. Figure **2–1** shows stages in the evolution of Western alphabets.

Numerous and often conflicting theories have been advanced about the origins of the alphabet; suggested sources include cuneiform, hieroglyphs, prehistoric geometric signs, and early Cretan pictographs.

Cretan pictographs

The Minoan civilization that existed on the Mediterranean island of Crete ranks behind only Egypt and Mesopotamia in its early level of advancement in the ancient Western world.

Minoan or Cretan picture symbols (see Fig. **2–1**) were in use as early as 2800 B.C. Short pictographic inscriptions written as early as 2000 B.C. have been found. About 135 pictographs survive; they include figures, arms, other parts of the body, animals, plants, and some geometric symbols. By 1700 B.C. these pictographs seem to have yielded to linear script writing, a possible precursor to the Greek alphabet.

One of the most interesting and perplexing relics of the Minoan civilization is the Phaistos Disk (Fig. **2–2**), which was unearthed on Crete in 1908. Lacking precedent or parallel, this flat terra-cotta disk, 16.5 centimeters (6 inches) in diameter, has pictographic and seemingly alphabetic forms imprinted on both sides in spiral bands. Typelike stamps were

Early Name	Probable Meaning	Greek Name	Cretan pictographs	Phoenician	Early Greek	Classical Greek	Latin	Modern English
Āleph	Ox	Alpha				A	A	A
Bēth	House	Bēta				B	B	B
Gimel	Camel	Gamma				Γ	C	C
Dāleth	Folding door	Delta				Δ	D	D
Hē	Lattice window	Epsilon				E	E	E
Wāw	Hook, nail						F	F
							G	G
Zayin	Weapon	Zeta				Z		
Hēth	Fence, Barrier	Ēta				H	H	H
Tēth	A winding (?)	Thēta				θ		
Yōd	Hand	Iōta				I	I	I
								J
Kaph	Bent Hand	Kappa				K	K	K
Lāmed	Ox-goad	Lambda				Λ	L	L
Mēm	Water	Mu				M	M	M
Nūn	Fish	Nu				N	N	N
Sāmek	Prop (?)	Xei				Ξ		
'Ayin	Eye	Ou				O	O	O
Pē	Mouth	Pei				Π	P	P
Sādē	Fish-hook (?)							
Kōph	Eye of Needle (?)	Koppa					Q	Q
Rēsh	Head	Rho				P	R	R
Shin, sin	Tooth	Sigma, san				Σ	S	S
Taw	Mark	Tau				T	T	T
								U
						Υ	V	V
								W
						X	X	X
							Y	Y
							Z	Z

2–1

2–2

2–1. This diagram displays several evolutionary steps of Western alphabets. The controversial theory linking early Cretan pictographs to alphabets is based on similarities in their appearance.

2–2. The Phaistos Disk, undated. The 241 signs include a man in a plumed headdress, a hatchet, an eagle, a carpenter's square, an animal skin, and a vase.

used to impress each character carefully into the wet clay; thus the principle of movable type was used in a Western culture as early as 2000 B.C. Just what the inscriptions say, who made them, and whether the stamps or types were used to make messages on papyrus or other perishable substrates may never be known. Along with all Cretan pictographs, the Phaistos Disk remains a great mystery. Some scholars have suggested an origin other than Crete, but there is no evidence to support or reject this theory.

Although the visual similarity between Cretan pictographs and early alphabet characters is striking, many paleographers question whether Cretan pictographs were the wellspring for the alphabet.

The North Semitic alphabet

While the alphabet's inventors are unknown, Northwest Semitic peoples of the western Mediterranean region—early Canaanites, Hebrews, and Phoenicians—are widely believed to be the source. The term *North Semitic writing* is used for early alphabetic writing found throughout this region. Because the earliest surviving examples are from ancient Phoenicia, a culture on the western shores of the Mediterranean Sea in what is now Lebanon and parts of Syria and Israel, these early scripts are often called the Phoenician alphabet. During the second millennium B.C. the Phoenicians became seafaring merchants. Their sailing ships, the fastest and best engineered in the an-

cient world, linked settlements throughout the Mediterranean region. Influences and ideas were absorbed from other areas, including Egypt and Mesopotamia.

Geography and commerce wield great influence upon the affairs of people. Even the development of the alphabet may have been an act of geography, for the Phoenician city-states became a hub in the ancient world and the crossroads of international trade. The Phoenicians absorbed cuneiform from Mesopotamia in the west and Egyptian hieroglyphics and scripts from the south. Possibly they had knowledge of Cretan pictographs and scripts and may have been influenced by them. Faced with this range of visible languages, they developed alternatives. Apparently the Phoenicians sought a writing system for their own Northern Semitic speech; evidence of a number of localized experiments has been unearthed.

Sui generis, a writing script developed in Byblos, the oldest Phoenician city-state, used pictographic signs devoid of any remaining pictorial meaning. Written about 2000 B.C., stone and bronze documents featuring this script have a syllabary of over a hundred characters and illustrate a major step toward the development of an alphabet.

Around 1500 B.C. Semitic workers in Egyptian turquoise mines in the Sinai desert area designed an achrophonic adaptation of hieroglyphics called *Sinaitic* script. *Achrophonic* means a pictorial symbol or hieroglyph was used to stand for the initial sound of the depicted object.

2–3. Ras Shamra script, c. 1500 B.C. Used for bureaucratic and commercial documents, myths and legends, the Ras Shamra script, reducing cuneiform to a mere thirty-two characters, has only recently been unearthed in the ruins of the ancient city of Ugarit.

2–4. The gestural curves of the Aramaic alphabet evolved into the Hebrew and Arabic alphabets.

2–5. The graphic forms of the Hebrew alphabet are squared, bold letters whose horizontal strokes are thicker than their vertical strokes.

2–6. Kufic characters are bold, elongated, and angular; their aesthetic properties are widely admired.

2–3

Ras Shamra script (Fig. **2–3**), a true Semitic alphabetical script, was found on clay tablets inscribed around 1500 B.C. It used thirty cuneiformlike characters to represent elementary consonant sounds. The signs were composed of wedge-shaped marks that resembled cuneiform because a similar stylus was used. There were no characters to signify vowels, which are connecting sounds that join consonants to make words, now represented by the letters *a, e, i, o,* and *u.* The alphabetical order of Ras Shamra script—the sequence in which the letters were memorized—was the same as those used in the later Phoenician and Greek alphabets.

The writing exported by the Phoenicians, a totally abstract and alphabetical system of twenty-two characters (see Fig. **2–1**), was in use by 1500 B.C. One of the oldest datable inscriptions in the Phoenician alphabet was carved along the side of the lid of the limestone sarcophagus of the Byblos king Ahiram (c. eleventh century B.C.). The Phoenicians' right-to-left writing may have developed because stonemasons carved inscriptions by holding a chisel in the left hand and a hammer in the right. Their early alphabet script was also written on papyrus with a brush or pen; unfortunately, their literature, including, for instance, one Byblos author's nine-book work on mythology, has perished.

Although North Semitic writing is the historical beginning of the alphabet, it may have descended from an earlier, lost prototype. Early alphabets branched into multiple directions, including the Phoenician alphabet that evolved further in Greece and Rome, as well as the Aramaic alphabet, which gave rise to Hebrew and Arabic writing elsewhere in the region.

The Aramaic alphabet and its descendants

The Aramaic alphabet (Fig. **2–4**), first used by tribes from Aram, a large area in what is now Syria, is a major early derivation from the North Semitic script. The oldest surviving specimen dates from about 850 B.C. The Aramaic alphabet of twenty-two letters for consonantal sounds was written from right to left. A wide pen held at a forty-five-degree angle often produced heavy horizontal and thin vertical strokes. This language and writing became dominant throughout the Near East. Examples have been found in Afghanistan, Egypt, Greece, and India. It is the predecessor of hundreds of scripts, including two major alphabets used today: modern Hebrew and Arabic. Both of these functional and beautifully designed letter systems are still written from right to left in the manner of their early Semitic predecessors.

The oldest known examples of the Early or Old Hebrew alphabet date from around 1000 B.C. When the Israelites returned to the western Mediterranean area following their Babylonian exile (586 to 516 B.C.), they discovered Aramaic writing had replaced Old Hebrew in the region. The Aramaic alphabet—possibly with influences from Old Hebrew—spawned the Square Hebrew alphabet, which evolved into modern Hebrew (Fig. **2–5**). Basically, the Hebrew alphabet consists of the twenty-two consonantal letters of the ancient North Semitic alphabet. Four letters are also employed to indicate long vowels, and five letters have a second form for use at the end of a word. As the language evolved, dots and dashes were added to characters to indicate vowels.

The curving calligraphic gestures of Arabic writing probably

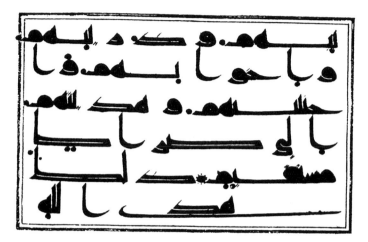

2–4

2–5

2–6

originated before A.D. 500. The twenty-two original sounds of the Semitic alphabet are supplemented by six additional characters added to the end. Three letters are also used as long vowels, and diacritical marks are added for short vowels and to distinguish consonant sounds. The two principle forms are Kufic, from the famous Muslim academy at Kufah in Mesopotamia, and Naskhi, which became the dominant Arabic script after about A.D. 1000. Kufic (Fig. **2–6**) is a bold inscriptional lettering with extended thick characters. Kufic has a majestic solidity and was widely used on coins, manuscripts, and inscriptions on metal and stone. It is still used for titles and decorative elements. The more cursive Naskhi style (Fig. **2–7**) is ideal for writing on papyrus and evolved into the modern Arabic scripts. Its vertical ascenders followed by horizontal curved strokes below convey a kinetic rhythm as it moves across the page.

The design of Arabic letters changes with the position within a word. All but six letters connect to the following letter with a small, upward-curving stroke when used in the middle of a word. Letters at the beginning or middle of a word are abbreviated; final letters and letters standing alone terminate in a bold flourish. These design alterations do not change the fundamental structure of the characters.

After the Latin alphabet, Arabic is the most widely used alphabet today. Arab conquests during the seventh and eighth centuries A.D. spread the Muslim religion and its holy book, the Qur'an, written in the Arabic alphabet, from North Africa and Spain on the Atlantic to India. Muslims believe the Qur'an (also spelled *Koran*) contains great truths revealed by Allah (God) to the prophet Muhammad (c. A.D. 570–632) through the Archangel Gabriel. Respect for these religious writings has elevated calligraphy to a high art in Muslim cultures.

The Aramaic alphabet is believed to be the predecessor of scripts used in India, apparently arriving around the seventh century B.C. Extensive elaboration was necessary to develop alphabets suitable for Indian spoken languages. The Indian subcontinent has a complex array of spoken and written language forms, and the specific origins of early writing in India and its neighboring nations are quite controversial. Both classical Sanskrit (Fig. **2–8**) and contemporary Indian writing have a vigorous horizontal and vertical structure, with the characters hanging from a strong horizontal stroke at the top. This horizontal stroke is believed to have originated from the scribal custom of writing beneath a ruled line, which gradually became part of the letter.

From North Semitic writing, the Aramaic alphabet and its descendants branched toward the East, forming a rich heritage of graphic forms remarkably different from their distant cousins, such as the Greek and Roman alphabets, that evolved in Western locales.

2–7

The Greek alphabet

Greek civilization laid the foundation for many of the accomplishments of the Western world—science, philosophy, and democratic government all developed in this ancient land. Art, architecture, and literature comprise a priceless part of the Greek heritage; it is fitting that the Greeks vastly improved the alphabet's beauty and utility after adopting it.

The Phoenician alphabet was adopted by the ancient Greeks and spread through their city-states around 1000 B.C. The oldest known inscriptions date from the eighth century B.C., but the Greek alphabet (Fig. **2–9**, and see Fig. 2–1), occupying a major position in the evolution of graphic communication, may have developed earlier. The Greeks took the Phoenician or North Semitic alphabet and changed five consonants to vowels. It is not known for certain who transported the alphabet from Phoenicia to Greece, but both mythology and tradition, which, in the ancient world, frequently became scrambled with oral history, point toward Cadmus of Miletus (dates unknown). According to various ancient accounts, Cadmus invented history, created prose, or designed some of the letters of the Greek alphabet. These alleged accomplishments raise the possibility that Cadmus may have brought the alphabet to Greece.

In an enigmatic parallel, early Greek mythology reports that Cadmus, king of Phoenicia, set forth to find his sister Europa after she was abducted by Zeus. During his journey King Cadmus killed a dragon that had slain his traveling companions. On the advice of Athena, he planted the dragon's teeth like seeds, and an army of fierce men sprang forth from them.

2–7. Musa Sa'id al Sa'idi al Najj, Quran manuscript, 1829–30. This manuscript is written in the cursive Naskhi style of Arabic calligraphy.

2–8. Indian Sanskrit type from a testament published in Calcutta, 1844. This type is based on a plain, scholarly hand known as Devanagari or town script.

2–9. Archaic Greek votive wheel, c. 525 B.C. A dedication to Apollo is clearly legible through the medium-green patina of this metal wheel, 16 centimeters (6 inches) in diameter, used for worship.

2–10. Timotheus, *The Persians*, papyrus manuscript, fourth century B.C. This excellent example of the Greek alphabet shows the symmetrical form and even visual rhythm that evolved. These qualities made the Greek alphabet the prototype for subsequent developments.

2–8

Tradition holds that King Cadmus brought the alphabet to Greece. Perhaps myth and oral history hint at a blinding truth: the power of Cadmus to raise armies from nowhere could be due to his command of the alphabet. Troop movements, scouting reports, and orders to the field could be delivered by writing. Cadmus's power to raise and direct armies came not from planting dragon's teeth but from using the alphabet as an information and communication tool.

Perhaps Cadmus's story is a myth and Phoenician traders brought the alphabet to Greece and other Mediterranean areas. Local Greek regions adapted the alphabet to their own needs until about 400 B.C., when Athens officially adopted a version that became standard throughout Greece.

The period around 700 B.C. saw a cultural renaissance in Greece. Achievements included Homer's *Odyssey* and *Iliad*, stone architecture, and human figures as major subjects on pottery. Large freestanding sculptures were only decades away. The city-state of Athens, cradle of representative government, organized surrounding towns into a unified political unit and moved toward an aristocratic republic by electing archons—the nine chief magistrates voted into one-year terms in 683 B.C. During this period the alphabet came into increasing use.

From a graphic design standpoint, the Greeks applied geometric structure and order to the uneven Phoenician characters, converting them into art forms of great harmony and beauty. The written form of Greek, as shown in *The Persians*, by Timotheus (Fig. **2–10**), has a visual order and balance as the letters move along a baseline in an even repetition of form and space, The letters and their component strokes are somewhat standardized because a system of horizontal, vertical, curved, and diagonal strokes is used. In the inscriptional form, such as on the fifth-century B.C. votive stela with four figures (Fig. **2–11**), the letters became symmetrical geometric constructions of timeless beauty. Stonecarvers took imaginative liberties with letterform design while maintaining the basic structure of the twenty-four-character alphabet that had stabilized by the classical period and is still used in Greece today. In this inscription, many letterforms, including the *E* and *M*, are based on a square, *A* is constructed from an equilateral triangle, and the design of the *O* is a near-perfect circle.

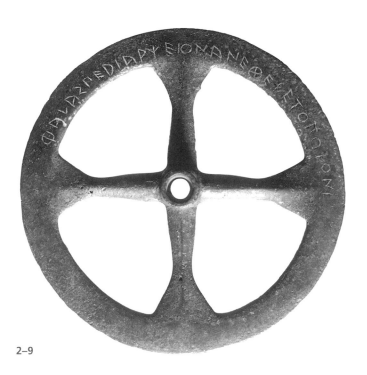

2–9

2–10

2–11

2–13

2–12

2–11. Votive stela with four figures, fifth century B.C. The design excellence of Greek inscriptions is clearly shown in this fragment. By using a three-sided square with a central dot for the *E* and a *V*-shaped horizontal in the *A*, the designer engaged in a personal inventiveness with form.

2–12. Greek wooden tablet with uncials, A.D. 326. The rounded uncials allowed an A to be made with two strokes instead of three, and an E to be made with three strokes instead of four.

2–13. Greek allotment tokens, c. 450–430 B.C. In the Greek city-state, some public officials were elected and others were selected by lot. These tokens were used in the selection process.

2–14. Greek juror's ballots, fourth century B.C. A juror voted "not guilty" with a ballot having a solid hub. A hollow-hubbed ballot was used to cast a "guilty" vote.

2–15. Greek signature seals, fifth century B.C. The leaping dolphin was photographed from a plaster impression made from the seal. The heron standing on one leg, the ewe rising from the ground, and the racehorse with broken reins were reproduced from the actual carvings.

Initially the Greeks adopted the Phoenician style of writing from right to left. Later they developed a writing method called *boustrophedon,* from the words meaning "to plow a field with an ox," for every other line reads in the opposite direction. Line one reads from right to left; then the characters do an about-face, and line two reads from left to right. The reader thus scans the text with a continuous back-and-forth eye movement, unhindered by the need to return to the opposite edge of the column to read each line. Finally the Greeks adopted the left-to-right reading movement that continues to this day in Western civilization.

As early as the second century A.D. the Greeks developed a more rounded writing style called *uncials* (Fig. 2–12). This script could be written more quickly, because its rounded letters were formed with fewer strokes. In addition to use on manuscripts, uncials were written on wood and soft materials such as wax tablets and clay. Uncials also demonstrated how writing tools and substrates influence written forms. Greek scribes made their pens from hard reeds, cut into nibs and split at the tip to aid ink flow. These pens gave their writing a totally different character than writing by Egyptian scribes, who used soft reeds to brush ink onto the substrate.

2–14

2–15

The Golden Age of Athens (c. 500 B.C.) was the high point of Greek culture. Democracy, or "people rule," was practiced. Aristotle called democracy "a state where freemen and the poor, being in a majority, are invested with the power of the State." (Freedom and equality did not extend to all people. The system was, in fact, based on slavery, because slave labor freed citizens to devote their time and energy to public affairs.) The vote of the majority became law. Visual communications played a secondary role in the oral culture of the Greek city-state. All citizens could attend the popular assembly and vote, and all elected officials were responsible to it. The orator who could speak persuasively to the assembly, the actor, and the lecturer were paramount in these city-states, where the total population, including the surrounding countryside, seldom exceeded ten thousand people. The historian or poet who wrote rather than spoke was less seriously regarded.

Nonetheless, the alphabet played a role in democracy; it enabled the use of allotment tokens when selecting citizens by lot for public service (Fig. **2–13**). Secret voting by jurors was possible through the use of metal ballots with alphabet inscriptions (Fig. **2–14**). To authorize and endorse documents, wealthy Greek citizens used signature seals, which could be stamped into wax or clay (Fig. **2–15**). Exquisite designs were engraved into the flat, oval bottom of a translucent, pale blue or gray variety of quartz. Animals were a favorite motif. The refined forms, harmonious balance, and wholeness of Greek sculpture were achieved in these small (about 2-centimeter, or 3/4-inch) signature seals used to impress a personal identification.

From the Macedonian city-state of Pella at the top of the Greek peninsula, Alexander the Great (356–323 B.C.) smashed the power of the Persian Empire and carried Hellenistic culture throughout the ancient world, including Egypt, Mesopotamia, and India. Reading and writing had become more important by this time, because the expansion of information and knowledge exceeded the ability of an oral culture to contain and document it. Alexander formed libraries, including a major one with several hundred thousand scrolls, in the colonial outpost of Alexandria in Egypt.

The design format of the papyrus scroll was usually 10.5 meters (about 35 feet) long, 24 centimeters (9 or 10 inches) high, and, when rolled, 4 to 6 centimeters (about 1 to 2 inches) in diameter. The text layout was in flush-left/random-right columns about 8 centimeters (3 inches) wide, with generous 2.5-centimeter (about 1-inch) ditches between them.

Unfortunately, most of the knowledge compiled by Greek civilization has been lost due to the fragile nature of papyrus scrolls and the damp Greek climate. Only thirty thousand scrolls survive, including only forty-three of the 330 plays by the great Greek playwrights.

After Alexander's death in Babylon at the age of thirty-two, his generals divided his empire into separate Hellenistic kingdoms. Greek civilization and its alphabet now became influential throughout the world. The Greek alphabet fathered the Etruscan, Latin, and Cyrillic alphabets and, through these ancestors, became the grandfather of alphabet systems used throughout the world today.

The Latin alphabet

The rise of Rome from a small village to the great imperial city that ruled much of the world, and the eventual collapse of its empire, constitutes one of the great sagas of history. Perhaps as early as 750 B.C. Rome existed as a humble village on the Tiber River in central Italy. By the first century A.D. the Roman Empire stretched from the British Isles in the north to Egypt in the south, and from Spain in the west to the Persian Gulf at the base of the ancient land of Mesopotamia in the east.

From a farm near Rome, the poet Horace (65–8 B.C.) wrote, "Captive Greece took Rome captive." After the Roman conquest of Greece in the second century B.C., scholars and whole libraries were moved to Rome. The Romans captured Greek literature, art, and religion, altered them to conform to the conditions of Roman society, and spread them throughout the vast Roman Empire.

The Latin alphabet (see Fig. 2–1) came to the Romans from Greece by way of the ancient Etruscans (Fig. **2–16**), a people whose civilization on the Italian peninsula reached its height during the sixth century B.C. After the letter *G* was designed by one Spurius Carvilius (c. 250 B.C.) to replace the Greek letter *Z* (zeta), which was of little value to the Romans, the Latin alphabet contained twenty-one letters: *A, B, C, D, E, F, G, H, I, K, L, M, N, O, P, Q, R* (which evolved as a variation of *P*), *S, T, V,* and *X*. Following the Roman conquest of Greece during the first century B.C., the Greek letters *Y* and *Z* were added to the end of the Latin alphabet because the Romans were appropri-ating Greek words containing these sounds. Three additional letters were added to the alphabet during the Middle Ages to arrive at the twenty-six letters of the contemporary English alphabet. The *J* is an outgrowth of *I,* which was lengthened in fourteenth-century manuscripts to indicate use with conso-nant force, particularly as the first letter of some words. Both *U* and *W* are variants of *V,* which was used for two different sounds in medieval England. At the beginning of the tenth century, *U* was designed to represent the soft vowel sound in contrast to the harder consonant sound of *V.* The *W* began as a ligature, which is a joining of two letters. In twelfth-century England two *V* letterforms were joined into *VV* to represent "double *U.*"

Rome took great pride in its imperial accomplishments and conquests, and created monumental letterforms for architec-tural inscriptions celebrating military leaders and their victo-ries. Roman inscriptions were designed for great beauty and permanence. The simple geometric lines of the *capitalis mon-umentalis* (monumental capitals) were drawn in thick and thin strokes, with organically unified straight and curved lines (Figs. **2–17** and **2–18**). Each letterform was designed to become one form rather than merely the sum of its parts. Careful attention was given to the shapes of spaces inside and between the letters. A Roman inscription became a sequence of linear geometric forms adapted from the square, triangle, and circle. Combined into an inscription, these letterforms molded the negative shapes around and between them into a measured graphic melody of spatial forms, achieving an eter-nal wholeness.

Much debate has centered on the elegant Roman *serifs,* which are small lines extending from the ends of the major strokes of a letterform. One theory holds that the serifs were originally chisel marks made by the "cleanup" strokes as the stonemason finished carving a letter. Others argue that the inscriptions were first drawn on the stone with a flat sign-writer's brush, and that the signwriter gave a short gesture before lifting the brush to sharpen the termination of the stroke. Regardless of which tool initiated the serif as a design element, we do know that the original letters were drawn on the stone with a brush and then carved into it. The shapes and forms defy mathematical analysis or geometrical con-struction. A letter found several times on an inscription will have subtle differences in width and proportion. In some inscriptions, lines with more letters will have both the letter-forms and the negative spaces between them slightly con-densed to accommodate the information. This represents an artistic judgment by the brushwriter rather than a measured calculation. Some Roman inscriptions even contain minute particles of red paint that have adhered to the stone through the centuries, leaving little doubt that the carved letters were

2–16

2–17

2–18

2–16. Etruscan Bucchero vase, seventh or sixth century B.C. A prototype of the educational toy, this rooster-shaped toy jug is inscribed with the Etruscan alphabet.

2–17. Carved inscription from the base of Trajan's column, c. A.D. 114. Located in Trajan's forum in Rome, this masterful example of *capitalis monumentalis* gives silent testimony to the ancient Roman dictum "the written word remains."

2–18. Detail, inscription on a tomb along the Appian Way, Rome. The controlled brush drawing of the forms on the stone combines with the precision of the stonemason's craft to create letterforms of majestic proportion and harmonious form.

painted with red pigment. Monumental capitals were carved as wedge-shaped troughs. The edges of the letterforms were not at sharp ninety-degree angles from the flat surface of the stone; rather, a more gentle, angled taper created a shallower edge that resisted chipping and wearing.

The Roman written hand took several forms. The most important was the *capitalis quadrata* (square capitals), a style widely used from the second century A.D. until the fifth century. Written carefully and slowly with a flat pen, square capitals (Fig. **2–19**) had stately proportions and clear legibility. The space between lines and letters was generous, but there was no space left between words. The letters were written between two horizontal baselines, and the *F* and *L* extended slightly above this line. The letter designs are quite similar to the letters we call *capitals* today. Serifs were added with the pen and strengthened the ends of the strokes.

The *capitalis rustica* (rustic capitals) were used during the same period (Fig. **2–20**). These condensed letterforms were written quickly and saved space. Parchment and papyrus were expensive, and the style enabled the writer to include half again as many letters on the page as was possible with square capitals.

As is evident from the ruins of Pompeii and Herculaneum, Roman brushwriters wrote notices (Fig. **2–21**), political campaign material, and advertising announcements on exterior walls, using both square and rustic capitals. Poster messages were also painted on reusable wooden panels placed in the streets. Placards and picture signboards were executed by professional letterers. Trademarks were widely used to identify the firm or place of origin of handcrafted products. Commercial records, documents of state, and literature were written on a variety of substrates. Papyrus from Egypt was supplemented by wood, clay, flat pieces of metal, and wax tablets held in wooden frames. Writing was scratched into wax with a stylus, the flat end of which was used to erase the writing in the soft wax so that the tablet could be used again.

Around 190 B.C. *parchment* came into common use as a substrate for writing. Tradition holds that Ptolemy V (ruled c. 205–181 B.C.) of Alexandria and King Eumenes II (ruled 197–160 B.C.) of Pergamum were engaged in a fierce library-building rivalry; therefore, Ptolemy placed an embargo on papyrus shipments to prevent Eumenes from continuing his rapid production of scrolls. Parchment, a writing surface made from the skins of domestic animals—particularly calves, sheep,

2–19

2–20

2–19. *Capitalis quadrata* (square capitals) from a manuscript, Vergil, c. A.D. 400. The flat pen held at an angle produced thick and thin strokes and serifs.

2–20. *Capitalis rustica* (rustic capitals) from a manuscript, Vergil, c. A.D. 400. The flat-nibbed pen was held in an almost vertical position, creating a staccato rhythm of thin verticals contrasting with elliptical round and arched diagonal strokes.

2–21. Wall writing from Pompeii, first century A.D. Over sixteen hundred messages ranging from passages from Vergil to crude obscenities were preserved under more than 3.6 meters (12 feet) of volcanic ash.

2–21

and goats—was invented to overcome the embargo. These refined leather sheets are made by first washing the skin and removing all hair or wool. Then the skin is stretched tightly on a frame and scraped to remove all traces of hair and flesh. After being whitened with chalk, it is smoothed with pumice. Larger, smoother, and more durable and flexible than papyrus sheets, parchment became very popular as a writing surface. *Vellum,* the finest parchment, is made from the smooth skins of newborn calves.

The *codex,* a revolutionary design format, began to supplant the scroll (called a *rotulus*) in Rome and Greece, beginning about the time of Christ. Parchment was gathered in signatures of two, four, or eight sheets. These were folded, stitched, and combined into codices with pages like a modern book. The parchment codex had several advantages over the papyrus scroll. The clumsy process of unrolling and rolling scrolls to look up information yielded to the quick process of opening a codex to the desired page. Papyrus was too fragile to be folded into pages, and the vertical strips on the back of a papyrus scroll made writing on both sides impractical. Both sides of the parchment pages in a codex could be used for writing; this saved storage space and material costs.

During the rise of Christianity, from after A.D. 1 until around A.D. 400, scrolls and codices were used concurrently. The durability and permanence of the codex appealed to Christians because their writings were considered sacred. With a whole pantheon of gods and little clear distinction between god and man, pagan scholars were less inclined to revere their religious writings. Traditionally, pagan writings were on scrolls. Christians were also involved in the comparative study of different texts. It is easy to have several codices open on a table but virtually impossible to have several scrolls unrolled for comparative reference. Christians sought the codex format to distance themselves from the pagan scroll; pagans clung to their scrolls in resistance to Christianity. Graphic format thereby became a symbol of religious belief during the late decades of the Roman Empire. Christianity, adopted as Rome's state religion in A.D. 325 by the Emperor Constantine (d. A.D. 337), elevated books and writing to a position of far greater importance than their previous roles in the ancient world.

In the first century A.D. Rome began to experience hostile actions from tribal peoples (called Barbarians by the Greeks) living beyond the Danube and Rhine rivers. In A.D. 325, Emperor Constantine moved the capital from Rome to the Greek town of Byzantium (later renamed Constantinople), located astride the mouth of the Black Sea. This weakened the western provinces, and the warlike Huns began to put great pressure on Rome's immediate neighbors. The Roman Empire was permanently divided in half in A.D. 395, and Rome itself was sacked by the Visigoths in A.D. 410. The emperor

moved his court to Ravenna, which became the capital of the Western Roman Empire until it fell in A.D. 476, marking the final dissolution of the Roman Empire. Rome's legacy includes architecture, engineering, language, law, and literature. Its alphabet became the design form for visible languages in the Western world.

The Korean alphabet

The Korean monarch Sejong (A.D. 1397–1450) introduced Hangul, the Korean alphabet, by royal decree in 1446. Hangul is one of the most scientific writing systems ever invented. Although the spoken Korean and Chinese languages are totally different, Koreans were using the complex Chinese characters for their written language. Sejong developed a simple vernacular alphabet of fourteen consonant and ten vowel signs to put literacy within the grasp of ordinary Korean citizens. He assembled a team of gifted young scholars to undertake a systematic study of existing writing systems and develop an innovative visible language.

Fourteen consonants (Fig. **2–22**) are represented by abstract depictions of the position of the mouth and tongue when they are spoken, and these are placed in five groups of related sounds. Ten vowels (Fig. **2–23**) are signified by dots positioned next to horizontal or vertical lines. The vertical line symbolizes a person, the horizontal line signifies the earth, and the round dot is seen as a symbol of heaven.

The Hangul alphabet is not written in a linear sequence in the manner of Greek and Roman alphabets; rather, letters are combined within an imaginary rectangle to form syllabic blocks. These syllables are made by combining at least a consonant and a vowel (Fig. **2–24**). Syllables containing a vertical vowel sign are composed and read horizontally from left to right, while those containing a horizontal vowel are composed and read vertically from top to bottom. Complex syllables are made by adding letters to the simple syllables or by combining elementary syllables into more complex configurations. Hangul's uniqueness among written languages stems in part from this system of clustering alphabet characters to construct syllables. In contemporary Korea the twenty-four letters are used to make over two thousand common syllables in everyday use.

Just as the invention of printing launched a quiet revolution in Chinese culture, alphabetic writing on papyrus slowly transformed Western society. Alphabetic writing was spread throughout the world by conquering armies, traders, and especially religious missionaries. Easy to write and learn, systems of simple signs for elementary sounds made literacy availableto large numbers of people. Alphabets are democratic writing; they put literacy within the reach of ordinary people, in contrast to the theocratic writing of the temple priests of Mesopotamia and Egypt. As scribes and priests lost their monopolies on written knowledge, their political power and influence declined. Secular and military leaders came to the fore as helmsmen in the classical world of Greece and Rome.

Alphabets remain one of humankind's grandest achievements. Alphabetic writing became the mortar binding whole communities against limitations imposed by memory, time, and place. Greater access to information permitted broader participation in public affairs.

	mouth	tongue-tip	tooth	velar	throat
Symbolization of the speech organs					
Basic letters	ㅁ	ㄴ	ㅅ	ㄱ	ㅇ
Addition of a stroke	ㅂ	ㄷ	ㅈ		
Addition of a stroke	ㅍ	ㅌ	ㅊ	ㅋ	ㅎ
Modification of basic letters		ㄹ			

2–22

2–22. Hangul consonants signify the structure of the mouth when speaking Korean.

2–23. Ten Hangul vowels are signified by the placement of dots adjacent to vertical or horizontal lines.

2–24. This matrix shows how individual Hangul characters are combined into blocks to correspond to spoken syllables in the Korean language.

Symbol of Man Vertical line	Symbol of Earth Horizontal line	Symbol of Heaven Round dot
│	▬	●
ㅏ	ㅗ	.
ㅑ	ㅛ	
ㅓ	ㅜ	
ㅕ	ㅠ	

2–23

consonants＼vowels	ㅏ	ㅑ	ㅓ	ㅕ	ㅗ	ㅛ	ㅜ	ㅠ	ㅡ	ㅣ
ㄱ	가	갸	거	겨	고	교	구	규	그	기
ㄴ	나	냐	너	녀	노	뇨	누	뉴	느	니
ㅇ	다	댜	더	뎌	도	됴	두	듀	드	디
ㄹ	라	랴	러	려	로	료	루	류	르	리
ㅁ	마	먀	머	며	모	묘	무	뮤	므	미
ㅂ	바	뱌	버	벼	보	뵤	부	뷰	브	비
ㅅ	사	샤	서	셔	소	쇼	수	슈	스	시
ㅇ	아	야	어	여	오	요	우	유	으	이
ㅈ	자	쟈	저	져	조	죠	주	쥬	즈	지
ㅊ	차	챠	처	쳐	초	쵸	추	츄	츠	치
ㅋ	카	캬	커	켜	코	쿄	쿠	큐	크	키
ㅌ	타	탸	터	텨	토	툐	투	튜	트	티
ㅍ	파	퍄	퍼	펴	포	표	푸	퓨	프	피
ㅎ	하	햐	허	혀	호	효	후	휴	흐	히

2–24

The Asian Contribution

3

Western civilization dawned from obscure sources along the banks of the Tigris and Euphrates rivers in Mesopotamia and along the course of the Nile River in Egypt. The origins of the extraordinary civilization that developed in the vast, ancient land of China are shrouded in similar mystery. Legend suggests that by the year 2000 B.C. a culture was evolving in virtual isolation from the pockets of civilization in the West. Among the many innovations developed by the ancient Chinese, some changed the course of human events. The compass made exploration and seafaring possible. Gunpowder, used by the Chinese for fireworks, fueled a warlike aspect of the human temperament and changed the nature of war. Chinese calligraphy, an ancient writing system, is used today by more people than any other visual language system. Paper, a magnificent and economical substrate for transmitting information, and printing, the duplication of words and images, made possible the wide communication of thought and deed. Europeans adopted these Chinese inventions and used them to conquer much of the world: The compass (which may have been developed independently in Europe) directed early explorers across the seas and around the globe; firearms enabled Europeans to subjugate the native populations of Africa, Asia, and the Americas; and printing on paper became the method for spreading European language, culture, religion, and law throughout the world.

Chinese calligraphy

Similar to Egyptian hieroglyphics and Mayan writing in Central America, the Chinese writing system is a purely visual language. It is not alphabetical, and every symbol is composed of a number of differently shaped lines within an imaginary square. Legend holds that Chinese was first written about 1800 B.C. by Tsang Chieh, who was inspired to invent writing by contemplating the claw marks of birds and footprints of animals. Tsang Chieh proceeded to develop elementary pictographs of things in nature. These images are highly stylized and composed of a minimum number of lines, but they are easily deciphered. The Chinese sacrificed the realism found in hieroglyphs for more abstract designs.

Aesthetic considerations seem to have interested the Chinese from the early beginnings of their writing. Simple nouns were developed first, and the written language slowly matured and became enriched as characters were invented to express feelings, actions, colors, sizes, and types. Chinese characters are logograms, graphic signs that represent an entire word. (The sign $, for instance, is a logogram representing the word *dollar*). Ideographs and phonetic loans—borrowing the sign of a similar-sounding word—were developed, but written Chinese was never broken down into syllable signs, like cuneiform, or alphabetic signs for elementary sounds. Therefore, there is no direct relationship between the spoken and written Chinese languages. Both are independent systems for conveying thought: a sound from the mouth to the ear, and a sign from the hand to the eye. Learning the total vocabulary of forty-four thousand characters was the sign of wisdom and scholarship. The Japanese adapted the Chinese logograms for their written language despite the great differences between the two spoken languages. Similarly, different spoken Chinese dialects are written with the same logograms.

The earliest known Chinese writing is called *chiaku-wen,* or "bone-and-shell" script (Figs. **3–1** and **3–2**), used from 1800 to 1200 B.C. It was closely bound to the art of divination, an effort to foretell future events through communication with the gods or long-dead ancestors. This ancient writing—as with hieroglyphics and cuneiform—was pictographic. Chinese pictographs are found incised on tortoise shells and large animals' flat shoulder bones, called oracle bones, which convey communications between the living and the dead. When one wished to consult an exalted ancestor or a god, the royal diviner was asked to inscribe the message on a polished animal bone. The diviner pushed a red-hot metal bar into a hole in the inscribed bone, and the heat produced an intricate web of cracks. The diviner then read or interpreted these cracks, which were believed to be messages from the dead.

The next phase of Chinese calligraphy, called *chin-wen,* or "bronze" script, consisted of inscriptions on cast-bronze objects, including food and water vessels, musical instruments, weapons, mirrors, coins, and seals. Messages were inscribed in the casting molds to preserve answers received

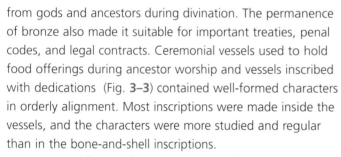

3–1

3–2

3–1. The top row of pictographs are *chiaku-wen,* or bone-and-shell script, attributed to the legendary Tsang Chieh. The lower row shows the same words from Li Ssu's unified *hsiao chuan,* or small-seal style. From left: sun, moon, water, rain, wood, and dog.

3–2. Oracle bone inscribed with *chiaku-wen,* or bone-and-shell script, c. 1300 B.C. The 128 characters inscribed on this scapula concern a diviner's predictions of calamities during the next ten-day period.

from gods and ancestors during divination. The permanence of bronze also made it suitable for important treaties, penal codes, and legal contracts. Ceremonial vessels used to hold food offerings during ancestor worship and vessels inscribed with dedications (Fig. **3–3**) contained well-formed characters in orderly alignment. Most inscriptions were made inside the vessels, and the characters were more studied and regular than in the bone-and-shell inscriptions.

Artists in different places developed different writing styles until Chinese calligraphy was unified under the powerful emperor Shih Huang Ti (c. 259–210 B.C.). During his reign Confucian scholars were buried alive and their books burned. Thousands of lives were sacrificed building the Great Wall of China to protect the emperor and his empire. But he also unified the Chinese people into one nation and issued royal decrees standardizing weights, measures, the axle length on carts, laws, and writing. Prime minister Li Ssu (c. 280–208 B.C.) was charged with designing the new writing style. This third phase in the design evolution of Chinese calligraphy is called *hsiao chuan,* or "small-seal" style (see Fig. **3–1**). The lines are drawn in thicker, more even strokes. More curves and circles are used in this graceful, flowing style, which is much more abstract than the earlier two styles. Each character is neatly balanced and fills its imaginary square primly.

The final step in the evolution of Chinese calligraphy is *chen-shu* (also, *kai-shu,* or "regular" style) (Fig. **3–4**), which has been in continuous use for nearly two thousand years. In regular style, every line, dot, and nuance of the brush can be controlled by the sensitivity and skill of the calligrapher. An infinite range of

design possibilities exists within every word. Structure, composition, shape, stroke thickness, and the relationship of strokes to each other and to the white spaces surrounding them are design factors determined by the writer. Regular-style calligraphy has an abstract beauty that rivals humanity's highest attainments in art and design. Indeed, it is considered the highest art form in China, more important even than painting. Oriental painting and calligraphy have close bonds. Both are executed with ink on paper or silk using gestured strokes of the brush.

The evolution of Chinese writing can be traced from its pictographic origins through one of the early characters—for example, the prehistoric character for the three-legged pot called a *li,* which is now the word for tripod (Fig. **3–5**). The *li* was an innovative product design, for the black discolorations on some surviving examples indicate that it stood in the fire to heat its contents rapidly. In the oracle-bone script, it was an easily recognized pictograph. In the 1000 B.C. bronze script, this character had evolved into a simpler form. The regular-style character echoes the three-part bottom and flat top of the earlier forms.

The painting of bamboo from the *Album of Eight Leaves* (Fig. **3–6**) by Li Fangying (A.D. 1695–1754) shows how the vividly descriptive strokes with a bamboo brush join calligraphy and painting, poem and illustration, into a unified communication. Nature is the inspiration for both, and every stroke and dot is given the energy of a living thing. Children begin their early training by drawing bamboo leaves and stems with the brush to learn the basic strokes.

Spiritual states and deep feelings can be expressed in calligraphy. Thick, languid strokes become mournful, and poems

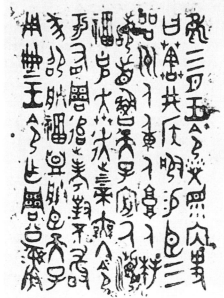

3–3

3–3. Four-handled vessel with *chin-wen,* or bronze script, inscription, eleventh century B.C. Bold, regular strokes are used to form the sixty-four characters of an eight-line dedication, which itself forms a rectangle in the vessel's bottom.

3–4. This actual-size detail from a Chinese poem is an excellent example of *chen-shu,* or regular-style, calligraphy. Two signature seals at lower left are chops, discussed later in this chapter.

3–4

3–5

3–6

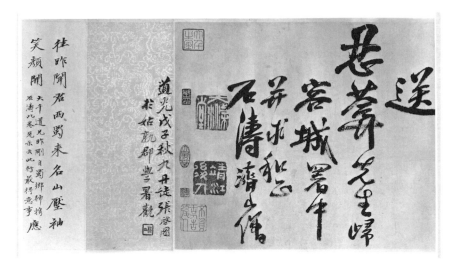

3–7

3–5. *Li* (three-legged pottery vessel), late Neolithic period. The evolution of the calligraphic character *Li* stemmed from this pot: oracle bone pictograph, bronze script, 1000 B.C., and regular style, 200 B.C.

3–6. Li Fangying, from *Album of Eight Leaves*, number six, 1744. The design of the total page, with the bamboo bending out into the open space in contrast to the erect column of writing, is striking.

3–7. Shitao Yuanji, *Mountain and River Landscape*, detail of scroll, Qing dynasty. The visual design qualities of calligraphy—from delicate and lacy to thunderous and bold—are contrasted in this scroll.

3–8. Chinese chop. The traditional Chinese identification stamp is inscribed into the bottom of a small decorative sculpture carved from soft stone.

written in celebration of spring have a light exuberance. A master calligrapher was once asked why he dug his ink-stained fingers so deeply into the hairs of his brush. He replied that only then could he feel the Tao (cosmic spirit that operates throughout the universe in animate and inanimate things) flow from his arm, into the brush, and onto the paper.

Calligraphy was said to have bones (authority and size), meat (the proportion of the characters), blood (the texture of the fluid ink), and muscle (spirit and vital force). The exuberant *Mountain and River Landscape* (Fig. **3–7**), by master calligrapher Shitao Yuanji (A.D. 1630–c. 1707), shows just how dynamic and inventive calligraphy can be, with broad strokes thrusting down the page in contrast to lively, delicate strokes of smaller characters. It demonstrates the ability of Chinese calligraphy to evoke natural objects, forming movement and energy into an organic whole.

The invention of paper

Dynastic records attribute the invention of paper to the eunuch and high governmental official Ts'ai Lun, who reported his invention to Emperor Ho in A.D. 105. Whether Ts'ai Lun truly invented paper, perfected an earlier invention, or patronized its invention is not known. He was, however, deified as the god of the papermakers.

In earlier times the Chinese wrote on bamboo slats or wooden strips using a bamboo pen with a dense and durable ink, the origins of which are obscure. Lampblack or soot was deposited on a dome-shaped cover over a vessel of oil with several burning wicks. The lampblack was collected, mixed thoroughly with a gum solution using a mortar and pestle, and then molded into sticks or cubes. For writing, such a stick or cube was returned to the liquid state by rubbing it in water on an inking stone. The strips of wood were used for short

3–8

messages; 23-centimeter (about 9-inch) pieces of bamboo tied together with leather strips or silk string were used for longer communications. Although these substrates were abundant and easy to prepare, they were heavy. After the invention of woven silk cloth, it too was used as a writing surface. However, it was very costly.

Ts'ai Lun's process for making paper continued almost unchanged until papermaking was mechanized in nineteenth-century England. Natural fibers, including mulberry bark, hemp fishnets, and rags, were soaked in a vat of water and beaten into a pulp with pounding mortars. A vat-man dipped a screen-bottomed, framelike mold into the pulp solution, taking just enough onto the mold for the sheet of paper. With skill and split-second judgment, the vat-man raised the mold from the vat while oscillating and shaking it to cross and mesh the fibers as the water drained through the bottom. Then the paper was couched, or pressed onto a woolen cloth, to which it adhered while it dried. The mold was free for immediate reuse. The couched sheets were stacked, pressed, and then hung to dry. The first major improvement in the process was the use of starch sizing or gelatin to stiffen and strengthen the paper and increase its ability to absorb ink.

In paper's early decades some ancient Chinese considered it a cheap substitute for silk or bamboo, but as time went on, its light weight, economical manufacture, and versatility overcame all reservations. The coarse, long-fibered quality of early paper caused no problems, because the hair brush, invented many centuries earlier, was the primary writing instrument. Scrolls for writing were made by gluing together sheets of paper, sometimes delicately stained slate blue, lemon yellow, or a pale, warm yellow. These sheets were rolled onto dowels of sandalwood or ivory that were sometimes tipped with jade or amber. In addition to writing on it, the Chinese used their new material as wrapping paper, wallpaper, toilet paper, and napkins.

The discovery of printing

Printing, a major breakthrough in human history, was invented by the Chinese. The first form was relief printing; the spaces around an image on a flat surface are cut away, the remaining raised surface is inked, and a sheet of paper is placed over the surface and rubbed to transfer the inked image to the paper. Two hypotheses have been advanced about the invention of printing. One is that the use of engraved seals to make identification imprints evolved into printing. As early as the third century B.C. seals or stamps were used to make impressions in soft clay. Often, bamboo or wood strips bearing writing were wrapped in silk, which was then sealed by clay stamped with an impression.

During the Han Dynasty (third century A.D.) seals called chops (Fig. **3–8**) were made by carving calligraphic characters into a flat surface of jade, silver, gold, or ivory. The user inked this flat surface by pressing it into a pastelike red ink made from cinnabar, then pressed onto a substrate to form an impression, as one does with present-day rubber stamps. The impression was a red shape with white characters. Around A.D. 500 chops came into use upon which the artisan had cut away the negative area surrounding the characters so that they could be printed in red surrounded by white paper (see Fig. **3–4**). The fundamental technique for block printing was now available. Yuan Chao Meng-fu's fourteenth-century painting of a goat and sheep (Fig. **3–9**) has both types of chops imprinted upon its surface: white characters reversed from a solid ground and solid characters surrounded by a white ground.

The second theory about the origins of printing focuses on the early Chinese practice of making inked rubbings from inscriptions carved in stone (Fig. **3–10**). Beginning in A.D. 165 Confucian classics were carved into stone to ensure an accurate, permanent record. The disadvantages of these stone

3–9

3–10

3–9. Yuan Chao Meng-fu, *A goat and sheep*, fourteenth century A.D. Chops were used to imprint the names of owners or viewers of a painting.

3–10. Buddhist dedicatory stela, c. A.D. 562. This votive limestone tablet illustrates the early Chinese practice of permanently and accurately rendering inscriptions by carving them on stone.

3–11. Chinese relief tomb sculpture and rubbing, northern Qi dynasty (A.D. 550–577). Illustrative images from the life of the deceased are captured in stone and with ink on paper.

"books" were their weight and the space they required. One historical work required thirteen acres for storage of the tablets, which were arranged like rows of tombstones. Soon, copies of these inscriptions were pulled by making ink rubbings. A damp sheet of thin paper was laid on the stone. The paper was pressed into the depressions of the inscription with a stiff brush. Then, an inked cloth pad was lightly rubbed over the surface to produce an ink image from the incised inscription. Although the ink was applied to the top of the paper rather than to the relief image in this method, the process is related to relief printing.

As early as the second century A.D. rubbings were also made from stone relief sculptures carved as offering shrines and tombs (Fig. **3–11**). In a sense, these reliefs were closer to painting than to sculpture, for the figures crowding the complex designs were handled as flat silhouettes with linear detail and very little spatial depth. In retrospect, these votive and tomb carvings resemble neither sculpture nor painting as much as they do relief woodblock printing plates.

3–11

Whether relief printing evolved from chops, rubbings from stone inscriptions, or a synthesis of both is not known. Just who invented relief printing and when and where it began remain a mystery. The route is marked by undated relics: printed fabrics, stencil pictures, and thousands of stamped impressions of the Buddha figure. By about A.D. 770, when the earliest existing datable relief printing was produced, the technique was well developed. Using a brush and ink, the material to be printed was prepared on a sheet of thin paper. Calligraphy was written, images were drawn. The block cutter applied this thin page to the smooth wooden block, image side down, after wetting the surface with a paste or sizing. When the paste or sizing was thoroughly dry, the paper was carefully rubbed off. A faint inked imprint of the image, which was now reversed, remained on the surface of the block.

Working with amazing speed and accuracy, the block cutter carved away the surface around the inked image, leaving it in high relief. The printer inked the raised surface, applied a sheet of paper over it, then rubbed the back of the paper with a rubber or stiff brush to transfer the ink to the page, which was then lifted from the block. So efficient was this method that a skilled printer could pull over two hundred impressions per hour.

During the eighth century Chinese culture and the Buddhist religion were exported to Japan, where the earliest surviving datable printing was produced. Mindful of the terrible smallpox epidemic three decades earlier, the Japanese empress Shotoku

decreed that one million copies of Buddhist *dharani* (charms) be printed and placed inside one million miniature pagodas about 11.5 centimeters (4 inches) tall (Fig. **3–12**). The empress was attempting to follow the teachings of Buddha, who had advised his followers to write seventy-seven copies of a *dharani* and place them in a pagoda, or place each one in its own small clay pagoda. This would lengthen one's life and eventually lead to paradise. Empress Shotoku's efforts failed, for she died about the time the charms were being distributed, rolled up in their little three-story wooden pagodas. But the sheer number produced, combined with their sacred value, enabled numerous copies to survive to this day.

The oldest surviving printed manuscript is the Diamond Sutra (Fig. **3–13**). It consists of seven sheets of paper pasted together to form a scroll 4.9 meters (16 feet) long and 30.5 centimeters (12 inches) high. Six sheets of text convey Buddha's revelations to his elderly follower Subhuti; the seventh is a complex linear woodcut illustration of the Buddha and his disciples. Buddha decreed that "whosoever repeats this text shall be edified." Apparently one Wang Chieh responded to the Buddha's charge, for the final lines of text declare that he made the Diamond Sutra for wide, free distribution to honor his parents on the date equivalent to 11 May, A.D. 868. The excellence of the printing indicates that the craft had advanced to a high level by the time it was produced.

During the early ninth century A.D. the Chinese government began to issue paper certificates of deposit to merchants who

3–12

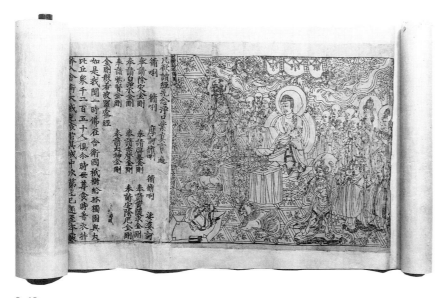

3–13

3–12. Buddhist charms called *dharani*, c. A.D. 770. Rolled up and inserted in little pagodas, these early specimens of relief printing had the text printed in Chinese calligraphy on one side and in Sanskrit on the other.

3–13. The Diamond Sutra, A.D. 868. Wang Chieh sought spiritual improvement by commissioning the duplication of the Diamond Sutra by printing; the wide spread of knowledge was almost incidental.

3–14. Chinese woodblock print, c. A.D. 950. A prayer text is placed below an illustration of Manjusri, the Buddhist personification of supreme wisdom, riding a lion.

3–15. Pages from the *Pen ts'ao,* A.D. 1249. In this illustrated wood block book on Chinese herbal medicine, generous margins and ruled lines bring order to the page.

deposited metal currency with the state. When a critical provincial shortage of iron money developed shortly before the year 1000, paper money was designed, printed, and used in lieu of metal coins. The government took control of the currency's production, and millions of notes per year were printed. Inflation and devaluation soon followed, as did efforts to restore confidence: money was printed on perfumed paper of high silk content, some money was printed on colored paper, and the penalty for counterfeiting was death. China thus became the first society in which ordinary people had daily contact with printed images. In addition to paper money, block prints bearing religious images and texts received wide distribution (Fig. **3–14**).

During the tenth century, errors in the Confucian classics came to light. Chinese prime minister Fang Tao became

deeply concerned and felt that new master texts should be made. Lacking the resources needed for extensive cutting of stone inscriptions, Fang Tao turned to the rapidly developing block-printing method for this monumental task. With the great scholars of the age as editors and a famous calligrapher overseeing the writing of the master copies, producing the 130 volumes of the nine Confucian classics with their commentaries took twenty-one years, A.D. 933–953. Although the original goal was not spreading knowledge to the masses but authenticating the texts, Fang Tao took a fairly obscure craft and thrust it into the mainstream of Chinese civilization.

The scroll was replaced with paged formats in the ninth or tenth century. First, folded books that opened accordion-style were made. These resembled scrolls that were folded like a railroad timetable instead of rolled. In the tenth or eleventh

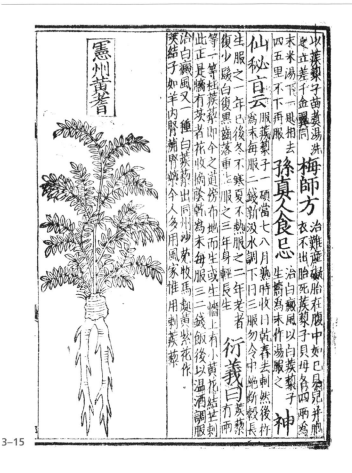

3–15

3–14

century stitched books were developed. Two pages of text were printed from one block. Then the sheet was folded down the middle with the unprinted side of the sheet facing inward and the two printed pages facing out. Sequences of these folded and printed sheets were gathered and sewn to make a codex-style book. The pages of the *Pen ts'ao* medical herbal (Fig. **3–15**) were assembled in this fashion. Illustrations and calligraphy were used for headings. A design used to separate the text into sections was shown in the center of the right-hand page.

Another early form of Chinese graphic design and printing was playing cards (Fig. **3–16**). These "sheet dice" were first printed on heavy paper cards about the time paged books were replacing manuscript scrolls.

A benchmark in block printing—reproducing beautiful calligraphy with perfection—was established in China by A.D. 1000 and has never been surpassed. The calligrapher was listed with the author and printer in the colophon. State printers were joined by private printers as histories and herbals, science and political science, poetry and prose were carved onto blocks of wood and printed. The quiet revolution that printing wrought upon Chinese intellectual life brought about a renaissance of learning and culture just as surely as Johann Gutenberg's invention of movable type in the West did more than five hundred years later.

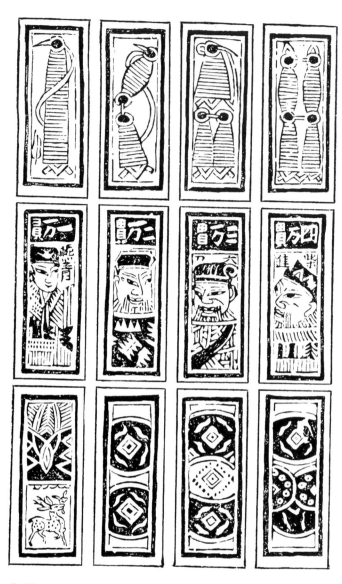

3–16

The invention of movable type

In a woodblock print, such as Figure 3–14, the wood around each calligraphic character is painstakingly cut away. Around A.D. 1045 the Chinese alchemist Pi Sheng (A.D. 1023–63) extended this process by developing the concept of movable type, an innovative process never used widely in Asia. If each character were an individual raised form, he reasoned, then any number of characters could be placed in sequence on a surface, inked, and printed. He made his types from a mixture of clay and glue. These three-dimensional calligraphic characters were baked over a straw fire until they hardened. To compose a text, Pi Sheng placed them side by side upon an iron plate coated with a waxy substance to hold the characters in place. The plate was gently heated to soften the wax, and a flat board was pressed upon the types to push them firmly in place and equalize their height from the surface of the form. After the wax cooled, the page of calligraphic types was printed exactly like a woodblock. After the printing was complete, the form was heated again to loosen the wax so that the characters could be filed in wooden cases.

Because Chinese writing is not alphabetical, types were organized according to rhymes. The large number of characters in Asian languages made filing and retrieving the characters difficult. Later, the Chinese cast letters in tin and cut them from wood (Fig. **3–17**), but movable type never replaced the handcut woodblock in the Orient.

A notable effort to print from bronze movable type began in Korea under government sponsorship in A.D. 1403. Characters cut from beech wood were pressed into a trough filled with fine sand, making a negative impression. A cover

3–17

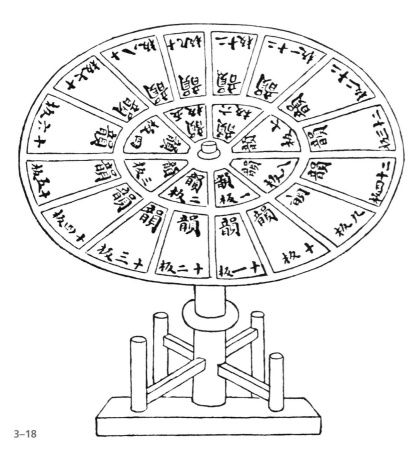

3–18

3–16. Chinese playing cards, undated. Many of the design conventions used here—numerical sequences of images signifying the suits and the depiction of royalty—survive in playing cards to this day.

3–17. Chinese movable types, c. 1300 B.C. This group of carved wood types ranges in size from about 1.25 to 2.5 centimeters (½ to 1 inch) in height.

3–18. Woodblock image of a revolving typecase, c. A.D. 1313. This quaintly stylized illustration shows the revolving case designed to make typesetting more efficient.

with holes was placed over the impression, and molten bronze was poured into it. After the bronze cooled, a type character was formed. These metal characters were, of course, less fragile than Pi Sheng's earthenware types.

It is curious that movable type was first invented in cultures whose written language systems numbered not in the hundreds but in the thousands of characters. With a total of more than 44,000 characters, it is not surprising that movable type never came into widespread use in the Far East. One interesting effort to simplify sorting and setting types was the invention of a revolving "lazy Susan" table with a spinning tabletop

2.13 meters (7 feet) in diameter (Fig. **3–18**). The compositor could sit at this table and rotate it to bring the section with the character within reach.

The Chinese contribution to the evolution of visual communications was formidable. During Europe's thousand-year medieval period, China's invention of paper and printing spread slowly westward, arriving in Europe just as the Renaissance began. This transitional period in European history began in fourteenth-century Italy and was marked by a rediscovery of classical knowledge, a flowering of the arts, and the beginnings of modern science. All were aided by printing.

Illuminated Manuscripts

4

The vibrant luminosity of gold leaf, as it reflected light from the pages of handwritten books, gave the sensation of the page being literally illuminated; this dazzling effect gave birth to the term *illuminated manuscript*. Today this name is used for all decorated and illustrated handwritten books produced from the late Roman Empire until printed books replaced manuscripts after typography was developed in Europe around A.D.1450. Two great traditions of manuscript illumination are the Eastern in Islamic countries and the Western in Europe, dating from classical antiquity. Sacred writings held great meaning for Christians, Jews, and Muslims. The use of visual embellishment to expand the word became very important, and illuminated manuscripts were produced with extraordinary care and design sensitivity.

Manuscript production was costly and time-consuming. Parchment or vellum took hours to prepare, and a large book might require the skins of three hundred sheep. Black ink for lettering was prepared from fine soot or lampblack. Gum and water were mixed with sanguine or red chalk to produce a red ink for headings and paragraph marks. A brown ink was formulated from "irongall," a mixture of iron sulfate and oak apples, which are oak galls caused by wasp larvae. Colors were created from a variety of mineral, animal, and vegetable matter. A vibrant, deep blue was made from lapis lazuli, a precious mineral mined only in Afghanistan that found its way to monasteries as far away as Ireland. Gold (and, less frequently, silver) was applied in two ways: sometimes it was ground into a powder and mixed into a gold paint, but this left a slightly grainy surface, so the preferred application method was hammering the gold into a fine sheet of gold leaf and applying it over an adhesive ground. Burnishing for texture, punching, and tooling with metalworking tools were often used on gold leaf for design effects. Books were bound between wooden boards usually covered with leather. Decorative patterns were applied by tooling the leather, and important liturgical manuscripts often had precious jewels, gold- and silverwork, enameled designs, or ivory carving on their covers.

During the early Christian era, nearly all books were created in the monastic *scriptorium*, or writing room. The head of the scriptorium was the *scrittori*, a well-educated scholar who understood Greek and Latin and functioned as both editor and art director, with overall responsibility for the design and production of the manuscripts. The *copisti* was a production letterer, who spent his days bent over a writing table penning page after page in a trained lettering style. The *illuminator*, or illustrator, was an artist responsible for the execution of ornament and image in visual support of the text. The word was supreme, and the scrittori controlled the scriptorium. He laid out the pages to indicate where illustrations were to be added after the text was written. Sometimes this was done with a light sketch, but often a note jotted in the margin told the illustrator what to draw in the space.

The *colophon* of a manuscript or book is an inscription, usually at the end, containing facts about its production. Often the scribe, designer, or, later, printer is identified. A number of colophons describe the work of the copisti as difficult and tiring. In the colophon of one illuminated manuscript, a scribe named George declared, "As the sailor longs for a safe haven at the end of his voyage, so does the writer for the last word." Another scribe, Prior Petris, described writing as a terrible ordeal that "dims your eyes, makes your back ache, and knits one's chest and stomach together" The reader was then advised to turn the pages carefully and to keep his finger far from the text.

In addition to preserving classical literature, the scribes working in medieval monasteries invented musical notation. Leo Treitler describes this in his book *With Voice and Pen: Coming to Know the Medieval Song and How It Was Made* (Oxford, 2003). As early as the ninth century punctuation marks were gradually used to denote pauses and pitch changes for chants, eventually arriving at the five line staff. Lance Hidy aptly noted that in addition to the Carolingian minuscule and the adaptation of Arabic numerals, musical notation is one of the most important contributions of medieval graphic design.

The illustration and ornamentation were not mere decoration. The monastic leaders were mindful of the educational value of pictures and the ability of ornament to create mystical and spiritual overtones. Most illuminated manuscripts were small enough to fit into a saddlebag. This portability enabled the transmission of knowledge and ideas from one region to another and one time period to another. Manuscript production over the thousand-year course of the medieval era created a vast vocabulary of graphic forms, page layouts, illustration and lettering styles, and techniques. Regional isolation and difficult travel caused innovation and influences to spread very slowly, so identifiable regional design styles emerged. Some of the more distinctive schools of manuscript production can be ranked as major innovations in graphic design.

The classical style

In classical antiquity, the Greeks and Romans designed and illustrated manuscripts, but few have survived. The Egyptian Book of the Dead was probably an influence. The fabulous Greek library at Alexandria, where late Egyptian culture met early classical culture, presumably contained many illustrated manuscripts. A fire during the time of Julius Caesar (100–44 B.C.) destroyed this great library and its seven hundred thousand scrolls. In the few surviving fragments of illustrated scrolls, the layout approach features numerous small illustrations drawn with a crisp, simple technique and inserted throughout the text. Their frequency creates a cinematic graphic sequence somewhat like the contemporary comic book.

The invention of parchment, which was so much more durable than papyrus, and the codex format, which could take thicker paint because it did not have to be rolled, opened new possibilities for design and illustration. Literary sources refer to manuscripts on vellum, with a portrait of the author as a *frontispiece*.

The earliest surviving illustrated manuscript from the late antique and early Christian era is the Vatican Vergil. Created in the late fourth century or early fifth century A.D., this volume contains two major works by Rome's greatest poet, Publius Vergilius Maro (70–19 B.C.): his *Georgics,* poems on farming and country life; and the *Aeneid*, an epic narrative about Aeneas, who left the flaming ruins of Troy and set out to found a new city in the west. In this illustration (Fig. **4–1**) two scenes depicting the demise of Laocoön, a priest punished by death for profaning the temple of Apollo, are shown in sequence within one image. At left, Laocoön calmly prepares to sacrifice a bull at the temple of Poseidon, oblivious to the approach of two serpents in the lake at the upper left corner. On the right, Laocoön and his two young sons are attacked and killed by the serpents.

A consistent design approach is used in the Vatican Vergil. The text is lettered in crisp rustic capitals, with one wide column on each page. Illustrations, framed in bright bands of color (frequently red), are the same width as the text column.

4–1

4–1. The Vatican Vergil, The death of Laocoön, early fifth century A.D. Two scenes from the life of Laocoön are shown in one illustration.

These are placed at the top, middle, or bottom of the page, adjacent to the passage illustrated. There are six full-page illustrations, and the illustrator neatly lettered the names of the major figures upon their pictures in the manner of present-day political cartoonists.

The Vatican Vergil is completely Roman and pagan in its conception and execution. The lettering is Roman, and the illustrations echo the rich colors and illusionistic space of the wall frescoes preserved at Pompeii. This pictorial and historical method of book illustration, so similar to late Roman painting, combined with rustic capitals, represents the *classical style*. It was used in many early Christian manuscripts and characterizes late Roman book design.

After the Western Roman Empire collapsed in A.D. 476, an era of dislocation and uncertainty ensued. Cities degenerated and became small villages; officials left their duties and moved to their country estates; government and law ceased to exist. Trade and commerce slumped and almost became nonexistent, for travel became extremely dangerous. Europe's regional languages, customs, and geographic divisions started to form in isolated areas during this period. The general population languished in illiteracy, poverty, and superstition.

The thousand-year medieval (meaning "middle") era lasted from the fifth-century fall of Rome until the fifteenth-century

INTERUOS CONQU
DENSUNUSDETU
ΛÇISTERΛOTULIƑI

4–2

deillodixicthrquemmrtæ
utavoqminonefcquraetpat
mufecfiliufaumdicitfiauc

4–3

4–2. Uncials from the Gospel of Saint Matthew, eighth century A.D. Rounded strokes were made with the pen held in a straight horizontal position.

4–3. Half-uncials, sixth century A.D. This specimen, written in a monastery in southern Italy, demonstrates the emergence of ascenders and descenders.

4–4. The Book of Durrow, the man, symbol of Matthew, A.D. 680. As flat as a cubist painting and constructed from simple geometric forms, this figure, facing the opening of the Gospel of Saint Matthew, wears a checkered pattern of red, yellow, and green squares and tilelike patterned textures.

The evolution of letter styles was based on a continuing search for simpler and faster letterform construction and writing ease. Two important new techniques came into prominence during the course of the late antique and early Christian period. Both were primarily used within the Christian church from the fourth until the ninth century A.D. and have retained this association. As mentioned earlier, the uncials (Fig. **4–2**), so named because they were written between two guidelines that were one *uncia* (the Roman inch) apart, were actually invented by the Greeks as early as the third century B.C. In a Greek wooden tablet from A.D. 326 (see Fig. **2–12**), the primary characteristics of uncials are seen. Uncials are rounded, freely drawn majuscule letters more suited to rapid writing than either square capitals or rustic capitals. The curves reduced the number of strokes required to make many letterforms, and the number of angular joints—which have a tendency to clog or close up with ink—was significantly reduced. Certain letters in the uncial style threatened to develop *ascenders* (strokes rising above the top guideline) or *descenders* (strokes dropping below the baseline), but the design remained that of a majuscule or capital letter. A step toward the development of minuscules (small or "lowercase" letterforms) was the semiuncial or half-uncial (Fig. **4–3**). Four guidelines instead of two were used, and strokes were allowed to soar above and sink below the two principal lines, creating true ascenders and descenders. The pen was held flatly horizontal to the baseline, which gave the forms a strong vertical axis. Half-uncials were easy to write and had increased legibility because the visual differentiation between letters was improved. Although some half-uncials appeared in the third century A.D., they did not flourish until the late sixth century.

Celtic book design

The period from the collapse of Rome until the eighth century was a time of migration and upheaval throughout Europe, as different ethnic tribes fought for territory. These unsettled times were the blackest decades of the medieval era. Wandering hordes of Germanic Barbarians did not invade the island of Ireland, tucked in the far corner of Europe, and the Celts living there enjoyed relative isolation and peace. In the early fifth century A.D., the legendary Saint Patrick and other missionaries began to rapidly convert the Celts to Christianity. In a fascinating melding of culture and religion, pagan temples were converted to churches and Celtic ornaments were applied to chalices and bells brought to Ireland by the missionaries.

Celtic design is abstract and extremely complex; geometric linear patterns weave, twist, and fill a space with thick visual textures, and bright, pure colors are used in close juxtaposition. This Celtic craft tradition of intricate, highly abstract decorative

Renaissance. The centuries following the decline of Rome saw Barbarian and Roman influences combine to produce a rich and colorful design vocabulary in the arts and crafts. Although the medieval era has been called the Dark Ages, there was nothing dark about the crafts of the period. The knowledge and learning of the classical world were almost entirely lost, but the Christian belief in sacred religious writings became the primary impetus for the preservation and making of books. Christian monasteries were the cultural, educational, and intellectual centers.

As early as the third century A.D., majestic page designs were achieved in early Christian manuscripts by dyeing parchment a deep and costly purple color and lettering the text in silver and gold. The monastic graphic artists who produced these works were severely reprimanded by St. Jerome (c. A.D. 347–420), who, in his preface to a manuscript Book of Job, blasted the practice as a useless and wasteful extravagance.

4–4

Countless hours of work were lavished upon individual pages, whose vibrant color and form are in stunning contrast to the stark, reclusive environment and rule of silence found in the monastic scriptorium.

Ornament was used in three ways: Ornamental frames or borders were created to enclose full-page illustrations (Fig. **4–4**); opening pages of each gospel and other important passages were singled out for illumination, particularly by the design of ornate initials (Fig. **4–5**); and full pages of decorative design called carpet pages were bound into the manuscript. This name developed because the densely packed design had the intricate patterning associated with oriental carpets. As a carpet page from the Lindisfarne Gospels shows (Fig. **4–6**), a seventh-century Celtic cross or other geometric motif became an organizing form that brought structure to the interlaces and lacertines filling the space. The *interlace* was a two-dimensional decoration formed by a number of ribbons or straps woven into a complex, usually symmetrical design. It is evident that drafting instruments were used to construct many of the designs in Celtic manuscripts. Interlaces created by animal forms were called *lacertines*. Most of the forms were either invented from imagination or based on earlier models. Careful observation of nature was not required of the Celtic designer or illustrator.

Large initials on the opening pages grew bigger in newer books as the decades passed. Integration of these initials with the rest of the text was a challenging design problem. The monks resolved it with a graphic principle called *diminuendo*, which is a decreasing scale of graphic information. On the opening page of the Gospel of Saint Mark in the Book of Durrow, the first letters of the word *Initium* create a large monogram thrusting down the page. The large double initial is followed in decreasing size by a smaller initial, the last four letters of the first word, the next two words, and the text. This descending scale unites the large initial to the text. Red S-shaped lines or dots link each text line to the initial and further unify the elements. The red dot pattern transforms the first three words into rectangles and contours the first letters of each verse. Ultimately, a harmonious design system is created. These red dots were used profusely, and watercolor washes often filled the negative spaces inside and between letters. Sometimes pigments were handled thickly and opaquely; at other times they were thin and as translucent as enamel.

In the Gospels the name of Christ is first mentioned in the eighteenth verse of the first chapter of Matthew. The illuminator created a graphic explosion using the monogram *XPI*. This letter combination—used to write Christ in manuscripts—is called the *Chi-Rho*, after the first two letters of the Greek word for Christ, chi *(X)* and rho *(P)*. The Chi-Rho in the

patterns was applied to book design in the monastic scriptoria, and a new concept and image of the book emerged. A series of manuscripts containing the four narratives of the life of Christ are the summit of Celtic book design. Written and designed around A.D. 680, the Book of Durrow is the earliest fully designed and ornamented Celtic book. The Book of Durrow was first assumed to have been created in Ireland. However, it is now thought to have come from the British Isles and written and decorated by Irish scribes.

The Lindisfarne Gospels, written by Eadfrith, Bishop of Lindisfarne, before A.D. 698, represents the full flowering of the Celtic style. The masterwork of the epoch is the Book of Kells, created at the island monastery of Iona around A.D. 800.

4–5. The Book of Durrow, opening page, the Gospel of Saint Mark, A.D. 680. Linked into a ligature, an *I* and an *N* become an aesthetic form of interlaced threads and coiling spiral motifs.

4–5

Book of Kells (Fig. 4–7) is composed of shimmering color and intricate, convoluted form blossoming over a whole page. The authors of the four gospels were signified by symbolic beings (Fig. 4–8). Having Saint Mark represented by a lion, Saint Luke by an ox, and Saint John by an eagle is part of a pagan tradition with its origin in Egyptian culture.

A radical design innovation in Celtic manuscripts was leaving a space between words to enable the reader to separate the string of letters into words more quickly. The half-uncial script journeyed to Ireland with the early missionaries and was subtly redesigned into the *scriptura scottica*—or *insular script* (see Figs. 4–5 and 4–9), as it is now called—to suit the local visual traditions. These half-uncials became the national letter-form style in Ireland and are still used for special writings and as a type style. Written with a slightly angled pen, the full, rounded characters have a strong bow, with ascenders bending to the right. A heavy triangle perches at the top of ascenders, and the horizontal stroke of the last letter of the word, particularly *e* or *t*, zips out into the space between words. The text page from the Book of Kells shows how carefully the insular script was lettered. Characters are frequently joined at the waistline or the baseline.

Ironically, these beautiful, carefully lettered half-uncials convey a text that is careless and contains misspellings and mis-

4–6

4–6. The Lindisfarne Gospels, carpet page facing the opening of Saint Matthew, c. A.D. 698. A mathematical grid buried under swirling lacertine birds and quadrupeds brings structure to the textured areas. A red, contoured cross with white circular "buttons" brings timeless stability to its churning energy.

readings. Even so, the Book of Kells is the culmination of Celtic illumination. Its noble design has generous margins and huge initial letters. Far more full-page illustrations than in any other Celtic manuscript are executed with a remark-able density and complexity of form; over 2,100 ornate capitals make every page a visual delight. Through the course of its 339 leaves, sentences intermittently bloom into full-page illuminations.

The magnificent Celtic school of manuscript design ended abruptly before the Book of Kells was completed. In A.D. 795 northern raiders made their first appearance on the Irish coast, and a period of intense struggle between the Celts and the Vikings followed. Both Lindisfarne and Iona, seats of two

of the greatest scriptoria in medieval history, were destroyed. When the invading Northmen swarmed over the island of Iona, where the Book of Kells was being completed in the monastic scriptorium, escaping monks took it to Kells and continued to work on it there. It can only be guessed whether or not majestic illuminated manuscripts were lost, or what magnificent volumes might have been designed had peace and stability continued for the Celts of Ireland.

The Caroline graphic renewal

When Charlemagne (A.D. 742–814), king of the Franks since 768 and the leading ruler of central Europe, rose from prayer

4–8

4–7. The Book of Kells, the Chi-Rho page, A.D. 794–806. Amidst intricate spirals and lacertines, the artist has drawn thirteen human heads, two cats, two mice calmly watching two other mice tug at a wafer, and an otter holding a salmon.

4–8. The Book of Kells, symbols for authors of the four Gospels, c. A.D. 794–806. Winged and stylized almost to abstraction, Matthew's man, Mark's lion, Luke's ox, and John's eagle float in four rectangles wrapped in a densely ornamented frame.

in Saint Peter's Cathedral in Rome on Christmas Day, A.D. 800, Pope Leo III (d. A.D. 816) placed a crown on his head and declared him emperor of what became known as the Holy Roman Empire. The whole of central Europe was united under Charlemagne in an empire that was neither Roman nor particularly holy. Nevertheless, it attempted to recapture the grandeur and unity of the Roman Empire in a Germanic and Christian federation. In addition to restoring the concept of empire to the West, Charlemagne introduced the feudal system, where landowning noblemen held dictatorial power over peasants who toiled in the fields, in an effort to bring order to chaotic medieval society.

Although by some reports he was illiterate except to sign his name, Charlemagne fostered a revival of learning and the arts. The England of the 700s had seen much intellectual activity, and Charlemagne recruited the English scholar Alcuin of York (c. A.D. 732–804) to come to his palace at Aachen and

establish a school. Except for the Celtic pattern-making tradition, book design and illumination had sunk to a low ebb in most of Europe. Illustrations were poorly drawn and composed, and writing had become localized and undisciplined in the hands of poorly trained scribes. Many manuscripts were difficult, if not impossible, to read. Charlemagne mandated reform by royal edict in A.D. 789. At the court in Aachen, a *turba scriptorium* ("crowd of scribes," as Alcuin called them) was assembled to prepare master copies of important religious texts. Then books and scribes were dispatched throughout Europe to disseminate the reforms.

Standardization of page layout, writing style, and decoration was attempted. Efforts to reform the alphabet succeeded. For a model, the ordinary writing script of the late antique period was selected, combined with Celtic innovations, including the use of four guidelines, ascenders, and descenders, and molded into an ordered uniform script called

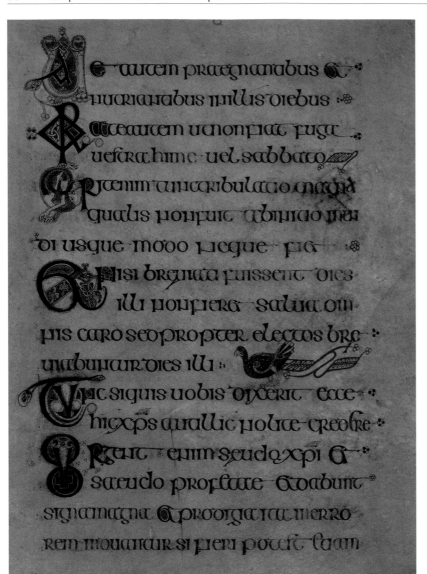

4–9. The Book of Kells, text page with ornamental initials, c. A.D. 794–806. The remarkable originality of the hundreds of illustrated initials is suggested by the variety of imaginative forms in the six initials on this one page.

4–10. Caroline minuscules from the Alcuin Bible, ninth century A.D. An economy of execution and good legibility characterized this new writing style.

4–11. Coronation Gospels, opening pages of Saint Mark's Gospel, c. A.D. 800. The author sits in a natural landscape on a page of deep crimson-stained parchment; the facing page is stained a deep purple with gold lettering.

Caroline minuscules (Fig. 4–10). The Caroline minuscule is the forerunner of our contemporary lowercase alphabet. This clear set of letterforms was practical and easy to write. Characters were set apart instead of joined, and the number of ligatures was reduced. Much writing had become a slurred scrawl; the new alphabet restored legibility. The Caroline minuscule became the standard throughout Europe for a time, but as the decades passed, writing in many areas veered toward regional characteristics. Roman capitals were studied and adopted for headings and initials of great beauty. These were not calligraphic but carefully drawn and built up with more than one stroke. The use of a dual alphabet was not fully developed in the sense that we use capital and small letters today, but a process in that direction had begun. In addition to graphic reforms, the court at Aachen revised sentence and paragraph structure as well as punctuation. The Carolingian revival of scholarship and learning stayed a serious loss of human knowledge and writings that had been occurring through the early medieval period.

When early manuscripts from the late antique period and Byzantine culture were imported for study, illuminators were shocked and stunned when they saw the naturalism and illusion of deep space in the illustrations. The two-dimensional style suddenly seemed passé in the face of this "picture-window" style, where space moved back into the page from a decorative frame and clothes seemed to wrap the forms of living human figures. Lacking the skill or basic knowledge of the antique artists, Carolingian illuminators began to copy these images with sometimes uneven results. The classical heritage was revived as accurate drawing and illusionistic techniques

4–10

4–11

were mastered by some illuminators. Figurative imagery and ornament, which had been scrambled together in earlier medieval illumination, separated into distinct design elements.

In a manuscript book such as the Coronation Gospels (Fig. **4–11**), designed and produced at the court of Charlemagne in the late eighth century A.D., a classical yet somewhat primitive elegance emerges. The two facing pages are unified by their exactly equal margins. Initial letters echo Roman monumental capitals, and the text appears to be closely based on the insular script of Ireland. Rustic capitals are used for supplementary materials, including chapter lists, introductory words, and prefaces. Whether this book was designed, lettered, and illu-

minated by scribes brought in from Italy, Greece, or Constantinople is not known. The creators of this book understood the lettering and painting methods of classical culture. Legend claims that in the year A.D. 1000, Emperor Otto III (A.D. 980–1002) of the Holy Roman Empire journeyed to Aachen, opened Charlemagne's tomb, and found him seated on a throne with the Coronation Gospels on his lap.

Spanish pictorial expressionism

On the Spanish peninsula, isolated from the rest of Europe by mountains, the scriptoria did not experience the initial impact of the Carolingian renewal. In A.D. 711, a Moorish

4–12

4–13

army under the Arab governor of Tangier crossed the Straits of Gibraltar and crushed the Spanish army. Even the Spanish king was among the missing in action. Moorish settlers mingled Islamic design motifs with Christian traditions to create unique manuscript designs.

A number of Islamic design motifs filtered into Spanish Christian manuscripts. Flat shapes of intense color were used. Sometimes they were sprinkled with stars, rosettes, polygons, or garlands in optically active contrasting colors. Flat, schematic drawing had prominent outlines. The two-dimensional aggressive color created a frontal intensity that obliterated any hint of atmosphere or illusion. A pagan tradition of totemlike animals dates back through Islamic northern Africa to Persia to ancient Mesopotamia, and these ghastly creatures reared their frightful heads in Spanish illumination. Decorative frames enclosed most illustrations, with intricate patterns evoking the richly colored geometric designs applied to Moorish architecture in tilework and molded and chiseled decorations.

There was a fascination with designs of intricate geometry and intense, pure color. In the commemorative labyrinth from Pope Gregory's *Moralia in Iob* (*Commentary on Job*) of A.D. 945, the scribe Florentius designed a *labyrinth page* (Fig. **4–12**) bearing the words *Florentius indignum memorare*, which modestly ask the reader to "remember the unworthy Florentius." Florentius's humility is belied by the dazzling graphic treatment and its position opposite the monogram of Christ. Labyrinth arrangements of commemorative messages date from ancient Greece and Rome and were quite popular in medieval manuscripts.

For the medieval faithful, life was but a prelude to eternal salvation, if the individual could triumph in the battle between good and evil raging on earth. Supernatural explanations were still assigned to natural phenomena that were not understood; eclipses, earthquakes, plague, and famine were seen as dire warnings and punishments. People believed a terrible destruction awaited the earth as foretold by the Biblical Book of Revelation. It suggested a date, "When the thousand years had ex-

4–14

4–12. Commemorative labyrinth from *Moralia in Iob*, A.D. 945. Starting in the center of the top line, the inscription reads down, left, and right, establishing a labyrinth of letterforms.

4–13. The Four Horsemen of the Apocalypse from the Beatus of Fernando and Sancha, A.D. 1047. Unlike other interpreters of the Apocalypse, Beatus saw the first horseman as God's envoy, whose arrows pierce the hearts of nonbelievers.

4–14. The fourth angel from the Beatus of Fernando and Sancha, A.D. 1047. Wing feathers are as sharp and menacing as daggers. The trumpet, wings, and tail bring an angular counterpoint to the horizontal bands of color.

pired," as a likely time for the Last Judgment. Many considered the year A.D. 1000 the probable end of the world; concern mounted as the year drew nigh. Among numerous interpretations of Revelation, the *Commentary of Beatus on the Apocalypse of Saint John the Divine* was widely read. The monk Beatus (A.D. 730–798) of Liebana in northern Spain wrote this harrowing interpretation in A.D. 776. Graphic artists gave visual form to the fearful end of the world in numerous copies penned and illustrated throughout Spain. The monastic dictum *Pictura est laicorum literatura* (The picture is the layman's literature) evidences the motivation for illustrations conveying information to the illiterate. Combining Christian prophecy with Moorish design influences, they succeeded admirably. The Book of Revelation is laced with rich, expressive imagery, and pictures assumed an importance rivaling the text's. Full-page illustrations appeared frequently.

Over sixty different passages are illustrated in twenty-three surviving copies. Stark, symbolic descriptions challenged the artist's mind as Beatus's interpretation of this prophecy was visualized. This is the most forceful interpretation of the Apocalypse in graphic art before Albrecht Dürer's intricate woodcut illustrations in the early 1500s (see Fig. 6–13).

On New Year's Eve, A.D. 999, many Europeans gathered to await the final judgment. Many reportedly spent the night naked on their cold rooftops waiting for the end. When nothing happened, new interpretations of the "thousand years" phrase were made, and manuscript copies of Beatus's *Commentary* continued to be produced. In the masterful Beatus of Fernando and Sancha of A.D. 1047, the scribe and illuminator Facundus drew schematic figures acting out the final tragedy in a hot and airless space created by flat horizontal bands of pure hue. The thick color is bright and clear. Chrome yellow, cobalt blue, red ocher, and intense green are slammed together in jarring contrasts. The Four Horsemen of the Apocalypse (Fig. 4–13), who are traditionally War, Famine, Pestilence, and Death, ride forth to unleash their terror upon the world.

Revelation 8:12 tells, "the fourth angel sounded, and the third part of the sun was smitten, and the third part of the moon, and the third part of the stars, so as the third part of them was darkened, and the day shown not for a third part of it, and the night likewise" (Fig. 4–14). The sun (labeled *sol*) and the moon (labeled *luna*) are one-third white and two-thirds red, to illustrate that one third of each had fallen away. A sinister eagle flies into the space screaming, "Woe, woe, woe to those who dwell on the earth." As an iconic symbol, this angel is worlds away from the pure white angel of hope in later Christian imagery. Inspired by words in the Apocalypse, "I am the alpha and the omega, the beginning and the end," Facundus designed the first page of the Beatus of Fernando and Sancha as a huge illuminated *A* (alpha, the first letter of the Greek alphabet), and the last page as a huge illuminated *O* (omega, the last letter).

During the early eleventh century A.D., the balance of power in Spain swung from the Moors to the Christians. Communications with other European countries improved, and Spanish graphic design tilted toward the continental mainstream that developed from the Carolingian style. The expressionistic graphics filling Bibles, commentaries, and most especially the *Commentary of Beatus* yielded to other graphic approaches.

Romanesque and Gothic manuscripts

The Romanesque period (c. A.D. 1000–1150) saw renewed religious fervor and even stronger feudalism. Europeans launched some ten crusades in a vigorous effort to conquer the Holy Lands. Monasticism reached its peak, and large liturgical books, including Bibles, Gospels, and psalters, were produced in the booming scriptoria. For the first time, universal design characteristics seemed possible, as visual ideas traveled back and forth on the pilgrimage routes. The illusionistic revival of the Carolingian era yielded to a new emphasis on linear drawing and a willingness to distort figures to meld with the overall design of the page. The representation of deep space became even less important, and figures were placed against backgrounds of gold leaf or textured patterns.

During the middle of the twelfth century the Romanesque period evolved into the Gothic, which lasted from A.D. 1150 until the European Renaissance began in fourteenth-century Italy. This transitional period saw the power of the feudal lords constrained by reasonable laws. Towns and villages grew into cities. Agriculture yielded to international trade as the foundation of political power, and money replaced land as the primary measure of wealth. European society was slowly transformed. Particularly in France and England, monarchies were supported by powerful noblemen, enabling more stable central governments to emerge. Uncertainty and fear, the daily companions of medieval peoples for centuries, diminished as the social and economic environment became more predictable, overcoming the wildly inconsistent conditions that prevailed in Romanesque times.

During the 1200s the rise of the universities created an expanding market for books. For example, twenty thousand of Paris's hundred thousand residents were students who flocked to the city to attend the university. Literacy was on the rise, and professional lay illuminators emerged to help meet the growing demand for books.

The Book of Revelation had a surge of unexplained popularity in England and France during the 1200s. A scriptorium at Saint Albans with high artistic standards seems to have figured prominently in this development. At least ninety-three copies of the Apocalypse survive from this period. A straightforward naturalism anchored in this world rather than a

4–15

future one supplanted the horror and anxiety of the earlier Spanish editions.

The Douce Apocalypse (Fig. **4–15**), written and illustrated around A.D. 1265, is one of the many masterpieces of Gothic illumination. Each of the hundred illustrated pages (three are now missing) has an illustration above two columns of beautifully lettered text. The scribe used a lettering style whose repetition of verticals capped with pointed serifs has been compared to a picket fence. *Textura* (from the Latin *texturum*, meaning woven fabric or texture) is the favored name for this dominant mode of Gothic lettering. Other terms, such as the French *lettre de forme* and the English *blackletter* and *Old English*, are vague and misleading. During its time, textura was called *littera moderna* (Latin for "modern lettering"). Textura was quite functional, for all the vertical strokes in a word were drawn first, then serifs and the other strokes needed to transform the group of verticals into a word were added. Rounded strokes were almost eliminated. Letters and the spaces between them were condensed in an effort to save

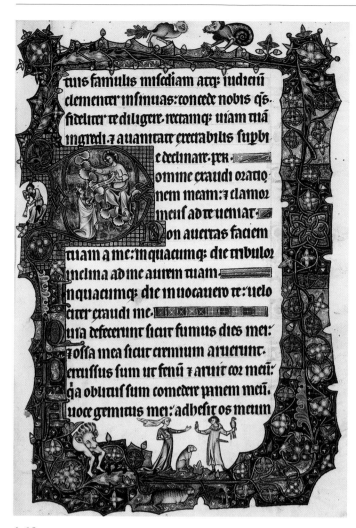

4–16

4–15. The multitude worshipping God, from the Douce Apocalypse, A.D. 1265. Saint John, the roving reporter of the final doom, is shown at the left of the scene, peering curiously into the rectangular image.

4–16. Page from the Ormesby Psalter, c. early 1300s A.D. Decoration, illustration, and initials are joined into a single complex text frame. Red and blue prevail in many late Gothic manuscripts.

the trend toward an international Gothic style that pervaded the late Gothic period. It is characterized by elongated figures that rise upward in a vertical movement, often wearing elegant, fashionable costumes or flowing robes. Even though the figures are pulled upward, there is a conviction of solid, almost monumental weight and an expression of human dignity. Increased naturalism was seen in human, animal, and botanical subjects. Elements from the national styles of various countries were combined, and growing numbers of commissions for private books, particularly from royal patrons, enabled scribes and illuminators to travel and disseminate artistic conventions and techniques.

Liturgical books of the late medieval era contained extraordinary designs. The Ormesby Psalter (Fig. **4–16**), created during the early 1300s in England, is a splendid example. Its generous 33.6-centimeter (about 13.5-inch) height allowed for illustrated capital initials containing biblical scenes on gold-leaf backgrounds. The large text is written in the textura writing style. The text area is surrounded by an intricate frame filled with decorative pattern capital initials and rich marginalia, which are thought to be visual clues suggesting appropriate parables and stories for the priest to tell the congregation after completing the scriptural reading. The page illustrated in Figure **4–16** has an owl/horse conferring with a man/snail at the top. At the bottom, a demon smugly watches a betrothal. The young maiden eagerly reaches for the falconer's engagement ring; the symbolic cat and mouse below the couple hint that someone is being victimized. The everyday life of the people had found its way into the margins of religious books. Some historians have seen this as an early indication of an approaching Renaissance humanism, with its concern for the quality of human life on earth.

space on the precious parchment. The overall effect is one of a dense black texture.

On each page of the Douce Apocalypse, an open square is left in the upper-left corner for an initial, but these letters were never added. Some illustrations, drawn but never painted, show an even line of great sensitivity and decisiveness. The illustrations are divided into segments by elaborate framing. In the illustration for the last passage of the seventh chapter of Revelation, the triumphant white-robed multitude who survived the great tribulation are shown surrounding a very human-looking God with his Lamb. Saint John's soft-blue robe and rust-brown cloak set the tone for a mellow palette of blues, greens, reds, browns, grays, and yellows.

The Douce Apocalypse represents a new breed of picture book that established the page design of the fifteenth-century woodblock books that emerged after printing came to Europe. The scribe and illuminator are not known; in fact, scholars have argued over whether this book was created in England or France. This blurring of national origin evidences

4–17

4–18

Judaic manuscripts

After the Babylonian Exile in 587 B.C., and again after the Romans crushed Jewish revolts in A.D. 70 and A.D. 135, the Jewish population in Israel was dispersed. Following the second revolt against the Romans, Israel ceased to exist as a political entity. The Jewish people, religion, and culture lived on in the *Diaspora* (Greek for "dispersion" or "scattering") throughout the known world. Surviving Judaic illuminated manuscripts produced across Europe during the medieval epoch are treasured masterworks of graphic design. The common belief that Judaic traditions rejected figurative art is not entirely true. Artistic embellishment for educational reasons or to adorn religious objects, including manuscripts, was encouraged as a means of expressing reverence for sacred objects and writings.

Many of the finest Judaic illuminated manuscripts are *Haggadot*, containing Jewish religious literature, including historical stories and proverbs—especially the saga of the Jewish exodus from Egypt. The Washington Haggadah (Fig. **4–17**) is an exemplary representative of the genre. It is one of eleven

known illuminated manuscripts created by the prolific artist and scribe Joel ben Simeon, who worked in Northern Italy and Germany during the late fifteenth century. Masterfully executed Hebrew calligraphy, often accompanied by gold initials on luminous blue ornamented plaques, occupies the center area of each page. The word was supreme; pictures played a supporting role and were pushed into generous margins at the sides or bottom of the space. Ben Simeon drew his illustrations using a delicately detailed pen-and-colored-ink technique. Drawings of people, animals, and birds are executed with great sensitivity.

Judaic illuminated manuscripts are relatively rare, but surviving copies evidence remarkable scholarship, meticulous illustrations, and calligraphic beauty.

Islamic manuscripts

Islam, one of the world's great religions, emerged from Muhammad's teachings as recorded in the Qur'an. This sacred book forms the divine authority for religious, social, and civil life in Islamic societies stretching south from the Baltic Sea to

4–19

4–17. Joel ben Simeon, page from the Washington Haggadah, c. A.D. 1478. The Messiah is heralded as he arrives on a donkey

4–18. Mustafa al-Khalil, frontispiece of a manuscript Qu'ran, 1739. Intricate patterns with interlocking forms and vibrant colors share design motifs with Islamic architectural decorations and carpets.

4–19. Muhammad Amin ibn Abi al-Husain Kazvini, Islamic manuscript called the Padishahnamah, early 1700s A.D. Indian Emperor Shah Jahan, who reigned from 1627 to 1658, holds court and makes ceremonial presentations.

(Fig. 4–18). Geometric shapes containing calligraphy are surrounded by rhythmic organic designs ranging from plant forms to abstract arabesques.

Figurative illustrations were not utilized because Islamic society embraced the principle of aniconism, which is religious opposition to representations of living creatures. This was based on a belief that only God could create life and that mortals should not make figures of living things or create images that might be used as idols. While this principle was strictly upheld in many Muslim areas, such as North Africa and Egypt, pictures were tolerated in some Islamic regions as long as they were restricted to private quarters and palace harems.

Probably before A.D. 1000, miniature paintings appeared in Persian books and became an important aspect of book illumination. Artists in Persia (now Iran) developed the defining attributes of illustrated Islamic manuscripts because the ruling Shahs patronized the creation of masterworks containing elaborate detail, precise patterns, and vibrant color. Some of the finest Islamic manuscripts were designed during the Safavid dynasty (A.D. 1502–1736); the influence of Persian artists spread to the Ottoman Empire (a domain founded by Turkish tribes, who conquered Constantinople in 1453 and ruled a vast empire for over four hundred years) and the Mughals (also called Moguls—Muslims from Mongol, Turkey, and Persia who conquered and ruled India from A.D. 1526 to 1857). Mughal emperors established a major school of Islamic illumination after bringing Persian artists to India in the sixteenth century to train local artists. Birds, animals, plants, and architecture native to the region were incorporated into Mughal manuscripts.

Figure 4–19 typifies the illustrated Islamic manuscript. The professional and personal life of Indian Mughal emperor Shah Jahan (reigned A.D. 1627–1658), who built masterworks of

equatorial Africa, and eastward from the Atlantic coast of Africa to Indonesia. Hundreds of thousands of manuscript copies of the Qur'an have been made, from small pocket-sized copies (see Fig. 2–7) to lavishly ornamented imperial editions. Muhammad called upon his followers to learn to read and write, and calligraphy quickly became an important tool for religion and government. His advocacy of women's literacy resulted in many important female calligraphers and scholars. A love of books permeates Islamic cultures; libraries were larger in Islamic regions and manuscript production was far more prolific than in Europe. From the eighth to the fifteenth century A.D. Islamic science was without peer, and over ten thousand scientific manuscripts from this epoch survive.

Islamic manuscript decoration emerged from modest origins. Early calligraphers who wrote seventh- and eighth-century copies of the Qur'an made their vowel marks ornate and drew rosettes to separate verses. Over the centuries, ornamentation became increasingly elaborate, with intricate geometric and arabesque designs filling the space to become transcendental expressions of the sacred nature of the Qur'an

architecture, including the Taj Mahal, is recounted and illustrated with full-page and double-page illustrations. Calligraphic writing is contained in intricate panels. Open spaces between the lines of calligraphy are filled with organic gold configurations determined by the word shapes. These negative spaces become concrete forms. Text and illustrations are framed with multiple lines and surrounded by complex ornamental borders ranging from floral arabesques to repetitive patterns and architectonic geometric structures.

The meticulously painted illustrations are in the great tradition of Persian painting, which was primarily a book illustrator's art beginning in the 1300s. Space is flat and shallow; ground and floor planes are parallel to the picture plane. Figures and objects are described by meticulous contour lines containing flat, or sometimes subtly modulated, planes of color. Tonal modulation and light-and-shadow patterns are usually minimal or nonexistent. Architecture is defined by geometric planes. Intricate decorative patterns are applied to carpets, clothing, and structures. Plants are drawn as schematic stylizations, with careful attention to detail and a profuse repetition of blossoms and leaves. Chromatic energy is achieved through warm/cool and light/dark color combinations.

Islamic manuscript design had a long and varied tradition, with numerous schools, influences, and aesthetic approaches. Geographic proximity with Asia in the east and Europe to the west permitted an assimilation of design ideas from other cultures. For over a thousand years Islamic manuscripts maintained traditions of artistic excellence, with production continuing long after typographic printing completely replaced manuscript books elsewhere. Major works were commissioned as recently as the nineteenth century.

Late medieval illuminated manuscripts

During the transitional decades, as the medieval era yielded to the European Renaissance, the production of illuminated manuscripts for private use became increasingly important. In the early 1400s the Book of Hours became Europe's most popular book. This private devotional volume contained religious texts for each hour of the day, prayers, and calendars listing the days of important saints. The pinnacle of the European illuminated book was reached in the early fifteenth century A.D., when a passionate lover of beautiful books, the French nobleman and brother of King Charles V, Jean, duc de Berry (1340–1416), who owned a vast portion of central France, installed the Limbourg brothers, of Dutch origin, in his castle to establish a private scriptorium. The duc de Berry owned one of the largest private libraries in the world at that time, with 155 books, including fourteen Bibles and fifteen Books of Hours.

Little is known about the brief lives of Paul, Herman, and Jean Limbourg. It is believed that all three were born after A.D.

4–20

1385. Sons of a Dutch wood sculptor, all three apprenticed as goldsmiths, then probably trained at an important Paris scriptorium after 1400. The duc de Berry employed Paul Limbourg in 1408 to head his workshop. Paul was probably the designer responsible for layout and design. Apparently a close rapport developed between patron and designer/illustrator, for on New Year's Day of 1411 the Limbourg brothers gave the duke a bogus book consisting of a wooden block bound in white velvet and locked with an enameled clasp decorated with his coat of arms.

In the early fifteenth century the Limbourgs were in the vanguard of an evolution in the interpretation of visual experience. The Gothic tendency toward abstraction and stylized presentation was reversed as they sought a convincing realism. Atmospheric perspective was used to push planes and volumes back in deep space, and a consistent effort toward achieving linear perspective was made. The Limbourgs' exceptional gifts of observation combined with remarkable painting skill enabled them to propel illuminated book design and illustration to its zenith. Their work conveys a strong sense of

4–21

4–20 and 4–21. The Limbourg brothers, January and February pages from *Les tres riches heures du duc de Berry,* 1413–16. Both pictorial and written information is presented with clarity, attesting to a high level of observation and visual organization.

mass and volume; in some illustrations highlights and cast shadows are created by a single light source.

The Limbourg brothers' masterpiece was *Les tres riches heures du duc de Berry* (Figs. **4–20** and **4–21**). The first twenty-four pages are an illustrated calendar. Each month has a double-page spread with a genre illustration relating to seasonal activities of the month on the left page and a calendar of the saints' days on the right. The illustrations are crowned with graphic astronomical charts depicting constellations and the phases of the moon. The winter farm scene for February includes a cutaway building with people warming themselves by a fire. The calendar page lists the saints' days and uses vibrant red and blue inks for the lettering. A pencil grid structure established the format containing the information.

Les tres riches heures is a pictorial book. Illustrations dominate the page layouts. Some pages have a mere four lines of text lettered in two columns under the illustrations. Decorated initials spin off whirling acanthus foliage, which is sometimes accompanied by angels, animals, or flowers in the generous margins.

Apprentices were kept busy grinding colors on a marble slab with a muller. The medium consisted of water mixed with arabic or tragacanth gum as a binder to adhere the pigment to the vellum and preserve the image. The Limbourg brothers used a palette of ten colors, plus black and white. The colors included cobalt and ultramarine blue and two greens, one made from a carbonate of copper, the other from iris leaves. Gold leaf and gold-powder paint were used in profusion. The minute detail achieved implies the use of a magnifying lens.

The Limbourg brothers did not live to complete this masterpiece, for all three died before February 1416, and the duc de Berry died on 15 July 1416; perhaps they were victims of a terrible epidemic or plague believed to have swept through France that year. The inventory of the duke's library, taken after his death, indicates that half his books were religious works, a third were history books, and volumes on geography, astronomy, and astrology rounded out the collection.

During the same years when the Limbourgs were creating handmade books, a new means of visual communication—woodblock printing—appeared in Europe. The invention of movable type in the West was but three decades away. The production of illuminated manuscripts continued through the fifteenth century A.D. and even into the early decades of the sixteenth century, but this thousand-year-old craft, dating back to antiquity, was doomed to extinction by the typographic book.

A Graphic Renaissance

Part II

The origins of European typography and design for printing

Printing Comes to Europe

5

1457 **Fust and Schoeffer,** *Psalter in Latin* **with two-color printed initials**

1276 **Paper mill established in Fabriano, Italy**

c 1450 **Gutenberg perfects typographic printing The Master of the Playing Cards perfects copperplate engraving**

c 1306 *Giotto completes the Arena Chapel frescoes*

c 1300 **Relief printing on textiles in Europe**

c 1460 **Blockbooks in use in the Netherlands**

1348 *Black Death decimates Florence, Italy*

c 1455 **Gutenberg and Fust complete** *42-line Bible*

1321 *Dante completes* The Divine Comedy

1484 *Botticelli,* Birth of Venus

1423 **Saint Christopher, early dated woodblock print**

1468 **Gutenberg dies**

The German Illustrated Book

6

1498 **Dürer,** *The Apocalypse*

1514–17 **de Brocar,** *Polyglot Bible*

1470 **Freiburger, Gering, and Kranz, 1st printing press in France**

1465 **Sweynheym and Pannartz, 1st Italian printing press; 1st printed music**

1486 **Reuwich illustrates trip to Holy Land**

1462 *Mainz, Germany, sacked by Adolf of Nassau*

c 1460 **Pfister, 1st printed book with illustrations**

1534 *Luther's first German-language Bible*

1493 **Koberger publishes** *The Nuremburg Cronicle*

1538 **1st printing press in Mexico**

1475 **Caxton, 1st English-language typographic book**

1528 **Albrecht Dürer dies**

Renaissance Graphic Design

7

1509 *Henry VIII becomes King of England*

1503 *da Vinci,* Mona Lisa

1505 **Geoffroy Tory returns to France from Italy**

1476 **Ratdolt:** *Calendarium* **has 1st complete title page**

1492 *Columbus sails to America*

1522 *Magellan's expedition circumnavigates the globe*

1470 **Jenson's roman typeface**

1517 *Luther launches the Reformation*

1494 *France invades Italy*

c 1530 **Garamond establishes an independent type foundry**

1469 **de Spira, 1st printing press in Venice**

1569–72 **Plantin,** *Polygot Bible*

1495 **Griffo designs and cuts Bembo type for Manutius**

1569 *Mercator, modern cartography*

1494 **Manutius establishes the Aldine Press in Venice**

1525 **Tory, 1st Book of Hours**

1594 *Shakespeare,* Romeo and Juliet

1501 **Griffo designs and cuts 1st italic type for Manutius' "pocket book"**

1512 *Michaelangelo completes Sistine Chapel ceiling*

1555 **Plantin establishes his press at Antwerp**

c 1557 **Granjon, Civilité type**

1522 **Arrighi's writing manual**

1529 **Tory,** *Champ Fleury*

1561 **Kerver, French version of** *Poliphili*

1527 *French army sacks Rome*

■ *1600*   ■ *1700*   ■ *1800*

1667 **Schipper, *Calvin's Commentary***   1721 *Bach, Brandenburg Concertos*

1621 ***Weekly Newes*, 1st English newspaper**

1605 *Cervantes*, Don Quixote; *Shakespeare*, Macbeth

1640 **Daye, *Whole Book of Psalmes***

An Epoch of Typographic Genius

8

1771 **Luce, *Essai d'une Nouvelle Typographique***

1776 *American Declaration of Independence*

1784 **Didot, true modern style type**

1737 **Fournier le Jeune standardized**   1789 *French Revolution begins, Bastille stormed*
type sizes; John Pine, *Opera of Horatii*

1790 **Bewick, *General History of Quadrupeds***

1726 *Swift*, Gulliver's Travels   1769 *Watt patents steam engine*

1742 **Fournier le Jeune, *Models des characteres de l'Imprimere***   1818 **Bodoni, *Manuale Tipograpfico***
(posthumous)

1789 **Blake, *Songs of Innocence***

c 1790 **Bodoni, typefaces bearing his name**

1760 *George III becomes King of England*

1702 **1st book printed with the Romain du Roi**   1770 *Boston Massacre*   1793 *Louis XVI beheaded*

1722 **Caslon, 1st Caslon Old Style font**   1774 *Louis XVI becomes King of France*

1700 *Sewall*, Story of Joseph, *1st American protest against slavery*

1784 *David*, Oath of the Horatii

1788 *Washington, 1st U.S. President*

1692 **Louis XIV commissions the Romain du Roi**   1764 **Fournier le Jeune, *Manuel Typographique***

1689 *Peter the Great becomes Czar of Russia*   1757 **Baskerville, *Vergil***   1799 *Napoleon rules France*

1719 *Daniel Defoe*, Robinson Crusoe

Printing Comes to Europe

5

*X*ylography is the technical term for the relief printing from a raised surface that originated in Asia. *Typography* is the term for printing with independent, movable, and reusable bits of metal or wood, each of which has a raised letterform on one face. This dry definition belies the immense potential for human dialogue and the new horizons for graphic design that were unleashed by this extraordinary invention in the mid-1400s by a restless German inventor whose portrait and signature are lost to the relentless passage of time. The invention of typography ranks near the creation of writing as one of the most important advances in civilization. Writing gave humanity a means of storing, retrieving, and documenting knowledge and information that transcended time and place; typographic printing allowed the economical and multiple production of alphabet communication. Knowledge spread rapidly and literacy increased as a result of this remarkable invention.

Several factors created a climate in Europe that made typography feasible. The demand for books had become insatiable. The emerging literate middle class and students in the rapidly expanding universities had seized the monopoly on literacy from the clergy, creating a vast new market for reading material. The slow and expensive process of bookmaking had changed little in one thousand years. A simple two-hundred-page book required four or five months' labor by a scribe, and the twenty-five sheepskins needed for the parchment were even more expensive than his labor.

In 1424, only 122 manuscript books resided in the university library at Cambridge, England, and the library of a wealthy nobleman whose books were his most prized and sought-after possessions probably numbered less than two dozen volumes. The value of a book was equal to the value of a farm or vineyard. The steady growth of demand had led independent merchants to develop an assembly-line division of labor, with specialists trained in lettering, decorative initialing, gold ornamentation, proofreading, and binding. Even this exploding production of manuscript books was unable to meet the demand.

Without paper, the speed and efficiency of printing would have been useless. Papermaking had completed its long, slow journey from China to Europe, so a plentiful substrate was available. Over six hundred years passed before papermaking, which spread westward along caravan routes from the Pacific Ocean to the Mediterranean Sea, reached the Arab world. After repelling a Chinese attack on the city of Samarkand in A.D. 751, the Arab occupation forces captured some Chinese papermakers. Abundant water and bountiful crops of flax and hemp enabled Samarkand to become a papermaking center, and the craft spread to Baghdad and Damascus and reached Egypt by the tenth century. From there it spread across North Africa and was introduced into Sicily in 1102 and into Spain by the Moors during the middle of the twelfth century. By 1276 a paper mill was established in Fabriano, Italy. Troyes, France, had a paper mill in 1348.

The watermark (Fig. **5–1**), a translucent emblem produced by pressure from a raised design on the mold and visible when the sheet of paper is held to the light, was used in Italy by 1282. The origin of this design device is unknown. Trademarks for paper mills, individual craftsmen, and perhaps religious symbolism were early uses. As successful marks were imitated, they began to be used as a designation for sheet and mold sizes and paper grade. Mermaids, unicorns, animals, flowers, and heraldic shields were frequent design motifs.

Early European block printing

The origins of woodblock printing in Europe are shrouded in mystery. After the Crusades opened Europe to Eastern influence, relief printing arrived on the heels of paper. Playing cards and religious-image prints were early manifestations. Circumstantial evidence implies that, like paper, relief printing from woodblocks also spread westward from China. By the early 1300s pictorial designs were being printed on textiles in Europe. Card playing was popular, and in spite of being outlawed and denounced by zealous clergy, this pastime stimulated a thriving underground block-printing industry, possibly before 1400.

In 1415 the Duke of Milan played cards with ivory slats bearing images painted by famous artists, and Flemish nobles used engraved silver plates. Throughout Europe,

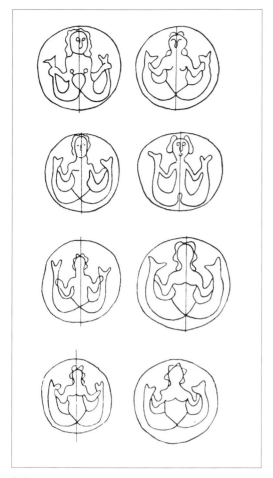

5–1

5–2

5–1. French watermark designs, fifteenth century. These mermaid designs were produced by bent wire attached to the mold used in making paper.

5–2. Jack of Diamonds, woodblock playing card, c. 1400. The flat, stylized design conventions of playing cards have changed little in over five hundred years. Visual signs to designate the suits began as the four classes of medieval society. Hearts signified the clergy; spades (derived from Italian *spada* [sword]) stood for the nobility; the leaflike club represented the peasantry; and diamonds denoted the burghers.

the working class gathered in taverns and by the roadside to play with grimy cards that were blockprinted and stenciled on coarse paper (Fig. **5–2**). Playing cards were the first printed pieces to move into an illiterate culture, making them the earliest European manifestation of printing's democratizing ability. The games of kings could now become the games of peasants and craftsmen. Because these cards introduced the masses to symbol recognition, sequencing, and logical deduction, their intrinsic value transcended idle entertainment.

The first known European block printings with a communications function were devotional prints of saints (Figs. **5–3** and **5–4**), ranging from small images fitting in a person's hand to larger images of 25 by 35 centimeters (about 10 by 14 inches). Image and lettering were cut from the same block of wood. These early prints evolved into block books (Figs. **5–5** and **5–6**), which were woodcut picture books with religious subject matter and brief text. Each page was cut from a block of wood and printed as a complete word and picture unit. Because most of the few surviving copies were printed in the Netherlands after 1460, it is not known whether the block book preceded the typographic book. Drawn in a simplified illustration style, with the visual elements dominant as in contemporary comic books, the block book was used for religious instruction of illiterates. This form gradually declined during the fifteenth century as literacy increased. Common subjects included the Apocalypse, a forewarning of the final doom and destruction of the world. *Ars moriendi* (manuals on the "art of dying") advised one on the preparation and meeting of the final hour. Europe's population was decimated by the great cycles of bubonic plague, called the Black Death, which claimed one fourth of the continent's inhabitants during the

5–3

5–4

5–5

5–6

5–7

5–3. Woodblock print of Saint Christopher, 1423. The unknown illustrator depicted the legendary saint, a giant who carried travelers safely across a river, bearing the infant Christ. The inscription below reads: "In whatsoever day thou seest the likeness of St. Christopher/in that same day thou wilt at least from death no evil blow incur/1423." One of the earliest dated European block prints, this image effectively uses changing contour-line width to show form.

5–4. Block print of the Annunciation, undated. The black area is an effective focal point unifying the two figures. The scroll, with a Latin inscription, serves the same communicative function as a "talk balloon." (The upper left corner of this print is missing.)

5–5. Block-book page from *The Story of the Blessed Virgin*, 1400s. This page attempts to justify the Immaculate Conception by a series of "logical" parallels: If the light of Venus's temple cannot be extinguished, if the moon is reflected in water, if a person can be changed into stone, and if man can be painted on stone, why should not the Blessed Virgin be able to generate?

5–6. Letter *K* from a grotesque alphabet, c. 1464. This page is from a twenty-four-page abecedarian block-book that presented each letter of the alphabet by composing figures in its shape.

5–7. Pages from an *ars moriendi*, 1466. A montage juxtaposes the deathbed scene with the subject's estate. One demon urges, "Provide for your friends," while the other advises, "Attend to your treasures." The densely textured text page recommends donating one's earthly goods to the Church.

fourteenth century and caused a thousand villages either to vanish totally or to be critically depopulated; death was an ever-present preoccupation.

In the *ars moriendi* shown (Fig. **5–7**), eleven illustrations depict the temptation of the devil and the comfort of the angel on subjects such as faith, impatience, vainglory, and the final hour of death. Thirteen pages are block-print text. While the apparent raison d'être of the *ars moriendi* was to help people meet death, it also must be considered an early example of printed propaganda, for it urges the dying to put aside the desire to provide for one's family and to will one's estate to the church. The *Biblia Pauperum* (Bible of the Poor) was a compendium of events in the life of Christ, including testimony about how Old Testament prophecy was fulfilled (Fig. **5–8**). Pages from *Ars Memorandi per Figuras Evangelistarum*, c. 1470 (Fig. **5–9**), demonstrate the graphic power of hand-painting fluid washes of watercolor to enliven a woodcut's symbolic imagery.

Most block books contained from thirty to fifty leaves. Some prints were hand-colored, and stencils were sometimes used to apply flat areas of color to textile, playing card, and later block-book woodcuts. In addition, some fifteenth-century prints exist where woodblocks were used to print paste

5–8. Page from a *Biblia Pauperum*, 1465. In this typical layout, a cross-shaped architectural structure brings order to a complex page. Bible verses appear in the upper corners; David and three prophets are above and below with a quotation from each on a scroll. Across the center, the creation of Eve, the Crucifixion of Christ, and Moses striking the rock for water are shown.

5–9. Pages from *Ars Memorandi per Figuras Evangelistarum*, (Book of Notable Religious Figures) c. 1470. Each image became a visual cue for the speaker and a symbolic illustration for the audience.

5–8

5–9

or gum, sprinkled with tinsel (minute sparkling fragments of metal), incrustation (minute quartz crystals with color), or flocking (powdered wool). These media were used as design elements to bring a vibrant tactile quality and luminosity to the image. The earliest block books were printed with a hand rubber in brown or gray ink; later versions were printed in black ink on a printing press. Because the hand rubber created too much indention to allow double-sided printing, the earliest block books are only printed on one side of the paper. Each double-page spread was followed by two blank pages, which were usually pasted together to preserve the visual flow of images and text. While the monastic designer might also cut his own woodblock, in the secular world the distinction between designer and cutter (*Formschneider*) was vigorously upheld by trade guilds. The cutters, who worked from the designer's ink layout on either paper or woodblock, were often members of carpentry guilds.

Movable typography in Europe

With the availability of paper, relief printing from woodblocks, and growing demand for books, the mechanization of book production by such means as movable type was sought by printers in Germany, the Netherlands, France, and Italy. In Avignon, France, goldsmith Procopius Waldfoghel was involved in the production of "alphabets of steel" around 1444, but with no known results. The Dutchman Laurens Janszoon Coster of Haarlem explored the concept of movable type by cutting out letters or words from his woodblocks for reuse. In his monumental book *Dutch Type* (2004), Jan Middendorp states that the Dutch

> managed to build up the Coster myth over several centuries. Eventually the Haarlem printer was believed to be Gutenberg's only serious competitor. Coster and his workshop were pictured by famous artists and praised by Italian historians; his ingenuity became a source of pride and confidence for the Dutch in general and for the Haarlem printing business in particular. In the nineteenth century, theatre pieces about the printer of genius were staged in Paris, Antwerp and London. In Haarlem, massive Coster festivals were organized in fierce competition with the Gutenberg centennial celebrations in Germany; on Haarlem's main square a bronze statue was installed in 1856 that is still there today.

The judgment of history, however, is that Johann Gensfleisch zum Gutenberg (b. late 14th century, d. 1468) of Mainz, Germany, first brought together the complex systems and subsystems necessary to print a typographic book around the year 1450. The third son of the wealthy Mainz patrician Friele Gensfleisch, Johann Gutenberg apprenticed as a goldsmith, developing the metalworking and engraving skills necessary

for making type. In September 1428 he was exiled from Mainz for his leadership role in a power struggle between the landed noblemen and the burghers of the trade guilds who sought a greater political voice. He relocated in Strasbourg, one hundred miles to the southwest, and became a successful and prosperous gem cutter and metalworker.

Early in 1438 Gutenberg formed a contractual partnership with Strasbourg citizens Andreas Dritzehen (who had received gem-cutting training from Gutenberg) and Andreas Hellmann (who owned a paper mill). He agreed to teach them a secret process for making mirrors to sell at an Aachen pilgrimage fair the following year. Mirrors were rare and difficult to manufacture. Molten lead was poured over glass, forming a reflective surface when it cooled; the difficulty was preventing the glass from cracking from the heat. When the fair was postponed until 1440, Gutenberg entered a new five-year contract to teach his partners another secret process.

When Dritzehen died in late 1438, his brothers Georg and Claus sued Gutenberg for either admission to the partnership or a refund. On 12 December 1439, the court ruled in Gutenberg's favor because his original contract specified that only one hundred florins would be paid to any partner's heirs. The record of this trial shows conclusively that Gutenberg was involved in printing. Several witnesses mention that the partners owned a press; woodturner Conrad Saspach testified that he had constructed the press. Testimony mentions type, a stock of lead and other metals, and a mysterious four-piece instrument secured by double handscrews (probably a type mold). Goldsmith Hans Dünne testified that as early as 1436 he had sold Gutenberg one hundred guilders' worth of material "solely for that which belonged to printing." In the mid-1440s Gutenberg moved back to Mainz, where he resolved the technical, organizational, and production problems that had plagued earlier typographic printing efforts. He had labored for ten years before his first printing and twenty years before printing the first typographic book, called the forty-two-line Bible (see Fig. 5–13).

Typographic printing did not grow directly out of block printing because wood was too fragile. Block printing remained popular among the Chinese because alignment between characters was not critical and sorting over five thousand basic characters was untenable. By contrast, the need for exact alignment and the modest alphabet system of about two dozen letters made the printing of text material from independent, movable, and reusable type highly desirable in the West.

A number of steps were necessary in the creation of typographic printing. A style of letter had to be selected. Gutenberg made the obvious choice of the square, compact textura lettering style commonly used by German scribes of his day. Early printers sought to compete with calligraphers by imitating their work as closely as possible. This typeface without subtle curves

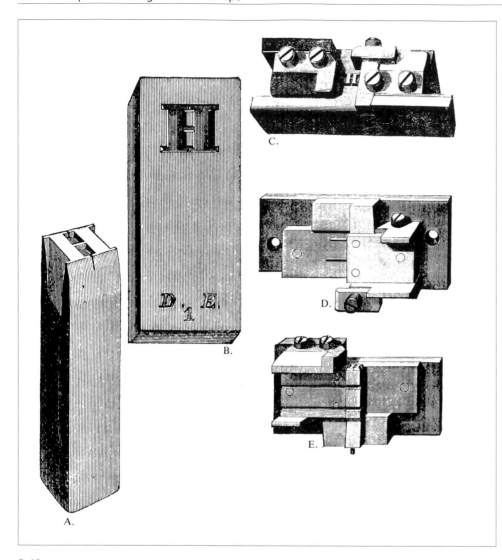

5–10. These early-nineteenth-century engravings illustrate Gutenberg's system for casting type. A steel punch is used to stamp an impression of the letterform into a softer brass matrix. After the matrix is slipped into the bottom of the two-part type mold, the mold is filled with the molten lead alloy to cast a piece of type. After the lead alloy cools, the type mold is opened and the type is removed.
A. Punch
B. Matrix
C. Type mold (with matrix removed to show a newly cast *H*)
D. and **E.** Type mold (opened so that the newly cast *H* can be removed)

5–10

was so well developed that the characters in the forty-two-line Bible are hardly distinguishable from good calligraphy. Next, each character in the font—small and capital letters, numbers, punctuation, ligatures—had to be engraved into the top of a steel bar to make a punch. This punch was then driven into a matrix of softer copper or brass to make a negative impression of the letterform.

The key to Gutenberg's invention was the type mold (Fig. **5–10**), used for casting the individual letters. Each character had to be plane parallel in every direction and the exact same height. Gutenberg's two-part type mold, which adjusted to accept matrixes for narrow characters (1) as well as wide ones (M), permitted large volumes of type to be cast with critical tolerances. Type required a metal that was soft enough to cast but hard enough to hold up for thousands of impressions, and that did not expand and contract when melted, poured into the type mold, then returned to a solid state as it cooled. As a metalsmith, Gutenberg knew that the silvery white metal antimony expands when it cools from a liquid to a solid state, in contrast

to most metals, which contract when cooled. He developed a unique alloy of 80 percent lead, 5 percent tin, and 15 percent antimony to maintain a constant mass throughout the process of manufacturing type. Gutenberg needed as many as fifty thousand single pieces of type in use at a time, so the speed, accuracy, and economy achieved by this type mold and its casting process were critical. The type was stored in compartmentalized cases and pulled out letter by letter to set the lines. After a page was printed, the type was returned to the compartments letter by letter.

The medieval block printer used a thin, watery ink made from oak gall. This ink worked fine on a woodblock, because the wood could absorb excess moisture, but it would run off or puddle on metal type. Gutenberg used boiled linseed oil colored with lampblack, which produced a thick, tacky ink that could be smoothly applied. To ink type, a dollop of ink was placed on a flat surface and smeared with a soft leather ball, coating the ball's bottom. The ball was then daubed onto the type for an even coating of ink.

A strong, sturdy press capable of sufficient force to pressure the ink from the type onto the paper surface was needed. Ample prototypes existed in presses used in making wine, cheese, and baling paper, and Gutenberg adapted their designs, which were based on a large screw lowering and raising a plate, to printing. Gutenberg's press and system were used for four hundred years with moderate improvements. This precision machine allowed tremendous printing speed and consistent quality, in contrast to the hand-rubbing method of the Orient and early European block printers. Later improvements included a frisket to protect margins and other unprinted areas, modification of the screw to lessen the energy needed to print, and a quick-release feature so that less energy was needed to lift the plate than to lower it. Eventually, a mechanical linkage replaced the screw. The graphic arts craftsmen involved in book production are illustrated in Figure **5–11**.

Early surviving examples of typographic design and printing include a German poem on the Last Judgment, four calendars, and a number of editions of a Latin grammar by Donatus. The earliest dated specimens are the 1454 letters of indulgence issued in Mainz (Fig. **5–12**). Pope Nicholas V issued this pardon of sins to all Christians who had given money to support the war against the Turks. Apparently the agents selling manuscript copies early in 1454 learned of Gutenberg's work and realized the value of printing this letter in quantity. Seven editions in two styles were ordered during 1454 and 1455 and numbered in the thousands.

Because the relentless expenses of research and development were a constant drain on Gutenberg's financial resources, in 1450 he found it necessary to borrow eight hundred guilders from Johann Fust (c. 1400–66), a wealthy Mainz burgher and merchant, to continue his work. The printing equipment was offered as collateral. At some point, Gutenberg conceived the idea of printing a Bible. Around 1452 he had to borrow another eight hundred guilders from Fust "for their common profit," establishing a partnership "in the production of books."

A heroic effort was required to produce this first typographic book, which is also one of the finest examples of the printer's art (Fig. **5–13**). The large 30 by 40.5–centimeter (11.75 by 15–inch) pages have two columns of type with a generous 2.9-centimeter (.75–inch) margin between them. The first nine pages have forty lines per column, the tenth page has forty-one lines per column, and the rest have forty-two lines per column. It is not known whether Gutenberg followed a manuscript like this or whether he began a forty-line Bible and then increased the number of lines per column for economy. With 1,282 pages in a two-volume work, the increase of two lines per column saved an additional sixty

pages. This fantastic project began with two presses, to which four were added. With lines of about thirty-three characters, each page had over 2,500 characters set from a font of 290 different characters. The generous number of alternate characters and ligatures enabled Gutenberg to achieve the richness and variety of the manuscript page. For further enrichment, blank spaces were left for decorative initials to be drawn in later by a scribe. A rigorous justification of the columns was possible because Latin words could be abbreviated freely. Up to six letters could be replaced by abbreviation symbols above the words. The edition of 210 copies consisted of 180 on paper and 30 on fine vellum, requiring 5,000 carefully prepared calfskins.

In 1455, as work neared completion, Fust suddenly sued Gutenberg for 2,026 guilders in payment of loans and interest. On 6 November 1455 the courts ruled in favor of Fust, with the requirement that he appear at the local monastery and swear before God that he was paying interest on some of the money he had loaned Gutenberg. Fust appeared and fulfilled the edict of court by taking the oath. Gutenberg did not attend. Instead, he sent two friends to beg Fust to give him more time. Fust declined and seized possession of Gutenberg's printing equipment and all work in progress; on the eve of completion of the immensely valuable forty-two-line Bible, which would have enabled him to pay all debts, Gutenberg was locked out of his printing shop.

Fust immediately entered into an agreement with Gutenberg's skilled assistant and foreman, Peter Schoeffer (c.1425–1502). An artist/designer experienced as an illuminator and manuscript dealer and a scribe at the University of Paris in 1449, Schoeffer quite possibly played a key role in the format development and type design for the forty-two-line Bible. If so, he may have been the first typeface designer. With Fust as business manager and Schoeffer in charge of printing, the firm of Fust and Schoeffer became the most important printing firm in the world, establishing a hundred-year family dynasty of printers, publishers, and booksellers. Schoeffer married Fust's daughter, Christina, around 1467. The new partnership's first venture was the completion of the forty-two-line Bible. As one of the forty-seven surviving copies bears a marginal notation that the hand rubrication, which is the application of red-ink initials and titles by a scribe, was completed on 24 August 1456, Fust probably acquired a nearly complete production when he foreclosed.

Sales of the forty-two-line Bible were brisk as Fust traveled widely to distribute them. An early author relates that Fust carried a parcel of Bibles to Paris and attempted to sell them as manuscripts. The forty-two-line Bible had no title page, no page numbers, nor other innovations to distinguish it from handmade manuscripts. Both Gutenberg and his customers

A.

B.

C.

D.

E.

5–11

F.

G.

H.

Forma plenissime absolutionis et remissionis in vita

Forma plenarie remissionis in mortis articulo

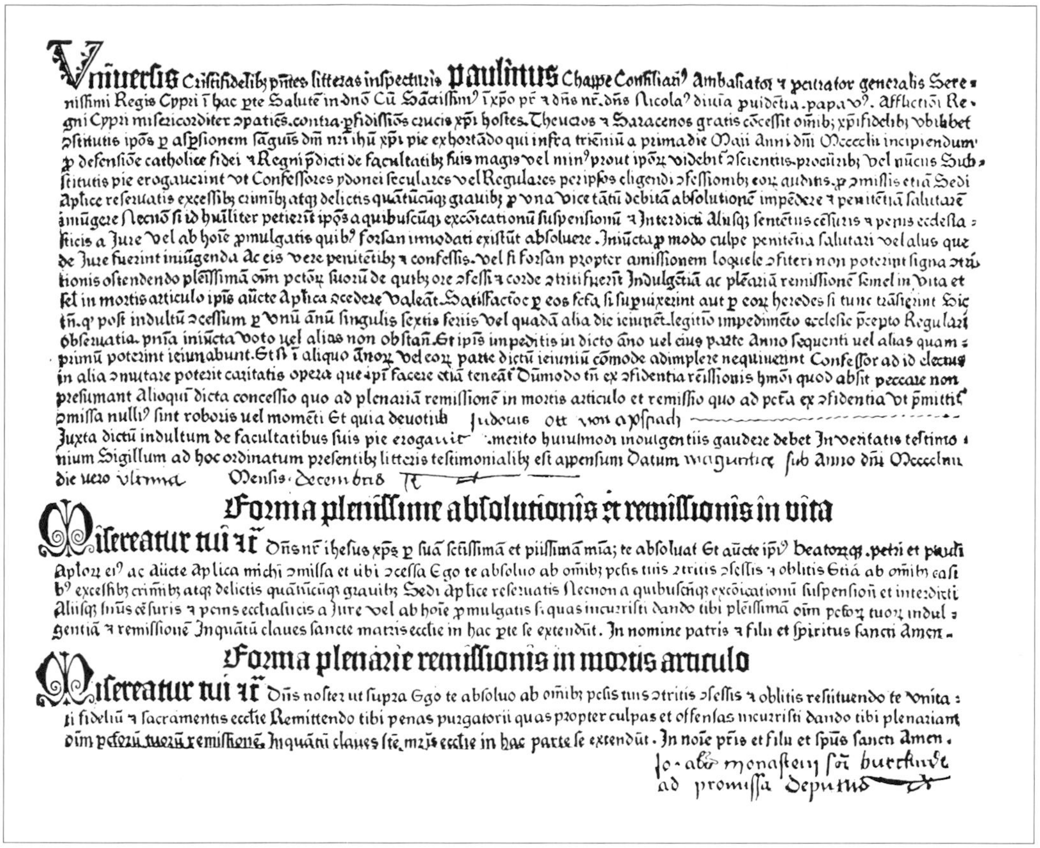

5–12

5–11. Jost Amman, woodcut illustrations for *Ständebuch* (Book of Trades), 1568. This little book presented over a hundred occupations, from the Pope to the scissors sharpener. Amman's crisp illustrations were accompanied by the prolific poet Hans Sachs's descriptive rhymes. The occupations of the graphic arts are shown here.

A. The parchment maker is shown scraping animal skins to produce a smooth surface after they have been washed, stretched, and dried.

B. The papermaker lifts his mold out of the vat as he forms each sheet by hand.

C. The typefounder is depicted pouring the melted lead into the type mold to cast a character. The foreground basket is filled with newly cast type.

D. One printer is shown removing a newly printed sheet from the press while the other one inks the type. In the background, compositors are shown setting type at typecases.

E. The designer is illustrated as he draws an image in preparation for a woodcut or copper engraving. (This is probably Amman's self-portrait.)

F. The woodblock cutter carefully cuts the drawing or design into a block of wood.

G. The illuminator, who originally applied gold leaf and color to manuscripts, continued his craft on the typographically printed page.

H. One bookbinder collates the pages of a volume by hand. The other prepares a book for the application of the covers.

5–12. Johann Gutenberg, thirty-one-line *Letters of Indulgence,* c. 1454. The written additions in this copy indicate that on the last day of December 1454, one Judocus Ott von Apspach was pardoned of his sins.

probably wanted it this way. When the French observed the number and conformity of the volumes, they thought witchcraft was involved. To avoid indictment and conviction, Fust was forced to reveal his secret. This event is alleged to be the basis for the popular story, related by several authors, of the German magician Dr. Faustus (Johann Faust in an early version), who grew dissatisfied with the limits of human knowledge and sold his soul to the devil in exchange for knowledge and power.

On 14 August 1457, Fust and Schoeffer published a magnificent psalter in Latin with a monumental 30.5 by 43.2–centimeter (12 by 17–inch) page size (Fig. **5–14**). The large red-and-blue initials were printed from two-part metal blocks that were either inked separately, reassembled, and printed with the text in one press impression, or stamped after the text was printed. These famous decorated two-color initials were a major innovation; their typographic vitality and elegance rival the most beautiful manuscript pages. The psalter in Latin was also the first book to bear a printer's trademark and imprint, printed date of publication, and colophon (Fig. **5–15**). A translation of the colophon reads: "This book of the Psalms, decorated with beautiful capitals, and with an abundance of rubrics, has been fashioned thus by an ingenious invention of printing and stamping without use of a pen. And to the worship of God it has been diligently brought to Completion by

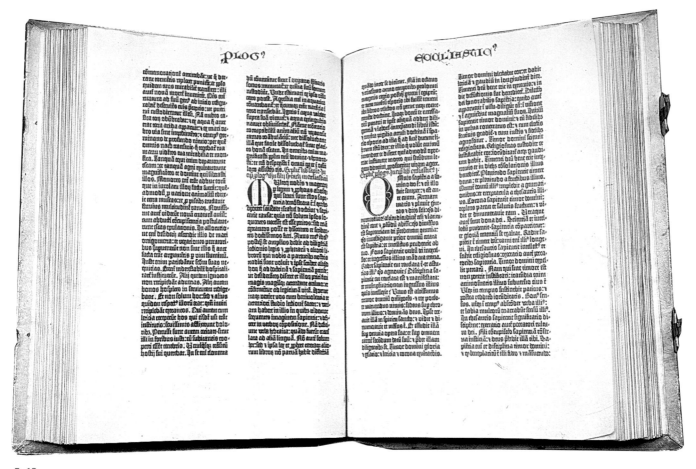

5–13

Johann Fust, a citizen of Mainz, and Peter Schoeffer of Gernsheim, in the year of Our Lord 1457, on the eve of the Feast of the Assumption."

Another important innovation appeared in Fust and Schoeffer's 1459 edition of *Rationale Divinorum Officiorum* (Rationale of Holy Duties) (Fig. **5–16**). This long volume explaining religious ceremonies was the first typographic book that employed a small-sized type style to conserve space and increase the amount of text on each page. This achieved significant economy in presswork, ink, and parchment.

Other major works included a beautiful Latin Bible (1462) and an edition of Cicero's *De officiis* (On Duty) (1465), which was the first printing of a classic from antiquity. Typographic printing spurred interest in ancient Greek and Roman culture. As knowledge from the ancient world and the medieval era began to spread through the printed word, the fusion became a catalyst for the creation of the modern world.

During a 1466 Paris trip to sell books, Johann Fust died, probably of plague. Peter Schoeffer and his associate, Conrad Henkis, who married Fust's widow the year after Fust died, continued this highly successful printing business, producing broadsheets, books, and pamphlets.

While Fust and Schoeffer were selling Bibles and printing psalters, Johann Gutenberg, who, like many innovators, was running a heartbeat ahead of his time, drifted into bankruptcy and in 1458 defaulted on interest payments for a 1442 loan. Although he was past sixty years of age and down and out, he had perfected his craft and completed his research. It is believed that with financial support from Mainz citizen Dr. Conrad Homery, Gutenberg was able to establish a new printing shop. Some scholars view him as the printer of the thirty-six-line Bible, a late-1450s reprint of the forty-two-line Bible with similar but less refined type. His *Catholicon*, an encyclopedic dictionary, was published in 1460 with a colophon—perhaps in Gutenberg's own words—stating that the work was published "with the protection of the Almighty, at whose will the tongues of infants become eloquent and who often reveals to the lowly what he hides from the wise." On 17 January 1465, Archbishop Adolf of Mainz appointed Gutenberg courtier with the rank of nobleman, entitling him to clothing, keep, and "twenty matter of corn and two fudder of wine each year." The flyleaf of a book owned by a Mainz priest bears an inscription stating that "the honorable Master Johann Gutenberg died 3 February 1468." Based on

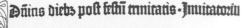

5–14   5–15

prior agreements, Dr. Homery petitioned the courts for ownership of the "forms, letters, instruments, tools, and other
things pertaining to the work of printing" that belonged to
the late Gutenberg. On 26 February 1468, the archbishop
transferred possession to Dr. Homery, who promised to keep
this equipment in Mainz and give first preference to Mainz
citizens in the event of future sale.

For a brief few years, printing was centered in Mainz, as
Fust and Schoeffer, Gutenberg, and former apprentices who
had established their own firms were located there. Ironically,
the swift spread of printing was hastened by a bloody conflict. German nobles were involved in power struggles that
erupted into full-scale war. Leading a sizable army, Adolf of
Nassau descended upon Mainz in 1462 and sacked the town.
Plundering and looting brought trade and commerce to a
halt. Warnings from other towns in Adolf's path enabled
many Mainz merchants and craftsmen to load everything possible on wagons and carts and flee. Many younger printers
and apprentices did not return. Rather, presses were soon
established as far away as France and Italy.

5–13. Johann Gutenberg, pages from the Gutenberg Bible,
1450–55. The superb typographic legibility and texture,
generous margins, and excellent presswork make this first
printed book a canon of quality that has seldom been
surpassed. An illuminator added the red and blue headers,
initials, and text by hand.

5–14. Fust and Schoeffer, page detail from *Psalter in Latin*,
1457. The red and blue initials are the earliest example of
color printing in Europe.

5–15. Fust and Schoeffer, colophon and trademark from
Psalter in Latin, 1457. The double crests are thought to
symbolize the two printers.

5–16

5–17

5–16. Jan Fust and Peter Schoeffer, page from *Rationale Divinorum Officiorum*, 1459. The innovative small type is combined with wonderfully intricate printed red and blue initials that evidence the early printer's efforts to mimic the design of the manuscript book.

5–17. The Master of the Playing Cards, *The Three of Birds*, c. 1450. Masterly design and placement of the images in the space enhanced the sureness of the drawing and use of line for tonal effects.

Copperplate engraving

During the same time and in the same section of Europe that Johann Gutenberg invented movable type, an unidentified artist called the Master of the Playing Cards created the earliest known copperplate engravings (Figs. **5–17**). Engraving is printing from an image that is incised or cut down into the printing surface. To produce a copperplate engraving, a drawing is scratched into a smooth metal plate. Ink is applied into the depressions, the flat surface is wiped clean, and paper is pressed against the plate to receive the ink image. The finest work of the Master of the Playing Cards is a set of playing cards using birds, animals, and wild men as images. The quality of his drawing suggests that he probably trained as an artist rather than as a goldsmith. The skilled execution implies that these playing cards were designed and engraved by someone who had already mastered engraving, not someone struggling to perfect a new graphic technique.

Scholars have speculated that Gutenberg, in addition to inventing typographic printing, may have been involved in the research and development of copperplate engraving. Images by the Master of the Playing Cards have now been associated with Mainz illuminators, including artists involved with Gutenberg's printing works during the 1450s. The links binding these early printing innovators together are illustrations of birds, animals, flowers, and figures duplicated in the engraved playing cards, an illuminated Bible produced in Mainz during the early 1450s, and the illumination added to a surviving copy of the forty-two-line Bible.

This circumstantial evidence raises exciting possibilities. Was Gutenberg striving to perfect the printing not just of scribes' lettering but of the magnificent ornamentation and illustration of the medieval manuscript as well? Was engraving pioneered as a means to print illustrations onto the typographic pages, which could then be hand-colored? Did Gutenberg explore using engraving plates as molds to cast relief versions so that illustrations could be printed with type? These provocative questions, still without definite answers, indicate that Gutenberg's research might have carried the printed book in a different direction from its subsequent development.

The German Illustrated Book

6

The Latin word *incunabula* means "cradle" or "baby linen." Its connotations of birth and beginnings caused seventeenth–century writers to adopt it as a name for books printed from Gutenberg's invention of typography until the end of the fifteenth century. (The date is completely arbitrary; this chapter traces the logical continuation of design and typography into the early 1500s.) Printing spread rapidly. By 1480 twenty-three northern European towns, thirty-one Italian towns, seven French towns, six Spanish and Portuguese towns, and one English town had presses. By 1500 printing was practiced in over 140 towns. It is estimated that over thirty-five thousand editions for a total of nine million books were produced. In 1450 Europe's monasteries and libraries housed a mere fifty thousand volumes. In addition, a vast array of ephemera, including religious tracts, pamphlets, and broadsides, was produced for free distribution or sale. Broadsides—single-leaf pages printed on one side—eventually evolved into printed posters, advertisements, and newspapers. Four years after printing came to Venice, a dismayed scribe complained that the city was "stuffed with books." The boom in this new craft led to overproduction and the proliferation of firms. From the ranks of over one hundred printing firms established in Venice before 1490, only ten survived until the end of the century.

Printing was resisted in some quarters. The scribes in Genoa banded together and demanded that the town council forbid printing in that town. They argued that greedy printers were threatening their livelihood. The council did not support the petition, and within two years Genoa joined the mushrooming list of towns with printers. Parisian illuminators filed suits in the courts in a vain attempt to win damages from printers who were engaged in unfair competition that caused the demand for manuscript books to decline. Some bibliophiles maintained that type was inferior to calligraphy and unworthy of their libraries. In 1492 a cardinal, who later became Pope Julius II, ordered scribes to hand-letter a copy of a typographic book for his library.

But typographic printing reduced a book's price to a fraction of its earlier cost, turning the serious shortage of books (and the knowledge they contained) into an abundance. The tide of progress could not be stayed, and manuscript production slowly declined. The philosopher Alfred N. Whitehead once observed how major advances in civilization are processes that all but wreck the society where they occur. Typography is the major communications advance between the invention of writing and twentieth-century electronic mass communications; it played a pivotal role in the social, economic, and religious upheavals that occurred during the fifteenth and sixteenth centuries. The modern nation developed as a result of the vigorous spirit of nationalism that swept over Europe and led to the American and French revolutions of the late eighteenth century. In addition to being a powerful vehicle for spreading ideas about human rights and the sovereignty of the people, printing stabilized and unified languages. People all across France, for example, were reading the same material in French, which formerly had many provincial idiosyncrasies of spelling and grammar. The French, English, and German languages became typographic mass media communicating to audiences of unprecedented size with one voice.

Illiteracy, the inability to read and write, began a long, steady decline. Literacy was of limited value to a medieval peasant who had no hope of gaining access to books. But tumbling book prices, the beginnings of such popular writing as romantic novels, and the proliferation of the ever-present broadside made reading desirable and increasingly necessary for Renaissance townspeople. The medieval classroom had been a scriptorium of sorts, where each student penned his own book. Typography radically altered education. Learning became an increasingly private, rather than communal, process. Human dialogue, extended by type, began to take place on a global scale that bridged time and space. Gutenberg's invention was the first mechanization of a skilled handicraft. As such, it set into motion, over the next three hundred years, the processes that would lead to the Industrial Revolution.

Renaissance innovators altered the perception of information by creating two visual systems. Painting evoked illusions of the natural world on flat surfaces through such means as the single light source and light-and-shadow modeling, the fixed viewpoint and linear perspective, and atmospheric perspective. Typography created a sequential and repeatable ordering of information and space. It led people toward linear thought and logic and toward a categorization and compartmentalization of information that formed the basis for empirical scientific inquiry. It fostered individualism, a dominant aspect of Western society since the Renaissance.

Publication of edition after edition of the Bible made increased study possible. People throughout Europe formulated their own interpretations instead of relying on religious leaders as the locus of truth. This led directly to the Reformation, which shattered Christianity into hundreds of sects. After Martin Luther (c. 1483–1546) posted his Ninety-five Theses for debate on the door of Castle Church in Wittenberg, Saxony, on 31 October 1517, his friends passed copies to printers. By December his proclamation had spread throughout central Europe. Within a few months, thousands of people all over Europe knew his views. Without typography, it is doubtful that the Protestant movement of the Reformation era could have happened. Both Luther and Pope Leo X used printed broadsides and tracts in a theological dispute before a mass audience throughout the continent.

By the end of the incunabula period, presses had been established throughout Europe, but very few printers at the time contributed to the development of graphic design. Most were content to print copies of manuscripts or earlier printed editions. Although the press replaced the copisti in producing running text, the same division of labor found in the scriptorium continued. Multicolor printing was used in Fust and Schoeffer's *Psalter in Latin*, but rubrication, decoration, and illumination in early incunabula were almost always by hand. Perhaps the difficulties of multicolor printing made it more expensive, or maybe enough political pressure was generated by the rubricators and illuminators to allow them to continue their crafts on typographic books.

Design innovation took place in Germany, where woodcut artists and typographic printers collaborated to develop the illustrated book and broadsheet. In Italy, the letter styles and format design inherited from illuminated manuscripts gave way to a design approach unique to the typographic book. Early printers followed the manuscript custom of putting the title and author at the top of the first page, in the same size and style of lettering as the text. A short space was skipped, then *Incipit* (here begins) launched the book. Early in the incunabula period, a printed *ex libris*, or bookplate (Fig. **6–1**), was pasted into the front of a book to identify the owner. As printing spread from Mainz, so did the use of the printer's trademark as a visual identifier.

Scribes and artists were often called upon to make exemplars, or layouts, for illustrated books and broadsides.

6–1

6–1. *Ex libris* design for Johannes Knabensberg, c. 1450s. One of the earliest extant bookplates, it bears an inscription, "Hans Igler that the hedgehog may kiss you. *Igler*, Knabensberg's nickname, is similar to the German word for hedgehog, making an early graphic pun.

Manuscript books have been discovered with editorial notes, marginal notes to indicate where typeset pages ended, inky fingerprints, and sketches for woodblocks. These indicate their use as layouts and manuscripts for printed books. In one such manuscript, the scribe's colophon is scratched out; in the printed book it is replaced by a typeset version.

Origins of the illustrated typographic book

Block printers and woodcarvers feared typographic printing as a serious threat to their livelihood, but early in the evolution of the typographic book, Bamberg printer Albrecht Pfister began to illustrate his books with woodblock prints. About 1460, he used five woodblocks (Fig. **6–2**) and the types from Gutenberg's thirty-six-line Bible to print his first edition of Johannes von Tepl's *Der Ackerman aus Böhmen* (*Death and the Plowman*); Pfister's nine editions of five books were popular literature, in contrast to the theological and scholarly works published by most other early printers. As the decades passed, typographic printers dramatically increased their use of woodblock illustrations. This created a booming demand for blocks, and the stature of graphic illustrators increased. Augsburg and Ulm, centers for woodblock playing-card and religious-print production, became centers for illustrated books. In the 1470s Günther Zainer (d. 1478) established a press in Augsburg, and his relative Johann Zainer established one about 70 kilometers (43 miles) to the east in Ulm. Both men were scribes and illuminators who had learned printing in Strasbourg.

6–2

.xiij.

De Marsepia & Lampedone reginis amazonū. C. xi

Arsepia seu marthesia & lampedo sorores
fuere Amazonum inuicem regine/ & ob il=
lustrem bellop gloriam sese martis vocaue
filias Quap qm pegrina sit historia paulo
altiꝰ assumēda est/ e scithia ergo ea tēpestate siluestri &
fere in accessa exteris regione/ & sub artheo se in occea
num vsꝗ ab eusino sinu ꝑtendente/ Siliscus & scolo
picus(vt aiunt)regij iuuenes factione maiop pulsi cū
parte ꝓlop ꝑ iuxta thermodobonté cappadocie amnem
deuene/& tirꝑs occupatis aruis raptu viuē & incolas
latrocinijs infestare cepē/ A quibus tractu temporis ꝑ
insidias fere omnes trucidati sunt homines, Qꝼ cum
egrefriēt viduate coniuges/ & in ardoré vindicte de=
uenissent feruide/ cum paucis qui supuixerint viris in
arma prorupere, Et primo impetu facto hostes a suis
demouere finibus/inde vltro circumstantibus intulere
bellum/demum arbitrantes huirutē potius ꝗ ꝺiugiū/
si exteris adbererent hoīnibus / & feminas solas posse

6–4

6–2. Albrecht Pfister (printer), illustration from the second edition
of *Der Ackerman aus Böhmen,* c. 1463. Death sits as a king on his
throne, flanked by a widower and his child on the left and the
deceased wife on the right.

6–3. Gunther Zainer (printer), illustration from *Spiegel des menschlichen Lebens,* 1475. In this illustration of a voice instructor, the triangular pattern on the tile floor introduces a lively tonal contrast.

6–4. Johann Zainer, page from *De Mulieribus Claris,* by Boccaccio,
1473. In this book about famous women, the woodcuts are all
designed in rectangles the width of the type column and dropped
in flush to it.

6–5. Anton Sorg, page from Aesop's *Vita et fabulae,* c. 1479. Sorg
used a wider column width than Zainer did in an earlier version of
Aesop's *Fables* and tried to compensate for the lack of alignment
between the woodcut and the type column by a margin of white
space above and below the illustration.

Das vierd puch   Das· xxxix.blat·

¶Die erst fabel von dem fuchs vmd dem trauben·

(H) In fuchs lieff für ein hohe weinreben vmd sahe daran hangen zeittig trauben·der begeret er zeessen/vmd süchet manigerley wege wie jm die traube werden mochten mit klimen vmd springen·Aber sy stunden so hoch das sy jm nit werden mochten·Do er daz mercket lief er hinweg vnd verkeret sein anfechtung vnd lust zu den traube in freude vmd sprache· Nun seind doch die trauben noch sawer·Ich wolt sy auch nit essen/ob ich sy wol mocht erlangen· ¶Dise fabel bedeütet das ein weiser man sol sich lassen beduncken/er wol vn müg des nit· das er nit gehaben mag.

¶Die ander fabel von der wisel vmd der müß.

6–5

Günther Zainer met resistance from the Augsburg woodcutter's guild when he wanted to illustrate his books with woodblocks. A 1471 agreement allowed Zainer to use woodblock illustrations as long as he commissioned them from members of the guild. His first illustrated books used a rounded Gothic type and woodblocks set into a type column of the same width. By 1475 his illustrated books, including *Spiegel des menschlichen Lebens* (The Mirror of Life), which analyzed the positive and negative aspects of various careers, used woodcuts with textured areas and some solid blacks (Fig. **6–3**). This introduced a greater tonal range to the page design. Fortune smiled upon Zainer, for the sale of about thirty-six thousand books printed in over a hundred editions made him one of Augsburg's most prominent and affluent citizens.

In Ulm, Johann Zainer used eighty woodcuts in his 1473 edition of *De Mulieribus Claris* (Of Famous Women) by Boccaccio (Fig. **6–4**). These illustrations have a very even line weight; the capital initials, printed rather than added later by hand, are

wonderful little woodblock letters formed by birds, snakes, and plants. Woodcuts were used over and over in different books. For example, the 175 woodcuts in Johann Zainer's 1476 edition of Aesop's *Vita et fabulae* (Life and Tales) appear again in the edition by Ulm printer Anton Sorg four years later (Fig. **6–5**). Many of these illustrations are not completely enclosed with rectangular borders, which allows white space to flow from the wide margins into the pictures. Simple outline initials extend this light design effect. Typographic paragraph marks leave nothing for the rubricator in this volume; the printed book was becoming independent of the manuscript.

The first illustrator to be identified as such in a book was Erhard Reuwich, for his work in *Peregrinationes in Montem Syon* (Travels in Mount Syon), printed with Schoeffer's types in 1486. The author of this first travel book, Bernardus de Breidenbach, dean of the Mainz Cathedral, departed for Jerusalem on 25 April 1483 and took Reuwich along to record the sights. When they returned to Mainz in January 1484, Breidenbach wrote a book about his journey; the published volume featured woodblocks cut from Reuwich's drawings. Reuwich was a careful observer of nature who introduced crosshatch illustration in this volume. His illustrations included regional maps, significant buildings, and views of major cities. This book was the first to have fold-out illustrations, including the four-page-wide view of Modon illustrated here (Fig. **6–6**), and a woodcut of Venice stretching almost meters (4 feet, 9 inches).

Nuremberg becomes a printing center

Because printing required a huge capital investment and large trained labor force, it is not surprising that Nuremberg, which had become central Europe's prosperous center of commerce and distribution, housed Germany's most esteemed printer, Anton Koberger (c. 1440–1513), by the end of the century. His firm was staffed by a hundred craftsmen operating twenty-four presses; it printed over two hundred editions, including fifteen Bibles. As a bookseller, Koberger owned sixteen shops and had agents throughout Europe. By the 1490s most printers had trouble selling large books and abandoned the huge format of the liturgical Bibles. Books with smaller page sizes were more convenient and affordable for private customers. Koberger, however, continued to publish and sell large books.

As a printer working in concert with master illustrators, he produced three masterpieces. The 1491 *Schatzbehalter* (Treasure Trove), a religious treatise, contains ninety-two full-page woodcuts by the painter and woodcut illustrator Michael Wolgemuth (1434–1519). Published in German and Latin versions in 1493, the six-hundred-page *Liber Chronicarum (Nuremberg Chronicle)* by Dr. Hartmann Schedel is an ambitious history of the world from the biblical dawn of creation (Fig. **6–7**) until

6–6

6–7

6–8

6–6. Erhard Reuwich (illustrator), illustration from *Peregrinationes in Montem Syon*, 1486. Panoramic vistas present accurate depictions of the cities visited on the journey.

6–7. Anton Koberger, pages from the *Nuremberg Chronicle*, 1493. The raised hand of God in the initial illustration is repeated over several pages retelling the biblical story of creation.

6–8. George Alt, title page for the *Nuremberg Chronicle*, 1493. This title reads, "Registry [index] for this Book of Chronicles with illustrations and portraits from the initiation of the world."

1493. One of the masterpieces of incunabula-period graphic design, the *Nuremberg Chronicle* has 1,809 woodcut illustrations in its complex, carefully designed 47.5 by 32.6–centimeter (18 by 12–inch) pages. The title page for the index is a full-page woodblock of calligraphy (Fig. **6–8**) attributed to George Alt (c. 1450–1510), a scribe who assisted Hartmann Schedel in lettering the Latin exemplar and who translated the Latin manuscript into German for that version.

The exemplars (handmade model layouts and manuscript texts used as guides for the woodcut illustrations, typesetting, page design, and makeup of books) for both editions survive and provide rare insight into the design and production process (Figs. **6–9** and **6–10**). The exemplars for the *Nuremberg Chronicle* are the work of several "sketch artists" and numerous scribes, whose lettering in the exemplar has the same character count as the type font to ensure an accurate conversion. The publishers contracted with Michael Wolgemuth and his stepson Wilhelm Pleydenwurff (d. 1494) to create the exemplars, draw the illustrations, and cut, correct, and prepare the woodblocks for printing. Also, one or the other had to be present at the printshop during typesetting and printing. For this work the artists were paid a one-thousand-guilder advance and guaranteed one half of the net profits. Because many woodcuts were used several times, only 645 different woodcuts were required. For example, 598 portraits of popes, kings, and other historical personages were printed from ninety-six blocks. Major cities of the world were illustrated (Figs. **6–11** and **6–12**); some woodblocks were used for more than one city.

Koberger's contract required him to order and pay for paper that was as good as, or better than, the sample he had supplied; print the book according to the exemplars in an acceptable type style; maintain the security of a locked room for the project; and provide a workroom for Wolgemuth and Pleydenwurff. Koberger was paid four guilders for every ream (five hundred sheets) of four-page sheets printed. During the months of production, Koberger could bill the publishers periodically for portions of the book that had been printed and gathered into three-sheet, twelve-page signatures.

Page layouts range from a full double-page illustration of the city of Nuremberg to unillustrated type pages. On some pages, woodcuts are inserted into the text; on others, woodcuts are lined into vertical columns. Rectangular illustrations are placed under or above type areas. When the layout threatens to become repetitive, the reader is jolted by an unexpected page design. The dense texture and rounded strokes of Koberger's sturdy Gothic types contrast handsomely with the tones of the woodcuts. The illustrators used their imagination to create unseen monstrosities, unvisited cities, and awful tortures, and to express the story of creation in graphic symbols.

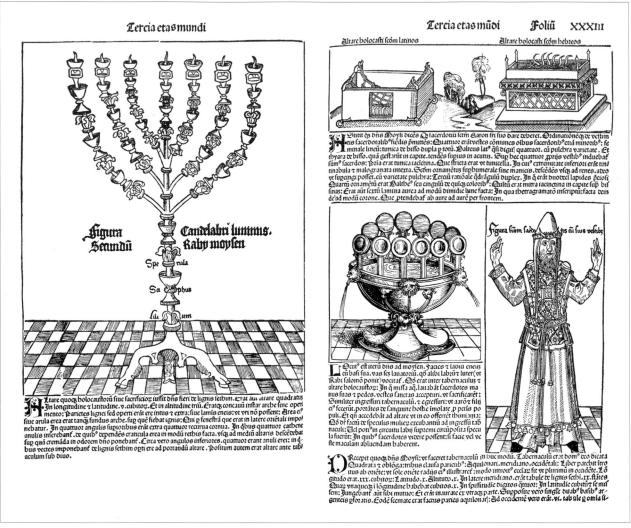

6–9

6–9. Anton Koberger, pages from the *Nuremberg Chronicle*, 1493. This complex layout is ordered by the use of rules around the illustrations. These convert the silhouette images into rectangles, which can be tightly fitted with the rectangles of type.

6–10. Studio of Michael Wolgemuth and Wilhelm Pleydenwurff, pages from the *Nuremberg Chronicle*, Latin exemplar, pre-1493. This layout and manuscript provided guidance for the compositors, although liberties were taken in the final layout.

Koberger was godfather to Albrecht Dürer (1471–1528), whose goldsmith father apprenticed him to Michael Wolgemuth for almost four years, beginning in 1486. Most likely the young Dürer, who grew up three houses down the street in Nuremberg from Wolgemuth's home and studio, assisted in the layout and illustration for the *Nuremberg Chronicle*.

In 1498 Dürer published Latin and German editions of *The Apocalypse* (Fig. **6–13**) illustrated by his monumental sequence of fifteen woodcuts. This thirty-two-page book, with 44.5 by 30.5–centimeter (16 by 12–inch) pages, has fifteen layouts with two columns of Koberger's type on the left facing one of Dürer's illustrations on the right. Dürer's *Apocalypse* has an unprecedented emotional power and graphic expressiveness. Volume and depth, light and shadow, texture and surface are created by black ink on white paper, which becomes a metaphor for light in a turbulent world of awesome powers. At age twenty-seven, Dürer earned renown throughout Europe.

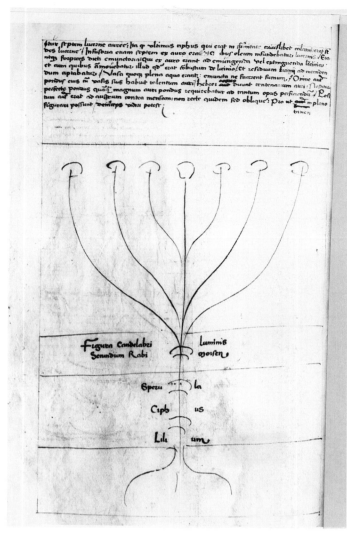

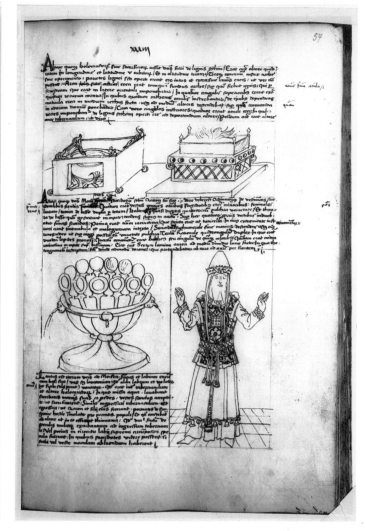

6–10

The colophon reads "Printed by Albrecht Dürer." Given his prodigious volume of prints, Dürer probably had a press in his workshop. As the types used are Koberger's, we don't know if Dürer acquired set type from his godfather and printed *The Apocalypse,* printed the woodblocks, and sent the sheets to Koberger's shop for typographic imprinting, or commissioned Koberger to print the edition under his own (Dürer's) supervision.

In 1511 Dürer issued a new edition of *The Apocalypse* and published two other large-format volumes, the *Large Passion* and *The Life of the Virgin* (Fig. **6–14**). In his mature work he achieved mastery in the use of line as tone. Dürer's broadsides were very popular, and at least eight editions of his *Rhinoceros* (Fig. **6–15**) went out of print. The text was undoubtedly edited to make the five lines of metal type form a perfect rectangle of tone aligning with the woodcut border.

Trips to Venice for six months at age twenty-three and for one-and-a-half years when he was thirty-four enabled Dürer to absorb the painting theory and technique, as well as the hu-

manist philosophy, of the Italian Renaissance. He became a major influence in the cultural exchange that saw the Renaissance spirit filter into Germany. He believed German artists and craftsmen were producing work inferior to that of the Italians because they lacked the theoretical knowledge of their fellow professionals to the south. This inspired his first book, *Underweisung der Messung mit dem Zirckel und Richtscheyt* (A Course in the Art of Measurement with Compass and Ruler), in 1525. The first two chapters are theoretical discussions of linear geometry and two-dimensional geometric construction. The third chapter explains the application of geometry to architecture, decoration, engineering, and letterforms. Dürer's beautifully proportioned Roman capitals, with clear instructions for their composition, contributed significantly to the evolution of alphabet design (Fig. **6–16**). Relating each letter to the square, Dürer worked out a construction method using a one-to-ten ratio of the heavy stroke width to height. This is the approximate proportion of the Trajan alphabet, but Dürer did not base his designs on any single source. Recognizing the

6–11

6–11 and 6–12. Anton Koberger, page from the *Nuremberg Chronicle*, 1493. Many woodblock book illustrations were hand-painted.

6–13. Albrecht Dürer, *The Four Horsemen of the Apocalypse*, 1498. Poised at a historical watershed as the medieval epoch evolved toward the German Renaissance, Dürer simultaneously achieved the spiritual power of the former and the artistic mastery of the latter.

6–14. Albrecht Dürer, title page for *The Life of the Virgin*, 1511. A linear sunburst creates a dazzling luminosity seldom achieved with black ink on white paper. The triangular shape of the title echoes angular lines radiating from the figures; the text (below) repeats the horizontal lines above it.

6–15. Albrecht Dürer, broadside, 1515. Dürer developed his woodcut illustration from a sketch and description sent from Spain, after the first rhinoceros in over a thousand years arrived in Europe.

6–12

6–13

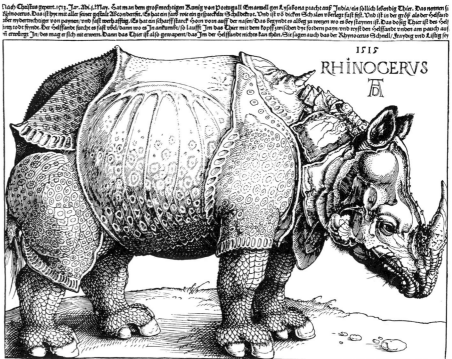

6–14

6–15

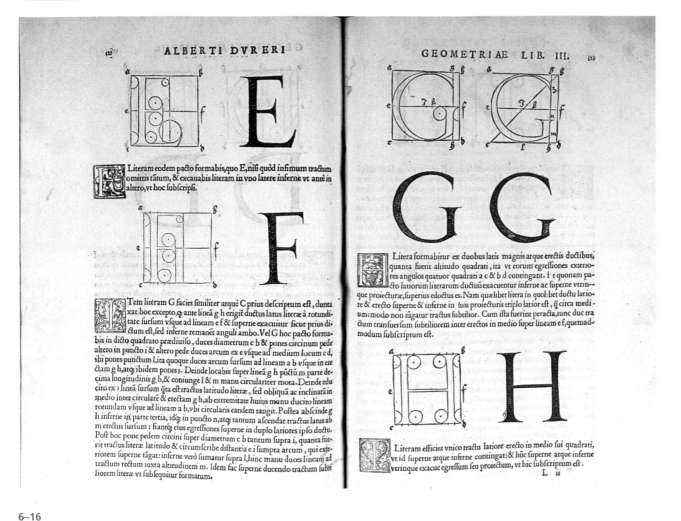

6–16

6–17

6–16. Albrecht Dürer, from *Underweisung der Messung*, 1525. Dürer presented variations for each character in the alphabet.

6–17. Albrecht Dürer, woodcut from *De Symmetria Partium Humanorum Corporum*, 1532. To assist his fellow artists, Dürer offers a "through-the-looking-grid" device as an aid to drawing.

6–18. Johann Schoensperger (printer), pages from *Teuerdank*, 1517. The flamboyant calligraphic gestures are appropriate for this romantic novel about chivalry. The swashes are carefully placed to animate the pages in the layout of the book.

value of art and perception as well as geometry, he advised his readers that certain construction faults could only be corrected by a sensitive eye and trained hand. The fourth chapter covers the construction of geometric solids, linear perspective, and mechanical aids to drawing.

The illustrated book *De Symmetria Partium Humanorum Corporum* (Treatise on Human Proportions) (Fig. **6–17**) first appeared in Nuremberg shortly after Dürer's death in 1528. It shared his tremendous knowledge of drawing, the human figure, and the advances of Italian artists with German painters and graphic artists.

The further development of the German illustrated book

While graphic artists and printers in Italy and France evolved toward Renaissance book design (discussed in chapter 7), German graphic design continued its tradition of textura typography and vigorous woodcut illustrations. One of Dürer's former students, Hans Schäufelein, was commissioned to design the illustrations for Pfintzing's *Teuerdank* (Fig. **6–18**), an adventure of chivalry and knighthood that was printed by Johann Schoensperger the Elder at Nuremberg in 1517. Commissioned by Emperor Maximilian to commemorate his marriage to Mary of Burgundy, this lavish book required five years to produce. The types for *Teuerdank*, designed by court calligrapher Vincenz Rockner, comprise one of the earliest examples of the Gothic style known as *Fraktur*. Some of the rigid, angular straight lines found in textura letterforms were replaced with flowing, curved strokes.

6–18

Rockner carried this design quality even further in an effort to duplicate the gestural freedom of the pen. As many as eight alternate characters were designed and cast for each letterform. These had sweeping calligraphic flourishes, some of which flowed deep into the surrounding space. When the book was published, other printers insisted that these ornamental letterforms must have been printed from woodblocks, for they refused to believe that it was possible to achieve these effects with cast metal types. (An inverted *i* in the 1517 edition, however, conclusively proves that metal types were used to print *Teuerdank*.)

Technically speaking, a *broadside* is a single leaf of paper printed on one side only. When both sides are printed, the page is frequently called a *broadsheet*; however, these terms are often used interchangeably. This ephemeral form of graphic communications became a major means for information dissemination from the invention of printing until the middle of the nineteenth century. Content ranged from announcements of deformed births to portraits of famous secular and religious leaders (see Fig. **6–21**). Festivals and fairs were advertised, and the sale of lottery tickets and indulgences was announced. Political causes and religious beliefs were expounded, and invasions and disasters were proclaimed. Folded printed sheets evolved into pamphlets, tracts, and, later, newspapers. The design of a broadside was often the task of the compositor, who organized the space and made typographic decisions while setting the type. Woodblock illustrations were commissioned from artists. Once available, a given woodblock might appear in a number of broadsides, or be sold or loaned to another printer.

As Martin Luther pressed the breach with the Catholic Church that began in 1517, his presence at the university in Wittenberg brought importance to the graphics produced there. Luther found a loyal friend and follower in the artist Lucas Cranach the Elder (1472–1553), who had been called to Wittenberg by the electors of Saxony. In addition to his studio, staffed by a number of well-trained assistants, Cranach operated a printing office, a bookshop, and a paper mill. He even found time to serve twice as mayor of Wittenberg. He turned his considerable energy to the Reformation by portraying the Reformers and their cause in books and broadsides. When Luther traveled to Worms for his celebrated trial in 1521, his portraits by Cranach filled the town on printed matter proclaiming his beliefs. And yet Cranach regularly accepted commissions for Madonnas and Crucifixions from Catholic clients, and many of the woodcuts he produced for the Luther Bible were also used in a subsequent Catholic edition. A most effective example of propaganda is Cranach's work for the *Passional Christi und Antichristi* (Passional of Christ and Antichrist) (Fig. **6–19**), printed by Grunenberg in

6–19

6–21

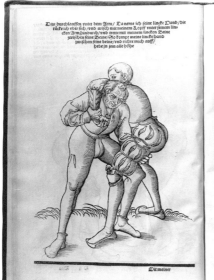

6–20

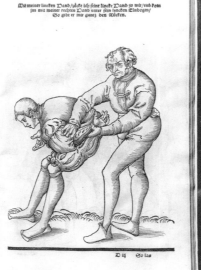

6–23

6–22

6–19. Grunenberg (printer) and Lucas Cranach the Elder (illustrator), pages from *Passional Christi und Antichristi*, 1521. In a biting satirical contrast, Christ labors under the weight of his cross while the Pope travels in style in a sedan chair.

6–20. Hans Lufft (printer) and Lucas Cranach the Younger (illustrator), pages from Auerswald's *Ringer-Kunst* (Art of Wrestling), 1539. Lufft printed Cranach's eighty-seven woodcuts without the usual border, enabling them to move dynamically on the page. The centered captions above and thick rule below restore balance in this predominantly pictorial book.

6–21. Lucas Cranach the Younger, broadside, 1551. This commemorative portrait of Martin Luther bears the identification of the illustrator (Cranach's flying snake device) and the block cutter, a craftsman named Jörg, who is identified typographically above the date.

6–22. Conrad Sweynheym and Arnold Pannartz, specimens of the first (top, 1465) and second (bottom, 1467) typefaces in the evolution toward Roman-style typefaces, shown near original size.

6–23. William Caxton and Colard Mansion, page from *The Game and Play of the Chesse*, c. 1476. The eccentric, jerky type used by Caxton ushered the era of the typographic book into the British nation.

1521. Inspired by Luther, scenes from the life of Christ and biting depictions of the papacy are juxtaposed in graphic contrast on facing pages. Both of Cranach's sons, Hans Cranach (d. 1537) and Lucas Cranach the Younger (1515–86), joined their father's studio; few examples of Hans's work remain, but the younger son continued to work in the family style for many years after his father's death (Figs. **6–20** and **6–21**).

Typography spreads from Germany

Italy, which was at the forefront of Europe's slow transition from the feudal medieval world to one of cultural and commercial renaissance, sponsored the first printing press outside Germany. Although fifteenth-century Italy was a political patchwork of city-states, monarchies, republics, and papal domains, it was at the zenith of its wealth and splendid patronage of the arts and architecture. In 1465 Cardinal Turrecremata of the Benedictine monastery at Subiaco invited two printers, Conrad Sweynheym (d. 1477) of Mainz, who had been employed by Peter Schoeffer, and Arnold Pannartz (d. 1476) of Cologne, to Subiaco to establish a press. The cardinal wished to publish Latin classics and his own writings.

The types designed by Sweynheym and Pannartz (Fig. **6–22**) marked the first step toward a Roman-style typography based on letterforms that had been developed by Italian scribes. These scholars had discovered copies of lost Roman classics written in ninth-century Caroline minuscules. They mistakenly thought they had discovered authentic Roman writing, in contrast to the black medieval lettering that they erroneously believed to be the writing style of "barbarians" who had destroyed Rome. Sweynheym and Pannartz created a typographic "double alphabet" by combining the capital letters of ancient Roman inscriptions with the rounded minuscules that had evolved in Italy from the Caroline minuscule. They tried to unify these contrasting alphabets by adding serifs to some of the minuscule letters and redesigning others. After three years in Subiaco, Sweynheym and Pannartz moved to Rome, where they designed a more fully Roman alphabet that became the prototype for the Roman alphabets still in use today. By 1473 the partnership had printed over fifty editions, usually in press runs of 275 copies. Ten other Italian cities also had printers publishing Latin classics, and the market could not absorb the sudden supply of books. The partnership of Sweynheym and Pannartz suffered a financial collapse and was dissolved.

Early volumes printed in Italy continued the pattern of the early German printed books. Initials, folios, headings, and paragraph marks were not printed. Space was left for these to be rubricated by a scribe with red ink. Often, a small letter would be printed in the space left for an illuminated initial to tell the scribe what initial to draw. In many incunabula, the paragraph marks were not drawn in the spaces provided. Eventually, the blank space alone indicated a paragraph.

After apprenticing in the English textile trade, William Caxton (c. 1421–91) left his native land for the textile center of Bruges in the Low Countries, where he set up his own business as a merchant and diplomat. In the early 1470s he spent a year and a half in Cologne, where he translated the *Recuyell of the Histories of Troy* from French into English and learned printing. On returning to Bruges, he enlisted the help of the illuminator and calligrapher Colard Mansion and set up a press in that city. In 1475 Caxton's translation became the first typographic English language book. In the epilogue to the third part, Caxton tells the reader, "my pen is worn, my hand is weary and shaky, my eyes are dimmed from too much looking at white paper"; thus he "practiced and learned at great expense how to print it."

The partners separated after printing an English translation of *The Game and Playe of the Chesse* (Fig. **6–23**) and two or three French-language books. Mansion remained in Bruges and printed twenty-seven editions before 1484, when he was forced to flee the city to escape his creditors. Caxton moved

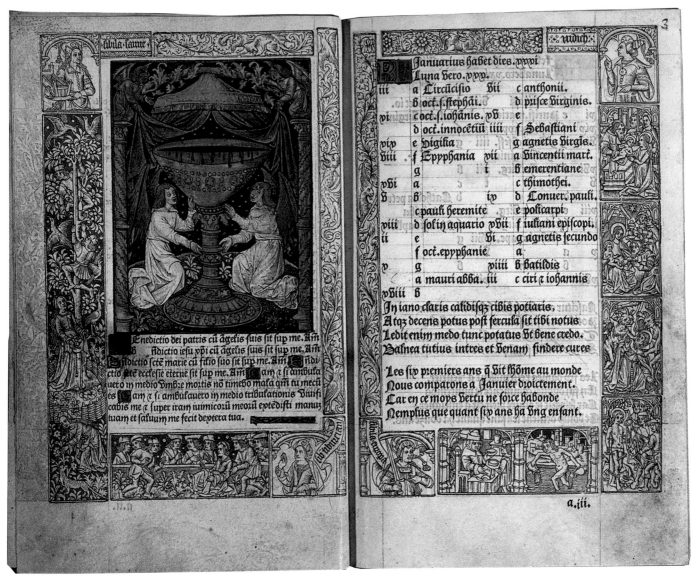

6–25

6–24. William Caxton, printer's trademark, after 1477.

6–25. Philippe Pigouchet, page from *Horae Beatus Virginis Mariae* (Hours of the Blessed Virgin Mary), 1498. The dense complexity of illustration, typography, and ornaments compressed into the space is typical of Pigouchet's book design.

6–26. Diego de Gumiel, title page for *Aureum Opus* (Great Works), 1515. The title almost becomes an afterthought in this title page. The use of white-on-black woodblocks and heraldic imagery is typical of early Spanish graphic design.

6–27. Arñao Guillen de Brocar, page from the Polyglot Bible, 1514–17. The grid system developed for this volume uses uneven columns to compensate for the different running lengths of the different languages.

his types and press across the English Channel and established the first press on English soil. He had printed the first book in English; now he printed the first book in England, at the Sign of the Red Pail in Westminster.

The roughly ninety books that he published in Westminster encompassed nearly all the major works of English literature up to the fifteenth century, including Chaucer's *Canterbury Tales* and Sir Thomas Malory's *Morte d'Arthur.* Caxton is a pivotal figure in the development of a national English language, for his typographic work stabilized and unified the constantly changing, diverse dialects in use throughout the islands. Primarily a scholar and translator, Caxton contributed little to the evolution of book design and printing, as his work had a crude vigor devoid of graphic elegance or refinement.

6–24   6–26   6–27

Woodcut illustrations from his volumes have a brash forceful-ness and are awkwardly drawn; the workmanship of his print-ing is inferior to continental printing of the same period. Caxton's printer's mark (Fig. **6–24**) evokes the carpets woven at Bruges. After Caxton's death, his foreman, Wynkyn de Worde, continued his work and published nearly four hundred titles over the following four decades.

Printing came to France in 1470 when three German print-ers—Michael Freiburger, Ulrich Gering, and Martin Kranz—were sponsored by the prior and the librarian of the Sorbonne to establish a press there. At first they used Roman letters inspired by Italian types to reprint classics, but after they lost their Sorbonne sponsorship in 1473 they began to print with Gothic types that were more familiar to their French audience. To a greater degree than in any other country, French block printers and typographic printers joined forces to duplicate the design of illuminated manuscripts. Late Gothic illumina-tion was the zenith of French art at that time, and early French printing surrounded its Gothic type and woodcut illus-trations with modular blocks that filled the space with flowers and leaves, birds and animals, patterns and portraits. Jean Dupré printed France's first outstanding typographic book, Augustine's *La cité de Dieu (The City of God),* in 1486.

Philippe Pigouchet's *Horae* (Book of Hours) established the graphic excellence of this popular form (Fig. **6–25**). Pigouchet appears to have introduced the *criblé* technique, in which the black areas of a woodblock are punched with white dots, giv-ing the page a lively tonality.

Spain also received three German printers, who arrived in Valencia in 1473 under the auspices of a major German import-export firm. The design sense of the Spanish, which favored dark masses balancing decorative detail, influenced their graphic design, particularly their large woodblock title pages (Fig. **6–26**). A particular masterpiece of Spanish typo-graphic design is Arñao Guillen de Brocar's Polyglot Bible (Fig. **6–27**) of 1514–17. Composed of correlated texts in multiple languages, this massive research project drew scholars from all over Europe to the University of Alcalá de Henares. The printer had to design a page format to accommodate five simultaneous typographic presentations.

During the remarkable first decades of typography, German printers and graphic artists established a national tra-dition of the illustrated book and spread the new medium of communication throughout Europe and even to the New World. Simultaneously, a cultural renaissance emerged in Italy and swept graphic design in unprecedented new directions.

Renaissance Graphic Design

7

The word renaissance means "revival" or "rebirth." Originally this term was used to denote the period that began in the fourteenth and fifteenth centuries in Italy, when the classical literature of ancient Greece and Rome was revived and read anew. However, the word is now generally used to encompass the period marking the transition from the medieval to the modern world. In the history of graphic design, the renaissance of classical literature and the work of the Italian humanists are closely bound to an innovative approach to book design. Type design, page layout, ornaments, illustration, and even the total design of the book were all rethought by Italian printers and scholars. The prototype roman alphabet designs of Sweynheym and Pannartz (see Fig. 6–22) and the coarse decorative borders of early

French books (see Fig. 6–24) were the first tentative steps toward unique Renaissance book designs. The flowering of a new approach to book design that was independent of the German illustrated book started in Venice and continued there during the last three decades of the fifteenth century.

Graphic design of the Italian Renaissance

It was not Florence, where the wealthy Medicis scorned printing as inferior to manuscript books, but Venice—the center of commerce and Europe's gateway to trade with the eastern Mediterranean nations, India, and the Orient—that led the way in Italian typographic book design. A Mainz goldsmith, Johannes de Spira. (d. 1470), was given a five-year monopoly on printing in Venice, publishing his first book, *Epistolae ad familiares* (Letter to Families), by Cicero, in 1469. His innovative and handsome roman type (Fig. **7–1**) cast off some of the Gothic qualities found in the fonts of Sweynheym and Pannartz; he claimed that it was an original invention. Printed in partnership with his brother, Vindelinus, de Spira's 1470 edition of Augustine's *De civitate Dei* was the first typographic book with printed page numbers. Vindelinus de Spira inherited his brother's press—but not the exclusive right to printing in Venice—upon Johannes's untimely death.

Nicolas Jenson (c. 1420–80), who had been Master of the Royal Mint of Tours, France, was a highly skilled cutter of dies used for striking coin. He established Venice's second press shortly after de Spira's death. In 1458 King Charles VII of France sent Jenson to Mainz to learn printing. It has been said that Jenson chose not to return to France after Louis XI ascended to the French throne in 1461. Jenson's fame as one of history's greatest typeface designers and punch cutters rests on the types first used in Eusebius's *De praeparatione evangelica* (Evangelical Preparation), which presents the full flowering of roman type design (Fig. **7–2**).

Part of the lasting influence of Jenson's fonts is their extreme legibility, but it was his ability to design the spaces

7–1

mortales colere uideantur: nec beatitudinis priuationem:ne i fateantur. Non ergo ad beatitudinem cósequendam omía fug pora: fed corruptibilia: grauia:moribunda:non qualia fecit pri

7–2

Hæc igitur ifpiciés diuinus ille uir mœnibus ferreis & íuiolabili a cæteris gétibus fepare nos uoluit:quo pacto facilius corpore a ímaculatos lógeq; ab huiufcemodi falfis opinioíbus remotos for

7–3   7–4   7–5

between the letters and within each form to create an even tone throughout the page that placed the mark of genius on his work. During the last decade of his life Jenson designed outstanding Greek and Gothic fonts and published approximately 150 books that brought him financial success and artistic renown. The characters in Jenson's fonts aligned more perfectly than those of any other printer of his time. Jenson and many other early printers designed trademarks to identify their books (Figs. **7–3** through **7–5**). As Lance Hidy has noted, these emblems bear witness to the revived attention to Egyptian hieroglyphics during the Renaissance. At the time, hieroglyphics were erroneously believed to be entirely ideographic and not phonetic. This resulted in the design of symbols and heraldry that are forerunners to those used in modern graphic design.

Renaissance designers loved floral decoration. Wildflowers and vines were applied to furniture, architecture, and the manuscript. The book continued to be a collaboration between the typographic printer—in the incunabula period typography was sometimes called artificial writing—and the illuminator, who added initials and ornaments. The logical next step was to print everything on a printing press. Erhard Ratdolt (1442–1528) took significant steps toward the totally printed book. A master printer from Augsburg, Germany, Ratdolt worked in Venice from 1476 until 1486. Working closely with his partners, Bernhard Maler and Peter Loeslein, Ratdolt's 1476 *Calendarium* (Record Book) by Regiomontanus had the first complete title page used to identify a book (Fig. **7–6**). In addition to this innovative title page, *Calendarium*

7–1. Johannes de Spira, typography from *De civitate Dei*, 1469. The vertical stress and sharp angles of textura that remained in Sweynheym and Pannartz's fonts yielded to an organic unity of horizontal, vertical, diagonal, and circular forms.

7–2. Nicolas Jenson, typography from Eusebius's *De praeparatione evangelica*, 1470. A new standard of excellence was established with wider letterforms, lighter tone, and a more even texture of black strokes on the white ground.

7–3. Attributed to Nicolas Jenson, mark for the Society of Venetian Printers, 1481. One of man's oldest symbols, the orb-and-cross motif is found in a chamber of Cheops's pyramid at Giza, where it was hewn into stone as a quarry mark. In Jenson's time it symbolized that "God shall reign over earth."

7–4. Laurentius de Rubeis, printer's mark, 1482. This orb and cross was designed in the town of Ferrara, located about 90 kilometers (55 miles) southwest of Venice.

7–5. Pere Miguel, printer's mark, 1494. Dozens of incunabula printers adopted an orb-and-cross mark. Miguel worked in Barcelona, Spain.

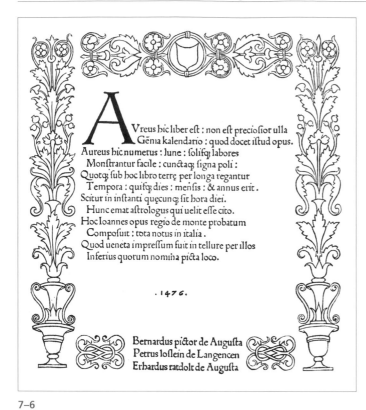

7–6

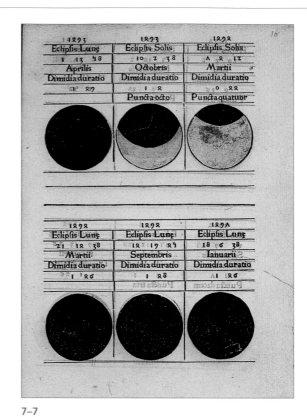

7–7

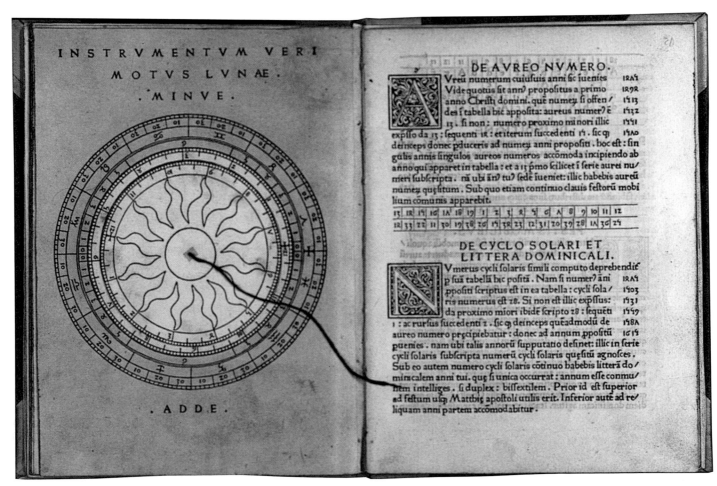

7–8

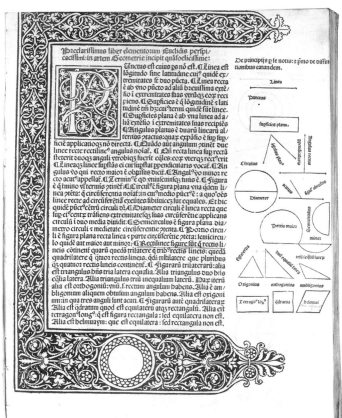

7–9

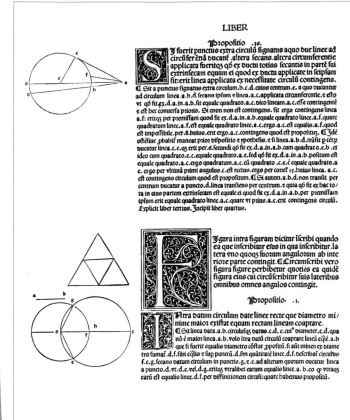

7–10

7–6. Erhard Ratdolt, Peter Loeslein, and Bernhard Maier, title page for *Calendarium*, by Regiomontanus, 1476. The title and author are identified in verse describing the book. The date and printers' names in Latin appear below.

7–7. Erhard Ratdolt, Peter Loeslein, and Bernhard Maier, page for *Calendarium*, by Regiomontanus, 1476. A grid of metal rules brings order and legibility to this record of past and future eclipses.

7–8. Erhard Ratdolt, Peter Loeslein, and Bernhard Maier, pages from *Calendarium*, by Regiomontanus, 1476. The two top circles are printed on heavy paper, cut out, and mounted over the larger woodcut with tape and a string. This may be the first "die-cut" and manual tip-in graphic material in a printed book.

7–9. Erhard Ratdolt, Peter Loeslein, and Bernhard Maier, title page for Euclid's *Geometriae elementa*, 1482. A dazzling white-on-black design brackets the text, and incredibly fine line diagrams in the wide margin visually define Euclid's terms.

7–10. Erhard Ratdolt, Peter Loeslein, and Bernhard Maier, page from Euclid's *Geometriae elementa*, 1482. The wide outer margin is maintained throughout the book for explanatory diagrams. Two sizes of initial letters denote sections and subsections.

contained sixty diagrams of solar and lunar eclipses printed in yellow and black. (Fig. **7–7**). Fear and superstition were being swept away as scientists began to understand natural phenomena, and printers disseminated this knowledge. Eclipses moved from black magic to predictable fact. In the rear of the book is a three-part mathematical wheel for calculating the solar cycles (Fig. **7–8**).

Yet another innovation by Ratdolt was the way woodcut borders and initials were used as design elements. These decorative features included naturalistic forms inspired by Western antiquity and patterned forms derived from the Eastern Islamic cultures. Bernhard Maier (also called Pictor) is assumed to be the designer of Ratdolt's borders. Both fine-line ornaments and reversed designs (white forms on a solid background) were used; sometimes these were printed in red ink. A three-sided woodcut border used on the title page for a number of Ratdolt's editions became a kind of trademark. It appears on the title page of Euclid's *Geometriae elementa* (Elements of Geometry) of 1482 (Fig. **7–9**). The format design uses a large outer margin about half as wide as the text column width (Fig. **7–10**). Small geometric figures, whose sheer delicacy of line represents a technical breakthrough, are placed in the margins adjacent to the supporting text.

7–11. Giovanni and Alberto Alvise, title page from *Ars Moriendi*, 1478. The vocabulary of graphic design possibilities was expanded by the design and casting of metal decorative ornaments that could be composed as part of the page along with type.

7–12. Manuscript book of Roberto Valturio's *De Re Militari*, undated. Freely drawn in brown pen-and-ink, the illustrations have brown and ocher washes applied.

7–13. Johannes Nicolai de Verona (printer), pages from Roberto Valturio's *De Re Militari*, 1472. Detail and gestural line quality are lost in the translation from manuscript original to printed volume, but the basic layout remains the same.

7–11

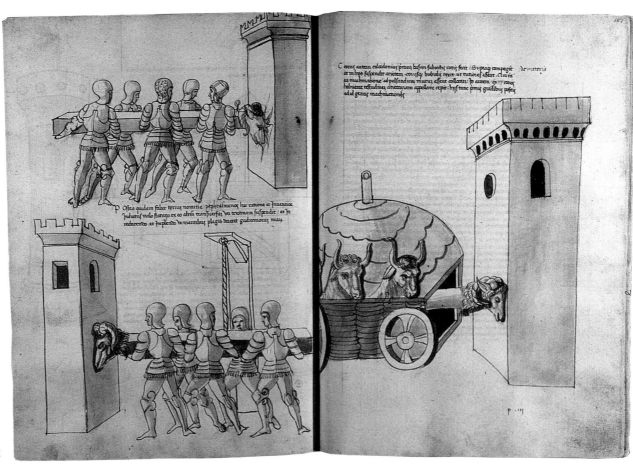

7–12

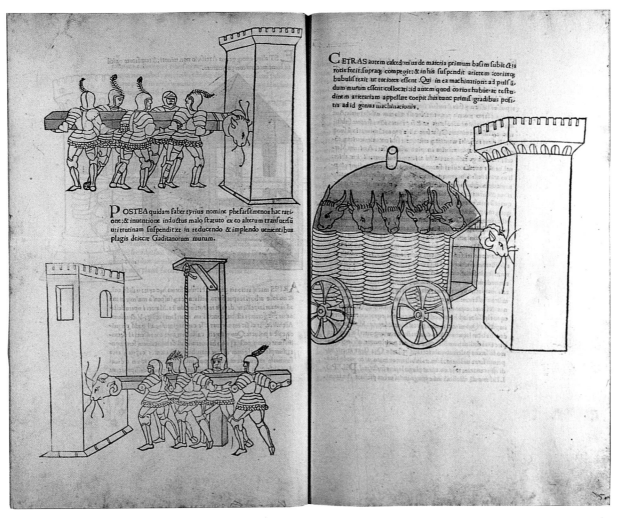

7–13

When Ratdolt left Venice and moved back to his native Augsburg, he publicized his return by issuing the first printer's type specimen sheet. This showed his range of typographic sizes and styles. Ratdolt remained an active printer until his death at age eighty-one. The innovations of Ratdolt and his partners during his decade in Venice were not immediately adopted by other Venetian printers. The full flowering of graphic decoration in the printed book did not begin until the turn of the century.

The *Ars Moriendi* (Art of Dying) was a best seller during the fifteenth century. At least sixty-five editions, including manuscripts, block books, and typographic books, were produced before 1501. An edition published on 28 April 1478 by the Italian printers Giovanni and Alberto Alvise in Verona is believed to be the first design that used *printers' flowers* (*fleurons*), which are decorative elements cast like type. The Verona *Ars Moriendi* used these as graphic elements in the title page design and as fillers in short lines that left blank areas in the text blocks (Fig. **7–11**).

It is quite possible that a printer identified as Johannes Nicolai de Verona, who printed a manual on warfare entitled *De Re Militari* (About Warfare), by Roberto Valturio, in 1472, was Giovanni Alvise. The light contour style of woodblock illustration used in *De Re Militari* initiated the fine-line style that became popular in Italian graphic design during the later decades of the fifteenth century.

A fascinating manuscript copy of *De Re Militari* (Figs. **7–12** and **7–13**) shows the relationship between the typographic book and the manuscript books used as exemplars or layouts. This manuscript book is written in semi-Gothic script but has marginal corrections in a roman hand. Because these corrections were incorporated by the printer, it is believed that this manuscript version was corrected by the author. Then, it was used as corrected copy by the compositors, as a layout by the blockcutters, and as a guide for page design and makeup by the pressman.

This extraordinary book is a compendium of the latest techniques and devices (many imaginary) for scaling walls, catapulting missiles, ramming fortifications, and torturing enemies. The text is set in a tight column with wide outer margins, and the freely shaped images spread across the pages in dynamic asymmetrical layouts. In the spread showing battering rams,

in quo quidem nolo ego te il-
irari ,quod uulgus folet:magnū
et tantas flammas,tam immen
poſt hominum memoriam ſem
iſſe, quo alerétur: quid eſt enim
ui coeli conuexa ; qui terras o-
m ſi naturam reſpicimus ; nihil
a eſt, quod mirum uoces: ſi rem.

7–14

POLIPHILO INCOMINCIA IL SECONDO LIBRO DI
LA SVA HYPNEROTOMACHIA. NEL QVALE PO-
LIA ET LVI DISERTABONDI, IN QVALE MODO ET
VARIO CASO NARRANO INTERCALARIAMEN-
TE IL SVO INAMORAMENTO.

NARRA QVIVI LA DIVA POLIA LA NOBILE ET
ANTIQVA ORIGINE SVA. ET COMO PER LI PREDE
CESSORI SVI TRIVISIO FVE EDIFICATO. ET DI QVEL
LA GENTE LELIA ORIVNDA. ET PER QVALE MO-
DO DISAVEDVTA ET INSCIA DISCONCIAMENTE
SE INAMOROE DI LEI IL SVO DILECTO POLIPHILO.

7–15

7–16

7–17

the repetition of the towers and rams' heads gives the pages a lively visual rhythm.

Medieval Christianity fostered a belief that the value of a human life was primarily its effect on God's judgment after death. A turning away from medieval beliefs toward a new concern for human potential and value characterized Renaissance humanism, a philosophy of human dignity and worth that defined man as capable of using reason and scientific inquiry to achieve both an understanding of the world and self-meaning. This new spirit was accompanied by a renewed study of classical writings from Greek and Roman cultures. An important humanist and scholar of the Italian Renaissance, Aldus Manutius (1450–1515), established a printing press in Venice at age forty-five to realize his vision of publishing the major works of the great thinkers of the Greek and Roman worlds. Important scholars and skilled technical personnel were recruited to staff his Aldine Press, which rapidly became known for its editorial authority and scholarship. From 1494 until 1498, a five-volume edition of Aristotle was published.

A most important member of the Aldine staff was Francesco da Bologna, surnamed Griffo (1450–1518). Manutius called this brilliant typeface designer and punch cutter to Venice, where he cut roman, Greek, Hebrew, and the first italic types for Aldine editions. His initial project in Venice was a roman face for *De Aetna* (Fig. **7–14**), by Pietro Bembo, in 1495. Griffo researched pre-Caroline scripts to produce a roman type that was more authentic than Jenson's designs. This style survives today as the book text face Bembo.

7–18

7–14. Aldus Manutius, from Pietro Bembo's *De Aetna*, 1495–96. As the model for Garamond in the sixteenth century, this typeface became the prototype for two centuries of European typographic design.

7–15. Aldus Manutius, typographic page from *Hypnerotomachia Poliphili*, 1499. The texture of the headings (set in all capitals), the text typography, and the outline initial have a subtle yet beautiful contrast. The one-line intervals of space separating the information into three areas introduces light and order into the page.

7–16. Aldus Manutius, illustrated spread from *Hypnerotomachia Poliphili*, 1499. The woodcut images represent the best illustrations of their period and are exquisitely blended with the typography, helping to produce a book of serenity and grace. Unfortunately, the designer of the woodcuts has never been identified.

7–17. Aldus Manutius, illustrated spread from *Hypnerotomachia Poliphili*, 1499. The illustrations, in the classic Venetian style, in both tone and weight are harmonius with the texture of the type.

7–18. Aldus Manutius, page from Juvenal and Persius, *Opera*, 1501. This was one of the first books using Griffo's new italic type. Note the unfilled space for a rubricated initial, the letter-spaced, all-capital heading, and the capital roman letter at the beginning of each line.

While in Germany the fifteenth century closed with Koberger and Dürer creating a technical and artistic masterpiece in *The Apocalypse*, in Italy Aldus Manutius ended the epoch with his 1499 edition of Fra Francesco Colonna's *Hypnerotomachia Poliphili* (*The Strife of Love in a Dream* or *The Dream of Poliphilus*) (Figs. **7–15** through **7–17**). This romantic and rather tedious fantasy tells of young Poliphilus's wandering quest for his lover, who has taken a vow to preserve her chastity; the journey takes him through classical landscapes and architectural environments. This celebration of paganism—with erotic overtones and a few explicit illustrations—probably escaped scandal only because of its high cost and limited Venetian audience.

This masterpiece of graphic design achieved an elegant harmony of typography and illustration that has seldom been equaled. The communicative coordination of the illustrations with the text and the exceptional integration of images and typography indicate that the printer, type designer, author, and artist worked in close collaboration. The name of the artist who designed the 168 delicate linear illustrations is unknown. Griffo designed new capitals for use with the Bembo lowercase. These capitals were based on the most precise research and study of Roman inscriptions available and used the one-to-ten (stroke weight to height) proportion advanced by leading

mathematicians of the era, whose search for mathematical laws of proportion included a study of Roman inscription lettering. Griffo made his lowercase ascenders taller than the capitals to correct an optical color problem—the tendency of capitals to appear too large and heavy in a page of text—that had plagued earlier Roman fonts. Griffo's typefaces became the model for the French type designers who perfected these letterforms during the following century. Exquisite chapter headings in capitals of the same size as those used in the text, large outline initials surrounded by stylized floral ornamentation, and an overall lightness to the page, combined with generous margins, fine paper, and meticulous presswork, excited printers and designers throughout Europe. *Poliphili* was Manutius's only illustrated book. After it was published, the Aldine staff turned their attention to scholarly editions.

In 1501 Manutius addressed the need for smaller, more economical books by publishing the prototype of the pocket book. This edition of Vergil's *Opera* (Works) had a 7.7 by 15.4–centimeter (3.75 by 6–inch) page size and was set in the first italic type font. Between the smaller size type and the narrower width of italic characters, a 50 percent gain in the number of characters in a line of a given measure was achieved over Jenson's fonts and Griffo's type for *De Aetna*. Italic (Fig. **7–18**) was closely modeled on the cancelleresca

7–19

CONTENTA.

❧CONTINETVR HIC ARISTOTELIS CA=
stigatissime recognitum opus metaphysicū a Clarissimo prin=
cipe Bessarione Cardinale Niceno latinitate foelici =
ter donatum/xiiij libris distinctum: cum adiecto
in xij primos libros Argyropyli Byzantij in=
terpretaméto/rarū proculdubio & hacte=
nus desideratū opus. Deus optimus
quisub nomine ipsius entis in hoc
opere celebratur:hoc ipsū fa=
ciat ad sui & laudem &
cognitionem om=
nibus studijs
proficu=
um.

THEOPHRASTI metaphysicorum liber   I

ITEM METAPHYSICA
introductio:quatuor
dialogorum li=
bris elu=
cida=
ta.

❧Venale habetur hoc eximium Aristotelis opus apud Henricum Stepha=
num e regione scholæ Decretorum.ex cuius officina accuratissime recognitū
prodijt Anno CHRISTI qui summum ens entium existit MDXV.
vicesima die mensis Octobris.

7–21

Graue' fatica non ti sia ad imparar fare' le'
littere' Maiuscule', quando nelle' pic=
cole' harai firmato bene'
la mano, et
eo maxime' ch'io ti ho
ditto che' li Dui'principij delle'
Piccole' sonno anchora quelli delle' Grandi
come' continuando il scriuere', da te'
medesimo uenerai
cognoscendo
Non ti'diro adunque' altro, Saluo che' te'
Sforzi' imparar fare' le' tue' Maiuscule'
Come' qui apresso ri=
trouerai per ese=
pio designato

7–20

7–19. Aldus Manutius, printer's trademark, c. 1500. The swiftest of sea creatures combines with an anchor to signify the epigram, "Make haste slowly."

7–20. Lodovico Arrighi, page from *La operina da imparare di scrivere littera cancellaresca*, 1522. The ample spaces between lines in Arrighi's writing leave room for the plume-shaped ascenders waving to the right in elegant counterpoint to the descenders sweeping gracefully to the left.

7–21. Henri Estienne, title page for Aristotle's *Metaphysics*, 1515. By setting the type in geometric shapes, Estienne achieved a distinctive graphic design with minimal means.

script, a slanted handwriting style that found favor among scholars, who liked its writing speed and informality.

On 14 November 1502, Manutius was granted a monopoly on Greek publishing and italic printing by the Venetian government, and shortly thereafter Griffo and Manutius quarreled and separated. Manutius wished to protect his huge investment in type design and production; Griffo found that he could not sell his original and popular typeface designs to other printers. With the parting of ways of this printer-publisher and his brilliant staff designer, graphic-design innovation in Venice ended.

Until his death in 1515, Manutius published numerous classical editions in the small format and italics of Vergil's *Opera*. These made the Aldine Press logo—a dolphin and anchor inspired by one of the illustrations in *The Dream of Poliphilus*—famous throughout Europe (Fig. **7–19**). Griffo returned to Bologna, where he vanished from the historical record after being charged for the murder of his son-in-law, who was bludgeoned with an iron bar in 1516.

The typographic book came to Italy from Germany as a manuscript-style book printed with types. A series of design innovations, including the title page, roman and italic type, printed page numbers, woodblock and cast metal ornaments, and innovative approaches to the layout of illustrations with type, enabled the Italian printers of the Renaissance to pass on to posterity the basic format of the typographic book as we know it today.

Italian writing masters

Ironically, the inevitable decline in manuscript writing that followed on the heels of typographic printing occurred while new opportunities opened for master calligraphers, almost as a side effect of printing. The rapid growth of literacy created a huge demand for writing masters to teach this fundamental skill, and the attendant expansion of government and commerce created a demand for expert calligraphers to draft important state and business documents. The first of many sixteenth-century writing manuals was created by Italian master calligrapher, printer, and type designer Lodovico Arrighi (d. c. 1527). His small volume of 1522, entitled *La operina da imparare di scrivere littera cancellaresca* (The First Writing Manual of the Chancery Hand) (Fig. **7–20**), was a brief course using excellent examples to teach the cancelleresca script. Arrighi's masterful writing was meticulously cut onto woodblocks by engraver Ugo da Carpi. Arrighi's directions were so clear and simple that the reader could learn this hand in a few days. *La operina . . . cancellaresca* sounded the death knell for the scriptorium as an exclusive domain for the few who could write; it rang in the era of the writing master and public writing skill. A follow-up 1523 volume, entitled *Il modo de temperare le penne*, pre-

sented a dozen handwriting styles. Among those influenced by Arrighi, Giovanni Battista Palatino (c. 1515–c. 1575) produced the most complete and widely used writing manuals of the sixteenth century.

The Italian Renaissance began to fade with the sack of Rome in 1527 by the combined forces of the Holy Roman Emperor Charles V and his Spanish allies. One of the victims of this outrage appears to have been Arrighi. He was working in Rome at the time, after which his name vanishes from the historical record.

Innovation passes to France

With dreams of conquest and empire, the French king Charles VIII (1470–98) crossed into Italy with a vast army in 1494 and attempted to gain control of the Kingdom of Naples, beginning a fifty-year effort by French kings to conquer Italy. Although vast outlays of money and men gained little except fleeting glory, the cultural vitality of the Italian Renaissance was imported to France. Francis I (1494–1547) ascended to the French throne on 1 January 1515, and under his patronage the French Renaissance flowered as he gave generous support to humanists, authors, and visual artists.

This cultural epoch was a fertile one for book design and printing, and the sixteenth century has become known as "the golden age of French typography." The initial design impetus was imported from Venice. Henri Estienne (d. 1520) was one of the early French scholar-printers (Fig. **7–21**) who became enthusiastic about Aldus's *Poliphilus*. Soon books printed in roman types, with title pages and initials inspired by the Venetians, were sprouting all over Paris. Estienne's untimely death left his wife with three young sons. The widowed mother quickly married Estienne's foreman, Simon de Colines (d. 1546), who ran the family business until his stepson, Robert Estienne (1503–59), was able to take over in 1526. At this time Simon de Colines opened his own firm. Robert Estienne became a brilliant printer of scholarly works in Greek, Latin, and Hebrew (Fig. **7–22**). His growing reputation as a publisher of great books, including a major Latin dictionary, enabled young Estienne to join his stepfather as one of the leading figures in this grand period of book design and printing.

Censorship became an increasingly difficult problem during the 1500s, as church and state sought to maintain their authority and control. Propagating ideas, not printing, was the main purpose of the scholar-printers, who often found their quest for knowledge and critical study in conflict with religious leaders and royalty. In spite of war and censorship, however, the humanist spirit took hold in France and produced both excellent scholarship and a notable school of book design. The leading printers produced books of fine proportions, outstanding legibility, beautiful typography, and elegant ornamentation. Two brilliant graphic artists, Geoffroy Tory (1480–1533) and the typeface designer and punch cutter Claude Garamond (c. 1480–1561), created visual forms that were embraced for two hundred years.

The term *renaissance man* is often used to identify a unique individual of genius whose wide-ranging activities in various philosophic, literary, artistic, or scientific disciplines result in important contributions to more than one field. Such a person was Geoffroy Tory. His range of accomplishments is astonishing: professor, scholar, and translator; poet and author; publisher, printer, and bookseller; calligrapher, designer, illustrator, and engraver. He translated, edited, and often published Latin

and Greek texts. As a reformer of the French language he introduced the apostrophe, the accent, and the cedilla. In the graphic arts he played a major role in importing the Italianate influence and then developing a uniquely French Renaissance school of book design and illustration.

Born of humble means in Bourges, Tory's brilliance captured the attention of the city's leading citizens, who made it possible for him to journey to Italy for study at the universities in Rome and Bologna. Returning to France in 1505, Tory became a lecturer in philosophy at the University of Paris, sometimes worked as a reader at Henri Estienne's printing office, and was active as a scribe and illuminator. His boundless enthusiasm for the visual forms of the Italian Renaissance included a deep love for roman letterforms. Tory's lettering, developed in Italy and used in the 1506 manuscript book *Les heures de Jean Lallemant* (The Hours of Jean Lallemant) (Fig. **7–23**), is a light roman with long ascenders and descenders. Some scholars believe that Tory designed early roman types used by Henri Estienne and Simon de Colines.

After a period of publishing with Simon de Colines, Tory made a second extended trip to Italy from 1516 until 1518 to improve his abilities as an artist and designer. Upon returning to Paris, Tory seems to have turned first to manuscript illumination for his livelihood, which quickly yielded to the design and engraving of woodblocks commissioned by printers. After Simon de Colines's 1520 marriage to Henri Estienne's widow, he began to commission borders, floriated letters, trademarks, and an italic typeface from Tory. This collaboration between the master printer and graphic artist established the new open, lighter style.

In sixteenth-century France, engravers were usually booksellers. In keeping with this tradition, Tory opened a Parisian bookselling firm on the Petit Pont under the sign of the Pot Cassé ("broken urn"), where he illustrated, published, bound, and—for several years—printed books. Tory sought out excellent craftsmen and trained them in his approach to book design, which helped to eliminate the dense, claustrophobic page layout and heavy Gothic typography in French printing.

7–22. Robert Estienne, title page for a Bible, 1540. As with many printers' marks of the era, Estienne's olive tree with a branch falling off became a pictorial illustration.

7–23. Geoffroy Tory, pages from the manuscript book *Les heures de Jean Lallemant*, 1506. The armorial frontispiece and forty vignettes have orderly rows of the Latin alphabet's twenty-three letterforms over a blue field with red and white stripes.

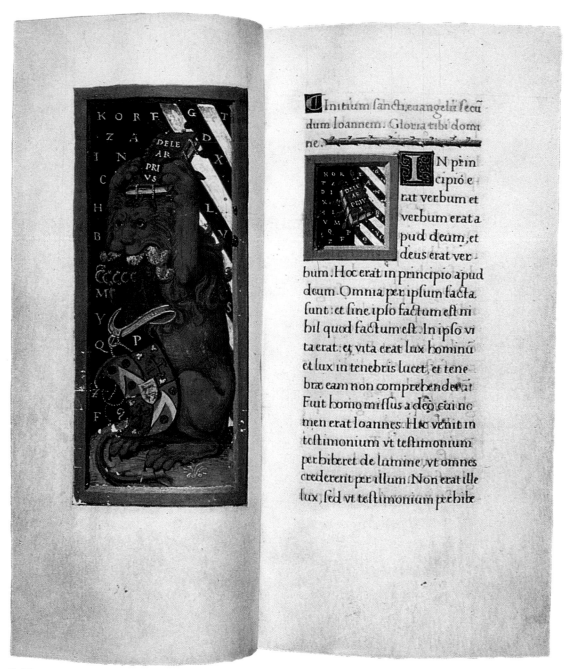

7–23

The origin of the *pot cassé* trademark (Fig. **7–24**), which quickly became a symbol for the fresh currents of the French Renaissance, is poignant. On 25 August 1522, Tory's ten-year-old daughter Agnes died suddenly. The devastated father wrote and published a poem in her memory. At the end of the text, the first engraving of the *pot cassé* appears. This shattered antique urn, chained to a closed, locked book and bearing the inscription *non plus* ("no longer," or "nothing more"), seems to symbolize the death of his daughter. This association is strengthened by the small winged figure in the upper right corner, a detail that had been cut away from the woodblock by the time this same cut was used in a book published by Tory a year later.

Nothing captured the imagination of French printers as did several series of initials designed by Tory. Roman capital initials (Fig. **7–25**) are set into black squares that come alive with meticulous floral designs and *criblé*. Along with matching printer's ornaments and headpieces, these initials were the perfect accompaniment for the lighter new roman types by Garamond. Tory's influence gained momentum in 1525, when he initiated a series of *Horae* (Book of Hours) (Fig. **7–26**), printed for him by Simon de Colines, that set the style for the era. A new clarity of thought, an innovative attitude toward form, and a precise harmony of the various elements—text, capital initials, borders, and illustrations—mark the 1525 *Horae* as a milestone in graphic design. The patchwork quilt of wood-

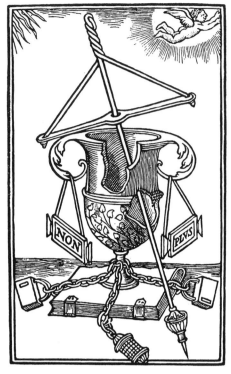

7–24

7–26

7–25

7–24. Geoffroy Tory, *pot cassé* emblem, 1524. Later, Tory explained that the broken jar symbolized one's body, the toret or auger symbolized fate, and the book held shut by three padlocked chains signified the book of a life after it is shut by death.

7–25. Geoffroy Tory, capital from a series of *criblé* initials, c. 1526. Engraved for Robert Estienne, this alphabet of roman capitals brought elegance and "color" to the pages of books printed at Estienne's press.

7–26. Geoffroy Tory, pages from *Horae in Laudem Beautissim ce Virginis Mariae* (Hours of Our Excellent Virgin Mary), 1541. A set of border components, filled with plant and animal motifs, are combined and recombined throughout the book. The open line quality facilitates the application of color by hand. The crowned *F* in the bottom center of the left-hand page is an homage to King Francis I.

7–27. Geoffroy Tory, pages from *Champ Fleury*, 1529. This double-page spread discusses how the Roman philosophers, poets, and orators live in spirit through the power of the Roman letters. It is illustrated by woodcuts of mythological subjects about which we have knowledge through the alphabet. The final paragraph of this "second book" introduces the "third book," the construction of roman letters, with an illustration showing the construction of an *A* from three *I*'s.

blocks filling the space of earlier Books of Hours became passé. A light, delicate effect was achieved in the complex illustrations and ornamental borders because Tory used a fine contour line with air flowing around and within his graceful curves. The texture and tone of these visual elements echo the typographic lightness. Tory selected a size and weight of initial that added just the right darker accent, and he used outline initials with his headings. He cut the woodblocks for these borders and illustrations himself. The creative momentum in publishing and graphic design had now passed to France, and King Francis I honored Tory's contribution by naming him *imprimeur du roi* (printer to the king) in 1530.

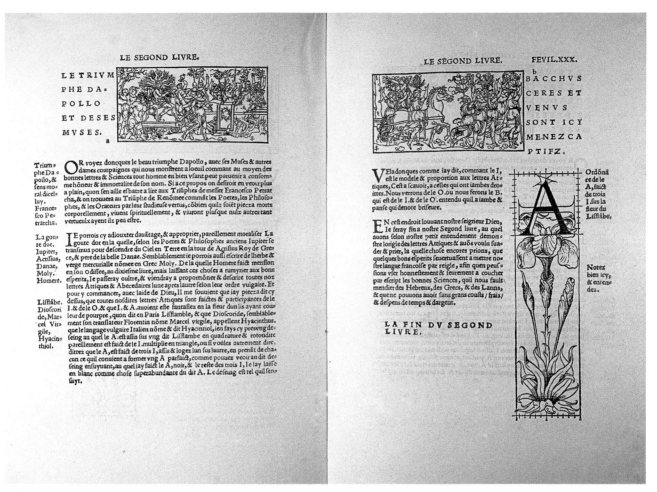

7–27

Tory's *Champ Fleury* (subtitled *The art and science of the proper and true proportions of the attic letters, which are otherwise called antique letters, and in common speech roman letters*), first published in 1529 (Fig. **7–27**), was his most important and influential work. It consists of three books. In the first, he attempted to establish and order the French tongue by fixed rules of pronunciation and speech. The second discusses the history of roman letters and compares their proportions with the ideal proportions of the human figure and face. Errors in Albrecht Dürer's letterform designs in the recently published *Underweisung der Messung* are carefully analyzed, then Dürer is forgiven his errors because he is a painter; painters, according to Tory, rarely understand the proportions of well-formed letters. The third and final book offers instructions in the geometric construction of the twenty-three letters of the Latin alphabet on background grids of one hundred squares (Fig. **7–28**). It closes with Tory's designs for thirteen other alphabets, including Greek, Hebrew, Chaldean, and his fantasy style made of hand tools (Fig. **7–29**).

Champ Fleury is a personal book written in a rambling conversational style with frequent digressions into Roman history and mythology. And yet its message about the Latin alphabet influenced a generation of French printers and punch cutters, and Tory became the most influential graphic designer of his century.

During the 1530s and 1540s, Robert Estienne achieved a wide reputation as a great printer (Fig. **7–30**), renowned for the scholarship and intellectual acumen that he brought to the editorial process. During the same time, Colines earned a similar reputation based on the elegance and clarity of his book designs (Fig. **7–31**). Illustrated title pages, typographic arrangements, ornaments and borders, and fine presswork contributed to this reputation.

Claude Garamond was the first punch cutter to work independently of printing firms. His roman typefaces (Fig. **7–32**) were designed with such perfection that French printers in the sixteenth century were able to print books of extraordinary legibility and beauty. Garamond is credited, by the sheer quality of his fonts, with a major role in eliminating Gothic styles from compositors' cases all over Europe, except in Germany. Around 1510 Garamond apprenticed as a punch cutter under Antoine Augereau. Just how much credit for the evolution of roman type should go to Augereau, whose religious beliefs led him to the gallows in 1534, to Geoffroy

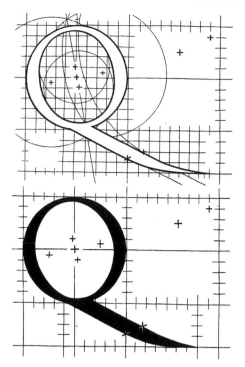

7–28

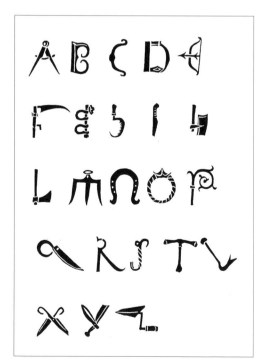

7–29

PAVLI IOVII NOVOCOMEN-
fis in Vitas duodeci m Vicecomitum Mediolani
Principum Præfatio.

ETVS TATEM nobi-
liffimæ Vicecomitum fami-
liæqui ambitiofius à præalta
Romanorū Cæfarum origi-
ne, Longobardífq; regibus
deducto ftemmate, repete-
re contédunt, fabulofis pe-
nè initiis inuoluere viden-
tur. Nos autem recentiora
illuftrioráque,vti ab omnibus recepta,fequemur:có-
tentíque erimus infigni memoria Heriprandi & Gal-
uanii nepotis, qui eximia cum laude rei militaris, ci-
uilífque prudentiæ, Mediolani principem locum te-
nuerunt.Incidit Galuanius in id tempus quo Medio-
lanum à Federico AEnobarbo deletū eft, vir fumma
rerum geftarum gloria, & quod in fatis fuit, infigni
calamitate memorabilis. Captus enim, & ad trium-
phum in Germaniam ductus fuiffe traditur: fed non
multo pòft carceris catenas fregit, ingentíque animi
virtute non femel cæfis Barbaris,vltus iniurias,patriā
reftituit.Fuit hic(vt Annales ferunt)Othonis nepos,
eius qui ab infigni pietate magnitudinéque animi,ca
nente illo pernobili claffico excitus, ad facrū bellum
in Syriam contendit,communicatis fcilicet confiliis
atque opibus cū Guliermo Montifferrati regulo,qui
à proceritate corporis, Longa fpatha vocabatur. Vo-
luntariorum enim equitum ac peditum delectæ no-
A.iii.

7–30

Tory, with whom Garamond worked around 1520, and to Garamond himself is somewhat unclear.

Around 1530 Garamond established his independent type foundry to sell to printers cast type ready to distribute into the compositor's case. This was a first step away from the "scholar-publisher-typefounder-printer-bookseller," all in one, that began in Mainz some eighty years earlier. The fonts Garamond cut during the 1540s achieved a mastery of visual form and a tighter fit that allowed closer word spacing and a harmony of design between capitals, lowercase letters, and italics. These types permit books such as the French-language *Poliphili*, printed by Jacques Kerver in 1546, to maintain their status as benchmarks of typographic beauty and readability to this day. The influence of writing as a model diminished in Garamond's work, for typography was evolving a language of form rooted in the processes of making steel punches, casting metal type, and printing instead of imitating forms created by hand gestures with an inked quill on paper. When Garamond died in poverty at age eighty-one, his widow sold his punches and matrixes. No doubt this contributed to the wide use of his fonts, which remained a major influence until the late 1700s.

Oronce Finé (1494–1555) was a mathematics professor and author whose abilities as a graphic artist complemented his scientific publications. In addition to illustrating his own mathematics, geography, and astronomy books, Finé became interested in book ornament and design. His contemporaries

De Natura ſtir-
PIVM LIBRI TRES,
Ioanne Ruellio authore.

Cum priuilegio
REGIS.

PARISIIS
Ex officina Simonis Colinæi.
1 5 3 6

7–31

7–28. Geoffroy Tory, construction of the letter *Q* from *Champ Fleury*, 1529. Tory used five compass centers in his effort to construct a geometrically ideal roman *O*, and he used an additional two compass centers to add a tail for the *Q*.

7–29. Geoffroy Tory, fantastic alphabet from *Champ Fleury*, 1529. The thirteen alphabets concluding this book (Hebrew, Greek, Persian, and so on) included this whimsical sequence of pictorial letterforms composed of tools. *A* is a compass, *B* is a fusy (steel used to strike a flint to start a fire), and *C* is a handle.

7–30. Robert Estienne, page from Paolo Giovio's *Vitae Duodecim Vicecomitum Mediolani Principum* (Biography of Twelve Early Milanese), 1549. Estienne used Garamond's roman fonts and Geoffroy Tory's initials in this book. Headings are set in one line of letterspaced capitals and two lines of lowercase.

7–31. Simon de Colines, title page for *De Natura Stirpium Libri Tres*, 1536. The typography is surrounded by an illustration that takes great liberties with natural scale and perspective to create a joyous interpretation of the natural bounty of the earth's flora.

had equal admiration for his contributions to science and graphic arts. He worked closely with printers, notably Simon de Colines, in the design and production of his books (Fig. **7–33**). Also, he made an excellent contribution as an editor and designer involved in numerous other titles. While Tory's inspiration is evident, Finé's mathematical construction of ornaments and the robust clarity of his graphic illustration are the work of an innovative graphic designer.

During the 1540s Robert Estienne was caught up in the turmoil of the Reformation. The protection King Francis I (1494–1547) provided for his "dear printer" ended with the king's death, and Estienne's work as a scholar and printer of "pagan-language" Latin, Greek, and Hebrew Bibles incurred the wrath of Catholic theologians at the Sorbonne, who sus-

pected that he was a heretic. After a 1549 visit to Geneva, Switzerland, to meet Protestant Reformation leader John Calvin (1509–64), Estienne began careful preparations to move his printing firm to that city the following year.

Comparison of the editions of *Poliphili* printed by Jacques Kerver (Figs. **7–34** and **7–35**) during the middle of the sixteenth century with Manutius's 1499 edition (see Figs. 7–15, 7–16, and 7–17) shows just how rapidly the French Renaissance printers expanded the range of book design. Manutius produced his *Poliphili* with a single size of roman type and used capitals as his only means of emphasis; Kerver had a large range of roman and italic type sizes for his page designs. Manutius used a set of ornamental initials and little starlike ornaments; Kerver selected from an elegant stock of

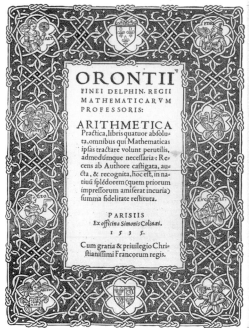

7–32   7–33   7–34

headpieces, tailpieces, and printers' flowers to embellish the printed page. The illustrations in Manutius's *Poliphili* used a monotone contour line; Kerver's illustrator achieved a broad range of tonal effects. A fully developed title page in the Kerver editions set the tone for his volume.

Early typographic books in each European country had an identifiable national style. The unified structure and tone of the French book produced during the golden age of French typography was admired throughout the continent. As Garamond-derived type fonts and Tory-inspired initials and ornaments became available throughout Europe, printers began to emulate the light elegance and ordered clarity of Parisian books. As a result, the first international style of typographic design flourished as the dominant graphic theme of the sixteenth century.

Basel and Lyons become design centers

Scholarship and book production flourished in many cities, but only a few—notably Nuremberg, Venice, and Paris— emerged as centers for design innovation. During the 1500s Basel, which became a part of Switzerland in 1501, and Lyons, a French city located 300 kilometers (180 miles) southwest of Basel, developed into major centers for graphic design. Printers in the two towns enjoyed a lively exchange. Types, woodcut borders, and illustrations from Basel were on many Lyons presses, and Lyons printers often produced editions for their busy Basel counterparts. Johann Froben (1460–1527) came to the sophisticated college town of Basel

to attend the university, then began to print there in 1491. He became Basel's leading printer and attracted the outstanding humanist scholar of the Northern Renaissance, Desiderius Erasmus (1466–1543), to the city. For eight years, beginning in 1521, Erasmus worked with Froben as author, editor, and adviser on matters of scholarship. Unlike most of his German contemporaries, Froben favored hearty, solid roman types rather than Gothics.

A twenty-three-year-old painter, Hans Holbein the Younger (1497–1543), arrived in Basel from Augsburg in the autumn of 1519. He was received as a master in the Zum Himmel guild and was engaged by Froben to illustrate books. His border designs were sculptural and complex and often included a scene from the Bible or classical literature. His prolific designs for title pages (Fig. **7–36**), headpieces, tailpieces, and sets of illustrated initials ranged from the humorous (peasants chasing a fox), to genre (dancing peasants and playing children), to a morbid series of initials depicting the Dance of Death. Before leaving for England in 1526, Holbein was probably already working on his greatest graphic work, the forty-one woodcuts illustrating *Imagines Mortis* (*The Dance of Death*) (Fig. **7–37**). The Dance of Death, a procession in which skeletons or corpses escort the living to their graves, was a major theme in the visual arts as well as in music, drama, and poetry. This use of art as an ominous reminder to the unfaithful of the inevitability of death originated in the fourteenth century, when the great waves of plague swept over Europe. By separating the procession into individual scenes, Holbein was able to intensify the suddenness

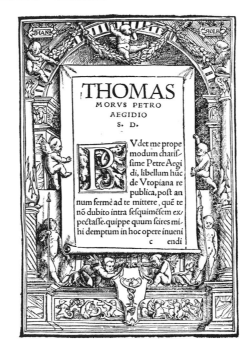

7–35   7–36

and personal tragedy of death. Numerous editions were printed from the blocks engraved by Hans Lutzelburger after Holbein's drawings.

After Froben's death, Johann Oporinus became Basel's leading printer. His masterpiece was the enormous 667-page folio *De Humani Corporis Fabrica* (Construction of the Human Body) (Fig. **7–38**) by the founder of modern anatomy from Brussels, Andreas Vesalius (1514–64). This important book is illustrated by full-page woodcuts of remarkable clarity and accuracy by artists working from dissected corpses under Vesalius's supervision. Many of the anatomical figures are gracefully posed in landscapes. Oporinus set Vesalius's turgid, wordy text in tight pages of roman type with precise page numbers, running heads, marginal notes in delicate italic type, and no paragraph indications. If imitation is the sincerest form of flattery, *De Humani Corporis Fabrica* ranks as a great book, for it was pirated, translated, reprinted, copied, and abridged by printers all across Europe. In fact, King Henry VIII of England ordered the production of an English pirated edition in 1545. Its carefully executed, copperplate-engraved illustrations—copied from the original woodcut title page and illustrations—mark this copy as the first successful book with engraved illustrations.

In Lyons, most of the forty printers churned out such routinely designed material as popular romances for the commercial market using Gothic type. In 1542 Jean de Tournes (1504–64) opened a firm in Lyons and began to use Garamond types with initials and ornaments designed by Tory.

7–32. Robert Estienne, opening page from *Illustrissimae Galliaru Reginae Helianorae* (Famous Gallic Queen Helianorae), 1531. It is believed that the types used in this book are made from Claude Garamond's early type punches and matrixes.

7–33. Simon de Colines (printer) and Oronce Finé (designer), title page for Finé's *Arithmetica*, 1535. In this title-page border, Finé used carefully measured strapwork, symbolic figures representing areas of knowledge, and a *criblé* background. De Colines's typography combines with this border to create a masterpiece of Renaissance graphic design.

7–34. Jacques Kerver, title page from *Poliphili*, 1561. A satyr and a nymph eyeing each other amidst an abundant harvest give the reader a glimpse of the pagan adventures within the book.

7–35. Jacques Kerver, typographic page from *Poliphili*, 1561. Bracketed by white space, Kerver's heading uses three sizes of capital and lowercase type, all capitals, and italic to bring variety to the design.

7–36. Johann Froben (printer) and Hans Holbein (illustrator), title page for Sir Thomas More's *Utopia*, 1518. Complex in image and tone, this title-page design unites the typography with the illustration by placing it on a hanging scroll.

7–37. Joannes Frellonius (printer) and Hans Holbein the Younger (illustrator), pages from *Imagines Mortis* (*The Dance of Death*), 1547. The terror of a child suddenly taken from his home by death is in striking contrast to the modest illustration size (6.65 centimeters, or 2 inches) and the understated elegance of Frellonius's typography.

7–38. Johann Oporinus (printer), page from *De Humani Corporis Fabrica*, 1543. Anatomical illustrations of skeletons and muscles in appear natural poses throughout.

7–37

But de Tournes was not content to imitate Parisian graphic design; he retained his fellow townsman, Bernard Salomon, to design headpieces, arabesques, *fleurons* (printers' flowers), and woodblock illustrations. The excellent book design of these collaborators was further enhanced (Fig. **7–39**) when they were joined by a Parisian type designer working in Lyons, Robert Granjon (d. 1579), who married Salomon's daughter Antoinette.

The most original of the designers inspired by Garamond's roman faces, Granjon created delicate italic fonts featuring beautiful italic capitals with swashes. Books set in italic lowercase had been using regular capitals. Granjon attempted to add a fourth major style—in addition to Gothic, roman, and italic—when he designed and promoted the *caractères de civilité* (characters of civility) (Fig. **7–40**), a typographic version of the French secretarial writing style then in vogue. The distinctive appearance of these typefaces with flamboyant cursive ascenders was insufficient compensation for their poor legibility. Therefore, *civilité* was just a passing fancy. The fleurons designed by Granjon were modular and could be put together in endless combinations to make headpieces, tailpieces, ornaments, and borders. Garamond's type designs were so beautiful and legible that for two hundred years, from about 1550 until the mid-1700s, most typeface designers followed Granjon by merely refining and altering Garamond's forms.

On 1 March 1562, a conflict between French troops and a reformed church congregation ended in a massacre. This began four decades of religious wars that effectively ended the golden age of French typography. Many Huguenot (French Protestant) printers fled to Switzerland, England, and the Low Countries to escape religious strife, censorship, and rigid trade laws. Just as the momentum for innovative graphic design had moved from Italy to France, it now passed from France into the Low Countries, especially the cities of Antwerp and Amsterdam.

A serious arm injury in the early 1550s ended the bookbinding career of Christophe Plantin (1514–89). Thus he changed his career to printing in midlife, and the Netherlands found its greatest printer. Plantin was born in a rural French village near Tours, apprenticed as a bookbinder and bookseller in Caen, then set up shop in Antwerp at age thirty-five. While de Tournes's dedication to quality and unsurpassed design standards have led many authorities to proclaim him the sixteenth century's best printer, Plantin's remarkable management sense and publishing acumen could earn him the same accolade for different reasons. Classics and Bibles, herbals and

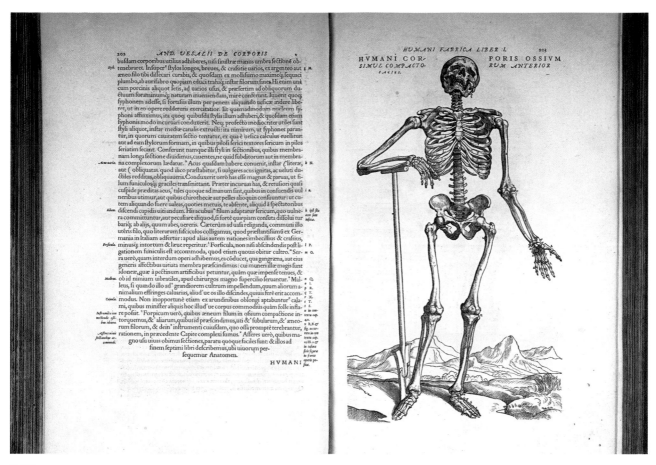

7–38

medicine books, music and maps—a full range of printed matter—poured from what became the world's largest and strongest publishing house. However, even Plantin got into trouble during this dangerous time for printers. While he was in Paris in 1562 his staff printed a heretical tract, and his assets were seized and sold. He recovered much of the money, however, and within two years was reorganized and again solvent. Plantin's design style (Fig. **7–41**) was a more ornamented, weightier adaptation of French typographic design.

Granjon was called to Antwerp for a period as type designer in residence. Plantin loved Granjon's fleurons and used them in profusion, particularly in his ever-popular emblem books. He published fifty emblem books containing illustrated verses or mottos for moral instruction or meditation. Plantin secured numerous punches and types at the estate sales of Colines and Garamond. Under the patronage of King Phillip II of Spain, he published the second great Polyglot Bible (Fig. **7–42**) between 1569 and 1572. This eight-volume work almost bankrupted him when the promised patronage was slow to materialize.

The use of copperplate engravings instead of woodcuts to illustrate his books was Plantin's main design contribution. He commissioned masters of this flourishing printmaking medium to design title pages and to illustrate books. Soon engraving was replacing the woodcut as the major technique for graphic images throughout Europe. After Plantin's death his son-in-law, John Moretus, continued the firm, which remained in the family until 1876, when the town of Antwerp purchased it and turned this amazing house and printing firm into a unique museum of typography and printing, containing two presses dating from Plantin's time.

The seventeenth century

After the remarkable progress in graphic design that took place during the brief decades of the incunabula and the exquisite typography and book design of the Renaissance, the seventeenth century was a relatively quiet time for graphic design innovation. An abundant stock of ornaments, punches, matrixes, and woodblocks from the 1500s was widely available, so there was little incentive for printers to commission new graphic materials. An awakening of literary genius occurred during the seventeenth century, however. Immortal works by gifted authors, including the British playwright and poet William Shakespeare (1564–1616) and the Spanish novelist, playwright, and poet Miguel de Cervantes Saavedra (1547–1616), were widely published. Unfortunately, similar

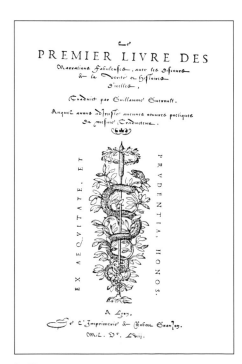

7–39

7–40

7–41

7–42

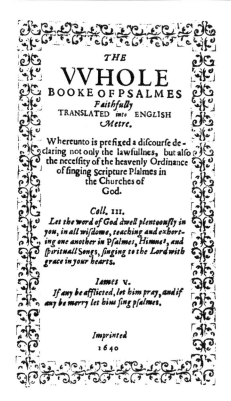

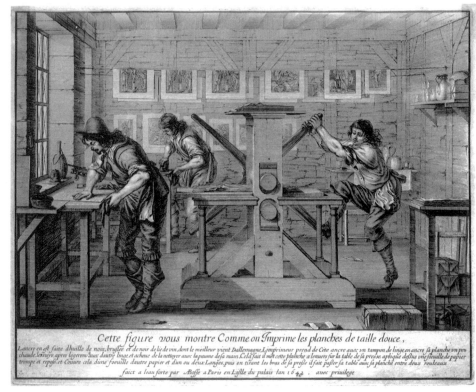

Cette figure vous montre Comme on Imprime les planches de taille douce,

7–43   7–44

innovation was lacking in the graphic arts. There were no important new layout approaches or typefaces to provide a distinctive format for outstanding new literature.

Printing came to the North American colonies when a British locksmith named Stephen Daye (c. 1594–1668) contracted with a wealthy dissenting clergyman, Reverend Jesse Glover, to sail with him to the New World and establish a printing press. Glover died during the sea voyage in the autumn of 1638 and was buried at sea. Upon arrival in Cambridge, Massachusetts, Glover's widow, Anne, set up the printing office assisted by Daye, and thus was the first printer in the colony. She later married the president of Harvard College and sold the press to Daye. The first printing was done in early 1639, and the first book to be designed and printed in the English American colonies was *The Whole Book of Psalmes* (now called *The Bay Psalm Book*) of 1640 (Fig. **7–43**). As the title page, with its dominant word *whole* and border of cast metal printers' flowers, demonstrates, the design and production of this volume was diligent but understandably lacking in refinement. Stephen's son Matthew, who was second in charge and had apprenticed in a Cambridge, England, printing shop before sailing to America, probably did the typesetting and took responsibility for the design of the broadsides, books, and other matter produced at this press.

In spite of strong censorship and a stamp tax on both newspapers and advertising, printing grew steadily in the

7–39. Jean de Tournes (printer) and Bernard Salomon (illustrator), pages from Ovid's *La vita et metamorfoseo* (Metamorphoses), 1559. Three tonal qualities—Salomon's border designs, his denser illustrations, and Granjon's italics echoing the borders' flowing curves—are used by de Tournes with just the right amount of white space.

7–40. Robert Granjon, title page for *Le premier livre des narrations fabuleuses* (The First Book of Fabulous Stories), 1558. The script letterforms are Granjon's caractères de civilité, which were used for the entire text of this 127-page book. The serpent device, elegantly bracketed by the motto in roman capitals, is Granjon's trademark.

7–41. Christophe Plantin, title page for *Centum Fabulae ex Antiquis* (A Hundred Old Stories), by Gabriello Faerno, 1567. Dignified and architectural, this title page is typical of the Plantin house style.

7–42. Christophe Plantin, page from the Polyglot Bible, 1569–72. A double-page format, with two vertical columns over a wide horizontal column, contained the Hebrew, Latin, Aramaic, Greek, and Syriac translations of the Bible.

7–43. Stephen and Matthew Daye, title page for *The Whole Booke of Psalmes*, 1640. In the title typography, a rich variety is achieved by combining three type sizes and using all capitals, all lowercase, and italics to express the importance and meaning of the words.

7–44. Abraham Bosse, *Printing Shop—The Plate Printer*, 1642. A convincing range of lights and darks is built from scratched lines.

Habit de Rôtisseur

7–45

COMMENTARIORUM
JOANNIS CALVINI
IN
EUANGELIUM
SECUNDUM JOANNEM
PRÆFATIO
Magnificis Dominis , Syndicis , Senatuique
Genevensi, Dominis suis vere observandis Joan. Calvinus Spi-
ritum prudentiæ & fortitudinis, prosperumque guber-
nationis successum à Domino precatur.

Uoties in mentem venit illa Christi sententia , qua tanti
æstimat quod hospitibus colligendis impenditur huma-
nitatis officium, ut in suas rationes acceptum ferat , simul
occurrit quam singulari vos honore dignatus sit , qui urbem vestram non unius vel paucorum , sed commune Ecclesiæ suæ ho-
spitium esse voluit. Semper apud homines profanos non modo
laudata , sed una ex præcipuis virtutibus habita fuit hospitalitas :
ac proinde in quibus extremam barbariem ac mores prorsus effe-
ratos damnare vellent, eos ἀξένους vel (quod idem valet) inhospitales
vocabant. Laudis autem vestræ longe potior est ratio , quod tur-
bulentis hisce miserisque temporibus Dominus vos constituit quo-
rum in fidem præsidiumque se conferent pii & innoxii homines ,
quos non sæva minus quam sacrilega Antichristi tyrannis è patriis
sedibus fugat ac dispellit. Neque id modo, sed sacrum etiam apud
vos domicilium nomini suo dicavit, ubi pure colatur. Ex his duo-
bus quisquis minimam partem vel palam rescindere , vel furtim
auferre conatur , non hoc agit modo ut nudatam præcipuis suis
ornamentis urbem vestram deformet , sed ejus quoque saluti ma-
ligne invidet. Quamvis enim quæ Christo & dispersis ejus mem-
bris præstantur hic pietatis officia, caninos impiorum latratus pro-
vocent, merito tamen hæc vobis una compensatio satis esse debet
quod è cælo Angeli & ex omnibus mundi plagis filii Dei benedi-

7–46

colonies. By 1775 there were about fifty printers in the thirteen colonies, and they fueled the revolutionary fever that was brewing. Just as printing had hurled Europe toward the Protestant Reformation during its early decades, it now pushed the American colonies toward revolution.

Copperplate engraving continued to grow in popularity as technical refinements greatly increased its range of tone, textures, and detail. Independent engraving studios were established, as shown in the combined etching and engraving by Abraham Bosse (1602–76) illustrating the plate printers in his printing shop (Fig. **7–44**). In addition to fulfilling commissions for copperplate engravings to be bound into books as illustrations, these studios produced engravings to hang on the wall. This enabled persons who were unable to afford oil paintings to have images in their homes. Broadsheets, advertising cards, and other printed ephemera were produced by the engraving studios. The wonderful imagination that was sometimes displayed is seen in the set of engravings called *The Trades* (Fig. **7–45**), originally created by N. de Larmessin in 1690. The tools or products of each trade were turned into lavish costumes on the figures. The nature of engraving—scratching fine lines into metal—encouraged the development of script letterforms of extreme fineness and delicacy, used with meticulously detailed illustrations.

During the seventeenth century the Netherlands prospered as a mercantile and seafaring nation. Books became an important export commodity as a result of the accomplishments of yet another dynasty of printers, founded by Louis Elzevir

7–45. After N. de Larmessin, "*Habit de rotisseur,*" (The Butcher's Clothes), from *The Trades,* 1690. A stately symmetry and somber reserve intensify the outrageous humor of this image.

7–46. Jan Jacob Schipper, page from Calvin's *Commentary*, 1667. Using types designed by Christoffel van Dyck, Schipper's mixture of sizes, letterspacing, and leading in the heading material is an excellent representation of the baroque sensibility.

(1540–1617). Their handy and practical little volumes had solid, legible Dutch type surrounded by economically narrow margins, and featured engraved title pages. Competent editing, economical prices, and convenient size enabled the Elzevirs to expand the book-buying market. Dutch, English, French, German, and Latin books were printed and exported throughout Europe. Their format designs were amazingly consistent, leading one prominent printing historian to declare that if you have seen one, you have seen them all. Many of their types were designed by the great Dutch designer and punch cutter Christoffel van Dyck. Designed to resist the wear and tear of printing, his types had stubby serifs with heavy bracketing (the connecting curves that unify the serif with the main stroke of the letter) and fairly stout hairline elements (Fig. **7–46**). Van Dyck's 111 matrixes and types were used continuously until 1810, when the fashion for the extreme thicks and thins of modern-style types unfortunately led the Haarlem foundry that owned them to melt them down to reuse the metal.

An Epoch of Typographic Genius

After the drought of graphic-design creativity during the 1600s, the eighteenth century was an epoch of typographic originality. In 1692 the French king Louis XIV, who had a strong interest in printing, ordered the establishment of a committee of scholars to develop a new type for the Imprimerie Royale, the royal printing office established in 1640 to restore the quality of earlier printing. The new letters were to be designed by "scientific" principles. Headed by mathematician Nicolas Jaugeon, the academicians studied all previous alphabets and studies on type design.

To construct the new roman capital letters, a square was divided into a grid of sixty-four units; each of these units was divided further into thirty-six smaller units for a total of 2,304 tiny squares. Italics were constructed on a similar grid. The new letter designs had fewer calligraphic properties inspired by the chisel and flat pen; a mathematical harmony was achieved by measurement and drafting instruments. However, these designs were not merely mechanical constructions, for the final decisions were made by the eye.

This *Romain du Roi*, as the new typeface was called, had increased contrast between thick and thin strokes, sharp horizontal serifs, and an even balance to each letterform. The master alphabets were engraved as large copperplate prints (Figs. **8–1** and **8–2**) by Louis Simonneau (1654–1727). Philippe Grandjean (1666–1714) cut the punches to convert the master alphabets into text type. The minute refinement on a 2,304-square grid proved absolutely worthless when reduced to text-size types.

Types designed for the Imprimerie Royale could only be used by that office for royal printing; other use constituted a capital offense. Other typefounders quickly cut types with similar characteristics, but they made sure the designs were sufficiently distinct to avoid confusion with Imprimerie Royale fonts.

In 1702 the *Médailles* folio was the first book to feature the new types. As the first important shift from the Venetian tradition of "old style" roman type design, the Romain du Roi (Fig. **8–3**) initiated a category of types called *transitional roman*. These break with the traditional calligraphic qualities, bracketed serifs, and relatively even stroke weights of Old Style fonts. The Romain du Roi (as William Morris observed in the late nineteenth century) saw the calligrapher replaced by the engineer as the dominant typographic influence.

Graphic design of the rococo era

The fanciful French art and architecture that flourished from about 1720 until around 1770 is called *rococo*. Florid and intricate, rococo ornament is composed of S- and C-curves with scrollwork, tracery, and plant forms derived from nature, classical and oriental art, and even medieval sources. Light pastel colors were often used with ivory white and gold in asymmetrically balanced designs. This lavish expression of the era of King Louis XV (1710–74) found its strongest graphic design impetus in the work of Pierre Simon Fournier le Jeune (1712–68), the youngest son of a prominent family of printers and typefounders. At age twenty-four, Fournier le Jeune established an independent type-design and foundry operation after studying art and apprenticing at the Le Bé foundry operated by his older brother, where he had cut decorative woodblocks and learned punch cutting.

Eighteenth-century type measurement was chaotic, for each foundry had its own type sizes, and nomenclature varied. In 1737 Fournier le Jeune pioneered standardization when he published his first table of proportions. The *pouce* (a now-obsolete French unit of measure slightly longer than an inch) was divided into twelve lines, each of which was divided into six points. Thus, his Petit-Romain size was one line, four points, or about equal to contemporary ten-point type; his Cicero size was two lines, or similar to contemporary twelve-point type.

Fournier le Jeune published his first specimen book, *Modèles des caractères de l'imprimerie* (Models of Printing Characters), shortly before his thirtieth birthday in 1742. It presented 4,600 characters. Over a six-year period he had both designed and cut punches for all of these by himself. His roman styles were transitional forms inspired by the Romain du Roi of 1702. However, his variety of weights and widths initiated the idea of a "type family" of fonts that are visually compatible and can be mixed. He personally designed and set the more complex pages, which were richly garlanded with his exquisite *fleurons,* used singly or multiplied for unlimited decorative effect. His explorations into casting enabled him to cast single-, double-, and triple-ruled lines up to 35.5 centimeters (about 14 inches) and to offer the largest metal type (equivalent to contemporary 84- and 108-point sizes) yet made. His decorative types (Fig. **8–4**)—outline, shaded, flowered, and exotic—worked remarkably well with his roman fonts, ornaments, and rules.

Printing has been called "the artillery of the intellect." It might be said that Fournier le Jeune stocked the arsenals of rococo printers with a complete design system (roman, italic, script, and decorative type styles, rules, and ornaments) of standardized measurement whose parts integrated both visually and physically (Fig. **8–5**). Because French law prevented typefounders from printing, Fournier le Jeune delivered made-up pages to Jean Joseph Barbou, the printer of his *Modèles des caractères,* whose nephew, Jean Gerard Barbou, was closely associated with him. In addition to publishing all of Fournier le Jeune's other books, the younger Barbou produced volumes of exceptional rococo design, combining Fournier le Jeune's decorative types and copperplate engravings by Charles Eisen (1720–78), who specialized in illustrations of graceful intricacy and sensual intimacy in vogue with royalty and the wealthy. Adding the talents of the engraver Pierre Philippe Choffard (1730–1809), who specialized in ornate tailpieces and spot illustrations, resulted in book designs such as Jean de La Fontaine's *Contes et nouvelles en vers* (Stories and Tales in Verse) of 1762 (Fig. **8–6**). In a small number of copies for a special audience, the engravings showing coy romantic escapades were replaced with other versions depicting explicit sexual conduct. In the *éditions de luxe,* the typefounder, printer, and illustrator combined their talents to project the psychology of the rococo era—showing the wealthy living extravagant, sensuous, and pastoral lives in a joyous fantasyland, oblivious to the growing militancy of the poverty-stricken masses. These wildly popular books remained in vogue until the French Revolution of 1789 brought the monarchy and the rococo era to an end.

Fournier le Jeune planned a four-volume *Manuel typographique* (Manual of Typography) (Fig. **8–7**) for many years, but only produced two volumes: *Type, Its Cutting and Founding,* 1764, and *Type Specimens* (originally planned as volume four), 1768. An improved measurement system based on the point (instead of the line and point) was introduced in the 1764 volume. He did not live to complete the other two volumes, one on printing and one on the great typographers' lives and work. Although his crowning achievement was only half completed, Fournier le Jeune made more typographic innovations and had a greater impact on graphic design than any other person of his era.

While even the most extravagant designs of Fournier le Jeune and his followers maintained the vertical and horizontal alignment that is part of the physical nature of metal typography, engravers were free to take tremendous liberties with

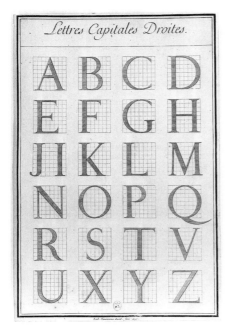

8–1

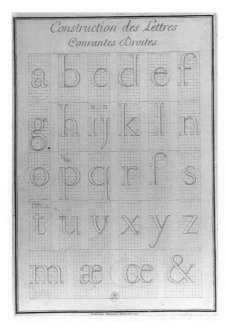

8–2

8–3

form. Basically, an engraving is a drawing made with a graver instead of a pencil as the drawing tool, and a smooth copperplate instead of a sheet of paper as the substrate. Because this free line was an ideal medium for expressing the florid curves of the rococo sensibility, engraving flourished throughout the 1700s. Delicate detail and fine lines made this medium much prized for labels, business cards, billheads, letterheads, and announcements. The renowned English writing master and engraver George Bickham (the elder, d. 1769) was the most celebrated penman of his time (Fig. **8–8**). In 1743 he published *The Universal Penman . . . exemplified in all the useful and ornamental branches of modern Penmanship, &c.; the whole embellished with 200 beautiful decorations for the amusement of the curious.* Bickham and other accomplished engravers prominently signed broadsheets, title pages, and large images for domestic walls that were frequently based on oil paintings.

As engravers became increasingly skillful, they even produced books independent of typographic printers by hand-engraving both illustrations and text. Englishman John Pine (1690–1756) was one of the best engravers of his time. His books, including the 1737 *Opera Horatii* (Works of Horace) (Fig. **8–9**) were sold by subscription before publication, and a list naming each subscriber was engraved in script in the front of the volume. Because the serifs and thin strokes of letterforms were reduced to the delicate scratch of the engraver's finest tool, the contrast in the text material was dazzling and inspired imitation by typographic designers. Each letter was inscribed by hand; thus the text has a slight vibration that gives it a handmade quality instead of a mechanical uniformity. In addition to book design and production, Pine was chief engraver of seals for the king of England, and he created portfolios of large etchings. One extraordinary set published in 1753 depicts the 1588 defeat of the Spanish Armada in 52 by 36–centimeter (20 by 14-inch) prints.

8–1 and **8–2**. Louis Simonneau, master alphabets for the Romain du Roi, 1695. These copperplate engravings were intended to establish graphic standards for the new alphabet.

8–3. Philippe Grandjean, specimen of Romain du Roi, 1702. Compared to earlier roman fonts, the crisp geometric quality and increased contrast of this first transitional typeface are clearly evident. The small spur on the center of the left side of the lowercase *l* is a device used to identify types of the Imprimerie Royale.

8–4. Pierre Simon Fournier le Jeune, specimen page of decorative types, 1768. Within each of Fournier's ornamental display letterforms is the structure of a well-proportioned roman letter.

8–5. Pierre Simon Fournier le Jeune, title page for *Ariette, mise en musique* (Ariette, Mode of Music), 1756. Vast numbers of floral, curvilinear, and geometric ornaments were needed to construct designs like this, which set the standard of excellence of the rococo period.

8–4

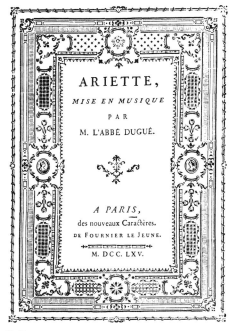

8–5

LE BÂT.

Un peintre étoit, qui jaloux de sa femme,
Allant aux champs, lui peignit un baudet
Sur le nombril, en guise de cachet.
Un sien confrere amoureux de la Dame,
La va trouver, & l'âne efface net,
Dieu sçait comment ; puis un autre en remet,
Au même endroit, ainsi que l'on peut croire.
A celui-ci, par faute de mémoire,
Il mit un Bât ; l'autre n'en avoit point.
L'époux revient, veut s'éclaircir du point.
Voyez, mon fils, dit la bonne commere ;
L'âne est témoin de ma fidélité.
Diantre soit fait, dit l'époux en colere,
Et du témoin, & de qui l'a bâté.

8–6

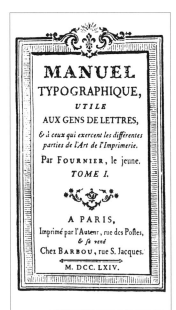

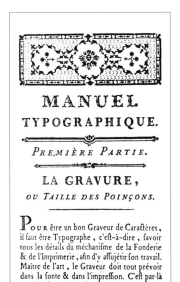

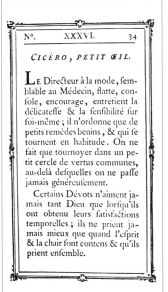

8–7

8–8

8–6. Joseph Gerard Barbou, pages from *Contes et nouvelles en vers* (Stories and Tales in Verse), by Jean de La Fontaine, 1762. To adorn a poem about a painter's romantic interlude with his subject, Barbou used Eisen's etching of the event, a topical tailpiece by Choffard, and Fournier le Jeune's ornamented type.

8–7. Pierre Simon Fournier le Jeune, pages from *Manuel typographique*, 1764 and 1768. In addition to showing the design accomplishments of a lifetime, Fournier's type manual is a masterwork of rococo design.

8–8. George Bickham, "A Poem, On the Universal Penman," by John Bancks, c. 1740. Bickham engraved his self-portrait above verses lauding his writing skills.

Caslon and Baskerville

For over two and a half centuries after the invention of movable type, England looked to the Continent for typography and design leadership. Civil war, religious persecution, harsh censorship, and government control of printing had created a climate that was not conducive to graphic innovation. Upon ascending to the throne in 1660, Charles II had demanded that the number of printers be reduced to twenty "by death or otherwise."

Type and design ideas were imported across the English Channel from Holland until a native genius emerged in the person of William Caslon (1692–1766). After apprenticing to a London engraver of gunlocks and barrels, young Caslon opened his own shop and added silver chasing and the cutting of gilding tools and letter stamps for bookbinders to his repertoire of engraving skills. The printer William Bowyer encouraged Caslon to take up type design and founding, which he did in 1720 with almost immediate success. His first commission was an Arabic font for the Society for Promoting Christian Knowledge. This was followed closely by the first

size of Caslon Old Style with italic (Fig. **8–10**) in 1722, and his reputation was made. For the next sixty years, virtually all English printing used Caslon fonts, and these types followed English colonialism around the globe. Printer Benjamin Franklin (1706–90) introduced Caslon into the American colonies, where it was used extensively, including for the official printing of the Declaration of Independence by a Baltimore printer.

Caslon's type designs were not particularly fashionable or innovative. They owed their tremendous popularity and appeal to an outstanding legibility and sturdy texture that made them "comfortable" and "friendly to the eye." Beginning with the Dutch types of his day, Caslon increased the contrast between thick and thin strokes by making the former slightly heavier. This was in direct opposition to fashion on the Continent, which was embracing the lighter texture of the Romain du Roi. Caslon's fonts have variety in their design, giving them an uneven, rhythmic texture that adds to their visual interest and appeal. The Caslon foundry continued under his heirs and was in operation until the 1960s.

124 Q. HORATII FLACCI

EPISTOLA XI.
AD BVLLATIVM.

VID tibi vifa Chios, Bullati, notaque
Lefbos?
Quid concinna Samos? quid Croefi regia
Sardis?
Smyrna quid, et Colophon? majora, minorane fama?
Cunctane prae Campo, et Tiberino flumine, fordent?
An venit in votum Attalicis ex urbibus una?   5
An Lebedum laudas,odio maris atque viarum?
Scis Lebedus quid fit: Gabiis defertior atque
Fidenis vicus: tamen illic vivere vellem,
Oblitufque meorum, oblivifcendus et illis,
Neptunum procul e terra fpectare furentem.   10
Sed neque, qui Capua Romam petit imbre lutoque
Adfperfus, volet in caupona vivere; nec, qui
Frigus collegit, furnos et balnea laudat,
Vt fortunatam plene praeftantia vitam;

8–9

ABCDEFGHIKLMN
OPQRSTUVWXYZJ
Quoufque tandem abutere,
Catilina, patientia noftra? qu
Quoufque tandem abutere, Ca-
tilina, patientia noftra? quam-

This new Foundery was begun in the Year 1720,
and finifh'd 1763; and will (with God's leave) be
carried on, improved, and inlarged, by WILLIAM
CASLON and Son, Letter-Founders in LONDON.

8–10

Caslon worked in a tradition of Old Style roman typographic design that had begun over two hundred years earlier during the Italian Renaissance. This tradition was bolstered by John Baskerville (1706–75), an innovator who broke the prevailing rules of design and printing in fifty-six editions produced at his press in Birmingham, England. Baskerville was involved in all facets of the bookmaking process. He designed, cast, and set type, improved the printing press, conceived and commissioned new papers, and designed and published the books he printed. This native of rural Worcestershire, who had "admired the beauty of letters" as a boy, moved to Birmingham as a young man and became established as a master writing teacher and stonecutter (Fig. **8–11**). While still in his thirties, Baskerville became a manufacturer of japanned ware. His frames, boxes, clock cases, candlesticks, and trays were made from thin sheet metal, often decorated with hand-painted fruit and flowers and finished with a hard, brilliant varnish. Manufacturing earned

Baskerville a fortune, and he built an estate, Easy Hill, near Birmingham. Around 1751, at the age of forty-four, he returned to his first love, the art of letters, and began to experiment with printing. As an artist who wanted to control all aspects of book design and production, he sought graphic perfection and was able to invest the time and resources necessary to achieve his goals. He was assisted by John Handy, a punch cutter, and Robert Martin, an apprentice who later became his foreman. Baskerville's type designs, which bear his name to this day, represent the zenith of the transitional style bridging the gap between Old Style and modern type design. His letters possessed a new elegance and lightness. In comparison with earlier designs, his types are wider, the weight contrast between thick and thin strokes is increased, and the placement of the thickest part of the letter is different. The treatment of serifs is new: they flow smoothly out of the major strokes and terminate as refined points. His italic fonts most clearly show the influence of master handwriting.

8–11

PUBLII VIRGILII

MARONIS

BUCOLICA,

GEORGICA,

ET

AENEIS.

BIRMINGHAMIAE:
Typis JOHANNIS BASKERVILLE.
MDCCLVII.

8–12

PARADISE
REGAIN'D.
A
POEM,
IN
FOUR BOOKS.
To which is added
SAMSON AGONISTES:
AND
POEMS upon SEVERAL OCCASIONS.
THE AUTHOR
JOHN MILTON.
From the Text of
THOMAS NEWTON, D. D.
BIRMINGHAM:
Printed by JOHN BASKERVILLE
For J. and R. TONSON in LONDON.
MDCCLVIII.

8–13

8–9. John Pine, page from Horace's *Opera* (Works), Volume II, 1737. Illustration and text were hand-engraved upon a copper printing plate and printed in one pass through the press.

8–10. William Caslon, specimens of Caslon roman and italic, 1734. The straightforward practicality of Caslon's designs made them the dominant roman style throughout the British Empire far into the nineteenth century.

8–11. John Baskerville, the Gravestone Slate, undated. This demonstration stone showed potential customers young Baskerville's carving skill and range of lettering styles.

8–12. John Baskerville, title page for Vergil's *Bucolica, Georgica, et Aeneis* (Pastorials, Farming, and Aeneis), 1757. Baskerville reduced the design to letterforms symmetrically arranged and letterspaced; he reduced content to author, title, publisher, date, and city of publication. Economy, simplicity, and elegance resulted.

8–13. John Baskerville, title page from *Paradise Regained*, 1758. The stately order of Baskerville's page design results from the harmony of elements and the spatial intervals that separate them.

As a book designer in a period of intricate, engraved title pages and illustrations and the generous use of printers' flowers, ornaments, and decorated initials, Baskerville opted for the pure typographic book (Figs. **8–12** and **8–13**). Wide margins and a liberal use of space between letters and lines were used around his magnificent alphabets. To maintain an elegant purity of typographic design, an unusually large percentage of each press run was rejected, and he melted down and recast his type after each printing.

Baskerville's improvements for his four presses, built in his own workshops, focused on perfect alignment between the inch-thick brass platen and the smooth stone press bed. The packing behind the sheet of paper being printed was unusually hard and smooth. As a consequence, he achieved even, overall impressions.

Trial and error led to the development of an ink composed of boiled linseed oil aged for several months after black or amber resin was added. Then, a fine lampblack—acquired

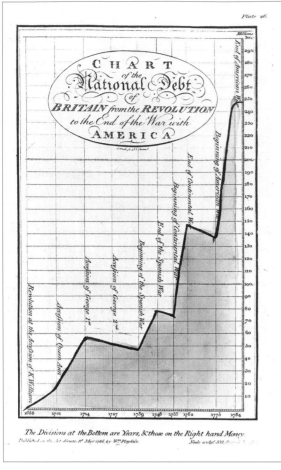

8–14

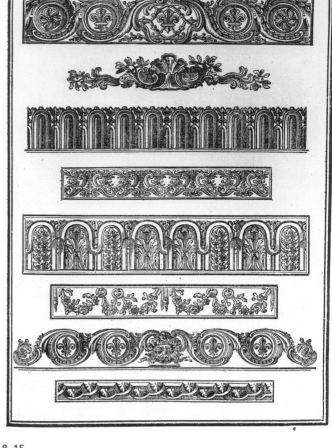

8–15

from "glass pinchers' and solderers' lamps"—was ground into it. The resin added a sheen to this unusually dense black ink, whose luster bordered on purple.

The smooth, glossy surface of the paper in Baskerville's books had not been seen before. It was achieved by using hot-pressed wove paper. Before Baskerville's *Vergil*, books were printed on laid paper, which has a textural pattern of horizontal lines. This pattern is created in manufacture by wires that form the screen in the papermaker's mold; the close parallel wires are supported by larger wires running at right angles to the thinner wires. The wove paper manufactured for Baskerville was formed by a mold having a much finer screen made of wires woven in and out like cloth. The texture of wire marks was virtually eliminated from this paper.

All handmade papers have a coarse surface. When paper is moistened before printing on a hand press, it becomes even coarser. Baskerville's desire for elegant printing led him to hot-press the paper after it was printed to produce a smooth, refined surface. How he hot-pressed or calendered his paper is controversial, because early sources give conflicting reports. One version is that Baskerville designed and constructed a

smoothing press with two copper rollers 21.6 centimeters (8 inches) in diameter and almost a meter (39 inches) long. A second version explains that Baskerville employed a woman and a little girl to operate a pressing or glazing machine that worked in a manner not unlike ironing clothes. Yet another version declares that as each page was removed from the press, it was sandwiched between two highly polished, heated copperplates that expelled moisture, set the ink, and created the glossy surface. Because Baskerville closely guarded his innovations, we can only guess which of these methods were employed. Realizing the potential market for mirror-smooth writing paper, he used his process to develop a steady stationery business through booksellers.

The net result of this effort was books of brilliant contrast, simplicity, and refinement. Professional jealousy caused Baskerville's critics to dismiss him as an "amateur," although his work set a standard of high quality. Some of his critics argued that reading Baskerville type hurt their eyes because of the sharpness and contrast. Benjamin Franklin, who admired Baskerville, wrote him a letter relating that he, Franklin, had torn the foundry name from a Caslon specimen

8–14. William Playfair, diagram from *Commercial and Political Atlas,* 1786. This hand-colored engraving uses a fever chart to depict the impact of wars upon Britain's soaring national debt.

8–15. Louis René Luce (designer) and Jean Joseph Barbou (printer), ornaments page from *Essai d'une nouvelle typographie,* 1771. These meticulously constructed cornices and borders express the authority and absolutism of the French monarchy.

sheet, told an acquaintance who was complaining about Baskerville's type that it was Baskerville's specimen sheet, and asked the man to point out the problems. The victim of Franklin's whimsy proceeded to pontificate on the problems, complaining that just looking at it gave him a headache.

Baskerville published fifty-six books, the most ambitious being a folio Bible in 1763. While he was met with indifference and even hostility in the British Isles, the design of his type and books became important influences on the Continent as the Italian Giambattista Bodoni (1740–1813) and the Didot family in Paris became enthusiastic about his work.

The origins of information graphics
The foundation for information graphics is analytic geometry, a branch of geometry developed and first used in 1637 by the French philosopher, mathematician, and scientist René Descartes (1596–1650). Descartes used algebra to solve geometry problems, formulate equations to represent lines and curves, and represent a point in space by a pair of numbers. On a two-dimensional plane, Descartes drew two perpendicular intersecting lines called axes: a horizontal line called the *x*-axis and a vertical line called the *y*-axis. Any point on the plane can be specified by two numbers. One defines its distance from the horizontal axis, and the other number defines its distance from the vertical axis; for example, $x = 2$, $y = 3$ denotes a point two units along the horizontal line and three units along the vertical line. These numbers are called Cartesian coordinates. The axes can be repeated at regular intervals to form a grid of horizontal and vertical lines called a Cartesian grid.

Cartesian coordinates and other aspects of analytic geometry were later used by the Scottish author and scientist William Playfair (1759–1823) to convert statistical data into symbolic graphics. A passionate man with strong opinions about trade and economics, Playfair worked hard to cham-

pion and spread his beliefs. In 1786, he published his *Commercial and Political Atlas.* This book was laden with statistical compilations and, in forty-four diagrams, introduced the *line* (or *fever*) graph (Fig. **8–14**) and the bar chart to graphically present complex information. Line graphs charted two lines whose x-axis represented the year and y-axis represented millions of pounds; these showed year-by-year imports and exports between England and its colonies, so trade surpluses and deficits could be seen at a glance.

Playfair calculated the area of descending sizes of circles to show the relative land area of European countries and to compare the populations of cities. These diagrams appeared in his 1801 *Statistical Breviary.* He introduced the first "divided circle" diagram (called a pie chart today) in his 1805 English translation of a French book, *The Statistical Account of the United States of America.* Playfair's diagram was a circle cut into wedge-shaped slices representing the area of each state and territory. Readers could see at a glance how vast the newly acquired western territories were in comparison with states such as Rhode Island and New Hampshire. In this way, Playfair created a new category of graphic design, now called information graphics. This field of design has gained importance because of our expanding base of knowledge, which requires graphics to present complex information in an understandable form.

The imperial designs of Louis René Luce
An imperial graphic design statement was achieved by a type designer and punch cutter at the Imprimerie Royale, Louis René Luce (d. 1773). During the three decades from 1740 until 1770, Luce designed a series of types that were narrow and condensed, with serifs as sharp as spurs. Engraved borders were being widely used and required a second printing; first the text was printed and then, in a second run of the same sheets, the borders. Luce created a large series of letterpress borders, ornaments, trophies, and other devices of impressive variety and excellent printing quality. These were designed with a mechanistic perfection that projects an air of imperial authority. Cast in modular sections, these ornaments were then assembled into the desired configuration by the compositor. The density of line in Luce's ornaments was carefully planned to be visually compatible with his typefaces and often had an identical weight so that they looked as if they belonged together in a design. In 1771 Luce published his *Essai d'une nouvelle typographie* (Essay on a New Typography), with ninety-three plates presenting the range of his design accomplishments (Fig. **8–15**).

Both Fournier le Jeune and Luce died before the French Revolution tore apart the world in which they lived and served, the *ancien régime* of the French monarchy. The opulent

8–16

8–18

8–17

8–16. Giambattista Bodoni, title page from *Saggio tipografico* (Typographic Essay), 1771. The tremendous influence of Fournier le Jeune upon Bodoni's earlier work is evident in this page design.

8–17. Giambattista Bodoni, section-heading page for Vergil's *Opera*, Volume II, 1793. In designs so pure and simple, every adjustment of letterspace and line space becomes critical to the overall design harmony.

8–18. Giambattista Bodoni, page from *Manuale tipografico*, 1818. The crisp clarity of Bodoni's letterforms are echoed by the scotch rules. Composed of double and triple thick-and-thin elements, these rules and borders echo the weight contrasts of Bodoni's modern types.

architectural, graphic, and interior designs patronized by royalty lost all social relevance in the world of democracy and equality that emerged from the chaos of revolution. Perhaps the ultimate irony occurred in 1790, when Romain du Roi typefaces commissioned by Louis XIV were used to print radical political tracts in support of the French Revolution.

The modern style

The son of an indigent printer, Giambattista Bodoni was born in Saluzzo in northern Italy. As a young man, he traveled to Rome and apprenticed at the Propaganda Fide, the Catholic press that printed missionary materials in native languages for use throughout the world. Bodoni learned punch cutting, but his interest in living in Rome declined after Ruggeri, his men-

tor and the director, committed suicide. Shortly thereafter, Bodoni left the Propaganda Fide with the idea of journeying to England and perhaps working with Baskerville. While visiting his parents before leaving Italy, twenty-eight-year-old Bodoni was asked to take charge of the Stamperia Reale, the official press of Ferdinand, Duke of Parma. Bodoni accepted the charge and became the private printer to the court. He printed official documents and publications desired by the duke in addition to projects he conceived and initiated himself. His initial design influence was Fournier le Jeune, whose foundry supplied type and ornaments to the Stamperia Reale after Bodoni took charge. The quality of Bodoni's design and printing, even though scholarship and proofreading were sometimes lacking, contributed to his growing international reputation. In 1790 the Vatican invited Bodoni to Rome to establish a press for printing the classics there, but the duke countered with an offer of expanded facilities, greater independence, and the privilege of printing for other clients. Bodoni elected to remain in Parma.

At about the same time, the cultural and political climate was changing. The revolt against the French monarchy led to a rejection of the lush designs so popular during the reigns of Louis XV and XVI. To fill the formal void, architects, painters, and sculptors enthusiastically embraced the classical forms of Greek and Roman antique art, which were captivating the public in the 1790s. All areas of design required a new approach to replace the outmoded rococo style; Bodoni led the way in evolving new typefaces and page layout. Figures

8–16, and **8–17** show Bodoni's evolution from Fournier le Jeune–inspired rococo to the modern style.

The term *modern*, which defines a new category of roman type, was first used by Fournier le Jeune in his *Manuel typographique* to describe the design trends that culminated in Bodoni's mature work. The initial impetus was the thin, straight serifs of Grandjean's Romain du Roi, followed by engraved pages by artists. Next came the letterforms and page layouts of Baskerville, particularly his practice of making the light strokes of his characters thinner to increase the contrast between thicks and thins. Also, Baskerville's rejection of ornament and his generous use of space were factors. Another trend, the design of narrower, more condensed letterforms, gave type a taller and more geometric appearance. Finally, all of these evolutionary trends were encouraged by a growing preference for a lighter typographic tone and texture.

Around 1790 Bodoni redesigned the roman letterforms to give them a more mathematical, geometric, and mechanical appearance. He reinvented the serifs by making them hairlines that formed sharp right angles with the upright strokes, eliminating the tapered flow of the serif into the upright stroke in Old Style roman. The thin strokes of his letterforms were trimmed to the same weight as the hairline serifs, creating a brilliant sharpness and a dazzling contrast not seen before. Bodoni defined his design ideal as cleanness, good taste, charm, and regularity. This regularity—the standardization of units—was a concept of the emerging industrial era of the machine. Bodoni decided that the letters in a type font should be created through combinations of a very limited number of identical units. This standardization of forms that could be measured and constructed marked the death of calligraphy and writing as the wellspring for type design and the end of the imprecise cutting and casting of earlier type design. Bodoni's precise, measurable, and repeatable forms expressed the vision and spirit of the machine age. It is noteworthy that as Bodoni was constructing alphabets of interchangeable parts, American inventor Eli Whitney was assembling firearms of interchangeable parts in his New Haven, Connecticut, factory, foreshadowing the mass-production techniques soon to revolutionize Western society.

In Bodoni's page layouts, the borders and ornaments of the earlier decorative work that had brought international fame to the Stamperia Reale were cast aside for an economy of form and efficiency of function. The severe purity of Bodoni's late graphic-design style has affinities with twentieth-century functional typography. Open, simple page design with generous margins, wide letter- and line-spacing, and large areas of white space became his hallmark. Lightness was increased by using a smaller x-height and longer ascenders and descenders. In some fonts, letters were cast on over-sized metal so the type could not be set solid. As a result, these fonts always had the appearance of generous leading.

A majority of books of this time, including most of the 345 books published by Bodoni, were new editions of Greek and Roman classics. Critics hailed Bodoni's volumes, including Vergil's *Opera* (Works) (Fig. **8–17**) as the typographic expression of neoclassicism and a return to "antique virtue." This is surprising, for Bodoni was breaking new ground. Bodoni designed about three hundred type fonts and planned a monumental specimen book presenting this work. After his death his widow and his foreman, Luigi Orsi, persisted with the project and published the two-volume *Manuale tipografico* (Manual of Type) (Fig. **8–18**) in 1818. This monumental celebration of the aesthetics of letterforms and homage to Bodoni's genius is a milestone in the history of graphic design. In 1872 the citizens of Saluzzo honored their native son by erecting a statue of Bodoni. Ironically, they carved his name in the base in Old Style roman letters.

A family dynasty of printers, publishers, papermakers, and typefounders began in 1713 when François Didot (1689–1757) established a printing and bookselling firm in Paris. In 1780 his son, Françoise-Ambroise Didot (1730–1804), introduced a highly finished, smooth paper of wove design modeled after the paper commissioned by Baskerville in England. The Didot typefoundry's constant experimentation led to *maigre* (thin) and *gras* (fat) type styles similar to the condensed and expanded fonts of our time. Around 1785 Françoise-Ambroise Didot revised Fournier's typographic measurement system and created the point system used in France today. He realized that the Fournier scale was subject to shrinkage after being printed on moistened paper, and even Fournier's metal master had no standard for comparison. Therefore, Didot adopted the official *pied de roi*, divided into twelve French inches, as his standard. Then each inch was divided into seventy-two points. Didot discarded the traditional nomenclature for various type sizes (Cicero, Petit-Romain, Gros-Text, and so on) and identified them with the measure of the metal type body in points (ten-point, twelve-point, and so on). The Didot system was adopted in Germany, where it was revised by Hermann Berthold in 1879 to work with the metric system. In 1886 the Didot system, revised to suit the English inch, was adopted as a standard point measure by American typefounders, and England adopted the point system in 1898. Fonts (Fig. **8–19**) issued from 1775 by François-Ambroise Didot possessed a lighter, more geometric quality, similar in feeling to the evolution occurring in Bodoni's designs under Baskerville's influence.

François-Ambroise had two sons: Pierre Didot (1761–1853), who took charge of his father's printing office, and Firmin Didot (1764–1836), who succeeded his father as head

AVIS

AUX SOUSCRIPTEURS

DE

LA GERUSALEMME

LIBERATA

IMPRIMÉE PAR DIDOT L'AÎNÉ

SOUS LA PROTECTION ET PAR LES ORDRES

DE MONSIEUR.

Les artistes choisis par Monsieur pour exécuter son édition de la Gerusalemme liberata demandent avec confiance aux souscripteurs de cet ouvrage un délai de quelques mois pour en mettre au jour la premiere livraison. Il est rarement arrivé qu'un ouvrage où sont entrés les ornements de la gravure ait pu être donné au temps préfix pour lequel il avoit été promis : cet art entraîne beaucoup de difficultés qui causent des retards forcés ; et certainement on peut regarder comme un empêchement insurmontable les jours courts et obscurs d'un hiver long et rigoureux. D'ailleurs la quantité d'ouvrages de gravure proposés actuellement par

8–19

8–21

of the Didot type foundry. Firmin's notable achievements included the invention of stereotyping. This process involves casting a duplicate of a relief printing surface by pressing a molding material (damp paper pulp, plaster, or clay) against it to make a matrix. Molten metal is poured into the matrix to form the duplicate printing plate. Stereotyping made longer press runs possible.

After the Revolution, the French government honored Pierre Didot by granting him the printing office formerly used by the Imprimerie Royale at the Louvre. There he gave the neoclassical revival of the Napoleonic era its graphic design expression in a series of *Éditions du Louvre* (Fig. **8–20**). Lavish margins surround Firmin Didot's modern typography, which is even more mechanical and precise than Bodoni's. Engraved illustrations by artists working in the neoclassical manner of the painter Jacques Louis David (1748–1825) have flawless technique and sharp value contrast. In seeking to imitate nature in her most perfect form, these artists created figures as ideally modeled as Greek statues, frozen in shallow picture boxes. A seldom-equaled, though brittle, perfection is achieved.

Bodoni and the Didots were rivals and kindred spirits. Comparisons and speculation about who innovated and who followed are inevitable. They shared common influences and the same cultural milieu. Their influence upon each other was reciprocal, for Bodoni and the Didots each attempted to push the modern style further than the other. In so doing, each pushed the aesthetics of contrast, mathematical construction, and neoclassical refinement to the ultimate possible level. Bodoni is credited with greater skill as a designer and printer, but the Didots possessed greater scholarship. Bodoni proclaimed that he sought only the magnificent and did not work for common readers. In addition to their extravagant folio editions, the Didots used their new stereotyping process to produce much larger editions of economical books for a broader audience. A year after the *Manuale tipografico* appeared, the 1819 *Spécimen des nouveaux caractères . . . de P. Didot l'aîné* (Specimens of New Characters . . . by P. Didot the elder) was published in Paris.

The illuminated printing of William Blake

During the waning years of the eighteenth century, an unexpected counterpoint to the severe typography of Bodoni and Didot appeared in the illuminated printing of the visionary English poet and artist William Blake (1757–1827). As a child, Blake reported seeing angels in a tree and the prophet Ezekiel in a field. After completing an engraving apprenticeship and

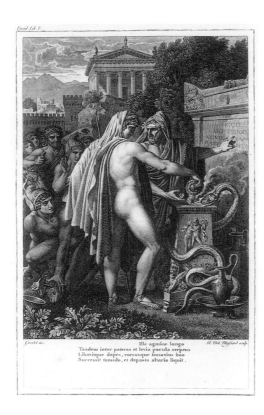

AENEIDOS

LIBER QUINTUS.

Interea medium Aeneas jam classe tenebat
Certus iter, fluctusque atros Aquilone secabat,
Mœnia respiciens, quæ jam infelicis Elissæ
Collucent flammis. Quæ tantum accenderit ignem
Causa latet; duri magno sed amore dolores
Polluto, notumque furens quid femina possit,
Triste per augurium Teucrorum pectora ducunt.
    Ut pelagus tenuere rates, nec jam amplius ulla
Occurrit tellus, maria undique et undique cœlum;
Olli cæruleus supra caput adstitit imber,
Noctem hiememque ferens; et inhorruit unda tenebris.
Ipse gubernator puppi Palinurus ab alta:
Heu! quianam tanti cinxerunt æthera nimbi?
Quidve, pater Neptune, paras? Sic deinde locutus,
Colligere arma jubet, validisque incumbere remis;
Obliquatque sinus in ventum, ac talia fatur:
Magnanime Aenea, non, si mihi Juppiter auctor

8–20

studying at the Royal Academy, Blake opened a printing shop at age twenty-seven, where he was assisted by his younger brother Robert. Upon Robert's death three years later, Blake reported that he saw Robert's soul joyfully rising through the ceiling. Blake informed friends that Robert appeared to him in a dream and told him about a way to print his poems and illustrations as relief etchings without typography.

Blake began to publish books of his poetry; each page was printed as a monochrome etching combining word and image. Blake and his wife then either hand-colored each page with watercolor or printed colors, hand-bound each copy in paper covers, and sold them at modest prices. The lyrical fantasy, glowing swirls of color, and imaginative vision that Blake achieved in his poetry and accompanying designs represent an effort to transcend the material of graphic design and printing to achieve spiritual expression. The 1789 title page from *Songs of Innocence* (Fig. **8–21**) shows how Blake integrated letterforms into illustrations. The swirls of foliage that spin from the serifs of the letters become leaves for the tree; small figures frolic among these letters set against a vibrant sky.

Blake's single-minded unworldliness and spiritual beliefs led some people to dismiss him as mad, and he died in poverty and neglect. His reaction against the neoclassical emphasis on

8–19. Françoise Ambroise Didot, typography from a prospectus for Tasso's *La Gerusalemme liberata* (Liberation of Jerusalem), 1784. Designed at the Didot foundry, the typeface used in this announcement for a forthcoming romantic novel is a very early presentation of a true modern-style letterform. Straight hairline serifs, extreme contrast between thick and thin strokes, and construction on a vertical axis are characteristics that mark this break with transitional letterforms.

8–20. Pierre Didot (printer), pages from Vergil's *Bucolica, Georgica, et Aeneis,* 1798. This double-page spread shows the splendid perfection, lavish margins, and cool understatement of neoclassical graphic design

8–21. William Blake, title page from *Songs of Innocence*, 1789. A joyful rainbow of color animates the sky on the title page for Blake's volume of gentle lyrics capturing the wonder of childhood.

reason and the intellect combined with his focus upon the imagination, introspection, and emotions as wellsprings for his work make Blake a harbinger of nineteenth-century romanticism. His bright colors and swirling organic forms are forerunners to expressionism, Art Nouveau, and abstract art.

8–22

In Albion's isle, when glorious Edgar reign'd,
He, wisely provident, from her white cliffs
Launch'd half her forests, and, with numerous fleets,
Cover'd his wide domain: there proudly rode,
Lord of the deep, the great prerogative
Of British monarchs. Each invader bold,
Dane and Norwegian, at a distance gazed,
And, disappointed, gnash'd his teeth in vain.
He scour'd the seas, and to remotest shores
With swelling sails the trembling corsair fled.
Rich commerce flourish'd; and with busy oars
Dash'd the resounding surge. Nor less, at land,
His royal cares; wise, potent, gracious prince!
His subjects from their cruel foes he saved,

8–22. Thomas Bewick, "Old English Hound," from the *General History of Quadrupeds*, 1790 *(left)*, and "The Yellow Bunting," from *British Birds*, 1797 *(right)*. Bewick achieved his dazzling tonal range by combining white-line-on-black techniques—much like drawing in chalk on a chalkboard—with a more usual black-line-on-white treatment in the lighter tonal areas.

8–23. Thomas Bewick (engraver) and William Bulmer (printer), page from William Somerville's *The Chase*, 1796. Simplicity becomes exquisite here, for the paper, type, printing, and engravings all reflect a perfection of craft.

8–23

The epoch closes

British national pride led to the establishment of the Shakespeare Press in 1786 to produce editions of splendor to rival the folio volumes of Paris and Parma. The state of English printing was such that a printing house, type foundry, and ink manufactory had to be established to produce work of the desired quality. Punch cutter William Martin (d. 1815), former apprentice to Baskerville and brother of Baskerville's foreman Robert Martin, was called to London to design and cut types "in imitation of the sharp and fine letter used by the French and Italian printers." His types combined the majestic proportions of Baskerville with the sharp contrasts of modern fonts. William Bulmer (1757–1830) was chosen by publishers John and Josiah Boydell and George and W. Nicol to print, in nine volumes, *The Dramatic Works of Shakespeare*, 1792–1802. These were followed by a three-volume edition of Milton.

As a boy in Newcastle, Bulmer had a close friend in Thomas Bewick (1753–1828), who is called the father of wood engraving (Fig. **8–22**). After apprenticing to engraver Ralph Beilby and learning to engrave sword blades and doorplates, Bewick turned his attention to wood-engraved illustrations. His "white-line" technique employed a fine graver to achieve delicate tonal effects by cutting across the grain on blocks of Turkish boxwood. Woodcuts were made by cutting

with the grain on softer wood. Publication of his *General History of Quadrupeds* in 1790 brought renown to Bewick and his technique, which became a major illustration method in letterpress printing until the advent of photomechanical halftones nearly a century later.

Bulmer used Martin's types and Bewick's wood engravings together in a series of volumes, including William Somerville's *The Chase* of 1796 (Fig. **8–23**), in which the clean, spacious design of Bodoni and Didot was tempered by a traditional English legibility and warmth. These gentle volumes might be called the lyrical envoi of a three-and-a-half-century period of graphic design and printing that began with Gutenberg in Mainz. Printing had been a handicraft, and graphic design had involved the layout of metal type and related material with illustrations printed from handmade blocks. The eighteenth century closed with stormy political revolutions in France and the American colonies. England was the nucleus for the gathering forces of the vast upheavals of the Industrial Revolution. The sweeping changes ushered in by the conversion of an agrarian, rural society with handicraft manufacture to the industrial society of machine manufacture shook Western civilization to its foundations. All aspects of the human experience, including visual communications, were transformed by profound and irrevocable changes.

Part III

The Bridge to the Twentieth Century

The Industrial Revolution:
The impact of industrial technology
upon visual communications

Graphic Design and the Industrial Revolution

9

1800 **Lord Stanhope, cast-iron press**
1812 *War of 1812 begins*　　　　　　　　　1831 *Henry, 1st electric motor*
1814 **Koenig, steam-powered press**　　　　　　　　　　　　　1848 *Marx, Communist Manifesto*
c 1765 **Cotterell, 12-line pica type**　　　1816 **Caslon, 1st sans-serif type**
1843 **Bufford, Boston lithography firm**
1803 **Thorne, 1st Fat Face type; 1st production paper machine**　　1845 **Besley, 1st Clarendon**
1804 *Napoleon crowned emperor*　　1827 **Wells, wood display type**　　1846 **Hoe, rotary lithographic press**
1815 *Napoleon defeated at Waterloo*　　　　　　　1851 *Melville, Moby Dick*
1800 *Library of Congress formed*　　　　　1828 *Democratic Party formed*
1833 **Figgins, 2-line Pearl, Outline**
1815 **Figgins, 1st Egyptian type**　　1834 **Berthold, Akzidenz Grotesk**
Leavenworth, pantagraph driven router
c 1822 **Niepce, 1st photolithographic print**
1821 *Champollion deciphers hieroglyphics*　1839 **Daguerre announces the daguerreotype process**
Talbot announces his photographic process
1806 *Webster, Dictionary*　　　　　　　　　1845 *Annexation of Texas*
1826 **Niepce, the 1st photograph from nature**　　1850 **Archer, wet-plate**
1808 *Beethoven, Fifth Symphony*　　1834 *Braille, writing system for blind*　　**collodion process**
1810 *Goya, Disasters of War*　　　　　　　　c 1843-45 **Hill & Adamson, early portrait photography**
1835 **Talbot, 1st photographic negative**
1796 **Senefelder invents lithography**　　1825 *Bolshoi Ballet starts in Moscow*　　1852 *Paxton, Crystal Palace*
1819 *Florida ceded to U.S.*　　　1837 *Victoria, Queen of United Kingdom*
1823 *Monroe Doctrine*　　1840 **Sharp introduces lithography to America**
1841 *British seize Hong Kong*
1844 *Morse, telegraph*

1847 **Pickering,** *The Elements of Euclid*

1834 **Morris is born**

1853 *Perry, treaty with Japan*

1765 **Harunobu, multicolor Ukiyo-e prints**
1682 **Moronobu,** *Young Man with Two Courtesans*

1830–32 **Hokusai,** *Thirty-Six Views of Mount Fuji*

1740 **Masanobu, linear perspective in Ukiyo-e prints**

Late 1700s **Utamaro, portraits of courtesans**

1900

1850s & '60s **Woodtype posters dominate the hoardings**
1856 **Prang opens Boston lithography firm**
1857 *Atlantic Monthly founded*   1893 *Ford's 1st motor engine*
1870s **Woodtype posters begin to decline as lithography becomes dominant**
1854 *Republican Party formed*   1871 *Boss Tweed indicted*   1886 **Mergenthaler, Linotype machine**
1887 **Lanston, Monotype machine**
1867 *Strauss, Blue Danube Waltz*
1880s **Dry plates replace wet plates**
1864–74 **Cameron, portrait photography**   1895 *Lumiere Brothers, Cinematographie*
1871 **Moss, commercially feasible photoengraving**
1867–69 **O'Sullivan geological expedition**
1861–65 **Brady & staff photograph U. S. Civil War**   1888 **Eastman Kodak camera makes photography "every person's art form"**
1879 **Greenaway, *Under the Window***
1880 **Horgan, experimental halftone screen**   1901 *Victoria dies*
1859 *Darwin, Origin of Species*   1881 **Ives, early halftone process**

1861 *U. S. Civil War begins* 1865 *Lincoln assassinated*   1885 **Ives, halftone screen**
1865 **Crane, his 1st children's book**   c 1877 **Muybridge, sequence photography**
1863 *Emancipation Proclamation*
1873 **Prang, English Christmas card**
1874 **Prang, 1st American Christmas card**
1862 **Nast joins *Harper's Weekly***
1884 *Twain, Huckleberry Finn*

The Arts and Crafts Movement and Its Heritage

10

1877 **Morris makes his 1st public lectures on design**   1902 **Ashbee, Essex House Psalter**
1882 **Century Guild is formed**   1903 **Doves Press Bible**
1883 **Mackmurdo, *Wren's City Churches* title page**
1884 ***Hobby Horse* published**
1891 *Edison, kinetoscopic camera*   1940 **Goudy, Typologia**
1893 **Morris, Chaucer type**   1918 **Koch forms workshop community**
1869 *Suez Canal opens*   1883 *Stevenson, Treasure Island*
1884 **Art Worker's Guild is formed**
1886 *Statue of Liberty*   1898 *Curie discovers radium*
1894 **Morris & Crane, *The Story of the Glittering Plain***
1894 *Nicolas II becomes Russian Czar*
1861 **Morris opens art-decorating firm**   1895 **Goudy's Camelot, his 1st typeface**
1896 **Morris, Kelmscott *Chaucer*; Pissarro founds Eragny Press;**
Rogers joins Riverside Press; Hornby starts Ashendene Press; Morris dies
1888 **Morris designs Golden type**
1896 *Sousa, Stars and Stripes Forever*

Art Nouveau

11

1876 *Bell, telephone*   1886 **Grasset, 1st poster**
1874 *Tiffany opens glassworks*   1889 *Van Gogh, Starry Night*
1891 **Toulouse-Lautrec, Moulin Rouge poster**
c 1856–59 **Hiroshige, *Evening Squall at Great Bridge near Atake***   1899 **Van de Velde, *Tropon* poster**
1896 ***Jugend,* 1st issue; *Steinlen, La Rue* poster; Ricketts begins Vale Press**
1883 **Grasset, *Historie des Quatre Fils Aymon***
1866 **Chéret, *La Biche au Bois poster***   1893 **Beardsley, *Mort D'Arthur*; Wright opens architectural office**

1879 *Edison, electric lamp*   1894 **Toorpp, *Delft Salad Oil Poster*; Mucha, *Gismonda* poster;**
1881 *Barnum & Bailey, circus*   **Rhead returns to America; Bradley, *Inland Printer* covers**
1895 **Bing, l'Art Nouveau gallery opens**
1890 **Chéret, Legion of Honor**
1898 **Behrens, *The Kiss***
1901 **Dudorvich, *Bitter Campar* poster**

The Genesis of Twentieth Century Design

12

1898 ***Ver Sacrum* begins publication; Berthold Foundry, Akzidenz Grotesk**
1899 **Moser, 5th Vienna Secession poster**
1898 *Curie discovers radium*
1896 **Wright designs *The House Beautiful***
1891 *Edison, kinetoscopic camera*   1907 **Deutscher Werkbund formed; Loeffler designs *Fledermaus* poster**
1900 **Behrens, sans serif running text; Klingspor issues Eckmannschrift**
1902 **Moser, 13th Vienna Secession poster; Wright, the 1st "prairie style" house**
1894 *Nicolas II becomes Russian Czar*
1895 **McNair and Macdonalds, Glasgow fine arts poster**
1897 **Vienna Secession formed**
1901 **Klingspor issues Behrensschrift**
1903 **Hoffmann & Moser, Vienna Workshops are established**
1904 **Lauweriks teaches geometric grid composition in Germany**

1909 **Behrens and Bernhard, AEG turbine hall**
1910 **Behrens, AEG lamp poster**

Graphic Design and the Industrial Revolution

9

Although it might be said that the Industrial Revolution first occurred in England between 1760 and 1840, it was a radical process of social and economic change rather than a mere historical period. Energy was a major impetus for this conversion from an agricultural society to an industrial one. Until James Watt (1736–1819) perfected the steam engine, which was deployed rapidly starting in the 1780s, animal and human power were the primary sources of energy. During the course of the nineteenth century, the amount of energy generated by steam power increased a hundredfold. During the last three decades of the century, electricity and gasoline-fueled engines further expanded productivity. A factory system with machine manufacturing and divisions of labor was developed. New materials, particularly iron and steel, became available.

Cities grew rapidly, as masses of people left a subsistence existence on the land and sought employment in the factories. Political power shifted away from the aristocracy and toward capitalist manufacturers, merchants, and even the working class. The growing body of scientific knowledge was applied to manufacturing processes and materials. People's sense of dominion over nature and faith in the ability to exploit the earth's resources for material needs created a heady confidence.

The capitalist replaced the landowner as the most powerful force in Western countries; investment in machines for mass manufacture became the basis for change in industry. Demand from a rapidly growing urban population with expanding buying power stimulated technological improvements. In turn, this enabled mass production, which increased availability and lowered costs. The cheaper, more abundant merchandise now available stimulated a mass market and even greater demand. As this supply-and-demand cycle became the force behind relentless industrial development, graphics played an important role in marketing factory output.

The giddy progression of the Industrial Revolution was not without its social costs. Workers who traded overpopulated rural areas for urban factories worked thirteen-hour days for miserable wages and lived in filthy, unsanitary tenements. This huge workforce of men, women, and children often suffered from shutdowns caused by overproduction, depressions, economic panics, business and bank failures, and the loss of jobs to newer technological improvements. On measure, the overall standard of living in Europe and America improved dramatically during the nineteenth century.

Nevertheless, critics of the new industrial age cried that civilization was shifting from an interest in humanist values toward a preoccupation with material goods and that people were losing their ties with nature, aesthetic experience, and spiritual values.

Greater human equality sprang from the French and American Revolutions and led to increased public education and literacy. The audience for reading matter proliferated accordingly. Graphic communications became more important and more widely available during this unsettled period of incessant change. As with other commodities, technology lowered unit costs and increased the production of printed materials. In turn, the greater availability created an insatiable demand, and the era of mass communications dawned.

Handicrafts greatly diminished as the unity of design and production ended. Earlier, a craftsman designed and fabricated a chair or pair of shoes, and a printer was involved in all aspects of his craft, from typeface design and page layout to the actual printing of books and broadsheets. Over the course of the nineteenth century, however, the specialization of the factory system fractured graphic communications into separate design and production components. The nature of visual information was profoundly changed. The range of typographic sizes and letterform styles exploded. The invention of photography—and, later, the means of printing photographic images—expanded the meaning of visual documentation and pictorial information. The use of color lithography passed the aesthetic experience of colorful images from the privileged few to the whole of society. This dynamic, exuberant, and often chaotic century witnessed an astonishing parade of new technologies, imaginative forms, and new functions for graphic design. The nineteenth century was an inventive and prolific period for new typeface designs, ranging from new categories such as Egyptian and sans serif to fanciful and outrageous novelty styles.

Innovations in typography

The Industrial Revolution generated a shift in the social and economic role of typographic communication. Before the nineteenth century, dissemination of information through books and broadsheets was its dominant function. The faster pace and mass-communication needs of an increasingly urban and industrialized society produced a rapid expansion of jobbing printers, advertising, and posters. Larger scale, greater visual impact, and new tactile and expressive characters were demanded, and the book typography that had slowly evolved from handwriting did not fulfill these needs.

It was no longer enough for the twenty-six letters of the alphabet to function only as phonetic symbols. The industrial age transformed these signs into abstract visual forms projecting powerful concrete shapes of strong contrast and large size. At the same time, letterpress printers faced increasing competitive pressure from lithographic printers, whose skilled craftsmen rendered plates directly from an artist's sketch and produced images and letterforms limited only by the artist's imagination. The letterpress printers turned to the typefounders to expand their design possibilities, and the founders were only too happy to comply. The early decades of the nineteenth century saw an outpouring of new type designs without precedent.

As in many other aspects of the Industrial Revolution, England played a pivotal role in this development; major design innovations were achieved by London typefounders. It might almost be said that the first William Caslon was the grandfather of this revolution. In addition to his heirs, two of his former apprentices who were dismissed for leading a workers' revolt, Joseph Jackson (1733–92) and Thomas Cotterell (d. 1785), became successful type designers and founders in their own right. Apparently Cotterell began the trend of sand-casting large, bold display letters as early as 1765, when his specimen book included, in the words of one of his amazed contemporaries, a "proscription, or posting letter of great bulk and dimension, as high as the measure of twelve lines of pica!" (about 5 centimeters, or 2 inches) (Fig. **9–1**).

Other founders designed and cast fatter letters, and type grew steadily bolder. This led to the invention of fat faces (Fig. **9–2**), a major category of type design innovated by Cotterell's pupil and successor, Robert Thorne (d. 1820), possibly around 1803. A fat-face typestyle is a roman face whose contrast and weight have been increased by expanding the thickness of the heavy strokes. The stroke width has a ratio of 1:2.5 or even 1:2 to the capital height. These excessively bold fonts were only the beginning, as Thorne's Fann Street Foundry began an active competition with William Caslon IV (1781–1869) and Vincent Figgins (1766–1844). The full range of Thorne's accomplishment as a type designer was documented after his death, when William Thorowgood—who was not a type designer, punch cutter, or printer, but who used lottery winnings to offer the top bid when Thorne's foundry was auctioned after his death—published the 132-page book of specimens that had been typeset and was ready to go onto the press when Thorne died.

9–1. Thomas Cotterell, twelve lines pica, letterforms, c. 1765. These display letters, shown actual size, seemed gigantic to eighteenth-century compositors, who were used to setting handbills and broadsides using types that were rarely even half this size.

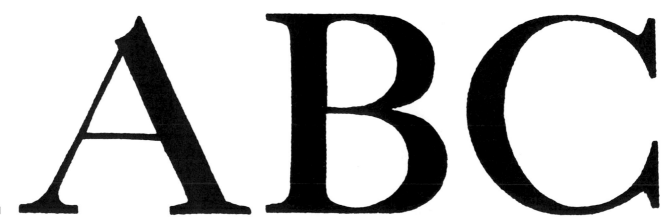

9–1

MINT
main.

Quousque tandem abutere, Catilina, patientia nostra? quamdiu nos etiam furor is te tuus eludet? quem after

CONSTANTINOPLE
£1234567890

9–2

ABCDEFGHIJ
KLMNOPQR
STUVWXYZ&,:;.-
£1234567890

9–3

Quosque tandem abutere Catilina patientia
FURNITURE 1820

**Quosque tandem abutere Catilina patientia nostra? quamdiu nos
W. THOROWGOOD.**

9–4

Quousque tandem abutere, Catilina, patientia nostra? quamdiu nos etiam furor iste tuus eludet? quem ad finem sese effrenata jactabit audacia? nihilne te nocturnum præsidium palatii, nihil urbis vigiliæ, nihil
ABCDEFGHIJKLMN
ABCDEFGHIJKLMNOPQR
£ 1234567890

9–5

Quousque tandem abutere Catilina, patientia nostra? quamdiu nos etiam furor iste tuus eludet? quem ad finem sese effrenata jactabit audacia? nihilne te nocturnum præsidium palatii, nihilne urbis vigiliæ, nihil timor populi, nihil consensus bonorum omnium, nihil hic munitissimus habendi senatus locus, nihil horum

£1234567890
SALES BY PUBLIC AUCTION.

9–6

9–7

9–2. Robert Thorne, fat-face types, 1821. Although the record dates these designs to William Thorowgood's 1821 publication of *New Specimen of Printing Types, Late R. Thorne's*, it is generally thought that Thorne designed the first fat faces in 1803.

9–3. Vincent Figgins, two lines pica, Antique, c. 1815. The inspiration for this highly original design, first shown by Figgins, is not known. Whether Figgins, Thorne, or an anonymous sign painter first invented this style is one of the mysteries surrounding the sudden appearance of slab-serif letterforms.

9–4. Robert Thorne, Egyptian type designs, 1821. Comparison with Figgins's design reveals subtle differences. Thorne based this lower-case on the structure of modern-style letters, but he radically modified the weight and serifs.

9–5. Henry Caslon, Ionic type specimen, mid-1840s. *Bracketing* refers to the curved transition from the main strokes of a letterform to its serif. Egyptian type replaced the bracket with an abrupt angle; Ionic type restored a slight bracket.

9–6. Robert Besley (designer, with Thorowgood), specimen of an early Clarendon, 1845. An adaptation of Ionic that was even more subtle than the development of Ionic from Egyptian, Clarendon styles were wildly popular after their introduction. When the three-year patent expired, numerous imitations and piracies were issued by other founders.

9–7. The top two specimens are typical Tuscan styles with ornamental serifs. They demonstrate the diversity of expanded and condensed widths produced by nineteenth-century designers. The bottom specimen is an Antique Tuscan with curved and slightly pointed slab-serifs. Note the care given to the design of negative shapes surrounding the letters.

One of Joseph Jackson's apprentices, Vincent Figgins, stayed with him and took full charge of his operation during the three years preceding Jackson's death in 1792. Figgins failed in his efforts to purchase his master's foundry because William Caslon III offered the highest bid. Undeterred, he established his own type foundry and quickly built a respectable reputation for type design and mathematical, astronomical, and other symbolic material, numbering in the hundreds of sorts. By the turn of the century Figgins had designed and cast a complete range of romans and had begun to produce scholarly and foreign faces. The rapid tilt in typographic design taste toward modern-style romans and new jobbing styles after the turn of the century seriously affected him, but he rapidly responded, and his 1815 printing

specimens showed a full range of modern styles, antiques (Egyptians)—the second major innovation of nineteenth-century type design (Fig. 9–3)—and numerous jobbing faces, including "three-dimensional" fonts.

The antiques convey a bold, machinelike feeling through slablike rectangular serifs, even weight throughout the letters, and short ascenders and descenders. In Thorowgood's 1821 specimen book of Thorne's type, the name Egyptian—which is still used for this style—was given to the slab-serif fonts shown (Fig. 9–4). Perhaps the name was inspired by the era's fascination with all aspects of ancient Egyptian culture, an interest that was intensified by Napoleon's 1798–99 invasion and occupation. Design similarities were seen between the chunky geometric alphabets and the visual qualities of some Egyptian artifacts. As early as the 1830s, a variation of Egyptian, having slightly bracketed serifs and increased contrast between thicks and thins, was called Ionic (Fig. 9–5). In 1845 William Thorowgood and Company copyrighted a modified Egyptian called Clarendon (Fig. 9–6). Similar to the Ionics, these letterforms were condensed Egyptians with stronger contrasts between thick and thin strokes and somewhat lighter serifs.

Figgins's 1815 specimen book also presented the first nineteenth-century version of Tuscan-style letters (Fig. 9–7). This style, characterized by serifs that are extended and curved, was put through an astounding range of variations during the nineteenth century, often with bulges, cavities, and ornaments.

It seems that the English typefounders were trying to invent every possible design permutation by modifying forms or proportions and applying all manner of decoration to their alphabets. In 1815 Vincent Figgins showed styles that projected the illusion of three dimensions (Fig. 9–8) and appeared as bulky objects rather than two-dimensional signs. This device proved very popular, and specimen books began to show perspective clones for every imaginable style. An additional variation was the depth of shading, which ranged from pencil-thin shadows to deep perspectives. Because contrivances—including perspectives, outline (Fig. 9–9), reversing (Fig. 9–10), expanding, and condensing—could multiply each typeface into a kaleidoscope of variations, foundries proliferated fonts with boundless enthusiasm. The mechanization of manufacturing processes during the Industrial Revolution made the application of decoration more economical and efficient. Designers of furniture, household objects, and even typefaces delighted in design intricacy. During the first half of the century, pictures, plant motifs, and decorative designs were applied to display letterforms (Fig. 9–11).

The third major typographic innovation of the early 1800s, sans-serif type, made its modest debut in an 1816 specimen book issued by William Caslon IV (Fig. 9–12). Buried among the

ABCDEFGH IJKLMNOP RSTUVWX.

9–8

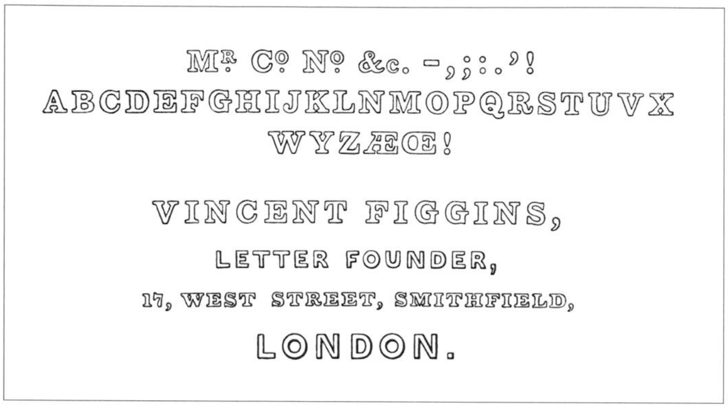

MR CO NO &c. -,;:.'!
ABCDEFGHIJKLNMOPQRSTUVX
WYZÆŒ!

VINCENT FIGGINS,

LETTER FOUNDER,

17, WEST STREET, SMITHFIELD,

LONDON.

9–9

MOLDER

9–10

9–11

W CASLON JUNR   LETTERFOUNDER

9–12

TWO-LINE GREAT PRIMER SANS-SERIF.

TO BE SOLD BY AUCTION, WITHOUT RESERVE ; HOUSEHOLD FURNITURE, PLATE, GLASS, AND OTHER EFFECTS. VINCENT FIGGINS.

9–13

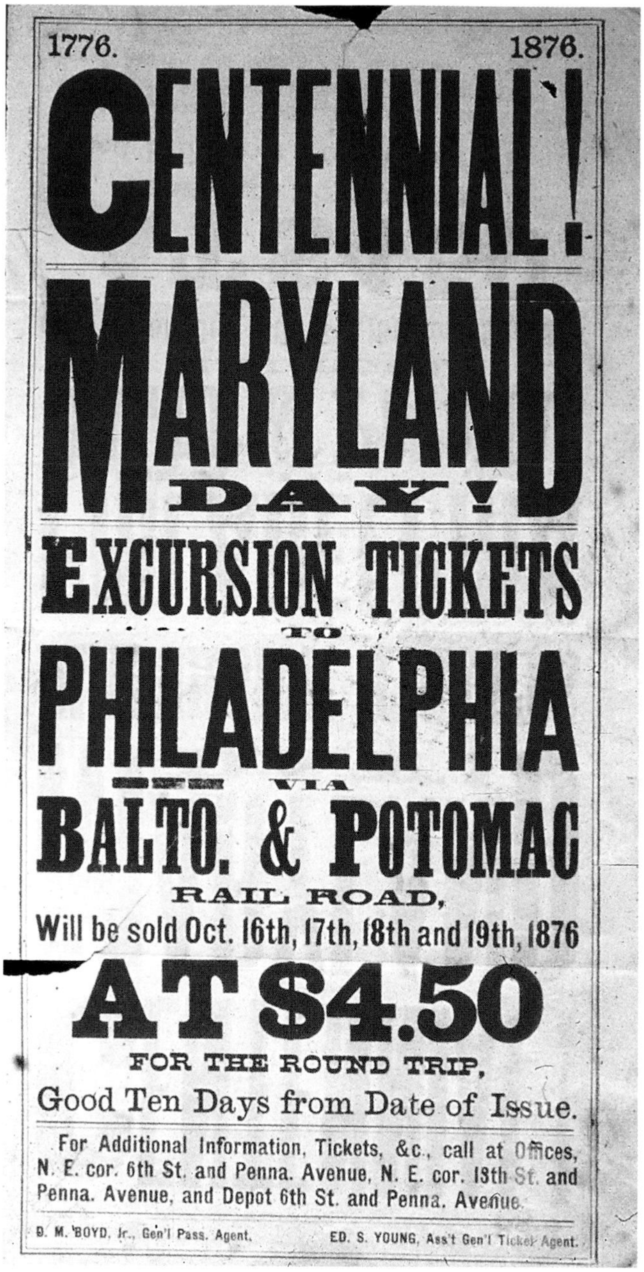

1776.   CENTENNIAL!   1876.
MARYLAND
DAY!
EXCURSION TICKETS
TO
PHILADELPHIA
VIA
BALTO. & POTOMAC
RAIL ROAD,
Will be sold Oct. 16th, 17th, 18th and 19th, 1876
AT $4.50
FOR THE ROUND TRIP,
Good Ten Days from Date of Issue.
For Additional Information, Tickets, &c., call at Offices, N. E. cor. 6th St. and Penna. Avenue, N. E. cor. 13th St. and Penna. Avenue, and Depot 6th St. and Penna. Avenue.
D. M. BOYD, Jr., Gen'l Pass. Agent.   ED. S. YOUNG, Ass't Gen'l Ticket Agent.

9–14

decorative display fonts of capitals in the back of the book, one line of medium-weight monoline serifless capitals proclaimed "W CASLON JUNR LETTER FOUNDER." It looked a lot like an Egyptian face with the serifs removed, which is probably how Caslon IV designed it. The name Caslon adopted for this style—Two Lines English Egyptian—tends to support the theory that it had its origins in an Egyptian style. (English denoted a type size roughly equivalent to today's fourteen-point; thus, Two Lines English indicated a display type of about twenty-eight points.)

Sans serifs, which became so important to twentieth-century graphic design, had a tentative beginning. The cumbersome early sans serifs were used primarily for subtitles

9–8. Vincent Figgins, five lines pica, In Shade, 1815. The first three-dimensional or perspective fonts were fat faces. Perhaps designers were seeking to compensate for the lightness of the thin strokes, which tended to reduce the legibility of fat faces at a distance.

9–9. Vincent Figgins, two-line Pearl, Outline, 1833. In outline and open fonts, a contour line of even weight encloses the alphabet shape, which usually appears black.

9–10. William Thorowgood, six-line Reversed Egyptian Italic, 1828. Types that appeared white against a printed black background enjoyed a brief popularity during the middle decades of the nineteenth century, then went out of fashion.

9–11. Woods and Sharwoods, letters from ornamented fonts, 1838–42. The wide fat-face letterforms provided a background for pictorial and decorative elements.

9–12. William Caslon IV, two-line English Egyptian, 1816. This specimen quietly introduced what was to become a major resource for graphic design.

9–13. Vincent Figgins, two-line Great Primer Sans-serif, 1832. Both the name and wide use of sans-serif typography were launched by awkward black display fonts in Figgins's 1832 Specimens of Printing Types.

9–14. Handbill for an excursion train, 1876. To be bolder than bold, the compositor used heavier letterforms for the initial letter of important words. Oversized terminal letterforms combine with condensed and extended styles in the phrase Maryland Day!

and descriptive material under excessively bold fat faces and Egyptians. They were little noticed until the early 1830s, when several typefounders introduced new sans-serif styles. Each designer and foundry attached a name: Caslon used Doric, Thorowgood called his grotesques, Blake and Stephenson named their version sans-surryphs, and in the United States, the Boston Type and Stereotype Foundry named its first American sans-serif faces Gothics. Perhaps the rich black color of these display types seemed similar to the density of Gothic types. Vincent Figgins dubbed his 1832 specimen sans serif (Fig. 9–13) in recognition of the font's most apparent feature, and the name stuck. German printers had a strong interest in sans serifs, and by 1830 the Schelter and Giesecke foundry issued the first sans-serif fonts with a lowercase alphabet. By midcentury, serifless alphabets were seeing increased use.

The wood-type poster

As display types expanded in size, problems multiplied for both printer and founder. In casting, it was difficult to keep the metal in a liquid state while pouring, and uneven cooling often created slightly concave printing surfaces. Many printers found large metal types to be prohibitively expensive, brittle, and heavy. An American printer named Darius Wells (1800–75) began to experiment with hand-carved wooden types and in 1827 invented a lateral router that enabled the economical mass manufacture of wood types for display printing. Durable, light, and less than half as expensive as large metal types, wood type rapidly overcame printers' initial objections and had a significant impact on poster and broadsheet design. Beginning in March 1828, when Wells launched the wood-type industry with his first specimen sheets, American wood-type manufacturers imported typeface designs from Europe and exported wood type. Soon, however, wood-type manufactories sprang up in European countries, and by midcentury American firms were creating innovative decorative alphabets of their own.

After William Leavenworth (1799–1860) combined the pantograph with the router in 1834, new wood-type fonts could be introduced so easily that customers were invited to send a drawing of one letter of a desired new style; the manufactory offered to design and produce the entire font based on the sketch without an additional charge for design and pattern drafting.

The impetus of this new display typography and the increasing demand for public posters by clients ranging from traveling circuses and vaudeville troupes to clothing stores and the new railroads led to poster houses specializing in letterpress display material (Fig. 9–14). In the eighteenth century, job printing had been a sideline of newspaper and book printers. The design of handbills, wood-type posters, and broadsheets at the poster houses did not involve a graphic designer in the twentieth-century sense. The compositor, often in consultation with the client, selected and composed the type, rules, ornaments, and wood-engraved or metal-stereotyped stock illustrations that filled the typecases. The designer had access to a nearly infinite range of typographic sizes, styles, weights, and novel ornamental effects, and the design philosophy was to use it. The need to lock all the elements tightly on the press enforced a horizontal and vertical stress on the design; this became the basic organizing principle.

Design decisions were pragmatic. Long words or copy dictated condensed type, and short words or copy were set in expanded fonts. Important words were given emphasis through the use of the largest available type sizes. There was a practical side to the extensive mixing of styles in job printing, because many fonts, each having a limited number of characters, were available at the typical print shop. Wood and metal types were used together freely.

The typographic poster houses that developed with the advent of wood type began to decline after 1870 as improvements in lithographic printing resulted in more pictorial and colorful posters by that process. Also, the importance of traveling entertainment shows—a mainstay among their clients—declined. The growth of magazines and newspapers with space advertising, and the legislative restrictions on posting, began to shift commercial communications away from posted notices, and the number of letterpress poster firms declined significantly by the end of the century.

A revolution in printing

The printing presses used by Baskerville and Bodoni were remarkably similar to the first one used by Gutenberg over three centuries earlier. Inevitably, the relentless progress of the Industrial Revolution radically altered printing. Inventors applied mechanical theory and metal parts to the hand press, increasing its efficiency and the size of its impression. Several improvements to make the hand press stronger and more efficient culminated in Lord Stanhope's printing press (Fig. **9–15**), constructed completely of cast-iron parts in 1800. The metal screw mechanism required approximately one-tenth the manual force needed to print on a wooden press, and Stanhope's press enabled a doubling of the printed sheet's size. William Bulmer's printing office installed and experimented with Lord Stanhope's first successful prototype. These innovations served to improve a partially mechanized handicraft.

The next step actually converted printing into a high-speed factory operation. Friedrich Koenig, a German printer who arrived in London around 1804, presented his plans for a steam-powered printing press to major London printers. Finally receiving financial support in 1807, Koenig obtained a patent in March 1810 for his press, which printed 400 sheets per hour in comparison to the hourly output of 250 sheets on the Stanhope hand press.

Koenig's first powered press was designed much like a hand press connected to a steam engine. Other innovations included a method of inking the type by rollers instead of the hand-inking balls. The horizontal movement of the type forms in the bed of the machine and the movement of the tympan and frisket were automated. This press was a prelude to Koenig's development of the stop-cylinder steam-powered press, which enabled much faster operation. In this design the type form was on a flat bed, which moved back and forth beneath a cylinder. During the printing phase the cylinder rotated over the type, carrying the sheet to be printed. It stopped while the form moved from under the cylinder to be inked by rollers. While the cylinder was still, the pressman fed a fresh sheet of paper onto the cylinder.

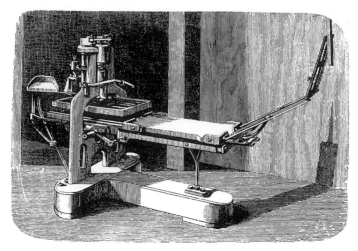

9–15

9–16

9–15. This engraved illustration depicts the printing press of all-iron parts invented in England by Charles, third Earl of Stanhope.

9–16. The first steam-powered cylinder press, 1814. Koenig's invention caused the speed of printing to skyrocket, while its price dropped considerably.

John Walter II of the *Times* in London commissioned Koenig to build two double-cylinder steam-powered presses (Fig. **9–16**). These were capable of printing 1,100 impressions an hour on sheets of paper that were 90 centimeters (35 inches) long and 56 centimeters (22 inches) wide. Fearing the sabotage that often destroyed new machinery when workers felt their jobs were endangered, Walter had the new presses moved to Printing House Square in absolute secrecy. Employees who had threatened Koenig and his invention were directed to wait for news from the Continent on the fateful morning of 29 November 1814. At six o'clock Walter entered the pressroom and announced, "The *Times* is already printed—by steam." The day's edition informed its readers, "Our Journal of this day presents to the public the practical result of the greatest improvement connected with printing since the discovery of the art itself. The reader of this paragraph now holds in his hand one of the many thousand impressions of The Times newspaper, which were taken off last night by a mechanical apparatus." An immediate savings resulted in the composing room, for the *Times* had been typesetting a duplicate of each edition so the two hand presses could print each page. Also, the news could be printed to reach subscribers several hours earlier.

In 1815 William Cowper obtained a patent for a printing press using curved stereotyped plates wrapped around a cylinder. This press achieved 2,400 impressions per hour, and it could be used to print 1,200 sheets on both sides. In 1827 the *Times* commissioned Cowper and his partner, Ambrose Applegath, to develop a four-cylinder steam-powered press using curved stereotyped plates made rapidly from papier-mâché molds. This press printed 4,000 sheets per hour, on both sides.

All across Europe and North America, book and newspaper printers began to retire their hand presses and replace them with steam-powered ones. The Applegath and Cowper steam-powered multiple-cylinder press produced thirty-two impressions for every one printed on the Stanhope hand press, and the cost of printing began to plunge downward as the size of editions soared upward. By the 1830s printing began its incredible expansion, as newspaper, book, and jobbing printers proliferated.

The value of high-speed steam-powered printing would have been limited without an economical and abundant source of paper. A young clerk in the Didot paper mill in France, Nicolas-Louis Robert, developed a prototype for a paper-making machine in 1798, but political turmoil in France prevented him from perfecting it. In 1801 English patent number 2487 was granted to John Gamble for "an invention for making paper in single sheets without seam or joining from one to twelve feet and upwards wide, and from one to forty-five feet and upwards in length." In 1803 the first production paper machine was operative at Frogmore, England. This machine, which was similar to Robert's prototype, poured a suspension of fiber and water in a thin stream upon a vibrating wire-mesh conveyor belt on which an unending sheet of paper could be manufactured. The rights were acquired by Henry and Sealy Fourdrinier, who invested their fortune financing and promoting what is called the Fourdrinier machine to this day. Ironically, although the

Fourdrinier brothers gave the world economical and abundant paper, they ruined themselves financially in the process.

The mechanization of typography

Setting type by hand and then redistributing it into the job case remained a slow and costly process. By the middle of the nineteenth century, presses could produce twenty-five thousand copies per hour, but each letter in every word in every book, newspaper, and magazine had to be set by hand. Dozens of experimenters worked to perfect a machine to compose type, and the first patent for a composing machine was registered in 1825. By the time Ottmar Mergenthaler (1854–99) perfected his Linotype machine in 1886, about three hundred machines had been patented in Europe and America, and several thousand patent claims were on file. Many people, including the writer Mark Twain, invested millions of dollars in the search for automatic typesetting. Before the Linotype was invented, the high cost and slow pace of composition limited even the largest daily newspapers to eight pages, and books remained fairly precious.

Mergenthaler was a German immigrant working in a Baltimore machine shop who struggled for a decade to perfect his typesetter. On 3 July 1886, the thirty-two-year-old inventor demonstrated his keyboard-operated machine (Fig. **9–17**) in the office of the *New York Tribune*. Whitelaw Reid, the editor of the *Tribune*, reportedly exclaimed, "Ottmar, you've done it! A line o' type." The new machine received its name from this enthusiastic reaction.

Many earlier inventors had tried to make a machine that would compose metal type mechanically by automating the traditional typecase. Others had tried a typewriter affair that pressed letters into a papier-mâché mold or attempted to transfer a lithographic image into a metal relief. Mergenthaler's brilliant breakthrough (Fig. **9–18**) involved the use of small brass matrixes with female impressions of the letterforms, numbers, and symbols. Ninety typewriter keys controlled vertical tubes that were filled with these matrixes. Each time the operator pressed a key, a matrix for that character was released. It slid down a chute and was automatically lined up with the other characters in that line. Melted lead was poured into the line of matrixes to cast a slug bearing the raised line of type.

In 1880 the New York newspapers offered over half a million dollars in prizes to any inventor who could create a machine that would reduce the compositor's time by 25 to 30 percent; Mergenthaler's Linotype machine could do the work of seven or eight hand compositors! The rapid deployment of the Linotype replaced thousands of highly skilled handtypesetters, and strikes and violence threatened many installations. But the new technology caused an unprecedented

9–17

9–18

explosion of graphic material, creating thousands of new jobs. The three-cent price of an 1880s newspaper plunged to one or two pennies, while the number of pages multiplied and circulation soared. Book publishing expanded rapidly, with fiction, biographies, technical books, and histories joining the educational texts and literary classics that were being issued. The Linotype led to a surge in the production of periodicals, and illustrated weeklies, including the *Saturday Evening Post* and *Collier's*, reached audiences of millions by the turn of the century. Another American, Tolbert Lanston (1844–1913), invented the Monotype machine, which cast single characters from hot metal, in 1887. It was a decade before the Monotype was efficient enough to be put into production.

Hand-set metal type faced a dwindling market. Since most text type was now machine set, less foundry type was needed. Devastating price wars and cutthroat competition featured discounts of 50 percent plus another 10 percent for cash payment. Consortiums, such as the 1892 merger of fourteen foundries into the American Type Founders Company, were formed in an effort to stabilize the industry by forcing weaker foundries out of business and thereby reducing surplus capac-

ity. Design piracy was rampant. After foundries released new typefaces, competitors immediately electroplated the new designs, then cast and sold types from the counterfeit matrixes. By century's end the type-foundry business stabilized. Hand-set metal typography found a smaller but significant niche providing display type for advertising and editorial headlines until the advent of phototypography in the 1960s.

Technological advances permitted machine-set typography to be printed on machine-manufactured paper with high-speed steam-powered printing presses. There was a global spread of words and pictures, and the age of mass communication arrived.

Photography, the new communications tool

Making pictorial images, and preparing printing plates to reproduce them, remained handwork processes until the arrival of photography. The concept behind the device used for making images by photochemical processes, the *camera obscura* (Latin for "dark chamber"), was known in the ancient world as early as the time of Aristotle in the fourth century B.C. A camera obscura is a darkened room or box with a small opening or lens in one side. Light rays passing through this aperture are

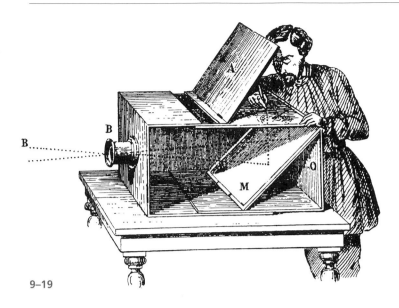

9–19

9–20

9–17. Ottmar Mergenthaler demonstrates the Blower Linotype, the first line-casting keyboard typesetter, to editor Whitelaw Reid on 3 July 1886.

9–18. The Model 5 Linotype became the workhorse of typesetting, with keyboards and matrixes available in over a thousand languages.

9–19. As this nineteenth-century box camera obscura demonstrates, the optical principles of photography were well understood and used by artists to aid in drawing.

9–20. Joseph Niepce, photolithographic print of Cardinal d'Ambroise, c. 1822. This routine portrait print is the first image printed from a plate that was created by the photochemical action of light rather than by the human hand.

projected onto the opposite side and form a picture of the bright objects outside. Artists have used the camera obscura as an aid to drawing for centuries. Around 1665, small, portable, boxlike camera obscuras were developed (Fig. **9–19**). The only additional element needed to "fix" or make permanent the image projected into a camera obscura was a light-sensitive material capable of capturing this image.

The inventors of photography

Photography and graphic communications have been closely linked beginning with the first experiments to capture an image of nature with a camera. Joseph Niepce (1765–1833), the Frenchman who first produced a photographic image, began his research by seeking an automatic means of transferring drawings onto printing plates. As a lithographic printer of popular religious images, Niepce searched for a way to make plates other than by drawing. In 1822 he coated a

pewter sheet with a light-sensitive asphalt, called *bitumen of Judea*, that hardens when exposed to light. Then he contact-printed a drawing, which had been oiled to make it transparent, to the pewter with sunlight. Niepce washed the pewter plate with lavender oil to remove the parts not hardened by light, and then he etched it with acid to make an incised copy of the original. Niepce called his invention *heliogravure* (sun engraving) (Fig. **9–20**).

In 1826 Niepce expanded his discovery by putting one of his pewter plates in the back of his camera obscura and pointing it out the window. This allowed him to make a picture directly from nature; the earliest extant photograph is a pewter sheet that Niepce exposed all day (Fig. **9–21**). When he removed it from the camera obscura and washed it with lavender oil, a hazy image of the sunlit buildings outside his workroom window was captured. Niepce continued his research with light-sensitive materials, including silver-coated

9–21

9–22

9–23

9–21. Joseph Niepce, the first photograph from nature, 1826. Looking out over the rear courtyard of the Niepce home, the light and shadow patterns formed by (from left to right) a wing of the house, a pear tree, the barn roof in front of the low bakehouse with its chimney, and another wing of the house are seen.

9–22 Louis Jacques Daguerre, Paris boulevard, 1839. In this early daguerreotype, the wagons, carriages, and pedestrians were not recorded because the slow exposure could only record stationary objects. On the lower left street corner, a man stopped to have his boots polished. He and the polisher were the first people ever to be photographed.

9–23. William Henry Fox Talbot, cameraless shadow picture of flowers, 1839. By sandwiching the flowers between his photographic paper and a sheet of glass and exposing the light-sensitive emulsion to sunlight, Talbot invented the photogram, later extensively used as a design tool by designers such as Laszlo Moholy-Nagy.

copper. A theatrical performer and painter who had participated in the invention of the diorama, Louis Jacques Daguerre (1799–1851), contacted him. Daguerre had been conducting similar research, Niepce warmed to him, and they shared ideas until Niepce died of a stroke in 1833.

Daguerre persevered, and on 7 January 1839 his perfected process was presented to the French Academy of Sciences. The members marveled at the clarity and minute detail of his *daguerreotype* prints (Fig. **9–22**) and the incredible accuracy of the images. In his perfected process, a highly polished silver-plated copper sheet was sensitized by placing it, silver side down, over a container of iodine crystals. After the rising iodine vapor combined with the silver to produce light-sensitive silver iodide, the plate was placed in the camera and exposed to light coming through the lens, to produce a latent

image. Placing the exposed plate over a dish of heated mercury formed the visible image. After the mercury vapors formed an alloy with the exposed areas of silver, the unexposed silver iodide was removed and the image was fixed with a salt bath. The bare metal appeared black in areas where no light had struck it. The luminous, vibrant image was a base relief of mercury and silver compounds that varied in intensity in direct proportion to the amount of light that had struck the plate during exposure. In one giant leap, the technology for making pictures by machine was realized. In one early year, a half-million daguerreotypes were made in Paris.

Daguerreotypes had limitations, for each plate was a one-of-a-kind image of predetermined size, and the process required meticulous polishing, sensitizing, and development. The polished surface had a tendency to produce glare, and unless it was viewed at just the right angle, the image had a curious habit of reversing itself and appearing as a negative.

Simultaneous research was conducted in England by William Henry Fox Talbot (1800–77), who pioneered a process that formed the basis for both photography and photographic printing plates. While sketching in the Lake Como region of Italy in 1833, Talbot became frustrated with his limited drawing ability and his difficulty in recording beautiful landscapes. He reflected on "how charming it would be if it were possible to cause these natural images to imprint themselves durably, and remain fixed upon the paper." After returning to England he began a series of experiments with paper treated with silver compounds, chosen because he knew silver nitrate was sensitive to light. In his early explorations he floated paper in a weak brine solution, let it dry, and then treated it with a strong solution of silver nitrate to form an insoluble light-sensitive silver-chloride compound in the paper. When he held a piece of lace or a leaf tight against the paper with a pane of glass and exposed it in sunlight, the paper around the object slowly darkened. Washing this image with a salt solution or potassium iodide would fix it somewhat by making the unexposed silver compounds fairly insensitive to light. Talbot called these images, made without a camera, *photogenic drawings* (Fig. **9–23**); today we call images made by manipulating with objects the light striking photographic paper *photograms*. The technique was often used by twentieth-century graphic designers.

During the course of his 1835 experiments Talbot began to use his treated paper in the camera obscura to create minute photographic images that had light areas rendered dark and dark areas appearing light. These images were mirror images of nature.

Talbot let his research drop and turned to other interests for almost three years, until the sudden international uproar over Daguerre. Talbot rushed his work to London, and on 31 January 1839, three weeks after Daguerre's announcement, Talbot presented a hastily prepared report to the Royal Society entitled, "Some account of the Art of Photogenic Drawing, or the process by which Natural Objects may be made to delineate themselves without the aid of the artist's pencil."

Upon learning about the research of Daguerre and Talbot, the eminent astronomer and chemist Sir John Herschel (1792–1871) tackled the problem. In addition to duplicating Talbot's results, he was first to use sodium thiosulfate to fix or make permanent the image by halting the action of light. On 1 February 1839 he shared this knowledge with Talbot. Both Daguerre and Talbot adopted this means of fixing the image. During that month Talbot solved the problem of the reversed image by contact printing his reverse image to another sheet of his sensitized paper in sunlight. Herschel named the reversed image a *negative* (Fig. **9–24**) and called the contact a *positive* (Fig. **9–25**). These terms and Herschel's later name for Talbot's invention, *photography* (from the Greek *photos graphos*, meaning "light drawing"), have been adopted throughout the world.

Late in 1840 Talbot managed to increase the light sensitivity of his paper, expose a latent image, then develop it after it was removed from the camera. He called his new process *calotype* (from the Greek *kalos typos,* meaning "beautiful impression") and also used the name *talbotype* at the suggestion of friends. In 1844 Talbot began publishing his book, *The Pencil of Nature*, in installments for subscribers (Fig. **9–26**; see also Fig. **9–40**); it featured twenty-four photographs mounted into each copy by hand. In the foreword he expressed a desire to present "some of the beginnings of the new art." As the first volume illustrated completely with photographs, *The Pencil of Nature* was a milestone in the history of books.

The crystal clarity of daguerreotypes was superior to the softness of calotype images. To make a positive calotype print, a sheet of the light-sensitive paper was tightly sandwiched underneath the calotype negative and placed in bright sunlight. Because the sun's rays were diffused by the fibers of the paper negative, the positive print was slightly blurred. But because a negative could be exposed to other light-sensitive materials to make an unlimited number of prints and could later be enlarged, reduced, and used to make photoprocess printing plates, Talbot's invention radically altered the course of both photography and later graphic design as well. In photography's earliest stages, however, Daguerre's process was dominant, because Talbot's potpourri of exclusive patents slowed the spread of his methods.

Although the softness of calotypes was not without character, having a textural quality similar to charcoal drawing, a search began for a suitable vehicle to adhere light-sensitive material to glass so that extremely detailed negatives and positive lantern slides could be made. A wet-plate process was announced by the English sculptor Frederick Archer (1813–57) in the March 1850 *Chemist*. By candlelight in a darkroom, a clear viscous liquid called *collodion* was sensitized with iodine compounds, poured over a glass plate, immersed in a silvernitrate bath, and exposed and developed in the camera while still wet. Photographers throughout the world adopted Archer's process. Because he did not patent his process, and it enabled much shorter exposure times than either daguerreotypes or calotypes, it almost completely replaced them by the mid-1850s.

The scope of photography was seriously limited by the need to prepare a wet plate immediately before making the exposure and to develop it immediately afterwards. Research finally led to the commercial manufacture of gelatin-emulsion

9–24

9–25

9–26

9–27

9–28

9–24. William Henry Fox Talbot, the first photographic negative, 1835. This image was made on Talbot's light-sensitive paper in the camera obscura, which pointed toward the leaded glass windows in a large room of his mansion, Lacock Abbey.

9–25. William Henry Fox Talbot, print from the first photographic negative. The sun provided the light source to contact-print the negative to another sheet of sensitized paper, producing this positive image of the sky and land outside the windows.

9–26. Pages from Talbot's *The Pencil of Nature,* 1844. This first book to be illustrated entirely with photographs had original prints mounted onto the printed page. Plate VII is a photogram. (The use of modern-style type with ornate initials is typical of early Victorian book design.)

9–27. Advertisement for the Kodak camera, c. 1889. George Eastman's camera, simple enough for anyone "who can wind a watch," played a major role in making photography every person's art form.

9–28. Illustration of Moss's photographic department, from *Scientific American*, 1877. When this major science journal reported on the rise of photoengraving, it revealed that, unknown to its readers, thousands of photoengravings had been used side by side with hand engravings during the 1870s with no recognizable differences.

dry plates by several firms in 1877. The three-decade heyday of the collodion wet plate rapidly yielded to the dry-plate method after 1880.

An American dry-plate manufacturer, George Eastman (1854–1932), put the power of photography into the hands of the lay public when he introduced his Kodak camera (Fig. 9–27) in 1888. It was an invention without precedent, for ordinary citizens now had the ability to create images and keep a graphic record of their lives and experiences.

The application of photography to printing

Beginning in the 1840s, the rising employment use of wood engraving that started with Thomas Bewick fostered an effective use of images in editorial and advertising communications. Because wood-engraving blocks were type-high and could be locked into a letterpress and printed with type, while copperplate and steel engraving or lithographs had to be printed as a separate press run, wood engraving dominated book, magazine, and newspaper illustration. However, the preparation of wood-engraved printing blocks was costly, and numerous inventors and tinkerers continued the search begun by Niepce to find an economical and reliable photoengraving process for preparing printing plates. Once a patent became a

matter of record, competitors searched for a loophole to circumvent the inventor's legal rights, making the identification of many inventors difficult.

In 1871 John Calvin Moss of New York pioneered a commercially feasible photoengraving method for translating line artwork into metal letterpress plates. A negative of the original illustration was made on a copy camera suspended from the ceiling by a rope to prevent vibration (Fig. 9–28). In a highly secret process, a negative of the original art was contact-printed to a metal plate coated with a light-sensitive gelatin emulsion, then etched with acid. After hand-tooling for refinement, the metal plate was mounted on a type-high block of wood. The gradual implementation of photoengraving cut the cost and time required to produce printing blocks and achieved greater fidelity to the original.

Before it was possible to print photographs, photography was used as a research tool in developing wood-engraved illustrations. The documentary reality of photography helped illustrators capture current events. During the 1860s and 1870s wood engravings drawn from photographs became prevalent in mass communications (Figs. 9–29 and 9–30). An example is found in the photograph *Freedmen on the Canal Bank in Richmond*, attributed to Mathew Brady. Arriving in Richmond, Virginia, shortly after the evacuation and destruction by fire of most of the business district on 2 April 1865, when the Union forces broke through the Confederate defenses of the city, Brady turned his camera upon a group of former slaves who suddenly found themselves freedmen. A moment in time was preserved; a historical document to help people understand their history was formed with the timeless immediacy of photography. As the means to reproduce this image was not yet available, *Scribner's* magazine turned to an illustrator to reinvent the image in the language of the wood engraving so that it could be reproduced.

Beginning with Talbot, researchers believed a photographic printing plate could print the subtle nuances of tone found in a photograph if a screen changed continuous tones into dots of varying sizes. Then, tones could be achieved in spite of the even ink application of the relief press. During the 1850s Talbot experimented with gauze as a way to break up tones.

Many individuals worked on the problem and contributed to the evolution of this process. A major breakthrough occurred on 4 March 1880, when the *New York Daily Graphic* printed the first reproduction of a photograph with a full tonal range in a newspaper (Figs. 9–31 and 9–32). Entitled *A Scene in Shantytown*, it was printed from a crude *halftone screen* invented by Stephen H. Horgan. The screen broke the image into a series of minute dots whose varying sizes created tones. Values from pure white paper to solid black ink were simulated by the amount of ink printed in each area of the image.

9–29

9–30

9–31

9–32

9–33

9–29. Attributed to Mathew Brady, photograph, "Freedmen on the Canal Bank at Richmond," 1865. The photographer supplied the visual evidence needed by the illustrator to document an event.

9–30. John Macdonald, wood engraving, *Freedmen on the Canal Bank at Richmond.* The tonality of the photographer's image was reinvented with the visual syntax of wood-engraved line.

9–31 and 9–32. Stephen H. Horgan, experimental photoengraving, 1880. This first halftone printing plate to reproduce a photograph in a newspaper heralded the potential of photography in visual communications.

9–33. David O. Hill and Robert Adamson, Reverend Thomas H. Jones, c. 1845. The painter's attention to lighting, characterization, placement of hands and head, and composition within the rectangle replaced the mug-shot sensibility of earlier photographers.

9–34. Julia Margaret Cameron, "Sir John Herschel," 1867. Moving beyond descriptive imagery, Cameron's compelling psychological portraits revealed her subjects' inner being.

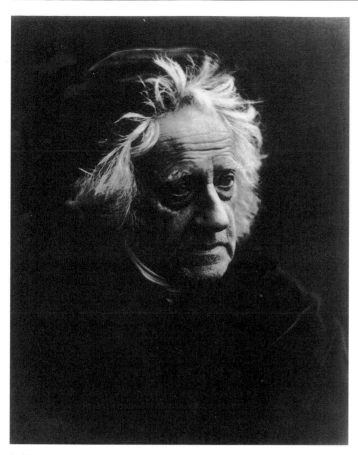

9–34

aration remained experimental until the end of the century. During the 1880s and 1890s, photomechanical reproduction began to rapidly make obsolete the highly skilled craftsmen who transferred artists' designs to handmade printing plates. Up to a week had been required to prepare a complex wood engraving; the photographic processes reduced the time from art to printing plate to one or two hours, with greatly reduced costs.

Defining the medium

During the same decades, when inventors were expanding photography's technical boundaries, artists and adventurers were exploring its image-making potential. Photography accurately reflects the external world, yielding a precise and repeatable image. However, merely isolating a single moment in time was not enough for some nineteenth-century photographers; they defined and extended the aesthetic and communicative frontiers of the new medium.

An early effort to introduce design concerns into photography began in May 1843, when the Scottish painter David Octavius Hill (1802–70) decided to immortalize the 474 ministers who withdrew their congregations from the Presbyterian Church and formed the Free Church of Scotland. Hill teamed up with Edinburgh photographer Robert Adamson (1821–48), who had been making calotypes for about a year. Using forty-second exposures, Hill posed the subjects in sunlight using all knowledge gained in two decades of portraiture (Fig. **9–33**). The resulting calotypes were lauded as superior to Rembrandt's paintings. Hill and Adamson also created landscape photographs that echoed the visual order found in landscape paintings of the period.

When Julia Margaret Cameron (1815–79) received a camera and the equipment for processing collodion wet plates as a forty-ninth birthday present from her daughter and son-in-law, the accompanying note said, "It may amuse you, Mother, to photograph." From 1864 until 1874, this wife of a high British civil servant extended the artistic potential of photography through portraiture that recorded "faithfully the greatness of the inner man as well as the features of the outer man." (Fig. **9–34**)

A lively contribution to photography was made by the Frenchman F. T. Nadar (1820–1910). His portraits of writers, actors (Fig. **9–35**), and artists have a direct and dignified simplicity and provide an invaluable historical record.

In 1886 the first photographic interview was published in *Le journal illustré* (Fig. **9–36**). Nadar's son Paul made a series of twenty-one photographs as Nadar interviewed the eminent hundred-year-old scientist Michel Eugène Chevreul. The elderly man's expressive gestures accompanied his answers to Nadar's questions.

Frederick E. Ives (1856–1937) of Philadelphia developed an early halftone process and worked on the first commercial production of halftone printing plates in 1881. The sum of all the minute dots produced the illusion of continuous tones. Later Ives joined brothers Max and Louis Levy to produce consistent commercial halftones using etched glass screens. A ruling machine was used to inscribe parallel lines in an acid-resistant coating on optically clear glass. After acid was used to etch the ruled lines into the glass, the indentations were filled with an opaque material. Two sheets of this ruled glass were sandwiched, face to face, with one set of lines running horizontally and the other set running vertically. The amount of light passing through each little square formed by the lines determined how big each dot would be. Halftone images could be made from these screens, and the era of photographic reproduction had arrived.

The first photomechanical color illustrations were printed in the 1881 Christmas issue of the Paris magazine *L'Illustration*. Complicated and time-consuming, photomechanical color sep-

9–35

9–36

9–35. F. T. Nadar, "Sarah Bernhardt," 1859. The famous actress took Paris by storm and became a major subject for the emerging French poster.

9–36. Paul Nadar, "Nadar Interviewing Chevreul," 1886. The words spoken by the one-hundred-year-old chemist were recorded below each photograph to produce a visual-verbal record of the interview.

9–37. Mathew Brady, "Dunker Church and the Dead," 1862. Made in the aftermath of the Battle of Antietam, the bloodiest battle of the Civil War, this photograph shows how visual documentation took on a new level of authenticity with the arrival of photography.

9–38. Timothy H. O'Sullivan, "Sand Dunes near Sand Springs, Nevada," 1867. The virgin territory of the American West was documented by expedition photographers. O'Sullivan's photography wagon—isolated by the almost Asian space of the sand dunes—becomes a symbol of these lonely journeys over vast distances.

9–39. Eadweard Muybridge, plate published in *The Horse in Motion*, 1883. Sequence photography proved the ability of graphic images to record time-and-space relationships. Moving images became a possibility.

Photography as reportage

The ability of photography to provide a historical record and define human history for forthcoming generations was dramatically proven by the prosperous New York studio photographer Mathew Brady (c. 1823–96). When the American Civil War began, Brady set out in a white duster and straw hat carrying a handwritten card from Abraham Lincoln reading "Pass Brady— A. Lincoln." During the war Brady invested a $100,000 fortune to send a score of his photographic assistants, including Alexander Gardner (1821–82) and Timothy O'Sullivan (c. 1840–82), to document the American Civil War. From Brady's photography wagons, called "Whatsit" by the Union troops, a great national trauma was etched forever in the collective memory. Brady's photographic documentation had a profound impact upon the public's romantic ideal of war (Fig. **9–37**). Battlefield photographs joined artist's sketches as reference materials for wood-engraved magazine and newspaper illustrations.

After the Civil War, photography became an important documentary and communications tool in the exploration of new territory and the opening of the American West. Photographers, including O'Sullivan, were hired by the federal government to accompany expeditions into the unexplored western territories (Fig. **9–38**). From 1867 until 1869, O'Sullivan accompanied the Geological Exploration of the Fortieth Parallel, beginning in western Nevada. Returned to the East and translated into illustrations for reproduction, images of the West inspired the great migratory wanderlust that eventually conquered all of North America.

9–37

9–38

9–39

An adventurous photographer, Eadweard Muybridge (1830–1904) lived in San Francisco and photographed Yosemite, Alaska, and Central America. Leland Stanford, a former governor of California and the president of the Central Pacific Railroad, commissioned Muybridge to document his belief that a trotting horse lifted all four feet off the ground simultaneously; a $25,000-dollar wager rested on the outcome. While working on the problem, Muybridge became interested in photographing a horse's stride at regular intervals. Success came in 1877 and 1878, when a battery of twenty-four cameras—facing an intense white background in the dazzling California sunlight—was equipped with rapid drop shutters that were slammed down by springs and rubber bands as a trotting horse broke threads attached to the shut-

ters. The resulting sequence of photographs arrested the horse's movement in time and space, and Stanford, a breeder and racer of trotters, won the bet (Fig. 9–39). The development of motion-picture photography, the kinetic medium of changing light passing through a series of still photographs joined together by the human eye through the persistence of vision, was the logical extension of Muybridge's innovation.

Nineteenth-century inventors like Talbot, documentalists like Brady, and visual poets like Cameron had a significant collective impact upon graphic design. By the arrival of the twentieth century, photography was becoming an increasingly important reproduction tool. New technologies radically altered existing ones, and both printing techniques and illustration changed dramatically. As photomechanical reproduction

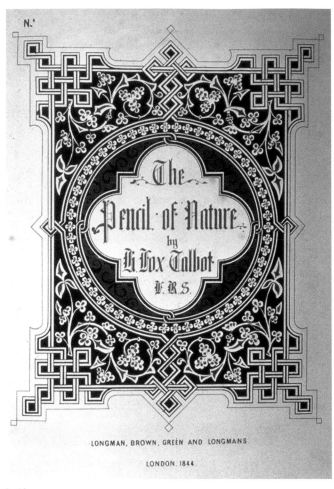

9–40

9–42

9–40. Title page for *The Pencil of Nature,* 1844. This design demonstrates the eclectic confusion of the Victorian era. Medieval letterforms, baroque plant designs, and Celtic interlaces are combined into a dense symmetrical design.

9–41. Sir Charles Barry with A. W. N. Pugin, The House of Lords in the British Houses of Parliament, constructed 1840–67. The Gothic Revival evolved from ornamental details inspired by Gothic architecture.

9–42. Owen Jones, color plate from *The Grammar of Ornament,* 1856. This plate shows patterns found in the arts and crafts of India.

replaced handmade plates, illustrators gained a new freedom of expression. Photography gradually monopolized factual documentation and pushed the illustrator toward fantasy and fiction. The textural and tonal properties of the halftone image changed the visual appearance of the printed page.

Popular graphics of the Victorian era

The reign of Victoria (1819–1901), who became queen of the United Kingdom of Great Britain and Ireland in 1837, spanned two-thirds of the nineteenth century. The Victorian era was a time of strong moral and religious beliefs, proper social conventions, and optimism. "God's in his heaven, all's right with the world" was a popular motto. The Victorians searched for a design spirit to express their epoch. Aesthetic confusion led to a number of often contradictory design approaches and philosophies mixed together in a scattered fashion (Fig. **9–40**). A fondness for the Gothic, which suited the pious Victorians, was fostered by the English architect A. W. N. Pugin (1812–52), who designed the ornamental details of the British Houses of

9–41

Parliament (Fig. **9–41**). The first nineteenth-century designer to articulate a philosophy, Pugin defined design as a moral act that achieved the status of art through the designer's ideals and attitudes; he believed the integrity and character of a civilization were linked to its design. Although Pugin said he looked to earlier periods—particularly the Gothic—not for style but for a principle, the net result of his influence was a wide mimicking of Gothic architecture, ornament, and letterforms.

The English designer, author, and authority on color Owen Jones (1809–74) became a major design influence at midcentury. During his mid-twenties Jones traveled to Spain and the Near East and made a systematic study of Islamic design. Jones introduced Moorish ornament to Western design in his 1842–45 book, *Plans, Elevations, Sections, and Details of the Alhambra.* His main influence was through his widely studied 1856 book of large color plates, *The Grammar of Ornament* (Fig. **9–42**). This catalog of design possibilities from Eastern and Western cultures, "savage" tribes, and natural forms became the nineteenth-century designer's bible of ornament. The Victorian love of exorbitant complexity was expressed by gingerbread woodwork applied to domestic architecture, ornate, extravagant embellishments on manufactured products from silverware to large furniture, and elaborate borders and lettering in graphic design.

In the 1850s the word Victorian began to be used to express a new consciousness of the industrial era's spirit, culture, and moral standards. In 1849 Prince Albert, husband of Queen Victoria, conceived the idea of a grand exhibition with hundreds of exhibitors from all industrial nations. This became the Great Exhibition of 1851, an important summation of the progress of the Industrial Revolution and a catalyst for future developments. Six million visitors reviewed the products of thirteen thousand exhibitors. This event is commonly called the Crystal Palace Exhibition, after the 800,000-square-foot steel and glass prefabricated exhibition hall that remains a landmark in architectural design.

Victorian graphic design captured and conveyed the values of the era. Sentimentality, nostalgia, and a canon of idealized beauty were expressed through printed images of children, maidens, puppies, and flowers. Traditional values of home, religion, and patriotism were symbolized with sentimentality and piety. The production medium for this outpouring of Victorian popular graphics was *chromolithography,* an innovation of the Industrial Revolution that unleashed a flood of colorful printed images.

The development of lithography

Lithography (from the Greek, literally "stone printing") was invented by Bavarian author Aloys Senefelder (1771–1834) in 1796. Senefelder sought a cheap way to print his own dra-

matic works by experimenting with etched stones and metal reliefs. He eventually arrived at the idea that a stone could be etched away around grease-pencil writing and made into a relief printing plate. His experiments, however, culminated in the invention of lithographic printing, in which the image to be printed is neither raised, as in relief printing, nor incised, as in intaglio printing. Rather, it is formed on the flat plane of the printing surface. Printing from a flat surface is called *planographic* printing.

Lithography is based on the simple chemical principle that oil and water do not mix. An image is drawn on a flat stone surface with oil-based crayon, pen, or pencil. Water is spread over the stone to moisten all areas except the oil-based image, which repels the water. Then an oil-based ink is rolled over the stone, adhering to the image but not to the wet areas of the stone. A sheet of paper is placed over the image and a printing press is used to transfer the inked image onto the paper. In the early 1800s Senefelder began experimenting with multicolor lithography, and in his 1819 book he predicted that one day this process would be perfected to allow reproduction of paintings.

Since the time of medieval block books, applying color to printed images by hand had been a slow and costly process. German printers spearheaded color lithography, and the French printer Godefroy Engelmann patented a process named *chromolithographie* in 1837. After analyzing the colors contained within the original image, the printer separated them into a series of printing plates and printed these component colors, one by one. Frequently, one printing plate (often black) established the image after separate plates printed other colors. The arrival of color printing had vast social and economic ramifications.

The Boston school of chromolithography

American chromolithography began in Boston, where several outstanding practitioners pioneered a school of lithographic naturalism. They achieved technical perfection and imagery of compelling realism.

In 1846 the American inventor and mechanical genius Richard M. Hoe (1812–86) perfected the rotary lithographic press (see Fig. **9–47**), which was nicknamed "the lightning press" because it could print six times as fast as the lithographic flatbed presses then in use. This innovation proved an important boost in lithography's competition with letterpress. Economical color printing, ranging from art reproductions for middle-class parlors to advertising graphics of every description, poured from the presses in millions of impressions each year.

The next major innovator of chromolithography in Boston was John H. Bufford (d. 1870), a masterly draftsman whose

9–43

9–43

9–43. John H. Bufford's Sons, "Swedish Song Quartett" poster, 1867. Arced words move gracefully above seven carefully composed musicians. Large capital letters point to the three soloists, establishing a visual relationship between word and image.

9–44. S. S. Frizzall (artist) and J. H. Bufford's Sons (printers), poster for the Cleveland and Hendricks presidential campaign, 1884. The loose style of the flags and other symbolic imagery framing the candidates emphasizes the extreme realism of the portraits.

9–44

crayon-style images achieved a remarkable realism. After training in Boston and working in New York, Bufford returned to Boston in 1840. Specializing in art prints, posters, covers, and book and magazine illustrations, Bufford often used five or more colors. The meticulous tonal drawing of his black stone always became the master plate. For an edition such as the c. 1867 "Swedish Song Quartett" [sic] poster (Fig. **9–43**), for example, the original master tonal drawing was precisely duplicated on a lithographic stone. Then, separate stones were prepared to print the flesh tones, red, yellow, blue, and the slate-gray background. Browns, grays, and oranges were created when these five stones were overprinted in perfect registration. The color range of the original was separated in component parts, then reassembled in printing. The near-photographic lithographic crayon drawing glowed with the bright underprinted yellows and reds of the folk costumes.

In 1864, Bufford's sons entered his firm as partners. The senior Bufford maintained artistic direction responsibilities until his death in 1870. Hallmarks of Bufford designs were

meticulous and convincing tonal drawing and the integration of image and lettering into a unified design. In their political campaign graphics, such as the poster for Grover Cleveland and Thomas A. Hendricks in the 1884 presidential campaign (Fig. **9–44**), a rich vocabulary of patriotic motifs, including eagles, flags, banners, columned frames, and Liberty clothed in the flag, were used to establish a patriotic tone. The Bufford firm folded in 1890. The two decades following the founder's death were a period of declining quality, cut-rate pricing, and emphasis on cheap novelties.

American lithography maintained its German heritage. Excellent Bavarian lithographic stones—and the highly skilled craftsmen who prepared them for printing—were exported from Germany to nations around the world. The Düsseldorf Academy of Art, with a curriculum based on rigorous academic drawing, was the major training school for artists who created images for lithographic printing. The four decades from 1860 until 1900 were the heyday of chromolithography as it dominated color printing. Victorian graphics found a most prolific innovator in a German immigrant to America, Louis Prang (1824–1909), whose work and influence were international. After mastering the complexities of his father's fabric-printing business, twenty-six-year-old Prang arrived in America in 1850 and settled in Boston. His knowledge of printing chemistry, color, business management, designing, engraving, and printing itself was of great value when he formed a chromolithography firm with Julius Mayer in 1856. Initially Prang designed and prepared the stones and Mayer did the printing on a single hand press. Prang's colorful work was very popular, and the firm grew rapidly. There were seven presses when Prang bought Mayer's share and changed its name to L. Prang and Company in 1860.

Popular narrative and romantic painting of the Victorian era was closely linked with the graphic illustration of chromolithographers, including Prang, who often commissioned art and held competitions to acquire subjects for printed images. In addition to art reproductions and Civil War maps and scenes, Prang produced literally millions of album cards called *scrap.* Collecting these "beautiful art bits" was a major Victorian pastime, and Prang's wildflowers, butterflies, children, animals, and birds became the ultimate expression of the period's love for sentimentalism, nostalgia, and traditional values.

Prang's meticulously drawn, naturalistic images followed in the tradition of Sharp and Bufford. He has been called the father of the American Christmas card for his pioneering work in holiday graphics. The earliest Christmas card, however, is thought to be an 1843 hand-tinted, dark sepia lithograph by British painter John Callcott Horsley (1817–1903).

After producing Christmas images suitable for framing in the late 1860s, Prang published an English Christmas card in 1873 and American Christmas cards the following year. Typical images included Santa Claus, reindeer, and Christmas trees. A full line of designs followed, and Easter, birthday, Valentine, and New Year's Day cards were produced annually by L. Prang and Company during the early 1880s. Prang sometimes used as many as forty stones for one design. Exceptional quality was achieved by dropping Bufford's master black plate in favor of a slow building and heightening of the image through the use of many plates bearing subtle colors.

Album cards evolved into advertising trade cards in the 1870s. Prang's distribution of twenty to thirty thousand business cards with floral designs at the 1873 Vienna International Exhibition popularized chromolithographic advertising cards. Sold in bulk, trade cards enabled merchants or manufacturers to imprint an advertising message on the back or in an open area on the front.

Prang made a lifelong contribution to art education after giving his daughter art lessons in 1856. Unable to find high-quality, nontoxic art materials for children, Prang began to manufacture and distribute watercolor sets and crayons. Finding a complete lack of competent educational materials for teaching industrial artists, fine artists, and children, he devoted tremendous energy to developing and publishing art-instruction books. On two occasions, he ventured into magazine publishing: *Prang's Chromo* was a popular art journal first published in 1868, and *Modern Art Quarterly,* published from 1893 until 1897, verified Prang's ability to grow and explore new artistic possibilities in his old age.

The design language of chromolithography

From Boston, chromolithography quickly spread to other major cities, and by 1860 about sixty chromolithography firms employed eight hundred people. Phenomenal growth put chromolithographers in every American city, and by 1890 over eight thousand people were employed by seven hundred lithographic printing firms. Figure **9–45** shows diverse chromolithographs produced by Prang and his competitors, including the label from a can of beans, a nursery catalogue cover, an early Christmas card, a die-cut friendship card album, and advertising trade cards.

Letterpress printers and admirers of fine typography and printing were appalled that the design was done on the artist's drawing board instead of the compositor's metal press bed. Without traditions and lacking the constraints of letterpress, designers could invent any letterform that suited their fancy and exploit an unlimited palette of bright, vibrant color never before available for printed communications.

The vitality of this graphic revolution stemmed from the talented artists who created the original designs, frequently working in watercolor, and the skilled craftsmen who traced the original art onto the stones. They translated designs into five, ten, twenty, or even more separate stones. Colored inks applied to these stones came together in perfect registration, recreating hundreds or even thousands of glowing duplicates of the original. The lithography firm, rather than the individual artists or craftsmen who created the work, was credited on chromolithographs, and the names of many designers are lost to history.

The Butterfly Brand can label and "peacock" trade card in Figure **9–45** demonstrate the integration of illustration with decorative patterns derived from *Jones's Grammar of Ornament.* The upper left corner of the "peacock" trade card is being peeled away to reveal a geometric pattern underneath. Trompe-l'oeil devices such as this delighted nineteenth-century graphic artists. In the premium booklet *Our Navy* (Fig. **9–46**), commissioned by the Allen & Ginter Company, montages use complex three-dimensional ornaments and ribbons as compositional devices unifying the layouts by tying disparate elements together as they move forward and backward in illusionistic space. A poster for the Hoe printing press (Fig. **9–47**) demonstrates a new freedom in lettering: lines of lettering become elastic, running in arcs or at angles, and even overlap images; blended and graduated colors flow on lettering and backgrounds; and ruled borders are free to notch and curve at will.

Traveling amusements such as circuses and carnivals commissioned large posters to herald their arrival. Producers of entertainment spectaculars favored dramatic illustrations with bold, simple lettering placed on brightly colored backgrounds and borders. The bright yellow band at the top of the Carry-Us-All carousel poster (Fig. **9–48**) was left blank to provide a place for local printers to imprint the dates and location of the carnival's visit. The Victorian passion for allegory and personification is seen in a Cincinnati Industrial Exposition poster

9–45

9–46

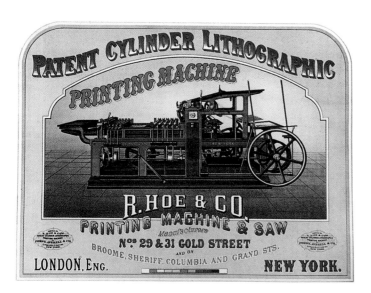

9–47

9–45. L. Prang and Company and others, c. 1880–early 1900s. This collection shows a range of graphic ephemera printed by chromolithography.

9–46. Schumacher & Ettlinger, lithographers, cover and pages from *Our Navy* premium booklet, 1888. Complex illusions are created by contrasting scale and perspective.

9–47. Forst, Averell & Co., poster for the Hoe printing press, 1870. This press made mass editions of chromolithographs possible.

9–48. The Riverside Print Company of Milwaukee, poster for C. W. Parker Company's Carry-Us-All portable carousels, undated. Parker's carousels, manufactured in Kansas, were very popular in midwestern nomadic carnivals.

9–49. Krebs Lithographing Company, poster for the Cincinnati Industrial Exposition, 1883. A buoyant optimism in industrial progress is conveyed.

9–48

9–49

(Fig. **9–49**). In a mythic scene in front of the exhibition hall, an allegorical figure representing the Queen City, as Cincinnati called itself, accepts machinery, agricultural products, and manufactured goods from symbolic figures representing the various states participating in the exhibition.

Complex montage designs promoting traveling shows, literary works, and theatrical performances (Fig. **9–50**) engaged viewers. Compared to contemporary posters, these advertisements were designed for greater viewing time because of the slower pace of nineteenth-century life and the relative lack of competition from other colorful images.

Labels and packages became important areas for chromolithography (Fig. **9–51**). Lithographing on tin sheets to make packages posed significant technical difficulties. Nonporous metal could not absorb printing inks, and sheet-metal and stone printing surfaces were equally hard and inflexible. At midcentury, transfer printing processes were developed. Reversed images were printed onto thin paper, then transferred onto sheet metal under great pressure. The paper backing was soaked off, leaving printed images on the tin plate. In 1875 Englishman Robert Barclay received a patent for offset lithographic printing on tin. Ink applied to an image drawn on a stone was picked up by a nonabsorbent cardboard impression cylinder, then immediately offset onto the sheet metal. Later Barclay used a rubber-coated cylinder to imprint the metal. Printed tin packages for food and tobacco products were widely used throughout Europe and North America during the late nineteenth and early twentieth centuries.

By century's end, the golden era of chromolithography was coming to a close. Changing public tastes and the development of photoengraving were making the use of chromolithography from hand-prepared stones obsolete. The decline can be marked by the year 1897, when Prang—mindful of the

revolution in design sensibilities and technology—merged his firm with Clark Taber & Company, a printing firm specializing in the new photographic-process reproduction of artwork. Also, the famous lithographic art reproduction firm of Currier & Ives went bankrupt shortly after the turn of the century.

The battle on the signboards

The letterpress poster and broadsheet were challenged in the middle of the nineteenth century by a more visual and pictorial poster. Lithography was the graphic medium allowing a more illustrative approach to public communication.

The letterpress printers responded to competition from the fluid and colorful lithographs being pasted on the signboards by midcentury with heroic and ingenious efforts to extend their medium. Witness, for example, the enormous multicolored woodcut poster designed by Joseph Morse of New York for the Sands, Nathan and Company Circus in 1856 (Fig. **9–52**). Large woodblocks were printed in sections to be assembled by the poster hangers.

9–50

9–50. W. J. Morgan and Co., Cleveland, lithographic theater poster, 1884. Montaged illustrations become overlapping planes with varied scale and spatial depth.

9–51. Package designs chromolithographed on tin for food and tobacco products used bright flat colors, elaborate lettering, and iconic images to create an emblematic presence for the product.

9–52. Joseph Morse, multicolored woodcut poster, 1856. The heroic scale—262 by 344 centimeters (8.5 by 11 feet)—permitted life-sized figures to tower before the headline "Five Celebrated Clowns Attached to Sands, Nathan Co.'s Circus."

9–53. Morris Pére et Fils (letterpress printers) and Emile Levy (lithographer), "Cirque d'hiver" poster, 1871. Performers are presented as surreal butterfly women.

9–54. Walter Crane, page from Walter Crane's *Absurd A.B.C.*, 1874. Animated figures are placed against a black background; large letterforms are integrated with the imagery.

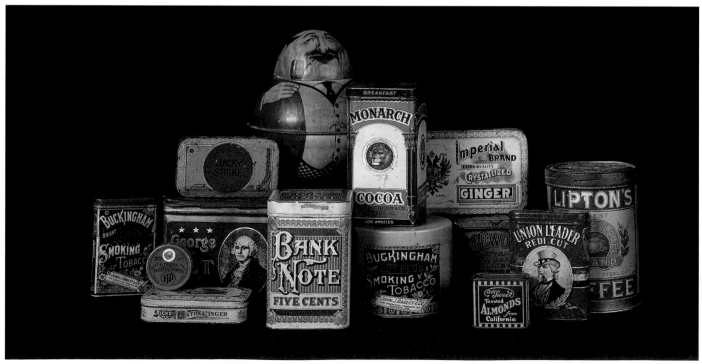

9–51

9–52

9–53

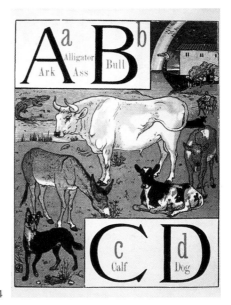

9–54

In his work from the 1860s, James Reilley of New York designed ingenious ways to increase the pictorial impact of the letterpress poster. The 1866 poster for John O'Brien's Consolidated Six Shows is an excellent example of Reilley's imaginative design solutions. In France, letterpress poster houses and lithographers collaborated as colorful lithographic illustrations were pasted onto large wood-type posters. A masterpiece of this genre is the 1871 "Cirque d'hiver" (Winter Circus) poster (Fig. **9–53**). The Morris Père et Fils printing firm commissioned a lithographer, Emile Levy, to illustrate an acrobatic dance act called Les Papillons (The Butterflies). The spectacular finale of this crowd-thrilling act featured two young female performers, one black and one white, being hurled through the air. Levy illustrated them as surreal butterfly women.

Images for children

Before the Victorian era, Western countries had a tendency to treat children as "little adults." The Victorians developed a more tender attitude, and this was expressed through the development of *toy books,* colorful picture books for preschool children. Several English artists produced books that were well designed and illustrated, with a restrained use of color, establishing an approach to children's graphics that is still in use today.

It is generally acknowledged that Walter Crane (1845–1915) was one of the earliest and the most influential designers of children's picture books (Fig. **9–54**). Apprenticed as a wood engraver as a teenager, Crane was twenty years old in 1865 when his *Railroad Alphabet* was published. A long series of his toy books broke with the traditions of printed material for children.

9–55

9–55. Randolph Caldecott, illustration from *Hey Diddle Diddle*, c. 1880. Oblivious to the outlandish elopement, Caldecott's dancing dinnerware moves to a driving musical rhythm.

9–56. Kate Greenaway, page from *Under the Window*, 1879. By leaving out the background, Greenaway simplified her page designs and focused on the figures.

9–57. Joseph A. Adams, page from *Harper's Illuminated and New Pictorial Bible*, 1846. In the first page of the Old and the New Testaments, the two-column format with a central margin for annotation was disrupted by centering the first few verses.

Earlier graphics for children insisted on a didactic or moral purpose, and always taught or preached to the young; Crane sought only to entertain. He was the first to be influenced by the Japanese woodblock and introduced it into Western art. After acquiring some Japanese prints from a British sailor in the late 1860s, Crane drew inspiration from the flat color and flowing contours. His unprecedented designs prompted numerous commissions for tapestries, stained-glass windows, wallpaper, and fabrics. Crane remained active into the twentieth century. He played an important role in the Arts and Crafts movement, discussed in chapter 10, and had a significant impact on art and design education.

As a bank clerk in his twenties, Randolph Caldecott (1846–86) developed a passion for drawing and took evening lessons in painting, sketching, and modeling. A steady stream of freelance assignments encouraged him to move to London and turn professional at the age of twenty-six. He possessed a unique sense of the absurd, and his ability to exaggerate movement and facial expressions of both people and animals brought his work to life. Caldecott created a world where dishes and plates are personified, cats make music, children are at the center of society, and adults become servants. His humorous drawing style became a prototype for children's books and later for animated films. (Fig. **9–55**).

Kate Greenaway's (1846–1901) expressions of the childhood experience captured the imagination of the Victorian era. As a poet and illustrator, Greenaway created a modest, small world of childhood happiness; as a book designer, she sometimes pushed her graceful sense of page layout to innovative levels (Fig. **9–56**). Silhouetted images and soft colors created pages of great charm, while the use of white space and asymmetrical balance broke with the Victorian tendency for clutter.

The clothes Greenaway designed for her models had a major influence on children's fashion design. Walter Crane, however, complained that Greenaway "overdid the big bonnet, and her little people are almost lost in their clothes." For Greenaway, childhood became an idealized fantasy world, and the Victorian love of sentiment and idealization made her an internationally renowned graphic artist whose books are still in print.

The rise of American editorial and advertising design
James (1795–1869) and John (1797–1875) Harper used modest savings—and their father's offer to mortgage the family farm if necessary—to launch a New York printing firm in 1817. Their younger brothers Wesley (1801–70) and Fletcher (1807–77) joined the firm in 1823 and 1825 respectively. Eighteen-year-old Fletcher Harper became the firm's editor when he became a partner, and the company's own publishing ventures grew dramatically over the decades. By midcentury, Harper and Brothers had become the largest printing and publishing firm in the world. In the role of senior editor and manager of publishing activities, Fletcher Harper shaped graphic communications in America for half a century.

Inventive book design was not a concern for most publishing firms in America and Europe, including Harper and Brothers, during most of the nineteenth century. With the rapid expansion of the reading public, and the economies resulting from new technologies, publishers focused on large press runs and modest prices. Modern-style fonts, often second-rate derivatives of Bodoni and Didot designs, were composed in workaday page layouts.

9–56

9–57

During the 1840s Harper and Brothers launched a monumental project that became the young nation's finest achievement of graphic design and book production to date. *Harper's Illuminated and New Pictorial Bible,* printed on presses specially designed and built for its production, contained 1,600 wood engravings from illustrations by Joseph A. Adams (Fig. **9–57**). Its publication in fifty-four installments of twenty-eight pages each was heralded by a carefully orchestrated advertising campaign. Each segment was hand-sewn and hand-bound in heavy paper covers printed in two colors.

During the preliminary preparations for this work, Adams invented an electrotyping process. This involved pressing the wood engraving into wax to make a mold, which was dusted with graphite to make it electroconductive. Then an electrodeposit of metal (usually copper) was made in the mold. The resulting thin shell was backed with lead, and this harder printing surface enabled Harper to publish fifty thousand copies in installments. A hardbound edition of twenty-five thousand copies with hand-tooled gold gilding on morocco leather binding was sold after the series of installments was

completed. The format consisted of two columns of text with a central margin bearing annotations. Illustrations included large images two columns wide, contained in ornate Victorian frames, and hundreds of spot illustrations dropped into the text. Every chapter opened with an illuminated initial.

The firm opened the era of the pictorial magazine in 1850 when the 144-page *Harper's New Monthly Magazine* (Fig. **9–58**) began publication with serialized English fiction and numerous woodcut illustrations created for each issue by the art staff. The monthly magazine was joined by a weekly periodical that functioned as a newsmagazine, *Harper's Weekly,* in 1857. *Harper's Bazar* [sic] for women was founded in 1867, and the youth audience was addressed by *Harper's Young People* in 1879. *Harper's Weekly* billed itself as "a journal of civilization" and developed an elaborate division of shop labor for the rapid production of woodblocks for printing cartoons and graphic reportage (Fig. **9–59**) based on drawings from artist/correspondents, including Thomas Nast (1840–1902).

Nast, a precociously talented artist, had switched from public school to art school after the sixth grade and began his

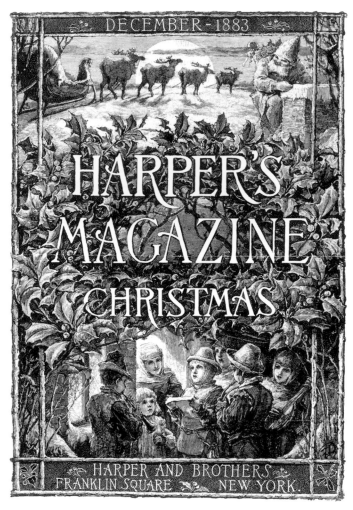

9–58

9–59

career as a four-dollar-per-week staff illustrator for *Leslie's Weekly* when he was fifteen years old. Fletcher Harper hired him when he was twenty-two to make battlefield sketches during the Civil War. The power of his work was such that President Abraham Lincoln called Nast "the best recruiting sergeant" and General Ulysses S. Grant declared that Nast had done as much as anyone to bring the conflict to a close. Public response to Nast's work was a major factor in propelling *Harper's Weekly*'s circulation from one hundred thousand to three hundred thousand copies per issue.

After the war Nast remained with *Harper's Weekly*, where he drew his images directly on the woodblock in reverse for the craftsmen to cut. His deep social and political concerns led him to strip away detail and introduce symbols and labels for increased communicative effectiveness in his work. He has been called the father of American political cartooning. The graphic symbols Nast popularized and focused include a number of important images: Santa Claus, John Bull (as a symbol for England), the Democratic donkey, the Republican elephant, Uncle Sam, and Columbia (a symbolic female signi-

fying democracy that became the prototype for the Statue of Liberty).

Nast also took on the governmental corruption of the political boss William Marcy Tweed, who controlled New York politics from infamous Tammany Hall. Tweed claimed that he did not care what the papers wrote because voters couldn't read, but "they could sure see them damn pictures." Nast's relentless graphic attack culminated on election day in a double-page cartoon of the "Tammany tiger" loose in the Roman Colosseum, devouring liberty, while Tweed as the Roman emperor surrounded by his elected officials presided over the slaughter (Fig. **9–60**). The opposition won the election.

After Fletcher Harper died in 1877, a more conservative editorial staff took over the magazine, leading Nast to declare that "policy always strangles individuals." President Theodore Roosevelt recognized the effectiveness of Nast's graphics for the Republican Party by appointing him consul general to Ecuador, where he died of yellow fever six months after his arrival.

Charles Parsons became the art editor of Harper and Brothers in 1863, and he helped raise the standard of picto-

9–60

9–61

9–58. Richard G. Tietze, poster for *Harper's Magazine*, 1883. An impressionistic quality is achieved in an illustration divided into three zones, with the middle holly area providing a background for the message while separating the images.

9–59. After A. H. Wald, cover for *Harper's Weekly*, 1864. Engraved after a sketch by a "visual journalist" in the field, this cover is a forerunner of newsmagazine coverage of current events.

9–60. Thomas Nast, political cartoon from *Harper's Weekly*, 1871. This double-page image was posted all over New York City on election day.

9–61. Charles Dana Gibson, poster for Scribner's, 1895. Although the exquisite beauty of the "Gibson Girls" was captured with facility and control, Gibson was unconcerned with the design of type and image as a cohesive whole. In this poster the printer added text in incompatible typefaces.

rial images in the company's publications. Parsons had a superb eye for young talent, and one illustrator he brought along was Charles Dana Gibson (1867–1944), whose images of young women (Fig. **9–61**) and square-jawed men established a canon of physical beauty in the mass media that endured for decades.

Among the many illustrators encouraged by Parsons, Howard Pyle (1853–1911) had the broadest influence. Pyle's own work and remarkable gifts as a teacher made him the major force that launched the period called the Golden Age of American Illustration. Spanning the decades from the 1890s until the 1940s, this period in the history of visual communications in America was largely dominated by the illustrator. Magazine art editors selected the illustrators, whose work overshadowed rather routine typographic formats. Advertising layouts often served as guides for the illustrator, indicating how much room to leave for the type.

Pyle published over 3,300 illustrations and two hundred texts ranging from simple children's fables to his monumental four-volume *The Story of King Arthur and His Knights*. The meticulous research, elaborate staging, and historical accuracy of Pyle's work (Fig. **9–62**) inspired a younger generation of graphic artists to carry forward the tradition of realism in America. The impact of photography, the new communications tool, on graphic illustration can be traced in Howard Pyle's career, which evolved with the new reproduction technologies. He was twenty-three years old when he received his first illustration commission from *Scribner's Monthly* in 1876. As with most magazine and newspaper illustration of the time, this ink-line drawing was turned over to a wood engraver to be cut into a relief block that could be locked in place with type and printed by letterpress.

A decade later, in 1887, Pyle was thirty-four years old when he received his first commission for a tonal illustration.

9–62

The new photomechanical halftone process made possible the conversion of the blacks, whites, and grays in Pyle's oil and gouache painting into minute black dots that were blended by the human eye to produce the illusion of continuous tone. In addition to this process's impact upon engravers, illustrators were faced with the need either to shift from pen-and-ink art to tonal, painted illustrations or to face a dwindling market for their work.

Another advance occurred for Pyle in 1893, when the forty-year-old illustrator created his first two-color illustration. The image was printed from two halftone plates. One impression was in black ink and the other—shot with a filter—separated the red tones from the blacks and grays. This plate was inked with a red ink closely matched to Pyle's red paint. Four years later, in 1897, Pyle had a first opportunity to apply his spectacular sense of color to a full-color illustration assignment. This image was printed by the developing four-color process system. All of Pyle's full-color illustrations were painted during the fourteen years from 1897 until his death at age fifty-eight in 1911.

Harper's Weekly's leading competitors in the magazine field were the *Century* magazine (1881–1930) and *Scribner's Monthly* (1887–1939). All three of these major periodicals

were printed by the printing firm of Theodore Low De Vinne (1824–1914). De Vinne and his staff gave a quiet, dignified, but rather dry layout to all three. In the *Century,* for example, text was set in two columns of ten-point type, and the wood engravings were dropped in adjacent to the appropriate copy. Article titles were merely set in twelve-point all capitals, and centered above the beginning page of the article. De Vinne was dissatisfied with the thin modern typefaces first used in this magazine, so he commissioned type designer Linn Boyd Benton to cut a blacker, more readable face, slightly extended with thicker thin strokes and short slab serifs. Now called Century, this unusually legible style is still widely used today. Its large x-height and slightly expanded characters have made it very popular for children's reading matter.

The rising tide of literacy, plunging production costs, and the growth of advertising revenues pushed the number of newspapers and magazines published in the United States from eight hundred to five thousand between 1830 and 1860. During the 1870s magazines were used extensively for general advertising.

Closely bound to the growth of magazines was the development of advertising agencies. In 1841 Volney Palmer of Philadelphia opened what is considered the first advertising agency. The advertising agency as a consulting firm with an array of specialized skills was pioneered by another Philadelphia advertising agent, N. W. Ayer and Son. In 1875 Ayer gave his clients an open contract that allowed them access to the real rates publications were charging the agencies. Then he received an additional percentage for placing the advertisements. In the 1880s Ayer provided services clients were not equipped to perform and publishers did not offer, such as copywriting. By the end of the century he was well on the way toward offering a complete spectrum of services: copywriting, art direction, production, and media selection.

Many of the conventions of persuasive selling were developed during the last two decades of the nineteenth century. Advertisements from the English and American magazines of the period demonstrate some of these techniques (Fig. **9–63**). The design of these pages demonstrate the makeup of Victorian advertising pages with little concern for a total design. By the end of the century, magazines, including *Cosmopolitan* and *McClure's*, were carrying over a hundred pages of advertisements in each monthly issue. Frequently an engraved illustration would have type set above or below it, and often the prevalent practice of chromolithography, superimposing lettering on top of a pictorial image, was adopted by engravers.

On 20 June 1877 the Pictorial Printing Company of Chicago launched a new graphic format when the first issue of *The Nickel Library* hit newsstands throughout America.

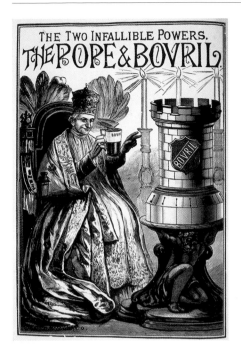

9–62. Howard Pyle, illustration from *The Merry Adventures of Robin Hood,* 1883. Pyle sought authenticity in every detail of setting, props, costume, and characterization.

9–63. Victorian advertisements, 1880–90. This potpourri ranges from small typographic ads to full-page ads with dominant illustrations.

9–63

Called nickel novels or story papers, the weekly publications in this series had action-filled covers interpreting tales of the Civil War and the Western frontier. The typical format was sixteen to thirty-two pages, set with two to four type columns per page. The 20.3 by 30.5–centimeter (8 by 12–inch) page size allowed the artists to create pictures that made a strong visual impact on the news dealer's shelf.

Victorian typography

As the Victorian era progressed, the taste for ornate elaboration became a major influence on typeface and lettering design. Early nineteenth-century elaborated types were based on letterforms with traditional structure. Shadows, outlines, and embellishments were applied while retaining the classical letter structure (see Fig. 9–49). In the second half of the century, advances in industrial technology permitted metal-type foundries to push elaboration, including the fanciful distortion

of basic letterforms, to an extreme degree. To produce more intricate types, punch cutters cut their designs in soft metal, then electroplated them to make a harder punch able to stamp the design into a brass matrix. Chromolithography, with its uninhibited lettering, was a major source of inspiration for foundries and letterpress printers seeking to maintain their share of a fiercely competitive graphic-arts industry.

Berlin-born Herman Ihlenburg (b. 1843) was a major Victorian typeface designer who spent most of his career from 1866 until after the turn of the century with the MacKellar, Smiths & Jordan foundry in Philadelphia, which became a major component of the American Type Founders Company when the monopoly was formed in 1892. MacKellar, Smiths & Jordan played a significant role in the design and production of Victorian display typefaces, and Ihlenburg was a leading member of their design staff. Before the end of the century he designed over eighty display typefaces and cut punches for

9–64

9–65

9–64. Herman Ihlenburg, typeface designs.

9–65. John F. Cumming, typeface designs. The bottom two typefaces show a marked shift in Cumming's design approach under the influence of the Kelmscott Press, which is discussed in chapter 10.

9–66. Trademark for Moss Engraving Company, 1872. Graphic complexity and slogans often embellished Victorian trademarks.

9–66

over thirty-two thousand typographic characters. This is all the more remarkable in light of the extreme complexity of many of his designs (Fig. **9–64**).

John F. Cumming (b. 1852) designed numerous elaborated typefaces for the Dickinson Type Foundry in Boston (Fig. **9–65**), but the passion for ornate Victorian typefaces began to decline in the 1890s, yielding to the revival of classical typography, inspired by the English Arts and Crafts movement (see chapter 10). Cumming rode the tides of change and designed faces derivative of Arts and Crafts designs.

Outlandish and fantasy lettering enjoyed great popularity, and many trademarks of the era reflect the Victorian love of

ornamental complexity (Fig. **9–66**). Typographic purists view the typeface designs of Ihlenburg, Cumming, and their contemporaries as aberrations in the evolution of typography, a commercial venture intended to give advertisers novel visual expressions to garner attention for their messages while providing foundries with a constant stream of original new typefaces to sell to printers.

The popular graphics of the Victorian era stemmed not from a design philosophy or artistic convictions but from the prevalent attitudes and sensibilities of the period. Many Victorian design conventions could still be found during the early decades of the twentieth century, particularly in commercial promotion.

The Arts and Crafts Movement and Its Heritage

As the nineteenth century wore on, the quality of book design and production became a casualty of the Industrial Revolution, with a few notable exceptions, such as the books by the English publisher William Pickering (1796–1854). At age fourteen Pickering apprenticed to a London bookseller and publisher; at age twenty-four he established his own bookshop specializing in old and rare volumes. Shortly thereafter, this young man with a deep love of books and outstanding scholarship began his publishing program. Pickering played an important role in the separation of graphic design from printing production. His passion for design led him to commission new woodblock ornaments, initials, and illustrations. He maintained control over the format design, type selection, illustrations, and all other visual considerations.

Pickering's books were produced by printers who worked under his close personal supervision. A cordial working relationship between publisher/designer and printer was established by Pickering and Charles Whittingham (1795–1876) of the Chiswick Press. Whittingham's excellent craftsmanship complemented Pickering's demands for quality. In books of prose and poetry, such as Pickering's fifty-three-volume series Aldine Poets, his designs moved toward classic simplicity. In collaboration with Whittingham, Pickering revived Caslon types, which he loved for their straightforward legibility. His liturgical books, including the 1844 Book of Common Prayer (Fig. **10–1**), are some of the finest examples of the revival of Gothic forms that permeated the nineteenth century.

Pickering's edition of Oliver Byrne's *The Elements of Euclid* (Fig. 10–2) is a landmark in book design. Diagrams and symbols are printed in brilliant primary colors with woodblocks; color replaced traditional alphabet labeling to identify the lines, shapes, and forms in the geometry lessons. The book's author claimed that with his approach, geometry could be learned in one-third the time needed with traditional textbooks, and that the learning was more permanent. The dynamic color and crisp structures anticipate geometric abstract art of the twentieth century.

In spite of the efforts of Pickering and others, the decline in book design continued until late in the century, when a book-design renaissance began. This revival—which first treated the book as a limited-edition art object, then influenced commercial production—was largely a result of the Arts and Crafts movement, which flourished in England during the last decades of the nineteenth century as a reaction against the social, moral, and artistic confusion of the Industrial Revolution. Design and a return to handicraft were advocated, and the "cheap and nasty" mass-produced goods of the Victorian era were abhorred. The leader of the English Arts and Crafts movement, William Morris (1834–96), called for a fitness of purpose, truth to the nature of materials and methods of production, and individual expression by both designer and worker.

The writer and artist John Ruskin (1819–1900) inspired the philosophy of this movement. Asking how society could "consciously order the lives of its members so as to maintain the largest number of noble and happy human beings," Ruskin rejected the mercantile economy and pointed toward the union of art and labor in service to society, as exemplified in the design and construction of the medieval Gothic cathedral. He called this the social order that Europe must "regain for her children." According to Ruskin, a process of separating art and society had begun after the Renaissance. Industrialization and technology caused this gradual severance to reach a critical stage, isolating the artist. The consequences were eclectic borrowing from historical models, a decline in creativity, and design by engineers without aesthetic concern. Underlying Ruskin's theories was his fervent belief that beautiful things were valuable and useful precisely because they were beautiful. In addition, Ruskin became concerned for social justice, advocating improved housing for industrial workers, a national education system, and retirement benefits for the elderly.

Among the artists, architects, and designers who embraced a synthesis of Ruskin's aesthetic philosophies and social consciousness, William Morris is a pivotal figure in the history of design. The eldest son of a wealthy wine importer, Morris grew up in a Georgian mansion on the edge of Epping

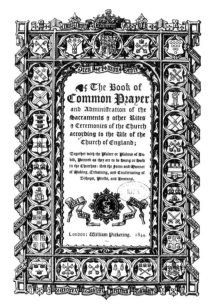

10–1

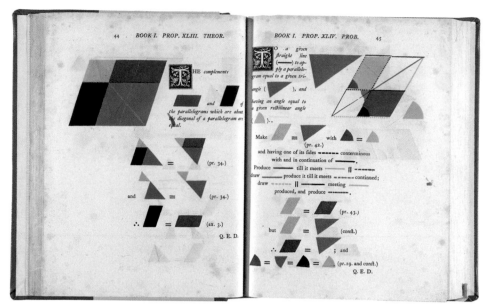

10–2

Forest, where the near-feudal way of life, ancient churches and mansions, and beautiful English countryside made a profound impression on him. In 1853 he entered Exeter College, Oxford, where he began his lifelong friendship with Edward Burne-Jones (1833–98). Both planned to enter the ministry, and their wide reading included medieval history, chronicles, and poetry. Writing became a daily activity for Morris, who published his first volume of poems at age twenty-four. Throughout his career he produced a steady flow of poetry, fiction, and philosophical writings, which filled twenty-four volumes when his daughter May (1862–1938) published his collected works after his death.

While traveling in France on a holiday in 1855, Morris and Burne-Jones decided to become artists instead of clergymen. After graduation Morris entered the Oxford architectural office of G. E. Street, where he formed a close friendship with his supervisor, the young architect Philip Webb (1831–1915). Morris found the routine of an architectural office stifling and dull, so in the fall of 1856 he left architecture and joined Burne-Jones in the pursuit of painting. Because Morris's family estate provided an ample income of nine hundred pounds a month, he could follow his ideas and interests wherever they led. The two artists fell under the influence of the Pre-Raphaelite painter Dante Gabriel Rossetti (1828–82). Morris struggled with his romantic paintings of medieval pageantry but was never fully satisfied with his work. He married his hauntingly beautiful model, Jane Burden, daughter of an Oxford stableman, and during the process of establishing their home, began to find his design vocation.

Red House, designed for them by Philip Webb, is a landmark in domestic architecture. Instead of featuring rooms in a rectangular box behind a symmetrical facade, the house had an L-shaped plan that grew out of functional interior space planning. When it came time to furnish the interior, Morris suddenly discovered the appalling state of Victorian product and furniture design. Over the next several years he designed and supervised the execution of furniture, stained glass, and tapestries for Red House.

As a result of this experience, Morris joined with six friends in 1861 to establish the art-decorating firm of Morris, Marshall, Faulkner and Company. Growing rapidly, the firm established London showrooms and began to assemble teams of craftsmen that eventually included furniture and cabinet-makers (Fig. **10–3**), weavers and dyers, stained glass fabricators, and potters and tile makers. Morris proved to be a brilliant two-dimensional pattern designer. He created over five hundred pattern designs for wallpapers, textiles, carpets, and tapestries. His 1883 fabric design Rose (Fig. **10–4**) demonstrates his close study of botany and drawing fluency; his willowy patterns wove decorative arabesques of natural forms. A similarly large number of stained glass windows were created under his supervision. Medieval arts and botanical forms were his main inspirations. The firm reorganized in 1875 as Morris and Company, with Morris as the sole owner.

Deeply concerned about the problems of industrialization and the factory system, Morris tried to implement Ruskin's ideas: the tastelessness of mass-produced goods and the lack of honest craftsmanship could be addressed by a reunion of art with craft. Art and craft could combine to create beautiful objects, from buildings to bedding; workers could find joy in their work once again, and the man-made environment—which had declined into industrial cities of squalid, dismal tenements filled

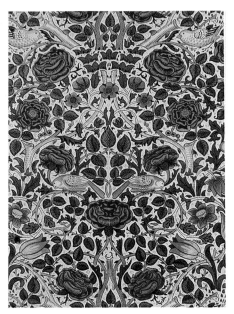

10–3

10–4

with tacky manufactured goods—could be revitalized.

A moral concern over the exploitation of the poor led Morris to embrace socialism. Dismay over the wanton destruction of the architectural heritage motivated him to found the Society for the Protection of Ancient Buildings, also called Anti-Scrape. Disgust at the false and misleading claims of advertising caused him to become involved in the Society for Checking the Abuses of Public Advertising, which confronted offenders directly.

During the 1880s and 1890s the Arts and Crafts movement was underpinned by a number of societies and guilds that sought to establish democratic artistic communities united for the common good. These ranged from exhibition cooperatives to communes based on socialist and religious ideals.

10–1. William Pickering, title page for the Book of Common Prayer, 1844. The intricacy of Gothic architecture and heraldic devices are convincingly depicted in this red and black title page.

10–2. William Pickering, pages from *The Elements of Euclid*, 1847. A system of color coding brought clarity to the teaching of geometry.

10–3. Cabinet design for Morris and Company, 1861. Paintings illustrating the honeymoon of the fifteenth-century Italian king René of Anjou by Ford Madox Brown, Edward Burne-Jones, and D. G. Rossetti grace this cabinet. The structure and ornamental carving allude to design from the medieval era.

10–4. William Morris, Rose fabric design, 1883.

The Century Guild

A twenty-six-year-old architect, Arthur H. Mackmurdo (1851–1942), met William Morris and was inspired by his ideas and accomplishments in applied design. On trips to Italy in 1878 and 1880, Mackmurdo filled his sketchbooks with studies of Renaissance architectural structure and ornament in addition to extensive drawings of botanical and other natural forms. Back in London, Mackmurdo led a youthful group of artists and designers who banded together in 1882 to establish the Century Guild. The group included designer/illustrator Selwyn Image (1849–1930) and designer/writer Herbert R Horne (1864–1916). The goal of the Century Guild was "to render all branches of art the sphere, no longer of the tradesman, but of the artist." The design arts were to be elevated to "their rightful place beside painting and sculpture." The group evolved a new design aesthetic as Mackmurdo and his

friends, who were about two decades younger than Morris and his associates, incorporated Renaissance and Japanese design ideas into their work. Their designs provide one of the links between the Arts and Crafts movement and the floral stylization of art nouveau.

Featuring the work of guild members, *The Century Guild Hobby Horse* began publication in 1884 as the first finely printed magazine devoted exclusively to the visual arts. The medieval passions of the Arts and Crafts movement were reflected in the graphic designs of Image and Horne. However, several designs contributed by Mackmurdo have swirling organic forms that are pure art nouveau in their conception and execution. He first explored abstract intertwining floral patterns in an 1881 carved chair back (Fig. **10–5**). The 1883 title page for his book *Wren's City Churches* (Fig. **10–6**)

10–5

10–6

10–7

10–8

10–10

10–11

10–9

10–5. Arthur H. Mackmurdo, chair, 1881. In developing this decorative pattern, Mackmurdo carefully considered visual design qualities and structural strength. Unifying construction and ornament became an important characteristic of art nouveau.

10–6. Arthur H. Mackmurdo, title page for *Wren's City Churches,* 1883. Mackmurdo's plant forms are stylized into flamelike, undulating rhythms that compress the negative space between them. This establishes a positive and negative interplay between black ink and white paper.

10–7. Arthur H. Mackmurdo, Peacock design, 1883. Mackmurdo applied forms and images similar to those on his famous title page to this printed cotton fabric.

10–8. Arthur H. Mackmurdo, trademark for the Century Guild, 1884. Flame, flower, and initials are compressed and tapered into proto–art nouveau forms.

10–9. Arthur H. Mackmurdo, design element from the *Hobby Horse,* 1884. The design is a reversal of the title-page design (see Fig. 10–6), for the stylized plant forms, undulating rhythms, animation of the space, and visual tension between positive and negative spaces are created by white forms on a black field instead of black forms on a white field.

10–10. Selwyn Image, title page to *The Century Guild Hobby Horse,* 1884. Packing it with detail, Image designed a "page within a page" that reflects the medieval preoccupation of the Arts and Crafts movement.

10–11. Selwyn Image, woodcut from *The Hobby Horse,* 1886. The potential of shape and pattern as visual means to express thought and feeling is realized in this graphic elegy for illustrator/engraver Arthur Burgess. A black bird flies toward the sun over mournful downturned tulips that hover above flamelike leaves.

was followed by fabric designs (Fig. **10–7**), the Century Guild trademark (Fig. **10–8**), and *Hobby Horse* graphics (Fig. **10–9**). In retrospect, these look like seminal innovations that could have launched a movement, but the designs were born before their time. Mackmurdo did not explore this direction further, and art nouveau did not explode into a movement until the following decade.

The Hobby Horse (Figs. **10–10** and **10–11**), which sought to proclaim the philosophy and goals of the Century Guild, was produced with painstaking care under the tutelage of Sir Emery Walker (1851–1933), the master printer and typographer at the Chiswick Press (Figs. **10–12** and **10–13**). Its careful layout and typesetting, handmade paper, and intricate woodblock illustrations made it the harbinger of the growing Arts and Crafts interest in typography, graphic design, and print-

ing. Mackmurdo, in addition to anticipating art nouveau, was a forerunner of the private press movement and the renaissance of book design. This private press movement should not be confused with amateur or hobby presses. Rather, it was a design and printing movement advocating an aesthetic concern for the design and production of beautiful books. It sought to regain the design standards, high-quality materials, and careful workmanship of printing that existed before the Industrial Revolution.

The Hobby Horse was the first 1880s periodical to introduce the British Arts and Crafts viewpoint to a European audience and to treat printing as a serious design form. Mackmurdo later recounted how he showed William Morris a copy of *Hobby Horse* and discussed with him the difficulties of typographic design, including the problems of proportions and margins, letterspacing and leading between lines, choosing paper, and typefaces. Reportedly Morris was filled with enthusiasm about the possibilities of book design as he admired the well-crafted typographic pages, generous margins, wide line spacing, and meticulous printing alive with handcut woodblock illustrations, head and tailpieces, and ornamented capitals. Original etchings and lithographs were printed as fine plates and bound into the quarterly issues.

In an article entitled "On the Unity of Art" in the January 1887 issue of *Hobby Horse*, Selwyn Image passionately argued that all forms of visual expression deserved the status of art. He suggested that "the unknown inventor of patterns to decorate a wall or a water-pot" who "employs himself in representing abstract lines and masses" deserves equal claim to being called an artist as the painter Raphael, who represented "the human form and the highest human interests." He chided the Royal Academy of Art by recommending that its name be changed to the Royal Academy of Oil Painting because it was so limited relative to the total range of art and design forms. In perhaps the most prophetic observation of the decade, Image concluded, "For when you begin to realize, that all kinds of invented Form, and Tone, and Colour, are alike true and honorable aspects of Art, you see something very much like a revolution looming ahead of you."

Although it received ample commissions, the Century Guild disbanded in 1888. Emphasis had been upon collaborative projects, but the members became more preoccupied with their individual work. Selwyn Image designed typefaces, innumerable illustrations, mosaics, stained glass, and embroidery. Mackmurdo focused on social politics and the development of theories to reform the monetary system, and Herbert Horne designed books with classic simplicity and restraint (Fig. **10–14**) . His educational background had included typesetting, and his layouts have a precise sense of alignment, proportion, and balance.

The Kelmscott Press

A number of groups and individuals concerned with the craft revival combined to form the Art Workers Guild in 1884. The guild's activities were expanded in 1888, when a splinter group formed the Combined Arts Society, elected Walter Crane as its first president, and planned to sponsor exhibitions. By the October 1888 opening of the first exhibition, the name had been changed to the Arts and Crafts Exhibition Society. Early exhibitions featured demonstrations and lectures. In 1888 these included William Morris on tapestry weaving, Walter Crane on design, and Emery Walker on book design and printing. In his lecture on 15 November, Walker showed lantern slides of medieval manuscripts and incunabula type design. Advocating a unity of design, Walker told his audience, "the ornament, whatever it is, picture or pattern-work, should form part of the page, should be part of the whole scheme of the book." Walker considered book design similar to architecture, for only careful planning of every aspect—paper, ink, type, spacing, margins, illustration, and ornament—could result in a design unity.

As Morris and Walker, who were friends and neighbors, walked home together after the lecture that autumn evening, Morris resolved to plunge into typeface design and printing. This was a possibility he had considered for some time, and he began work on his first typeface design that December. Incunabula typefaces were photographically enlarged to five times their original size so that he could study their forms and counterforms. His decision to tackle graphic design and printing is not surprising, for he had long been interested in books. His library included some magnificent medieval manuscripts and incunabula volumes. Earlier, Morris had made a number of manuscript books, writing the text in beautifully controlled scripts and embellishing them with delicate borders and initials with flowing forms and soft, clear colors.

Morris named his first typeface Golden (Fig. **10–15**), because his original plan was to print *The Golden Legend,* by Jacobus de Voragine, as his first book, working from William Caxton's translation. Golden was based on the Venetian roman faces designed by Nicolas Jenson between 1470 and 1476 (see Fig. 7–2). Morris studied large photographic prints of Jenson's letterforms, then drew them over and over. Punches were made and revised for the final designs, which captured the essence of Jenson's work but did not slavishly copy it. Typefounding of Golden began in December of 1890. Workmen were hired, and an old handpress rescued from a printer's storeroom was set up in a rented cottage near Kelmscott Manor in Hammersmith, which Morris had purchased as a country home. Morris named his new enterprise Kelmscott Press (Fig. **10–16**; see also Fig. 12–16), and its first production was *The Story of the Glittering Plain* by William Morris, with illustrations by Walter Crane (Fig.

10–17). Initially, twenty copies were planned, but as word of the enterprise spread, Morris was persuaded to increase the press run to two hundred paper copies and six on vellum. From 1891 until the Kelmscott Press disbanded in 1898, two years after Morris's death, over eighteen thousand volumes of fifty-three different titles were produced.

Careful study of the incunabula Gothic types of Peter Schoeffer (see Fig. 5–14), Anton Koberger (see Figs. 6–7 through 6–11), and Günther Zainer informed Morris's design of Troy, the remarkably legible blackletter typeface designed for *The Story of the Glittering Plain*. Morris made the characters wider than most Gothic types, increased the differences between similar characters, and made the curved characters rounder. A smaller version of Troy, called Chaucer, was the last of Morris's three typeface designs. These stirred a renewed interest in Jenson and Gothic styles and inspired a number of other versions in Europe and America.

The Kelmscott Press was committed to recapturing the beauty of incunabula books. Meticulous hand-printing, hand-made paper, handcut woodblocks, and initials and borders similar to those used by Ratdolt turned the picturesque cottage into a time machine swinging four centuries back into the past. The book became an art form.

The Kelmscott design approach was established in its early books. William H. Hooper (1834–1912), a master craftsman lured from his retirement to work at the press, engraved decorative borders and initials designed by Morris on wood. These have a wonderful visual compatibility with Morris's types and wood block illustrations cut from drawings by Burne-Jones, Crane, and C. M. Gere. Morris designed 644 blocks for the press, including initials, borders, frames, and title pages. First he lightly sketched the main lines in pencil; then, armed with white paint and black ink, he worked back and forth, painting the background in black and, over it, the pattern in white. The entire final design would be developed through this fluid process, for Morris believed that meticulous copying of a preliminary drawing squeezed the life from a work.

The most outstanding volume from the Kelmscott Press is the ambitious 556-page *Works of Geoffrey Chaucer* (Figs. **10–18** and **10–19**). Four years in the making, the Kelmscott Chaucer has eighty-seven woodcut illustrations from drawings by Burne-Jones and fourteen large borders and eighteen smaller frames around the illustrations cut from designs by Morris. In addition, Morris designed over two hundred initial letters and words for use in the Kelmscott Chaucer, which was printed in black and red in large folio size. An exhaustive effort was required by everyone involved in the project. This edition, 425 copies on paper and 13 on vellum, was the final achievement of Morris's career. On 2 June 1896, the bindery delivered the first two copies to the ailing designer. One was

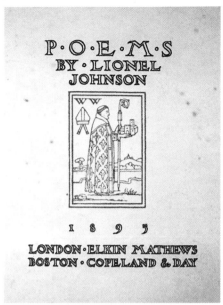

10–12   10–13   10–14

THE ARTS AND CRAFTS OF TODAY.
BEING AN ADDRESS DELIVERED IN
EDINBURGH IN OCTOBER, 1889. BY
WILLIAM MORRIS.
'Applied Art' is the title which the Society has
chosen for that portion of the arts which I have to
speak to you about. What are we to understand by
that title? I should answer that what the Society
means by applied art is the ornamental quality
which men choose to add to articles of utility. Theoretically this ornament can be done without, and
art would then cease to be 'applied'... would exist
as a kind of abstraction, I suppose. But though this
ornament to articles of utility may be done without,
man up to the present time has never done without
it, and perhaps never will; at any rate he does not
propose to do so at present, although, as we shall

10–16

10–15

for Burne-Jones, the other for Morris. Four months later, on 3 October, William Morris died at age sixty-two.

The paradox of William Morris is that as he sought refuge in the handicraft of the past, he developed design attitudes that charted the future. His call for workmanship, truth to materials, making the utilitarian beautiful, and fitness of design to function are attitudes adopted by succeeding generations who sought to unify not art and craft but art and industry. Morris taught that design could bring art to the working class, but the exquisite furnishings of Morris and Company and the magnificent Kelmscott books were available only to the wealthy.

10–12. Herbert Horne, trademark for the Chiswick Press, c. 1895. The Aldine dolphin joined a heraldic lion on the press's emblem.

10–13. Walter Crane, trademark for the Chiswick Press, c. 1898. The medieval overtones of Crane's version of the Chiswick mark, in contrast to the simplified version by Horne, demonstrate the divergent viewpoints of the period.

10–14. Herbert Horne, title page for *Poems,* by Lionel Johnson, 1895. Symmetry, outline type, letterspacing, and alignment are the design qualities of Horne's work. The letterforms are a perfect companion for the illustration.

10–15. William Morris, Golden typeface, 1888–90. This font inspired renewed interest in Venetian and Old Style typography.

10–16. William Morris, trademark for the Kelmscott Press, 1892.

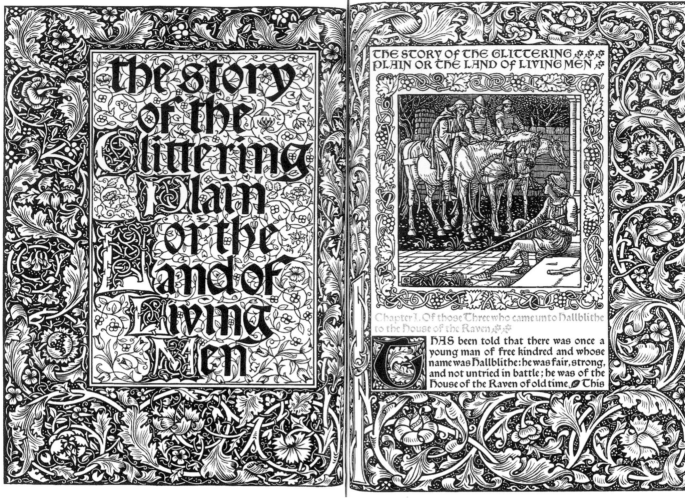

10–17

10–17. William Morris (designer) and Walter Crane (illustrator), title-page spread for *The Story of the Glittering Plain*, 1894. Operating on his compulsion to ornament the total space, Morris created a luminous range of contrasting values.

10–18. William Morris, illustrated page from *The Works of Geoffrey Chaucer*, 1896. A system of types, initials, borders, and illustrations were combined to create the dazzling Kelmscott style.

10–19. William Morris, text page from *The Works of Geoffrey Chaucer*, 1896. Beautiful pages of texture and tone contain an order and clarity that make the author's words legible and accessible.

The influence of William Morris and the Kelmscott Press upon graphic design, particularly book design, was evidenced not just in the direct stylistic imitation of the Kelmscott borders, initials, and typestyles; Morris's concept of the well-made book, his beautiful typeface designs based on earlier models, and his sense of design unity, with the smallest detail relating to the total concept, inspired a whole new generation of book designers (Fig. **10–20**). Ironically, this crusader for handicraft became the inspiration for a revival of fine book design that lasted well into the twentieth century and filtered into commercial printing.

The complexity of Morris's decorations tends to draw attention away from his other accomplishments. His books achieved a harmonious whole, and his typographic pages—which formed the overwhelming majority of the pages in his books—were conceived and executed with readability in mind. Morris's searching reexamination of earlier typestyles and graphic design history touched off an energetic redesign process that resulted in a major improvement in the quality and variety of fonts available for design and printing.

One final irony is that while Morris was returning to printing methods of the incunabula period, he used initials, borders, and ornaments that were modular, interchangeable, and repeatable. A basic aspect of industrial production was applied to the printed page.

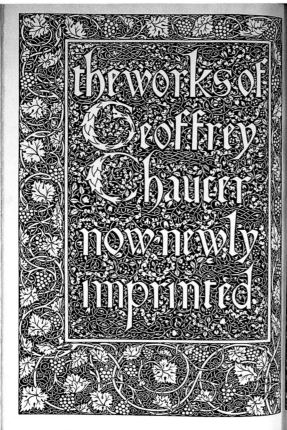

10–18

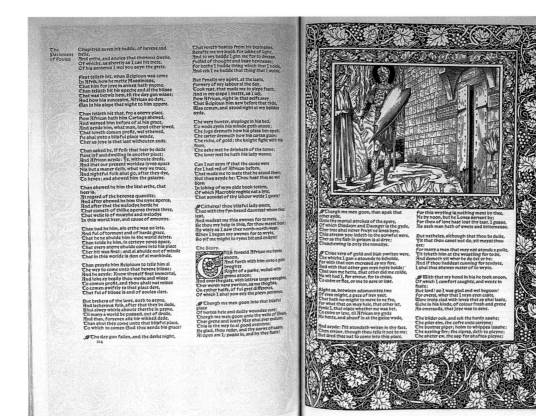

10–19

10–20

10–20. Walter Crane, layout sketches from *The Bases of Design*, 1898. Crane used these sketches to demonstrate the relationship of two pages that form a double-page unit, and how the margins can be used for decorative effect.

10-21. Charles R. Ashbee, the Essex House Press emblem, c. 1902. This full-page woodcut, metaphorically relating the Guild of Handicraft with the bee seeking a flower, appears on the colophon page of the Essex House Psalter.

10-22. Charles R. Ashbee, page from the Essex House Psalter, 1902. Hand-cut woodblock initials, calligraphic type, handmade paper, and handpress printing combine to recreate the quality of the incunabula.

The private press movement

Architect, graphic designer, jeweler, and silversmith, the indefatigable Charles R. Ashbee (1863–1942) founded the Guild of Handicraft in 1888 with three members and only fifty pounds British sterling as working capital. Although William Morris was dubious and threw "a great deal of cold water" upon Ashbee's plan, the guild met with unexpected success in its endeavors. Its School of Handicraft unified the teaching of design and theory with workshop experience. Ashbee sought to restore the holistic experience of apprenticeship, which had been destroyed by the subdivision of labor and machine production. About seven hundred students received a dualistic education with practical skill development supplemented by readings from Ruskin and study of the application of art principles to materials. Able neither to secure state support nor to compete with the state-aided technical schools, the School of Handicraft finally closed on 30 January 1895. The Guild of Handicraft, on the other hand, flourished as a cooperative where workers shared in governance and profits. It was inspired by both socialism and the Arts and Crafts movement.

In 1890 the guild leased Essex House, an old Georgian mansion in what had declined into a shabby and desolate section of industrial London.

After the death of William Morris, Ashbee opened negotiations with the executors of his estate to transfer the Kelmscott Press to Essex House. When it became known that the Kelmscott woodblocks and types were to be deposited in the British Museum with the stipulation that they not be used for printing for a hundred years, Ashbee resolved to hire key personnel from the Kelmscott Press, to purchase the equipment that was available for sale, and to form the Essex House Press (Fig. **10–21**). The Psalter of 1902 was the design masterpiece of the Essex House Press (Fig. **10–22**). The text is in vernacular sixteenth-century English from the c. 1540 translation of Archbishop Thomas Cranmer of Canterbury. Ashbee developed a graphic program for each psalm consisting of a roman numeral, the Latin title in red capitals, an English descriptive title in black capitals, an illustrated woodcut initial, and the body of the psalm. Verses were separated by woodcut leaf ornaments printed in red.

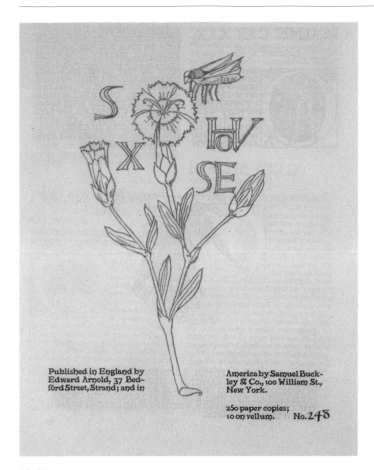

10–21

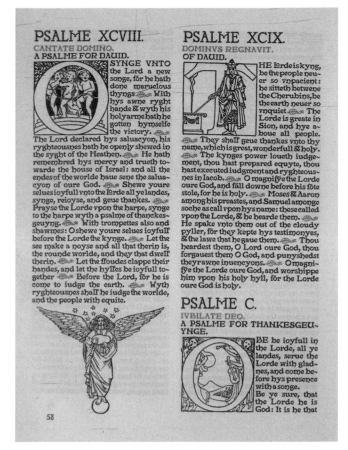

10–22

In 1902 the guild moved to the rural village of Chipping Campden and began the ambitious task of turning the village into a communal society for guild workers and their families. The large costs involved, combined with the expenses of maintaining the guild's retail store on Brook Street in London, forced the guild into voluntary bankruptcy in 1907. Many of the craftsmen continued to work independently, and the undaunted Ashbee returned to his architectural practice, which had lain fallow during his experiments over two decades. Although he was a leading design theorist and a follower of the ideals of Ruskin and Morris at the turn of the century, after World War I Ashbee questioned whether industrial manufacturing was inherently evil and formulated a design policy relevant to the industrial age. Thus, the Ruskin follower who went furthest in establishing an idyllic workshop paradise became a major English voice calling for integration of art and industry in a later era.

In 1900 the bookbinder T. J. Cobden-Sanderson (1840–1922) joined Emery Walker in establishing the Doves Press at Hammersmith. They set out to "attack the problem of pure Typography" with the view that "the whole duty of Typography is to communicate to the imagination, without loss by the way, the thought or image intended to be conveyed by the Author." Books from the Doves Press, including its monumental masterpiece, the 1903 Doves Press Bible (Fig. **10–23**), are remarkably beautiful typographic books. Illustration and ornament were rejected in the approximately fifty volumes produced there using fine paper, perfect presswork, and exquisite type and spacing. The five-volume Bible used a few striking initials designed by Edward Johnston (1872–1944). This master calligrapher of the Arts and Crafts movement had been inspired by William Morris and abandoned his medical studies for the life of a scribe. Johnston's study of pen techniques and early manuscripts, as well as his teaching activities, made him a major influence on the art of letters.

Established in 1895, the Ashendene Press, directed by C. H. St. John Hornby of London, proved an exceptional private press (Fig. **10–24**). The type designed for Ashendene was inspired by the semi-Gothic types used by Sweynheym and Pannartz in Subiaco. It possessed a ringing elegance and straightforward

THE FIRST BOOK OF MOSES CALLED GENESIS

IN THE BEGINNING

GOD CREATED THE HEAVEN AND THE EARTH. ❡AND
THE EARTH WAS WITHOUT FORM, AND VOID; AND
DARKNESS WAS UPON THE FACE OF THE DEEP, & THE
SPIRIT OF GOD MOVED UPON THE FACE OF THE WATERS.
❡And God said, Let there be light: & there was light. And God saw the light,
that it was good: & God divided the light from the darkness. And God called
the light Day, and the darkness he called Night. And the evening and the
morning were the first day. ❡And God said, Let there be a firmament in the
midst of the waters, & let it divide the waters from the waters. And God made
the firmament, and divided the waters which were under the firmament from
the waters which were above the firmament: & it was so. And God called the
firmament Heaven. And the evening & the morning were the second day.
❡And God said, Let the waters under the heaven be gathered together unto
one place, and let the dry land appear: and it was so. And God called the dry
land Earth; and the gathering together of the waters called he Seas: and God
saw that it was good. And God said, Let the earth bring forth grass, the herb
yielding seed, and the fruit tree yielding fruit after his kind, whose seed is in
itself, upon the earth: & it was so. And the earth brought forth grass, & herb
yielding seed after his kind, & the tree yielding fruit, whose seed was in itself,
after his kind: and God saw that it was good. And the evening & the morning
were the third day. ❡And God said, Let there be lights in the firmament of
the heaven to divide the day from the night; and let them be for signs, and for
seasons, and for days, & years: and let them be for lights in the firmament of
the heaven to give light upon the earth: & it was so. And God made two great
lights; the greater light to rule the day, and the lesser light to rule the night: he
made the stars also. And God set them in the firmament of the heaven to give
light upon the earth, and to rule over the day and over the night, & to divide
the light from the darkness: and God saw that it was good. And the evening
and the morning were the fourth day. ❡And God said, Let the waters bring
forth abundantly the moving creature that hath life, and fowl that may fly
above the earth in the open firmament of heaven. And God created great
whales, & every living creature that moveth, which the waters brought forth
abundantly, after their kind, & every winged fowl after his kind: & God saw
that it was good. And God blessed them, saying, Be fruitful, & multiply, and
fill the waters in the seas, and let fowl multiply in the earth. And the evening
& the morning were the fifth day. ❡And God said, Let the earth bring forth
the living creature after his kind, cattle, and creeping thing, and beast of the
earth after his kind: and it was so. And God made the beast of the earth after
his kind, and cattle after their kind, and every thing that creepeth upon the

27

10–23

AL NOME DEL NOSTRO SIGNORE
GESU CRISTO CROCIFISSO E DELLA
SUA MADRE VERGINE MARIA.

IN QUESTO LIBRO SI CONTENGONO
CERTI FIORETTI, MIRACOLI, ED
ESEMPLI DIVOTI DEL GLORIOSO
POVERELLO DI CRISTO, MESSER
SANTO FRANCESCO, E DALQUANTI
SUOI SANTI COMPAGNI, A LAUDE
DI GESU CRISTO. AMEN.

CAPITOLO PRIMO.   Capitolo 1

IN PRIMA E DA CON-
siderare che il glorioso
Messer Santo Francesco
in tutti gli atti della vita
sua fu conforme a Cristo
benedetto: che come Cristo nel princípio
della sua predicazione elesse dodici Apostoli, a dispregiare ogni cosa mondana, a
seguitare lui in povertate, & nell'altre vir-
tudi; così Santo Francesco elesse dal prin-
cipio del fondamento dell'Ordine dodici
Compagni, possessori dell'altissima po-
vertade, e come uno de' dodici Apostoli di
Cristo, riprovato da Dio, finalmente s'impiccò per la gola; così uno de' dodici
Compagni di Santo Francesco, ch'ebbe nome
Frate Giovanni dalla Cappella, apostatò, e finalmente s'impiccò se medesimo per la gola. E questo agli eletti è grande assempro & materia di
umiltade e di timore; considerando che nessuno
è certo di dovere perseverare alla fine nella grazia
di Dio. E come que' Santi Apostoli furono al tut-
to maravigliosi di santitade e di umiltade, e pieni

b   1

10–24

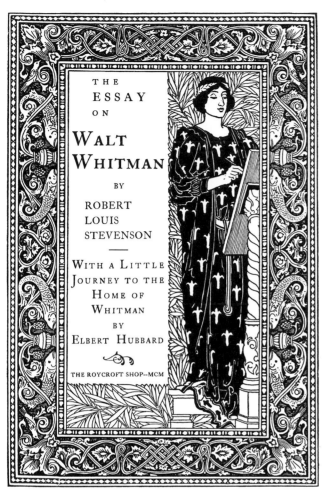

10–25

> On, still on, I wandered on,
> And the sun above me shone;
> And the birds around me winging
> With their everlasting singing
> Made me feel not quite alone.
>
> In the branches of the trees
> Murmured like the hum of bees
> The low sound of happy breezes,
> Whose sweet voice that never ceases
> Lulls the heart to perfect ease.

10–26

10–23. T. J. Cobden-Sanderson and Emery Walker, pages from the Doves Press Bible, 1903. This book's purity of design and flawless perfection of craft have seldom been equaled.

10–24. C. H. St. John Hornby, pages from Saint Francis of Assisi's *Legend*, 1922. A liberal use of all-capital type and initial words printed in color brought distinction to Ashendene Press page layouts.

10–25. Louis Rhead, title page for *The Essay on Walt Whitman*, 1900. The Roycroft Press commissioned this design from a prominent graphic designer.

10–26. Lucien Pisssarro, Brook type, 1903. A specimen from *Verses* by Christina G. Rosetti shows the roman structure, slab serifs, and decorative details of Pissarro's private press typeface.

legibility with modest weight differences between the thick and thin strokes and a slightly compressed letter.

A curious twist in the unfolding of the Arts and Crafts movement is the case of the American Elbert Hubbard (1856–1915), who met William Morris in 1894. Hubbard established his Roycroft Press (printing) and Roycroft Shops (handicrafts) in East Aurora, New York. The Roycroft community became a popular tourist attraction where four hundred employees produced artistic home furnishings, copperware, leather goods, and printed material. Hubbard's books (Fig. **10–25**), inspirational booklets, and two magazines had the appearance of Kelmscott volumes.

Although Hubbard died in 1915 aboard the ill-fated *Lusitania*, the Roycrofters continued until 1938. Hubbard's critics claim he tarnished the whole movement, while his defenders believe the Roycrofters brought beauty into the lives of ordinary people who otherwise would not have had an opportunity to enjoy the fruits of the reaction against industrialism's mediocre products. His detractors included May Morris, who declined an invitation to visit "that obnoxious imitator of my dear father" during her American visit.

Lucien Pissarro (1863–1944) learned drawing from his father, the impressionist painter Camille Pissarro, then apprenticed as a wood engraver and illustrator under the renowned book illustrator Auguste Lepère. Disillusioned with the response to his work in France, and learning of a revival of interest in wood-engraved illustrations in England, Pissarro moved to Wiltshire, England, to participate in this movement. In 1892 Lucien married Esther Bensusan (1870–1951). Captivated by Kelmscott books, Lucien and Esther established the Eragny Press (named after the Normandy village where he was born and studied with his father) in 1894.

Lucien and Esther Pissarro collaborated on designing, wood engraving, and printing Eragny Press books; many had three- and four-color woodblock prints produced from his artwork. He designed his Brook typeface (Fig. **10–26**) for their press, drawing inspiration from Nicolas Jenson. Unlike older members of the Arts and Crafts movement, the Pissarros were inspired by both the past and the present; their books (Fig. **10–27**) combined the traditional sensibilities of the private press movement with an interest in the blossoming art nouveau movement (discussed in chapter 11) and expressionism.

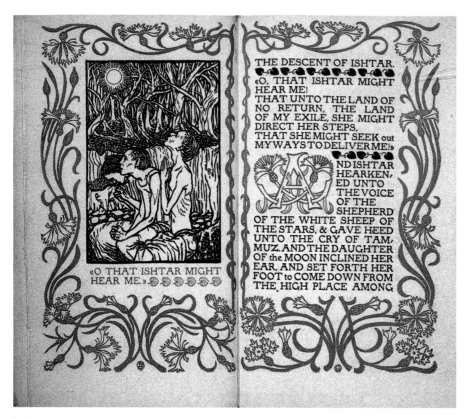

THE DESCENT OF ISHTAR.
«O, THAT ISHTAR MIGHT HEAR ME! THAT UNTO THE LAND OF NO RETURN, THE LAND OF MY EXILE, SHE MIGHT DIRECT HER STEPS, THAT SHE MIGHT SEEK out MY WAYS TO DELIVER ME!»

AND ISHTAR HEARKEN-ED UNTO THE VOICE OF THE SHEPHERD OF THE WHITE SHEEP OF THE STARS, & GAVE HEED UNTO THE CRY OF TAM-MUZ. AND THE DAUGHTER OF the MOON INCLINED HER EAR, AND SET FORTH HER FOOT to COME DOWN FROM THE HIGH PLACE AMONG

«O THAT ISHTAR MIGHT HEAR ME.»

10–27

10–27. Lucien and Esther Pissarro, pages from *Ishtar's Descent to the Nether World*, 1903. Image, color, and ornament combine to generate an intense expressionistic energy.

10–28. S. H. De Roos, pages from *Hand and Soul*, by Dante Gabriël Rossetti, published by De Heuvelpers (The Hill Press), 1929.

A book-design renaissance

The long-range effect of Morris was a significant upgrading of book design and typography throughout the world. In Germany, this influence inspired a renaissance of arts-and-crafts activities, wonderful new typefaces, and a significant improvement in book design.

In the Netherlands the traditional vanguard was led by Sjoerd H. De Roos (1877–1962) and the brilliant Jan van Krimpen (1892–1958). They were followed by J. F. van Royen (1878–1942) and two master printer-publishers from Maastricht, Charles Nypels (1895–1952) and A. A. M. Stols (1900–1973). They too wanted to foster a renaissance in Dutch typography, and, like Morris, they did not consider the Industrial Revolution a blessing. On the contrary, mass production was viewed as a necessary evil, cautiously tolerated, principally for economic reasons.

They sought to revive the printing arts through a return to traditional standards. Their guidelines included symmetrical layouts, tranquil harmony and balance, careful margin proportions, proper letter and word spacing, single traditional typefaces in as few sizes as possible, and skillful letterpress printing. They believed a typographer should serve the text first and otherwise stay in the background.

First trained in lithography, from 1895 until 1898 De Roos took a general course in art at the Rijksacademie in Amster-

dam. At the age of twenty-three he was hired as an assistant draftsman by Het Binnenhuis, a progressive industrial and interior design firm. It was during this period that he became aware of the low level of contemporary Dutch typography, and reviving book design soon became his lifelong passion.

De Roos left Het Binnenhuis in 1903, and in the same year was asked to design the book *Kunst en maatschappij* (Art and Society), a translation of a collection of essays by William Morris. Legibility was a top priority, and the book was set in the relatively new face designed by and named for the Swiss-French architect and typographic designer Eugène Grasset. This was the only book designed by De Roos in the art nouveau style, and because of its simplicity it was unique for Dutch book design at that time. This was a watershed in De Roos's career and resulted in his being hired as artistic assistant for the Type Foundry Amsterdam, where he would remain until 1941.

De Roos was convinced that the typeface was the foundation of sound book design and that ideally it should be practical, beautiful, and easily readable. In his opinion no indigenous typeface in the Netherlands satisfied these requirements, and in January 1912, the Type Foundry Amsterdam issued De Roos's Hollandsche Mediaeval, a text face in ten sizes based on fifteenth-century Venetian types. This was the first typeface designed and produced in the Netherlands for over a century, and

BEFORE ANY KNOWLEDGE OF PAINTING WAS BROUGHT TO FLORENCE, THERE WERE ALREADY PAINTERS IN LUCCA, AND PISA, AND AREZZO, WHO FEARED GOD AND LOVED THE ART. THE WORKMEN FROM Greece, whose trade it was to sell their own works in Italy and teach Italians to imitate them, had already found in rivals of the soil a skill that could forestall their lessons and cheapen their labours, more years than is supposed before the art came at all into Florence. The pre-eminence to which Cimabue was raised at once by his contemporaries, and which he still retains to a wide extent even in the modern mind, is to be accounted for, partly by the circumstances under which he arose, and partly by that extraordinary purpose of fortune born with the lives of some few, and through which it is not a little thing for any who went before, if they are even remembered as the shadows of the coming of such an one, and the voices which prepared his way in the wilderness. It is thus, almost exclusively, that the painters of whom I speak are now known. They have left little, and but little heed is taken of that which men hold to have been surpassed; it is gone like time gone,–a track of dust and dead leaves that merely led to the fountain.

6

Nevertheless, of very late years and in very rare instances, some signs of a better understanding have become manifest. A case in point is that of the triptych and two cruciform pictures at Dresden, by Chiaro di Messer Bello dell' Erma, to which the eloquent pamphlet of Dr. Aemmster has at length succeeded in attracting the students. There is another still more solemn and beautiful work, now proved to be by the same hand, in the Pitti gallery at Florence. It is the one to which my narrative will relate.

THIS Chiaro dell' Erma was a young man of very honourable family in Arezzo; where, conceiving art almost for himself, and loving it deeply, he endeavoured from early boyhood towards the imitation of any objects offered in nature. The extreme longing after a visible embodiment of his thoughts strengthened as his years increased, more even than his sinews or the blood of his life; until he would feel faint in sunsets and at the sight of stately persons. When he had lived nineteen years, he heard of the famous Giunta Pisano; and, feeling much of admiration, with perhaps a little of that envy which youth always feels until it has learned to measure success by time and opportunity, he determined that he would seek out Giunta, and, if possible, become his pupil.

7

10–28

for at least ten years was one of the most popular faces available. This was followed by eight more type designs from which De Roos derived considerable status. A prolific writer, between 1907 and 1942 he published 193 articles on type design and typography. One of his exceptional designs was Hand and Soul for De Heuvelpers in 1929 (Fig **10–28**). For the book he designed the layout, the typeface Meidoorn, and the initial letters. Also, an important client from this period was the progressive Rotterdam publisher W.L. and J. Brusse who asked De Roos to give their publications a new look.

Jan van Krimpen, born in Gouda, attended the Royal Academy of Fine Arts in The Hague, and soon became the preeminent book designer of his generation in the Netherlands. In 1920 the publication of *Deirdre en de zonen van Usnach* (Deirdre and the Sons of Usnach) by A. Roland Hoist inaugurated the twenty-one-book Palladium series dedicated to contemporary poets (Fig. **10–29**). *Het zatte hart* (The Drunken Heart) (1926), by Karel van de Woestijne, demonstrated his deft drawing and use of initial letters and is the only book in the Palladium series set in his own face, Lutetia (Fig. **10–30**). Cut in 1923–24, this was the first typeface he designed during

his thirty-five-year association with the Haarlem printer Enschedé. For Van Krimpen, no typography existed other than that of the book, and all of his typefaces were designed for this purpose. He viewed advertising as well as the people connected with it with contempt. For him, the reader should never even be conscious of typography; the designer's one purpose was to make reading as pleasurable as possible and never come between the reader and the text. Fortunately, though, he usually broke away to some degree from his own rules, and each of his books has something subtly different to offer. Until his death in 1958, the fiery Van Krimpen would continue to relentlessly oppose anything and everyone that, in his opinion, was harmful to book typography.

Charles Nypel's ties to the printing profession in Maastricht spanned several generations. In 1914 he began working as an apprentice to De Roos at the Type Foundry Amsterdam, and in 1917 he was officially hired by his family firm Leiter-Nypels, becoming a partner in 1920. Nypels had a fresh approach, evidenced by his title and text pages, his use of color, and his initial letters. The finest example of his earlier work is the 1927 Constantijn Huygens's *Het Voorhout ende 't kostelijke*

10–29

10–29. Jan van Krimpen, pages from *Deirdre & de zonen van Usnach* (Deirdre and the Sons of Usnach), by A. Roland Holst, Paladium Series, 1920.

10–30. Jan van Krimpen, pages from *Het zatte hart* (The Drunken Heart), by Karel van de Woestijne, Paladium no. 25, 1926.

10–31. Charles Nypels, pages from *Het Voorhout ende 't kostelijke mal*, by Constantin Huygens, typeface Grotius and initial designed by De Roos, 1927.

10–32. Charles Nypels, pages from *Don Quichotte,* by Miguel de Cervantes 1929 – 1931.

10–33. A. A. M. Stols, pages from *Nieuwe loten* (New Cuttings), by Marie Cremers, third book in the Trajectum ad Mosam series, 1923.

10–30

mal (The Voorhout and the Delightful Comedy) (Fig. **10–31**). De Roos's red and blue initial letters turn many of the pages into scintillating typographic symphonies of color. Published in four sections between 1929 and 1931, *Don Quichotte* shows Nypels at his elegant best, and the exceptional initials by De Roos added the finishing touch (Fig. **10–32**). This book was considered to be far too costly and eventually resulted in Nypels having to leave the firm. Afterward he worked as a freelance designer for firms such De Gemeenschap in Utrecht.

Like Nypels, A. A. M. (Sander) Stols was born into a Maastricht printing family. While Stols was studying law in Amsterdam in 1921, he and his younger brother Alphonse decided to enter the family publishing business, Boosten & Stols. Both were critical of the firm's past quality and were committed to high design standards. Stols's doctrine was simplicity and maximum legibility, and his work was noted for its constrained classical typography and craftsmanship (Fig. **10–33**). He preferred typefaces such as Garamond and Bembo, but on a number of

10–31

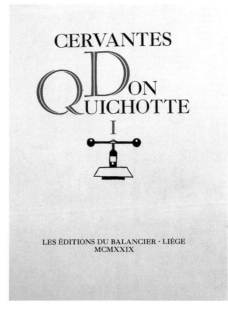

10–32

10–33

occasions he used De Roos's typefaces Hollandsche Mediaeval and Erasmus Mediaeval. Like Van Krimpen, Stols described the designer's role in terms that were clear and to the point:

> Providing the form in which a book will be printed . . . the designer must never-the-less satisfy a number of requirements for the book, knowledge of its history and technology, artistry and taste, and in-sight as to production costs. In short all those factors which make it possible to make a written text into a printed book that satisfy the greatest demands of legibility.

Jean François van Royen was born in Arnhem in 1878 and died at the German concentration camp in Amersfoort in 1942. Although a book designer and private publisher, Van Royen made his principal contribution to graphic design in the Netherlands through his position as general secretary of the Dutch PTT (Post, Telephone and Telegraph), and it would be impossible to evaluate his contribution outside this context.

CHEOPS

NA ZIJN ONTVANGST,
na te zijn opgenomen
in de doorluchte drom,
men en den ftoet
der ſmetteloos verrezenen, die dreven
door alle hemelen, het groot gevolg,
dat vergezelt en toch is ver gebleven
en nimmer naderde de onontwijde
Openenden, de Hooge Heerſchers, Zij,
achter wier ſlippen en wier laatſte tred
toeſloeg een blikſemend verſchiet; te midden
der ſtrengeling, het menigvuldig winden,
dat afliep in een rulle effening
of krimpend zich in eigen krinkelbocht
verſtrikte, wiſſelende in een rythme
van heffingen, die naar het zenith klommen,
van zinkingen, waarin werd uitgevierd
het diepſte zwichten; in den breeden ſleep,
die omvoer door de ruimten en de verten
aantaſtte en veegde al de banen door
des ongemetenen, in deze weidſche vlucht
de koning CHEOPS. ¶ Stil in zijnen zin
en wachtende had hij zich toegevoegd
en ingeſchikt en zich terecht gevonden
in deze nieuwe orde, het zich richten

6

naar anderen en de ontwende plicht
van zich te minderen, terug te dringen
den eigen ſcherpen wil, het gaan begeven
verdwenen in de menigte, het deelen
in dezen ijver en afhankelijkheid
der velen en het zijnen dienſt verrichten
als begeleider en als wegtrawant.

EN mede ging hij met den ommegang
den eeuwigen, die in geen tijd geboren,
die heenſtreek door den weergaloozen luiſter
der hemelcreaturen, door de zalen,
de leege hoven, die in doodſche nacht
zoo roerloos en zoo ſtrak geopend waren
en uitgezet, alsof zij allen ſtonden
onder één hooge koepeling, een dak,
dat werd getild op fonkelend gebint
van ſtalen flitſen; dan de donkerten
de ruig gevulde, waar het wereldſtof
aanvankelijk geſtrooid en zwevend was
in doffen ſtilſtand of al aangevat
door plotſeling bezinken ſchoksgewijs
bijeen liep en ging vloeien in gebogen
bedding, die ijlings tot een ronden kolk,
een boezem werd, een in zich opgeſloten
holte, een kom opzwellende ten boorde
en eindelijk een volle moederſchoot,
wier zwoegende arbeid, wier bedwongen nooden
en zware ſpanning klimmend was, totdat

7

10–34

Halbfette
Deutſche Schrift

Eine
deutſche Schrift

Schmale deutſche Schrift
mit Schwungbuchſtaben
und Initialen

10–35

DENN EINE JEGLICHE KUNST
ODER WERK ✦ WIE KLEIN
SIE SEIEN ★ DAS SIND ALLE
SAMT GNADEN ✦ UND WIR
KET SIE ALLESAMT DER HEI +
LIGE GEIST ✦ ZU NUTZ UND
ZU FRUCHT DER MENSCHEN
+ WÄRE ICH NICHT EIN PRIE
STER ✦ UND WÄRE UNTER
EINER VERSAMMLUNG + ICH
NÄHME ES FÜR EIN GROSSES
DING ★ DASS ICH SCHUHE MA
CHEN KÖNNTE ✦ UND ICH
WOLLTE AUCH GERNE MEIN
BROT MIT MEINEN HÄN
DEN VERDIENEN ✦ KINDER
★ DER FUSS NOCH DIE HAND
DIE SOLLEN NICHT DAS AUGE
SEIN WOLLEN ✦ EIN JEGLI
CHER SOLL SEIN AMT TUN ✦
DAS IHM GOTT ZUGEFÜGT.

10–36

His own book designs were limited in quantity, and he probably would not have been remembered beyond a small circle for this role alone.

After receiving his doctorate in law from the University of Leiden in 1903, Van Royen worked for a year with the publishing firm of Martinus Nijhoff at The Hague before assuming the minor position of clerical aide in the legal section of the PTT in 1904. In 1912 Van Royen joined De Zilverdistel (The Silver Thistle), a private press at The Hague. Two typefaces were specifically commissioned for De Zilverdistel. The first was De Roos's Zilvertype, basically an updated version of Hollandsche Mediaeval. The second, Disteltype, a modern interpretation of the Carolingian minuscule, was designed by Lucien Pissarro.

In 1916, *Cheops,* designed by Van Royen, was printed in Zilvertype with the initial letters and titles also cut by De Roos following Van Royen's suggestions (Fig. **10–34**). Van Royen had an exotic side, and his easily distinguishable titles, initials, and vignettes are far more extravagant than those of Van Krimpen and De Roos. In 1923, Van Royen changed the name of De Zilverdistel to De Kunera Pers (The Kunera Press), and it continued until his death in 1942.

The most important of the German type designers was Rudolf Koch (1876–1934), a powerful figure who was deeply mystical and medieval in his viewpoints. A devout Catholic, Koch taught at the Arts and Crafts School in Offenbach am Main, where he led a community of writers, printers, stonemasons, and metal and tapestry workers in a creative community. He regarded the alphabet as a supreme spiritual achievement of humanity. Basing his pre–World War I work on pen-drawn calligraphy, Koch sought the medieval experience through the design and lettering of handmade manuscript books. But he did not merely seek to imitate the medieval scribe; he tried to build upon the calligraphic tradition by creating an original, simple expression from his gestures and

materials. After the war, Koch turned to hand-lettered broadsides and handicrafts, then became closely associated with the Klingspor Type Foundry. His type designs ranged from original interpretations of medieval letterforms (Fig. **10–35**) to unexpected new designs, such as the rough-hewn chunky letterforms of his Neuland face (Fig. **10–36**).

In America, the influence of the Arts and Crafts movement on the revitalization of typography and book design moved forward in the hands of two young men from the Midwest who fell under the spell of the Kelmscott Press during the 1890s. Book designer Bruce Rogers (1870–1956) and typeface designer Frederic W. Goudy (1865–1947), each inspired for a lifetime of creative work, had long careers filled with a love of books and diligent work. They carried their exceptional sense of book design and production well into the twentieth century.

Even as a boy in Bloomington, Illinois, Frederic Goudy had a passionate love of letterforms. He later recalled cutting over three thousand letters from colored paper and turning the walls of the church he attended into a multicolored environment of Biblical passages. Goudy was working in Chicago as a bookkeeper in the early 1890s when he embraced printing and publicity. Books from the Kelmscott Press, including the *Works of Geoffrey Chaucer,* and from other private presses represented in the rare book department of the A. C. McClurg Bookstore fired Goudy's imagination. He became interested in art, literature, and typography on "a higher plane than mere commercialism."

In 1894 Goudy started the Camelot Press with a friend, but he returned to bookkeeping the following year when disagreements developed. In 1895 he set up the short-lived Booklet Press, then designed his first typeface, Camelot, during the period of unemployment that followed. His pencil drawing of capitals was mailed to the Dickinson Type Foundry of Boston with an offer to sell the design for five dollars. After a week or two, a check for ten dollars in payment for the design arrived. In 1899 Goudy became a freelance designer in Chicago, specializing in lettering and typographic design. A printing venture modeled on the private-press handicraft ideal (Fig. **10–37**), the Village Press, was moved first to Boston, then to New York, where a terrible fire completely destroyed it in 1908. That same year marked the end of Goudy's efforts as a printer; he turned his energy to the design, cutting, and casting of typefaces and began a long association with the Lanston Monotype Company, which commissioned some of his finest fonts. Goudy designed a total of 122 typefaces by his own count (he counted roman and italic variations as separate faces), including a few faces that were never produced. A staunch traditionalist, Goudy based many of his faces on Venetian and French Renaissance type designs (Fig. **10–38**).

10–34. J. F. van Royen, double page spread from *Cheops,* by J.H. Leopold, initials and titles by S. H. de Roos, published by De Zilverdistel 1916.

10–35. Rudolf Koch, Halbfette Deutsche Schrift (Semibold German Script), 1911–13; Deutsche Schrift (German Script), 1906–10; and Schmale Deutsche Schrift (Condensed German Script), 1910–13. Koch's Gothic revivals achieved unusual legibility, striking typographic color and spatial intervals, and many original forms and ligatures.

10–36. Rudolf Koch, specimen of Neuland, 1922–23. A dense texture is achieved in this intuitively designed typeface with unprecedented capital *C* and *S* forms. The woodcut-inspired ornaments are used to justify this setting into a crisp rectangle.

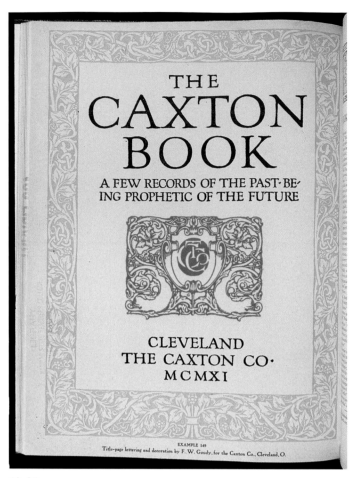

10–37

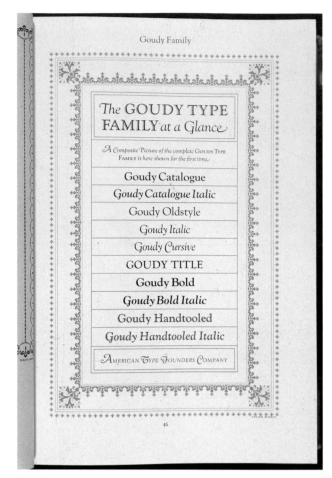

10–38

With an amiable and witty personality and wonderful writing ability, Goudy linked everyday printers to William Morris and his ideals. His readable books include *The Alphabet* (1908), *Elements of Lettering* (1921), and *Typologia* (1940). The two journals he edited, *Ars Typographica* and *Typographica*, impacted the course of book design. In 1923 Goudy established the Village Letter Foundry in an old mill on the Hudson River, where he became a successful anachronism—an independent type designer who cut matrixes, then cast and sold type. In 1939 a second disastrous fire burned the mill to the ground, destroying about seventy-five original type designs and thousands of matrixes. Undaunted, Goudy continued to work until his death at age eighty-two.

A student of Goudy's at the turn of the century named William Addison Dwiggins (1880–1956) proved a highly literate book designer who established a house style for the Alfred A. Knopf publishing company and designed hundreds of volumes for this firm. During the early 1920s Dwiggins first used the term *graphic designer* to describe his professional activities. In 1938 he designed one of the most widely used book faces in America, Caledonia.

Albert Bruce Rogers of Lafayette, Indiana, evolved from his Kelmscott roots in the 1890s and became the most important American book designer of the early twentieth century. After graduating from college, where he was active as a campus artist, Rogers became a newspaper illustrator in Indianapolis. Dismayed by the ambulance-chasing school of pictorial reportage, with its frequent trips to the local morgue, Rogers tried landscape painting, worked for a Kansas railroad, and did book illustrations. After a close friend, J. M. Bowles, showed Kelmscott books to Rogers, his interest immediately shifted toward the total design of books. Bowles was running an art supply store and editing a small magazine called *Modern Art*. Louis Prang became interested in this periodical and invited Bowles to move to Boston and edit what then became an L. Prang and Company periodical. A typographic designer was needed, so Rogers was hired at fifty cents an hour with a twenty-hour-per-week guarantee.

Rogers joined the Riverside Press of the Houghton Mifflin Company in 1896 and designed books with a strong Arts and Crafts influence. In 1900 Riverside established a special department for high-quality limited editions with Rogers as its

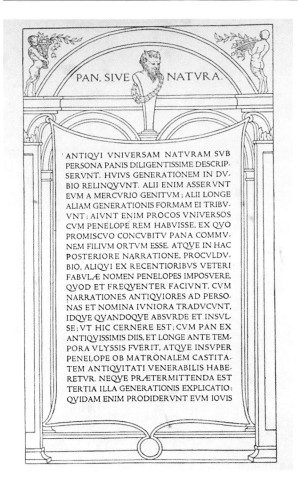

10–39

10–40

designer for sixty limited editions over the next twelve years. Beatrice Warde wrote that Rogers "managed to steal the Divine Fire which glowed in the Kelmscott Press books, and somehow be the first to bring it down to earth." Rogers applied the ideal of the beautifully designed book to commercial production, becoming very influential and setting the standard for the twentieth-century book. He has been called an allusive designer, for his work recalls earlier designs. For inspiration, he shifted from the sturdy types and strong woodblock ornaments of Jenson and Ratdolt to the lighter, graceful lettering of the French Renaissance (Fig. **10–39**).

In 1912 Rogers left the Riverside Press to become a freelance book designer. In spite of some difficult years, he needed freedom to be able to realize his full potential as a graphic artist. His 1915 typeface design Centaur is one of the finest of the numerous fonts inspired by Jenson. It was first used in *The Centaur,* by Maurice de Guerin, one of Rogers's most elegant book designs (Fig. **10–40**). In 1916 he journeyed to England for an unsuccessful effort to collaborate with Emery Walker, then stayed on as a consultant to the Cambridge University Press until 1919. Rogers worked in

10–37. Frederic W. Goudy, booklet cover, 1911. The ideals of the Arts and Crafts movement were actualized in printing for commerce.

10–38. Page 45 from American Type Founders' *Specimen Book and Catalogue 1923* presented the Goudy series of Old Style fonts, including fonts designed by others.

10–39. Bruce Rogers, typographic page of classical typography. Venetian in concept, this design uses a similar line weight in the type strokes and frame lines.

10–40. Bruce Rogers, page from *The Centaur,* by Maurice de Guerin, 1915. The headpiece, initial, and page layout echo the wonderful graphic designs of the French Renaissance.

England again from 1928 through 1932; his design commissions included the monumental Oxford Lectern Bible.

Very much an intuitive designer, Rogers possessed an outstanding sense of visual proportion and of "rightness" (Fig. **10–41**). Design is a decision-making process; the culmination of subtle choices about paper, type, margins, leading between

PRINTING AND THE RENAIS-
SANCE : A PAPER READ BEFORE
THE FORTNIGHTLY CLUB OF
ROCHESTER NEW YORK BY
JOHN ROTHWELL SLATER.

NEW YORK
William Edwin Rudge
1921

10–41

EPICURUS
THE EXTANT REMAINS OF
THE GREEK TEXT TRANS-
LATED BY CYRIL BAILEY
WITH AN INTRODUCTION
BY IRWIN EDMAN

NEW YORK
THE LIMITED EDITIONS CLUB
MCMXLVII

10–42

lines, and so on can combine to create either a unity or a disaster. Rogers wrote, "the ultimate test, in considering the employment or the rejection of an element of design or decoration, would seem to be: does it look as if it were inevitable, or would the page look as well or better for its omission?" So rigorous were Rogers's design standards that when he compiled a list of successful books from among the seven hundred he designed, he only selected thirty. The first book on his list was predated by more than a hundred earlier ones. While Rogers was a classicist who revived the forms of the past, he did so with a sense of what was appropriate for outstanding book design (Fig. **10–42**). Like Frederic Goudy, he lived a long life and was honored for his accomplishments as a graphic designer.

Morris, the Arts and Crafts movement, and the private presses inspired a vigorous revitalization of typography. The passion for Victorian typefaces started to decline in the 1890s, as imitations of Kelmscott typefaces were followed by revivals of other classical typeface designs. Garamond, Plantin, Caslon, Baskerville, and Bodoni—these typeface designs of past masters were studied, recut, and offered for hand and keyboard composition during the first three decades of the twentieth century.

In the United States, the American Type Founders Company (ATF) established an extensive typographic research library and played an important role in reviving past designs. Its head of typeface development, Morris F. Benton (1872–1948), designed important revivals of Bodoni and Garamond. Benton's collaborator on ATF's Garamond (Fig. **10–43**) was Thomas Maitland Cleland (1880–1964), a designer whose borders, type, and images were inspired by the Italian and French Renaissance. Cleland played a major role in making Renaissance design and its resource, the design arts of ancient Rome, dominant influences on American graphics during the first three decades of the twentieth century.

Benton's revival of Nicolas Jenson's type was issued as the Cloister family. From 1901 to 1935 Benton designed approximately 225 typefaces, including nine additional members of the Goudy family and over two dozen members of the Cheltenham family, which began as one typeface by architect Bertram Goodhue. Benton carefully studied human perception and reading comprehension to develop Century Schoolbook, designed for and widely used in textbooks. Figure **10–44** shows examples from seven of Benton's type families.

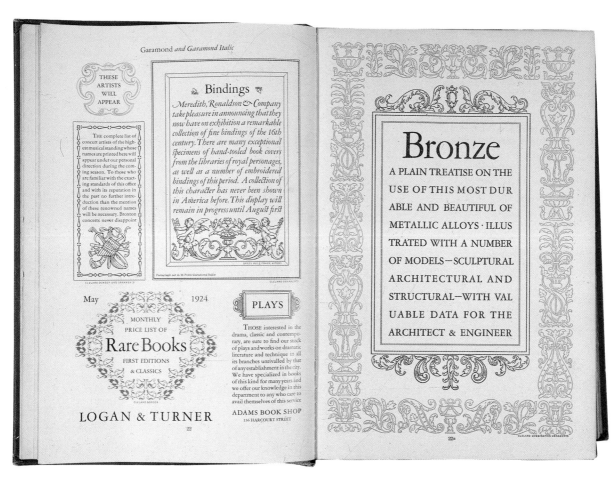

10–43

10–44

10–41. Bruce Rogers, title page from *Printing and the Renaissance: A Paper Read before the Fortnightly Club of Rochester New York by John Rothwell Slater,* published by William Edwin Rudge, New York, 1921.

10–42. Bruce Rogers, title page for *Epicurus,* Limited Edition Club, New York, 1947.

10–43. Pages from American Type Founders' *Specimen Book and Catalogue 1923* display printing demonstrations of its Garamond revival with Cleland ornaments.

10–44. Morris F. Benton, typeface designs: Alternate Gothic, 1906; Century Schoolbook, 1920; Clearface, 1907; Cloister Bold, 1913; Franklin Gothic, 1905; News Gothic, 1908; Souvenir, 1914; Stymie Medium, 1931.

The legacy of the Arts and Crafts movement extends beyond visual appearances. Its attitudes about materials, function, and social value became an important inspiration for twentieth-century designers. Its positive impact on graphic design continues a century after William Morris's death through the revivals of earlier typeface designs, the continued efforts toward excellence in book design and typography, and the private press movement that continues to this day.

Art Nouveau

11

Increased trade and communication between Asian and European countries during the late nineteenth century caused a cultural collision; both East and West experienced change as a result of reciprocal influences. Asian art provided European and North American artists and designers with new approaches to space, color, drawing conventions, and subject matter that were radically unlike Western traditions. This revitalized graphic design during the last decade of the nineteenth century.

The influence of ukiyo-e

Ukiyo-e means "pictures of the floating world" and defines an art movement of Japan's Tokugawa period (1603–1867). This epoch was the final phase of traditional Japanese history; it was a time of economic expansion, internal stability, and flourishing cultural arts. Fearful of the potential impact of European colonial expansion and Christian missionaries on Japanese culture, the shogun (a military governor whose power exceeded the emperor's) issued three decrees in the 1630s excluding foreigners and adopted an official policy of national seclusion. Japanese citizens were barred from traveling overseas or returning from abroad; foreign trade was restricted to approved Dutch and Chinese traders sailing to the Nagasaki seaport. During this period of national isolation, Japanese art acquired a singular national character with few external influences.

Ukiyo-e blended the realistic narratives of *emaki* (traditional picture scrolls) with influences from decorative arts. The earliest ukiyo-e works were screen paintings depicting the entertainment districts—called "the floating world"—of Edo (modern Tokyo) and other cities. Scenes and actors from Kabuki theatrical plays, renowned courtesans and prostitutes, and erotica were early subjects.

Ukiyo-e artists quickly embraced the woodblock print. Hishikawa Moronobu (1618–94) is widely respected as the first master of the ukiyo-e print (Fig. **11–1**). This son of a provincial embroiderer began his career by making designs for embroidery. After moving to Edo in the middle of the seventeenth century, Moronobu became a book illustrator who used Chinese woodcut techniques and reached a large audience. In addition to actors and courtesans, his work presented the everyday life of ordinary people, including crowds on the street and peddlers. Prints surpassed screen paintings in importance as artists exploited a growing interest in images depicting urban life.

Japanese woodblock prints (Fig. **11–2**) were a careful collaboration between publisher, artist, block cutter, and printer. The publisher financed the production of a print and coordinated the work of the other three partners. The artist supplied a separate drawing for each color. These were pasted onto woodblocks, and the negative or white areas were cut away, destroying the original drawing in the process. After all the blocks for a print were cut, printing began. Water-based inks and subtle blends were used, requiring great skill and speed by the printers. Only after all colors were printed could the artist see the whole design.

11–1

11–2

11–3

Working within an evolving tradition, several Japanese artists made major contributions to the genre. Okumura Masanobu (1686–1764) was among the first artists to move from hand-coloring single-color woodcuts to two-color printing, and Suzuki Harunobu (c. 1725–70) introduced full-color prints from numerous blocks, each printed in a different color, in 1765.

Contemporaries of Kitagawa Utamaro (c. 1753–1806) heralded him as an unrivaled artist in portraying beautiful women; he has been called the supreme poet of the Japanese print. His loving observation of nature and human expression resulted in prints of insects, birds, flowers, and women possessing great beauty and tenderness (Fig. **11–3**). His images of Edo's most renowned beauties were identified by name. Rather than repeating stereotypes of conventional beauty, Utamaro conveyed his subjects' feelings, based on careful observation of their physical expressions, gestures, and emotional states. His warm yellow and tan backgrounds emphasized delicate, lighter-toned skin.

In 1804 Utamaro was jailed for three days, then forced to wear handcuffs for fifty days, after making prints depicting the wife and concubines of deposed military ruler Toyotomi Hideyoshi. This crushed his spirit and his work declined; two years after this torture Utamaro died, at age fifty-three.

The most renowned and prolific ukiyo-e artist was Katsushika Hokusai (1760–1849), who produced an estimated 35,000 works during seven decades of ceaseless artistic cre-

11–1. Hishikawa Moronobu, *Young Man with Two Courtesans*, 1682. The earliest ukiyo-e prints presented scenes from daily life in a simple narrative manner.

11–2. Artist unknown, woodblock print from a book about roses, after 1868. Pattern and naturalistic depiction coexist in a print illustrating a mountain rose that blooms in May, attracting a species of water bird.

11–3. Kitagawa Utamaro, portrait of a courtesan, late 1700s. Restrained color palette and exquisitely simple composition characterized Utamaro's prints of tall, graceful women.

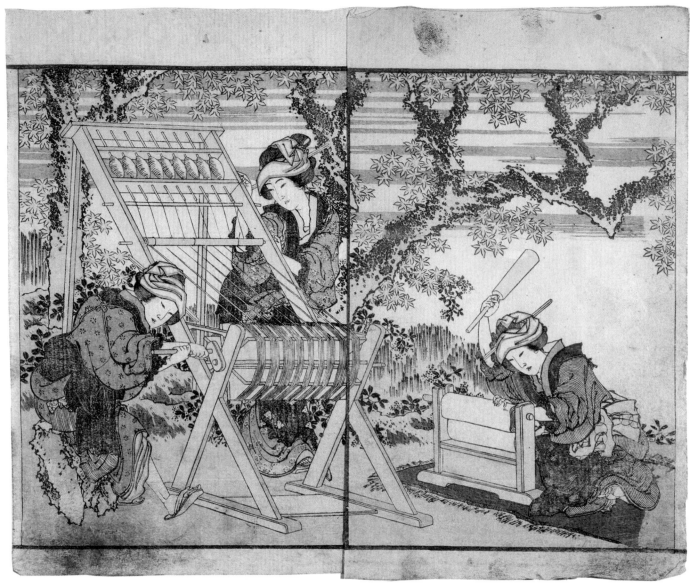

11–4

ation. In his teens Hokusai worked at a lending bookstore and was apprenticed to a woodblock engraver before turning to drawing and painting. At age nineteen his first published prints of Kabuki actors appeared. Hokusai's work spanned the gamut of ukiyo-e subjects: album prints; genre scenes; historical events; illustrations for novels; landscape series including views of rivers, mountains, waterfalls, and bridges; nature studies of flowers, birds, shells, and fish; paintings on silk; sketchbooks; and privately commissioned prints for special occasions, called *surimono*. His model books for amateur artists were very popular, as were his caricatures of occupations, customs, and social behavior.

Book illustration was a major form of popular art. Hokusai, like most ukiyo-e artists, began his career illustrating *yellowbacks*—cheap novelettes so named for the color of their cov-

ers—then moved into illustrations for the major novelists of the day. From age twenty until the year of his death, Hokusai illustrated over 270 titles, including several books of his art (Fig. **11–4**), including *Hokusai Gashiki* (Hokusai's Drawing Style, 1819) and *Hokusai Soga* (Hokusai's Rough Sketches, 1820). These were produced both in black and white and in three colors. Japanese book illustrators developed a superb feeling for the kinetic rhythm of a book, using scale, density, texture, and dramatic action to achieve a dynamic sequence of images.

Single-leaf polychrome prints were considered the summit of ukiyo-e art. Hokusai, who called himself "the old man mad with painting," produced numerous suites of prints. He was in his seventies when he designed the series *Thirty-Six Views of Mount Fuji* (Fig. **11–5**). Mount Fuji occupies a special place in Japanese culture; the ancient Japanese were sun worshipers,

11–5

11–6

and this 3,776-meter (12,000-foot) volcano first catches the rising sun's rays. Hokusai's Mount Fuji prints took the Japanese landscape print to a high level of expression through the grandeur of their conception and their inventive portrayal of natural forms. They depict the external appearances of nature and symbolically interpret the vital energy forces found in the sea, winds, and clouds.

Ando Hiroshige (1797–1858) was the last great master of the Japanese woodcut. A rival of Hokusai, he inspired the European impressionists with his brilliant spatial composition and ability to capture the transient moments of the landscape. In the series *Fifty-Three Stages of the Tokaido*, Hiroshige illustrated the fifty-three way stations (Fig. **11–6**) along the Eastern Sea Road from Edo to Kyoto, capturing subtle nuances of light, atmosphere, and season. He not only

observed and captured the poetic splendor of nature but related it to the lives of ordinary people as well. This is seen in the brilliant spatial compositions of the series *Famous Places in Edo: A Hundred Views* (Fig. **11–7**). Hiroshige's death during an 1858 cholera epidemic came as the collision of Asian and

11–4. Attributed to Katsushika Hokusai, c. 1820. Scenes of everyday life, such as these women working thread, were published in pictorial books of Hokusai's art.

11–5. Katsushika Hokusai, *South Wind, Clear Dawn,* c. 1830–32. This woodcut of Mount Fuji struck by early morning light is also called *Red Fuji.*

11–6. Ando Hiroshige, *Evening Snow at Kanbara,* 1832–34. The soft quietude of a wintry evening is captured in a poetic range of grays.

11-7

drawing, abstraction and simplification of natural appearances, flat color and silhouettes, unconventional use of bold black shapes, and decorative patterns. Subjects often became emblematic symbols, reduced to graphic interpretations conveying their essence. Landscape and interior environments were frequently presented as suggestive impressions rather than detailed depictions. Too often, ukiyo-e has been venerated for its catalytic impact on Western art rather than for its independent major achievements in graphic illustration and design.

Art nouveau

Art nouveau was an international decorative style that thrived roughly during the two decades (c. 1890–1910) that girded the turn of the century. It encompassed all the design arts—architecture, furniture and product design, fashion, and graphics—and consequently embraced posters, packages, and advertisements; teapots, dishes, and spoons; chairs, door frames, and staircases; factories, subway entrances, and houses. Art nouveau's identifying visual quality is an organic, plantlike line. Freed from roots and gravity, it can either undulate with whiplash energy or flow with elegant grace as it defines, modulates, and decorates a given space. Vine tendrils, flowers (such as the rose and lily), birds (particularly peacocks), and the human female form were frequent motifs from which this fluid line was adapted.

The term *art nouveau* arose in a Paris gallery run by art dealer Samueal Bing, which opened in 1895 as the Salon de l'Art Nouveau. In addition to Japanese art, "new art" by European and American artists was displayed and sold there. This gallery became an international meeting place where many young artists were introduced, among them the American glass artist Louis Comfort Tiffany, whose work had a sizable influence in Europe. Art nouveau soon embraced all areas of the arts: architecture, painting, commercial art, ceramics, furniture, ornament, and book design.

Nikolaus Pevsner's book *Pioneers of Modern Design,* which appeared in 1936, 1949, and 1960, was one of the first to give art nouveau a significant position in the development of 20th century art and architecture. He saw the movement's principal characteristics as "the long sensitive curve, reminiscent of the lily's stem, an insect's feeler, the filament of a blossom or occasionally a slender flame, the curve undulating, flowing and interplaying with others, sprouting from corners and covering asymmetrically all available surfaces."

To dismiss art nouveau as surface decoration is to ignore its pivotal role in the evolution of all aspects of design. Art nou-

European cultures was about to have a major influence on Western art and design. The treaties resulting from American commodore Matthew C. Perry's naval expeditions to Japan, beginning in 1853, led to the collapse of Japan's traditional isolationist policies and opened trade with the West. A mid-nineteenth-century revolution overthrew the last shogun in 1867 and restored supreme power to the Meiji emperor the following year. Japan's leaders began building a modern nation with economic and military similarities to Western nations. A centralized constitutional government, industrialization, and a strong military were developed.

The late-nineteenth-century Western mania for all things Japanese is called *Japonisme.* Japanese artifacts streamed into Europe, and several books on Japanese art and ornament were published during the 1880s. Although ukiyo-e practitioners were considered mere artisans in Japan, they captivated European artists, who drew inspiration from the calligraphic line

veau is the transitional style that evolved from the historicism that dominated design for most of the nineteenth century. By replacing this almost servile use of past forms and styles, art nouveau became the initial phase of the modern movement, preparing the way for the twentieth century by rejecting the anachronistic approaches of the nineteenth century.

This was a vital period in architecture and the applied arts, because it formed a bridge between Victorian clutter and modernism. The Victorians sought solutions through established historical approaches. The modernists, though, adopted a new international ornamental style, using elegant motifs aligned with nature and often distinguished by free and graceful lines. Although expressions of this new style varied from country to country, they were all part of the same family.

Ideas, processes, and forms in twentieth-century art bear witness to this catalytic function. Modern architecture, graphic and industrial design, surrealism, and abstract art have roots in art nouveau's underlying theory and concepts. In art nouveau graphics, the organic linear movements frequently dominate the spatial area and other visual properties, such as color and texture. In earlier three-dimensional design, ornaments often were mere decorative elements applied to the surface of a building or object, but in art nouveau objects, the basic forms and shapes were formed by, and evolved with, the design of the ornament. This was a new design principle unifying decoration, structure, and intended function. Because art nouveau forms and lines were often invented rather than copied from nature or the past, there was a revitalization of the design process that pointed toward abstract art. Perhaps the seminal genius of the movement was Belgian architect Baron Victor Horta (1861–1947). His 1892 townhouse for Emile Tassel was unified by tendrilous curvilinear networks unlike anything yet seen in England or on the Continent.

During this period there was a close collaboration between visual artists and writers. The French symbolist movement in literature of the 1880s and 1890s, with its rejection of realism in favor of the metaphysical and sensuous, was an important influence, and led artists to symbolic and philosophic attitudes. In a skeptical era with scientific rationalism on the rise and traditional religious beliefs and social norms under assault, art was seen as a potential vehicle to a much-needed spiritual rejuvenation. Birth, life, and growth; death and decay—these became symbolic subject matter. The complexity of this era and movement has allowed contradictory interpretations: because of its decorativeness, some observers see art nouveau as an expression of late-nineteenth-century decadence; others, however, noting art nouveau's quest for spiritual and aesthetic values, see it as a reaction against the retrogression and materialism of this epoch.

Art nouveau graphic designers and illustrators attempted to make art a part of everyday life. Their fine-arts training had educated them about art forms and methods developed primarily for aesthetic considerations. At the same time they enthusiastically embraced applied-art techniques that had evolved with the development of commercial printing processes. As a result, they were able to upgrade significantly the visual quality of mass communications. The international character of art nouveau was expedited by advances in transportation and communications technology. Contact between artists in various nations through print media and international exhibitions allowed cross-fertilization to take place. The many art periodicals of the 1890s served this purpose while simultaneously introducing the new art and design to a larger audience.

The numerous sources often cited for art nouveau are diffuse and wide-ranging. They include William Blake's book illustration, Celtic ornament, the rococo style, the Arts and Crafts movement, Pre-Raphaelite painting, Japanese decorative design, and especially ukiyo-e woodblock prints. Important inspiration also came from European painting in the late 1880s, which had fallen under the Asian spell. The swirling forms of Vincent Van Gogh (1853–90), the flat color and stylized organic contour of Paul Gauguin (1848–1903), and the work of the Nabis group of young artists all played a role. The Nabis explored symbolic color and decorative patterns, concluding that a painting was, first of all, an arrangement of color in two-dimensional patterns.

Chéret and Grasset

The transition from Victorian graphics to the art nouveau style was a gradual one. Two graphic artists working in Paris, Jules Chéret (1836–1933) and Eugène Grasset (1841–1917), played important roles in the transition. In 1881 a new French law concerning freedom of the press lifted many censorship restrictions and allowed posters anywhere except on churches, at polls, or in areas designated for official notices. This new law led to a booming poster industry employing designers, printers, and afficheurs. The streets became an art gallery for the nation, and respected painters felt no shame at creating advertising posters. The Arts and Crafts movement was creating a new respect for the applied arts, and Jules Chéret showed the way.

Now acclaimed as the father of the modern poster, Chéret was the son of an indigent typesetter who paid four hundred francs to secure a three-year lithographic apprenticeship for his son at age thirteen. The teenager spent his weekdays lettering backwards on lithographic stones and his Sundays absorbing art at the Louvre.

After completing his apprenticeship he worked as a lithographic craftsman and renderer for several firms and took

11–8

11–9

drawing classes. At the age of eighteen he went to London but could only find work making catalogue drawings of furniture, so he returned to Paris after six months.

Chéret was convinced that pictorial lithographic posters would replace the typographic letterpress posters that filled the urban environment, but he could not convince advertisers of this. At the age of twenty-two he produced a blue and brown poster for Offenbach's operetta *Orphée aux Enfers* (Orpheus in Hades) (Fig. **11–8**). When further commissions were not forthcoming, he returned to London, where he soon mastered the more advanced English color lithography. A poster commission for a family of clowns he had befriended was the turning point, leading to label commissions from the philanthropist and perfume manufacturer Eugene Rimmel. Several years of close association and friendship with Rimmel were marked by extensive design and production experience, culminating in Rimmel financing Chéret's establishment of a printing firm in Paris in 1866. The latest English technology and custom-crafted, oversized lithographic stones were purchased, and Chéret was poised to begin the process of running letterpress typography from signboards. Still very Victorian in approach, the first poster from his shop (Fig. **11–9**) was a monochromatic design for the theatrical production *La biche au bois* (The Doe in the Woods), starring the twenty-two-year-old Sarah Bernhardt. Both artist and actress took Paris by storm, as Bernhardt became the leading actress of her day and Chéret pioneered the visual poster.

During the 1870s Chéret evolved away from Victorian complexity, simplifying his designs and increasing the scale of

his major figures and lettering. In 1881 he sold his printing company to the larger printing firm Imprimerie Chaix and became its artistic director, a move that gave him more time for art and design. He drew from a model in the mornings, then spent the afternoons painting at his easel, drawing with pastels, and working on his huge lithographic stones. By 1884 some Chéret posters were produced in sizes of up to two meters (about seven feet) tall by printing the images in sections, which were joined on the wall by the afficheurs. The total annual press run of his designs was almost 200,000 copies. At least eight French printers specialized in posters, and Chéret was joined by a score of other poster designers.

Chéret's artistic influences included the idealized beauty and carefree lifestyle painted by Watteau and Fragonard, the luminous color of Turner, and the winding movement of Tiepolo, whose figures expressed energy and movement through twisting torsos and extended limbs. Chéret worked directly on the stone, in contrast to the standard practice, whereby an artist's design was executed on the stones by craftsmen. During the 1880s he used a black line with the primary colors (red, yellow, and blue). He achieved a graphic vitality with these bright colors, and subtle overprinting allowed an astonishing range of colors and effects; stipple and crosshatch, soft watercolorlike washes and bold calligraphic chunks of color, scratching, scraping, and splattering—all were used in his work. His typical composition is a central figure or figures in animated gesture, surrounded by swirls of color, secondary figures or props, and bold lettering that often echoes the shapes and gestures of the figure. His unending production for music halls and the theater,

11–10

11–11

beverages and medicines, household products (Fig. **11–10**), entertainers, and publications transformed the walls of Paris (Fig. **11–11**).

The beautiful young women he created, dubbed "Chérettes" by an admiring public, were archetypes—not only for the idealized presentation of women in mass media but for a generation of French women who used their dress and apparent lifestyle as inspiration. One pundit dubbed Chéret "the father of women's liberation" because he introduced a new role model for women in the late Victorian era. Options for women were limited, and the proper lady in the drawing room and the trollop in the bordello were stereotyped roles, when into this dichotomy swept the Chérettes. Neither prudes nor prostitutes, these self-assured, happy women enjoyed life to the fullest, wearing low-cut dresses, dancing, drinking wine, and even smoking in public. While Chéret preferred the large format, saying that because "a well-made woman is about 150 centimeters [five feet], a poster 240 centimeters [about 7.9 feet] in length affords ample space for drawing a figure full length," his output ranged from life-size images to the diminutive.

11–8. Jules Chéret, poster for *Orphée aux Enfers,* 1879. Chéret evolved toward larger, more animated figures and greater unity of word and image.

11–9. Jules Chéret, poster for *La biche au bois* (The Doe in the Wood), 1866. Chéret's early green and black poster used the multiple image format so popular in the 1860s. The lettering is a harbinger of the swirling forms marking his mature style.

11–10. Jules Chéret, poster, "L'aureole du midi," Pétrole de Sureté, 1893.

11–11. Jules Chéret, "Èlysée Montmartre bal masqué" (Masked Ball) poster, 1896. Parisian elegance, a carefree grace, and astounding technical mastery are present. The figures create a lively play of angles, linking the top and bottom lettering.

Chéret was named to the Legion of Honor by the French government in 1890 for creating a new branch of art that advanced printing and served the needs of commerce and industry. He designed over a thousand posters by the turn of

11–12

11–13

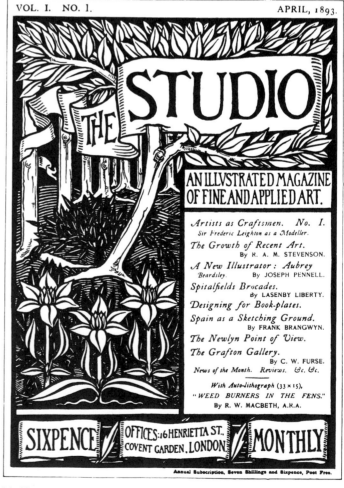

11–14

11–15

11–16

11–12. Eugéne Grasset, title page for *Histoire des quatre fils Aymon,* 1883. Dividing the space into zones, Grasset unified lettering, illustration, and decorative patterns into a total page design.

11–13. Eugéne Grasset, chapter title page and text page from *Histoire des quatre fils Aymon,* 1883. A structural unity of type, image, and ornament is achieved.

11–14. Eugéne Grasset, exhibition poster, c. 1894. Quietly demure instead of exuberant, Grasset's figures project a resonance very different from that of the Chérette.

11–15. Aubrey Beardsley, first cover for *The Studio,* 1893. Beardsley's career was launched when editor C. Lewis Hine featured his work on this cover and reproduced eleven of his illustrations in the inaugural issue.

11–16. Jan Toorop, *The Three Brides,* 1893. In this pencil and colored crayon drawing on brown paper, the undulating flow of stylized ribbons of hair symbolizes sound pouring forth from the bells. Toorop's curvilinear drawing inspired his contemporaries.

the century, when his poster production nearly ceased and he spent more time on pastels and paintings. He retired to Nice, where the Jules Chéret Museum opened, preserving his work, shortly before his death at age ninety-seven.

Swiss-born Grasset was the first illustrator/designer to rival Chéret in public popularity. Grasset had studied medieval art intensely, and this influence, mingled with a love of exotic oriental art, was reflected strongly in his designs for furniture, stained glass, textiles, and books. A bellwether achievement, both in graphic design and printing technology, was the 1883 publication of *Histoire des quatre fils Aymon* (History of Four Young Men of Aymon) (Figs. **11–12** and **11–13**), designed and illustrated by Grasset. It was printed in an aquatint-grain/color-photo relief process from plates made by Charles Gillot, who transformed Grasset's line and watercolor designs into subtle, full-color printed book illustrations. Grasset and Gillot collaborated closely on this two-year project, with Grasset working extensively on the plates. The design is important for its total integration of illustrations, format, and typography. Grasset's design ideas were rapidly assimilated after publication, including the decorative borders framing the contents, the integration of illustration and text into a unit, and the design of illustrations so that typography was printed over skies and other areas. Spatial segmentation was used as an expressive component in the page layouts.

In 1886 Grasset received his first poster commission. His willowy maidens, who wore long, flowing robes and struck static poses to advertise inks, chocolates, and beer, soon began to grace French streets. Figure **11-14** illustrates what has been called his "coloring-book style" of thick black contour drawing

locking forms into flat areas of color in a manner similar to medieval stained-glass windows. His figures echo Botticelli and wear medieval clothing; his stylized, flat cloud patterns reflect his knowledge of Japanese woodblocks. Grasset's formal composition and muted color contrasted strongly with Chéret's informally composed, brightly colored work. In spite of Grasset's tradition-bound attitude; his flowing line, subjective color, and ever-present floral motifs pointed toward French art nouveau. His oeuvre included wallpaper and fabric design, stained-glass windows, typefaces, and printer's ornaments

English art nouveau

In England the art nouveau movement was primarily concerned with graphic design and illustration rather than architectural and product design. Its sources, in addition to those listed earlier, included Gothic art and Victorian painting. A strong momentum toward an international style was created by the April 1893 inaugural issue of *The Studio,* the first of nearly a dozen new 1890s European art periodicals. The April issue reproduced the work of Aubrey Beardsley (1872–98) (Fig. **11–15**); *The Three Brides,* by the Dutch artist Jan Toorop (1858–1928), was included in the September issue (Fig. **11–16**). Early issues of *The Studio* also included work by Walter Crane (an early innovator in the application of Japanese ornamental pattern and Eastern interpretations of nature to the design of surface pattern) and furniture and textiles produced for the Liberty and Company store.

Aubrey Beardsley was the *enfant terrible* of art nouveau, with his striking pen line, vibrant black-and-white work, and shockingly exotic imagery. A strange cult figure, he was

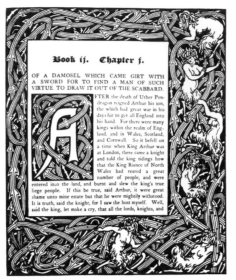

11–17

11–18

11–19

11–17. Aubrey Beardsley, full page illustration, *Morte d'Arthur,* 1893. This image shows Beardsley's emerging ability to compose contour line, textured areas, and black and white shapes into powerful compositions. The contrast between geometric and organic shapes reflects the influence of the Japanese print.

11–18. Aubrey Beardsley, chapter opening, *Morte d'Arthur,* 1893. William Morris's lyrical bouquets were replaced by rollicking mythological nymphs in a briar border design.

11–19. William Morris, page from *The Recuyell of the Historyes of Troye,* 1892. Comparison of page designs by Morris and Beardsley reveals that their differences reflect a dichotomy of philosophy, lifestyle, and social values.

11–20. Aubrey Beardsley, illustration for Oscar Wilde's *Salomé,* 1894. John the Baptist and Salomé, who was given his head on a platter by Herod after her dance, are remarkable symbolic figures. The dynamic interplay between positive and negative shapes has seldom been equaled.

11–21. Charles Ricketts, title page for *The Sphinx,* 1894. Ricketts's unconventional title page, dominated by an illustration, is placed on the left rather than the right. The text is set in all capitals.

11–22. Charles Ricketts, pages from *The Sphinx,* 1894. The white space and typography printed in rust and olive-green ink are without precedent.

positions based on a dominant black form. Japanese block prints and William Morris were synthesized into a new idiom. Beardsley's unique line was reproduced by the photoengraving process, which, unlike the hand-cut woodblock, retained complete fidelity to the original art.

Morris was so angry when he saw Beardsley's *Morte d'Arthur* that he considered legal action. Beardsley had, to Morris's mind, vulgarized the design ideas of the Kelmscott style (Fig. **11–19**) by replacing the formal, naturalistic borders with more stylized, flat patterns. Walter Crane, always ready with an unequivocal viewpoint, declared that Beardsley's *Morte d'Arthur* had mixed the medieval spirit of Morris with a weird "Japanese-like spirit of deviltry and the grotesque," which Crane thought fit only for the opium den.

In spite of Morris's anger, the enthusiastic response to Beardsley's work resulted in numerous commissions. He was named art editor for *The Yellow Book,* a magazine whose bright yellow cover on London newsstands became a symbol for the new and outrageous. In 1894 Oscar Wilde's *Salomé* received widespread notoriety for the obvious erotic sensuality of Beardsley's illustrations (Fig. **11–20**). Late-Victorian English society was shocked by this celebration of evil, which reached its peak in Beardsley's work for an edition of Aristophanes's *Lysistrata.* Banned by English censors, it was widely circulated on the Continent.

During the last two years of his life, Beardsley was an invalid. When he could work, the flat patterns and dynamic curves of art nouveau yielded to a more naturalistic tonal quality, and dotted contours softened the decisive line of his earlier work. Even as he waned toward a tragically early death, Beardsley's lightning influence penetrated the design and illustration of Europe and North America.

intensely prolific for only five years and died of tuberculosis at age twenty-six. He became famous at age twenty, when his illustrations for a new edition of Malory's *Morte d'Arthur* (Figs. **11–17** and **11–18**) began to appear in monthly installments, augmenting a strong Kelmscott influence with strange and imaginative distortions of the human figure and powerful black shapes. "The black spot" was the name given to com-

11–20

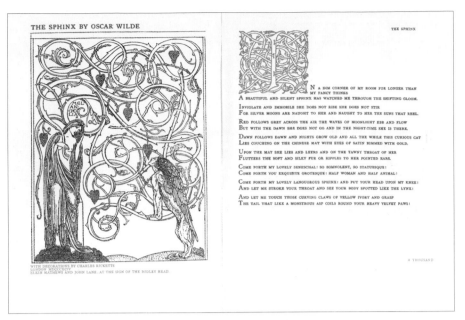

11–21

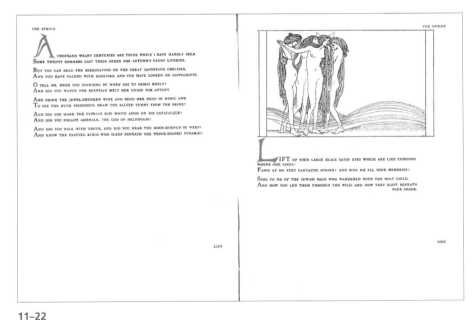

11–22

Beardsley's leading rival among English graphic designers working in the wake of the Arts and Crafts movement and on the crest of art nouveau was Charles Ricketts, who maintained a lifelong collaboration with his close friend Charles Shannon (1863–1931). Ricketts began as a wood engraver and received training as a compositor; therefore, his work was based on a thorough understanding of print production. While Beardsley tended to approach his works as illustrations to be inserted between pages of typography, Ricketts approached the book as a total entity, focusing upon a harmony of the parts: binding, end sheets, title page, typography, ornaments, and illustrations (which were frequently com-

missioned from Shannon). After working as an engraver and designer for several printing firms, Ricketts established his own studio and publishing firm.

In 1893 Ricketts's first total book design appeared, and the following year he produced his masterly design for Oscar Wilde's exotic and perplexing poem, *The Sphinx* (Fig. **11–21** and Fig. **11–22**) Although Ricketts owed a debt to Morris, he usually rejected the density of Kelmscott design. His page layouts are lighter, his ornaments and bindings more open and geometric (Fig. **11–23**), and his designs have a vivid luminosity. The complex, intertwining ornament of Celtic design and the flat, stylized figures painted on Greek vases, which he

11–23

11–24

studied in the British Museum, were major inspirations. From them, Ricketts, like Beardsley, learned how to indicate figures and clothing with minimal lines and flat shapes with no tonal modulation.

In 1896 Ricketts launched the Vale Press. Unlike Morris, Ricketts did not own a press or do his own printing and instead placed his typesetting and presswork with printing firms who followed his exacting requirements. When Morris was shown Vale Press books during his final illness, he cried in admiration of the great beauty of Ricketts's volumes.

The further development of French art nouveau

During the 1880s Grasset was a regular at Rodolphe Salis's Le Chat Noir nightclub, a gathering place for artists and writers that opened in 1881. There he met and shared his enthusiasm for color printing with younger artists: Georges Auriol (1863–1939), Henri de Toulouse-Lautrec (1864–1901), and fellow Swiss artist Théophile-Alexandre Steinlen (1859–1923).

Even Jules Chéret had to concede that Lautrec's 1891 poster "La Goulue au Moulin Rouge" broke new ground in poster design (Fig. **11–24**). A dynamic pattern of flat planes— black spectator's silhouettes, yellow ovals for lamps, and the stark white undergarments of the notorious cancan dancer, who performed with transparent or slit underwear—move horizontally across the center of the poster. In front of this is the profile of the dancer Valentine, known as "the boneless one" because of his amazing flexibility. In this milestone of poster design, simplified symbolic shapes and dynamic spatial relationships form expressive and communicative images.

The son of the count of Toulouse, Toulouse-Lautrec had turned obsessively to drawing and painting after breaking both hips in an accident at age thirteen. Further growth of his legs was stunted, leaving him crippled. He became a master draftsman in the academic tradition after moving to Paris two years later. Japanese art, impressionism, and Degas's design and contour excited him, and he haunted Paris cabarets and

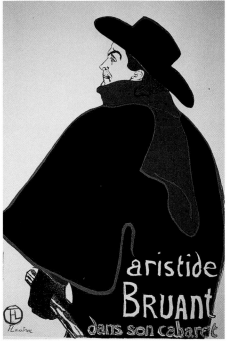

11–25   11–26   11–27

bordellos, watching, drawing, and developing a journalistic, illustrative style that captured the night life of *la belle epoque* ("the beautiful era"), a term used to describe glittering late-nineteenth-century Paris (Fig. **11–25**). Primarily a printmaker, draftsman, and painter, Toulouse-Lautrec produced only thirty-one posters (Figs. **11–24, 11–25, 11–26, 11–27**), the commissions for which were negotiated in the cabarets in the evenings, and a modest number of music- and book-jacket designs. Drawing directly on the lithographic stone, he often worked from memory with no sketches and used an old toothbrush that he always carried to achieve tonal effects through a splatter technique.

There is an affinity, in the fluid reportorial line and flat color, between the posters and prints of Steinlen and those of his friend and sometime rival for commissions, Toulouse-Lautrec. The debate over which one influenced the other is irrelevant, because Steinlen and Lautrec drew inspiration from similar sources and each other. Steinlen arrived in Paris at age twenty-two with his young wife, a great love of drawing, and a mania for cats. His first Paris commissions were cat drawings for Le Chat Noir (Fig. **11–28**). Steinlen was a prolific illustrator during the 1880s and 1890s, and his radical political views, socialist affiliations, and anticlerical stance led him toward a social realism depicting poverty, exploitation, and the working class. His black-and-white lithographs often had color printed by a stencil process. His vast oeuvre included over two thousand magazine covers and interior illustrations, nearly two

11–23. Charles Ricketts, binding design for *Poems of Adoration,* by Michael Fields, c. 1900. Christian symbolism is abstracted into elemental forms, with rigorous rectangles punctuated by a few well-placed circles and arches.

11–24. Henri de Toulouse-Lautrec, poster, "La Goulue au Moulin Rouge," 1891. Shapes become symbols; in combination, these signify a place and an event.

11–25. Henri de Toulouse-Lautrec, poster for *Reine de joie,* 1892. The banker Rothchild thought his own likeness had been used for the main character in the book being advertised and attempted to prevent distribution of the poster.

11–26. Henri de Toulouse-Lautrec, poster for Aristide Bruant, 1893. The influence of the Japanese print is clearly evident in the flat silhouette, unmodulated color, and stylized curvilinear drawing.

11–27. Henri de Toulouse-Lautrec, poster for Jane Avril, 1893. The gestural expressiveness of Toulouse-Lautrec's drawing on the lithographic stone captures the vitality of the dancer. This poster was created from sketches made during a performance.

hundred sheet-music covers, over a hundred book-illustration assignments, and three dozen large posters.

Although his first color poster was designed in 1885, his legacy is based on masterworks of the 1890s. His 305 by 228–centimeter (10 by 7–foot) multipanel poster for the printer Charles Verneau (Fig. **11–29**) mirrored the pedestrians on adjacent Parisian sidewalks in nearly life-sized,

11–28

11–29

11–30

11–31

11–32

environmental scale. Remarkable tenderness was displayed in a dairy poster illustrating his hungry cats demanding a share of his daughter Colette's bowl of milk (Fig. **11–30**).

The young Czech artist Alphonse Mucha (1860–1939) had shown remarkable drawing ability when he was growing up in the small Moravian village of Ivancice. After journeying to Paris at age twenty-seven, Mucha spent two years of study supported by a benefactor. This financial support ended suddenly, and a period of dire poverty ensued. But Mucha gained steady acceptance as a dependable illustrator with strong drawing skills.

On Christmas Eve 1894, Mucha was at the Lemercier's printing company, dutifully correcting proofs for a friend who had taken a holiday. Suddenly the printing firm's manager burst into the room, upset because the famous actress Sarah Bernhardt was demanding a new poster for the play *Gismonda* by New Year's Day. As Mucha was the only artist available, he received the commission. Using the basic pose from Grasset's earlier poster for Bernhardt in *Joan of Arc* (Fig. **11–31**) and sketches of Bernhardt made at the theater, Mucha elongated Grasset's format, used Byzantine-inspired mosaics as background motifs, and produced a poster totally distinct from any of his prior work (Fig. **11–32**). The bottom portion of this poster was unfinished because only a week was available for design, printing, and posting. Because of its complexity and muted colors, Mucha's work lacked Chéret's impact from afar. But once they stepped closer, Parisians were astounded.

On New Year's Day 1895, as Mucha began his meteoric rise, a number of influences throughout Europe were converging into what would be labeled art nouveau. Although Mucha resisted this label, maintaining that art was eternal and could never be new, the further development of his work and of the visual poster are inseparably linked to this diffuse international movement and must be considered part of its development. Just as the English Arts and Crafts movement was a special influence on that country's art nouveau, the light and fanciful flowing curves of eighteenth-century French rococo were a special resource in France. The new art was hailed as *le style moderne* until December 1895, when Samuel Bing, a long-time dealer in Far Eastern art and artifacts who fostered the growing awareness of Japanese work, opened his new gallery, Salon de l'Art Nouveau, to exhibit art and crafts by young artists working in new directions. Bing commissioned the Belgian architect and designer Henri Clemens van de Velde (1863–1957) to design his interiors, and exhibited painting, sculpture, glasswork, jewelry, and posters by an international group of artists and designers.

Graphic design, more ephemeral and timely than most other art forms, began to move rapidly toward the floral phase of art nouveau as Chéret, Grasset, Toulouse-Lautrec, and especially Mucha developed its graphic motifs. From 1895 until 1900, art nouveau found its most comprehensive statement in Mucha's work. His dominant theme was a central female figure surrounded by stylized forms derived from plants and flowers, Moravian folk art, Byzantine mosaics, and even magic and the occult. So pervasive was his work that by 1900, *le style Mucha* was often used interchangeably with *l'art nouveau*. (The new art was called *Jugendstil*, after the magazine *Jugend* [Youth] in Germany, *Sezessionstil*, after the Vienna Secession art movement in Austria; *stile floreale* or *stile Liberty* after textiles and furnishings from the London department store in Italy; *modernismo* in Spain, and *nieuwe kunst* in the Netherlands.)

Mucha's women project an archetypal sense of unreality. Exotic, sensuous, and yet maidenlike, they express no specific age, nationality, or historical period. His stylized hair patterns (Fig. **11–33** and **11–34**) became a hallmark of the era in spite of detractors who dismissed this aspect of his work as "noodles and spaghetti." Sarah Bernhardt, who had not been pleased with Grasset's Joan of Arc poster or many other posters for her performances, felt that Mucha's *Gismonda* poster expressed her so well graphically that she signed him to a six-year contract for sets, costumes, jewelry, and nine more posters. The sheer volume of Mucha's output was astounding. For example, the 134 lithographs for the book *Ilsée, princesse de Tripoli* (Fig. **11–35**), printed in a limited edition of 252 copies, were produced in three months. In addition to graphics, Mucha designed furniture, carpets, stained-glass windows, and manufactured objects. His pattern books—including *Combinaisons ornementales* (Ornamental Combinations) (Fig. **11–36**), produced in collaboration with Maurice Verneuil (1869–after 1934) and Georges Auriol (1863–c. 1938)—spread art

11–28. Théophile Alexandre Steinlen, poster, "Tournee du chat noir" de Rodolphe Salis, 1896.

11–29. Théophile Alexandre Steinlen, poster for Charles Verneau's printing firm, 1896. A cross section of Parisian society—a mother and baby, a washerwoman, two workers, Steinlen's daughter Colette with her nanny, a businessman, and sophisticated shoppers—promenades in a nearly life-sized echo of the adjacent sidewalks.

11–30. Théophile Alexandre Steinlen, poster for Guillot Brothers sterilized milk, c. 1897. The red dress functions graphically in a manner similar to Beardsley's "black spot."

11–31. Eugéne Grasset, poster for Sarah Bernhardt as Joan of Arc, 1894. A medieval figure stands before sky patterns inspired by ukiyo-e prints.

11–32. Alphonse Mucha, *Gismonda* poster, 1894. The life-size figure, mosaic pattern, and elongated shape created an overnight sensation.

11–33

11–34

11–35

11–36

11–37

11–38

11–39

11–33. Alphonse Mucha, poster for Job cigarette papers, 1898. Mucha delighted in filling the total space with animated form and ornament.

11–34. Alphonse Mucha, illustration from *Ilsée, princesse de Tripoli,* 1901. This masterly example of Mucha's page design has contour lines printed in dark blue-gray. Five other lithographic stones printed light blue-gray, metallic gold, pink, yellow, and brown.

11–35. Alphonse Mucha, cover for *Wiener Chic* (Vienna Chic), 1906. This fashion-magazine cover shows Mucha's ornamental patterns and interplay between organic areas for typography and illustration.

11–36. Maurice Verneuil, page from *Combinaisons ornementales,* 1900. Art nouveau was spread by pattern books for artists and designers.

11–37. Emmanuel Orazi, poster for La Maison Moderne (The Modern House), 1905. Furniture, objects, clothing, jewelry, and even the woman's hair evidence the totality of the movement.

11–38. A. L. Rich, trademark for General Electric, c. 1890. This design satisfies the requirements of a successful trademark: it is unique, legible, and unequivocal, which explains why it has survived decades of fluctuating design approaches. (A registered trademark of General Electric Company, used by permission.)

11–39. Eugène Grasset, cover for *Harper's Magazine,* 1892. Grasset's work, combining flowing contours and flat color with an almost medieval flavor, captured the American imagination.

nouveau. There were also numerous Dutch books that provided instructive patterns in the art nouveau style.

In 1904, at the height of his fame, Mucha left Paris for his first American visit. His last major art nouveau work was executed in 1909. After Czechoslovakia became an independent nation in 1917, Mucha's time and work were centered there. His *Slav Epic,* a series of twenty large murals, depicted the history of his people. After Germany partitioned Czechoslovakia in 1939, Mucha was one of the first people arrested and interrogated by the Gestapo, and he died a few months later.

Although Emmanuel Orazi (1860–1934) came to prominence as a poster designer in 1884, when he designed a poster for Sarah Bernhardt, it was not until his static style yielded to the influences of Grasset and Mucha a decade later that he produced his best work. His La Maison Moderne poster (Fig. 11–37) was designed for a gallery competing with Bing's Salon de l'Art Nouveau. A sophisticated young lady, drawn in an almost Egyptian profile, is posed before a counter bearing objects from the gallery. The logo centered in the window typifies the many applications of art nouveau letterforms to trademark design. Many trademarks of art nouveau origin (Fig. 11–38) have been in continuous use since the 1890s.

Art nouveau comes to America

British and French graphic art soon joined forces to invade America. In 1889, and again in 1891 and 1892, Harper's magazines commissioned covers from Eugène Grasset (Fig. 11–39). These first presentations of a new approach to graphic design were literally imported, for Grasset's designs were printed in Paris and shipped by boat to New York to be bound onto the magazines. The visual poster was adopted by the American publishing industry, and colorful placards began to appear at the newsstands advertising the new books and major magazines, including *Harper's, Scribner's,* and *Century.*

British-born Louis Rhead (1857–1926) studied in England and Paris before emigrating to America in 1883. After eight years in New York as an illustrator, he returned to Europe for three years and adopted Grasset's style. Upon his return to America, a prolific flow of posters, magazine covers (Fig. 11–40), and illustrations enabled him to join the self-taught American William H. Bradley (1868–1962) as one of the two major American practitioners of art nouveau–inspired graphic design and illustration.

While Rhead embraced Grasset's willowy maidens, contour line, and flat color, he rejected his pale colors in favor of vibrantly unexpected combinations, such as red contour lines on bright blue hair before an intense green sky. Rhead's eclectic style sometimes mixed a profusion of influences. Decorative embellishments from Victorian designs, forms inspired by the Arts and Crafts movement, and curving, abstract linear patterns were sometimes combined in his designs.

While Rhead adopted the French poster as his model, the energetic and enormously talented Will Bradley was inspired by English sources. After his father died from wounds received in the Civil War, nine-year-old Bradley moved with his mother from Massachusetts to Ishpeming, Michigan, to live with relatives. His early training in graphic arts began at age eleven, when he became an apprentice for the *Iron Agitator* (later the *Iron Ore*) newspaper. When Bradley was seventeen, he used his fifty-dollar savings to go to Chicago and apprentice at Rand-McNally as an engraver. Realizing that engravers did not design or illustrate, and that illustrators and designers did not engrave, he returned briefly to Ishpeming. But Chicago soon beckoned again, and he became a typographic designer at the Knight & Leonard printing company when he was nineteen.

Unable to afford art lessons, Bradley became a voracious student of magazines and library books. As with Frederic Goudy and Bruce Rogers, William Morris and his ideals had an enormous impact on Bradley. By 1890 his Arts and Crafts–inspired pen-and-ink illustrations were bringing regular commissions. In early 1894 Bradley became aware of Beardsley's work, which led him toward flat shapes and stylized contour. Beginning in 1894, Bradley's work for the *Inland Printer* and the

11–40

11–41

Chap Book (Figs. **11–41, 11–42, 11–43**) ignited art nouveau in America. His detractors dismissed him as "the American Beardsley," but Bradley used Beardsley's style as a stepping-stone to fresh graphic technique and a visual unity of type and image that moved beyond imitation. He made innovative use of photomechanical techniques to produce repeated (Fig. **11–43**), overlapping, and reversed images.

Bradley was inventive in his approach to typographic design and flouted all the prevailing rules and conventions. Type became a design element to be squeezed into a narrow column or letterspaced so that lines of many and few letters all became the same length and formed a rectangle. Inspired by the Kelmscott Press, Bradley established the Wayside Press after moving from Chicago to Springfield, Massachusetts, in late 1894. He produced books and advertisements and began publication of an art and literary periodical, *Bradley: His Book* (Fig. **11–44**), in 1896. Both the magazine and the press were critical and financial successes, but the rigors and many roles involved in running them—editor, designer, illustrator, press manager—threatened Bradley's health. In 1898 he sold

11–42

11–43

11–44

11–40. Louis Rhead, cover for *Harper's Bazar,* 1894. Dazzling linear patterns animate the background. Note the intensity of Rhead's colorful advertisement for Royal Baking Powder on the back cover, in contrast to the other three more typical ads.

11–41. Will Bradley, covers for *The Inland Printer*, 1894–95. Bradley's graphic vocabulary ranged from delicate contour line for an overall light effect, complex full-tone drawing, and reduction of the image to black-and-white silhouette masses.

11–42. Will Bradley, cover for *The Inland Printer,* 1895. Figures are reduced to organic symbols in dynamic shape relationships.

11–43. Will Bradley, poster for *The Chap Book,* 1895. Repetition of the figure in a smaller size, overlapping the larger figure, enabled Bradley to create a complex set of visual relationships.

11–44. Will Bradley, poster for *Bradley: His Book,* 1898. Medieval romanticism, Arts and Crafts–inspired patterns, and art nouveau are meshed into a compressed frontal image.

Wayside Press to the University Press in Cambridge and accepted a position there.

During an 1895 visit to the Boston Public Library, Bradley studied its collection of small, crudely printed books from colonial New England called *chapbooks,* after the traveling peddlers known as chapmen who sold them. The vigor of these works, with their Caslon types, wide letterspacing, mix of roman, italic, and all-capital type, sturdy woodcuts, and plain rules, inspired the beginnings of a new direction in graphic arts that became known as the chapbook style. After

the turn of the century Bradley became a consultant to the American Type Founders, designing typefaces and ornaments. He wrote and designed their series of twelve little books, *The American Chap-Book* (Fig. **11–45**). A growing passion for type design and layout led Bradley to become art editor of *Collier's* magazine in 1907. During the last decades of his career he made significant contributions to the evolution of twentieth-century editorial design.

Ethel Reed (b. 1876) was the first America woman to achieve national prominence as a graphic designer and

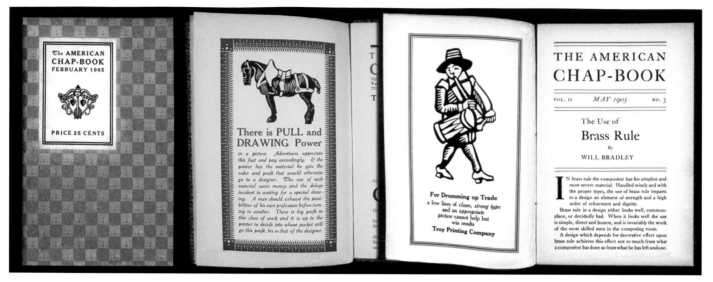

11–45

11–46

11–47

11–48

illustrator (Fig. **11–46**). Born and raised in Massachusetts, she became well known as a book illustrator and poster designer at age eighteen. For four brief years (1894–98) she created posters and illustrations for Boston publishers Copeland & Day and Lamson, Wolffe and Company. Reed's career ended abruptly after she traveled to England and produced her last poster in London in 1898. Her disappearance from the historical record at age twenty-two remains a mystery.

An art director for Harper and Brothers publications from 1891 until 1901, Edward Penfield (1866–1925) enjoyed a reputation rivaling Bradley's and Rhead's. His monthly series of posters for *Harper's* magazine from 1893 until 1898 were directed toward the affluent members of society, frequently depicting them reading or carrying an issue of the magazine. His first poster for *Harper's* was designed for the January 1894 issue and featured a naturalistic watercolor illustration

showing a sophisticated young man purchasing a subscription (Fig. **11–47**). During the course of that year, Penfield evolved toward his mature style of contour drawing with flat planes of color. By eliminating the background, he forced the viewer to focus on the figure and lettering. Penfield drew with a vigorous, fluid line, and his flat color planes were often supplemented by a masterly stipple technique. In a humorous 1894 poster for the July issue (Fig. **11–48**), a young lady is so preoccupied by her reading that she lights a string of fireworks without even looking at them; the absorbing enjoyment of reading *Harper's* is conveyed. In an 1897 poster (Fig. **11–49**), everyone on a train, including the conductor, is reading *Harper's*. This campaign was wildly successful in promoting the magazine, and competitive publications commissioned imitative designs showing the reading public absorbed in their magazines. William Carqueville (1871–1946) created similar

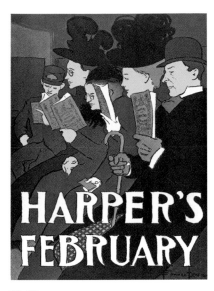

11–49   11–50   11–51

11–45. Will Bradley, covers and spreads from *The American Chap-Book,* 1905. Designers, compositors, and printers drew ideas and possibilities from Bradley's demonstration designs and ornaments.

11–46. Ethel Reed, poster for the book *Folly or Saintliness,* 1895. In an imaginative use of three-color printing, the white face with red lips glows against an otherwise black and orange-brown poster.

11–47. Edward Penfield, poster for *Harper's,* 1894. Traditional tonal modeling creates this image; he shifted to line and flat color later that year.

11–48. Edward Penfield, poster for *Harper's,* 1894. Figurative letterforms and a dramatic sense of expectation the moment before the fireworks begin create a whimsical concept.

11–49. Edward Penfield, poster for *Harper's,* 1897. Spatial compression similar to a telephoto lens converts five overlapping figures into a rhythmic two-dimensional pattern.

11–50. Will Carqueville, poster for *Lippincott's,* 1895. Both the style and concept of Penfield's poster from the preceding Fourth of July are imitated.

11–51. Maxfield Parrish, poster for *Scribner's* magazine, 1897. Parrish created an elegant land of fantasy with his idealized drawing, pristine color, and intricate composition.

posters for *Lippincott's* magazine, including one for the July 1895 issue featuring a girl dropping her *Lippincott's* after a young boy startles her with a firecracker (Fig. **11–50**)

Several younger artists of the 1890s poster movement were to become major illustrators for magazines and books during the twentieth century. Maxfield Parrish (1870–1966) was rejected as a student by Howard Pyle, who told young Parrish that there was nothing more that Pyle could teach him

and that he should develop an independent style. Parrish expressed a romantic and idealized view of the world (Fig. **11–51**) in book, magazine, and advertising illustrations during the first three decades of the twentieth century before turning to painting landscapes for reproduction.

Innovation in Belgium and the Netherlands

Belgium experienced the beginnings of creative ferment during the 1880s, when the Cercle des XX (Group of Twenty) formed to show progressive art ignored by the salon establishment, including paintings by Gauguin in 1889 and Van Gogh in 1890. The cover design for a Les Vingt (The Twenty) exhibition catalogue by Georges Lemmen (1865–1916) in 1891 demonstrates that Belgian artists were at the vanguard in the movement toward a new art (Fig. **11–52**). By the mid-1890s Belgian art nouveau became a significant force, as architect Baron Victor Horta and designer Henri van de Velde were influencing developments throughout Europe.

Van de Velde, an architect, painter, designer, and educator, synthesized sources such as the Japanese print, French art nouveau, the English Arts and Crafts movement, and, later, the Glasgow School into a unified style. After exploring postimpressionism, including pointillism, he studied architecture and joined the Cercle des XX. Morris's example inspired his increasing involvement in design, and Van de Velde soon abandoned painting. Interiors, book design, bookbinding, jewelry, and metalwork became major activities. In 1892 Van de Velde wrote an important essay, "Déblaiement d'art," calling for a new art that would be contemporary in concept and form but possess the vitality and ethical integrity of the great decorative and applied arts of the past. The ornaments and initials designed for a reprint of this essay and for the periodical *Van nu en straks* (Of Today and Tomorrow) approach pure abstraction

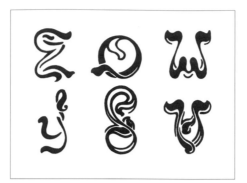

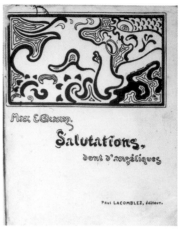

11–52

11–53

11–54

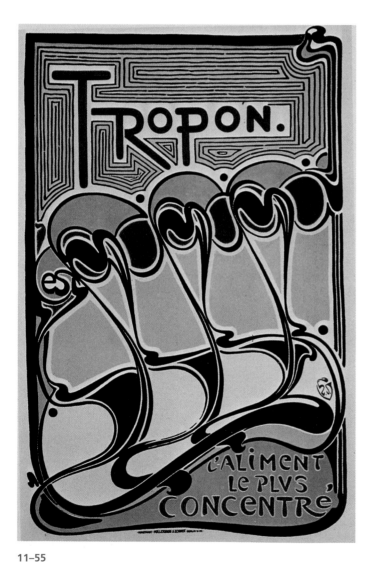

11–55

11–52. Georges Lemmen, cover design for a Les Vingt (The Twenty) exhibition catalogue, 1891. A rising sun, symbolic of the group, ascends over a rhythmic sea of swirling lines.

11–53. Henri van de Velde, initials from *Van nu an straks,* c. 1896. Typography was pushed here toward an expression of pure form.

11–54. Henri van de Velde, *Salutations* book cover, 1893. Illustration and lettering are unified by corresponding forms and line weights.

11–55. Henri van de Velde, poster for Tropon food concentrate, 1899. This swirling configuration may have been inspired by the separation of egg yolks from egg whites.

11–56. Henri van de Velde, title pages for *Also Sprach Zarathustra,* 1908. In this monumental art nouveau book design, bold graphic shapes fill the pages.

11–57. Henri van de Velde, text pages from *Also Sprach Zarathustra,* 1908. Gold ornaments cap each column of type. The chapter heading design is in the center of the left page, and a chapter section is indicated high on the right page.

(Fig. **11–53**), for the basic letter structures are transfigured by dynamic linear rhythms. Van de Velde's work can be seen as a serious effort to develop new forms for the era. In book design he broke creative ground, drawing dynamic linear forms that embrace their surrounding space and the intervals between them. His work evolved from forms inspired by symbols and plant motifs to rhythmic linear patterns (Fig. **11–54**). In applying this approach to graphic design, Van de Velde became a precursor of twentieth-century painting, foretelling the coming of Kandinsky and abstract expression in the twentieth century. His only poster was for a concentrated food product, Tropon, for which he created labeling and advertising in 1899 (Fig. **11–55**). Rather than communicating information about the

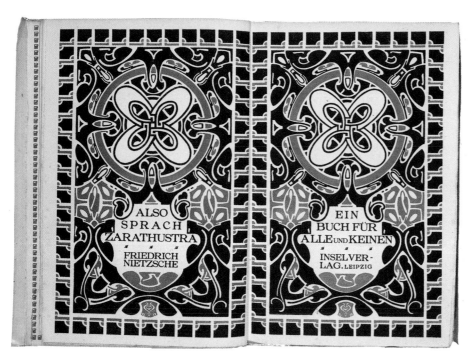

11–56

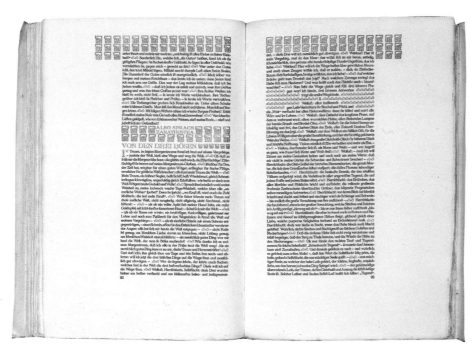

11–57

product or depicting people using it, Van de Velde engaged the viewer with symbolic form and color. His 1908 book design for Friedrich Nietzsche's *Also Sprach Zarathustra* and *Ecce Homo* was a masterwork (Figs. **11–56**, and **11–57**).

Although Van de Velde became an innovator of art nouveau, he was far more interested in furthering the Arts and Crafts philosophy than in visual invention as an end in itself. After the turn of the century, his teaching and writing (*The Renaissance in Modern Applied Art,* 1901; *A Layman's Sermons on Applied Art,* 1903) became a vital source for the development of twentieth-century architecture and design theory. He taught that all branches of art—from painting to graphic design and from industrial design to sculpture—share a common language of form and are of equal importance to the human community. Appropriate materials, functional forms, and a unity of visual organization were demanded. He saw ornament not as decoration but as a means of expression that could achieve the status of art.

11–58. Privet Livemont, Rajah Coffee poster, 1899. The steam from the coffee cup and the product name are entwined in a fascinating interplay of forms.

11–59. Gisbert Combaz, La Libre Esthetique poster, 1898. The sinuous art nouveau line acquires the mechanistic precision of a French curve.

11–60. J. H. and J. M. de Groot, *Driehoeken bij ontwerpen van ornament* (Triangles in the Design of Ornament), published by Joh. G. Stemler & Cz., Amsterdam, 1896.

11–61. Chris Lebeau, binding for *De stille kracht* (The Quiet Power) by Louis Couperus, published by Van Holkema en Warendorf, Amsterdam, 1900.

11–58

11–59

Machine-made objects, Van de Velde argued, should be true to their manufacturing process instead of trying, deceitfully, to appear handmade. After the grand duke of Saxe Weimar called Van de Velde to Weimar as an art and design adviser in 1902, he reorganized the Weimar Arts and Crafts Institute and the Weimar Academy of Fine Arts, a preliminary step toward Walter Gropius's formation of the Bauhaus in 1919 (see chapter 16). When World War I broke out, Van de Velde returned to his native country. In 1925 the Belgian government expressed their appreciation by naming Van de Velde director of the Institut Supérieur des Arts Décoratifs in Brussels.

Other 1890s Belgian graphic designers added their own variations to the new art. After six years in Paris, Privat Livemont (1861–1936) returned to his native Belgium. This teacher and painter produced nearly three dozen posters, strongly inspired by Mucha's idealized women, their tendrilous hair, and their lavish ornament. His major innovation was a double contour separating the figure from the background. A dark contour was outlined by a thick, white band, which increased the image's impact when posted on billboards (Fig. **11–58**). Gisbert Combaz (1869–1941) turned from the practice of law to become an artist and art historian specializing in the Far East. He was a leading member of La Libre Esthetique,

the organization that evolved from the Cercle des XX in 1893. His many exhibition posters for this group feature intense color and pushed the art nouveau arabesque into an almost mechanical, tense line (Fig. **11–59**).

Nieuwe Kunst in the Netherlands spanned roughly the 14 years between 1892 through 1906. Through Nieuwe Kunst many young Dutch artists sought new vistas with energy and enthusiasm, encouraged by fresh, optimistic, and progressive ideals. They brought about an important artistic revival in the Netherlands that provided the seeds for future movements such as De Stijl, art deco, and what is now known as the Wendingen style.

The book was one of the principal expressive mediums of Nieuwe Kunst. Some special qualities of the movement's book design are unpredictability, eccentricity, openness, and innovation. It also reflects a love for order and geometry, balanced by a penchant for the primitive and independence from accepted norms.

In comparison to art nouveau book design in other European countries, Nieuwe Kunst was more playful and diverse. Although they ignored the actual relationship of plant and flower forms to the picture plane, some artists were faithful to nature in depicting these forms. Eventually there

11–60

11–61

emerged an abstract approach where undulating and swerving lines were united into intricate patterns. After 1895, mathematics was seen as a creative source in itself, with symmetry and rationalism each playing a part.

Of particular importance to the Nieuwe Kunst movement were influences from the Dutch East Indies (now Indonesia). The Dutch had a bond with their overseas colonies that was quite different from that of other colonial powers. Dutch artists readily assimilated East Indian motifs and techniques.

The interest in natural and mathematical forms engendered a number of books on adapting these to stylized decoration. One of the most popular was *Driehoeken bij ontwerpen van ornament* (Triangles in the Design of Ornament), by J. H. de Groot, a teacher at the Quellinus arts and crafts school in Amsterdam, and his sister Jacoba M. de Groot. Published in a large edition in 1896, it reached a broad audience and exerted much influence. Providing artists with vivid instructions for the construction of abstract forms based on nature, in fifty plates accompanied by descriptive texts it demonstrated that almost any imaginable figure could be created from variations of 30- and 45-degree triangles. It is no coincidence that theosophy, where geometry is seen as an ordering principle of the cosmos, was popular in the Netherlands during this period (Fig. **11–60**).

The introduction of batik as a contemporary design medium was one of the important contributions of the Netherlands to the international art nouveau movement. Batik-making had long been a traditional craft for women in the Dutch East Indies. The lush and organic designs of Javanese batik greatly inspired artists such as Chris Lebeau and Jan Toorop, and this flat-pattern design soon evolved into a distinctive Dutch national style.

Chris Lebeau produced some of the most striking and complex designs in batik and was successful in assimilating traditional patterns and colors of the East Indies into his own work. In 1900 the publisher Lambertus Jacobus Veen commissioned Lebeau to design the binding for *De stille kracht* (The Quiet Power), the most heavily East Indian of all the novels by The Hague writer Louis Couperus (Fig. **11–61**). In October 1900, the definitive design for *De stille kracht* was produced in batik and then stamped in gold before being made into the binding. On the back both the binder and the batik studio are cited, an unusual gesture in this period. Although the design suggests flowers, it was actually made according to a mathematical system based on diamond shapes. *De stille kracht* was a large edition that reached thousands of readers, and as a result Lebeau and Veen were largely responsible for the popularity of batik in the Netherlands.

11–62

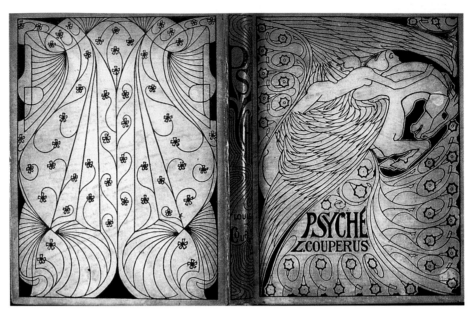

11–63

Jan Toorop (1858–1928) was born on the Dutch East Indies island of Java and at the age of thirteen left to study in the Netherlands. He eventually studied at the polytechnic school at Delft, the Amsterdam Academy, and the École des Arts Décoratifs in Brussels. For Toorop Javanese culture was a natural source of inspiration. His use of the silhouette, his linear style, and the forms, expressions, and hair styles of his female figures are derived from Javanese wajan shadow puppets. This Javanese influence is clear in his 1895 poster for Delftsche Slaolie (Delft Salad Oil), dominated by two enigmatic female figures, a design that brought him acclaim in decorative art circles (Fig. **11–62**).

Veen was a personal friend of Toorop and gave him many binding commissions. His 1898 binding for *Psyche*, one of the many designs for Couperus, shows his skill in combining text with illustration. The design is filled with Toorop's "whiplash" lines, and the lettering, especially on the spine, blends in with the illustration (Fig. **11–63**).

And last, there were those exacting designers who found refuge in the familiar solidity of geometry. Here decorative ornaments are derived predominantly from mathematics, and books such as *Driehoeken bij ontwerpen van ornament* were sources of inspiration. An outstanding example is *De vrouwen kwestie, haar historische ontwikkeling en haar economische kant* (The Woman Question, Her Historical Development and Her Economical Side), by Lily Braun, designed in 1902 by S. H. de Roos (Fig. **11–64**).

By 1903, the glory and excitement of the experimental period of nieuwe kunst showed clear signs of having run its course as the movement assumed an established form, and by 1910 nieuwe kunst had sadly digressed into mainly vapid commercial devices. In the end, the original discoveries were taken over by those who only saw their superficial appeal and continued to exploit them as fashionable decorative styles, easy to manipulate and applicable to almost any goal.

The German Jugendstil movement

When art nouveau arrived in Germany, as mentioned earlier, it was called *Jugendstil* (youth style) after a new magazine, *Jugend* (Youth), that began publication in Munich in 1896. From Munich, Jugendstil spread to Berlin, Darmstadt, and all over Germany. German art nouveau had strong French and British influences, but it still retained strong links to traditional academic art. The German interest in medieval letterforms—Germany was the only European country that did not replace Gutenberg's textura type with the roman styles of the Renaissance—continued side by side with art nouveau motifs.

During *Jugend*'s first year, its circulation climbed to thirty thousand copies per week, and the magazine soon attracted a readership of 200,000 per week. Art nouveau ornaments and illustrations were on virtually every editorial page. Full double-page illustrations, horizontal illustrations across the top of a page, and decorative art nouveau designs brought rich variety to a format that was about half visual material

11–64

11–65

11–66

and half text. One unprecedented editorial policy was to allow each week's cover designer to design a masthead to go with the cover design (Fig. **11–65**). Over the course of a year, the *Jugend* logo appeared variously as giant textura letters, tendrilous art nouveau lettering, or just as the word *Jugend* set in twenty-four-point typography above the image because that week's designer had ignored or forgotten the need to include the logotype in the design. In the cover design for October 1899 by Hans Christiansen (1866–1945), a leading artist associated with *Jugend*, the simple, sans-serif letterforms are drawn in constrained, pale colors (Fig. **11–66**); the images are contrasting planes of warm and cool colors. Large-scale ornamentation ranged from Peter Behrens's (1868–1940) abstract designs (Fig. **11–67**) inspired by ancient Egyptian artifacts to stylized floral designs (Fig. **11–68**)

Along with Otto Eckmann (1865–1902), Behrens became widely known for large, multicolor woodblock prints (Fig. **11–69**) inspired by French art nouveau and the Japanese print. In addition to five cover illustrations and numerous decorative borders for *Jugend*, Eckmann designed jewelry, objects, furniture, women's fashions, and an important typeface called Eckmannschrift. He became a designer and consultant for the Allgemeine Elektrizitäts-Gesellschaft (General Electric Company), or AEG, and explored the application of Jugendstil ornament to the graphic and product needs of industry (Fig. **11–70**).

The Klingspor Foundry was the first German typefoundry to commission new fonts from artists, and in 1900 it released

11–62. Jan Toorop, poster for Delftsche Slaolie (Delft Salad Oil), 1894. Printed in yellow and lavender, this poster becomes kinetic through its undulating linear rhythms and close-valued complementary colors.

11–63. Jan Toorop, binding for *Psyche,* by Louis Couperus, published by L. J. Veen, Amsterdam, 1898. *Psyche* is a symbolic, tragic, and erotic fairy tale of Princess Psyche, Prince Eros, and the winged stallion Chimera. Psyche was a princess from the Land of Today and longed for the Land of Tomorrow. She was born with two useless little wings with which she wished to soar to other realms. One day while at her father's palace, she saw in the ephemeral cloud shapes a knight on the blond winged steed called Chimera. As depicted on the binding, Chimera eventually became reality and in Psyche's death carried her off through the wind and stars to the lands of her dreams.

11–64. S. H. de Roos, design for *De vrouwen kwestie, haar historische ontwikkeling en haar economische kant* (The Woman Question, Her Historical Development and Her Economical Side), by Lily Braun, published by A. B. Soep, Amsterdam, 1902.

11–65. Otto Eckmann, *Jugend* cover, 1896. Jugendstil graphics often blended curvilinear stylization with traditional realism.

11–66. Hans Christiansen, *Jugend* cover, 1899. The stylized curves of the letterforms echo the curves of the illustration's flat shapes.

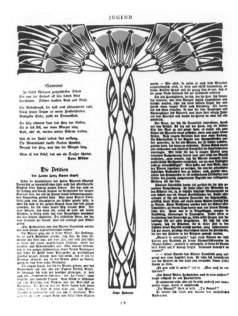

11–67

11–68

11–69

11–70

11–71

Eckmann's Eckmannschrift (Fig. **11–71**; see also Fig. 12–32), which created a sensation and thrust this small regional foundry into international prominence. Drawn with a brush instead of a pen, Eckmannschrift was a conscious attempt to revitalize typography by combining medieval and roman. As the new century opened, Eckmann seemed poised to play a major role in the further evolution of design, but in 1902 this thirty-seven-year-old designer succumbed to the tuberculosis that had plagued him for years.

In addition to his work for *Jugend*, Peter Behrens experi-

mented with ornaments and vignettes of abstract design through two other publications, *Der Bunte Vogel* and *Die Insel*. He became artistic advisor to *Die Insel* and its publisher, Insel-Verlag, for which he designed one of the finest Jugendstil trademarks (Fig. **11–72**). *Die Insel* was not illustrated, and Behrens gave it a consistent typographic format and program using Old Style typefaces.

The primary German contribution was not Jugendstil, however, but the innovations that developed in reaction to it after the turn of the century as architects and designers, including

11–72

11–74

11–73

Peter Behrens, became influenced by the ideals of the Arts and Crafts movement, purged of its medieval affectations. Designers in Germany, Scotland, and Austria moved rapidly from the floral phase of art nouveau toward a more geometric and objective approach. This accompanied a shift from swirling organic line and form to a geometric ordering of space. (The birth of this modernist design sensibility is discussed in chapter 12.)

The Italian pictorial tradition

At the turn of the century, Italian posters were characterized by a sensuous exuberance and elegance rivaling that of *la belle epoque* in France. For twenty-five years, the Milan firm of Giulio Ricordi, previously known for publishing opera librettos, produced most of the masterpieces of Italian poster design. Ricordi's director was the German born Adolfo Hohenstein (1854–1928), and like Chéret in France, Hohenstein is seen as the father of poster design in Italy (Fig. **11–73**). Working under him were some of the best poster artists in Italy, including Leopoldo Metlicovitz (1868–1944) (Fig. **11–74**), Giovanni Mataloni (1869–1944)

11–67. Peter Behrens, page design for *Jugend,* 1904. Evoking peacock feathers and Egyptian lotus designs, an abstract column rises between two columns of textura-inspired type.

11–68. Hans Christiansen, page design for *Jugend,* 1899. Decorative motifs created lyrical environments for poetry.

11–69. Peter Behrens, *The Kiss,* 1898. This six-color woodcut, controversial for its androgynous imagery, was first reproduced in *Pan* magazine.

11–70. Otto Eckmann, cover for an Allgemeine Elektrizitäts-Gesellschaft catalogue, 1900. Brush-drawn lettering and ornaments express the kinetic energy of electricity.

11–71. Otto Eckmann, title page for *Eckmann Schriftprobe,* 1901. The blending of contradictory influences—medieval, oriental, and art nouveau—produced a wildly popular typeface.

11–72. Peter Behrens, trademark for Insel-Verlag, 1899. The ship in a circle perched on art nouveau waves typifies *Jugendstil* trademark design.

11–73. Adolfo Hohenstein, Bitter Campari poster, 1901.

11–74. Leopoldo Metlicovitz, Calzaturificio di Varese poster, 1913. This classic Metlicovitz poster exudes an optimistic elegance.

11–75

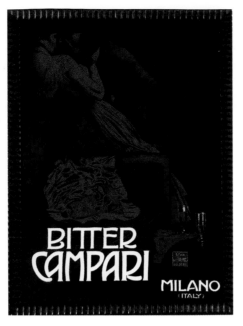

11–76

11–77

11–78

11–75. Giovanni Mataloni, Brevetto Auer poster, 1895.

11–76. Marcello Dudovich, Bitter Campari poster, 1901. The message is unambiguous as Dudovich equates sensual pleasure with that derived from Bitter Campari.

11–77. Franz Laskoff, Monte Tabor poster, 1900.

11–78. Leonetto Capiello, E.A. Mele & C. poster, 1903.

(Fig. **11–75**), and Marcello Dudovich (1878–1962) (Fig. **11–76**). Dudovich was an eclectic designer who eventually arrived at a unique colorful style. Like Hohlwein in Germany, he preferred elegant subjects presented in flat areas of color. Together with artists such as the Polish-born Franz Laskoff (1869–1918) (Fig. **11-77**) and Leonetto Capiello (1875–1942) (Fig. **11–78**), he was a popular designer for the fashionable Mele department store in Naples, an important Ricordi client that commissioned over 120 posters.

The English art historian Herbert Read once suggested that the life of any art movement is like that of a flower. A budding

in the hands of a small number of innovators is followed by full bloom; then the process of decay begins as the influence becomes diffused and distorted in the hands of imitators who understand merely the stylistic manifestations of the movement rather than the driving passions that forged it. After the turn of the century, this was the fate of art nouveau. Early art nouveau objects and furniture had been primarily one-of-a-kind or limited-edition items. But as the design of posters and periodicals brought art nouveau to an ever-widening circle, far greater quantities were produced. Some manufacturers focused on the bottom line by turning out vast amounts of merchandise and graphics with lower design standards. Lesser talents copied the style, while many innovators moved on in other directions. Art nouveau slowly declined until it vanished in the ashes of World War I, the political and nationalist forces thrusting Europe toward global war having made its aesthetic *joie de vie* irrelevant.

Art nouveau's legacy is a tracery of the dreams and lifestyles of a brief Indian summer in the human saga. Its offspring were twentieth-century designers who adopted not its surface appearance, but its attitudes toward materials, processes, and value.

The Genesis of Twentieth Century Design

12

The turn of a century invites introspection. As one century closes and a new one begins, writers and artists begin to question conventional wisdom and speculate on new possibilities for changing the circumstances of culture. For example, the end of the eighteenth century gave birth to a new category of typeface design, which is still called the modern style (see Figs. 8–17, 8–18, and 8–19) two hundred years later. At that same time, the neoclassical revival of Greco-Roman forms in architecture, clothing, painting, and illustration (see Fig. 8–20) replaced baroque and rococo design. As the nineteenth century drew to a close and the twentieth century began, designers across the disciplines of architectural, fashion, graphic, and product design searched for new forms of expression. Technological and industrial advances fed these concerns. The new design vocabulary of art nouveau had challenged the conventions of Victorian design. Art nouveau proved that inventing new forms, rather than copying forms from nature or historical models, was a viable approach. The potential of abstract and reductive drawing and design was explored by designers in Scotland, Austria, and Germany who moved away from the serpentine beauty of organic drawing as they sought a new aesthetic philosophy to address the changing social, economic, and cultural conditions at the turn of a century.

Frank Lloyd Wright and the Glasgow School

During the final years of the nineteenth century, the work of the American architect Frank Lloyd Wright (1867–1959) was becoming known to European artists and designers. Clearly, he was an inspiration for the designers evolving from curvilinear art nouveau toward a rectilinear approach to spatial organization. In 1893 Wright began his independent practice. He rejected historicism in favor of a philosophy of "organic architecture," with "the reality of the building" existing not in the design of the facade but in dynamic interior spaces where people lived and worked. Wright defined organic design as having *entity*, "something in which the part is to the whole as the whole is to the part, and which is all devoted to a purpose. . . . It seeks that completeness in idea in execution that is absolutely *true* to method, *true* to purpose, *true* to character."

Wright saw *space* as the essence of design, and this emphasis was the wellspring of his profound influence upon all areas of twentieth-century design. He looked to Japanese architecture and design for a model of harmonious proportion and visual poetry; in pre-Columbian architecture and art he found lively ornament restrained by a mathematical repetition of horizontal and vertical spatial divisions. Wright's repetition of rectangular zones and use of asymmetrical spatial organization were adopted by other designers. In addition to architecture, his design interests included furniture, graphics, fabrics, wallpapers, and stained-glass windows (see Fig. 15–1). At the turn of the century he was at the forefront of the emerging modern movement.

As a young man, Wright operated a basement printing press with a close friend. This experience taught him to incorporate white or blank space as an element in his designs, to establish and work within parameters, and to combine varied materials into a unified whole. During his long career, Wright periodically turned his hand to graphic design. Throughout the winter of 1896–97, Wright collaborated with William H. Winslow in the production of *The House Beautiful* (Fig. **12–1**), by Rev. William C. Gannett, printed on a handpress using handmade paper at the Auvergne Press in an edition of ninety copies. Wright's border designs were executed in a fragile freehand line describing a lacy pattern of stylized plant forms.

The Studio and its reproductions of work by Beardsley and Toorop had a strong influence on a group of young Scottish artists who became friends at the Glasgow School of Art in the early 1890s. Headmaster Francis H. Newbery pointed out affinities between the work of two architectural apprentices taking evening classes—Charles Rennie Mackintosh (1868–1928) and J. Herbert McNair (1868–1955)—and the work of two day students—sisters Margaret (1865–1933) and Frances Macdonald (1874–1921). The four students began to collaborate and were soon christened "The Four." Artistic collaboration and friendship led to matrimony, for in 1899 McNair married Frances Macdonald. The following year, Mackintosh and Margaret Macdonald married.

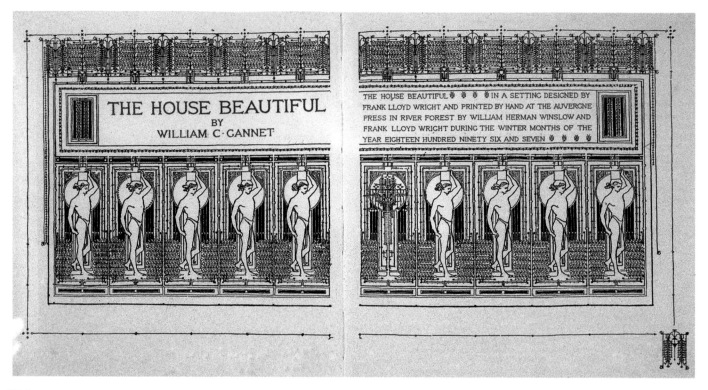

12–1

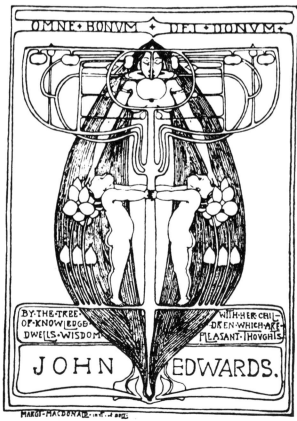

12–2

These young collaborators, more widely known as the Glasgow School, developed a unique style of lyrical originality and symbolic complexity. They innovated a geometric style of composition by tempering floral and curvilinear elements with strong rectilinear structure. The Macdonald sisters held strong religious beliefs and embraced symbolist and mystical ideas. The confluence of architectural structure with the sisters' world of fantasy and dreams produced an unprecedented transcendental style that has been variously described as feminine, a fairyland fantasy, and a melancholy disquietude.

Designs by The Four are distinguished by symbolic imagery (Fig. **12–2**) and stylized form. Bold, simple lines define flat planes of color. A poster for the Glasgow Institute of the Fine Arts (Fig. **12–3**), designed by Margaret and Frances Macdonald in collaboration with J. Herbert McNair, demonstrates the rising verticality and integration of flowing curves with rectangular structure that are hallmarks of their mature work. Abstract interpretations of the human figure, such as Mackintosh's Scottish Musical Review poster (Fig. **12–4**), had not been seen in Scotland before; many observers were outraged. But the editor of *The Studio* was so impressed that he visited Glasgow and published two articles on the new group in 1897. He reminded *Studio* readers, "The purpose of a poster is to attract notice, and the mildest eccentricity would not be out of place provided it aroused curiosity and so riveted the attention of passers-by. . . .

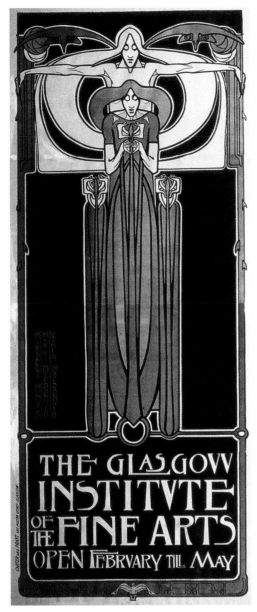

12–3

12–1. Frank Lloyd Wright, title page for *The House Beautiful*, 1896–97. An underlying geometric structure imposed a strong order upon the intricacy of Wright's textural design

12–2. Margaret Macdonald, bookplate design, 1896. Reproduced in *Ver Sacrum* in 1901 as part of an article on the Glasgow group, this design depicts Wisdom protecting her children within the leaflike shelter of her hair before a symbolic tree of knowledge, whose linear structure is based on Macdonald's metalwork.

12–3. Margaret and Frances Macdonald with J. Herbert McNair, poster for the Glasgow Institute of the Fine Arts, 1895. The symbolic figures have been assigned both religious and romantic interpretations.

12–4. Charles Rennie Mackintosh, poster for *The Scottish Musical Review,* 1896. In this towering image that rises 2.46 meters (over 8 feet) above the spectator, complex overlapping planes are unified by areas of flat color. The white ring and birds around the figure create a strong focal point.

12–4

12–5

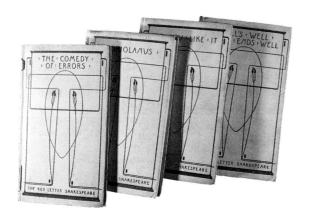

12–6

12–7

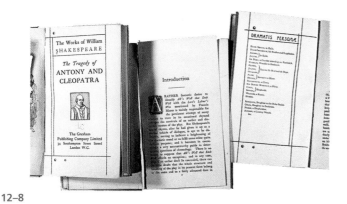

12–8

12–5. Jessie Marion King, double title pages for William Morris's *The Defence of Guenevere,* 1904. Vigorous energy and fragile delicacy, seemingly contradictory qualities, characterize King's work.

12–6. Talwin Morris, bindings for the Red Letter Shakespeare series, c. 1908. A standardized format and subtle graphic lyricism were achieved in economical commercial editions.

12–7. Talwin Morris, page ornaments from the Red Letter Shakespeare series, c. 1908. The name for this small, modestly priced set derives from its two-color printing with character names in red. Between the introduction and the play, each volume had a graceful black ornament with a red oval.

12–8. Talwin Morris, pages from the Red Letter Shakespeare series, c. 1908. The standard format used rigorous linear structures and graceful ornamented capitals.

There is so much decorative method in his perversion of humanity that despite all the ridicule and abuse it has excited, it is possible to defend his treatment." German and Austrian artists learned of Glasgow's countermovement to mainstream art nouveau through these articles. The Four were celebrated on the continent, particularly in Vienna, but often ignored in the British Isles. In 1896 the organizers at the annual Arts and Crafts Exhibition in London invited them to participate. So dismayed were the hosts, however, that no further invitations were extended.

Mackintosh made notable contributions to the new century's architecture, and major accomplishments were realized in the design of objects, chairs, and interiors as total environments. The Four pioneered interior designs with white walls bathed in light and furnished with a few carefully placed pieces, in contrast to the complex interiors prevailing at the time. Mackintosh's main design theme is rising vertical lines, often with subtle curves at the ends to temper their junction with the horizontals. Tall and thin rectangular shapes and the counterpoint of right angles against ovals, circles, and arcs characterize his work. In his furniture, simple structure is accented with delicate decorative ornaments. In the interior designs, every small detail was carefully designed to be visually compatible with the whole. The work of The Four and their influence on the Continent became important transitions to the aesthetic of the twentieth century.

Among those who drew inspiration from The Four, Jessie Marion King (1876–1949) achieved a distinctive personal statement (Fig. **12–5**) with medieval-style fantasy illustrations accompanied by stylized lettering. Her grace, fluidity, and romantic overtones widely influenced fiction illustration throughout the twentieth century. Newbery recognized the poetic nature of King's work; in lieu of conventional drawing courses, he wisely assigned her independent study to nurture her emerging individuality. After working in architectural offices and serving as assistant art director for *Black and White* magazine in London, Talwin Morris (1865–1911) became art director of the Glasgow publishing firm of Blackie's after answering an 1893 want ad in the *London Times*. Shortly after moving to Glasgow, Morris established contact with The Four and embraced their ideas. Blackie's—a volume printer of large editions of popular books for the mass market, including novels, reprints, and encyclopedias—provided Morris with a forum for applying the geometric spatial division and lyrical organic forms of the Glasgow group to mass communications.

Morris often developed formats for series that could be used over and over again with subtle variations (Figs. **12–6**, **12–7**, and **12–8**). The sheer volume of his work was a major factor in introducing the English public to the emerging ideas and visual forms of modern architecture and design.

The Vienna Secession

In Austria, *Sezessionstil*, or the Vienna Secession, came into being on 3 April 1897, when the younger members of the Künstlerhaus, the Viennese Creative Artists' Association, resigned in stormy protest. Technically, the refusal to allow foreign artists to participate in Künstlerhaus exhibitions was the main issue, but the clash between tradition and new ideas emanating from France, England, and Germany lay at the heart of the conflict, and the young artists wanted to exhibit more frequently. Painter Gustav Klimt (1862–1918) was the guiding spirit who led the revolt; architects Joseph Maria Olbrich (1867–1908) and Josef Hoffmann (1870–1956) and artist-designer Koloman Moser (1868–1918) were key members. Like the Glasgow School, the Vienna Secession became a countermovement to the floral art nouveau that flourished in other parts of Europe.

Benchmark posters for the Vienna Secession's exhibitions demonstrate the group's rapid evolution from the illustrative allegorical style of symbolist painting (Fig. **12–9**) to a French-inspired floral style (Fig. **12–10**) to the mature Vienna Secession style (see Fig. 12–23), which drew inspiration from the Glasgow School. (Compare, for instance, Figure 12–3 and Figure 12–4 with Figure 12–23.) Figure 12–9 is the first Vienna Secession exhibition poster. Klimt referred to Greek mythology to show Athena, goddess of the arts, watching Theseus deliver the deathblow to the Minotaur. Athena and her shield, which depicts Medusa, form simultaneous profile and frontal symbolic images. This is an allegory of the struggle between the Secession and the Künstlerhaus. The trees were overprinted later after the male nude outraged the Vienna police, but this controversy only fueled public interest in the artists' revolt. Figure 12–10, by Moser, demonstrates how quickly the central idealized figures and swooping floral forms of French art nouveau were absorbed. A major difference is the Secession artists' love of clean, simple, sans serif lettering, ranging from flat, blocky slabs to fluidly calligraphic forms.

For a brief period, as the new century opened, Vienna was the center for creative innovation in the final blossoming of art nouveau, as represented by the Vienna Secession's elegant *Ver Sacrum* (Sacred Spring), published from 1898 until 1903. *Ver Sacrum* was more a design laboratory than a magazine. A continuously changing editorial staff, design responsibility handled by a rotating committee of artists, and unpaid contributions of art and design were all focused on experimentation and graphic excellence. In 1900 the journal had only three hundred subscribers and a press run of six hundred copies, but it enabled designers to develop innovative graphics as they explored the merger of text, illustration, and ornament into a lively unity.

The magazine had an unusual square format: The 1898–99 issues were 28 by 28.5 centimeters (11 by 11¼ inches) and the

12–9

12–10

12–9. Gustav Klimt, poster for the first Vienna Secession exhibition, 1898. The large open space in the center is unprecedented in Western graphic design.

12–10. Koloman Moser, fifth Vienna Secession exhibition poster, 1899. A metallic gold bronze figure and olive green background are printed on yellow tone paper that forms the contour lines.

12-11. Alfred Roller, cover design for *Ver Sacrum,* initial issue, 1898. Roller used an illustration of a tree whose growth destroyed its pot, allowing it to take root in firmer soil, to symbolize the Secession.

12–12. Alfred Roller, cover design for *Ver Sacrum,* 1898. A stipple drawing of leaves becomes a frame for the lettering, which sits in a square that gives the impression of a collage element.

1900–03 issues were reduced to 23 by 24.5 centimeters (9 by 9¾ inches). Secession artists preferred vigorous linear art, and *Ver Sacrum* covers often combined hand-lettering with bold line drawing (Figs. **12–11**, **12–12**, and **12–13**) printed in color on a colored background. Decorative ornaments, borders, headpieces (Fig. **12–14** and Fig. **12–15**), and tailpieces were used generously, but the overall page layouts (Fig. **12–16**) were refined and concise, thanks to ample margins and careful horizontal and vertical alignment of elements into a unified whole.

Ver Sacrum's use of white space in page layouts, sleek-coated stock, and unusual production methods achieved an original visual elegance. Color plates were tipped in, and 55 original etchings and lithographs as well as 216 original woodcuts were bound into the issues during the magazine's six years of publication. Sometimes signatures were printed in color combinations, including muted brown and blue-gray, blue and green, brown with red-orange, and chocolate with gold. When signatures were bound together, four colors, instead of two, appeared on the double spreads. The Vienna Secession artists did not hesitate to experiment: A poem was printed in metallic gold ink on translucent paper; a photograph of an interior was printed in scarlet ink; and in one

12–11   12–12   12–13

12–14

12–15

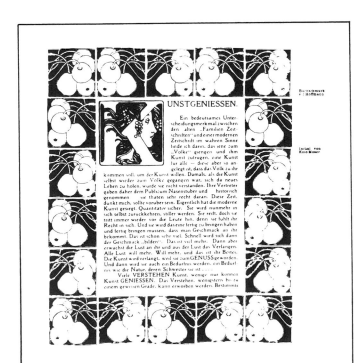

12–16

12–13. Koloman Moser, cover design for *Ver Sacrum,* 1899. A stencil-effect technique for creating images has an affinity, in its reduction of the subject to black and white planes, with high-contrast photography.

12–14. Josef Hoffmann, headpiece from the premiere issue of *Ver Sacrum,* 1898. Berries, drawn in the free contour line favored by many Secession artists, flow around a plaque that proclaims "Association of Visual Artists of Austria. Secession."

12–15. Joseph Olbrich, frame for *Ver Sacrum* article title, 1899. The fluid repetition of forms and symmetry in this decorative botanical frame, with its dense black color, bring lively contrast to the typographic page.

12–16. Josef Hoffmann (border) and Koloman Moser (initial), page from *Ver Sacrum,* 1898. Hoffmann's modular berry motif and Moser's figurative initial combine to produce an elegant page.

12–17

12–18

12–19

12–20

issue, a linear design by Koloman Moser was embossed on silky-smooth coated white stock in what may have been the first white-on-white embossed graphic design.

Design aesthetics were so important that advertisers were required to commission their advertising designs (Fig. **12–17**) from the artists and designers contributing to each issue to ensure a visual design unity. The exceptional linear and geometric design elements gracing *Ver Sacrum*'s pages became an important design resource as the Vienna Secession style evolved.

Editorial content included articles about artists and their work, poems contributed by leading writers of the day (Figs. **12–18** and **12–19**), and an illustrated monthly calendar (Fig. **12–20**). Critical essays were published, including a famous article entitled "Potemkin City" by the polemic Austrian architect Adolf Loos (1870–1933). Because Viennese building façades were cast-concrete fronts mimicking Renaissance and baroque palaces, Loos accused Vienna of being like the artificial towns of canvas and pasteboard erected in the Ukraine to deceive the Russian empress Catherine. All areas of design were challenged by Loos, whose other writings roundly condemned both historicism and *Sezessionstil* as he called for a functional simplicity that banished "useless decoration in any form." Standing alone at the turn of the century, Loos blasted the nineteenth-century love of decoration and abhorrence of empty spaces. To him, "organic" meant not curvilinear but the use of human needs as a standard for measuring utilitarian form.

12–17. Alfred Roller, Koloman Moser, and Frederick Koenig, inside front cover advertisements for *Ver Sacrum,* 1899. All of the ads and the makeup of the whole page are carefully designed to avoid the graphic clutter and clash usually present when small ads are clustered together.

12–18. Adolf Bohm, page from *Ver Sacrum,* 1898. The lyrical contours of trees reflected on a lake provide an appropriate environment for a poem about autumn trees.

12–19. Koloman Moser, illustration of a duchess and a page for R. M. Rilke's poem "Vorfrühling" (Early Spring) from *Ver Sacrum,* 1901. Elemental geometric forms are repeated, building complex kinetic patterns

12–20. Alfred Roller (designer and illustrator), *Ver Sacrum* calendar for November 1903. An exuberant border brackets a seasonal illustration, "Letzte Blätter" (Last Leaves), and hand-lettered, rectangular numbers and letters.

While the personal monograms by Secession artists convey a communal aesthetic (Fig. **12–21**), various members specialized in one or more disciplines: architecture, crafts, graphic design, interior design, painting, printmaking, and sculpture. Moser played a major role in defining the approach to graphic design. His Fromme's Calendar poster (Fig. **12–22**) combined mystical symbols with simplified two-dimensional space. The transcendental overtones of the Glasgow School yielded to a fascination

12–21

12–22

12–23

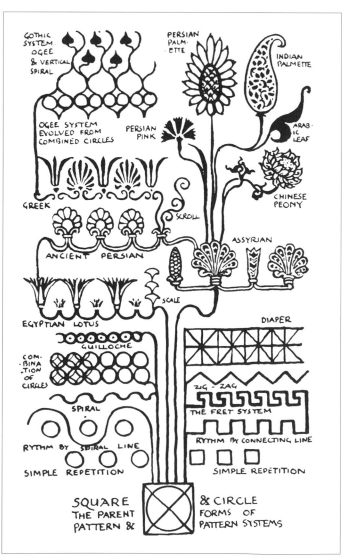

12–24

12–25

with geometry. Moser's poster (Fig. **12–23**) for the thirteenth Vienna Secession exhibition is a masterpiece of the mature phase. This evolution toward elemental geometric form was diagrammed by Walter Crane in his book *Line and Form* (Fig. **12–24**). When Vienna Secession artists rejected the French floral style, they turned toward flat shapes and greater simplicity. Design and craft became increasingly important as this metamorphosis culminated in an emphasis on geometric patterning and modular design construction. The resulting design language used squares, rectangles, and circles in repetition and combination. Decoration and the application of ornament depended on similar elements used in parallel, nonrhythmic sequence. This geometry was not mechanical and rigid but subtly organic.

Alfred Roller (1864–1935) made significant innovations in graphic design with a masterly control of complex line, tone, and form (Fig. **12–25**). A set designer and scene painter for theater, Roller's principal work as a graphic designer and illustrator was for *Ver Sacrum* and Secession exhibition posters. Cubism and art deco are anticipated in his 1902 poster for the fourteenth Vienna Secession exhibition (Fig. **12–26**). His poster for the sixteenth exhibition, later that same year (Fig. **12–27**), sacrificed legibility in order to achieve an unprecedented textural density. Berthold Löffler (1874–1960) also anticipated later developments with his reductive symbolic images of thick contours and simple geometric features. Figures in his posters and illustrations became elemental significations rather than depictions (Fig. **12–28**).

By the turn of the century, both Moser and Hoffmann had been appointed to the faculty of the Vienna School for Applied Art. Their ideas about clean, geometric design, formed when they stripped the Glasgow influence of its virgins, symbolic roses, and mystical overtones, captured the imagination of their students. With financing from the industrialist Fritz Wärndorfer, Hoffmann and Moser launched the Wiener Werkstätte (Vienna Workshops) in 1903 (Figs. **12–29** and **12–30**). An outgrowth of Sezessionstil, this spiritual continuum of Morris's workshops sought a close union of the fine and applied arts in the design of lamps, fabrics, and similar objects for everyday use, including books, greeting cards, and other printed matter (Fig. **12–31**). Originally formed to produce designs by Moser and Hoffmann, the Vienna Workshops flourished, and many other collaborators participated. The goal was to offer an alternative to poorly designed, mass-produced articles and trite historicism. Function, honesty to materials, and harmonious proportion were important concerns; decoration was used only when it served these goals and did not violate them. Master carpenters, bookbinders, metalsmiths, and leatherworkers were employed to work with the designers in the effort to elevate crafts to the standards of fine arts. Moser left the Vienna Workshops in 1907, and his death at age fifty in 1918 cut short the career of a major design innovator.

After 1910 the creative momentum in Vienna declined. But the gulf between nineteenth-century ornament and art nouveau on the one hand and the rational functionalism and geometric formalism of the twentieth century on the other had been bridged. The Vienna Workshops survived the chaos of World War I and flourished until the Depression era, when financial difficulties forced their closing in 1932.

12–28

12–26. Alfred Roller, poster for the fourteenth Vienna Secession exhibition, 1902. Dense geometric patterns animate the space.

12–27. Alfred Roller, poster for the sixteenth Vienna Secession exhibition, 1902. Letters were reduced to curved corner rectangles with slashing curved lines to define each character.

12–28. Berthold Löffler, poster for a theater and cabaret, c. 1907. Masklike faces were simplified into elemental linear signs.

12–29. The registered trademark and monogram applied to products of the Vienna Workshops demonstrate the harmony of proportion, lyrical geometry, and clarity of form that characterize its designs.

12–30. Josef Hoffmann, Wiener Werkstätte exhibition poster, 1905. A repetitive blue geometric pattern was created by a hand-stencil technique after the lettering and two lower rectangles were printed by lithography. This lettering was combined with other patterns in an advertisement and other posters.

12–31. Josef Hoffmann, bookplate design, 1903. In a large series of figure studies, Hoffmann reduced the image to elongated contours and simple shapes signifying hair or hats.

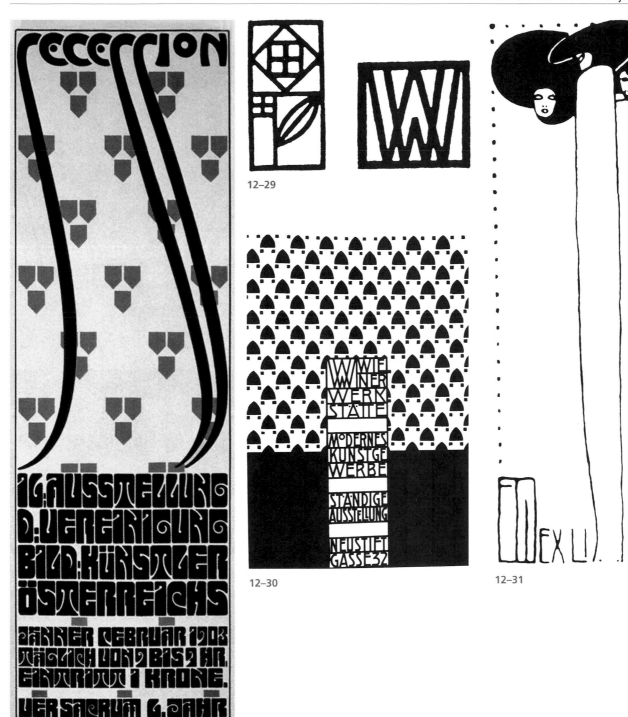

12–29

12–30

12–31

12–27

Peter Behrens and the New Objectivity

The German artist, architect, and designer Peter Behrens played a major role in charting a course for design in the first decade of the new century. He sought typographic reform, was an early advocate of sans-serif typography, and used a grid system to structure space in his design layouts. He has been called "the first industrial designer" in recognition of his designs for such manufactured products as streetlamps and teapots. His work for the Allgemeine Elektrizitäts-Gesellschaft,

or AEG, is considered the first comprehensive visual identification program. In architecture, his early buildings pioneered non-load-bearing glass curtain walls spanning the spaces between support girders.

Behrens was orphaned at age fourteen. The substantial inheritance from his father's estate provided financial autonomy, which assisted in the evolution of his work. He chose art for his career and studied in Hamburg, then moved to Munich, where a renaissance in German arts and crafts was

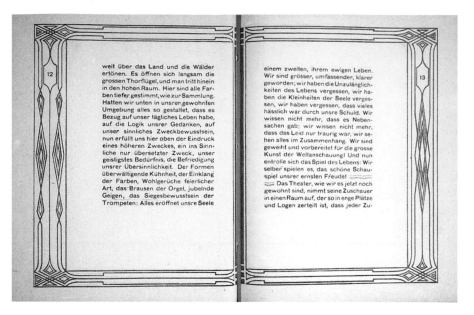

12–32

12–33

12–34

beginning. Although his early paintings were of the poor and the industrial landscape, Behrens later abandoned social realism and embraced the 1890s German Jugendstil movement.

In 1900 the grand duke of Hessen, who sought to "fuse art and life together," established a new Darmstadt artist's colony, hoping to encourage cultural and economic growth in light manufacturing, such as furniture and ceramics. The colony's seven artists, including Behrens and Vienna Secession architect Olbrich, all had experience in the applied arts. Each was granted land to build a home; Behrens designed his own house and all its furnishings, from furniture to cutlery and china, an important experiment in total design.

German art critics of the period were interested in the relationship of art and design forms to social, technical, and cultural conditions. Behrens was concerned about these issues as well and believed that, after architecture, typography provided "the most characteristic picture of a period, and the strongest testimonial of the spiritual progress" and "development of a people." His typographic experiments were a deliberate attempt to express the spirit of the new era. In 1900 Behrens set his twenty-five-page booklet, *Celebration of Life and Art: A Consideration of the Theater as the Highest Symbol of a Culture*, in sans-serif type (Fig. **12–32**). According to German typographic historian Hans Loubier, this booklet may

ABCDEFGHIJKLMNOPQRSTUVWXYZ
abcdefghijklmnopqrstuvwxyz

ABCDEFGHIJKLMNOPQRSTUVWXYZ
abcdefghijklmnopqrstuvwxyz

ABCDEFGHIJKLMNOPQRSTUVWXYZ
abcdefghijklmnopqrstuvwxyz

ABCDEFGHIJKLMNOPQRSTUVWX
abcdefghijklmnopqrstuvwxyz

12–35

12–32. Peter Behrens, text pages for *Celebration of Life and Art: A Consideration of the Theater as the Highest Symbol of a Culture,* 1900. Blue-gray borders and red initials surrounded by rust-colored decorations frame the unprecedented sans-serif running text.

12–33. Peter Behrens, title and dedication pages for *Celebration of Life and Art,* 1900. A sharp angularity characterizes the title page (left), framed by caryatids. On the right, a dedication to the Darmstadt artists' colony is ornamented with controlled curvilinear rhythms.

12–34. Peter Behrens, cover for *Dokumente des Modernen Kunstgewerbes . . .* (Documents of Modern Applied Arts . . .), 1901. This decorative geometric design and sans-serif lettering based on a square foreshadow art deco design of the 1920s and 1930s.

12–35. Berthold Foundry, Akzidenz Grotesk typefaces, 1898–1906. An elegant system of weight contrast is achieved in these pioneering letterforms.

12–36. Typefaces released by the Klingspor Type Foundry. Top to bottom: Otto Eckmann's Eckmannschrift, 1900; Peter Behrens's Behrensschrift, an attempt to innovate typographic forms for the new era, 1901; Behrens Kursiv, Behrens's italic version of Behrensschrift, 1907; Behrens Antiqua, his attempt to recapture the clarity and authority of Roman inscriptions, 1908; and Behrens Medieval, his personal interpretation of Renaissance forms, 1913.

12–36

represent the first use of sans-serif type as running book text. Furthermore, all-capital sans-serif type is used in an unprecedented way on the title and dedication pages (Fig. **12–33**). The following year Behrens explored formal geometric design motifs with modular sans-serif characters based on a square (Fig. **12–34**).

Behrens was not alone in his interest in sans-serif typography at the turn of the century. The Berthold Foundry designed a family of ten sans serifs that were variations on one original font. This Akzidenz Grotesk (called Standard in the United States) type family (Fig. **12–35**) had a major influence on twentieth-century typography. In addition to the four weights shown in Figure 12–35, Berthold released three expanded and three condensed versions. Akzidenz Grotesk permitted compositors to achieve contrast and emphasis within one family of typefaces. It was a major step in the evolution of the uni-

fied and systematized type family. The designers of Akzidenz Grotesk achieved a remarkable harmony and clarity, and inspired the sans-serif typefaces of the post–World War II era.

A sense of urgency existed in the German art and design community. A new century was at hand, and the need to create new forms for a new era seemed pressing. Typographic reform was one of Behrens's major interests. After struggling with a conservative typefounder in an effort to develop a new typeface, Behrens contacted thirty-two-year-old Dr. Karl Klingspor (b. 1868) of the Klingspor Foundry. He agreed to manufacture and release Behrens's first typeface, Behrensschrift (Fig. **12–36**), in 1901. Klingspor had just enjoyed unexpected success with the wildly popular Eckmannschrift (Fig **12–36**; see also Fig. 11–71). Behrensschrift was an attempt to reduce any poetic flourish marking the forms, and so to make them more universal.

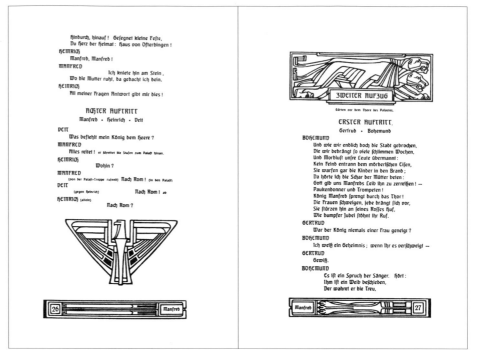

12–37

Unlike the ornate Victorian, art nouveau, and medieval typefaces dominating new type design at the time, Behrens standardized the strokes used to construct his letterforms. He consciously sought to innovate a typographic image for the new century and to create a uniquely German type by combining the heavy, condensed feeling of black letter, the letter proportions of roman inscriptions, and his standardized letterform construction. Horizontals and verticals are emphasized and diagonals replaced by curved strokes in letters such as *W* and *V.* Some typographic authorities were outraged by Behrensschrift, but its feather-stroke serifs and clarity, strikingly different from the dense black letter and ornate art nouveau typefaces used extensively in Germany at the time, made it a resounding success for both book (Fig. **12–37**) and job-printing typography. In the promotional booklet for Behrensschrift, Behrens compared the act of reading text type to "watching a bird's flight or the gallop of a horse. Both seem graceful and pleasing, but the viewer does not observe details of their form or movement. Only the rhythm of the lines is seen by the viewer, and the same is true of a typeface."

In 1903 Behrens moved to Düsseldorf to become director of the Düsseldorf School of Arts and Crafts. There, innovative preparatory courses preceded study in specific disciplines, such as architectural, graphic, and interior design. Behrens's purpose was to go back to the fundamental intellectual principles of all form-creating work, allowing such principles to be rooted in the artistically spontaneous and their inner laws of perception rather than directly in the mechanical aspects of the work. Students drew and painted natural forms in different media, then made analytical studies to explore linear movement, pattern, and geometric structure. These introductory courses were precursors for the Bauhaus Preliminary Course, where two of Behrens's apprentices, Walter Gropius and Ludwig Mies van der Rohe, served as directors.

A dramatic transformation occurred in Behrens's work in 1904, after the Dutch architect J. L. Mathieu Lauweriks (1864–1932) joined the Düsseldorf faculty. Lauweriks was fascinated by geometric form and had developed an approach to teaching design based on geometric composition. His grids began with a square circumscribed around a circle; numerous permutations could be made by subdividing and duplicating this basic structure (Fig. **12–38**). The geometric patterns thus developed could be used to determine proportions, dimensions, and spatial divisions in the design of everything from chairs to buildings (Fig. **12–39**) and graphics (Fig. **12–40**). Behrens's application of this theory proved catalytic in pushing twentieth-century architecture and design toward using rational geometry as an underlying system for visual organization. His work from this period is part of the tentative beginnings of constructivism in graphic design, where realistic or even stylized depictions are replaced by architectural and geometric structure. Sometimes Behrens used square formats, but more frequently he used rectangles in ratios such as 1 square wide by 1.5 or 2 squares high.

In 1907 Emil Rathenau, director of the AEG, appointed Behrens its artistic advisor. After Rathenau purchased

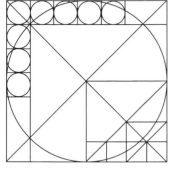

12–38

12–39

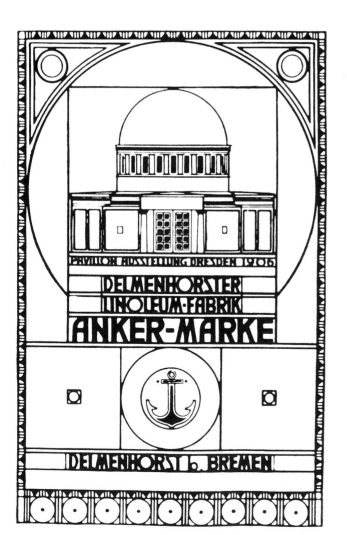

12–40

12–37. Peter Behrens, pages from *Manfred*, by Georg Fuchs, 1903. Behrensschrift is used systematically with headpieces, tailpieces, and folios.

12–38. These diagrams illustrate Dutch architect J. L. M. Lauweriks's compositional theory elaborating grid systems from a square circumscribed around a circle.

12–39. Peter Behrens, Anchor Linoleum exhibition pavilion, 1906. Classical forms and proportions are combined with mathematically derived geometric structure and pattern in a search for a twentieth-century language of form.

12–40. Peter Behrens, poster for the Anchor Linoleum exhibition pavilion, 1906. Lauweriks's grid theory is applied to graphic design.

European manufacturing rights to Thomas A. Edison's patents in 1883, the firm became one of the world's largest manufacturing concerns.

Rathenau was a visionary industrialist who sought to give a unified visual character to the company's products, environments, and communications. In 1907 the electrical industry was high technology; electric teakettles were as advanced as digital electronics are today. As design adviser to the AEG, Behrens began to focus on the design needs of industry, with responsibilities ranging from large buildings to stationery and electric fans.

The year 1907 also marked the founding, in Munich, of the Deutsche Werkbund (German Association of Craftsmen), which advocated a marriage of art with technology. Behrens

12–41

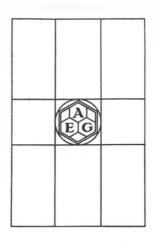

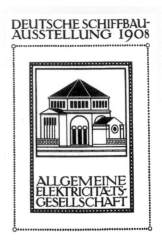

12–42

played a major role in this first organization created to inspire high-quality design in manufactured goods and architecture. The group's leaders, including Hermann Muthesius, Henry van de Velde, and Behrens, were influenced by William Morris and the English Arts and Crafts movement, but with significant differences: While Morris was repulsed by the products of the machine age and advocated a return to medieval craftsmanship in romantic protest against the industrial revolution, the Werkbund recognized the value of machines and advocated design as a way to give form and meaning to all machine-made things, including buildings.

With visionary zeal these designers advanced a philosophy of *Gesamkultur,* that is, a new universal culture existing in a totally reformed man-made environment. Design was seen as the engine that could propel society forward to achieve Gesamkultur. Soon after the Werkbund formed, two factions emerged. One, headed by Muthesius, argued for the maximum use of mechanical manufacturing and standardization of design for industrial efficiency. This group believed form should be determined solely by function and wanted to eliminate all ornament. Muthesius saw simplicity and exactness as being both functional demands of machine manufacture and symbolic aspects of twentieth-century industrial efficiency and power. A union of artists and craftsmen with industry, he believed, could elevate the functional and aesthetic qualities of mass production, particularly in low-cost consumer products. The other faction, led by Van de Velde, argued for the primacy of individual artistic expression. Behrens attempted to mediate the two extremes, but his work for AEG showed strong tendencies toward standardization. A design philosophy is merely an idle vision until someone creates artifacts that make it a real force in the world, and Werkbund members consciously sought a new design language to realize

their goals. Behrens's work for AEG became an early manifestation of Werkbund ideals, and he was sometimes called "Mr. Werkbund."

Behrens's AEG designs represent a synthesis of two seemingly contradictory concepts: neoclassicism and *Sachlichkeit* (loosely translated, commonsense objectivity). His neoclassicism grew from a careful study of art and design from ancient Greece and Rome. Rather than merely copying the stylistic aspects of such work, he found in it the formal language of harmony and proportion needed to achieve a unity of the parts to the whole. Sachlichkeit was a pragmatic emphasis on technology, manufacturing processes, and function, in which artistic conceits and questions of style were subordinate to purpose. In concert, these two concepts guided Behrens in his quest for forms to achieve Gesamkultur.

On 31 January 1908, copyright application was made for Behrens's hexagonal AEG trademark (Fig. **12–41**). This pictographic honeycomb design containing the firm's initials signifies mathematical order while functioning as a visual metaphor relating the complexity and organization of a twentieth-century corporation to a beehive. Behrens's guide booklet for the AEG pavilion for the 1908 German Shipbuilding Exhibition was an early application of the trademark and corporate typeface (Fig. **12–42**). The AEG graphic identity program made consistent use of three linchpin elements that would be present in corporate identity programs as the genre evolved half a century later: a logo, a typeface, and a consistent layout of elements following standardized formats.

Behrens designed a typeface for AEG's exclusive use to bring unity to its printed materials. At a time when German graphic design was dominated by traditional black-letter and decorative Victorian and art nouveau styles, Behrens designed a roman-style letterform inspired by classical Roman inscrip-

12–43

tions. Initially this was not available in type, so display type on all AEG printed graphics was hand-lettered. In 1908 a typeset variation named Behrens-Antiqua (see Fig. 12–36) was released by Klingspor Foundry, first for the exclusive use of AEG, then later for general use. Behrens had three important goals in designing this new type: It differentiated AEG communications from all other printed matter; its forms were universal rather than individualized by the touch of a specific artist's hand; and it strove for a monumental character that could evoke positive connotations of quality and performance. Behrens-Antiqua has the solemn, monumental quality of roman letterforms. Behrens designed ornaments inspired by ancient Greek and Roman ceramic and brass craft objects, whose geometric properties satisfied his belief that geometry could make ornament universal and impersonal.

The consistent use of graphic devices gave AEG graphics a unified image (Fig. **12–43**). These devices, in addition to modular divisions of space using Lauweriks's grid, included framing the space with a medium-weight rule; central placement of static elements; exclusive use of Behrens-Antiqua type; use of analogous colors (often two or three sequential colors on the color wheel); and simple, objective photographs and drawings with subjects isolated from their environments.

The industrial products designed by Behrens ranged from electric household products, such as teakettles and fans, to streetlamps and industrial products such as electric motors. He brought the formal eye of the painter and the structural approach and professional ethics of the architect to product

12–41. Peter Behrens, AEG trademark, 1907. The new mark was consistently applied to buildings, stationary, products, and graphics.

12–42. Peter Behrens, guidebook covers for the AEG pavilion at the German Shipbuilding Exhibition, 1908. A translation drawing reduces the architectural structure to flat planes. The lettering used here became a basis for the AEG visual identification system.

12–43. Peter Behrens, covers for *Mitteilungen Der Berliner Elektricitaets Werke* (Berlin Electric Works Magazine), 1908. Each issue used a different geometric pattern on the front cover, and the graphic theme was echoed by the back cover calendar design.

design. The combination of visual form, working method, and functional concern in his work for AEG products enabled him to produce the body of work that has led some to proclaim Behrens the first industrial designer. An innovative use of standardization is seen in the design of AEG teakettles with interchangeable parts (Fig. **12–44**): three basic kettle forms, two lids, two handles, and two bases. These were made in three materials: brass, copperplate, and nickelplate; and three finishes: smooth, hammered, and rippled. All components were available for assembly in three sizes; all of these teakettles used the same heating elements and plugs. This system of interchangeable components made it theoretically possible to configure 216 different teakettles, but only about 30 were actually brought to market.

12–44

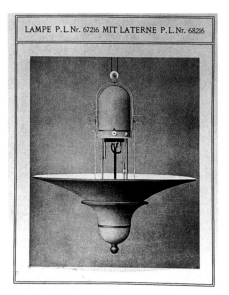

12–45

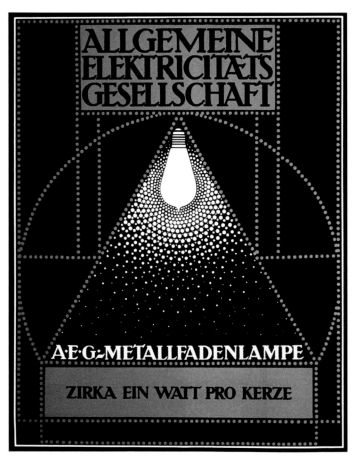

12–46

12–47

Beginning in early 1907 Behrens designed a large series of AEG arc lamps (Fig. **12–45**) that produced intense light by passing an electrical current between two carbon electrodes. These were three hundred times brighter, more energy efficient, and safer than gas lamps of the time. Because the carbon rods had to be replaced every eight to twenty hours, convenient exterior clips were designed for quick dismantling. Their forms and proportions suggest Lauweriks's grid, while the overall shapes evoke the harmonious design and graceful curves of Greek vases. The arc lamps were widely used in factories, railway stations, and other public buildings.

Behrens sought neutrality and standardization in product designs for machine manufacture. His streetlamps and teaket-

12–48

12–49

tles have simple forms shorn of decoration, with connotations of social class and wealth stripped away. His work pointed toward a new design sensibility that would mature in the 1920s. This rational approach announced the need for form to emerge from function rather than being an added embellishment.

An electric lamp poster (Fig. **12–46**) designed by Behrens for AEG around 1910 demonstrates the typographic and spatial parameters of the mature AEG corporate identification program; it realizes Behrens's quest for a twentieth-century language of form. The AEG corporate design program included applications to architecture ranging from storefronts (Fig. **12–47**) to his massive Turbine Hall (Fig. **12–48**). This major architectural design—with its twenty-two giant exposed exterior steel girders along the sides, glass curtain walls, and form determined by function—became a prototype for future design evolution. In addition to Gropius and Mies van der Rohe, mentioned earlier, Behrens's apprentices during this period included Le Corbusier and Adolf Meyer. Given these designers' later importance, Behrens's philosophy and the studio shop talk were surely catalysts for future ideas.

At the 1914 Werkbund annual conference (Fig. **12–49**), the debate between Muthesius's rationalism and standardization and Van de Velde's expressionism was soundly determined in

12–44. Peter Behrens, catalogue page for AEG teakettles, 1908. Permutations of the modular system of shapes, handles, materials, and textures are shown. Note the spatial division by rules to create zones of information.

12–45. Peter Behrens, AEG arc lamp catalogue page, 1907. Shape and proportion are inspired by ancient Greek vases.

12–46. Peter Behrens, AEG electric lamp poster, c. 1910. Geometric elements structure the space and signify the radiant energy of illumination.

12–47. Peter Behrens, AEG retail store in Berlin, 1910. Lettering inscribed on white marble, dark wooden framing echoing the geometric divisions of AEG graphics, and the door-glass trademark convey the corporate image. Posters were often hung on the three-panel screen behind the window display.

12–48. Peter Behrens (designer) and Karl Bernhard (structural engineer), AEG Turbine Hall, 1909. Except for the identifying logo and name on the end of the roof, there is neither ornament nor embellishment. The structure and proportions are designed to suggest its function—a massive industrial factory engineered for the assembly of giant steam turbines.

12–49. Peter Behrens, poster for a Deutsche Werkbund exhibition, 1914. The designer is an allegorical torchbearer, in keeping with the Werkbund view that design is an enlightening and humanizing social force. The subtitle reads, "Art in Craft, Industry, and Commerce—Architecture."

12–51

ABCDEFGHIJKLMNOPQRSTUVWXYZ
abcdefghijklmnopqrstuvwxyz
&£1234567890.,;:-!?'""""/()

12–50

12–50. Edward Johnston, Johnston's Railway Type, 1916. These elemental letterforms were prototypes for reductive design.

12–51. The London Underground symbol, revised by Edward Johnston in 1918, is shown in the 1972 version used today.

favor of Muthesius's approach. Up until this 1914 meeting, Behrens played a key role among designers who revolted against Victorian historicism and art nouveau design and advocated a Spartan approach, stripped of decoration. The austere orthodoxy of the International style, discussed in chapters 18 and 20, was the evolutionary extension of these beliefs.

Behrens began to accept architectural commissions from other clients in 1911. Graphic and product design occupied less of his time. In 1914 Behrens's contract with AEG was terminated, although he continued to work on AEG projects from time to time. Until his death in 1940, Behrens's design practice centered upon architecture. His work during the opening decades of the century crystallized advanced thinking about design while planting seeds for future developments.

Design for the London Underground

In 1890 the world's first underground electric railway system opened in London. During the first two decades of the twentieth century, the Underground Electric Railways of London, Ltd., consolidated much of London's urban transportation sys-

tem. Just as AEG director Emil Rathenau was the catalyst for that firm's comprehensive design program, a statistician and attorney named Frank Pick (1878–1941) provided the vision necessary to lead the Underground Group to the forefront of innovative publicity and design.

Pick had been a vocal critic of his employer's promotional efforts; publicity was added to his areas of responsibility around 1908. Although lacking artistic training, Pick had acquired a passion for art and design. He responded to the jumble of advertisers' posters competing with transportation information and publicity by designating poster boards at station entrances for Underground posters and maps, then limited advertisers' posters to gridded spaces inside stations and on platforms. Underground station signs introduced in 1908 had a solid red disk with a blue bar across the middle bearing the station name in white sans-serif letters. These bright, simple designs stood out against the urban clutter.

Underground publicity posters were eclectic, wide-ranging, and evolved over the decades. The focus was usually on destination rather than transportation. Urban transit by bus, streetcar, and subway was presented as the heartbeat of the city, providing access to movies and museums, sports and shops. To boost off-peak evening and weekend use, posters encouraged travel to leisure destinations, including theaters, the zoo, parks, and the countryside. Pick took personal responsibility for selecting artists and approving designs. Designers were given little direction beyond a general theme or subject. Underground posters ranged in style from lyrical romanticism to the beginnings of mass-media modernism.

Dissatisfaction with the typography on Underground printed material prompted Pick to commission the eminent calligrapher Edward Johnston (1872–1944) to design an exclusive, patented typeface for the Underground in 1916. Pick requested a typeface possessing the bold simplicity shown by distinctive letters from preceding epochs, but with an indisputably twentieth-century quality. Johnston responded to this apparent contradiction by crafting a sans-serif typeface (Fig. **12–50**) whose strokes have consistent weight; however, the letters have the basic proportions of classical Roman inscriptions. Johnston sought absolute functional clarity by reducing his characters to the simplest possible forms: the *M* is a perfect square whose forty-five-degree diagonal strokes meet in the exact center of the letter; the *O* is a perfect circle; all of the letters have a similar elemental design. The lowercase *l* has a tail to avoid confusion with the capital *I*.

Johnston designed a new version of the station signage and logo, using his new typeface on a blue bar in front of a red circle instead of a solid disk. This London Underground logo is still used today (Fig. **12–51**), incorporating refinements made in 1972.

As Pick ascended within the Underground management, his design advocacy expanded to include signage, station architecture, and product design, including train and bus design. Station platforms and coach interiors were carefully planned for human use and design aesthetics. Over the first four decades of the Underground's existence, Pick's design patronage made a positive contribution to the environment and became an international model for corporate design responsibility.

In the late nineteenth and early twentieth centuries, pioneering designers in Germany, Scotland, and Austria broke with art nouveau to chart new directions in response to personal and societal needs. Their concern for spatial relationships, inventive form, and functionality formed the groundwork for design in the new century.

The Modernist Era

Part IV

Graphic design in the first half
of the twentieth century

1900

The Influence of Modern Art

13

1897 **Mallarme,** *Un Coup de Des*

1901 *Queen Victoria dies*

1894 **Beggarstaffs agency founded**

c 1909-1912 **Analytical Cubism**
1909 **Marinetti,** *Manifesto of Futurism;*
Braque, *Pitcher and Violin*
1905 *Einstein,* Theory of Relativity
1911 **The Blue Rider expressionist group**
1913 *New York Armory Show*

1910 **Kandinsky,** *Concerning*
the Spiritual in Art
1905 **The Bridge expressionist group**
1903 *The Wright Brothers, first airplane flight*
1908 *Model "T" Ford*
c 1911 **Kandinsky, nonobjective paintings**
1909 *NAACP is formed*
c 1913-1914 **Synthetic Cubism**
1906-1907 **Picasso, influenced by**
Cézanne and African art

1918 **Housmann & Höch, photomontages**
1919 **Schwitters, Merz exhibition**
Heartfield, Grosz &
others found Berlin Dada;
Léger, *La Fin du Monde...*
1916 **Dada founded; Arp "chance" in art**
1918 *Czar Nicolas II executed*
1915 **Marinetti, "Mountains + Valleys + Streets x Joffre"**
1914 **de Chirico,** *Departure of the Poet*
1914 *Kafka,* The Trial

1917 **Ball, Dada sound poems; Coburn,** *Vortographs*
1918 **Apollinaire,** *Calligrammes* **published**

Pictorial Modernism

14

1844 **Beggarstaffs agency founded**

1908 **Hohlwein,** *PKZ poster*

1905 **Bernhard, Priester matches poster**
1911 **Erdt,** *Opel poster*

1915 **Leete, Kitchener "wants you" poster**
1918 **Kauffer, Daily Herald poster**
1915 *Griffith,* The Birth of a Nation
1918 *World War I ends*
1914 *World War I begins*
1917 **Klinger, 8th war loan campaign poster;**
Flagg *"Uncle Sam"* **poster**

A New Language of Form

15

1910 **Mondrian learns of Cubism**

1916 **Van der Leck,**
Batavier Line **poster**
c 1913 **Malevich, first Suprematist paintings**
1917 **De Stijl movement & journal begin**
1912 **Wright, Coonley house**
with geometric stained
glass windows
1919 **Lissitzky,** *Beat the Whites*
with the Red Wedge **poster;**
1917 *Russian Revolution begins*

1918 **Van Doesburg,** *Composition XI*
1918 *Wendingen* **magazine is founded**

The Bauhaus and the New Typography

16

1919 **Gropius, founds Weimar**
Bauhaus & publishes
manifesto

1916 **Johnston, Railway Type**

■ *1930*

1933 **Nazis raid Heartfield's apartment**
1924 **Breton,** *Manifesto of Surrealism* 1930 *Gandhi leads protest against salt tax*

1922 *USSR is formed*   1934 **Heartfield, "Yuletide" poster**
1927 **Depero,** *Dinamo Azari*

1929 **Man Ray,** *Sleeping Woman*
1923 **Schwitters,** *Merz* **magazine**
Kollwitz, *The Survivors...* **poster**

1924 *Mussolini and Facists consolidate their power in Italy*
1923 *Hitler,* Mein Kampf

1920 *U.S. women gain vote*
1923 **Binder, Vienna Music and Theater posters**   c 1936-1943 **Hohlwein, designs for Nazis**
1927 *Lindbergh, solo flight across the Atlantic; Stalin rules Russia*   Late 30s **Binder, Carlu, Cassandre, & Kauffer to the U. S.**
1925 **Cassandre,** *L'Intransiegeant* **poster**
1925 *Fitzgerald,* The Great Gatsby   1932 **Cassandre,** *Dubonnet* **poster**
1927 **Cassandre,** *Etoile du Nord* **poster**   1936 *Roosevelt reelected*
1931 *Empire State Building*   1940s **Games, World War II posters**

1920's **Vladimir Lebeder becomes father of the 20th century Russian picture book**
1929 *Stock market crash*   1939 **Sutnar emigrates to U. S.**
1924 **Rodchenko, serial covers,** *Mess Mend*   1939 *Germany invades Poland, World War II begins*
1932 *Low point of Depression; Roosevelt elected President*
1924 **Rietveld, Schroeder house**   1930 **Gustav Klutis extols Soviet accomplishments**   1944 **Mondrian dies**
in photomontage posters   1941 **Lissitzky dies**
1923 **Mayakovsky & Lissitzky,** *For the Voice*   1933 *Hitler, German Chancellor*   1948 *Gandhi assassinated*
1928 *Warner Brothers, 1st sound motion picture*
1922 **Berlewi, mechano-faktura theory**   1934 *Mao Tse-tung leads "Long March"*   1943 *Mass production of penicillin*
1929 **Lissitzky,** *Russische Ausstellung* **poster**
1924 **Lissitzky,** *The Isms of Art*
1931 **Van Doesburg dies,** *De Stijl* **journal ends**

1928 **Gropius, Moholy-Nagy, & Bayer leave Bauhaus; Tschichold,** *Die Neue Typographie;*   1947 *The Marshall Plan*
1922 **Kandinsky joins Bauhaus**   **Zwart, NKF catalogue; Koch, Kabel**
1920 **Klee joins Bauhaus**   1930 **Mies van der Rohe moves Bauhaus to Berlin**   1940 *Churchill, "blood, toil, tears, and sweat" speech*
1923 **Moholy-Nagy replaces Itten at Bauhaus;**   1945 *United Nations formed*
Bauhaus exhibition, Tschichold attends;   1931 **Gill, Essay on** *Typography*   1939 *New York World's Fair*   1946 *Nuremberg war trials*
Werkman, 1st *Next Call*   1932 **Morison, Times New Roman**   1947 **Tschichold joins Penguin books**
1927 **Renner, Futura**   1933 **Nazis close Bauhaus; arrest Tschichold**   1949 *Mao Tse-tung's communist*
1933 **Beck, London Underground map**   *forces capture China*
1925 **Bauhaus moves to Dessau; Bayer, universal**   1935 **Matter,** *Pontresina* **poster**   1956 **Sandberg,** *experimenta*
alphabet; Tschichold, *elementare typographie*   *typographica*

The Modern Movement in America

17   1934 **Brodovitch art directs** *Harper's Bazaar*   1951 **Brodovitch,** *Portfolio* **magazine**
1935 *Rural Electric Administration*   1950 **CCA "Great Ideas" ads begin**
1940 **Kauffer, Greek resistance poster**
c 1928 **Agha becomes art director of** *Vogue*   1941 **Carlu,** *American's answer! Production* **poster**

Late 1930s **Bauhaus masters Albers, Bayer,**   1939 **Binder, New York World's Fair poster; Moholy-Nagy, School of Design**
Breuer, Gropius, Mies van der Rohe,
1924 **Erte,** *Harper's Bazaar* **covers**   **& Moholy-Nagy emigrate to U. S.**   1945 **CCA Allied Nations advertisements**
1945 *A-bombs dropped; World War II ends*

1935 **WPA hires artists for design projects**
1936 **Jacobson, design director for CCA**   1950 *Korean War begins*
1936 *Spanish Civil War begins*   1948 **Matter, Knoll chair ads**

c 1937 **Beall, REA posters**   1944 **Sutnar, Catalog Design**
1937 *Picasso,* Guernica

1943 **Alexander Liberman becomes art**
director of Vogue Magazine

The Influence of Modern Art

13

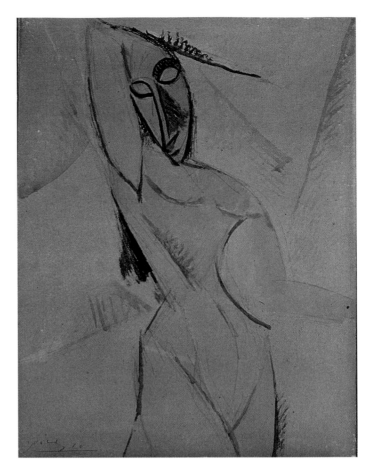

13–1

The first two decades of the twentieth century were a time of ferment and change that radically altered all aspects of the human condition. The social, political, cultural, and economic character of life was caught in fluid upheaval. In Europe, monarchy was replaced by democracy, socialism, and communism. Technology and scientific advances transformed commerce and industry. Transportation was radically altered by the coming of the motorcar (1885) and the airplane (1903). The motion picture (1896) and wireless radio transmission (1895) foretold a new era of human communications. Beginning in 1908 with the Turkish revolution that restored constitutional government and the Bulgarian declaration of independence, colonized and subjugated peoples began to awaken and demand independence. The slaughter during the first of two global wars, fought with the destructive weapons of technology, shook the traditions and institutions of Western civilization to their foundations.

Amidst this turbulence, it is not surprising that visual art and design experienced a series of creative revolutions that questioned long-held values and approaches to organizing space as well as the role of art and design in society. The traditional objective view of the world was shattered. The representation of external appearances did not fulfill the needs and vision of the emerging European avant-garde. Elemental ideas about color and form, social protest, and the expression of Freudian theories and deeply personal emotional states occupied many artists. Some of these modern movements, such as fauvism, had a limited effect on graphic design. Others, such as cubism

and futurism, Dada and surrealism, De Stijl, suprematism, constructivism, and expressionism directly influenced the graphic language of form and visual communications in this century. The evolution of twentieth-century graphic design closely relates to modern painting, poetry, and architecture.

Cubism

By introducing a design concept independent of nature, cubism began a new artistic tradition and way of seeing that challenged the four-hundred-year Renaissance tradition of pictorial art. The genesis of this movement was a series of works by the Spanish painter Pablo Picasso (1881–1973) that applied elements of ancient Iberian and Africa tribal art to the human figure (Fig. **13–1**). Boldly chiseled geometric planes of African sculpture, masks (Fig. **13–2**), and fabrics were an exciting revelation for Picasso and his friends. Another major influence was the French postimpressionist painter Paul Cézanne (1839–1906), who observed that the painter should "treat nature in terms of the cylinder and the sphere and the cone." The drawings and paintings of these artists demonstrate the new approach to handling space and expressing human emotions. Figures are abstracted into geometric planes, and classical norms for the human figure are broken. The spatial illusions

13–2

13–3

of perspective give way to an ambiguous shifting of two-dimensional planes. Some figures are simultaneously seen from more than one viewpoint.

Over the next few years, Picasso and his close associate Georges Braque (1881–1963) developed cubism as the art movement that replaced the rendering of appearances with the endless possibilities of invented form. *Analytical cubism* (Fig. **13–3)** is the name given to their work from about 1910–1912. During this period they analyzed the planes of the subject matter, often from several points of view, and used these perceptions to construct a painting composed of rhythmic geometric planes. The real subject is shapes, colors, textures, and values used in spatial relationships. Analytical cubism's compelling fascination grows from the unresolved tension of the sensual and intellectual appeal of the pictorial structure in conflict with the challenge of interpreting the subject matter. Cubism has a strong relationship with the process of human vision. Our eyes shift and scan a subject; our minds combine these fragments into a whole.

Picasso and Braque introduced paper collage elements into their work in 1912. Collage allowed free composition independent of subject matter and declared the reality of the painting as two-dimensional object. The texture of collage ele-

13–1. Pablo Picasso, *Nude,* c. 1906–07. The seeds of cubism are contained in the fragmentation of the figure and background spaces into abstracted geometric planes.

13–2. Lege African mask, from what is now the Republic of Congo, undated. Abstracted geometric forms showed European artists a different approach to art and design.

13–3. Pablo Picasso, *Man with Violin,* 1911–12. In the analytical cubism phase, Picasso and Braque studied the planes of a subject from different vantage points, fractured them, and pulled them forward toward the canvas surface. The planes shimmer vibrantly in ambiguous positive and negative relationships one to another.

ments could signify objects. To denote a chair, for example, Picasso glued oilcloth printed with a chair cane pattern into a painting. Often letterforms and words from newspapers were incorporated as visual form and for associated meaning.

In 1913 cubism evolved into *synthetic cubism*. Drawing on past observations, the cubists invented forms that were signs rather than representations of the subject matter. The essence of an object and its basic characteristics, rather than its outward appearance, were depicted. Juan Gris (1887–1927) was a major painter in the development of synthetic cubism. His

13–4

13–5

paintings, such as the 1916 *Fruit Bowl* (Fig. **13–4**), combined composition from nature with an independent structural design of the picture space. First he planned a rigorous architectural structure using golden section proportions and a modular composition grid; then he "laid the subject matter" on this design scheme. Gris had a profound influence on the development of geometric art and design. His paintings are a kind of halfway house between an art based on perception and an art realized by the relationships between geometric planes.

Among the artists who clustered around Picasso and Braque and joined the cubist movement, Fernand Léger (1881–1955) moved cubism away from the initial impulses of its founders. From around 1910, Léger took Cézanne's famous dictum about the cylinder, sphere, and cone far more seriously than any other cubist. Motifs such as nudes in a forest were transformed into fields of colorful stovepipe sections littering the picture plane. Léger's work might have evolved toward an art of pure color and shape relationships, but his four years of military service among working-class French citizens and the heightening of his visual perception during the war turned him toward a style that was more recognizable, accessible, and populist. He moved closer to his visual experi-

ence in paintings like *The City* (Fig. **13–5**). Perceptions of the colors, shapes, posters, and architecture of the urban environment—glimpses and fragments of information—are assembled into a composition of brightly colored planes. The letterforms in Léger's paintings and graphic work for Blaise Cendrars's book *La fin du monde, filmée par l'Ange Notre-Dame (The End of the World, filmed by the Angel of Notre-Dame),* an antiwar book describing God's decision to destroy life on earth due to humans' warlike nature (Figs. **13–6** and **13–7**), pointed the way toward geometric letterforms. His almost pictographic simplifications of the human figure and objects were a major inspiration for modernist pictorial graphics that became the major thrust of the revived French poster art of the 1920s. Léger's flat planes of color, urban motifs, and the hard-edged precision of his machine forms helped define the modern design sensibility after World War I.

By developing a new approach to visual composition, cubism changed the course of painting and to some extent graphic design as well. Its visual inventions became a catalyst for experiments that pushed art and design toward geometric abstraction and new attitudes toward pictorial space.

Futurism

Futurism was launched when the Italian poet Filippo Marinetti (1876–1944) published his Manifesto of Futurism in the Paris newspaper *Le Figaro* on 20 February 1909. Marinetti's stirring words established futurism as a revolutionary movement in which all the arts were to test their ideas and forms against the new realities of scientific and industrial society:

We intend to sing the love of danger, the habit of energy and fearlessness. Courage, audacity, and revolt will be es-

13–6   13–7

sential elements of our poetry. . . . We affirm that the world's magnificence has been enriched by a new beauty: the beauty of speed . . . a roaring car that seems to ride on grapeshot is more beautiful than the *Victory of Samothrace*. . . . Except in struggle, there is no more beauty. No work without an aggressive character can be a masterpiece. The manifesto voiced enthusiasm for war, the machine age, speed, and modern life. It shocked the public by proclaiming, "We will destroy museums, libraries, and fight against moralism, feminism, and all utilitarian cowardice."

Marinetti and his followers produced an explosive and emotionally charged poetry that defied correct syntax and grammar. In January 1913, Giovanni Papini (1881–1956) began publication of the journal *Lacerba* in Florence, and typographic design was pulled onto the artistic battlefield. The June 1913 issue published Marinetti's article calling for a typographic revolution against the classical tradition. Harmony was rejected as a design quality because it contradicted "the leaps and bursts of style running through the page." On a page, three or four ink colors and twenty typefaces (*italics* for quick impressions, **boldface** for violent noises and sounds) could redouble words' expressive power. Free, dynamic, and piercing words could be given the velocity of stars, clouds, airplanes, trains, waves, explosives, molecules, and atoms. A new and painterly typographic design, called *parole in libertá* or "words in freedom," was born on the page (Figs. **13–8** through **13–12**).

Noise and speed, two dominant conditions of twentieth-century life, were expressed in futurist poetry. Marinetti wrote that a man who has witnessed an explosion does not stop to connect his sentences grammatically but hurls shrieks and words at his listeners. He urged poets to liberate themselves

13–4. Juan Gris, *Fruit Bowl,* 1916. Cubist planes move forward and backward in shallow space, while the vertical and diagonal geometry of a grid imposes order.

13–5. Fernand Léger, *The City,* 1919. This monumental composition of pure, flat planes signifying the geometry, color, and energy of the modern city led its creator to say that "it was advertising that first drew the consequences" from it.

13–6. Fernand Léger, pages from *La fin du monde,* 1919. The destruction of the earth begins when the angel on Notre Dame Cathedral blows her trumpet; mayhem is illustrated by falling names.

13–7. Fernand Léger, page from *La fin du monde,* 1919. A whirlwind tour of the re-creation of the earth after the fall of man is illustrated by a pinwheel of lettering spelling "accelerated slow motion cinema."

from servitude to grammar and open new worlds of expression. Since Gutenberg's invention of movable type, most graphic designs used a vigorous horizontal and vertical structure, but the futurist poets cast these constraints to the wind. Freed from tradition, they animated their pages with a dynamic, nonlinear composition achieved by pasting words and letters in place for reproduction from photoengraved printing plates.

The futurist concept that writing and/or typography could become a concrete and expressive visual form has been a sporadic preoccupation of poets dating back at least to the work of the Greek poet Simias of Rhodes (c. 33 B.C.). Called pattern poetry, the verse that explored this idea often took the shape of objects or religious symbols. In the nineteenth century, the German poet Arno Holz (1863–1929) reinforced intended

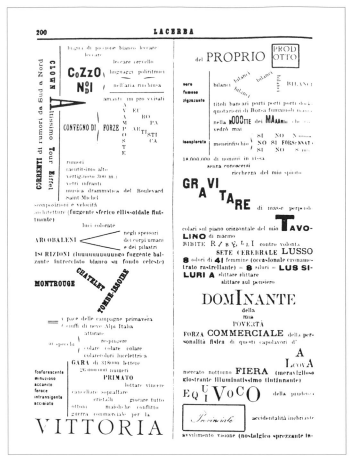

13–8

13–9

13–10

13–11

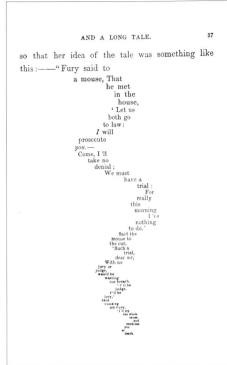

13–12

13–13

auditory effects by such devices as omitting capitalization and punctuation, varying word spacing to signify pauses, and using multiple punctuation marks for emphasis. Lewis Carroll's *Alice's Adventures in Wonderland* used descending type sizes and pictorial shape to construct a mouse's tail as part of the mouse's tale (Fig. **13–13**).

In 1897 the French symbolist poet Stéphane Mallarmé (1842–98) published the poem "Un coup de dés" ("A Throw of the Dice," Fig. **13–14**), composed of seven hundred words on twenty pages in a typographic range: capital, lowercase, roman, and italic. Rather than surrounding a poem with white, empty margins, Mallarmé dispersed this "silence" through the work as part of its meaning. Instead of stringing words in linear sequence like beads, he placed them in unexpected positions on the page to express sensations and evoke ideas. Moreover, he was successful in relating typography to the musical score—the placement and weight of words relate to intonation, stress, and rhythm in oral reading.

Another French poet, Guillaume Apollinaire (1880–1918), was closely associated with the cubists, particularly Picasso, and was involved in a rivalry with Marinetti. Apollinaire had championed African sculpture, defined the principles of cubist painting and literature, and once observed that "catalogs, posters, advertisements of all types, believe me, they contain the poetry of our epoch." His unique contribution to graphic design was the 1918 publication of a book entitled *Calligrammes*, poems in which the letterforms are arranged to form a visual design,

13–8. Carlo Carrà, "Parole in libertà" (free word composition), 1914. The futurist poets believed that the use of different sizes, weights, and styles of type allowed them to weld painting and poetry, because the intrinsic beauty of letterforms, manipulated creatively, transformed the printed page into a work of visual art.

13–9. Filippo Marinetti, "Montagne + Vallate + Strade x Joffre" (Mountains + Valleys + Streets x Joffre), 1915. This poem "depicts" Marinetti's journey, which included the war front (lower left), France (upper left), and a visit to Léger (top right).

13–10. Ardengo Soffici, "Bifszf + 18 Simultaneitè Chimismi lirici," 1915. Traditional verse is composed against clusters of modulating letterforms used as pure visual form. Diagonal rules link the units and create rhythms from page to page.

13–11. Filippo Marinetti, poem from *Les mots en liberté futuristes* (Futurist Words-in-Freedom), 1919. Here, the confusion, violent noise, and chaos of battle explode above the girl reading her lover's letter from the front. Marinetti's experience in the trenches of war inspired this poem.

13–12. Filippo Marinetti, "Une assemblée tumultueuse" (A Tumultuous Assembly). Foldout from *Les mots en liberté futuristes*, 1919.

13–13. Lewis Carroll, typographic image, 1866. Unexpected and totally different from the rest of *Alice's Adventures in Wonderland*, this graphic experiment in figurative typography has received both design and literary acclaim.

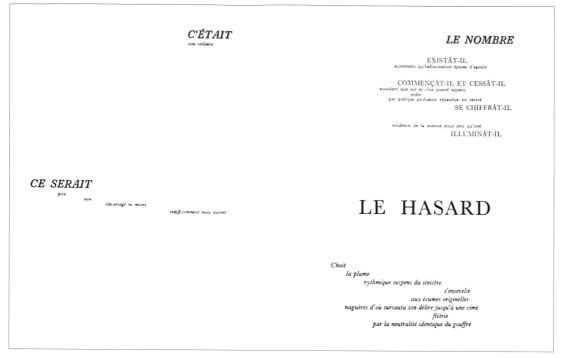

13–14

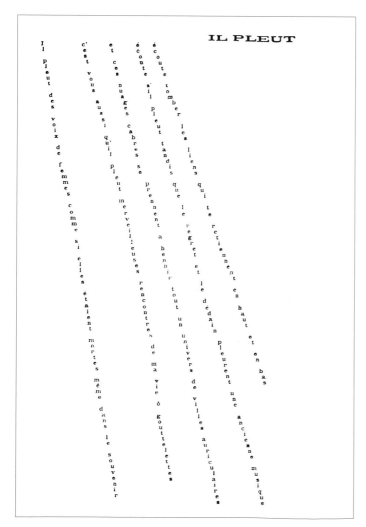

13–15

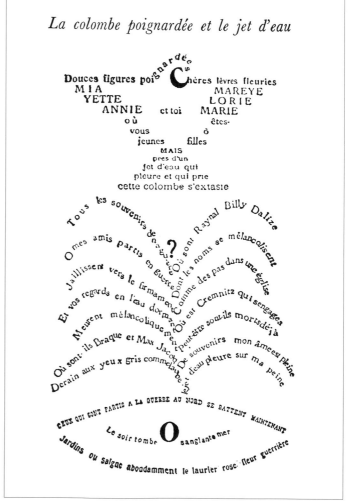

13–16

13–17

13–18

figure, or pictograph (Figs. **13–15** and **13–16**). In these poems he explored the potential fusion of poetry and painting, introducing the concept of simultaneity to the time- and sequence-bound typography of the printed page.

On 11 February 1910, five artists who had joined Marinetti's futurist movement published the Manifesto of the Futurist Painters. Umberto Boccioni (1882–1916), Carlo Carrà (1881–1966), Luigi Russolo (1885–1947), Giacomo Balla (1871–1958), and Gino Severini (1883–1966) declared their intent to "Destroy the cult of the past. . . . Totally invalidate all kinds of imitation. . . . Elevate all attempts at originality. . . . Regard art critics as useless and dangerous. . . . Sweep the whole field of art clean of all themes and subjects that have been used in the past. . . . Support and glory in our day-to-day world, a world which is going to be continually and splendidly transformed by victorious Science." The futurist painters were strongly influenced by cubism, but they also attempted to express motion, energy, and cinematic sequence in their work (Fig. **13–17**). They first used the word *simultaneity* in a visual-art context to express concurrent existence or occurrence, such as the presentation of different views in the same work of art.

The Manifesto of Futurist Architecture was written by Antonio Sant'Elia (1888–1916). He called for construction based on technology and science and for design that addressed the unique demands of modern life (Fig. **13–18**).

13–14. Stéphane Mallarmé, pages from "Un coup de dés" (A Throw of the Dice), 1897. Mallarmé anticipated the formal and expressive typographic concerns that emerged in the twentieth century, when poets and painters became interested in the creative potential of the printed page.

13–15. Guillaume Apollinaire, "Il pleut" (It's Raining), from *Calligrammes*, 1918. Letterforms sprinkle figuratively down the page, relating visual form to poetic content.

13–16. Guillaume Apollinaire, poem from *Calligrammes*, 1918. The typography becomes a bird, a water fountain, and an eye in this expressive design.

13–17. Giacomo Balla, *Dynamism of a Dog on a Leash,* 1912. The futurist painters sought to introduce dynamic motion, speed, and energy to the static, two-dimensional surface.

13–18. Antonio Sant'Elia, drawing for the new city of the future, 1914. These drawings were reproduced with Sant'Elia's manifesto in *Lacerba*. After the war, many of his ideas about form developed in architecture, product, and graphic design.

He declared decoration to be absurd and used dynamic diagonal and elliptic lines because their emotional power was greater than horizontals and verticals. Tragically, Sant'Elia was killed on the battlefield, but his ideas and visionary drawing influenced the course of modern design, particularly art deco.

13–19

13–20

13–21

Among the artists who applied futurist philosophy to graphic and advertising design, Fortunato Depero (1892–1960) produced a dynamic body of work in poster (Fig. **13–19**), typographic, and advertising design. This young painter shifted from social realism and symbolism to futurism in 1913 after seeing a copy of the futurist paper *Lacerba*. In 1927 Depero published his *Depero futurista* (Figs. **13–20** and **13–21**), a compilation of his typographical experiments, advertisements, tap-

estry designs, and other works. *Depero futurista* is a precursor of the artist's book, published by an artist as a creative expression independent of the publishing establishment. From September 1928 until October 1930, Depero worked in New York and designed covers for magazines such as *Vanity Fair, Movie Makers,* and *Sparks,* as well as print advertising. Although limited to a sophisticated and cosmopolitan audience, the appearance of his futurist work in American graphic communications proved somewhat influential in America's movement toward modernism. Futurism became a major influence on other art movements, and its violent, revolutionary techniques were adopted by the Dadaists, constructivists, and De Stijl. The futurists initiated the publication of manifestos, typographic experimentation, and publicity stunts (on 8 July 1910, 800,000 copies of Marinetti's leaflet *Against Past-Loving Venice,* were dropped from a clock tower onto Venice crowds), forcing poets and graphic designers to rethink the very nature of the typographic word and its meaning.

Dada

Reacting against the carnage of World War I, the Dada movement claimed to be anti-art and had a strong negative and destructive element. Dada writers and artists were concerned with shock, protest, and nonsense. They bitterly rebelled against the horrors of the world war, the decadence of European society, the shallowness of blind faith in technological progress, and the inadequacy of religion and conventional moral codes in a continent in upheaval. Rejecting all tradition, they sought complete freedom.

KARAWANE

jolifanto bambla ô falli bambla
grossiga m'pfa habla horem
égiga goramen
higo bloiko russula huju
hollaka hollala
anlogo bung
blago bung
blago bung
bosso fataka
ü üü ü
schampa wulla wussa ólobo
hej tatta gôrem
eschige zunbada
ɯulubu ssubudu uluɯ ssubudu
tumba ba- umf
kusagauma
ba - umf

(1917)
Hugo Ball

13–22

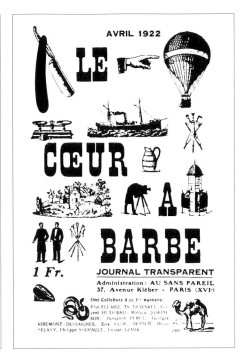

13–23

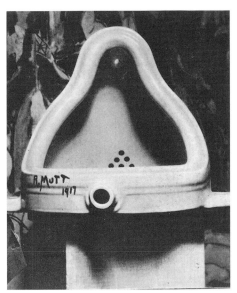

13–24

The Dada movement developed spontaneously as a literary movement after the poet Hugo Ball (1886–1927) opened the Cabaret Voltaire in Zurich, Switzerland, as a gathering place for independent young poets, painters, and musicians. Dada's guiding spirit was a young and volatile Paris-based Rumanian poet, Tristan Tzara (1896–1963), who edited the periodical *DADA* beginning in July 1917. Tzara joined Ball, Jean Arp (1887–1966, also known as Hans Arp), and Richard Huelsenbeck (1892–1974) in exploring sound poetry (Fig. **13–22**), nonsense poetry, and chance poetry. He wrote a steady stream of Dada manifestos and contributed to all major Dada publications and events. Chance placement and absurd titles characterized their graphic work (Fig. **13–23**). Dadaists did not even agree on the origins of the name *Dada*, such was the anarchy of the movement. One version says the movement was named when dadaists opened a French-German dictionary and randomly selected the word *dada*, a child's hobbyhorse.

The French painter Marcel Duchamp (1887–1968) joined the Dada movement and became its most prominent visual artist. Earlier, cubism had influenced his analysis of subjects as geometric planes, while futurism inspired him to convey time and motion. To Duchamp, Dada's most articulate spokesman, art and life were processes of random chance and willful choice. Artistic acts became matters of individual decision and selection. This philosophy of absolute freedom allowed Duchamp to create ready-made sculpture, such as a bicycle wheel mounted on a wooden stool, and exhibit found objects, such as a urinal, as art (Fig. **13–24** and Fig. **13–25**).

13–19. Fortunato Depero, New Futurist Theater Company poster, 1924. Flat planes of vibrant color, diagonal composition, and angular repetitive forms produce kinetic energy.

13–20. Fortunato Depero, cover for *Depero futurista*, 1927. Bound by massive chrome bolts, this book expresses its status as a physical object.

13–21. Fortunato Depero, page from *Depero futurista*, 1927.

13–22. Hugo Ball, Dada poem, 1917. Sound and sight poems such as this expressed the Dadaist desire to replace man's logical nonsense with an illogical nonsense.

13–23. Dada magazine cover for *The Bearded Heart*, 1922. A casual organization of space has found illustrations randomly dispersed about the page with no particular communicative intent.

13–24. Alfred Stieglitz, photograph of *The Fountain*, by Marcel Duchamp, 1917. When an object is removed from its usual context, we suddenly see it with fresh eyes and respond to its intrinsic visual properties.

The public was outraged when Duchamp painted a mustache on a reproduction of the *Mona Lisa*. This act was not intended, however, as an attack on the *Mona Lisa*. Rather, it was an ingenious assault on tradition and a public that had lost the humanistic spirit of the Renaissance.

Dada quickly spread from Zurich to other European cities. Dadaists said they were not creating art but mocking and defaming a society gone insane; even so, several Dadaists

13–25

13–26

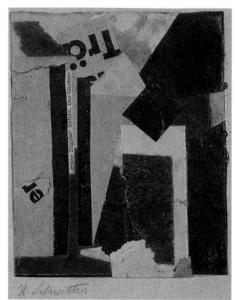

13–27

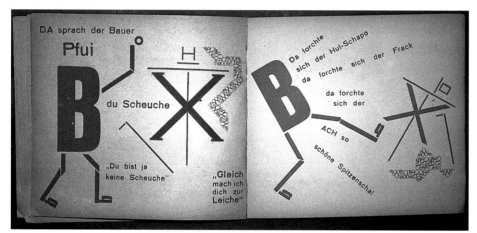

13–29

W W
P B D
Z F M
R F   R F
T Z P F   T Z P F
M W T
R F M R
R K T   P C T
S W   S W
K P T
F   G
K P T
R   Z
K P T
R Z L
T Z P F   T Z P F
H F T L

13–28

priimiitittii.

priimiitittii tisch
tesch
priimiitittii tesch
tusch
priimiitittii tischa
tescho
priimiitittii tescho
tuschi
priimitii
priimiitittii
priimiitittii too
priimiitittii taa
priimiitittii too
priimiitittii taa
priimiitittii tootaa
priimiitittii tootaa
priimiitittii tuutaa
priimiitittii tuutaa
priimiitittii tuutaatoo
priimiitittii tuutaatoo
priimiitittii tootaatuu
priimiitittii tootaatuu

13–30

13–31

13–25. Marcel Duchamp, 1917. Cover of *La septième face du dé* (The Seventh Face of the Die), by Georges Hugnet, 1936.

13–26. Hannah Höch, *Da—dandy,* collage and photomontage, 1919. Images and materials are recycled, with both chance juxtapositions and planned decisions contributing to the creative process.

13–27. Kurt Schwitters, untitled (*Grüne Zugabe*), probably 1920s. Material gathered from the streets, alleys, and garbage cans was washed and cataloged according to size and color for use as the raw material of art.

13–28. Kurt Schwitters, *W W priimiitittii,* 1920. The Dada poets separated the word from its language context; these two poems are intended to be seen as pure visual form and read as pure sound. Intuitive but highly structured typography grew out of the initial random chance of early Dada poetry.

13–29. Kurt Schwitters, Théo van Doesburg, and Kate Steinitz, page from *Die Scheuche* (The Scarecrow), 1922. In this modern fairy tale, type and image are wedded literally and figuratively as the *B* overpowers the *X* with verbiage.

13–30. Kurt Schwitters, pages from *Merz* 11, 1924. Ads for Pelikan tusche and inks demonstrate Schwitters's growing interest in constructivism during the 1920s.

13–31. John Heartfield, poster attacking the press, 1930. A surreal head wrapped in newspaper appears over a headline: "Whoever reads the bourgeois press turns deaf and blind. Away with these stupidity-causing bandages!"

produced meaningful visual art and influenced graphic design. Dada artists claimed to have invented photomontage (Fig. **13–26**), the technique of manipulating found photographic images to create jarring juxtapositions and chance associations. Both Raoul Hausmann (1886–1977) and Hannah Höch (1889–1978) were creating outstanding work in the medium as early as 1918.

Kurt Schwitters (1887–1948) of Hanover, Germany, created a nonpolitical offshoot of Dada that he named *Merz,* coined from the word *Kommerz* (commerce) in one of his collages. Schwitters gave Merz meaning as the title of a one-man art movement. Beginning in 1919, his Merz pictures were collage compositions using printed ephemera, rubbish, and found materials to compose color against color, form against form, and texture against texture (Fig. **13–27***)*. His complex designs combined Dada's elements of nonsense, surprise, and chance with strong design properties. When he tried to join the Dada movement as "an artist who nails his pictures together," he was refused membership for being too bourgeois.

Schwitters wrote and designed poetry that played sense against nonsense (Fig. **13–28***)*. He defined poetry as the interaction of elements: letters, syllables, words, sentences. In the early 1920s, constructivism (discussed in chapter 17) became an added influence in Schwitters's work after he made contact with El Lissitzky (1890–1941) and Théo van Doesburg (1883–1931), who invited Schwitters to Holland to promote Dada. Schwitters and Van Doesburg collaborated on a book in which typographic forms were depicted as characters (Fig. **13–29**). Between 1923 and 1932 Schwitters published twentyfour issues of the periodical *Merz* (Fig. **13–30**), whose eleventh issue was devoted to advertising typography. During this time Schwitters ran a successful graphic design studio with Pelikan (a manufacturer of office equipment and supplies) as a major client, and the city of Hanover employed him as typography consultant for several years. When the German political situation deteriorated in the 1930s, Schwitters began spending more time in Norway, and he moved to Oslo in 1937. After Germany invaded Norway in 1940 he fled to the British Isles, where he spent his last years and reverted to traditionalist painting.

In contrast to the artistic and constructivist interests of Schwitters, the Berlin Dadaists John Heartfield (1891–1968), Wieland Herzfelde (b. 1896), and George Grosz (1893–1959) held vigorous revolutionary political beliefs and oriented many of their artistic activities toward visual communications to raise public consciousness and promote social change. John Heartfield is the English name adopted by Helmut Herzfelde as a protest against German militarism and the army in which he served from 1914 to 1916. A founding member of the Berlin Dada group in 1919, Heartfield used the harsh disjunctions of photomontage as a potent propaganda weapon and introduced innovations in the preparation of mechanical art for offset printing. The Weimar Republic and the growing Nazi party were his targets in posters (Figs. **13–31**, **13–32**, and **13–33**), book and magazine covers (Figs. **13–34** to **13–37**), political illustrations, and cartoons. His montages are the most urgent in the history of the technique. Heartfield did not take photographs or retouch images but worked directly with glossy prints acquired from magazines and newspapers. Occasionally he commissioned a needed image from a photographer. After storm troopers occupied his apartment-studio in 1933, Heartfield fled to Prague, where he continued his graphic propaganda and mailed postcard versions of his graphics to Nazi leaders. In 1938 he learned that he was on a secret Nazi list of enemies and fled to London. He settled in Leipzig, East Germany, in 1950, where he designed theater sets and posters. Before his death in 1968, he produced photomontages protesting the Vietnam War and calling for world peace. "Unfortunately Still Timely" was the title of one retrospective of his graphic art.

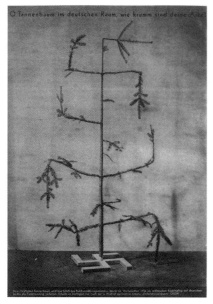

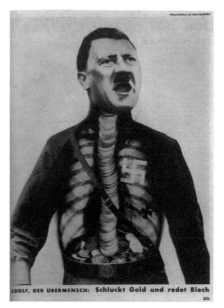

13–32

13–33

13–35

13–34

Heartfield's younger brother, Wieland Herzfelde, was a poet, critic, and publisher who edited the journal *Neue Jugend* (New Youth), which was designed by Heartfield (Fig. **13–38**). After being jailed in 1914 for distributing communist literature, Wieland started the Malik Verlag publishing house, an important avant-garde publisher of Dada, left-wing political propaganda, and experimental literature. The painter and graphic artist George Grosz was closely associated with the Herzfelde brothers. He attacked a corrupt society with satire and caricature (Fig. **13–39**) and advocated a classless social system. His drawings project the angry intensity of deep political convictions in what he perceived to be a decadent, degenerate milieu.

Having inherited Marinetti's rhetoric and assault on all artistic and social traditions, Dada was a major liberating movement that continued to inspire innovation and rebellion. Dada was born in protest against war, and its destructive and exhibitionist activities became more absurd and extreme after the war ended. In 1921 and 1922, controversy and disagreement broke out among its members, and the movement split into factions. French writer and poet André Breton (1896–1966), who was associating with the Dadaists, emerged as a new leader who believed that Dada had lost its relevance, making new directions necessary. Having pushed its negative activities to the limit, lacking a unified leadership, and with its members facing the new ideas that eventually led to surrealism, Dada foundered and ceased to exist as a cohesive movement by the end of 1922. However, Schwitters and Heartfield continued to evolve and produced their finest work after the movement's demise. Dada's rejection of art and tradition enabled it to enrich the visual vocabulary started by futurism.

13–36

13–37

13–38

13–39

13–32. John Heartfield, Yuletide poster, 1934. Under the headline, "Oh Tannenbaum in Germany, how crooked are your branches," a sickly tree symbolizes the ethos of the Third Reich.

13–33. John Heartfield, anti-Nazi propaganda poster, 1935. The headline, "Adolf, the Superman: Swallows gold and talks tin," is visualized by a photomontage X-ray of Hitler showing an esophagus of gold coins.

13–34. John Heartfield, cover for *Deutschland Deutschland über alles,* by Kurt Tucholsky, 1927.

13–35. John Heartfield, "Der Sinn des Hitlergrusses" (The Meaning of the Hitler Salute), cover for *AIZ,* 1932.

13–36. John Heartfield, "Der Sinn von Genf: Wo das Kapital lebt, kann der friede nicht leben" (The Meaning of Geneva: Where Capital Lives, Peace Cannot Live), cover for *AIZ,* 1932. In Geneva crowds of demonstrators against fascism were shot with machine guns.

13–37. John Heartfield, cover for *AIZ,* 1934. Shells form a cathedral to symbolize the mentality of military expansion and the arms race. A swastika, dollar mark, and pound sign top the towers.

13–38. John Heartfield, page from *Neue Jugend,* 1917. Pages of this radical tabloid have a visual vitality of Dadaist origin.

13–39. George Grosz, cover for *Der Blutige Ernst* (Dead Serious), 1919. A couple before a collage of cabaret ads signify postwar decadence.

13–40

Through a synthesis of spontaneous chance actions with planned decisions, Dadaists helped to strip typographic design of its traditional precepts. Also, Dada continued cubism's concept of letterforms as concrete visual shapes, not just phonetic symbols (Fig. **13–40**).

Surrealism

With roots in Dada and in a group of young French writers and poets associated with the journal *Littérature,* surrealism entered the Paris scene in 1924, searching for the "more real than real world behind the real"—the world of intuition, dreams, and the unconscious realm explored by Freud. Apollinaire had used the expression "surreal drama" in reviewing a play in 1917. The poet André Breton, founder of surrealism, imbued the word with all the magic of dreams, the spirit of rebellion, and the mysteries of the subconscious in his 1924 Manifesto du Surrealisme: "*Surrealism,* noun, masc. pure psychic automatism by which it is intended to express, either verbally or in writing, the true function of thought. Thought dictated in the absence of all control exerted by reason, all aesthetic or moral preoccupations."

Tristan Tzara came from Zurich to join Breton, Louis Aragon (1897–1982), and Paul Eluard (1895–1952). He stirred the group on toward scandal and rebellion. These young poets rejected the rationalism and formal conventions dominating postwar creative activities in Paris. They sought ways to make new truths, to reveal the language of the soul. Surrealism (or "super reality") was not a style or a matter of aesthetics; rather, it was a way of thinking and knowing, a way of feeling, and a way of life. Where Dada had been negative, destructive, and perpetually exhibitionist, surrealism professed a poetic faith in man and his spirit. Humanity could be liberated from social and moral conventions. Intuition and feeling could be freed. The writers experimented with stream-of-consciousness writing, or automatism, to seek an uninhibited truth.

The impact of the surrealist poets and writers has been limited to French literary and scholarly circles; it was through the movement's painters that surrealism affected society and visual communications. While surrealists often created works so personal that communication became impossible, they also produced images whose emotional content, symbolism, or fantasy triggered a collective, universal response in large numbers of people. Breton and his friends speculated about the possibility of surreal painting. They discovered the work of Giorgio de Chirico (1888–1978) and declared him the first surrealist painter. A member of the short-lived Italian metaphysical school of painting, De Chirico painted hauntingly empty vistas of Italian Renaissance palaces and squares that possess an intense melancholy (Fig. **13–41**). Vacant buildings, harsh shadows, deep tilted perspective, and enigmatic images convey emotions far removed from ordinary experience.

Of the large number of artists who joined the surrealist movement, several significantly influenced visual communications, with a major impact on photography and illustration. Max Ernst (1891–1965), a restless German Dadaist, used a

13–41

13–42

13–43

number of techniques that have been adopted in graphic communications. Fascinated by the wood engravings in nineteenth-century novels and catalogues, Ernst reinvented them by using collage techniques to create strange juxtapositions (Fig. **13–42**). These surreal collages have had a strong influence on illustration. His *frottage* technique involved using rubbings to compose directly on paper. As he looked at his rubbings, Ernst's imagination invented images in them, much as one sees images in cloud formations. Then he developed the rubbings into fantastic pictures. *Decalcomania,* Ernst's process of transferring images from printed matter to a drawing or painting, enabled him to incorporate a variety of images into his work in unexpected ways. This technique has been used extensively in illustration, painting, and printmaking.

Figurative surrealist painters have been called "naturalists of the imaginary" by French art historians. Space, color, perspective, and figures are rendered in careful naturalism, but the image is an unreal dreamscape. The Belgian surrealist René Magritte (1898–1967) used jolting and ambiguous scale changes, defied the laws of gravity and light, created unexpected juxtapositions, and maintained a poetic dialogue between reality and illusion, truth and fiction (Fig. **13–43**). His prolific body of images inspired many visual communications.

13–44

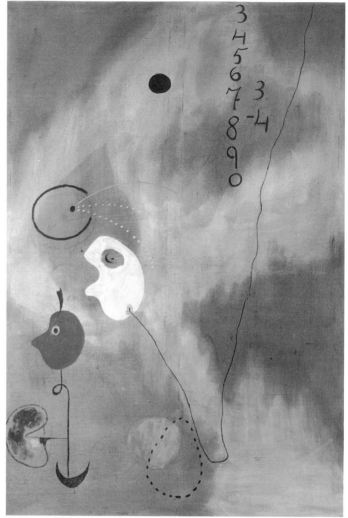

13–45

13–44. Salvador Dali, *Le grand paranoiac* (The Great Paranoid), 1936. The viewer simultaneously sees figures groping in a landscape and a large human head.

13–45. Joan Miró, *Painting* (called *The Addition*), 1925. Miró often worked with little conscious direction of his brush, creating paintings that are intuitive, spontaneous expressions of the subconscious mind.

13–46. Käthe Schmidt Kollwitz, "The Survivors Make War on War!" poster, 1923. This powerful antiwar statement was commissioned by the International Association of Labor Unions in Amsterdam.

13–47. Wassily Kandinsky, *Improvisation No. 29,* 1912. Kandinsky defined an improvisation as a spontaneous expression of inner character having spiritual nature.

The theatrical Spanish painter Salvador Dali (1904–1989) influenced graphic design in two ways. His deep perspectives inspired designers to bring vast depth to the flat, printed page; his naturalistic approach to simultaneity (Fig. **13–44**) has been frequently imitated in posters and editorial images.

Another group of surrealist painters, the emblematics, worked with a purely visual vocabulary. Visual automatism (intuitive stream-of-consciousness drawing and calligraphy) was used to create spontaneous expressions of inner life in the work of Joan Miró (1893–1983) and Jean Arp. Miró explored a process of metamorphosis through which he intuitively developed his motifs into cryptic, organic shapes (Fig.

13–45). As early as 1916, Arp explored chance and unplanned harmonies in works such as *Squares Arranged According to the Laws of Chance.* The biomorphic forms and open composition of these artists were incorporated into product and graphic design, particularly during the 1950s.

Surrealism's impact on graphic design has been diverse. It provided a poetic example of the liberation of the human spirit. It pioneered new techniques and demonstrated how fantasy and intuition could be expressed in visual terms. Unfortunately, the ideas and images of surrealism have been exploited and trivialized frequently in the mass media.

Expressionism

In early-twentieth-century art, the tendency to depict not objective reality but subjective emotions and personal responses to subjects and events was called *expressionism,* which emerged as an organized movement in Germany before World War I. Color, drawing, and proportion were often exaggerated or distorted, and symbolic content was

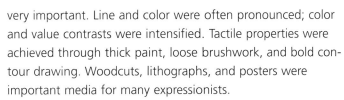

13–46

13–47

very important. Line and color were often pronounced; color and value contrasts were intensified. Tactile properties were achieved through thick paint, loose brushwork, and bold contour drawing. Woodcuts, lithographs, and posters were important media for many expressionists.

Revolting against conventional aesthetic forms and cultural norms, expressionists felt a deep sense of social crisis, especially during the years prior to World War I. Many German expressionists rejected the authority of the military, education, government, and Hohenzollern rule. They felt deep empathy for the poor and social outcasts, who were frequent subjects of their work. Intense idealism fueled the expressionists' belief in art as a beacon pointing toward a new social order and improved human condition.

German artists formed two early expressionist groups: *Die Brücke* (The Bridge) originated in Dresden in 1905, and *Der Blaue Reiter* (The Blue Rider) began in Munich in 1911. Expressionists consciously sought new approaches to art and life. Die Brücke artists declared their independence in transforming their subject matter until it conveyed their own unexpressed feelings; by contrast, Der Blaue Reiter redefined art as an object without subject matter, but with perceptual properties that were able to convey feelings. Die Brücke's figurative paintings and woodblock prints were forged with thick, raw strokes, often becoming bold statements about alienation, anxiety, and despair. German expressionism extended into theater, film, and literature, for example in such works as Franz Kafka's *Metamorphosis* and *The Trial*.

Outstanding examples of the expressionist concern for the human condition and its representation in easily understood graphic imagery are found in drawings, prints, sculpture, and posters by Käthe Schmidt Kollwitz (1867–1945). Married to a physician who ran a clinic in a Berlin working-class district, Kollwitz gained firsthand knowledge about the miserable conditions of the working poor. She documented their plight in figurative works of great emotional power. Great empathy for the suffering of women and children is conveyed by her posters (Fig. **13–46**).

Founding members of Der Blaue Reiter included Russian émigré Wassily Kandinsky (1866–1944) and the Swiss artist Paul Klee (1879–1940). Less inclined to express the agony of the human condition, they sought a spiritual reality beyond the outward appearances of nature and explored problems of form and color. Kandinsky led the group and became the leading advocate of art that could reveal the spiritual nature of people through the orchestration of color, line, and form on the canvas. Kandinsky's book *Concerning the Spiritual in Art* (1910) was an early argument for nonobjective art capable of conveying emotions from the artist to the observer through purely visual means without subject matter or literal symbols. Kandinsky compared color and form to music and its ability to express deep human emotion. This belief in the autonomy and spiritual values of color led to the courageous emancipation of his painting from motifs and representational elements (Fig. **13–47**).

13–48

13–49

Klee synthesized elements inspired by all the modern movements as well as children's and naive art, achieving intense subjective power while contributing to the objective formal vocabulary of modern art (Fig. **13–48**). His subject matter was translated into graphic signs and symbols with strong communicative power. Klee's *Pedagogical Sketchbook* (1925) defined the elements of art, their interaction, motion, and spatial depth. His published lectures are the most complete explication of modern design by any artist.

In France the *fauves* (wild beasts), led by Henri Matisse (1869–1954), shocked proper French society with their jarring color contrasts and spirited drawing in the first decade of the century. Except for Georges Rouault (1871–1958), the fauves were more involved with color and structural relationships than expressions of spiritual crisis.

The techniques and subject matter of expressionism influenced graphic illustration and poster art; the emphasis on social and political activism continues to provide a viable model for graphic designers addressing problems of the human condition and environment. Inspiration was drawn from art by children, unschooled artists, non-European cultures, and tribal arts. Theories about color and form advanced by Kandinsky and Klee became important foundations for design and design education through their teaching at the Bauhaus, discussed in chapter 16.

Photography and the modern movement

It was inevitable that the new visual language of the modern movements, with its concern for point, line, plane, shape, and texture, and for the relationships between these visual elements, would begin to influence photography, just as it had affected typography in the futurist and Dadaist approaches to graphic design.

Francis Bruguiere (1880–1945) began to explore multiple exposures in 1912, pioneering the potential of light recorded on film as a medium for poetic expression. In his photographic abstractions, the play of light and shadow becomes the subject (Fig. **13–49**). Another photographer who extended his vision into the realm of pure form was Alvin Langdon Coburn (1882–1966). By 1913 his photographs of rooftops and views from tall buildings focused on the pattern and structure found in the world instead of depicting objects and things (Fig. **13–50**). Coburn's kaleidoscope patterns, which he called *vortographs* when the series began in 1917, are early nonobjective photographic images. Coburn praised the beautiful design seen through a microscope, explored multiple exposure, and used prisms to split images into fragments.

An American artist from Philadelphia, Man Ray (born Emanuel Rabinovitch, 1890–1976), met Duchamp and fell under the Dada spell in 1915. After moving to Paris in 1921, Man Ray joined Breton and others in their evolution from

13–50

13–51

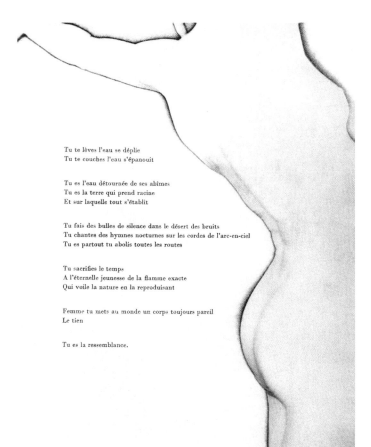

13–52

13–48. Paul Klee, *Fish Magic,* 1925. Images are reinvented into potent signs; color, form, and texture are delicately balanced into a cohesive composition; and the whole transmits a quiet poetry from a world invented by the artist's imagination.

13–49. Francis Bruguiere, *Light Abstraction,* c.1930. By cutting and bending paper, Bruguiere composed a photographic composition of forms moving in and out of space.

13–50. Alvin Langdon Coburn, *The Octopus,* 1912. The visual design patterns of shape and tone became Coburn's subject as he viewed the world from unexpected vantage points.

13–51. Man Ray, *Sleeping Woman,* 1929. In this surreal image, solarization is used not just as a visual technique but as a mean to plumb the psychic experience.

13–52. Man Ray, page from *Facile* (Easy), by Paul Eluard, 1936.

Dada toward surrealism, with its less haphazard investigation of the role played by the unconscious and chance in artistic creation. During the 1920s he worked as a professional photographer while applying Dada and surrealism to photography, using both darkroom manipulation and bizarre studio setups. He was the first photographer to explore the creative potential of solarization (Fig. **13–51**), the reversal of the tonal sequence in the denser areas of a photographic negative or print, which adds strong black contours to the edges of major shapes. (Fig. **13–52**). Solarization is achieved by giving a latent or developing photographic image a second exposure to light. Man Ray's cameraless prints, which he called *rayographs* (Fig. **13–53**), were more complex than schadographs. Man Ray frequently made his exposures with moving beams of light and

combined experimental techniques such as solarization with the basic technique of placing objects on the photographic paper. He also used distortion, printing through textures, and multiple exposures as he searched for dreamlike images and new interpretations of time and space, applying surrealism to graphic design (Fig. **13–54**) and photography assignments.

The concepts, images, and methods of visual organization from cubism, futurism, Dada, surrealism, and expressionism have provided valuable insights and processes for graphic designers. The innovators of these movements, who dared to walk into a no-man's-land of unexplored artistic possibilities, continue to influence artists, designers, and illustrators to this day.

13–53. Man Ray, *Gun with Alphabet Squares,* 1924. In this *rayograph,* multiple exposures and a shifting light source transform the photographic record of the gun and stencil letters into a new order of visual form.

13–54. Man Ray, London Underground poster, 1932. The visual analogy between trademark and planet permits an unexpected application of surrealist dislocation to visual communications. Dual posters were often used on underground boardings.

13–53

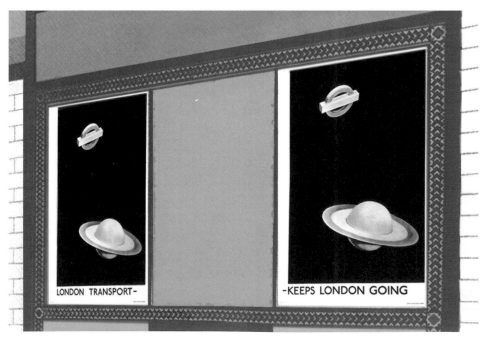

13–54

Pictorial Modernism

14

14–1

14–1. The Beggarstaffs, poster for Kassama Corn Flour, 1894. Their straightforward style was firmly established in one of their earlier posters.

The European poster during the first half of the twentieth century was a continuation of the 1890s poster, but in the second decade of the century its course was strongly affected by modern-art movements and altered by the communication needs of world war. Although influenced by cubism and constructivism, poster designers were cognizant of the need to maintain a pictorial reference if their posters were to communicate persuasively with the general public; they walked a tightrope between the creation of expressive and symbolic images on the one hand and concern for the total visual organization of the picture plane on the other. This dialogue between communicative imagery and design form generates the excitement and energy of pictorial graphics influenced by modern art.

One of the most remarkable moments in the history of graphic design is the brief career of the Beggarstaffs. James Pryde (1866–1941) and William Nicholson (1872–1949) were brothers-in-law who had been close friends since art school. Respected academic painters, they decided to open an advertising design studio in 1894 and felt it necessary to adopt pseudonyms to protect their reputations as artists. One of them found a sack of corn in a stable labeled The Beggarstaff Brothers, and they adopted the name, dropping the "Brothers." During their brief collaboration they developed a new technique, later named collage. Cut pieces of paper were moved around, changed, and pasted into position on board. The resulting style of absolutely flat planes of color had sensitive edges "drawn" with scissors (Fig. **14–1**). Often, an incomplete image challenged the viewer to participate and decipher the subject (Fig. **14–2**). The Beggarstaffs ignored the prevalent trend toward floral art nouveau as they forged this new working method into posters of powerful colored shapes and silhouettes.

Unfortunately, their work was an artistic success but a financial disaster. They attracted few clients, and only a dozen of their designs were printed. One of their most famous posters, for Sir Henry Irving's production of *Don Quixote* at the Lyceum Theater (Fig. **14–3**), was never printed, because Irving decided it was a bad likeness. They billed him for only fifty pounds; he paid them twice that. Later, the poster was published in a limited edition, in reduced size, for collectors.

When it became economically advisable for Nicholson and Pryde to terminate the partnership, each returned to painting and received some measure of recognition. Nicholson also de-

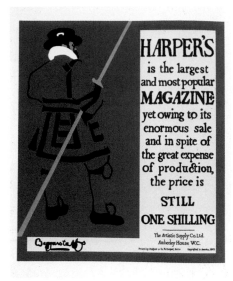

14–2

14–3

14–4

veloped a woodcut style of illustration that maintained some of the graphic economy of Beggarstaff posters (Fig. **14–4**).

Like Nicholson and Pryde, British painter and illustrator Dudley Hardy (1866–1922) also turned to poster and advertising design. He was instrumental in introducing the graphic pictorial qualities of the French poster to London billboards during the 1890s. Hardy developed an effective formula for theatrical poster work: lettering and figures appear against simple flat backgrounds. His poster for the play *The Gaiety Girl* (Fig. **14–5**) provided Londoners with a media icon (the Gaiety Girl) akin to Parisians' Chérette.

Plakatstil

The reductive, flat-color design school that emerged in Germany early in the twentieth century is called *Plakatstil* (poster style). In 1898, fifteen-year-old Lucian Bernhard (1883–1972) attended the Munich Flaspalast Exhibition of Interior Decoration and was overwhelmed by what he saw. Returning home "just drunk with color" from this avant-garde design show, Bernhard began to repaint the proper nineteenth-century decor of his family's home while his father was away on a three-day business trip. Walls, ceilings, and even furniture traded drabness for a wonderland of brilliant color. Upon his return home, the elder Bernhard was not amused. Lucian was called a potential criminal and severely rebuked. He ran away from home that very day and never returned.

In Berlin, Bernhard was trying unsuccessfully to support himself as a poet when he saw an advertisement for a poster contest sponsored by Priester matches. The prize was two hundred marks (about fifty dollars at the time), so Bernhard, who had excelled at art in school, decided to enter. His first design showed a round table with a checked tablecloth, an ashtray holding a lighted cigar, and a box of matches. Feeling that the image was too bare, Bernhard painted scantily clad dancing girls in the background.

Later that day, he decided that the image was too complex and painted the girls out. When a friend dropped by and asked if it was a poster for a cigar, Bernhard painted out the cigar. Then, deciding that the tablecloth and ashtray stood out too prominently, Bernhard painted them out as well, leaving a pair of matches on a bare table. Because the entries had to be postmarked by midnight on that date, Bernhard hastily painted the word Priester above the matches in blue, wrapped the poster, and sent it off.

Later Bernhard learned that the jury's immediate reaction to his poster was total rejection. But a tardy juror, Ernst Growald of the Hollerbaum and Schmidt lithography firm, rescued it from the trashcan. Stepping back to study the image, Growald proclaimed, "This is my first prize. Here is a genius." Growald convinced the rest of the jury, and Bernhard's first poster was the now-famous Priester matches poster (Fig. **14–6**), which reduced communication to one word and two matches.

This self-taught young artist probably did not realize it at the time, but he had moved graphic communications one step further in the simplification and reduction of naturalism into a visual language of shape and sign. Toulouse-Lautrec had started the process and the Beggarstaffs had continued it, but Bernhard established the approach to the poster of using flat color shapes, the product name, and product image (Fig. **14–7**). He repeated this approach over and over during the next two decades. In addition, he designed over three hundred packages for sixty-six products, using similar elementary graphics.

The outstanding Berlin lithography firm of Hollerbaum and Schmidt recognized that an important direction for German

14–5

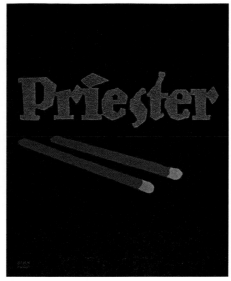

14–6

14–7

poster art was developing in the hands of Bernhard and other young artists. It signed exclusive contracts with six of them, including Bernhard, Hans Rudi Erdt (1883–1918), Julius Gipkens (1883–1968), and Julius Klinger (1876–1950). This farsighted business decision effectively forced anyone wishing to commission designs from these artists to work with the Hollerbaum and Schmidt printing firm. Comparison of the Stiller shoes poster by Bernhard and Erdt's "Never Fail" and Opel motorcar posters (Figs. **14–8** and **14–9**) demonstrate how well Erdt was able to apply the Bernhard formula: flat background color; large, simple image; and product name. Gipkens, like Bernhard, was a self-taught graphic designer who developed a large clientele in Berlin. His fluid, linear drawing gave a nervous wiggle to both his lettering and images and became a trademark in his work (Fig. **14–10**).

Born and educated in Vienna, Julius Klinger had been associated with the Vienna Secession artists. He eventually moved to Berlin, where his style veered from floral art nouveau toward decorative shapes of bright, clear color and concise, simple lettering (see Fig. **14–19**). His designs were less reductive than works by Bernhard and Erdt.

During the early years of Bernhard's poster design career, he developed a sans-serif lettering style painted in broad brushstrokes. At first he did not employ any particular concept, but over time dense alphabets of unique character gradually developed. This lettering impressed a staff member from the Berthold Type Foundry in Berlin, and a typeface design was based on it (Fig. **14–11**). When the typeface was released

14–2. The Beggarstaffs, poster for *Harper's Magazine,* 1895. The viewer brings closure by combining fragments into a symbolic image.

14–3. The Beggarstaffs, poster for *Don Quixote,* 1896. Cut paper shapes produce a graphic image whose simplicity and technique were ahead of their time.

14–4. William Nicholson, illustration from *An Alphabet,* 1897. The reductive simplicity of Beggarstaff posters is maintained.

14–5. Dudley Hardy, theatrical poster for *The Gaiety Girl,* 1898. The actor and play title stand out dramatically against the red background.

14–6 Lucien Bernhard, poster for Priester matches, c. 1905. Color became the means of projecting a powerful message with minimal information.

14–7. Lucian Bernhard, poster for Stiller shoes, 1912. Against the brown background, dark letterforms, and black shoe, the inside of the shoe is intense red and the front of the heel is bright orange.

in 1910, Bernhard was quite surprised to see his personal lettering style cast in metal for the entire world to use. His sense of simplicity was also applied to trademark design. For Hommel Micrometers, in 1912, Bernhard constructed a little mechanical man holding one of the client's sensitive measuring devices (Fig. **14–12**). For Manoli cigarettes, in 1911, Bernhard reduced the firm's trademark to an elemental letter within a geometric form printed in a second color (Figs. **14–13** and **14–14**).

Bernhard was a pivotal designer. His work might be considered the logical conclusion of the turn-of-the-century poster movement. At the same time, his emphasis on reduction,

14–8

14–9

INNEN-DEKORATION
VERLAG UND REDAKTION

14–11

14–12

14–10

minimalist form, and simplification anticipated the constructivist movement. As time went on, Bernhard tackled interior design, then studied carpentry to learn furniture design and construction. This led to a study of architecture; during the 1910s Bernhard designed furniture, rugs, wallpapers, and lighting fixtures as well as office buildings, factories, and houses.

A visit to America in 1923 excited Bernhard, and he returned to live in New York. His work was far too modern to gain acceptance in America; it took him five years to establish himself as a graphic designer. During that time he worked as an interior designer. In 1928 Bernhard contracted with American Type Founders to design new typefaces, producing a steady stream of new fonts that captured the sensibilities of the era.

Switzerland and the *Sach plakat*

In Switzerland, a land with three principle languages, poster design was affected by German, French, and Italian cultures. Like the Netherlands, Switzerland is a small country amidst large neighbors, and many outside influences are also apparent there. The country has long been a popular vacation spot, and travel posters filled a natural need. With his 1908 poster of Zermatt (Fig. **14–15**), Emil Cardinaux (1877–1936) created the

14–13

14–14

14–8. Hans Rudi Erdt, poster for Never Fail safes, 1911. The military bearing of the security guard reflects the reliability of the company.

14–9. Hans Rudi Erdt, poster for Opel automobiles, 1911. Pose, expression, and clothing signify the affluent customer for this automobile.

14–10. Julius Gipkens, poster for Heinemann's wicker furniture, undated. The dog and checkered cushion suggest hearth and home.

14–11. Berthold Type Foundry, Block Type, 1910. Early twentieth-century German sans-serif typefaces were based on Bernhard's poster lettering.

14–12. Lucian Bernhard, trademark for Hommel Micrometers, 1912. Every shape and form comprising this figure is derived from Hommel's products.

14–13. Lucian Bernhard, trademark for Manoli cigarettes, 1910. A simple *M* in a circle suggests the minimalism of future trademarks.

14–14. Lucian Bernhard, poster for Manoli, 1910. Bernhard designed a number of posters for Manoli cigarettes. The name *Manoli* was derived from the name of the company owner's wife, Ilona Mandelbaum, in reverse.

14–15. Emil Cardinaux, Zermatt poster, 1908. The Matterhorn emerges in all its splendor above the landscape and simple lettering below.

14–15

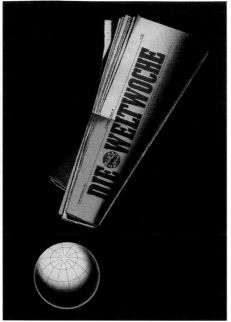

14–16

14–17

14–18

14–16. Niklaus Stoecklin, BiORO poster, 1941. Combined with a pair of sunglasses, the tube of sunscreen lotion becomes a nose.

14–17. Herbert Leupin, poster for *Die Weltwoche,* 1949. A globe and a rolled up newspaper together form an exclamation point.

14–18. Otto Baumberger, poster for the department store PKZ, 1923.

14–19. Julius Klinger, poster for Germany's eighth bond drive, 1917. Eight arrows piercing a dragon remind citizens that their contributions have helped wound the enemy.

14–20. Lucian Bernhard, poster for a war-loan campaign, 1915. A sharp militaristic feeling is amplified by the Gothic inscription, "This is the way to peace—the enemy wills it so! Thus subscribe to the war loan!"

14–21. Lucian Bernhard, "Frauen!" (Women!), poster, 1918. The women's liberation movement had already been active in Germany , but the war increased its momentum. This poster announced the first elections in Germany open to women.

first modern Swiss poster, sharing many characteristics with the Plakatstil in Germany. Even after modern production procedures such as offset printing began to be used in most poster production, traditional lithographic crafts were retained in what was known as Basel realism. This style was promoted by Niklaus Stoecklin (1896–1982) (Fig. **14–16**), Otto Baumberger (1889–1961), and later Herbert Leupin (1914–99) (Fig. **14–17**), whose *Sachplakate* (object posters) were characterized by a simple, laconic, and sometimes hyper-realistic approach. Baum-

berger's 1923 poster for the PKZ department store consists of a life-size drawing of a coat showing the actual hairs of the fabric with the text restricted to "PKZ" (Fig. **14–18**).

The poster goes to war

The poster reached the zenith of its importance as a communications medium during World War 1 (1914–18). Printing technologies had advanced rapidly, while radio and other electronic means of public communication were not yet in widespread use. In this global conflict, governments turned to the poster as a significant medium of propaganda and visual persuasion. Armies had to be recruited and public morale had to be boosted to maintain popular support for the war effort. In this first conflict fought with the armaments of technology—airplanes, zeppelins, heavy artillery, and tanks—fund-raising drives were used to collect vast amounts of money to finance the war. As resources were diverted to the war effort, public support for conservation and home gardening was required to lessen the risk of acute shortages. Finally, the enemy had to be assailed for its barbarism and threat to civilization.

The posters produced by the Central Powers (led by Germany and Austria-Hungary) were radically different from those made by the Allies (led by France, Russia, and Great Britain, joined by the United States in 1917). In Austria-Hungary and Germany, war posters continued the traditions of the Vienna Secession and the simplicity of the Plakatstil pioneered by Bernhard. Words and images were integrated, and the essence of the communication was conveyed by simplifying images into powerful shapes and patterns. In expressing this design philos-

14–21

14–19   14–20

ophy, Julius Klinger observed that the United States flag was the best poster America had. Klinger's war posters expressed complex ideas with simple pictographic symbols (Fig. **14–19**). Curiously, Bernhard adopted a medieval approach in several war posters, such as the hand-drawn red-and-black lithographic Seventh War Loan poster (Fig. **14–20**). In an almost primeval expression of the ancient Germanic spirit, Bernhard depicted a clenched fist in medieval armor thrusting from the top right corner of the space. His 1918 poster "Frauen" was designed for the first elections in German open to women (Fig. **14–21**).

Gipkens (Fig. **14–22**) often contrasted stark graphic shapes boldly against the white ground. When it became evident after 1916 that submarine warfare was the only possible way Germany could break the English blockade, Erdt (Fig. **14–23**) celebrated underwater heroes and rallied the public behind them. Showing the destruction of enemy symbols or flags was a frequent propaganda device. A most effective example is Cologne designer Otto Lehmann's (b. 1865) poster depicting industrial workers and farmers holding on their shoulders a soldier taking down a torn British flag (Fig. **14–24**).

The Allies' approach to graphic propaganda was more illustrative, using literal rather than symbolic imagery to address propaganda objectives. British posters stressed the need to protect traditional values, the home, and the family. Perhaps the most effective British poster of the war years is the widely imitated 1915 military recruiting poster by Alfred Leete (1882–1933) showing the popular Lord Horatio Kitchener, British Secretary of War, pointing directly at the viewer (Fig. **14–25**). This image originally appeared as the 5 September 1914 cover of

London Opinion magazine above the headline "Your Country Needs You." Some posters appealed directly to sentimentality, such as Saville Lumley's (d. 1950) 1914 image, "Daddy, What Did YOU do During the Great War?" (Fig. **14–26**).

Public patriotism ran high when the United States entered the war to "make the world safe for democracy" in "the war to end all wars." Illustrator Charles Dana Gibson offered his services as art director to the Division of Pictorial Publicity, a federal agency that produced over seven hundred posters and other propaganda materials for fifty other governmental agencies. Working without charge, leading magazine illustrators turned to poster design and grappled with the change in scale from magazine page to poster. Persuasive propaganda replaced narrative design, and suddenly the illustrators had to integrate lettering with images. James Montgomery Flagg (1877–1960), whose sketchy painting style was widely known, produced forty-six war posters during the year and a half of American involvement in the war, including his American version of the Kitchener poster, a self-portrait of Flagg himself (Fig. **14–27**).

Joseph C. Leyendecker (1874–1951) was America's most popular illustrator between the World War I era and the early 1940s. Leyendecker followed Gibson by creating a canon of idealized physical beauty in the mass media. His career received a boost from his popular posters. Asked to honor the role of Boy Scouts in the Third Liberty Loan Campaign (Fig. **14–28**), Leyendecker combined common visual symbols— Liberty clad in the flag, holding an imposing shield, and taking a "Be Prepared" sword from a scout—that promoted patriot-

14–22

14–23

14–24

14–25

14–26

14–27

ism within all levels of American society. His ability to convey the iconic essence of a subject was emerging. This skill held Leyendecker in good stead after the war, for his 322 covers for the *Saturday Evening Post* and countless advertising illustrations, notably for Arrow Shirts and Collars during the 1920s, effectively captured the American experience and attitudes during the two decades between the world wars.

Honoring soldiers and creating a cult around national leaders or symbolic figures were two important functions of the poster; ridiculing or disparaging the leaders of the enemy forces was another. In Paul Verrees's attempt at humor (Fig. **14–29**), a strategy seldom seen in propaganda posters, the Kaiser is "canned."

Many posters emphasized the public's contribution to the war effort by appealing to patriotic emotions. In a poster for the American Red Cross (Fig. **14–30**) by Jesse Willcox Smith (1863–1935), the viewer is asked if he or she has a service flag, which signifies that the household has supported the

14–28

14–29

14–30

14–22. Julius Gipkens, poster for an exhibition of captured air-planes, 1917. A symbolic German eagle sits triumphantly upon the indicia of a captured allied aircraft.

14–23. Hans Rudi Erdt, poster heralding German submarines, c. 1916. A powerful structural joining of type and image pro-claimed, "U-Boats Out!"

14–24. Otto Lehmann, poster for a war-loan campaign, undated. The lettering translates, "Support our men in field gray. Crush England's might. Subscribe to the war loan."

14–25. Alfred Leete, poster for military recruiting, c. 1915. This printed sheet confronts the spectator with a direct gaze.

14–26. Saville Lumley, "Daddy, What Did YOU Do in the Great War?," poster, 1914

14–27. James Montgomery Flagg, poster for military recruiting, 1917. Five million copies of Flagg's poster were printed, making it one of the most widely reproduced posters in history.

14–28. Joseph C. Leyendecker, poster celebrating a successful bond drive, 1917. Leyendecker's painting technique of slablike brush strokes makes this poster distinctive.

14–29. J. Paul Verrees, poster promoting victory gardens, 1918. Public action—the raising of one's own food—is tied directly to the defeat of the enemy.

14–30. Jesse Willcox Smith, poster for the American Red Cross, 1918. Public display of graphic symbols showing support for the war effort were encouraged.

Red Cross effort. Smith shared a studio with Elizabeth Shippen Green (1871–1954) and Violet Oakley (1874–1961), both of whom she met while studying with Howard Pyle. The three were very active as illustrators specializing in magazine and children's book illustrations portraying children, mother-hood, and the everyday life of the times.

The maverick from Munich

A leading Plakatstil designer, Ludwig Hohlwein (1874–1949) of Munich began his career as a graphic illustrator with work commissioned by *Jugend* magazine as early as 1904. During the first half of the century, Hohlwein's graphic art evolved with changing social conditions. The Beggarstaffs were his initial in-spiration, and in the years before World War I Hohlwein took great delight in reducing his images to flat shapes. Unlike the Beggarstaffs and his Berlin rival Bernhard, however, Hohlwein applied a rich range of texture and decorative pattern to his im-ages (Fig. **14–31**). Many of his early posters were for clothing manufacturers and retail stores, and it seemed that Hohlwein never repeated himself. In the posters that he designed during World War I, Hohlwein began to combine his simple, powerful shapes with more naturalistic imagery (Fig. **14–32**).

As evidenced in a poster (Fig. **14–33**) for a Red Cross col-lection to benefit the recovering war wounded, Hohlwein's work straddles the line between the symbolic posters of other Central Powers graphic designers and the Allies' pictorial posters. After the war Hohlwein received numerous advertis-ing poster commissions. His work became more fluid and painterly, with figures frequently arranged on a flat white or color ground and surrounded by colorful lettering.

14–31

14–33

14–34

14–32

After an unsuccessful attempt to seize power in the Munich Putsch of 1923, Adolf Hitler was sent to prison, where he spent his time writing *Mein Kampf*, which set forth his political philosophy and political ambitions for Germany. He wrote that propaganda "should be popular and should adapt its intellectual level to the receptive ability of the least intellectual" citizens. Hitler was convinced that the more artistically designed posters used in Germany and Austria during World War I were "wrongheaded" and the slogans and popular illustrations of the Allies more effective.

Hitler had an almost uncanny knack for visual propaganda. When he rose on the German political scene, the swastika was adopted as the symbol for the Nazi party. Uniforms consisting of brown shirts with red armbands bearing a black swastika in a white circle began to appear throughout Germany as the Nazi party grew in strength and numbers. In retrospect, it seems almost inevitable that the Nazi party would commission posters from Hohlwein, for the evolution of his work coincided closely with Hitler's concept of effective propaganda. As Hitler delivered passionate radio addresses to the nation about the German "master race" and the triumphant superiority of German athletes and culture, Hohlwein posters conveyed these images all across the nation (Figs. **14–34** and **14–35**). As the Nazi dictatorship consolidated its power and World War II approached, Hohlwein moved toward a bold imperial and militaristic style of tight, heavy forms and strong tonal contrasts (Fig. **14–36**). Hohlwein's oeuvre evolved with changing political and social currents, and his reputation as a designer was seriously tarnished by his collaboration with the Nazis.

Postcubist pictorial modernism

After World War I, the nations of Europe and North America sought a return to normalcy. The war machinery was turned toward peacetime needs, and a decade of unprecedented prosperity dawned for the victorious Allies. Faith in the machine and technology was at an all-time high. This ethic gained expression through art and design. Léger's celebration of mechanical, machine-made, and industrial forms became an important design resource, and cubist ideas about spatial

14–35   14–36

organization and synthetic imagery inspired an important new direction in pictorial images. Among the graphic designers who incorporated cubism directly into their work, an American working in London, Edward McKnight Kauffer (1890–1954), and a Ukrainian immigrant to Paris, A. M. Cassandre (born Adolphe Jean-Marie Mouron, 1901–68), played major roles in defining this new approach.

The term *art deco* is used to identify popular geometric works of the 1920s and 1930s. To some extent an extension of art nouveau, it signifies a major aesthetic sensibility in graphics, architecture, and product design during the decades between the two world wars. The influences of cubism, the Bauhaus (see chapter 16), and the Vienna Secession commingled with De Stijl and suprematism (discussed in chapter 15), as well as a mania for Egyptian, Aztec, and Assyrian motifs. Streamlining, zigzag, moderne, and decorative geometry—these attributes were used to express the modern era of the machine while still satisfying a passion for decoration. (The term *art deco*, coined by British art historian Bevis Hillier in the 1960s, derives from the title of the Exposition Internationale des Arts Décoratifs et Industriels Modernes, a major design exhibition held in Paris in 1925. It was not used for the title of this chapter because graphic designs not encompassed by the term, such as Plakatstil and the wartime propaganda posters, are also discussed here.)

Kauffer was born in Great Falls, Montana. His formal education was limited to eight years of grammar school because his itinerant fiddler father abandoned the family when Kauffer was three. At age twelve Kauffer began to work at odd jobs

14–31. Ludwig Hohlwein, poster for men's ready-made clothing, 1908. The interplay between organic/geometric form and figurative/abstract images fascinated Hohlwein.

14–32. Ludwig Hohlwein, Starnbergersee poster, 1910.

14–33. Ludwig Hohlwein, fund-raising poster, 1914. A graphic symbol (the red cross) combines with a pictorial symbol (a wounded soldier) in an appeal with emotional power and strong visual impact.

14–34. Ludwig Hohlwein, poster for the Deutsche Lufthansa, 1936. A mythological winged being symbolizes the airline, German victory in the Berlin Olympics, and the triumph of the Nazi movement.

14–35. Ludwig Hohlwein, concert poster, 1938. A Teutonic she-warrior looms upward, thanks to a low viewpoint and a light source striking her from below.

14–36. Ludwig Hohlwein, recruiting poster, early 1940s. In one of Hohlwein's last Nazi posters, a stern and somber soldier appears above a simple question, "And you?"

to supplement the family income. At age sixteen he traveled to San Francisco and worked in a bookstore while taking night-school art classes and painting on weekends. On his way to New York late in 1912, he stopped in Chicago for several months to study at the Art Institute. There he saw the famous Armory Show, which traveled to Chicago from New York in 1913. This first American exposure to modern art caused an uproar. The 16 March 1913 *New York Times* headline proclaimed "Cubists and Futurists Make Insanity Pay."

14–37   14–38   14–39

Twenty-two-year-old Kauffer responded intuitively to the strength of the work, decided his Chicago teachers were not on top of recent developments in art, and moved to Europe. After living in Munich and Paris, he journeyed to London in 1914 when war broke out. Kauffer's famous 1918 *Daily Herald* poster (Fig. **14–37**), although flawed somewhat by the type choice and placement, showed how the formal idiom of cubism and futurism could be used with strong communications impact in graphic design. Winston Churchill even suggested that Kauffer design an emblem for the Royal Flying Corps. For the next quarter of a century, a steady stream of posters and other graphic design assignments enabled him to apply the invigorating principles of modern art, particularly cubism, to the problems of visual communication. He designed 141 posters for the London Underground Transport (Figs. **14–38** and **14–39**). Many of these promoted weekend pleasure travel to rural areas at the end the lines. Kauffer achieved visual impact with landscape subjects on posters by reductive design, editing complex environments into interlocking shapes. Later his posters tended to display art deco attributes (Fig. **14–40**).

In a March 1937 *PM* magazine article, Aldous Huxley observed that in contrast to the predominant use of money and sex in advertising for everything from scents to sanitary plumbing, Kauffer "prefers the more difficult task of advertising products in terms of forms that are symbolical only to those particular products. . . . He reveals his affinity with all artists who have ever aimed at expressiveness through simplification, distortion, and transposition, and especially the

Cubists," producing "not a copy, but a simplified, formalized and more expressive symbol." When World War II began, Kauffer returned to his native America, where he worked until his death in 1954.

At age fourteen A. M. Cassandre immigrated to Paris from Ukraine, where he had been born to a Russian mother and French father. He studied at the École des Beaux Arts and Académie Julian. His graphic design career began at age twenty-two fulfilling poster commissions (Fig. **14–41**) from the Hachard & Cie printing firm to earn money for art study and living expenses. From 1923 until 1936 he revitalized French advertising art through a stunning series of posters. Cassandre's bold, simple designs emphasize two-dimensionality and are composed of broad, simplified planes of color. By reducing his subjects to iconographic symbols, he moved very close to synthetic cubism. His love of letterforms is evidenced by an exceptional ability to integrate words and images into a total composition. Cassandre achieved concise statements by combining telegraphic copy, powerful geometric forms, and symbolic imagery created by simplifying natural forms into almost pictographic silhouettes. A poster for the Paris newspaper *L'Intransigeant* (Fig. **14–42**) is a masterful composition. Cassandre cropped the paper's name as it thrust toward the upper right-hand corner, leaving the often-used shortened version.

Many of Cassandre's finest works were for railways (Figs. **14–43** and **14–44**) and steamship lines. In his poster for the ocean liner *L'Atlantique* (Fig. **14–45**), Cassandre exaggerated the scale difference between the ship and the tugboat to

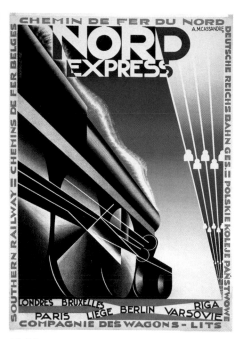

14–40

14–43

14–44

14–41

14–42

14–37. E. McKnight Kauffer, poster for the *Daily Herald,* 1918. This bellwether poster was based on the designer's earlier futurist- and cubist-inspired print of flying birds.

14–38. E. McKnight Kauffer, London Underground poster, 1930. Lyrical muted colors capture the idyllic quality of the rural location.

14–39. E. McKnight Kauffer, poster for the London Underground, 1924. The essence of the subject is distilled into dynamic colored planes.

14–40. E. McKnight Kauffer, poster for the London Underground. Art deco is dominant in this poster suggesting the power of the London Underground.

14–41. A. M. Cassandre, poster for the furniture store Au Bucheron, 1923. Cassandre's first poster used a repetition of orange and yellow geometric planes.

14–42. A. M. Cassandre, poster for the Paris newspaper *L'Intransigeant,* 1925. A pictographic image of Marianne, the symbolic voice of France, urgently shouts news received over telegraph wires.

14–43. A. M. Cassandre, poster for the North Star Paris-to-Amsterdam night train, 1927. A magnificent abstract design conveys an intangible aspect of travel: distant destinations offer new experiences and hope for the future. Amsterdam hosted the Olympic Games in 1928, and this poster advocated rail travel for that event.

14–44. A. M. Cassandre, Express Nord poster, 1927. The spirit of art deco is clearly expressed by the image of the locomotive.

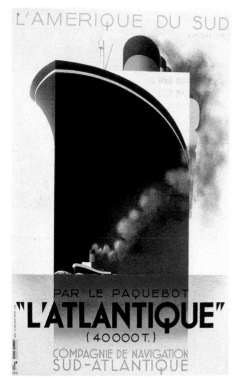

14–45

14–48

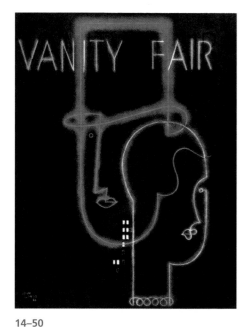

14–50

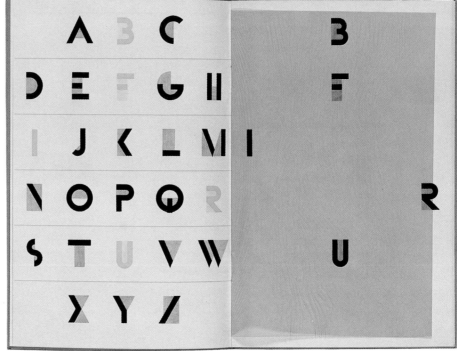

14–47

14–46

14–49

achieve a monolithic quality signifying safety and strength. The severe geometry is softened by the smoke and fading reflection. The iconography of his cinematic sequence of word and image was used to advertise the liqueur Dubonnet (Fig. **14–46**) for over two decades. Consumption of the beverage transforms the line drawing into a full-color painting. The figure became a popular trademark used in formats ranging from notepads to press advertisements and billboards. In the

1964 book *Language of Vision* the designer and design historian Gyorgy Kepes described Cassandre's method: "One unifying device employed by Cassandre was the use of a contour line common to various spatial units. The double outline takes on a double meaning, similar to a visual pun. It refers to inside and outside space simultaneously, . . . [and] the spectator is therefore forced into intensive participation as he seeks to resolve the apparent contradiction. But the equivocal contour

14–45. A. M. Cassandre, poster for the ocean liner *L'Atlantique,* 1931. The ship is constructed on a rectangle, echoing the poster's rectangular edges.

14–46. A. M. Cassandre, poster for Dubonnet, 1932. DUBO (doubt): the man eyes his glass uncertainly; DU BON (of some good): the beverage is tasted; and DUBONNET: the product is identified as the glass is refilled.

14–47. A. M. Cassandre, Bifur typeface, 1929. Strokes from each letter are omitted; a linear shaded area restores the basic silhouette.

14–48. A. M. Cassandre, Acier Noir typeface, 1936. In this unique design, each letter is half solid and half outlined.

14–49. A. M. Cassandre, Peignot typeface, 1937. This thick-and-thin sans serif replaces lowercase with small capitals having ascenders and descenders.

14–50. Jean Carlu, *Vanity Fair* cover, 1930. Stylized geometric heads evoke neon lights and cubism as they glow against a night sky.

line does more than unify different spatial data. It acts like a warp, weaving the threads of color planes into one rhythmical unity. The rhythmical flow of the line injects the picture surface with a sensual intensity."

For the Deberny and Peignot type foundry, Cassandre designed typefaces with daring innovations. In the quintessential art deco display type Bifur (Fig. **14–47**), the eye is able to fill in the missing parts and read the characters. Acier Noir (Fig. **14–48**) contrasts outline and solid black portions of the letters, while Peignot (Fig. **14–49**) represents the attempt to revolutionize the alphabet by reviving an earlier roman form. All lowercase letters are small capitals, except the *b, d,* and *f.* The small *H, K,* and *L* have ascending strokes.

During the late 1930s Cassandre worked in the United States for such clients as *Harper's Bazaar*, Container Corporation of America, and N. W. Ayer. After returning to Paris in 1939, he turned to painting and design for the ballet and theater, which were his major areas of involvement over the next three decades.

In addition to Kauffer and Cassandre, many other graphic designers and illustrators incorporated concepts and images from cubism in their work. Jean Carlu (1900–89), a promising eighteen-year-old French architectural student, fell under the wheels of a Paris trolley car; his right arm was severed from his body. His survival was miraculous, and during long days of recovery he thought intensely about the world and his future. World War I had turned northern France into a vast burial ground, and the country struggled for economic recovery in the face of devastation. Having to abandon his dream of architecture, young Carlu vowed to become an artist and apply his talents to the needs of his country, and with commitment and concentration, he taught himself to draw with his left hand.

Carlu understood the modern movements and applied this knowledge to visual communication (Fig. **14–50**). Realizing the need for concise statements, he made a dispassionate, objective analysis of the emotional value of visual elements. Then he assembled them with almost scientific exactness. Tension and alertness were expressed by angles and lines; feelings of ease, relaxation, and comfort were transmitted by curves. Carlu sought to convey the essence of the message by avoiding the use of "two lines where one would do" or expressing "two ideas where one will deliver the message more forcefully." To study the effectiveness of communications in the urban environment, he conducted experiments with posters moving past spectators at varying speeds so that message legibility and impact could be assessed and documented.

In 1940 Carlu was in America completing an exhibition entitled "France at War" for the French Information Service display at the New York World's Fair. On 14 June 1940 German troops marched into Paris, and Carlu was stunned to learn that his country was capitulating to Hitler. He decided to remain in America for the duration of the war; this sojourn extended to thirteen years. Some of his best work was created during this period, notably his posters designed for the American and Allied war efforts (see Fig. 17–24). In his finest designs, word and image are interlocked in terse messages of great power.

Paul Colin (1892–1989) started his career as a graphic designer in 1925, when an acquaintance from the trenches of World War I asked the thirty-three-year-old painter if he would like to become the graphics and set designer for the Théâtre des Champs-Elysées in Paris. In program covers and posters, Colin often placed a figure or object centrally before a colored background and type or lettering above and/or below it. These strong, central images are animated by a variety of techniques: creating a double image, often with different drawing techniques and scale changes; using the transparency of overlapping images as a means to make two things into one; adding color shapes or bands behind or to the side of the central figure to counteract its static placement. Vibrant color, informal compositions, and energetic linear drawings expressed joy in life (Fig. **14–51**).

Colin's simple, sketchy design tendencies enabled him to produce a substantial oeuvre. Estimates of the number of posters he created range from one to two thousand, and some sources credit him with as many as eight hundred set designs. Whatever the exact numbers, Colin was the most prolific and enduring French designer of his generation. He produced propaganda posters during World War II until the fall of France, and new Colin posters were still being commissioned, printed, and posted throughout Paris during the early 1970s.

A direct application of cubism to graphic design was made by Austin Cooper (1890–1964) in England. In a series of three

14–51

14–52

collage-inspired posters, he attempted to spark memories of the viewer's earlier Continental visits by presenting fragments and glimpses of landmarks (Fig. **14–52**). Lively movement is achieved by shifting planes, sharp angles, and the superimposition of lettering and images. In 1924 Cooper made an interesting foray into the use of pure geometric shape and color to solve a communications problem for the London Underground (Figs. **14–53** and **14–54**). Geometric forms rising from the bottom to the top of each poster change in a color spectrum from warm to cool to symbolize the temperature changes as one leaves the cold street in winter—or the hot street in summer—for the greater comfort of the underground railway.

In Vienna, Joseph Binder (1898–1972) studied at the Vienna School of Applied Art, which was under the direction of Alfred Roller, from 1922 until 1926. While still a student, Binder combined various influences, including Koloman Moser

and cubism, into a pictorial graphic design style with strong communicative power. The hallmarks of his work were natural images reduced to basic forms and shapes, like the cube, sphere, and cone, and two flat color shapes used side by side to represent the light and shadow sides of a figure or object. His award-winning poster for the Vienna Music and Theater Festival (Fig. **14–55**) is an early manifestation of the uniquely Viennese approach to art deco. Binder traveled widely, settling in New York City in 1935. As with so many immigrants to America, his work evolved in his changed environment (see Figs. 17–17 and 17–18). He developed a highly refined and stylized naturalism in posters and billboards advertising throat lozenges, beer, travel, and public services.

Between the world wars, Germany became a cultural hub as advanced ideas in all the arts flowed across its borders from other European countries. Geometric pictorial images

14–53

14–54

14–55

inspired by cubism and French advertising art—along with lettering, typography, and spatial organization from the Russian constructivist and Dutch De Stijl movements (discussed in chapter 15)—combined with vigorous Teutonic forms in a unique national approach. Superb printing technology and rigorous art training institutes enabled German graphic designers to achieve a high level of excellence. Schulz-Neudamm, staff designer for motion picture publicity at Universum-Film Aktiengesellschaft, is prominent among the many German designers who created memorable graphics during this period (Fig. **14–56**).

In England, Abram Games (1914–96) extended the philosophy and spatial ideas of postcubist pictorial modernism through World War II and well into the second half of the twentieth century. He began his career on the eve of World War II and produced educational, instructional, and propaganda graphics during the war. About his philosophy, Games wrote, "the message must be given quickly and vividly so that interest is subconsciously retained. The discipline of reason conditions the expression of design. The designer constructs, winds the spring. The viewer's eye is caught, the spring released." Games's poster for the Emergency Blood Transfusion Service (Fig. **14–57**) asks the viewer, "If he should fall, is your blood there to save him?" Ordinary images of a hand, a bottle, and a foot soldier are combined in a compelling statement that provokes an emotional response from the observer.

14–51. Paul Colin, travel poster for Paris, 1935. Informal color shapes move in counterpoint to simple contour illustrations in an open composition.

14–52. Austin Cooper, poster for the Southern Railway, undated. Cubist rhetoric operates symbolically for mass communications, with fragments and glimpses of a Paris trip.

14–53. Austin Cooper, poster for the London Underground, 1924. Color conveys the comfort of warmer temperatures in the underground railway during winter.

14–54. Austin Cooper, poster for the London Underground, 1924. Color conveys the comfort of cooler temperatures in the underground railway during the summers.

14–55. Joseph Binder, poster for the Vienna Music and Theater Festival, 1924. Figures are reduced to flat, geometric shapes, but the proportions and light-and-shadow planes retain a sense of naturalism.

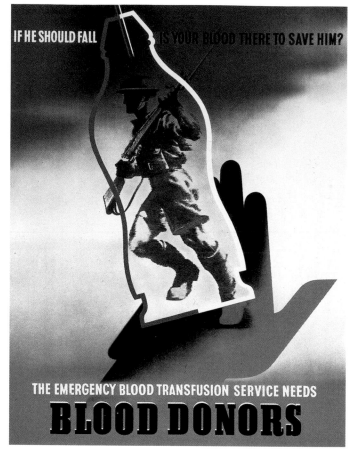

14–57

14–56. Schulz-Neudamm, cinema poster for *Metropolis*, 1926. The art deco idiom often conveyed unbridled optimism for machines and human progress, but here it turns darkly toward a future where robots replace people.

14–57. Abram Games, poster to recruit blood donors, c. 1942. Placing the soldier inside the diagram of the blood bottle cements the connection between the donor's blood and the soldier's survival.

14–56

Modernist pictorial graphics in Europe focused on the total integration of word and image, which became one of the most enduring currents of twentieth-century graphic design. The approach began with Bernhard's 1905 Priester matches poster, responded to the communications needs of World War I and the formal innovations of cubism and other early modern-art movements, and emerged after the war to play a major role in defining the visual sensibilities of the 1920s and 1930s. It retained sufficient momentum to provide graphic solutions to communications problems during World War II and beyond.

A New Language of Form

15

During the postwar years, when Kauffer and Cassandre were applying synthetic cubism's planes to the poster in England and France, a formal typographic approach to graphic design emerged in Holland and Russia, where artists saw clearly the implications of cubism. Visual art could move beyond the threshold of pictorial imagery into the invention of pure form. Ideas about form and composing space from the new painting and sculpture were quickly applied to problems of design. It would be a mistake, however, to say that modern design is a stepchild of the fine arts. As discussed in chapter 12, Frank Lloyd Wright (Fig. **15–1**), the Glasgow group, the Vienna Secession, Adolf Loos, and Peter Behrens were all moving a heartbeat ahead of modern painting in their consciousness of plastic volume and geometric form at the turn of the century. A spirit of innovation was present in art and design, and new ideas were in abundance. By the end of World War I, graphic designers, architects, and product designers were energetically challenging prevailing notions about form and function.

Russian suprematism and constructivism

Russia was torn by the turbulence of World War I and then the Russian Revolution in the second decade of the twentieth century. Czar Nicholas II (1868–1918) was overthrown and executed together with his family. Russia was ravaged by civil war, and the Red Army of the Bolsheviks emerged victorious by 1920. During this period of political trauma, a brief flowering of creative art in Russia had an international influence on twentieth-century graphic design. Beginning with Marinetti's

Russian lectures, the decade saw Russian artists absorb cubism and futurism with amazing speed and then move on to new innovations. The Russian avant-garde saw common traits in cubism and futurism and coined the term *cubo-futurism*. Experimentation in typography and design characterized their futurist publications, which presented work by the visual and literary art communities. Symbolically, the Russian futurist books were a reaction against the values of czarist Russia. The use of coarse paper, handicraft production methods, and handmade additions expressed the poverty of peasant society as well as the meager resources of the artists and writers. The poet Vladimir Mayakovsky's autobiographical play was printed in a dissonant futurist style designed by David and Vladimir Burliuk (Fig. **15–2**), becoming a model for works by others, including Ilya Zdanevich (Figs. **15–3** and **15–4**).

Kasimir Malevich (1878–1935) founded a painting style of basic forms and pure color that he called *suprematism*. After working in the manner of futurism and cubism, Malevich created an elemental geometric abstraction that was new and totally nonobjective. He rejected both utilitarian function and pictorial representation, instead seeking the supreme "expression of feeling, seeking no practical values, no ideas, no promised land." Malevich believed the essence of the art experience was the perceptual effect of color and form. To demonstrate this, perhaps as early as 1913 he made a composition with a black square on a white background (Fig. **15–5**), asserting that the feeling this contrast evoked was the essence of art. In works such as the 1915 *Suprematist Composition* (Fig. **15–6**) and the cover of *Pervyi tsikl lektsii (First Circle of Lectures)* (Fig. **15–7**), Malevich created a construction of concrete elements of color and shape. The visual form became the content, and expressive qualities developed from the intuitive organization of the forms and colors.

The Russian movement was actually accelerated by the revolution, for art was given a social role rarely assigned to it. Leftist artists had been opposed to the old order and its conservative visual art. In 1917 they turned their energies to a massive propaganda effort in support of the revolutionaries, but by 1920 a deep ideological split developed concerning the role of the artist in the new communist state. Some artists, including Malevich and Kandinsky, argued that art must remain an essentially spiritual activity apart from the utilitarian needs of society. They rejected a social or political role, believing the sole aim of art to be realizing perceptions of the world by inventing forms in space and time. Led by Vladimir Tatlin (1885–1953) and Alexander Rodchenko (1891–1956), twenty-five artists advanced the opposing viewpoint in 1921, when they renounced "art for art's sake" to devote themselves to industrial design, visual communications, and applied arts serving the new communist society. These constructivists called on the artist to stop

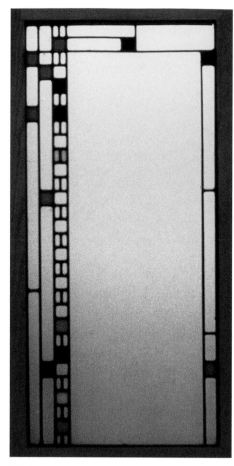

15–1

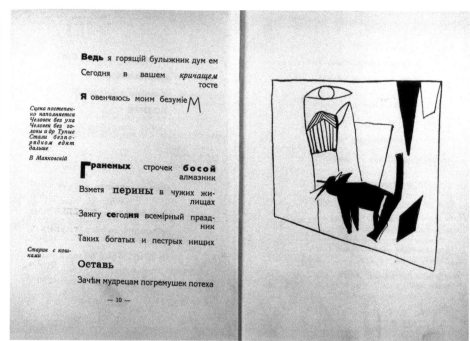

15–2

15–4

15–3

15–5

15–6

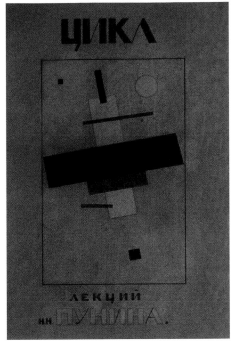

15–7

15–1. Frank Lloyd Wright, stained-glass window for the Coonley House, 1912. Space is organized as geometric planes; squares of red, orange, and blue create a vibrant counterpoint to white panes separated by dark strips of lead.

15–2. David and Vladimir Burliuk, pages from *Vladimir Mayakovsky: A Tragedy,* 1914. In an effort to relate visual form to meaning, Russian futurist graphic design mixed type weights, sizes, and styles.

15–3. Ilya Zdanevich, insert cover of *Milliork,* by Aleksei Kruchenykh, 1919.

15–4. Ilya Zdanevich, pages from *Le-Dantyu as a Beacon,* 1923. The Burliuk brothers and the Dadaists inspired Zdanevich's playscript design, the lively movements of which are created by mixing type sizes and styles, and building letters with letterpress ornaments.

15–5. Kasimir Malevich, *Black Square,* c. 1913. A new vision for visual art is as far removed as possible from the world of natural forms and appearances.

15–6. Kasimir Malevich, *Suprematist Composition,* 1915. A symphonic arrangement of elemental shapes of luminous color on a white field becomes an expression of pure feeling.

15–7. Kasimir Malevich, cover of *Pervyi tsikl lektsii* (First Circle of Lectures), by Nikolai Punin. A suprematist composition is combined with typography, 1920.

producing useless things such as paintings and turn to the poster, for "such work now belongs to the duty of the artist as a citizen of the community who is clearing the field of the old rubbish in preparation for the new life." Tatlin turned from sculpture to the design of a stove that would give maximum heat from minimum fuel; Rodchenko forsook painting for graphic design and photojournalism.

An early attempt to formulate constructivist ideology was the 1922 brochure *Konstruktivizm* by Aleksei Gan (1893–1942). He criticized abstract painters for their inability to break the umbilical cord connecting them to traditional art and boasted that constructivism had moved from laboratory work to practical application. Gan wrote that tectonics, texture, and construction were the three principles of constructivism. *Tectonics* represented the unification of communist ideology with visual form; *texture* meant the nature of materials and how they are used in industrial production; and *construction* symbolized the creative process and the search for laws of visual organization.

The constructivist ideal was best realized by the painter, architect, graphic designer, and photographer El (Lazar Markovich) Lissitzky. This indefatigable visionary profoundly influenced the course of graphic design. At age nineteen, after being turned down by the Petrograd Academy of Arts because of ethnic prejudice against Jews, Lissitzky studied architecture at the Darmstadt, Germany, school of engineering and architecture. The mathematical and structural properties of architecture formed the basis for his art.

15–8

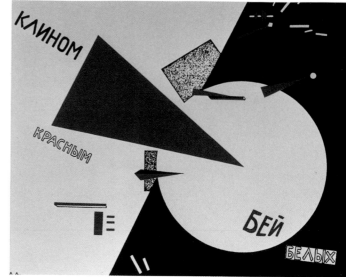

15–9

15–8. El Lissitzky, *PROUN 23*, no. 6, 1919. Lissitzky developed visual ideals about balance, space, and form in his paintings, which became the basis for his graphic design and architecture.

15–9. El Lissitzky, *Beat the Whites with the Red Wedge*, 1919. The Bolshevik army emblem, a red wedge, slashes diagonally into a white sphere signifying A. F. Kerensky's "white" forces. The slogan's four words are placed to reinforce the dynamic movement.

15–10. El Lissitzky, cover art for *Veshch*, 1921–22. Mechanical drawing instruments were used to construct geometric letterforms in a different style for each title; small typeset type was pasted in for plating.

15–11. El Lissitzky, title page for *Veshch*, 1922. Lissitzky searched for a geometric organizational system relating type, geometric elements, and photographs as elements in a whole. These goals were achieved by 1924.

15–12. El Lissitzky, layout for a *Broom* cover, vol. 5, no. 3, 1922. Isometric perspective letterforms are upside down and backward in the second title presentation, achieving a subtle vitality in a rigorously symmetrical design.

In 1919 Marc Chagall, principal of the art school in Vitebsk, located about 250 miles east of Moscow, asked Lissitzky to join the faculty. Malevich was teaching there and became a major influence on Lissitzky, who developed a painting style that he called *PROUNS* (an acronym for "projects for the establishment [affirmation] of a new art"). In contrast to the absolute flatness of Malevich's picture plane, PROUNS (Fig. **15–8**) introduced three-dimensional illusions that both receded (negative depth)

behind the picture plane (naught depth) and projected forward (positive depth) from the picture plane. Lissitzky called PROUNS "an interchange station between painting and architecture." This indicates his synthesis of architectural concepts with painting; it also describes how PROUNS pointed the way to the application of modern painting concepts of form and space to applied design. This is seen in his 1919 poster "Beat the Whites with the Red Wedge" (Fig. **15–9**). The space is dynamically divided into white and black areas. Suprematist design elements are transformed into political symbolism that even a semiliterate peasant can supposedly understand: Support for the "red" Bolshevik against the "white" forces of Kerenski is symbolized by a red wedge slashing into a white circle.

Lissitzky saw the October 1917 Russian Revolution as a new beginning for mankind. Communism and social engineering would create a new order, technology would provide for society's needs, and the artist/designer (he called himself a constructor) would forge a unity between art and technology by constructing a new world of objects to provide mankind with a richer society and environment. This idealism led him to put increasing emphasis on graphic design, as he moved from private aesthetic experience into the mainstream of communal life.

In 1921 Lissitzky traveled to Berlin and the Netherlands, where he made contact with De Stijl, the Bauhaus, Dadaists, and other constructivists. In addition, he met the architect Hendricus Theodorus Wijdeveld (1885–1987) and designed a cover for the magazine *Wendingen* in 1922 (see Fig. 15–60). Postwar Germany had become a meeting ground for eastern and western advanced ideas in the early 1920s. Access to excellent German printing facilities enabled Lissitzky's typo-

15–10   15–11   15–12

graphic ideas to develop rapidly. His tremendous energy and range of experimentation with photomontage, printmaking, graphic design, and painting enabled him to become the main conduit through which suprematist and constructivist ideas flowed into Western Europe. Editorial and design assignments for several publications were important vehicles by which his ideas influenced a wider audience.

During the early 1920s the Soviet government offered official encouragement to the new Russian art and even sought to publicize it through an international journal (Figs. **15–10** and **15–11**). Editor Ilya Ehrenburg was joined by Lissitzky in creating the trilingual journal *Veshch* (Russian)/*Gegenstand* (German)/*Objet* (French). The title (meaning "object") was chosen because the editors believed that art meant the creation of new objects, a process for building a new collective international approach led by young European and Russian artists and designers. The first cover (Fig. 15–10) shows how Lissitzky constructed his designs on a dynamic diagonal axis with asymmetrical balancing of elements, the weight placed high on the page. Lissitzky and Ehrenburg realized that parallel yet isolated art and design movements had evolved during the seven-year period of separation when Europe and Russia were bled by revolution and war; they saw *Veshch as* a meeting point for new works from different nations.

Lissitzky's Berlin period enabled him to spread the constructivist message through frequent Bauhaus visits, important articles, and lectures. Major collaborations included the joint design and editing of a special double issue of *Merz* with Schwitters in 1924. The editors of *Broom*, a radical American magazine covering advanced literature and art, commissioned

title pages and other graphics from Lissitzky. A *Broom* cover layout (Fig. **15–12**) shows Lissitzky's practice of making layouts on graph paper, which imposed the modular structure and mathematical order of a grid upon his designs. Advertisements and displays were commissioned by the Pelikan Ink Company (Figs. **15–13** and **15–14**). Rebelling against the constraints of metal typesetting, Lissitzky often used drafting-instrument construction and paste-up to achieve his designs. In 1925 he predicted that Gutenberg's system of printing would become a thing of the past and that photomechanical processes would replace metal type and open new horizons for design as surely as radio had replaced the telegraph.

As a designer, Lissitzky did not decorate the book—he constructed it by visually programming the total object. In a 1923 book of Vladimir Mayakovsky's poems, *For the Voice,* also translated as *For Reading Out Loud* (Figs. **15–15**, **15–16**, and **15–17**), Lissitzky designed exclusively with elements from the metal typecase, set by a German compositor who knew no Russian. He said his intent was to interpret the poems as "a violin accompanies a piano." A die-cut tab index along the right margin helped the reader find a poem. Each poem's title spread is illustrated with abstract elements signifying its content. Spatial composition, contrast between elements, the relationship of forms to the negative space of the page, and an understanding of such printing possibilities as overlapping color were important in this work.

One of the most influential book designs of the 1920s was *The Isms of Art 1914–1924* (Fig. **15–18**), which Lissitzky edited with the Dadaist Hans Arp. Lissitzky's format for this book was an important step toward the creation of a visual program for

15–13 15–14 15–15

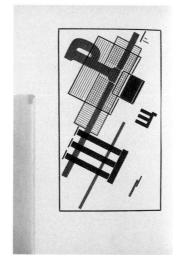

15–16 15–17

15–13. El Lissitzky, advertisement for Pelikan carbon paper, 1924. Typewriter type, the manufacturer's signature, and stamped letters express the product's use. Overlapping planes convey the sandwiching of material to make carbon copies.

15–14. El Lissitzky, poster for Pelikan ink, 1924. This photogram was produced in the darkroom by placing objects directly on the photographic paper, then making the exposure by flashing a light held to the left.

15–15. El Lissitzky, cover of *For the Voice,* by Mayakovsky, 1923. In contrast to the *Veshch* cover, constructed on a diagonal axis, here a rigid right angle is animated by the counterbalance of the *M* and circles.

15–16. El Lissitzky, pages from *For the Voice,* by Mayakovsky, 1923. The poem "Our March" begins, "Beat your drums on the squares of the riots, turned red with the blood of revolution." The title type has staccato cadences of a drumbeat; the red square signifies the blood-stained town squares.

15–17. El Lissitzky, pages from *For the Voice,* by Mayakovsky, 1923. The poem title "Order for the Army of the Arts" appears on the right page opposite a dynamic constructivist design.

15–18. El Lissitzky, book cover for *The Isms of Art,* 1924. Complex typographic information is organized into a cohesive whole by the construction of structural relationships.

15–18

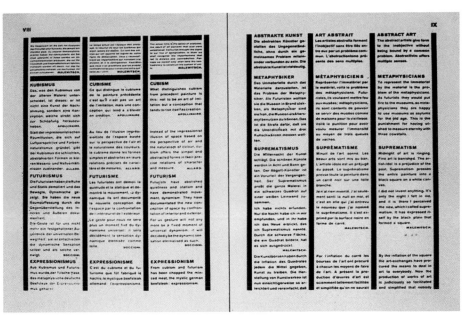

15–20

15–19

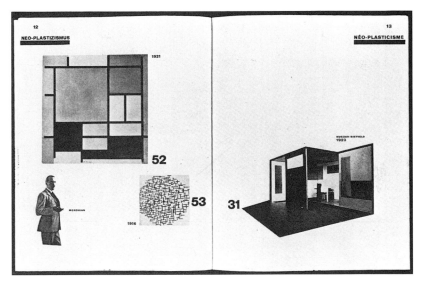

15–21

15–19. El Lissitzky, title page for *The Isms of Art,* 1924. The graphic spirit achieved by medium-weight sans-serif type, mathematical division of the space, white areas, and bold rules established a typographic standard for the modern movement.

15–20. El Lissitzky, text format for *The Isms of Art,* 1924. Rigorous verticals separate German, French, and English texts, and horizontal bars emphasize an important introductory quotation.

15–21. El Lissitzky, pictorial spread from *The Isms of Art,* 1924. The grid systems of the preceding typographic pages are echoed in the placement of the images, which are one, two, and three columns wide.

organizing information. The three-column horizontal grid structure used for the title page (Fig. **15–19**), the three-column vertical grid structure used for the text (Fig. **15–20**), and the two-column structure of the contents page became an architectural framework for organizing the forty-eight-page pictorially illustrated portfolio (Fig. **15–21**). Asymmetrical balance, silhouette halftones, and a skillful use of white space are other important design considerations. By using large, bold sans-serif numbers to link the pictures to captions listed earlier, Lissitzky allows these numbers to become compositional elements. This treatment of sans-serif typography and bold rules is an early expression of the modernist aesthetic.

15–22

15–24

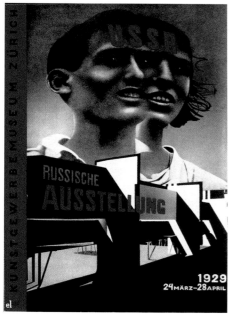

15–23

Lissitzky utilized montage and photomontage for complex communications messages (Fig. **15–22**). On a poster for a Russian exhibition in Switzerland, the image (Fig. **15–23**) gives equal position to the female and the male, a significant symbolic communication in a traditionally male-dominated society.

After returning to Russia in 1925, Lissitzky spent increasing amounts of time with large exhibition projects for the Soviet government (Fig. **15–24**) in addition to publications, art direction, and some architectural design projects. His eighteen-year battle with tuberculosis had begun two years before.

In December 1941, six months after Germany invaded Russia, Lissitzky died. Through his social responsibility and commitment to his people, his mastery of technology to serve his goals, and his creative vision, El Lissitzky set a standard of excellence for the designer. Later, typographer Jan Tschichold wrote, "Lissitzky was one of the great pioneers. . . . His indirect influence was widespread and enduring. . . . A generation that has never heard of him . . . stands upon his shoulders."

Alexander Rodchenko was an ardent communist who brought an inventive spirit and willingness to experiment to typography, montage, and photography. His early interest in descriptive geometry lent an analytical precision and definition of form to his paintings. In 1921 Rodchenko abandoned painting and turned to visual communication because his social views called for a sense of responsibility to society instead of to personal expression. Collaborating closely with the writer Mayakovsky, Rodchenko produced page designs with strong geometric construction, large areas of pure color, and concise, legible lettering. His heavy sans-serif hand-lettering engendered the bold sans-serif types that were widely used in the Soviet Union.

In 1923 Rodchenko began to design a magazine for all fields of the creative arts, entitled *Lef* (Figs. **15–25**, **15–26**, and **15–27**). A design style based on strong, static horizontal and vertical forms placed in machine-rhythm relationships emerged. Overprinting, precise registration, and photomontage were regularly employed in *Novyi lef*. Rodchenko delighted in contrasting bold, blocky type and hard-edged shapes against the softer forms and edges of photomontages. His interest in photomontage (Figs. **15–25** through **15–29**) was a

15–25   15–26   15–27   15–28

conscious effort to innovate an illustration technique appropriate to the twentieth century. The beginning of Russian photomontage coincided with the development of montage in film—a new conceptual approach to assembling cinematic information—and shared some of its vocabulary. Common techniques included showing simultaneous action; superimposing images; using extreme close-ups and perspective images, often together; and rhythmically repeating an image.

The concept of serial painting—a series or sequence of independent works unified by common elements or an underlying structure—was applied to graphic design by Rodchenko. In 1924 his series of ten covers for the Jim Dollar (pseudonym for the well-known Soviet author Marietta Shaginian) "Miss Mend" books (Fig. **15–29**) used a standard geometric format printed in black and a second color. The title, number, second color, and photomontage change with each edition, conveying the uniqueness of each book. The standardized elements bring consistency and economy to the whole series. As seen in the work of Salomon Telingater (1903–69), a dash of Dadaist vitality was often mixed into constructivist designs (Fig. **15–30**). A witty originality informed Telingater's use of typography and montage elements.

Georgii (1900–33) and Vladimir Augustovich (1899–1982) Stenberg were talented brothers who collaborated on theatrical designs and film posters (Figs. **15–31**, **15–32**, and **15–33**). Mindful of the reproduction difficulties with photographs at the time, they made meticulously realistic drawings for their posters by enlarging film-frame images via projection and grid methods. These three-dimensional illusions were contrasted with flat forms of bright color in dynamic, well-designed posters conveying strong, direct messages.

The master of propaganda photomontage was Gustav Klutsis (1895–1944), who referred to the medium as "the art construction for socialism." Employing monumental and heroic images, Klutsis used the poster as a means for extolling Soviet

15–22. El Lissitzky, cover of *Zapisky poeta* (Notes of a Poet), by Ilia Selvinskii, 1928.

15–23. El Lissitzky, exhibition poster, 1929. In this stark, powerful image, the youth of a collective society are cloned into an anonymous double-portrait above the exhibition structure designed by Lissitzky.

15–24. El Lissitzky, exhibition design for Pressa, 1928. Light, sound, and motion become design elements. Belts symbolic of web printing are in continuous movement in this publishing-industry design.

15–25. Alexander Rodchenko, cover for *Lef*, no. 1, 1923. The logo is printed in tight registration, with the top half of the letterforms red and the bottom half black.

15–26. Alexander Rodchenko, cover for *Lef*, no. 2, 1923. In this early photomontage, a crossout overprinting the montage negates the old order; young children symbolize the new society.

15–27. Alexander Rodchenko, cover for *Lef*, no. 3, 1923. A biplane bearing the magazine logo drops a fountain-pen bomb at a gorilla representing the traditional arts of the czarist regime.

15–28. Alexander Rodchenko, poster, 1937. Lenin looms above, larger than life, yet his hand makes symbolic contact with the masses. The "podium" is a *Rabochii* newspaper proclaiming "Peace! Bread! Land!"

accomplishments. His work has often been compared to John Heartfield's powerful political statements. It is highly likely that Klutsis was familiar with Heartfield's work, which was exhibited in Russia during the 1930s. Klutsis was convinced that photomontage was the medium of the future and that it had rendered all other forms of artistic realism obsolete. Although most of his posters celebrated the achievements of Stalin, Klutsis's uncompromising avant-garde approach eventually caused him to be arrested in 1938 during the Stalinist purges. He perished in the labor camps in 1944 (Figs. **15–34**, **15–35**, **15–36**, and **15–37**).

15–29

15–31

15–30

Another Soviet artist associated with Tatlin and the constructivists who profoundly influenced Russian modernism was Vladimir Vasilevich Lebedev (1891–1967). He embraced Bolshevism and designed bold, flat, neoprimitivist agitational propaganda posters for ROSTA, the Soviet telegraph agency. This work proved to be excellent preparation for designing picture books for boys and girls. Lebedev learned to simplify, to reduce forms to their basic geometric shapes and use only brilliant primary colors, and to tell a story visually and in sequence. "In the twenties," he explained, "we fought for mastery and purity of art; we wanted fine art to be descriptive, not illustrative. Cubism gave us discipline of thought, without which there is neither mastery nor purity of professional language." With the growth of the Soviet children's book industry under Lenin's New Economic Policy of the 1920s, Lebedev became the father of the twentieth-century Russian picture book. In such graphic masterpieces as *Prikliucheniya chuch-lo* (The Adventures of the Scarecrow, 1922) (Figs. **15–38** and **15–39**), *Azbuka* (Alphabet Book, 1925), *Morozhenoe* (Ice Cream, 1925), *Okhota* (The Hunt, 1925), *Tsirk* (Circus, 1925) (Figs. **15–40** and **15–41**),

15–32

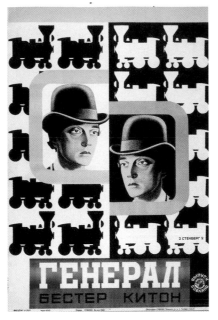

15–33

15–34

15–35

15–36

15–37

15–29. Alexander Rodchenko, paperback book covers, 1924. Consistency is achieved through standardized format; montages illustrate each story.

15–30. Salomon Telingater, covers for *Slovo predstavliaetsia Kirsanovu* (The Word Belongs to Kirsanov), by K. Kirsanov, 1930. The author's whimsy is reflected in Telingater's rollicking typography, which changes tune, tempo, and key as it flows down the page.

15–31. Georgy and Vladimir Augustovich Stenberg, film poster, undated. Spatial dislocation is achieved by extreme perspective, circular type, and the fragmented figure.

15–32. Georgy and Vladimir Augustovich Stenberg "The Eleventh Year of the Revolution," poster, 1928

15–33. Georgy and Vladimir Augustovich Stenberg, "The General," poster, 1929.

15–34. Gustav Klutsis, *Spartakiada* postcard, 1928

15–35. Gustav Klutsis, "We Will Repay the Coal Debt to the Country," poster, 1930

15–36. Gustav Klutsis, "Everyone Must Vote in the Election of Soviets" series, poster, 1930

15–37. Gustav Klutsis, "Building Socialism under the Banner of Lenin," poster, 1931

15–39

15–38

15–40

15–38. Vladimir Vasilevich Lebedev, book spread, *Prikliucheniya chuch-lo* (The Adventures of the Scarecrow), 1922.

15–39. Vladimir Vasilevich Lebedev, book spread, *Prikliucheniya chuch-lo* (The Adventures of the Scarecrow), 1922.

15–40. Vladimir Vasilevich Lebedev, book spread, *Tsirk* (Circus), 1928.

15–41. Vladimir Vasilevich Lebedev, book spread, *Tsirk* (Circus), 1928.

Vchera i segodnya (Yesterday and Today, 1925), and *Bagazh* (Baggage, 1926), often in collaboration with the poet Samuil Marshak, Lebedev devised a flexible, modernist shorthand for figures that he reduced to their simplest shapes against a vast white background and relieved only by bright, flat harmonious color and some contrasting texture. Like his French contempo-

raries, Lebedev cultivated "infantilism" in his work by borrowing the fresh, spontaneous, naïve techniques of children's art. "When I make drawings for children," he explained, "I try to recall my own consciousness as a child." He was also extraordinarily inventive with various typefaces. Lebedev, more than anyone else, brought the picture book up to date.

ПОД СВИСТ И ЩЕЛКАНЬЕ БИЧЕЙ, ПОД ГРОХОТ БАРАБАНА

ЛЕТИТ ОТЧАЯННЫЙ ЖОКЕЙ— ДОН ПЕДРО ОБЕЗЬЯНА.

МАМЗЕЛЬ ФРИКАСЕ

НА ОДНОМ КОЛЕСЕ.

15–41

Freeing his designs of any gratuitous detail, Lebedev illustrated little Marxist parables on the superiority of the Soviet system to capitalism. Lebedev was always an agitational propagandist at heart. But a good communist, he insisted, "doesn't deny the necessity of an individual approach to illustrations. And the more the artist shows his personality in his work, the more effective will his art be, the deeper it will influence the reader, the closer it will bring him to art." The Communist Party thought otherwise. During the Great Purges of the 1930s, *Pravda* denounced Lebedev's picture books for their "formalism"; and he was forced to capitulate to the dictates of the state-supported style, socialist realism, by replacing his hard-edged designs with lush, benign fluff. He always regretted the compromise.

During the years immediately following the 1917 revolution, the Soviet government tolerated advanced art while more urgent problems commanded its attention, but by 1922, having turned hostile, it accused experimental artists of "capitalist cosmopolitanism" and advocated social-realist painting. Although constructivism lingered as an influence in Soviet graphic and industrial design, painters like Malevich who did not leave the country drifted into poverty and obscurity. Like Klutsis, many artists vanished into the gulag. However, this artistic movement underwent further development in the West, and innovative graphic design in the constructivist tradition continued through the 1920s and beyond.

De Stijl

The De Stijl movement was launched in the Netherlands in the late summer of 1917. Its founder and guiding spirit, Théo van Doesburg, was joined by painters Piet Mondrian (1872–1944), Bart Anthony van der Leck (1876–1958), and Vilmos Huszár (1884–1960), the architect Jacobus Johannes Pieter Oud (1890–1963), and others. Working in an abstract geometric style, De Stijl sought universal laws of equilibrium and harmony for art, which could then be a prototype for a new social order.

Mondrian's paintings are the wellspring from which De Stijl's philosophy and visual forms developed. By 1911 Mondrian had evolved from traditional landscape painting to a symbolic style influenced by Van Gogh and expressing the forces of nature. It was then that he first saw cubist paintings. In early 1912 he relocated in Paris and began to introduce the vocabulary of cubism into his work. Over the next few years, Mondrian purged his art of all representative elements and moved cubism toward a pure, geometric abstraction. When war broke out in 1914, Mondrian was in Holland, and he remained there during the war.

The philosopher M. H. J. Schoenmakers decisively influenced Mondrian's thinking. Schoenmakers defined the horizontal and the vertical as the two fundamental opposites shaping our world, and called red, yellow, and blue the three principal colors. Mondrian began to paint purely abstract paintings composed of horizontal and vertical lines. He believed the cubists had not accepted the logical consequences of their discoveries; this was the evolution of abstraction toward its ultimate goal, the expression of pure reality. Mondrian believed true reality in visual art "is attained through dynamic movement in equilibrium . . . established through the balance of unequal but equivalent oppositions. The clarification of equilibrium through plastic art is of great importance for humanity. . . . It is the task of art to express a clear vision of reality."

For a time in the late 1910s, paintings and designs by Mondrian, Van der Leck, and Van Doesburg were quite similar (see Figs. **15–42**, **15–43**, and **15–44**). They reduced their visual vocabulary to the use of primary colors (red, yellow, and blue) with neutrals (black, gray, and white), straight horizontal and vertical lines, and flat planes limited to rectangles and squares.

With their prescribed visual vocabulary, De Stijl artists sought an expression of the mathematical structure of the universe and the universal harmony of nature. They were deeply concerned with the spiritual and intellectual climate of their time and wished to express the "general consciousness of their age." They believed the war was expunging an obsolete age, and science, technology, and political developments would usher in a new era of objectivity and collectivism. This attitude was widespread during World War I, for many European philosophers, scientists, and artists believed prewar values had lost their relevance. De Stijl sought the universal laws that govern visible reality but are hidden by the outward appearance of things. Scientific theory, mechanical production, and the rhythms of the modern city formed from these universal laws.

In the Dutch language, *schoon* means both "pure" and "beautiful." De Stijl adherents believed beauty arose from the absolute purity of the work. They sought to purify art by

15–42

15–43

15–42. Piet Mondrian, *Composition with Red, Yellow, and Blue,* 1922. The search for universal harmony becomes the subject, and the concrete presence of painted form on canvas becomes the vehicle for expressing a new visual reality.

15–43. Théo van Doesburg and Laszlo Moholy-Nagy, book cover, 1925. The essence of De Stijl is conveyed.

15–44. Bart van der Leck, layout for a Batavier Line poster, 1915–16. In a series of preliminary layouts, Van der Leck struggled to bring order to the design by dividing the space into rectangles.

15–45. Bart van der Leck, Batavier Line poster, 1916. Flat pure color and bold horizontal and vertical spatial divisions build the design.

15–46. Vilmos Huszár, cover design for *De Stijl,* 1917. Huszár combined his composition with type and Van Doesburg's logo to create a concise rectangle in the center of the page.

15–47. Vilmos Huszár, title pages for *De Stijl,* 1918. Huszár presented a positive/negative figure/ground study in spatial relationships. Restrained typography marked Apollinaire's death.

banning naturalistic representation, external values, and subjective expression. The content of their work was to be universal harmony, the order that pervades the universe. Mondrian produced a body of paintings of incomparable spiritual and formal quality. His compositions of asymmetrical balance, with tension between elements, achieved absolute harmony (Fig. **15–42**). The implications for modern design proved to be immense.

A 1925 cover (Fig. **15–43**) by Van Doesburg in collaboration with Hungarian artist Laszlo Moholy-Nagy (1895–1946) for the former's book *Grundbegriffe der neuen gestaltenden* (Basic Concepts of Form-making) shows the direct application of the De Stijl vocabulary to graphic design. Even before the movement formed, Van der Leck used flat, geometric shapes of pure color and created graphic designs with flat color images and simple black bars organizing the space (Figs. **15–44** and **15–45**).

Van Doesburg applied De Stijl principles to architecture, sculpture, and typography. He edited and published the journal *De Stijl* from 1917 until his death in 1931. Primarily funded with his own limited resources, this publication spread the movement's theory and philosophy to a larger audience. *De Stijl* advocated the absorption of pure art by applied art. The spirit of art could then permeate society through architectural, product, and graphic design. Under this system, art would not

15–44

15–45

15–46

15–47

be subjugated to the level of the everyday object; the everyday object (and, through it, everyday life) would be elevated to the level of art. *De Stijl* became a natural vehicle for expressing the movement's principles in graphic design. Huszár designed a logo with letters constructed from an open grid of squares and rectangles (Fig. **15–46**) and also designed some of the early title pages (Fig. **15–47**). In 1921 Van Doesburg developed a new horizontal format (Figs. **15–48** and **15–49**) that was used until the last issue, published in 1932. (Mondrian stopped contributing articles to the journal in 1924, after Van Doesburg developed his theory of elementarism, which declared the diago-

nal to be a more dynamic compositional principle than horizontal and vertical construction.)

In designs of alphabets and posters, Van Doesburg applied horizontal and vertical structure to letterforms and the overall layout (Fig. **15–50**). Curved lines were eliminated and sans-serif typefaces were favored. Type was often composed in tight rectangular blocks. The square was used as a rigorous module for letterform design. A harmony of form was achieved, but banishing curved and diagonal lines diminished character uniqueness and legibility. Asymmetrically balanced layouts were composed on an open implied grid. Color was

15–48

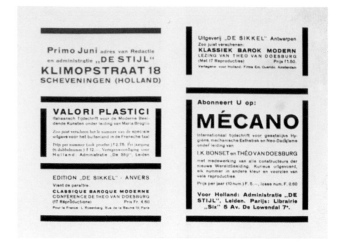

15–49

15–50

15–51

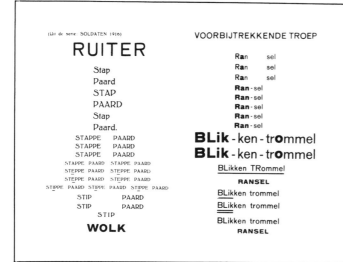

15–52

15–48. Théo van Doesburg, cover for *De Stijl,* 1922. Type is asymmetrically balanced in the four corners of an implied rectangle. *De Stijl* is combined with the letters *N* and *B,* which indicated *Nieuwe Beelden* (New Images).

15–49. Théo van Doesburg, advertisements and announcements from *De Stijl,* 1921. Five messages are unified by a system of open bars and sans-serifs typography.

15–50. Théo van Doesburg, exhibition poster, 1920. Original lettering was executed in ink in a poster for The Golden Section: International Exhibition of Cubists and Neo-Cubists.

15–51. Théo van Doesburg and Kurt Schwitters, "Kleine Dada Soirée," poster, 1922.

15–52. Théo van Doesburg, Dadaist poetry from *De Stijl,* 1921. Type size, weight, and style can be interpreted vocally when reading the poem aloud.

15–53. El Lissitzky, cover and page from *De Stijl,* 1922. Van Doesburg invited Lissitzky to design and edit a double issue of *De Stijl* that reprinted "A Tale of Two Squares" in Dutch.

15–54. Gerrit Rietveld, the Schroeder House, Utrecht, 1924. A new architecture is composed of planes in a square.

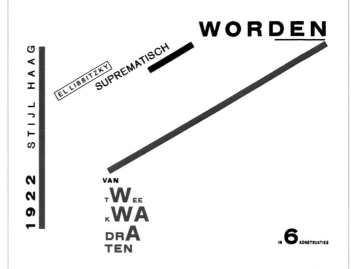

15–53

15–54

used not as an afterthought or decoration but as an important structural element. Red was favored as a second color in printing because, in addition to its graphic power to compete with black, it signified revolution.

Van Doesburg comprehended the liberating potential of Dada and invited Kurt Schwitters to Holland to campaign for it. They collaborated on typographic design projects (see Fig. **15–51**), and Van Doesburg explored Dada typography and poetry, which he published in *De Stijl* under the pseudonym I. K. Bonset (Fig. **15–52**). He saw Dada and De Stijl as opposite but complementary movements: Dada could destroy the old order, then De Stijl could build a new order on the razed site of prewar culture. In 1922 he convened an International Congress of Constructivists and Dadaists in Weimar. One of

the constructivists attending was El Lissitzky, who designed an issue of *De Stijl* (Fig. **15–53**).

In architectural experiments, Van Doesburg constructed planes in space with dynamic asymmetrical relationships. De Stijl architectural theory was realized in 1924 when Gerrit Rietveld (1888–1964) designed the celebrated Schroeder House in Utrecht (Fig. **15–54**). This house was so radical that neighbors threw rocks, and the Schroeder children were taunted by their classmates at school. The following year, Oud designed the Café de Unie (Fig. **15–55**) with an asymmetrical facade, projecting De Stijl's vision of order on an environmental scale.

Because Van Doesburg, with his phenomenal energy and wide-ranging creativity, *was* De Stijl, it is understandable that De Stijl as an organized movement did not survive his death in 1931 at age forty-seven. However, others continued to use its visual vocabulary for many years; for example, Bart van der Leck's open compositions of forms constructed of horizontal, vertical, and diagonal lines and shapes separated by spatial intervals are found in works ranging from early posters (Figs. **15–56** and **15–57**) to book designs and illustrations of the 1940s.

In 1918, the Dutch architect Wijdeveld initiated the magazine *Wendingen.* It started as a monthly publication devoted to architecture, construction, and ornamentation, but during its thirteen years of existence it represented all sectors of the visual arts. Wijdeveld constructed his letters from existing typographic material and used the same technique in his *Wendingen* covers, stationery designs, and posters. In the design of the *Wendingen* pages, Wijdeveld used solid and heavy borders constructed from right angles, typographic counterparts to the brick architecture of the Amsterdam School. This is amply evident in the design of his covers for the Frank Lloyd Wright issues of *Wendingen* (Fig. **15–58**) and his 1929 poster announcing an

15–55

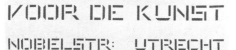

15–56

15–57

15–59

International Exhibition on Economics at the Stedelijk Museum in Amsterdam (Fig. **15–59**). Wijdeveld contributed only four *Wendingen* covers, and the others were designed by various architects, sculptors, painters, and designers. The 1922 cover by El Lissitsky (Fig. **15–60**) and the 1929 cover by Huszár (Fig. **15–61**) are striking examples.

The spread of constructivism

During World War I, Russian suprematism and the Dutch De Stijl movements were apparently completely isolated from one another, yet both groups pushed cubism to a pure geometric art. After the war their ideas were adopted by artists in other countries, including Czechoslovakia, Hungary, and Poland. The Polish designer Henryk Berlewi (1894–1967) was decisively influenced by Lissitzky's 1920 Warsaw lectures. In 1922 and 1923, Berlewi worked in Germany and began to evolve his *Mechano-faktura* theory. Believing that modern art was filled with illusionistic pitfalls, he mechanized painting and graphic design (Fig. **15–62**) into a constructed abstraction that abolished any illusion of three dimensions. This was accomplished by mathematical placement of simple geometric forms on a ground. The mechanization of art was seen as an expression of industrial society.

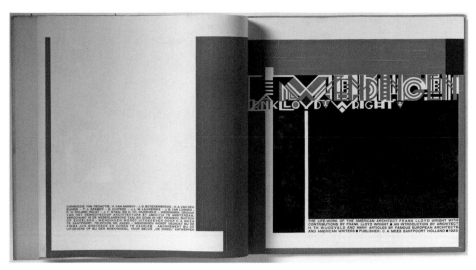

15–58

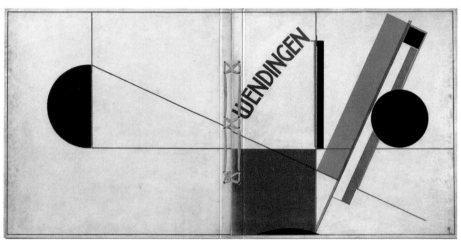

15–60

15–61

15–55. J. J. P. Oud, Facade of the Café de Unie, Rotterdam, 1925. Oud successfully resolved problems of structure, signage, and identification. Architectural and graphic forms of contrasting color and scale are ordered into a harmonious balance.

15–56. Bart Anthony van der Leck, exhibition poster, 1919. Moored in pictorial art, Van der Leck diverted De Stijl's vocabulary toward elemental images.

15–57. Bart Anthony van der Leck, "Het vlas" (The Flax), 1941.

15–58. H. T. Wijdeveld, title page for *Wendingen,* no. 7-3, "The Lifework of Frank Lloyd Wright, part IV," after a design by Frank Lloyd Wright.

15–59. H. T. Wijdeveld, Internationale Economisch-Historische Tentoonstelling (International Economic Historical Exhibition), poster, 1929.

15–60. El Lissitsky, cover for *Wendingen,* no. 4-1, 1921. Lithograph after a drawing by El Lissitsky. El Lissitsky came to Germany from Russia at the end of 1921, and there is no indication that he came to the Netherlands before the end of 1922. It is possible that Dr. Adolph Behne, a close friend of El Lissitsky living in Berlin, asked Wijdeveld to give El Lissitsky this commission due to his dire straits at that time.

15–61. Vilmos Huszár, "The Paintings of Diego (de la) Rivera," cover for *Wendingen,* no. 10-3, 1929. The forms on this cover are inspired by Aztec architecture, and the colors are those of the Mexican national flag.

15–62

15–63

15–64

15–65

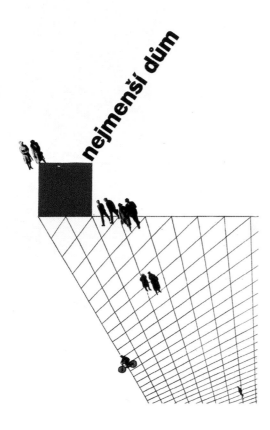

sutnar

nejmenší dům

15–66

15–62. Henryk Berlewi, exhibition poster, 1925. This early application of Mechano-faktura principles to graphic design is for an exhibition held in a Warsaw automobile showroom.

15–63. Henryk Berlewi, Putos Chocolates brochure, page 6, 1925. Copywriter Aleksander Wat closely collaborated with Berlewi to integrate text and form.

15–64. Ladislav Sutnar, cover design for *Getting Married,* 1929. The triangle creates a strong focal point, unifies the silhouette figures, and becomes the main structural element in a delicately balanced composition.

15–65. Ladislav Sutnar, cover design for *Samuel hledaá* (Samuel the Seeker), 1931.

15–66. Ladislav Sutnar, cover of *Nejmensi dum* (Minimum Housing), 1931.

In 1924 Berlewi joined the futurist poets Aleksander Wat and Stanley Brucz in opening a Warsaw advertising firm called Roklama Mechano. They introduced modern art forms to Polish society in industrial and commercial advertisements. Their brochure stated that advertising design and costs should be governed by the same principles that govern modern industry and the laws of economy. Advertising copy was reorganized for conciseness and impact, and visual layout was adapted to this text (Fig. **15–63**). Berlewi hoped that commercial advertising could become a vehicle for abolishing the division between the artist and society.

In Czechoslovakia, Ladislav Sutnar (1897–1976) became the leading supporter and practitioner of functional design. He advocated the constructivist ideal and the application of design principles to every aspect of contemporary life. In addition to graphics, this prolific Prague designer created toys, furniture, silverware, dishes, and fabrics. The publishing house Druzstevni Prace retained Sutnar as design director. His book jackets and editorial designs evinced an organizational simplicity and typographic clarity, giving graphic impact to the communication (Figs. **15–64**, **15–65**, and **15–66**).

Karel Teige (1900–51), also from Prague, was initially trained as a painter but early in his career began working in typography and photomontage as an enthusiastic advocate of international modernism. He was an active participant in Devûtsil (Nine Forces), a group of avant-garde poets, designers, architects, performance artists, and musicians, and designed many of their publications using what was available in the letterpress printer's type case. Founded in 1920, Devûtsil would eventually have as many as eighty members. Teige believed that the untrained practitioner could contribute a fresh and innovative approach to design, and from 1922 until 1938 he designed over one hundred books and periodicals. His constructivist approach involved an expressive use of type, montage, collage, and borrowed clips from silent films. He was the editor of several avant-garde magazines, including *Disk* (Fig. **15–67**), *Zeme sovetu, Stavba,* and *ReD.* A social idealist, he believed that good design could help resolve the differences between capitalist America and the communist Soviet Union. After his own country fell to communism in 1948, the new authorities considered him to be too egalitarian and cosmopolitan. For this reason he was banned from

15–67

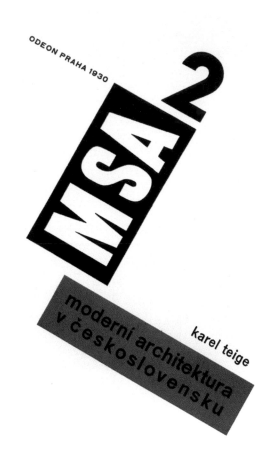

15–68

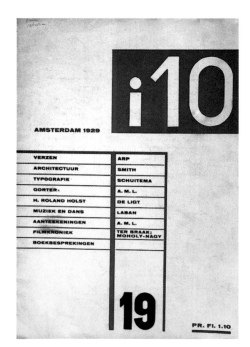

15–69

15–70

working as a writer and designer, and he died three years later (Fig. **15–68**).

In 1919, after completing law studies in Budapest, Hungarian artist Laszlo Moholy-Nagy turned to nonrepresentational painting influenced by Malevich. In 1921 he moved to Berlin, where Lissitzky, Schwitters, and Van Doesburg were frequent visitors to his studio. His design for Arthur Müller Lehning's Amsterdam-based avant-garde publication *i10*—one of the purest examples of De Stijl principles applied to typography—demonstrates the collaboration of constructivism, De Stijl, and Merz. De Stijl member César Domela (b. 1900) assisted Moholy-Nagy in the cover design (Fig. **15–69**). The printer was initially disturbed by the complete disregard for the rules of typography, as shown in the opening page of the premiere issue (Fig. **15–70**), but eventually he came to understand and appreciate the design. (In 1980, *i10* publisher/editor Lehning told Philip B. Meggs that, although the *i10* cover is often attributed to Domela, Lehning's recent retrieval of Moholy-Nagy's cover layouts indicates major responsibility should be credited to him.)

The quest for a pure art of visual relationships that began in the Netherlands and Russia remained a major influence for the visual disciplines throughout the twentieth century. One of the dominant directions in graphic design has been the use of geometric construction in organizing the printed page. Malevich and Mondrian used pure line, shape, and color to create a universe of harmoniously ordered, pure relationships. This was seen as a visionary prototype for a new world order. The unification of social and human values, technology, and visual form became a goal for those who strove for a new architecture and graphic design.

15–67. Karel Teige, cover for *Disk*, no. 1, 1923.

15–68. Karel Teige, cover for *Moderni architektura v Ceskoslovensku,* 1930.

15–69. Laszlo Moholy-Nagy, cover design for *i10*, 1927. The designer saw type as form and texture to be composed with a rectangle, lines, and spatial intervals to achieve dynamic equilibrium. Clarity of communication and harmony of form are achieved.

15–70. Laszlo Moholy-Nagy, title page spread for *i10*, 1927. The printer was deeply disturbed by this design, with its words running vertically, bold sans-serif type placed into serif text for emphasis, bullets separating paragraphs, and bold bars by page numbers.

The Bauhaus and the New Typography

16

"It is obvious," wrote Aldous Huxley in 1928, "that the machine is here to stay. Whole armies of William Morrises and Tolstoys could not now expel it. . . . Let us then exploit them to create beauty—a modern beauty, while we are about it." Ideas from all the advanced art and design movements were explored, combined, and applied to problems of functional design and machine production at a German design school, the Bauhaus (1919–33). Twentieth-century furniture, architecture, product design, and graphics were shaped by the work of its faculty and students, and a modern design aesthetic emerged.

On the eve of world war in 1914, the Belgian art nouveau architect Henri van de Velde, who directed the Weimar Arts and Crafts School, resigned his position to return to Belgium. Thirty-one-year-old Walter Gropius (1883–1969) was one of three possible replacements he recommended to the grand duke of Saxe-Weimar. During the war years the school was closed, and it was not until after the war that Gropius, who had already gained an international reputation for factory designs using glass and steel in new ways, was confirmed as the new director of an institution formed by merging the applied arts–oriented Weimar Arts and Crafts School with a fine arts school, the Weimar Art Academy. Gropius was permitted to name the new school Das Staatliche Bauhaus (literally translated, The State Home for Building). It opened on 12 April 1919, when Germany was in a state of severe ferment. Its catastrophic defeat in "the war to end all wars" led to economic, political, and cultural strife. The prewar world of the Hohenzollern dynasty was over, and a quest to construct a new social order pervaded all aspects of life.

The Bauhaus Manifesto, published in German newspapers, established the philosophy of the new school:

> The complete building is the ultimate aim of all the visual arts. Once the noblest function of the fine arts was to embellish buildings; they were indispensable components of great architecture. Today the arts exist in isolation. . . . Architects, painters, and sculptors must learn anew the composite character of the building as an entity. . . . The artist is an exalted craftsman. In rare moments of inspiration, transcending his conscious will, the grace of heaven may cause his work to blossom into art. But proficiency in his craft is essential to every artist. Therein lies the prime source of creative imagination.

Recognizing the common roots of both the fine and applied visual arts, Gropius sought a new unity of art and technology as he enlisted a generation of artists in a struggle to solve problems of visual design created by industrialism. It was hoped that the artistically trained designer could "breathe a soul into the dead product of the machine," for Gropius believed that only the most brilliant ideas were good enough to justify multiplication by industry.

The Bauhaus was the logical consequence of a German concern for design in industrial society that began in the opening years of the century. As discussed in chapter 14, the Deutsche Werkbund worked to elevate standards of design and public taste, attracting architects, artists, public and industry officials, educators, and critics to its ranks. The Werkbund attempted to unify artists and craftsmen with industry to elevate the functional and aesthetic qualities of mass production, particularly in low-cost consumer products.

Gropius had served a three-year assistantship in Peter Behrens's architectural office beginning in 1907. Behrens's advocacy of a new objectivity and theories of proportion had an impact on the development of the young Gropius's thinking. Henri van de Velde was also an important influence. During the 1890s Van de Velde declared the engineer to be the new architect and called for logical design using new technologies and materials of science: reinforced concrete, steel, aluminum, and linoleum.

The Bauhaus at Weimar

The Bauhaus years in Weimar (1919–24) were intensely visionary and drew inspiration from expressionism (Figs. **16–1** and **16–2**). Characterized by the utopian desire to create a new spiritual society, the early Bauhaus sought a new unity of artists and craftsmen to build for the future. Stained glass, wood, and metal workshops were taught by an artist and a craftsman and were organized along medieval Bauhütte lines—master,

16–1

16–2

16–1. Lyonel Feininger, *Cathedral*, 1919. This woodcut was printed on the title page of the Bauhaus Manifesto.

16–2. Attributed to Johannes Auerbach, first Bauhaus seal, 1919. The style and imagery of this seal—chosen in a student design competition—express the medieval and craft affinities of the early Bauhaus.

journeyman, apprentice. The Gothic cathedral represented a realization of people's longing for a spiritual beauty that went beyond utility and need; it symbolized the integration of architecture, sculpture, painting, and crafts. Gropius was deeply interested in architecture's symbolic potential and the possibility of a universal design style as an integrated aspect of society.

Advanced ideas about form, color, and space were integrated into the design vocabulary when Der Blaue Reiter painters Paul Klee and Wassily Kandinsky joined the staff in 1920 and 1922 respectively. Klee integrated modern visual art with the work of non-Western cultures and children to create drawings and paintings that are charged visual communication (see Fig. 13–48). Kandinsky's belief in the autonomy and spiritual values of color and form had led to the courageous emancipation of his painting from the motif and from representational elements (see Fig. 13–47). At the Bauhaus, no distinction was made between fine and applied art.

The heart of Bauhaus education was the preliminary course, initially established by Johannes Itten (1888–1967). His goals

were to release each student's creative abilities, to develop an understanding of the physical nature of materials, and to teach the fundamental principles of design underlying all visual art. Itten emphasized visual contrasts and the analysis of Old Master paintings. With his methodology of direct experience, he sought to develop perceptual awareness, intellectual abilities, and emotional experience. In 1923 Itten left the Bauhaus because of disagreement about the conduct of this course. The Bauhaus was evolving from a concern for medievalism, expressionism, and handicraft toward more emphasis on rationalism and designing for the machine. Gropius began to consider Itten's mysticism to be an "otherworldliness" inconsistent with the search for an objective design language capable of overcoming the dangers of past styles and personal taste.

As early as the spring of 1919, Bauhaus teacher Lyonel Feininger (1871–1956) learned about De Stijl and introduced it to the Bauhaus community. The Bauhaus and De Stijl had similar aims. In late 1920 Van Doesburg established contacts with

16–3

16–4

16–3. Oscar Schlemmer, later Bauhaus seal, 1922. Comparison of the two seals demonstrates how graphic designs express ideas; the later seal connotes the emerging geometric and machine orientation.

16–4. Joost Schmidt, Bauhaus exhibition poster, 1923. Echoes of cubism, constructivism, and De Stijl provide evidence that the Bauhaus became a vessel in which diverse movements were melded into new design approaches. This poster shows the influence of Oscar Schlemmer, then a master at the Bauhaus. The opening of the exhibition was postponed until August, and two pieces of paper were pasted on with the corrected dates. This example is the original version.

16–5. Herbert Bayer, cover design, *Staatliches Bauhaus in Weimar, 1919–1923,* 1923. Geometrically constructed letterforms printed in red and blue on a black background are compressed into a square.

16–6. Laszlo Moholy-Nagy, title page, *Staatliches Bauhaus in Weimar.* This page structure is based on a rhythmic series of right angles. Stripes applied to two words create a second spatial plane.

16–7. Laszlo Moholy-Nagy, proposed title page for *Broom,* 1923. This inventive design for the avant-garde magazine shows how thoroughly Moholy-Nagy understood cubism and Lissitzky.

the Bauhaus, and he moved to Weimar the following year. He desired a teaching position, but Gropius believed Van Doesburg was too dogmatic in his insistence on strict geometry and an impersonal style. Gropius opposed creating a Bauhaus style or imposing a style on the students. But even as an outsider, Van Doesburg exerted a strong influence by allowing his home to become a meeting place for Bauhaus students and faculty. He lived in Weimar until 1923, teaching courses in De Stijl philosophy primarily attended by Bauhaus students. Furniture design and typography were especially influenced by De Stijl; this influence among faculty and students probably supported Gropius's efforts to lessen Itten's role.

Continuing conflicts between the Bauhaus and the Thuringian government led the authorities to insist that the Bauhaus mount a major exhibition to demonstrate its accomplishments. By the time the school launched this 1923 exhibition—attended by 15,000 people and internationally acclaimed—romantic medievalism and expressionism were being replaced by an applied-design emphasis, causing Gropius to replace the slogan "A Unity of Art and Handicraft" with "Art and Technology, a New Unity." A new Bauhaus symbol reflected this shift (Fig. **16–3**). Joost Schmidt's poster for this exhibition combines geometric and machine forms (Fig. **16–4**), reflecting the reorientation occurring at the Bauhaus.

The impact of Laszlo Moholy-Nagy

In this same year, Itten's replacement as head of the preliminary course was the Hungarian constructivist Laszlo Moholy-Nagy. A restless experimenter who studied law before turning to art, Moholy-Nagy explored painting, photography, film, sculpture, and graphic design. New materials such as acrylic resin and plastic, new techniques such as photomontage and the photogram, and visual means including kinetic motion, light, and

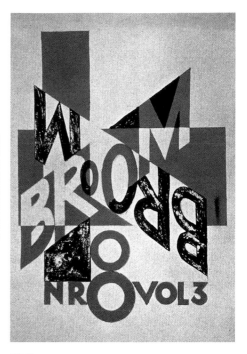

16–5   16–6   16–7

transparency were encompassed in his wide-ranging investigations. Young and articulate, Moholy-Nagy had a marked influence on the evolution of Bauhaus instruction and philosophy, and he became Gropius's "prime minister" at the Bauhaus as the director pushed for a new unity of art and technology.

Gropius and Moholy-Nagy collaborated as editors for *Staatliches Bauhaus in Weimar, 1919–1923,* the catalogue for the 1923 exhibition. The cover (Fig. **16–5**) for this record of the first years was designed by a student, Herbert Bayer (1900–85), while the interior was designed by Moholy-Nagy (Fig. **16–6**). Moholy-Nagy contributed an important statement about typography, describing it as "a tool of communication. It must be communication in its most intense form. The emphasis must be on absolute clarity.... Legibility—communication must never be impaired by *a priori* esthetics. Letters must never be forced into a preconceived framework, for instance a square." In graphic design, he advocated "an uninhibited use of all linear directions (therefore not only horizontal articulation). We use all typefaces, type sizes, geometric forms, colors, etc. We want to create a new language of typography whose elasticity, variability, and freshness of typographical composition [are] exclusively dictated by the inner law of expression and the optical effect." (Fig. **16-7**)

In 1922 and 1923, Moholy-Nagy ordered three paintings from a sign company. These were executed from his graph-paper layouts in colors selected from the firm's porcelain-enamel color chart, in keeping with his theory that the essence of art and design was the concept, not the execution, and that the two could be separated. Moholy-Nagy acted on

this belief beginning in 1929, when he retained an assistant, Gyorgy Kepes (1906–2002), to complete the execution of his commissions. Kepes would later be known as the founder of the Center for Advanced Visual Studies at the Massachusetts Institute of Technology, an association designed to promote creative collaboration between artists and scientists.

Moholy-Nagy's passion for typography and photography inspired a Bauhaus interest in visual communications and led to important experiments in the unification of these two arts. He saw graphic design, particularly the poster, as evolving toward the *typophoto.* He called this objective integration of word and image to communicate a message with immediacy "the new visual literature." Moholy-Nagy's 1923 Pneumatik poster (Fig. **16–8**) is an experimental typophoto. In that year he wrote that photography's objective presentation of facts could free the viewer from depending on another person's interpretation. He saw photography influencing poster design—which demands instantaneous communication—by techniques of enlargement, distortion, dropouts, double exposures, and montage. In typography he advocated emphatic contrasts and bold use of color. Absolute clarity of communication without preconceived aesthetic notions was stressed.

As a photographer, Moholy-Nagy used the camera as a tool for design. Conventional compositional ideas yielded to unexpected organization, primarily through the use of light (and sometimes shadows) to design the space. The normal viewpoint was replaced by worm's-eye, bird's-eye, extreme close-up, and angled viewpoints. An application of the new language of vision to forms seen in the world characterizes his

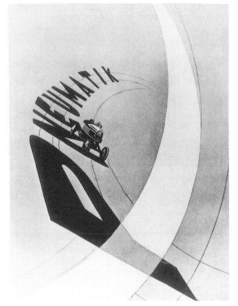

16–8

16–9

16–10

16–11

regular photographic work. Texture, light and dark interplay, and repetition are qualities of such works as *Chairs at Margate* (Fig. **16–9**). In his growing enthusiasm for photography, Moholy-Nagy antagonized the Bauhaus painters by proclaiming the ultimate victory of photography over painting.

In 1922 he began to experiment with photograms; the following year he began to make photomontages, which he called *photoplastics*. Moholy-Nagy believed the photogram, because it allowed an artist to capture a patterned interplay

of light and dark on a sheet of light-sensitive paper without a camera, represented the essence of photography (Fig. **16–10**). The objects he used to create photograms were chosen for their light-modulating properties, and any reference to the objects forming the black, white, and gray patterns or to the external world vanished in an expression of abstract pattern. Moholy-Nagy saw his photoplastics (Fig. **16–11**) not just as the results of a collage technique but as manifestations of a process for arriving at a new expression that could become

16–12

16–13

both more creative and more functional than straightforward imitative photography. Photoplastics could be humorous, visionary, moving, or insightful, and usually had drawn additions, complex associations, and unexpected juxtapositions.

The Bauhaus at Dessau

Tension between the Bauhaus and the government in Weimar had existed from the beginning; it intensified when a new, more conservative regime came to power and tried to impose unacceptable conditions on the school. On 26 December 1924, the director and masters all signed a letter of resignation, effective 1 April 1925, when their contracts expired. Two weeks later, the students signed a letter to the government informing it that they would leave with the masters. Gropius and Dessau mayor Dr. Fritz Hesse negotiated moving the Bauhaus to this small provincial town. In April 1925, some of the equipment was moved with faculty and students from Weimar to Dessau, and work began immediately in temporary facilities. A new building complex was designed and occupied in the fall of 1926 (Fig. **16–12**), and the curriculum was reorganized.

During the Dessau period (1925–32) the Bauhaus identity and philosophy came to full fruition. The De Stijl (Fig. **16–13**) and constructivist underpinnings were obvious, but the Bauhaus did not merely copy these movements. Rather, it developed clearly understood formal principles that could be applied intelligently to design problems. The Bauhaus Corporation, a business organization, was created to handle the sale of workshop prototypes to industry. Abundant ideas flowed from the Bauhaus to influence twentieth-century life: designs for furniture and other products, functional architecture, environmental spaces (Fig. **16–14**), and typography. The masters were now called professors, and the medieval master/journeyman/apprentice system was abandoned. In 1926 the Bauhaus was renamed Hochschule für Gestaltung (High

16–8. Laszlo Moholy-Nagy, typophoto poster for tires, 1923. Letterforms, photography, and design elements are integrated into an immediate and unified communication.

16–9. Laszlo Moholy-Nagy, *Chairs at Margate,* 1935. The juxtaposition of two images creates a contrast of pattern and texture and introduces a process of change into the two-dimensional image.

16–10. Laszlo Moholy-Nagy, *Photogram,* 1922. Light itself becomes a malleable medium for generation design and form.

16–11. Laszlo Moholy-Nagy, *The World Foundation,* 1927. In this satirical photoplastic, Moholy-Nagy shows "quack-clacking super-geese [pelicans]" observing "the simplicity of the world constructed as a leg show."

16–12. Walter Gropius, Dessau Bauhaus building, 1925–26. This architectural landmark has a series of parts—workshop (shown here), classroom, dormitory, and administrative structures—unified into a whole.

16–13. Herbert Bayer, symbol for the Kraus stained-glass workshop, 1923. A square is divided by a horizontal line into two rectangles. The top rectangle has the three-to-five ratio of the golden mean. Each rectangle formed is then divided with a vertical to form a square and a smaller rectangle. A harmony of proportion and balance is achieved by minimal means with the obvious influence of De Stijl.

School for Form), and the influential *Bauhaus* magazine (Fig. **16–15**) began publication.

This magazine, and the series of fourteen *Bauhausbücher* (Bauhaus books, Fig. **16–16**), became important vehicles for disseminating advanced ideas about art theory and its application to architecture and design. Kandinsky, Klee, Gropius, Mondrian, Moholy-Nagy, and Van Doesburg (see Fig. 15–43) were editors or authors of volumes in the series. Moholy-Nagy designed twelve of the books and eight of the jackets (Fig. **16–17**). The jacket for book 12 was printed on translucent

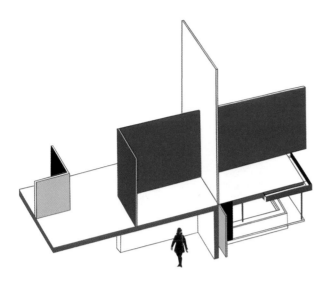

16–14

16–15

16–14. Herbert Bayer, proposed streetcar station and newsstand, 1924. A concise modular unit, designed for economical mass production, combines an open waiting area, newsstand, and rooftop advertising panels.

16–15. Herbert Bayer, cover for *Bauhaus* magazine, 1928. A page of typography joins the designer's tools and basic geometric forms in a photographic still life. Composed before a camera instead of at a drawing board, this cover achieves a rare integration of type and image.

16–16. Laszlo Moholy-Nagy, brochure cover for the series of fourteen Bauhaus books, 1929. Two photoprints of metal type are collaged together to create an unusual spatial configuration. Colored ink is printed on the upper numeral 14.

16–17. Laszlo Moholy-Nagy, dust jackets for four Bauhaus books, 1924–30. Jackets for volumes 5 and 10 evidence close ties with De Stijl; 12 and 14 represent modern architecture.

16–18. Herbert Bayer, banknote for the State Bank of Thuringia, 1923. Germany's rampant postwar inflation necessitated large-denomination banknotes. Black type overprints a red triangle, lines, and a textural repetition of the denominations.

tracing paper. It presented Gropius's modular housing proposals for industrial fabrication to combine economy with social purpose and structural functionalism with aesthetic concerns. Properties of modern architecture were expressed on book 14's jacket by a photograph of typography printed on glass whose shadow falls onto a red plane.

Five former students were appointed masters, including Josef Albers (1888–1976), who taught a systematic preliminary course investigating the constructive qualities of materials; Marcel Breuer (1902–81), the head of the furniture work-

shop, who invented tubular-steel furniture; and Herbert Bayer, who became professor of the newly added typography and graphic design workshop. In Weimar, Gropius had observed Bayer's interest in graphics and encouraged it with periodic assignments (Fig. **16–18**; see also Fig. 16–5), so Bayer's typographic preoccupation preceded the move to Dessau.

In addition to soliciting printing orders from Dessau businesses to help balance the Bauhaus budget, Bayer's workshop made striking typographic design innovations along functional and constructivist lines. Sans-serif fonts were used almost exclusively, and Bayer designed a universal type that reduced the alphabet to clear, simple, and rationally constructed forms (Fig. **16–19**). This was consistent with Gropius's advocacy of form following function. Bayer omitted capital letters, arguing that the two alphabets (capitals and lowercase) are incompatible in design, with two totally different signs (i.e., capital *A* and small *a*) expressing the same spoken sound. He experimented with flush-left, ragged-right typesetting without justification, which is the squaring or flushing of both left and right edges of a type

16–17

16–16

16–18

column by adding word or letter spacing. Extreme contrasts of type size and weight were used to establish a visual hierarchy of emphasis determined by an objective assessment of the relative importance of the words. Bars, rules, points, and squares were used to subdivide the space, unify diverse elements, lead the viewer's eye across a page, and call attention to important elements. Elementary forms and the use of black with one bright, pure hue were favored. Open composition on an implied grid and a system of sizes for type, rules, and pictorial images brought unity to the designs. Dynamic composition with strong horizontals and verticals (and, on occasion, diagonals) characterize Bayer's Bauhaus period.

These properties are clearly seen in Bayer's poster for Kandinsky's sixtieth birthday exhibition (Fig. **16–20**). A visual hierarchy developed from a careful analysis of content, permitting a functional sequence of information. Careful horizontal and vertical alignments were made, then the entire contents rotated diagonally to achieve a dynamic yet balanced architectural structure. With the text controlled by a seven-column

grid, Bayer's poster for a 1927 exhibition of European arts and crafts is even more architectural in its organization (Fig. **16–21**).

The final years of the Bauhaus

In 1928 Walter Gropius resigned his post to resume private architectural practice. At the same time, Bayer and Moholy-Nagy both left for Berlin, where graphic design and typography figured prominently in the activities of each. Former student Joost Schmidt (1893–1948) followed Bayer as master of the typography and graphic-design workshop (Fig. **16–21**). He moved away from strict constructivist ideas and stocked the workshop with a larger variety of type fonts. Exhibition design (Fig. **16–22**) was outstanding under Schmidt, who brought unity to this form through standardized panels and grid-system organization. The directorship of the Bauhaus was assumed by Hannes Meyer (1889–1954), a Swiss architect with strong socialist beliefs, who had been hired to set up the architectural program in 1927. By 1930 conflicts with the municipal authorities forced Meyer's resignation. Ludwig Mies van der Rohe

16–19

16–20

16–19. Herbert Bayer, universal alphabet, 1925. This experiment in reducing the alphabet to one set of geometrically constructed characters maximizes differences between letters for greater legibility. The lower letterforms show different weights. Later variations include the bold, condensed, typewriter, and handwriting styles shown here.

16–20. Herbert Bayer, exhibition poster, 1926. Type and image are arranged in a functional progression of size and weight from the most important information to supporting details.

16–21. Herbert Bayer, "Europäisches Kunstgewerbe 1927" (European Arts and Crafts 1927), poster, 1927.

16–22. Joost Schmidt, *Bauhaus* magazine cover, 1929. This format allows effective use of varying image size and shape in the lower two-thirds of the cover.

16–23. Jan Tschichold, hand-lettered advertisement for the Leipzig Trade Fair, 1922. Symmetry and historical letterforms characterize Tschichold's youthful work.

(1886–1969), a prominent Berlin architect whose design dictum "less is more" became a major tenet of twentieth-century design, became director.

In 1931 the Nazi party dominated the Dessau City Council; it canceled Bauhaus faculty contracts in 1932. Mies van der Rohe tried to run the Bauhaus from an empty telephone factory in Berlin-Steglitz, but Nazi harassment made continuance untenable. The Gestapo demanded the removal of "cultural Bolsheviks" from the school, with Nazi sympathizers as replacements. The faculty voted to dissolve the Bauhaus, and it closed on 10 August 1933, with a notice to students that faculty would be available for consultation if needed. Thus ended one of the most important design schools of the twentieth century. The growing cloud of Nazi persecution led many Bauhaus faculty members to join the flight of intellectuals and artists to America. In 1937 Gropius and Marcel Breuer were teaching architecture at Harvard University, and Moholy-Nagy established the New Bauhaus (now the Institute of Design) in Chicago. A year later, Herbert Bayer began the American phase of his design career. This transatlantic exodus influenced the course of American design after World War II.

The accomplishments and influences of the Bauhaus transcend its fourteen-year life, thirty-three faculty members, and about 1,250 students. It created a viable, modern design movement spanning architecture, product design, and visual communications. A modernist approach to visual education was developed, and the faculty's class-preparation and teaching methods made a major contribution to visual theory. In dissolving fine and applied art boundaries, the Bauhaus tried to bring art into a close relationship with life by way of design, which was seen as a vehicle for social change and cultural revitalization.

16–21

16–22

16–23

In a 1961 prose poem entitled "homage to gropius,"
Herbert Bayer wrote:

for the future
the bauhaus gave us assurance
in facing the perplexities
    of work;
it gave us the know-how to
    work.
a foundation in the crafts,
an invaluable heritage of timeless principles
as applied to the
    creative process.
it expressed again that we are
    not to impose aesthetics
on the things we use, to the
    structures we live in,
but that purpose and form must
    be seen as one.
that direction emerges when one
    considers
    concrete demands,
special conditions, inherent
    character
of a given problem.
but never losing perspective

that one is, after all,
    an artist.
the bauhaus existed for a short
    span of time
but the potentials,
inherent in its principles
have only begun to be realized.
its sources of design remain
    forever full
of changing possibilities.

Jan Tschichold and die neue Typographie
(the new typography)

Much of the creative innovation in graphic design during the
first decades of the century occurred as part of the modern-
art movements and at the Bauhaus, but these explorations
toward a new approach to graphic design were often seen
and understood only by a limited audience outside the mainstream of society. The person who applied these new design
approaches to everyday design problems and explained them
to a wide audience of printers, typesetters, and designers was
Jan Tschichold (1902–74). The son of a designer and sign
painter in Leipzig, Germany, Tschichold developed an early
interest in calligraphy, studied at the Leipzig Academy, and
joined the design staff of Insel Verlag as a traditional calligrapher (Fig. **16–23**). In August 1923, twenty-one-year-old

16–24

16–25

16–28

16–26

16–27

Tschichold attended the first Bauhaus exhibition in Weimar and was deeply impressed. He rapidly assimilated the new design concepts of the Bauhaus and the Russian constructivists into his work (Fig. **16–24**) and became a practitioner of the new typography. For the October 1925 issue of *Typographische Mitteilungen* (typographic impartations), Tschichold designed a twenty-four-page insert entitled "Elementare Typographie" (Figs. **16–25**, **16–26**, and **16–27**), which explained and demonstrated asymmetrical typography to printers, typesetters, and designers. It was printed in red and black and featured avant-garde work along with Tschichold's lucid commentary. Much German printing at this point still used medieval textura and symmetrical layout. Tschichold's insert was a revelation and generated much enthusiasm for the new approach.

His 1928 book, *Die neue Typographie,* vigorously advocated the new ideas. Disgusted with "degenerate typefaces and arrangements," he sought to wipe the slate clean and find a new asymmetrical typography to express the spirit, life, and visual sensibility of the day. His objective was functional design by the most straightforward means. Tschichold declared the aim of every typographic work to be the delivery

16–24. Jan Tschichold, display poster for a publisher, 1924. One of the Tschichold's earliest attempts to apply modern design principles, printed in black and gold, proclaims, "Books by Philobiblon are available here in Warsaw."

16–25. Jan Tschichold, cover for "Elementare Typographie" insert, 1925. A sparse, open functionalism is achieved.

16–26. Jan Tschichold, pages from "Elementare Typographie," 1925. Bold rules punctuate the space, and Tschichold's essay explains the new approach.

16–27. Jan Tschichold, pages from "Elementare Typographie," 1925. Illustrated by Lissitzky's work, Russian constructivist design is explained.

16–28. Jan Tschichold, brochure for his book *Die neue Typographie,* 1928. This brochure functions as a remarkable didactic example of the principles Tschichold was advocating.

of a message in the shortest, most efficient manner. He emphasized the nature of machine composition and its impact on the design process and product.

Tschichold's brochure for the book illustrates this radical new typography (Fig. **16–28**), which rejected decoration in

16–29

16–30

16–29. Jan Tschichold, advertisement, 1932. Asymmetrical balance, a grid system, and a sequential progression of type weight and size determined by the words' importance to the overall message are aspects of this design.

16–30. Jan Tschichold, cinema poster for *Die Hose* (The Trousers), 1927. The space is divided into dynamic red and white planes, with forms aligned and balanced on a diagonal axis.

16–31. Jan Tschichold, poster for *Der Berufsphotograph* (The Professional Photographer), 1938.

16–32. Jan Tschichold, exhibition poster for Konstructivism (Constructivism), 1937. Black type and a sand-colored circle are used to achieve an economy of means and perfection of balance appropriate to the subject.

favor of rational design planned for communicative function. Functionalism, however, is not completely synonymous with the new typography; Tschichold observed that although plain utilitarianism and modern design had much in common, the modern movement sought spiritual content and a beauty more closely bound to the materials used, "but whose horizons lie far beyond."

A dynamic force should be present in each design, he argued, for type should be set in motion rather than at rest. Symmetrical organization was artificial because it placed pure form before the meaning of the words. Tschichold favored headlines flush to the left margin, with uneven line lengths. He believed a kinetic asymmetrical design of contrasting elements expressed the new age of the machine. Types should be elementary in form without embellishment; thus, sans-serif type, in a range of weights (light, medium, bold, extra-bold, italic) and proportions (condensed, normal, expanded), was declared to be the modern type. Its wide range of value and texture in the black-and-white scale allowed the expressive,

abstract image sought by modern design. Stripped of unessential elements, sans-serif type reduced the alphabet to its basic elementary shapes. Designs were based on an underlying horizontal and vertical structure. Spatial intervals were seen as important design elements, with white space given a new role as a structural component. Rules, bars, and boxes were often used for structure, balance, and emphasis. The precision and objectivity of photography were preferred for illustration. Tschichold showed how the modern-art movement could relate to graphic design by synthesizing his practical understanding of typography and its traditions with the new experiments. The essence of the new typography was clarity, not simply beauty; its objective was to develop form from the functions of the text. Tschichold's own prolific design practice set the standard for the new approach in books, job printing, advertisements (Fig. **16–29**), and posters (Figs. **16–30**, **16–31**, and **16–32**).

In March 1933, armed Nazis entered Tschichold's flat in Munich and arrested him and his wife. Accused of being a

16–31

16–32

"cultural Bolshevik" and creating "un-German" typography, he was denied his teaching position in Munich. After six weeks of "protective custody" Tschichold was released; he quickly took his wife and four year-old son to Basel, Switzerland, where he worked primarily as a book designer. In Switzerland, Tschichold began to turn away from the new typography and to use roman, Egyptian, and script styles in his designs. The new typography had been a reaction against the chaos and anarchy in German (and Swiss) typography around 1923, and he now felt that it had reached a point where further development was not possible.

In 1946 he wrote that the new typography's "impatient attitude conforms to the German bent for the absolute, and its military will to regulate and its claim to absolute power reflect those fearful components of the German character [that] set loose Hitler's power and the Second World War." Tschichold began to feel that graphic designers should work in a humanist tradition that spans the ages and draws from the knowledge and accomplishments of master typographers of the past. He continued to feel that the new typography was suitable for publicizing industrial products and communication about contemporary painting and architecture, but also believed it was folly to use it for a book of baroque poetry, for example, and he called reading long pages of sans serif "genuine torture."

During the 1940s, particularly with his 1947–49 work as a typographer for Penguin Books in London, Tschichold led an international revival of traditional typography (Fig. **16–33**). After World War II, he believed designers should draw upon the whole history of design to create solutions expressing con-

tent (Fig. **16–34**). While much of his later work used symmetrical organization and classical serif type styles, he advocated freedom of thought and artistic expression. He even endorsed the occasional use of ornamental typography as having "a refreshing effect, like a flower in rocky terrain." He observed that perhaps a person must first lose his freedom (as he had) before one could discover its true value.

Tschichold continued to design and write in Switzerland until his death in 1974. Because he saw the value of the new typography as an attempt at purification, clarity, and simplicity of means, he was able to bring typographic expression to fruition for the twentieth century. His revival of classical typography restored the humanist tradition of book design, and he made an indelible mark on graphic design.

Typeface design in the first half of the twentieth century

The passion for the new typography created a spate of sans-serif styles during the 1920s. An earlier sans serif, Johnston's Railway Type (see Fig. 12–50), inspired the Gill Sans series (Fig. **16–35**), which was designed by Edward Johnston's friend and former student, Eric Gill (1882–1940), and issued between 1928 and 1930. This type family, which eventually included fourteen styles, does not have an extremely mechanical appearance because its proportions stem from the roman tradition.

An architectural apprentice dropout tutored by Johnston at the turn of the century, Eric Gill was a complex and colorful figure who defies categorization in the history of graphic design. His activities encompassed stonemasonry, inscription

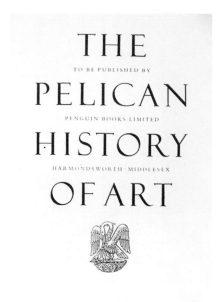

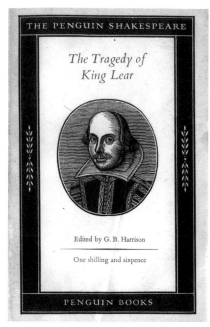

Gill Sans Light

Gill Sans Light Italic

Gill Sans

Gill Sans Italic

Gill Sans Bold

Gill Sans Bold Italic

Gill Sans Extrabold

Gill Sans Ultrabold

16–33   16–34   16–35

carving for monuments, sculpture, wood engraving, typeface design, lettering, book design, and extensive writing. His 1913 conversion to Catholicism intensified his belief that work has spiritual value and that the artist and craftsman serve a human need for beauty and dignity. Around 1925, in spite of his earlier polemics against machine manufacture, he was persuaded by Stanley Morison (1889–1967) of the Monotype Corporation to accept the challenge of type design. His first type, Perpetua, is an antique roman face inspired by the inscription on Trajan's column but subtly redesigned to accommodate the needs of typecasting and printing. Gill's embrace of historical influences—including the Trajan capitals, letters used in medieval manuscripts and the incunabula, Baskerville, and Caslon—threatened to make him a historicist, but his highly original vision and opinions enabled him to transcend these influences in much of his work. His work for *The Four Gospels* (Fig. **16–36**) demonstrates this synthesis of old and new. The Golden Cockerel type that Gill created for this book is a revitalized roman incorporating both Old Style and Transitional qualities. His woodcut illustrations have an archaic, almost medieval quality. However, his total design integration of illustration, capitals, headings, and text into a dynamic whole is strikingly modem.

In his highly personal and poetic little volume *Essay on Typography* (Fig. **16–37**), Gill first advanced the concept of unequal line lengths in text type. He argued that the uneven word spacing of justified lines posed greater legibility and design problems than the use of equal word spacing and a ragged-right margin. From late 1928 until his death, he worked at Hague and Gill, Printers, using a handpress, hand-set type, handmade paper, and types he designed exclusively for the press. This was not, however, a private press in the Arts and Crafts tradition, for Gill said a private press "prints solely what it chooses to print, whereas a public press prints what its customers demand of it."

Beginning with Bayer's universal alphabet (see Fig. 16–19) and Jakob Erbar's c. 1925 typeface Erbar, many geometrically constructed sans-serif typefaces were designed during the 1920s. Futura (Figs. **16–38** and **16–39**) was designed by Paul Renner (1878–1956) for the Bauer foundry in Germany. Futura had fifteen alphabets, including four italics and two unusual display fonts, and became the most widely used geometric sans-serif family. As a teacher and designer, Renner fought tirelessly for the notion that designers should not merely preserve their inheritance and pass it on to the next generation unchanged; rather, each generation should try to solve inherited problems and attempt to create a contemporary form true to its own time. Even the mystical medievalist Rudolf Koch (see Fig. 10–35) designed a very popular geometric sans-serif typeface, Kabel (Fig. **16–40**), which was enlivened by unexpected design subtleties.

Morison, typographic adviser to the British Monotype Corporation and the Cambridge University Press, supervised the design of a major twentieth-century newspaper and magazine typeface commissioned by the *Times* of London in 1931. Named Times New Roman (Fig. **16–41**), this typeface—with short ascenders and descenders and sharp, small serifs—was introduced in the 3 October 1932 edition of London's newspaper of record. The typographic appearance of one of the world's preeminent newspapers was radically changed

FORASMUCH AS MANY HAVE TAKEN IN HAND
TO SET FORTH IN ORDER A DECLARATION OF
THOSE THINGS WHICH ARE MOST SURELY BE-
LIEVED AMONG US, EVEN AS THEY DELIVERED
them unto us, which from the beginning were eyewitnesses,
and ministers of the word; It seemed good to me also, having
had perfect understanding of all things from the very first,
to write unto thee in order, most excellent Theophilus, That
thou mightest know the certainty of those things, wherein
thou hast been instructed.

THERE WAS IN THE DAYS OF HEROD, THE KING OF JUDÆA, A CERTAIN PRIEST NAMED ZACHARIAS, OF THE COURSE OF ABIA: AND HIS WIFE WAS OF THE DAUGHTERS OF Aaron, and her name was Elisabeth. And they were both righteous before God, walking in all the commandments and

131

16–36

22 whole world to play with and dopes him with the idea that in serving it he is serving his fellow-men.
¶ Therefore Industrialism will compromise with the Humane, and the Humane will dally with Industrialism. We shall have machine-made ornament (tho' in the near future there will mercifully be less than in the immediate past) and we shall have motor-buses tearing along country roads. We shall have imitation handicrafts in London shops, & cows milked by machinery even on small farms, and cottage larders stocked with canned foods. "Whole-hogging" is not the ordinary man's strong point.
¶ Nevertheless, the positive good & the positive dignity of Industrialism will undoubtedly achieve an almost complete ascendancy in men's minds to-morrow, and this ascendancy will purge even the Humane of its foibles. The two worlds will grow more distinct and will recognize each other without the present confusion. The hard and logical development of Industrialism will impose, even upon its enemies, a very salutary hardness and logicality. Fancy lettering will be as distasteful to the artist as it will be to the engineer—in fact it is more than probable that it will be the artists who

16–37

FUTURA Light
FUTURA Light italic
FUTURA Book
FUTURA Medium
FUTURA Medium Italic
FUTURA Demibold
FUTURA Demibold italic
FUTURA Bold
FUTURA Bold italic
FUTURA Bold condensed
Futura Display
Futura Black

16–39

16–38

LEICHTE
KABEL von formvollendeter Gestalt
für die gute Werbedrucksache
für den feinen Bilder-Katalog
für die Gebrauchsdrucksache

GEBR. KLINGSPOR · OFFENBACH AM MAIN
Unsere vollständige Schriftprobe wird auf Verlangen an Interessenten kostenlos abgegeben

16–40

16–33. Jan Tschichold, brochure cover for *The Pelican History of Art,* 1947. The classical symmetry of this design has a power and subtlety rivaling Roman inscriptions and the best work of Baskerville and Bodoni.

16–34. Jan Tschichold, paperback book cover, 1950. This series format evokes designs and prints of Shakespeare's era.

16–35. Eric Gill, the Gill Sans type family, 1928–30. This family has been widely used, especially in England.

16–36. Eric Gill, page from The Four Gospels, 1931. Descending type sizes, all capitals on opening lines, unjustified right margins, and initial capitals integrated with illustrations are forged into a unified whole.

16–37. Eric Gill, page from *Essay on Typography,* 1931. Gill spoke of industrialism, humanism, letterforms, and legibility, while demonstrating his belief in unjustified typography.

16–38. Paul Renner, folder for Futura, 1927. This early version of Futura was more abstract than the fonts released in America. The structural relationships in this layout typify the new typography.

16–39. Paul Renner, Futura typefaces, 1927–30. The extensive range of sizes and weights provided vigorous contrasts for printers and designers who adopted the new typography.

16–40. Rudolf Koch, Kabel light, c. 1928. A series of ads introduced Kabel's range of weights to German designers and printers.

16–41. Stanley Morison (typographic adviser), the *London Times,* 3 October 1932. Even the 120-year-old masthead fell victim to the redesign that introduced Times New Roman.

16–42. Otto Neurath and the Vienna Method, "Geburten und Sterbefalle in Wein" (Births and Deaths in Vienna) chart, c. 1928. Neurath called the Isotype a "language picture" that enabled the reader to make connections. The impact of World War I on mortality and births is dramatically evident.

16–43. Gerd Arntz and Otto Neurath, "Gesellschaftsgliederung in Wien" (Social Stratification in Vienna) chart, 1930.

16–44. Henry C. Beck, map for the London Underground, 1933. By depicting a schematic concept of the subway lines rather than a conventional map, Beck simplified the communication of information for the subway rider.

16–41

overnight, and the traditionally conservative readers warmly applauded the legibility and clarity of the new typeface. Times New Roman became one of the most widely used typefaces of the twentieth century. Its popularity has been attributed to its legibility, handsome visual qualities, and the economy achieved by moderately condensed letterforms. By making the stems and curves slightly thicker than in most roman-style letterforms, the designers gave Times New Roman a touch of the robust color that is associated with Caslon type.

The Isotype movement

The important movement toward developing a "world language without words" began in the 1920s, continued into the 1940s, and still has important influences today. The Isotype concept involves the use of elementary pictographs to convey information. The originator of this effort was Vienna sociologist Otto Neurath (1882–1945). As a child, Neurath marveled at the way ideas and factual information could be conveyed by visual means. Egyptian wall frescoes in a Vienna Museum and diagrams and illustrations in his father's books fired his imagination. Neurath felt that the social and economic changes following World War I demanded clear communication to assist public understanding of important social issues relating to housing, health, and economics. A system of elementary pictographs to present complex data, particularly

statistical data, was developed (Fig. **16–42**). His charts were completely functional and shorn of decorative qualities. Neurath had ties with the new typography movement, for Tschichold assisted him and his collaborators briefly in the late 1920s, and Renner's new Futura typeface was adopted for Isotype designs immediately after it became available.

Originally called the Vienna Method, the name Isotype (International System of Typographic Picture Education) was selected after Neurath moved to Holland in 1934. The Transformation Team, headed by scientist and mathematician Marie Reidermeister (1898–1959), converted verbal and numerical data compiled by statisticians and researchers into layout form. These layouts were handed over to graphic artists for final execution. One problem was the need to produce large quantities of symbols for charts. Initially the pictographs were individually drawn or cut from paper. After woodcut artist Gerd Arntz (1900–88), whose constructivist-inspired prints included archetypal geometric figures, joined the group in 1928, he designed most of the pictographs (Fig. **16–43**).

Often reduced to as little as one-half-centimeter tall, these pictographs were designed to express subtleties such as a drunken man, an unemployed man, or an emigrant man in charts and diagrams. Arntz cut the pictographs on linoleum blocks, after which they were printed on a letterpress and then pasted into the finished artwork. An inventory of 1,140

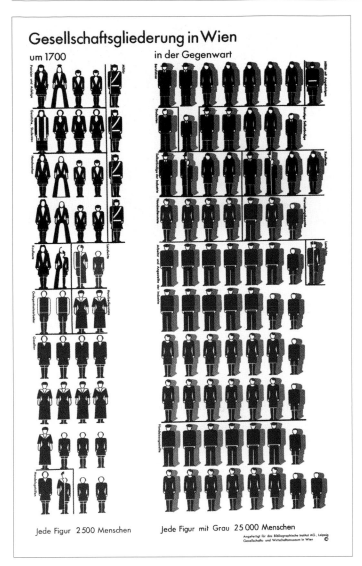

16–43

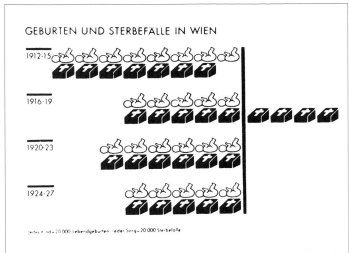

16–42

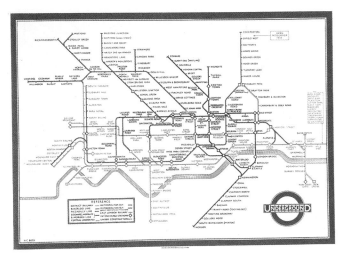

16–44

pictographs was designed by 1940, when the Isotype group fled to England. Pictographs were now duplicated by means of type-high letterpress line blocks. Because of their Germanic background, Neurath and Reidermeister were interned briefly, then were allowed to resume their work in England. In 1942 they were married.

Important among Neurath's many assistants was Rudolf Modley (1906–76), who came to America during the 1930s and established Pictorial Statistics, Inc., which later became the Pictographic Corporation. This organization became the North American branch of the Isotype movement. Modley believed a symbol should follow principles of good design, be effective in both large and small sizes, have unique characteristics to distinguish it from all other symbols, be interesting, function well as a statistical unit for counting, and work in outline or in silhouette.

The Isotype group's contribution to visual communications is the set of conventions they developed to formalize the use of pictorial language. This includes a pictorial syntax (a system of connecting images to create an ordered structure and meaning) and the design of simplified pictographs. The impact of their work on post–World War II graphic design includes research toward the development of universal visual-language systems and the extensive use of pictographs in signage and information systems.

The prototype for the modern map

The London Underground also sponsored a major graphic design innovation when it made a trial printing of a new subway system map (Fig. **16–44**) in 1933. Draftsman Henry C. Beck (1903–74) submitted an unsolicited design proposal that replaced geographic fidelity with a diagrammatic interpretation.

16–45

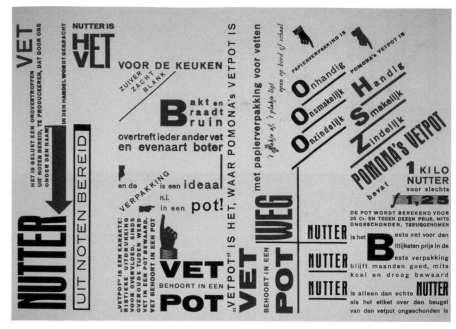

16–46

The central portion of the map, showing complex interchanges between routes, was enlarged in proportion to outlying areas. Meandering geographic lines were drawn on a grid of horizontals, verticals, and forty-five-degree diagonals. Bright color coding identified and separated the routes. Although cautious about the value of Beck's proposal, the publicity department printed the trial run and invited public response. When the public found the new map extremely functional, it was developed and employed throughout the system. In preparing the camera-ready art for the first trial printing of his map, Beck hand-lettered over 2,400 characters in Johnston's Railway Type! Beck's development and revisions of the London Underground maps over twenty-seven years made a significant contribution to the visual presentation of diagrams and networks, for his discoveries inspired many variations around the world.

Independent voices in the Netherlands

In the Netherlands, several designers were influenced by the modern movements and the new typography, but they were very personal and original in their visions. The Dutch designer Piet Zwart (1885–1977) created a synthesis from two apparently contradictory influences: the Dada movement's playful vitality and De Stijl's functionalism and formal clarity. By the time Zwart began graphic design projects at age thirty-six, he had trained as an architect, designed furniture and interiors, and worked in Jan Wils's (1891–1972) architectural office. Zwart's interior designs moved toward functionalism and clarity of form after his communication with de Stijl began in 1919; however, he never joined the movement, because

although he agreed with its basic philosophy, he found it too dogmatic and restrictive.

By happenstance, in the early 1920s Zwart received his first typographic commissions (Fig. **16–45**) from Laga, a flooring manufacturer. As his work evolved, he rejected both traditional symmetrical layout and De Stijl's insistence on strict horizontals and verticals. After making a rough layout, Zwart ordered words, rules, and symbols from a typesetter and playfully manipulated them on the surface to develop the design. The fluid nature of collage technique joined with a conscious concern for functional communication. Zwart designed the space as a "field of tension" brought alive by rhythmic composition, vigorous contrasts of size and weight, and a dynamic interplay between typographic form and the background page (Figs. **16–46** and **16–47**). Zwart's catalogue designs for N. V. Nederlandsche Kabelfabriek (NKF) (Dutch Cable Manufactory) have a dynamic spatial integration of type and images (Figs. **16–48** and **16–49**).

Rejecting the dull grayness of conventional typography, Zwart created dynamic and arresting layouts. He fractured tradition by taking a new look at the material from which graphic designs are made. With no formal training in typography or printing, he was uninhibited by rules and methods of traditional professional practice. The need for typography to be in harmony with its era and available production methods was an important concern for Zwart. Realizing that twentieth-century mass printing made typographic design an important and influential cultural force, he had a strong sense of social responsibility and concern for the reader. Zwart considered

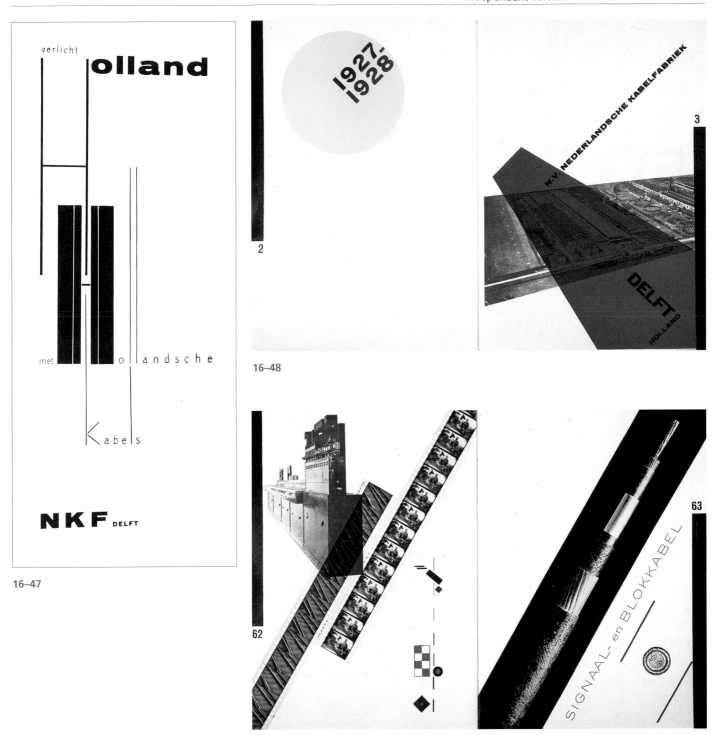

16–47

16–48

62

16–49

16–45. Piet Zwart, advertisement for the Laga Company, 1923. The influence of De Stijl principles is evident in Zwart's earliest graphics.

16–46. Piet Zwart, folder, 1924. Order is achieved in a complex communication by the rhythmic repetition of diagonals, words, letters, rules, and the dingbat hand.

16–47. Piet Zwart, advertisement for the NKF cableworks, 1926. Structured on dynamic verticals, this design is an example of how Zwart, functioning as his own copywriter, developed simultaneous visual and verbal solutions to the client's communication problem.

16–48. Piet Zwart. Pages from the NKF cableworks catalogue, 1928. Equilibrium is achieved by a yellow circle balancing a red wedge crossing the blue halftone of the NKF plant. The NKF plant area, overprinted by the red, becomes a purple halftone on a red background.

16–49. Piet Zwart, pages from the NKF cableworks catalogue, 1928. This layout demonstrates Zwart's use of photographs as compositional shapes.

16–50

16–51

16–52

16–53

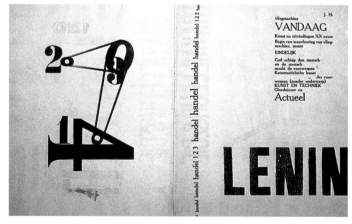

16–54

the function of time as an aspect of the reader's experience as he planned his page designs; he recognized that twentieth-century citizens were inundated with communications and could not afford the luxury of wading through masses of reading matter. Brief slogans with large letters in bold type and diagonal lines were used to attract the attention of the reader (Fig. **16–50**), who could quickly grasp the main idea or content. Explanatory matter was organized to make it easy to isolate essential information from secondary material.

Zwart's activities over a long and illustrious career included photography, product and interior design, and teaching. Zwart once called himself a *typotekt*. This play on words, which expresses his position as an architect who had become a typographic designer, has a deeper meaning, for it also expresses

the working process of the new typography. The way that Zwart (as well as Lissitzky, Bayer, and Tschichold) constructed a design from the material of the typecase is analogous to the manner in which an architect's design is constructed from glass, steel, and concrete. His personal logo (Fig. **16–51**) is a visual/verbal pun, for the Dutch word *zwart* means "black."

The end of 1933 witnessed a change in Zwart's work, as he became more involved with teaching and industrial and interior design. After twelve years of ascendancy in graphic design, he never again attained the level of his earlier achievements. Yet during that period, he ranked among the modern masters of this profession.

Another Dutch artist, Hendrik N. Werkman (1882–1945) of Groningen, is noted for his experimentation with type, ink,

GEDEELTE WIJZERPLAAT OP WARE GROOTTE

ELKE STREEP 5 GRAM

DUIDELIJK

ZOO

KLEIN

2.0
C.M.

MODEL Z

16–55

16–50. Piet Zwart, pages from the English-language NKF cable-works catalogue, 1926. Repetition and contrast reinforce the verbal message.

16–51. Piet Zwart, personal logo, 1927.

16–52. H. N. Werkman, page 1 of *The Next Call*, no. 2, October 6, 1923. The impression from a lock plate from the side of a door suggests an upper-case E.

16–53. H. N. Werkman, pages 2 and 3 of *The Next Call*, no. 4, January 24, 1924. Printed to commemorate Lenin soon after his death, the columns of *O*s and *M*s suggest soldiers guarding a casket.

16–54. H. N. Werkman, pages 4 and 5 of *The Next Call*, no. 4.

16–55. Paul Schuitema, brochure cover for the Berkel Model Z scales, before 1929. Arrows moving from the large word *ZOO* (meaning "So") create a double headline: "So clear—every dash 5 grams" and "So small—20 centimeters [wide]." This brochure was printed by letterpress from typographic material assembled on the press bed from Schuitema's layout.

and ink rollers for purely artistic expression. After his large printing company foundered in 1923 as a result of his indifference toward business matters and the economic situation in Europe following World War I, Werkman established a small job-printing firm in an attic space above a warehouse. Beginning in 1923 he used type, rules, printing ink, brayers, and a small press to produce monoprints which he referred to as *druksels* (prints). In September 1923 he began publication of *The Next Call,* a small magazine of typographic experiments and texts (Figs. **16–52, 16–53,** and **16–54**). The printing press became a layout pad as Werkman composed wood type, wood blocks, and even parts of an old lock directly on the letterpress bed. He loved printing and took joy in beautiful paper, wood textures, and the unique qualities of each nicked and dented piece of wood type. His process of building a design from ready-made components can be compared to the creative process of the Dadaists, particularly in collage. Like Lissitzky, Werkman explored type as concrete visual form as well as alphabet communication. A few days before the city

of Groningen was liberated by the Canadian army in April 1945, Werkman was executed by the Nazis. After his arrest, much of his work was confiscated and taken to the headquarters of the Security Police, and it was destroyed when the building burned during the fighting.

Another important Dutch graphic constructivist designer from the province of Groningen, Paul Schuitema (1897–1973), was educated as a painter during World War I and then turned to graphic design in the early 1920s. Schuitema's most important clients were the P. van Berkel Meat Company, the Van Berkel Patent Scale and Cutting Machine Factory, and the printer C. Chevalier, all three based in Rotterdam. He designed the Van Berkel trademark, as well as brochures, advertisements, stationery, and exhibitions. Over the next five years his work for this company would open new vistas in advertising typography (Fig. **16–55**). Other clients included the Dutch PTT (Post, Telephone and Telegraph) (Fig. **16–56**). He made significant use of overprinting and organized his space with rigorous horizontal, vertical, and diagonal movements. Objective photography was

16–57

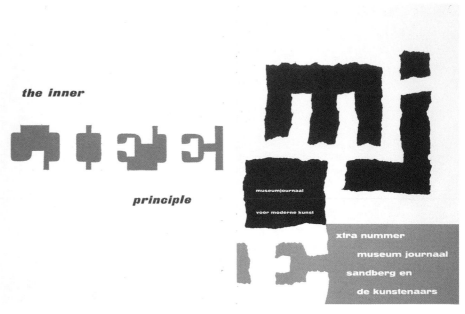

16–58

16–59

16–56

16–60

16–56. Paul Schuitema, "Koopt A.N.V.V. Postzegels, Steunt het werk der Alg. Ned. Ver. Voor Vreemdelingen verkeer, een landsbelang," poster, 1932. The text promotes the sale of postage stamps in support of Dutch tourism.

16–57. Willem Sandberg, page from *Experimenta typographica,* 1956. To illustrate the utility of jugs, Sandberg transformed the *u* in *Kruges* (jugs) into a vessel filled with blue letters.

16–58. Willem Sandberg, page from *Experimenta typographica,* 1956. Sandberg's sensitive exploration of the negative space between letterforms became enormously influential with a generation of designers.

16–59. Willem Sandberg, cover for *Museum journaal voor moderne kunst,* 1963. Sandberg designed contrasts between scale (large/small), color (red/blue/white), and edge (torn/sharp).

16–60. Willem Sandberg, Cover for *Nu* (Now), 1959.

16–61. Willem Sandberg, pages from *Nu* (Now), 1959.

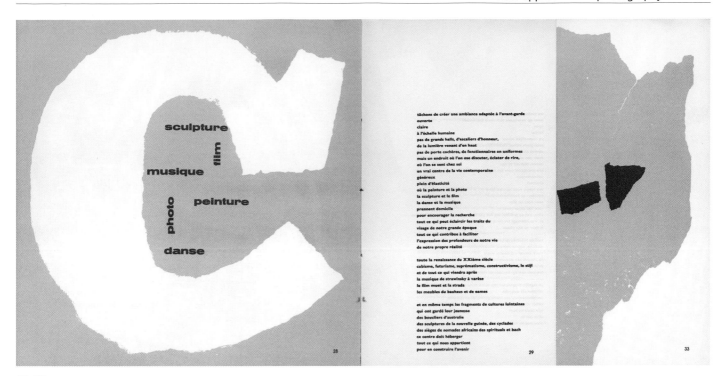

16–61

integrated with typography as part of a total structure. For thirty years Schuitema taught at the Koninklijke Academie van Beeldende Kunsten (Royal Academy of Fine Arts) at The Hague, where he inspired several generations of designers.

Willem Sandberg (1897–1984), director of the Stedelijk Museum in Amsterdam from 1945 until 1963, emerged as a highly original practitioner of the new typography after World War II. During the war, while hiding and working for the Resistance, he created his *experimenta typographica*, a series of probing typographic experiments in form and space that was finally published in the mid-1950s (Figs. **16–57** and **16–58**) and inspired his later work. Sandberg was an explorer; his text settings were often completely unjustified, and sentence fragments were arranged freely on the page, with ultrabold or delicate script introduced for accent or emphasis. He rejected symmetry and liked bright primary colors and strong contrasts, as well as muted hues and subtle juxtapositions. Crisp sans-serif type was combined with large torn paper collage letterforms with rough edges. Exhibition catalogue text was often printed on coarse brown paper, in contrast to the coated enamel pages interspersed for halftones.

In the *Museum journaal voor moderne kunst* (Museum Journal of Modem Art) cover (Fig. **16–59**), contrasts of scale, color, and edge are used in a seemingly casual but highly structured layout. The white negative areas around the *m* and *j* interact dynamically with the red letters. The torn edges contrast with the crisp type and sharp-edged blue bar, which has

an *E* torn from it. In the 1957 cover for the Stedelijk Museum's library catalogue, the first six letters of the word *bibliotheek* (library) are also made from torn paper, denoting a fascination with serendipity inherited from Werkman. Sandberg's work demonstrates that many of the underlying design ideas of the new typography remained vital after World War II (Figs. **16–60** and **16–61**).

New approaches to photography

The new typography emphasized objective communication and was concerned with machine production. The camera was seen as a vital tool for image making. Much of the photography used in conjunction with the new typography was straightforward and neutral. The role of photography as a graphic communications tool was expanded by Swiss designer/photographer Herbert Matter (1907–84). While studying painting in Paris under Léger, Matter became interested in photography and design. In the early 1930s he worked with the Deberny and Peignot type foundry as a photographer and typographic designer; also, he assisted Cassandre in poster design. At age twenty-five Matter returned to his native Switzerland and began to design posters for the Swiss National Tourist Office. Matter thoroughly understood modernism's new approaches to visual organization and its techniques, such as collage and montage. Like Laszlo Moholy-Nagy, Matter applied this knowledge to photography and graphic design. His posters of the 1930s use montage, dynamic scale changes, and an effective

16–62

16–63

integration of typography and illustration. Photographic images become pictorial symbols removed from their naturalistic environments and linked together in unexpected ways.

Matter pioneered extreme contrasts of scale and the integration of black-and-white photography, signs, and color areas (Fig. **16–62**). In his travel poster proclaiming that all roads lead to Switzerland, three levels of photographic information combine in a majestic expression of space (Fig. **16–63**). In the foreground, a cobblestone road photographed from ground level thrusts back into the space. Its motion is stopped by a ridge bearing the famous Swiss roadway that twists and winds over the mountains. Finally, a majestic mountain peak soars up against the blue sky. A tourism poster for Pontresina (Fig. **16–64**) uses uncommon camera angles and an extreme scale change from the large head to the small skier.

Another Swiss graphic designer showing great expertise in the use of photography in graphic design during the 1930s was Walter Herdeg (1908–95) of Zurich. In publicity materials for Swiss resorts, Herdeg achieved design vitality through the selection and cropping of photographic images. In designs for the St. Moritz ski resort (Fig. **16–65**), Herdeg created a graphic unity through the consistent application of a stylized sun symbol and a logotype derived from handwriting. During World War II, Herdeg launched a bimonthly international graphic design magazine entitled *Graphis*. For forty-two years and 246 issues, he published, edited, and designed this publication, which sparked an unprecedented dialogue among graphic designers throughout the world.

The new language of form began in Russia and Holland, crystallized at the Bauhaus, and found one of its most articu-

16–64

16–65

late spokesmen in Jan Tschichold. The rational and scientific sensibilities of the twentieth century gained graphic expression. The new typography enabled designers of vision to develop functional and expressive visual communications, and it continued to be an important influence well into the late twentieth century.

16–62. Herbert Matter, Swiss tourism poster, 1934. Angular forms and linear patterns convey a sense of movement appropriate to winter sports.

16–63. Herbert Matter, Swiss tourism poster, 1935. The photographic montage has a graphic vigor signifying the spatial experience of mountain height.

16–64. Herbert Matter, poster for Pontresina, 1935. High and low camera angles accompany dramatic scale contrasts.

16–65. Walter Herdeg, poster for St. Moritz, 1936. Light and shadow create a lively composition conveying the thrills of skiing. St. Moritz's sun trademark becomes part of the photograph.

The Modern Movement in America

17–1

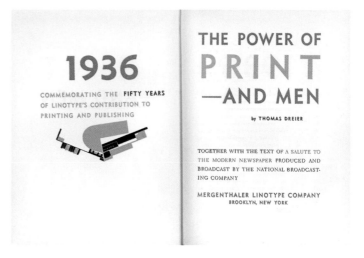

17–2

The modern movement did not gain an early foothold in the United States. When the fabled 1913 Armory Show introduced modernism to America, it generated a storm of protest and provoked public rejection of modern art and design. Modernist European design did not become a significant influence in America until the 1930s. As the billboards in a Walker Evans (1903–75) photograph demonstrate (Fig. **17–1**), American graphic design during the 1920s and 1930s was dominated by traditional illustration. However, the modern approach slowly gained ground on several fronts: book design, editorial design for fashion and business magazines catering to affluent audiences, and promotional and corporate graphics.

When Tschichold's "Elementare Typographie" insert was publicized in American advertising and graphic arts venues, it caused considerable excitement and turmoil. Editors and writers savagely attacked it as "typographic fireworks" and a "typographic revolution" of "insane jugglings of type by a band of crazy, foreign type anarchists." But a small number of American typographers and designers recognized the vitality and functionalism of the new ideas. In 1928 and 1929 new typeface designs, including Futura and Kabel, became available in America, spurring the modern movement forward. A number of book designers, including William Addison Dwiggins (1880–1956), were transitional designers whose work ranged from the classical tradition of Goudy and Rogers to the new typography of Tschichold. After two decades in advertising design, Dwiggins began designing books for Alfred A. Knopf in 1926. He established Knopf's reputation

17–1. Walker Evans, untitled, 1936. Evans's Atlanta photograph contrasting decaying homes and Depression-era movie posters documents a chasm between reality and graphic fantasy.

17–2. William Addison Dwiggins, title pages from *The Power of Print and Men,* 1936. This title shows Dwiggins's ornaments, his Metro and Electra typefaces, and his passion for subtle color combinations.

17–3. S. A. Jacobs, title page for *Christmas Tree,* by e.e. cummings, 1928. Typography implies an image, which joins with rules and ornaments to suggest a landscape.

17–4. Merle Armitage, title page for *Modern Dance,* by Merle Armitage, 1935. Sans-serif capitals are letterspaced and separated by hairline rules.

17–5. Lester Beall, cover for *PM,* 1937. This cover is evidence of Beall's growing interest in European modernism, and the color and diagonal typography suggest the influence of the Bauhaus and constructivism. However, his use of the nineteenth-century typeface on the lower left gives the design its own dimension. This issue contained an article on Beall's own graphic design.

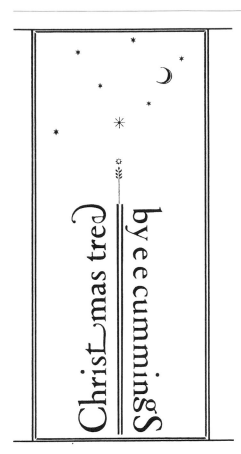

17–3

17–4

17–5

for excellence in book design, experimenting with uncommon title-page arrangements and two-column book formats. His stenciled ornaments (Fig. **17–2**) combining the sensibility of the cubist collage with the grace of traditional ornament. His eighteen typeface designs for Mergenthaler Linotype include Caledonia (1938), a graceful text face; Electra (1935), a modern design with reduced thick-and-thin contrast; and Metro (1929), Linotype's geometric sans serif designed to compete with Futura and Kabel.

Other important book designers of the period include S. A. Jacobs, whose prolific oeuvre includes several books of e. e. Cummings's poetry (Fig. **17–3**), and Merle Armitage (1893–1975), whose typographic expressions ranged from Renaissance-inspired designs to books for avant-garde music and dance that helped define the modernist design aesthetic in America (Fig. **17–4**).

Lester Beall (1903–69) was a Kansas City native who moved to Chicago and earned an art history degree in 1926. Beall was primarily self-taught; his extensive reading and curious intellect formed the basis for his professional development. After gaining experience in the late 1920s and early 1930s as a graphic designer whose work broke with traditional American advertis-

ing layout, Beall moved his studio to New York in 1935. In the challenging social and economic environment of the Depression era, he attempted to develop strong, direct, and exciting visual forms. Beall understood Tschichold's new typography and the Dada movement's random organization, intuitive placement of elements, and use of chance in the creative process (Fig. **17–5**). Admiring the strong character and form

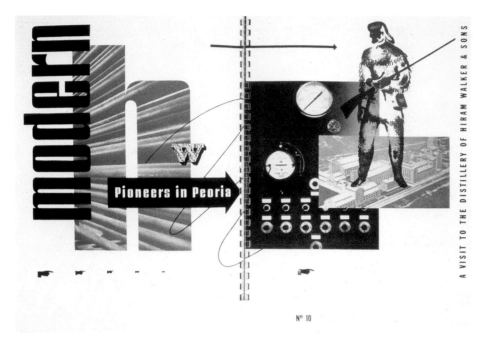

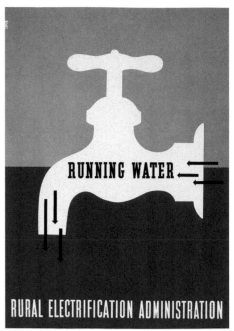

17–6

17–7

17–8

17–9

of nineteenth-century American wood types, Beall delighted in incorporating them into his work during this period. Often, flat planes of color and elementary signs such as arrows were combined with photography, as Beall sought visual contrast and a high level of informational content. The design of Figure **17–6** has strong horizontal movements contrasting with a rhythm of verticals. Images are layered in space; here a transparent illustration of a pioneer overprints two photographs. Beall's posters for the Rural Electrification Administration, a federal agency

charged with bringing electricity to the less populated areas of America, reduced pro-electrification messages to elemental signs (Fig. **17–7**). One poster series combined photomontage with the red and white stripes of the American flag (Fig. **17–8**).

In 1951 Beall moved his studio from New York City to his country home at Dumbarton Farms in Connecticut. In this new environment, and in response to client and social changes, Beall became increasingly involved in the emerging corporate design movement of the 1950s and 1960s (see chapter 20).

17–10

17–6. Lester Beall, title pages from a promotional brochure, c. 1935. Victorian wood type contrasts with sans-serif type, and photography contrasts with drawing.

17–7. Lester Beall, poster for the Rural Electrification Administration, c. 1937. The benefits of electricity were presented through signs understandable to illiterate and semiliterate audiences.

17–8. Lester Beall, poster for the Rural Electrification Administration, c. 1937. Patriotic graphics and happy farm children imply a rural life improved by government programs.

17–9. Erté, Harper's Bazaar covers, July 1929; July 1934; and January 1935. Erté's covers projected a sophisticated, continental image on the newsstand.

17–10. Martin Munkacsi, editorial photograph from Harper's Bazaar, 1934. Rejecting the conventions of the studio, Munkacsi allowed outside locations and the natural movements of his models to suggest innovative possibilities.

Immigrants to America

A migratory process began slowly, then reached a crescendo by the late 1930s, as cultural leaders from Europe, including many graphic designers, came to America. The design language they brought with them, and the changes imposed on their work by their American experience, forms an important phase of the development of American graphic design.

It is a curious coincidence that four individuals—Erté (born Romain de Tirtoff, 1892–1990), Dr. Mehemed Fehmy Agha (1896–1978), Alexey Brodovitch (1898–1971), and Alexander Liberman (1912–1999)—who brought European modernism to American graphic design were Russian-born, French-educated immigrants who worked in editorial design for fashion magazines. Erté was a Russian admiral's son, born in St. Petersburg. After becoming a prominent Paris illustrator and set designer working in the art deco manner, he was signed to an exclusive contract from 1924 until 1937 to design covers and fashion illustrations for Harper's Bazaar magazine (Fig. 17–9). Renowned for his fashion designs, set designs, illustrations, and graphics, Erté became a major proponent of the art deco sensibility. His work combined the stylized drawing of synthetic cubism, an exotic decorativeness, and the elegance of high fashion.

Dr. Agha was the first art director trained in modern design to guide the graphic destiny of a major American periodical. Born in Ukraine to Turkish parents, Agha studied art in Kiev and received advanced degrees in languages in Paris. After working in Paris as a graphic artist, he moved to Berlin and was there in 1928 when he met Condé Nast, who had come to close down the unprofitable Berlin edition of Vogue maga-

zine and was seeking a new art director for the American Vogue. Impressed with Agha's graphics, Nast persuaded him to come to New York as Vogue's art director. Energetic and uncompromising, Agha soon took over design responsibilities for Vanity Fair and House & Garden as well. He overhauled Condé Nast's stuffy, dated approach to editorial design by introducing bleed photography, machine-set sans-serif type, white space, and asymmetrical layouts.

At the rival Harper's Bazaar, which had been purchased by newspaperman William Randolph Hearst in 1913 and rejuvenated through the use of photography, Carmel Snow became editor in 1933. She was keenly interested in the visual aspects of the magazine and hired Hungarian Martin Munkacsi (1896–1963) as a staff photographer. Long-held conventions of editorial photography were slapped in the face by Munkacsi's new compositions (Fig. 17–10). Munkacsi was one of a new breed of editorial and advertising photographers who combined the visual dynamic learned from Moholy-Nagy and Man Ray with the fresh approach to photography made possible by the new 35mm Leica "miniature" camera. Invented by an employee of the Leitz Company of Germany in 1913, this small portable camera was introduced much later, because its production was delayed by World War I. With the addition of faster, higher-resolution films, photography became an extension of the photographer's vision.

Snow invited Alexey Brodovitch (1898–1971) to become art director of Harper's Bazaar, where he remained from 1934 until 1958. Brodovitch, a Russian who had fought in the czar's cavalry during World War I, immigrated to Paris and established himself as a leading contemporary designer there before heading

17–11

17–12

17–13

17–14

17–15

to the United States in 1930. With an affinity for white space and sharp type on clear, open pages, he rethought the approach to editorial design (Figs. **17–11** and **17–12**). He sought "a musical feeling" in the flow of text and pictures. The rhythmic environment of open space balancing text was energized by the art and photography he commissioned from major European artists, including Henri Cartier-Bresson, Cassandre, Dali, and Man Ray. In addition, Brodovitch taught designers how to use photography. His cropping, enlargement, and juxtaposition of images and his exquisite selection from contact sheets were all accomplished with extraordinary intuitive judgment (Fig. **17–13** and **17–14**). He saw contrast as a dominant tool in editorial design and paid close attention to the graphic movement through the editorial pages of each issue.

17–16 **17–17** **17–18**

Born in Kiev, Russia, Alexander Liberman (1912–99) spent his early years in Paris and studied at the École des Beaux Arts. After working for Cassandre he was hired as a layout designer by the French weekly magazune *Vu* and in 1933 was appointed as its director (Fig. **17–15**). In 1940 he emigrated to the United States, where he joined the design section at Condé Nast. Initially a layout designer for *Vogue,* he succeeded Agha as the magazine's art director in 1943. Using photographers such as Irving Penn, Cecil Beaton, and Lee Miller, he enlivened *Vogue* with current images. He was appointed editorial director of all Condé Nast publications in 1961 and remained in that position until his retirement thirty years later (Fig. **17-16**).

Joseph Binder came to the United States in 1934 for a series of lectures and workshops and soon received wide acclaim. Encouraged by the response to his work, he settled in New York the following year. In America, Binder's technique became more refined, partly because he had begun to use the airbrush to achieve highly finished forms. His strong cubist beginnings eventually yielded to a stylized realism.

In Binder's 1939 New York World's Fair poster (Fig. **17–17**), the trylon and perisphere, emblems of the fair, combine with spotlights, a skyline, and modern transportation images to symbolize America's coming of age on the eve of World War II. World events would soon force the United States to cast aside its neutrality, traditionalism, and provincialism; the new embrace of modernist design was part of this process. Traces of cubism remained in Binder's work, as can be seen in his 1939 poster for iced coffee (Fig. **17–18**), where two-dimensional

17–11. Alexey Brodovitch (art director) and Man Ray (photographer), pages from *Harper's Bazaar*, 1934. The figure's oblique thrust inspired a dynamic typographic page with several sizes and weights of geometric sans serifs.

17–12. Alexey Brodovitch (art director) and Man Ray (photographer), pages from *Harper's Bazaar*, 1934. The forms and texture of the experimental photograph are amplified and complemented by the typographic design.

17–13. Alexey Brodovitch, photography by Herbert Matter, *Harper's Bazaar* cover, June 1940. Brodovitch often used repetition as a design device, as with the round forms on the butterfly wings and the eyes of the model.

17–14. Alexey Brodovitch, cover for *Harper's Bazaar,* June 1951. In this striking cover the feeling of summer is captured by the bold colors. The cropping of the image draws attention to the beach clothing rather than the model herself.

17–15. Alexander Liberman, cover for *VU,* 1933. *VU* was one of the first publications where photography played a leading role and was the inspiration for magazines such as *Life* and *Look* in the United States.

17–16. Alexander Liberman, *Vogue* cover, 1945. With surrealistic overtones Liberman fuses an appeal for the Red Cross with high fashion.

17–17. Joseph Binder, poster for the New York World's Fair, 1939. America's embrace of modernism, technology, and global power is signified.

17–18. Joseph Binder, poster for A & P Coffee, 1939. Flat shapes and airbrushed modulations create strong value contrasts, requiring the viewer to fill in the details of Binder's edited naturalism.

planes support the illustrative content. During his Vienna period (see Fig. 14–55). Binder had constructed images from planes; now the subject matter became dominant, and design qualities were subordinated to pictorial imagery.

The Works Progress Administration Poster Project

As part of the New Deal of President Franklin Delano Roosevelt, the federal government created the Works Progress Administration (WPA) in 1935. Direct relief for the unemployed was replaced by work opportunities, and billions of dollars were inserted into the economy as an average of more than two million workers were paid from fifteen to ninety dollars per month from 1935 until 1941. Launched in the fall of 1935, the WPA Federal Art Project enabled actors, musicians, visual artists, and writers to continue their professional careers. A poster project was included among the various cultural programs. Sculptors and painters joined unemployed illustrators and graphic designers in the studios. As many designs were by artists, it is not surprising that the project took a strong aesthetic approach to typography, used as both compositional element and message communicator.

From 1935 until 1939, when the Federal Art Project was abolished, over two million copies of approximately 35,000 poster designs were produced. Most of the designs were silkscreened. Silk-screen printing's characteristic flat color combined with influences from the Bauhaus, pictorial modernism, and constructivism to produce a modernist result that contrasted with the traditional illustration dominating much of American mass-media graphics of the era. Government-sponsored cultural events, including theatrical performances and art exhibitions, were frequent subjects for the poster project, as were public-service communications about health, crime prevention, housing, and education.

The flight from fascism

The rise of Nazism in Europe created one of the greatest transnational migrations of intellectual and creative talent in history. Scientists, authors, architects, artists, and designers left Europe for the haven of North America during the late 1930s. Among them were the artists Ernst, Duchamp, and Mondrian. When the Nazis closed the Bauhaus in 1933, faculty, students, and alumni dispersed throughout the world and made modern design a truly international movement. Gropius, Mies van der Rohe, and Breuer transplanted the functionalist architectural movement to the United States, and Bayer and Moholy-Nagy brought their innovative approaches to graphic design. Other European graphic designers who came to America and made significant contributions to design include Will Burtin (1908–72), Jean Carlu, George Giusti (1908–90), Herbert Matter, and Ladislav Sutnar.

Sponsored by the Association of Arts and Industries, Moholy-Nagy arrived in Chicago in 1937 and established the New Bauhaus. This closed after just one year due to inadequate financial support, but Moholy-Nagy managed to open the School of Design in 1939. The primary source of financial support came from Moholy-Nagy himself and other faculty members, many of whom agreed to teach without pay if necessary. Both Carlu and Bayer also found it difficult to find clients who comprehended their work during their first months in America.

Burtin, recognized as one of Germany's outstanding designers, fled Germany in 1938 after refusing to work for the Nazi regime. His work combined a graphic clarity and directness with a lucid presentation of the subject matter. The "Design Decade" *Architectural Forum* cover (Fig. **17–19**) demonstrates his ability to bring together structural form and symbolic information in a cohesive whole. The dates, printed on acetate, combine with the architect's tools to signify design during the preceding decade; shadows become integral forms in the design. Burtin's keen understanding of science is reflected in designs for the Upjohn pharmaceutical company, interpreting such complex subjects as bacteriology (Fig. **17–20**). In 1943 Burtin left Upjohn to work on government training manuals, followed by three years as art director of *Fortune* magazine. In 1948 he became a design consultant for Upjohn and other companies, making a major contribution to the visual interpretation of graphic information.

A patron of design

A major figure in the development of American modern design beginning in the 1930s was a Chicago industrialist, Walter P. Paepcke (1896–1960), who founded the Container Corporation of America (CCA) in 1926. Paepcke pioneered the manufacture of paperboard and corrugated-fiber containers. Acquisitions and expansion enabled CCA to become a national company and the nation's largest producer of packaging materials. Paepcke was unique among the large industrialists of his generation, for he recognized that design could both serve a pragmatic business purpose and become a major cultural thrust on the part of the corporation. His interest was inspired by his wife, artist Elizabeth Nitze Paepcke (1902–94), who prompted her husband to hire perhaps the first corporate design director in America. In 1936 Egbert Jacobson (1890–1966) was selected as the first director of CCA's new department of design. As with Behrens's design program for AEG early in the century, CCA's new visual signature (and its implementation) was based on two ingredients: the vision of the designer and a supportive client. Jacobson had an extensive background as a color expert, and this knowledge was put to use as mill and factory interiors were transformed from drab industrial grays

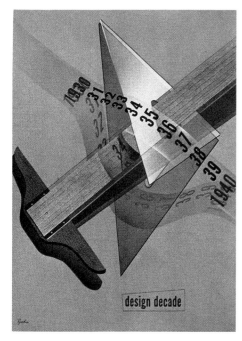

17–19   **17–20**   **17–22**

17–21

17–19. Will Burtin, cover for *Architectural Forum,* 1940. Burtin gave graphic form to abstract ideas, such as passage of time.

17–20. Will Burtin, cover for the first issue of *Scope,* 1941. To signify new "miracle drugs" under development, a color illustration is superimposed over a black-and-white photograph of a test tube.

17–21. Egbert Jacobson, logo for Container Corporation of America (CCA),1936. This logical symbol, combining an image of the major product with a map suggesting the national scope of the firm, was innovative for its time.

17–22. A. M. Cassandre, advertisement for CCA, 1938. A strong statement—"Research, experience, and talent focused on advanced paperboard packaging"—is illustrated with near hypnotic impact.

and browns to bright colors. A new trademark was applied to stationery, checks (Fig. **17–21**), invoices, vehicles, and signage. A consistent format used sans-serif type and a standard color combination of black and shipping-carton tan.

Paepcke was an advocate and patron of design. He had maintained a long-standing interest in the Bauhaus, perhaps as a response to the school's experiments with paper materials and structures. Moved by Moholy-Nagy's commitment and determination, Paepcke provided much-needed moral and financial support to the Institute of Design. By the time of Moholy-Nagy's tragic early death from leukemia on 24 November 1946, the institute was on a firm educational and organizational footing.

CCA's advertising agency was N. W. Ayer, where art director Charles Coiner (1898–1989) made a major contribution. Beginning in May 1937, Cassandre was commissioned to design a series of CCA advertisements that defied American advertising conventions. The traditional headline and body copy were replaced by a dominant visual that extended a simple statement about CCA (Fig. **17–22**). In contrast to the long-winded copywriting of most 1930s advertising, many CCA advertisements only had a dozen words.

Cassandre was also commissioned by Brodovitch to design covers for *Harper's Bazaar* (Fig. **17–23**). When Cassandre returned to Paris in 1939, CCA continued his basic approach by commissioning advertisements from other artists and designers of international stature, including Bayer (who was retained as a consulting designer by Jacobson, then served as chairman of CCA's department of design from 1956 to 1965), Léger, Man Ray, Matter, and Carlu.

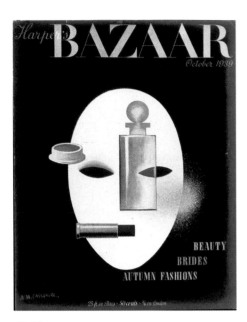

17–23

17–24

The war years

While the trauma of war disrupted the ability of many governments to produce graphic propaganda, a diverse group of painters, illustrators, and designers received commissions from the U. S. Office of War Information. America's wartime graphics ranged from brilliantly conceived posters to informational training materials and amateurish cartoons.

In 1941, as America's entry into the global conflict seemed inevitable, the federal government began to develop propaganda posters to promote production. Charles Coiner became its art consultant as America's colossal defense buildup began. He commissioned Carlu to create one of the finest designs of his career, the famous "America's answer! Production" poster (Fig. **17–24**). Over 100,000 copies were distributed throughout the country, and Carlu was recognized with a top award by the New York Art Director's Club Exhibition.

Intense feelings about Hitler, Pearl Harbor, and the war seemed to pull powerful communications from the graphic designers, illustrators, and fine artists commissioned to create posters for the Office of War Information. Illustrator John Atherton (1900–52), creator of numerous *Saturday Evening Post* covers, penetrated to the heart of the problem of careless talk, gossip, and discussion of troop movements as a source of enemy information (Fig. **17–25**). Binder's poster proposal for the U.S. Army Air Corps (Fig. **17–26**) is potent in its simplicity, signifying the essence of the air corps through minimal means. Impact is achieved by dramatic contrasts of color and scale. Kauffer was commissioned to design posters to

boost the morale of the Allied nations (Fig. **17–27**); an image of Hermes, the classical Greek messenger of the Gods, combines with an American flag to make a powerful graphic symbol. The social realist Ben Shahn (1898–1969), whose paintings addressed political and economic injustice during the Depression, reached a larger audience in posters conveying Nazi brutality (Fig. **17–28**). He achieved communicative power with intense graphic forms: the implication of a prison by closing the space with a wall; the hood masking the victim's identity; the simple, straightforward headline; and the factual urgency of a telegram.

The posters Bayer produced during and after the war were surprisingly illustrative compared to his constructivist approach during the Dessau Bauhaus period. His 1939/40 cover for PM was one of the last designs he made before this change in his design approach became evident (Fig. **17–29**). Sensitive to his new audience and oriented toward communications problem solving, Bayer painted illustrations with a simplified realism, then combined these with the hierarchy of information and strong underlying composition he pioneered at Dessau. In his poster promoting egg production, the large white egg centered against the black sky becomes a strong focal point (Fig. **17–30**). The headline to the left balances the flaming town to the right, and the diagonal subheading echoes the shadow cast by the egg.

When one compares Bayer's 1949 poster for polio research (Fig. **17–31**) with his 1926 poster for the Kandinsky Jubilee Exhibition (see Fig. 16–20), these two designs are clearly worlds

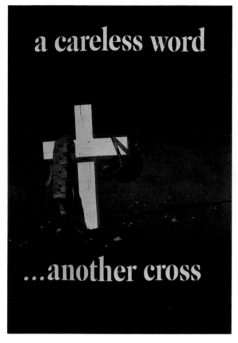

17–25

17–26

17–27

17–28

17–23. A. M. Cassandre, cover for *Harper's Bazaar,* 1939. A perfume-bottle nose, lipstick mouth, and powder-puff cheek achieve simultaneity.

17–24. Jean Carlu, poster for the Office of Emergency Management, 1941. Visual and verbal elements are inseparably interlocked into an intense symbol of productivity and labor.

17–25. John Atherton, poster for the U.S. Office of War Information, 1943. The placement of the two-part headline implies a rectangle; this symmetry is animated by the off-center placement of the white cross.

17–26. Joseph Binder, poster proposal for the U.S. Army Air Corps, 1941. Extreme spatial depth is conveyed by the scale change between the close-up wing and aircraft formation.

17–27. E. McKnight Kauffer, poster promoting Allied unity, c. 1940. The Portuguese headline translates, "We Fight for the Liberty of All."

17–28. Ben Shahn, poster for the U.S. Office of War Information, 1943. A dire crisis is conveyed using the most direct words and imagery possible.

apart. The Kandinsky poster was designed by a twenty-six-year-old typography teacher at a young school optimistically hoping to build a new social order by design; the polio research poster is the work of a forty-eight-year-old designer living in a foreign land, after a European war in which twenty-six million people were killed. The photography and typography of Bayer's Bauhaus period yielded to hand-painted illustration and hand-

lettering, but the commitment to functional communication, the integration of letterforms and imagery, and the asymmetrical balance remained constant.

During World War II, CCA innovated uses for paperboard packaging, which freed metals and other strategic materials for the war effort. A "Paperboard Goes to War" advertising campaign (Figs. **17–32** and **17–33**) continued the design

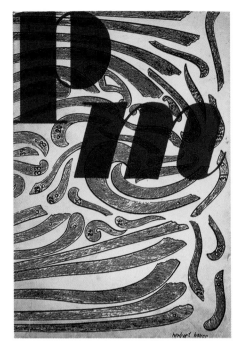

17–29

17–30

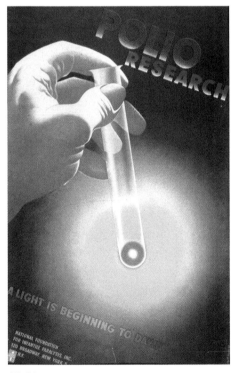

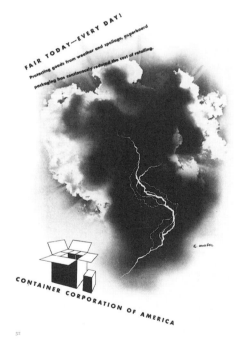

17–31

17–32

17–33

experimentation of the earlier institutional ads. Before the war there was still a degree of public concern about the strength of paperboard; this campaign prepared the way for its extensive use after the war. Each advertisement showed a specific use of a CCA product in the war effort. Bayer, Carlu, and Matter joined Jacobson in creating powerful economical statements directly striking the essence of the communications problem. Strong visuals were used with two or three lines of typography, often placed diagonally in counterpoint to compositional lines from the illustration or montage.

After the war

The United States demobilized millions of troops and converted industry from wartime needs to consumer markets after World War II. Seeking another institutional advertising campaign using fine art, CCA decided to commission paint-

17–34   17–35   17–36

ings by artists from each of the then forty-eight states (Fig. **17–34**). A simple copy line appeared under each full-color painting, followed by the CCA logotype. The series served to advance a Bauhaus ideal: the union of art with life. Once selected, artists were allowed the freedom of their artistic convictions. A major corporate art collection, now housed in the Smithsonian Institution, was assembled.

After the state series was completed, CCA developed one of the most brilliant institutional campaigns in the history of advertising. Elizabeth and Walter Paepcke were attending the Great Books discussion group conducted in Chicago by Robert M. Hutchins and Mortimer Adler. These two scholars were also editing the Great Books of the Western World series, which included two volumes discussing the ideas contained in the series. Walter Paepcke approached Adler with the possibility of an institutional ad campaign presenting the great ideas of Western culture. Each would present an artist's interpretation of a great idea selected by Adler and his colleagues. The Paepckes joined Bayer and Jacobson to form a jury to select the visual artists who would be asked to bring graphic actualization to these abstract concepts. Beginning in February 1950, this unprecedented institutional campaign transcended the bounds of advertising, as ideas about liberty, justice, and human rights were conveyed to an audience of business leaders, investors, prospective employees, and molders of public opinion. The campaign ran over three decades, with 157 visual artists creating artwork for almost two hundred "Great Ideas" advertisements. Art ranged from painted and sculptural portraits to geometric abstraction, symbolic interpretations (Fig. **17–35**), and collage (Fig. **17–36**).

17–29. Herbert Bayer, cover for *PM,* December 1939/January 1940. This issue included articles on Bayer's work, his design philosophy, and his ideas about typography.

17–30. Herbert Bayer, poster to encourage egg production, c. 1943. Black and white predominate, intensifying the muted primary colors.

17–31. Herbert Bayer, poster supporting polio research, 1949. The diagonal shaft of the test tube leads the eye from the red and blue headline to the flowing yellow light that is beginning to dawn, linking the elements in the same manner as the thick black bars of Bayer's Bauhaus work.

17–32. Herbert Matter, advertisement for CCA, 1942. A thunderstorm amplifies the copy concept of paperboard packaging protecting goods from weather and spoilage.

17–33. Herbert Matter, advertisement for CCA, 1943. A unified complex of images suggests global scope, paperboard boxes, and food for troops in harsh environmental conditions.

17–34. Ben Cunningham (artist), Leo Lionni (art director), N. W. Ayer & Son (agency), CCA advertisement honoring Nevada, 1949. Artists commissioned to interpret their native state were given complete artistic freedom.

17–35. Herbert Bayer, CCA "Great Ideas" advertisement, 1954. Protection from injustice and oppression is asserted by hands warding off arrows penetrating into the page.

17–36. Herbert Bayer, CCA "Great Ideas" advertisement, 1960. Theodore Roosevelt's admonition about threats to America found expression in a collage depicting affluence and decadence.

17–37   17–38

Just as CCA set the standard of excellence for institutional advertising in the postwar era, Brodovitch remained the pre-eminent designer for magazines. In addition to his skills as an editorial designer, Brodovitch developed an exceptional gift for identifying and assisting new talent. Photographers Richard Avedon (1923–2004) and Irving Penn (b. 1917) both received early commissions and advice from Brodovitch. Art Kane (1925–95) was another Brodovitch protégé. Kane worked as a photo retoucher and art director of *Seventeen* magazine before turning to photography. He was a master of symbolism, multiple exposure, and the reduction of photography to essential images needed to convey the essence of content with compelling conviction.

During the early 1950s Brodovitch designed the short-lived visual arts magazine *Portfolio* (Fig. **17–37**). At the height of his graphic powers, Brodovitch gave this publication a seldom matched elegance and visual flow through pacing, the cropping of images, and use of color and texture. Large images, dynamic space, and inserts on colored and rough-textured papers (Fig. **17–38**) contrast with smooth, coated white paper. A 138-centimeter (4-foot) foldout photographic essay (Fig. **17–39**) on the Mummer's Parade, punctuated with vertical columns of filmstrips, is sequential and kinetic.

In addition to freelance design commissions for CCA, Matter received design and photographic assignments from other clients, including *Vogue, Fortune*, and *Harper's Bazaar.* Matter's editorial design solutions deftly exploited photography, as shown in his cover for the October issue of *Fortune* (Fig. **17–40**). In 1946 he began a twenty-year period as graphic-de-

sign and photography consultant to the Knoll Associates furniture design and manufacturing firm, and he produced some of his finest work for this design-oriented client. Advertisements for molded-plastic chairs by Eero Saarinen are remarkable in their dynamic composition (Fig. **17–41**). Biomorphic shapes, while quite fashionable during the late 1940s and early 1950s in painting, furniture, and other design forms, became trapped in this time frame and are now associated with the sensibilities of the period. It is a tribute to Matter's strong grasp of design fundamentals that the advertising series he created for Saarinen furniture has maintained its vitality long after the forms of the era have become dated.

During the 1950s Matter turned toward more purely photographic solutions. His ability to convey concepts with images is shown in the folder (also used as advertisements on two consecutive right-hand magazine pages) unveiling a new line of molded-plastic pedestal furniture (Fig. **17–42**). Matter's "Chimney Sweeper" proved to be the most enduring advertisement in the history of the company (Fig. **17–43**).

At other times Matter developed almost purely typographic designs. In his catalogue cover for an Alexander Calder exhibition at the Guggenheim Museum in New York, the suspended letters of Calder's name are used to imply the mobile sculptures (Fig. **17–44**).

With his powerful shapes and well-defined subjects, Joseph Binder remained a force on the American design scene until the 1960s. His ubiquitous military recruiting posters (Fig. **17–45**) were among the last manifestations of pictorial modernism and became ingrained in the American consciousness

17–39

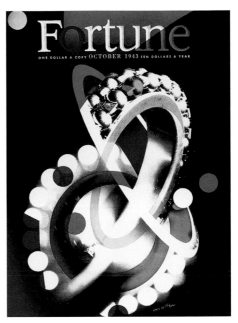

17–40

17–41

17–42

17–37. Alexey Brodovitch, cover for *Portfolio,* 1951. Screen tints produce the illusion that translucent rectangles of pink and blue-gray have been placed on the stencil logo slashing down the back cover.

17–38. Alexey Brodovitch, pages from *Portfolio,* 1951. A masterful scale shift occurs in the transition from the small, scattered cattle brands around the bull to the large cattle brands of the portfolio's first page.

17–39. Alexey Brodovitch, pages from *Portfolio,* 1951. Two pages from the Mummer's Parade fold out to reveal a dynamic cropping and juxtaposition of images.

17–40. Herbert Matter, cover for *Fortune,* October, 1943. Here photograms and geometric shapes are combined with photographs of ball bearings to construct a forceful image.

17–41. Herbert Matter, advertisement for Knoll Associates, 1948. Photographs of organic chair components combine with flat yellow "shadows" to generate the energy of a Calder mobile.

17–42. Herbert Matter, brochure covers introducing a Knoll chair, 1956. When the translucent cover page is turned, the strange wrapped object is revealed to be a chair.

17–43

17–44

17–45

during the 1950s. The geometric and symbolic shapes of pictorial modernism were converted into monolithic masses symbolizing military might and the technological accomplishments of a new era of sophisticated weaponry.

Born to Italian and Swiss parents, George Giusti worked in both Italy and Switzerland before coming to New York City in 1938 and opening a design office. He possessed a unique ability to reduce forms and images to a simplified, minimal essence. His images become iconographic and symbolic. Giusti's freely drawn images included evidence of process in his work; an image painted in transparent dyes has areas of flooded and blotted color, and his three-dimensional illustrations often include the bolts or other fasteners used to assemble the elements. Beginning in the 1940s and continuing well into the 1960s, Giusti received frequent commissions for his bold, iconographic images for advertising campaigns and for cover designs of *Holiday* (Fig. **17–46**) and *Fortune* magazines.

Informational and scientific graphics

Sutnar came to New York as design director of the Czechoslovakian Pavilion at the New York World's Fair in 1939, the year Hitler seized his country. Sutnar remained in New York and became a vital force in the evolution of modern design in the United States. A close association with Sweet's Catalog Service enabled Sutnar to place an indelible mark on the design of industrial product information. A new trademark (Fig. **17–47**) established the typographic character of Sweet's printed matter.

Since 1906 Sweet's had provided a compendium of architectural and industrial product information. Working closely with Sweet's research director, Knut Lönberg-Holm, Sutnar

developed a system for structuring information in a logical and consistent manner. In two landmark books, *Catalog Design* and *Catalog Design Progress* (Fig. **17–48**), they documented and explained their approach to a generation of designers, writers, and clients. Informational design was defined as a synthesis of function, flow, and form. *Function* is utilitarian need with a definite purpose: to make information easy to find, read, comprehend, and recall. *Flow* means the logical sequence of information. Sutnar felt the basic unit was not the page but the "visual unit," that is, the double-page spread. He rejected traditional margins and used bleeds extensively. He used shape, line, and color as functional elements to direct the eye as it moved through the design seeking information. The format of *Catalog Design Progress* itself has a coding system (Fig. **17–49**) of signs, numbers, and words, with a triangle at the bottom of title pages pointing the reader forward.

As Sutnar approached problems of form, static and uniform arrangements of catalog information gave way to dynamic information patterns and clear, rational organization. Each catalogue has a unifying graphic theme, and visual articulation of type—underlining, size and weight contrasts, spacing, color, and reversing—aided searching, scanning, and reading. A simple visualization language with emphasis on graphic charts, diagrams, and pictures clarified complex information and saved reading time. The upper-right corner is each visual unit's point of entrance and contains the identifying title (Fig. **17–50**). Optical unity resulted from a systematic use of line, shape, color, and type. These elements were combined into *visual traffic signs* to assist the user in the search for information.

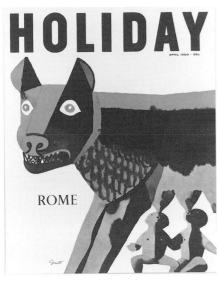

17–46

17–47

17–48

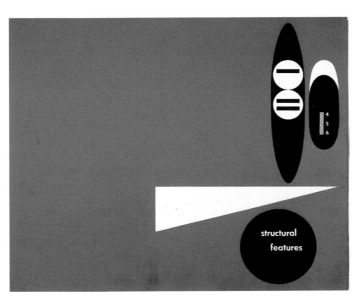

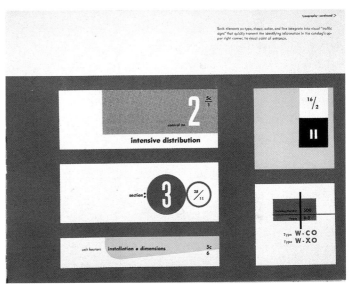

17–49

17–50

17–43. Herbert Matter, "Chimney Sweeper" advertisement for Eero Saarinen's womb chair, ca. 1955. This was Knoll's longest running advertisement, appearing in the New Yorker from 1958 until 1971.

17–44. Herbert Matter, catalogue cover for an Alexander Calder exhibit, 1964. The letters of Calder's name hang from the sky as pieces of sculpture.

17–45. Joseph Binder, recruiting poster for the U.S. Navy, c. 1954. Echoes of Cassandra's steamship posters remain, but the strength expressed is more powerful and forbidding.

17–46. George Giusti, cover for *Holiday*, 1960. Part cubism and part expressionism, this simplified image depicts the legend of Romulus, the founder of Rome, who was raised by a wolf with his twin Remus.

17–47. Ladislav Sutnar, trademark for Sweet's Catalog Service, 1942. Disarmingly simple, this mark has a beautifully harmonious figure-ground relationship.

17–48. Ladislav Sutnar, title page for *Catalog Design Progress,* 1950. Bars and rectangles containing type become compositional elements to be balanced in dynamic equilibrium.

17–49. Ladislav Sutnar, section divider page from *Catalog Design Progress,* 1950. Signs and shapes declare "part one, section two, topics four, five, and six: structural features."

17–50. Ladislav Sutnar, page from *Catalog Design Progress,* 1950. These upper-right-hand corner designs are from five different catalogue systems.

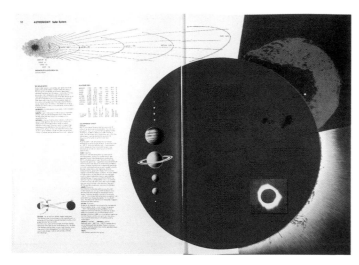

17–51

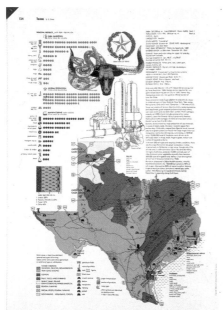

17–52

17–53

17–51. Herbert Bayer, pages from the *World Geo-Graphic Atlas,* 1953. Planets are in scale with respect to each other and the sun; a photograph of a solar eruption and illustration of a solar eclipse appear on the right.

17–52. Herbert Bayer, page from the *World Geo-Graphic Atlas,* 1953. Color coding, symbols, cross sections, maps, and illustrations provide a visual inventory of earth resources.

17–53. Herbert Bayer, page from the *World Geo-Graphic Atlas,* 1953. Immediate visual comparisons about population and energy use can be made.

An important milestone in the visual presentation of data was the publication of the *World Geo-Graphic Atlas* by CCA in 1953. In an introduction, Paepcke spoke of a need for "a better understanding of other peoples and nations." The designer and editor, Bayer, labored for five years on the project. Once again, Paepcke behaved unlike the conventional businessman, for CCA published a 368-page atlas filled with 120 full-page maps of the world supported by 1,200 diagrams, graphs, charts, symbols, and other graphic communications about the planet. This atlas was distributed to clients, suppliers, libraries, and museums. Bayer assembled information from multiple scientific disciplines, including geography, astronomy (Fig. **17–51**), climatology, economics, and sociology, and presented it through symbols, charts, and diagrams. Detailed information about states and countries was presented (Fig. **17–52**). Bayer and his assistants delivered each page to the printer as a single gouache painting with Futura type pasted onto an acetate overlay.

Bayer was ahead of his time in his effort to inventory earth resources and study the planet as a series of interlocking geophysical and life systems. Prophetically, the final section of the *World Geo-Graphic Atlas* discusses the conservation of resources, addressing population growth and resource depletion. Bayer used R. Buckminster Fuller's Dymaxion Projection, a map that shows the globe in two dimensions without distortion, as a base for pictographs representing population and rectangles of black dots symbolizing energy consumption (Fig. **17–53**). It demonstrated that North America had only 8 percent of the world's population but consumed 73 percent of its energy.

Many of the immigrants who brought European design concepts to the United States arrived virtually penniless and with minimal possessions, but they were armed with talent, ideas, and a strong belief in design as a valuable human activity that could contribute to the improvement of human communication and the human condition. The American experience was greatly enriched by their presence.

Part V | The Age of Information

Graphic design in the global village

The International Typographic Style

18

1944 **Herdeg,** *Graphis 1st* issue
1945 *A-bombs dropped; World War II ends*
1947 **Ruder and Hofmann join Basel School of Design faculty**
1940 *Churchill, "blood, toil, tears, and sweat" speech*
1949 *Mao Tse-tung's communist forces capture China*
1942 **Bill,** *Moderne Schweizer Architektur*
1930s **Bill, Stankowski, and others, constructivist graphic design**
1948 **Huber,** *Gran premio dell' Autodrome* poster

1952 **de Harak opens New York studio**
1953 **Stankowski, Standard Elektrik Lorenz AG logo**
1950 **Ulm School of Design planned; Odermatt opens studio; Zapf designs Palatino**
1954 **Frutiger, Univers designed**
1955 **Casey joins MIT**
1957 **Miedinger, Haas Grotesque (later named Helvetica by Stempel foundry)**
1959 *Neue Grafik Design begins publication* **Hofmann,** *Giselle* poster
1960 **Müller-Brockmann,** *der Film* poster

1967 **Ruder,** *Typography: A Manual of Design*
1968 **Ulm School of Design closes; Stankowski, Berlin design program; Zapf,** *Manuale Typographicum*

The New York School

19

1940s **Rand,** *Directions* covers
1940 *Print* magazine, 1st issue
1947 **Rand,** *Thoughts on Design*
1945 *United Nations founded*
1939 **Thompson, his 1st** *Westvaco Inspirations*
1945 **Lustig, New Directions book covers**
1941 *Japan attacks Pearl Harbor*

1950 **Alvid Eisenman creates graphic design rogram at Yale University**
1952 *Korean War ends*
1949 **Doyle Dane Bernbach founded**
1953 **Wolf, art directs** *Esquire*
1954 *Senate censures McCarthy*
1950s **Brodovitch's editorial design classes inspire a generation**
1955 **Bass,** *Man with the Golden Arm* graphics

1957 **Brownjohn, Chermayeff, & Geismar formed**
1960s **Lois,** *Esquire* "statement" covers
1959 **Brodovitch retires, Wolf art directs** *Bazaar; Communication Arts,* 1st issue
1958 **Storch, redesigns** *McCall's*
1968-71 **Lubalin,** *Avant Garde* magazine

Corporate Identity and Visual Symbols

20

1946 **Dorfsman joins CBS**
1943 *mass production of penicillin*
1940 **Golden becomes art director of CBS**
1945 **Olden joins CBS**
1947 **Pintori joins Olivetti**
1950 *Korean War begins*
1948 *Gandhi assassinated*
1952 *Eisenhower elected President*
1951 **Golden, CBS symbol**

1956 **Rand, IBM logo; Pintori, Olivetti Electrosumma 22 poster**
1954 **Matter, New Haven railroad program New York and Hartford**
1959 **Golden dies**
1959 *Castro ousts Batista from Cuba*
1962 **Aicher & staff, Lufthansa identity system**

1960 **Chermayeff & Geismar, Chase Manhattan identity; Beall, International Paper logo**
1964 **Mobil identity program**
1962 *Cuban missile crisis*
1968 **Wyman, Mexico City Olympics**
1965 *Watts riots*

The Conceptual Image

21

1953 **Trepkowski, "Nie!" poster**
1954 **Testa, Pirelli graphics Push Pin Studios forms**
1959 *Twen* magazine launched
1958 *Supreme Court orders school desegregation*
1956 **Trepkowski dies; Tomaszewski leads Polish movement, evolves toward a colorful collage approach**

1960 *Kennedy elected President*
c 1962 **Berg joins CBS Records**

1964 **Massin designs** *The Bald Soprano*
c 1967 **Wilson & Moscoso, psychadelic posters; Glaser,** *Dylan* poster
1966 **Kieser, Alabama Blues poster**
1968 **Grapus founded**

1963 **Tanaka design studio opens Total Design opens in Amsterdam**
1964 *Tonkin Gulf Resolution escalates Vietnam War*
1962 **Fletcher, Forbes, & Gill founded**
1965 **Oxenaar, 1st new Dutch currency**
1964 **Kamekura,** *Tokyo Olympics* posters

23

1966 **Solomon, Sea Ranch environmental graphics**
1962 **Venturi, Grand's Restaurant supergraphics**
1968 **Weingart joins Basel School of Design faculty**
1964 **Tissi E. Lutz advertisements**

The Digital Revolution and Beyond

24

c 1969 **Engelbart, 1st mouse**
1951 *UNIVAC I, 1st mass produced computer*
1969 *Compuserve, 1st commercial online service*
1981 *First space shuttle mission*
1980 *CNN 24-hour cable news*
1983 **Kare and Adkinson, MacPaint interface design**
1984 **Macintosh computer; Vander Lans,1st issue,** *Émigré* magazine
1985 **Apple laser printer Pagemaker software Licko, digital typefaces**

1987 *Stock market crashes*
1987 **Stone, Stone type family; Greiman, bitmapped** *Design Quarterly;* **Fella, Detroit Focus graphics**
1992 **Carson,** *Ray Gun*
1990 **Macintosh II color computer; Adobe, multiple master typefaces; Bernes-Lee, HTML programming language**

1994 *33% of U. S. households have computers*
1994 **Helfand, Discovery Channel Website; Carter, Big Caslon typeface**
1994 **Wired publishes its first issue**

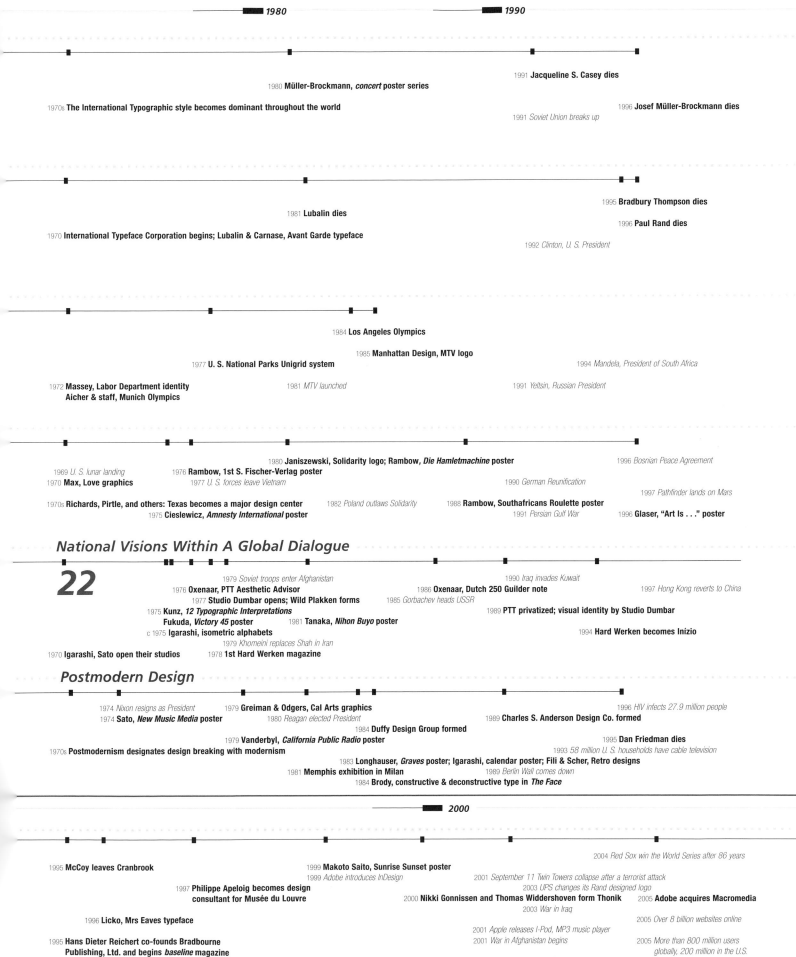

1980

1990

1991 **Jacqueline S. Casey dies**

1980 **Müller-Brockmann,** *concert* **poster series**

1970s **The International Typographic style becomes dominant throughout the world**

1996 **Josef Müller-Brockmann dies**

1991 *Soviet Union breaks up*

1995 **Bradbury Thompson dies**

1981 **Lubalin dies**

1996 **Paul Rand dies**

1970 **International Typeface Corporation begins; Lubalin & Carnase, Avant Garde typeface**

1992 *Clinton, U. S. President*

1984 **Los Angeles Olympics**

1985 **Manhattan Design, MTV logo**

1977 **U. S. National Parks Unigrid system**

1994 *Mandela, President of South Africa*

1972 **Massey, Labor Department identity**
Aicher & staff, Munich Olympics

1981 *MTV launched*

1991 *Yeltsin, Russian President*

1980 **Janiszewski, Solidarity logo; Rambow,** *Die Hamletmachine* **poster**

1996 *Bosnian Peace Agreement*

1969 *U. S. lunar landing*
1970 **Max, Love graphics**

1976 **Rambow, 1st S. Fischer-Verlag poster**

1977 *U. S. forces leave Vietnam*

1990 *German Reunification*

1997 *Pathfinder lands on Mars*

1970s **Richards, Pirtle, and others: Texas becomes a major design center**

1982 *Poland outlaws Solidarity*

1988 **Rambow, Southafricans Roulette poster**

1975 **Cieslewicz,** *Amnesty International* **poster**

1991 *Persian Gulf War*

1996 **Glaser, "Art Is . . ." poster**

National Visions Within A Global Dialogue

22

1979 *Soviet troops enter Afghanistan*

1990 *Iraq invades Kuwait*

1976 **Oxenaar, PTT Aesthetic Advisor**

1986 **Oxenaar, Dutch 250 Guilder note**

1997 *Hong Kong reverts to China*

1977 **Studio Dumbar opens; Wild Plakken forms**

1985 *Gorbachev heads USSR*

1975 **Kunz,** *12 Typographic Interpretations*
Fukuda, *Victory 45* **poster**

1981 **Tanaka,** *Nihon Buyo* **poster**

1989 **PTT privatized; visual identity by Studio Dumbar**

c 1975 **Igarashi, isometric alphabets**

1994 **Hard Werken becomes Inízio**

1979 *Khomeini replaces Shah in Iran*

1970 **Igarashi, Sato open their studios**

1978 **1st Hard Werken magazine**

Postmodern Design

1974 *Nixon resigns as President*

1979 **Greiman & Odgers, Cal Arts graphics**

1996 *HIV infects 27.9 million people*

1974 **Sato,** *New Music Media* **poster**

1980 *Reagan elected President*

1989 **Charles S. Anderson Design Co. formed**

1984 **Duffy Design Group formed**

1979 **Vanderbyl,** *California Public Radio* **poster**

1995 **Dan Friedman dies**

1970s **Postmodernism designates design breaking with modernism**

1993 *58 million U. S. households have cable television*

1983 **Longhauser,** *Graves* **poster; Igarashi, calendar poster; Fili & Scher, Retro designs**

1981 **Memphis exhibition in Milan**

1989 *Berlin Wall comes down*

1984 **Brody, constructive & deconstructive type in** *The Face*

2000

1995 **McCoy leaves Cranbrook**

2004 *Red Sox win the World Series after 86 years*

1999 **Makoto Saito, Sunrise Sunset poster**

1999 *Adobe introduces InDesign*

2001 *September 11 Twin Towers collapse after a terrorist attack*

1997 **Philippe Apeloig becomes design**
consultant for Musée du Louvre

2003 *UPS changes its Rand designed logo*

2000 **Nikki Gonnissen and Thomas Widdershoven form Thonik**

2005 **Adobe acquires Macromedia**

2003 *War in Iraq*

1996 **Licko, Mrs Eaves typeface**

2005 *Over 8 billion websites online*

2001 *Apple releases I-Pod, MP3 music player*

1995 **Hans Dieter Reichert co-founds Bradbourne**
Publishing, Ltd. and begins *baseline* **magazine**

2001 *War in Afghanistan begins*

2005 *More than 800 million users*
globally, 200 million in the U.S.

1997 *Over 30 million Internet users globally*

2002 **Max Kisman founds Holland Fonts**

The International Typographic Style

During the 1950s a design movement emerged from Switzerland and Germany that has been called Swiss design or, more appropriately, the International Typographic Style. The objective clarity of this design movement won converts throughout the world. It remained a major force for over two decades, and its influence continues into the twenty-first century.

The visual characteristics of this international style include a unity of design achieved by asymmetrical organization of the design elements on a mathematically constructed grid; objective photography and copy that present visual and verbal information in a clear and factual manner, free from the exaggerated claims of propaganda and commercial advertising; and the use of sans-serif typography set in a flush-left and ragged-right margin configuration. The initiators of this movement believed sans-serif typography expresses the spirit of a more progressive age and that mathematical grids are the most legible and harmonious means for structuring information.

More important than the visual appearance of this work is the attitude developed by its early pioneers about their profession. These trailblazers defined design as a socially useful and important activity. Personal expression and eccentric solutions were rejected, while a more universal and scientific approach to design problem solving was embraced. In this paradigm, the designers define their roles not as artists but as objective conduits for spreading important information between components of society. Achieving clarity and order is the ideal.

Pioneers of the movement

More than any other individual, the quality and discipline found in the Swiss design movement can be traced to Ernst Keller (1891–1968). In 1918 Keller joined the Zurich Kunstgewerbeschule (School of Applied Art) to teach the advertising layout course and develop a professional course in design and typography. In teaching and in his own lettering, trademark, and poster design projects, Keller established a standard of excellence over the course of four decades. Rather than espousing a specific style, Keller believed the solution to the design problem should emerge from its content. Fittingly, his work encompassed diverse solutions. His poster for the Rietburg Museum (Fig. **18–1**) demonstrates his interest in symbolic imagery, simplified geometric forms, expressive edges and lettering, and vibrant contrasting color. A gentle and unassuming man, Keller initiated a climate of excellence in Swiss graphic design.

The roots of the International Typographic Style are to a large extent found in the curriculum advanced at the School of Design in Basel. The development of this curriculum has its basis in fundamental geometric exercises involving the cube and the line. This foundation, begun in the nineteenth century and thus independent of De Stijl and the Bauhaus, was the basis for the 1908 formation of the school's *Vorkurs* (foundation course) and remained relevant to the design program in the 1950s.

Théo Ballmer (1902–65), who studied briefly at the Dessau Bauhaus under Klee, Gropius, and Meyer in the late 1920s, applied De Stijl principles to graphic design in an original way, using an arithmetic grid of horizontal and vertical alignments. In 1928 Ballmer's poster designs achieved a high degree of formal harmony as he used an ordered grid to construct visual forms. In his "Büro" poster (Fig. **18–2**), both the black word and its red reflection are carefully developed on the underlying grid. The other lettering on this poster shows the influence of Van Doesburg's experiments with geometric letterforms. However, Ballmer's lettering is more refined and graceful than the ungainly types of Van Doesburg. While the grid used to build the forms in the "Büro" poster is invisible, in Ballmer's "Norm" poster (Fig. **18–3**) the grid itself is openly displayed.

Max Bill's (1908–94) work encompassed painting, architecture, engineering, sculpture, and product and graphic design. After studying at the Bauhaus with Gropius, Meyer, Moholy-Nagy, Albers, and Kandinsky from 1927 until 1929, Bill moved to Zurich. In 1931 he embraced the concepts of *art concret* and began to find his way clearly. Eleven months before Van Doesburg died in April 1930, he formulated a manifesto of *Art Concret*, calling for a universal art of absolute clarity based on controlled arithmetical construction. *Art concret* paintings were totally constructed from pure, mathematically exact

18–1   18–2   18–3

visual elements—planes and colors. Because these elements have no external meanings, the results are purely abstract. Graphic design is the antithesis of this concept in one sense, as design without symbolic or semantic meaning ceases to be a graphic communication and becomes fine art. However, *art concret* concepts can nonetheless be applied to the structural aspect of graphic design.

As the 1930s gave way to the war years and Switzerland maintained its neutrality, Bill constructed layouts of geometric elements organized with absolute order. Mathematical proportion, geometric spatial division, and the use of Akzidenz Grotesk type (particularly the medium weight) are features of his work of this period (Fig. **18–4**). He further explored the use of the ragged-right margin and indicated paragraphs by an interval of space instead of a paragraph indent in some of his 1940s book designs. His American architecture exhibition poster, constructed with an intricate grid (Fig. **18–5**), demonstrates his strategy of designing a mathematical structure to contain the elements. The evolution of Bill's art and design was based on the development of cohesive principles of visual organization. Important concerns include the linear division of space into harmonious parts; modular grids; arithmetic and geometric progressions, permutations, and sequences; and the equalization of contrasting and complementary relationships into an ordered whole. In 1949 he concluded, "It is possible to develop an art largely on the basis of mathematical thinking."

In 1950 Bill became involved in the planning of the curriculum and buildings for the Hochschule für Gestaltung (Institute

18–1. Ernst Keller, poster for the Rietberg Museum, 1952. Emblematic images are energized by repetitive geometric elements.

18–2. Théo Ballmer, poster for an office professions exhibition, 1928. Traces of the grid squares used to construct this poster remain as the thin white lines between the letters.

18–3. Théo Ballmer, poster for a traveling exhibition of industrial standards, 1928. Absolute mathematical construction is used, rather than the asymmetrical horizontals and verticals of De Stijl.

of Design) in Ulm, Germany. This school, which operated until 1968, attempted to establish a center of research and training to address the design problems of the era with educational goals similar to those of the Bauhaus. Among the cofounders, Otl Aicher (1922–91) played a major role in developing the graphic design program (see Figs. 20–31 through 20–34). Bill left the Ulm directorship in 1956, and the school evolved using scientific and methodological approaches to design problem solving. English typographer Anthony Froshaug (1918–84) joined the Ulm faculty as professor of graphic design from 1957 until 1961 and set up the typography workshop. Froshaug's design of the Ulm journal's first five issues (Fig. **18–6**) is paradigmatic of the emerging movement.

The Ulm Institute of Design included a study of semiotics, the philosophical theory of signs and symbols, in its curriculum. Semiotics has three branches: *semantics*, the study of the

18–4

18–5

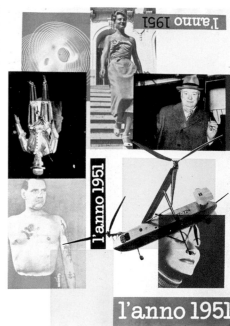

18–7

18–6

18–8

meaning of signs and symbols; *syntactics*, the study of how signs and symbols are connected and ordered into a structural whole; and *pragmatics,* the study of the relation of signs and symbols to their users. Also, principles of Greek rhetoric were reexamined for application to visual communications.

In counterpoint to Bill's evolution toward a purist approach to graphic design from the 1930s to the 1950s, there was also a strong tendency toward complexity in this period. During the same era, Max Huber (1919–92) brought a vitality and intricacy to his work. After studying the formal ideas of the Bauhaus and experimenting with photomontage as a student at the Zurich School of Arts and Crafts, Huber moved south to Milan, Italy, and began his career. Returning to his native Switzerland during the war, Huber collaborated with Bill on exhibition design projects. After his return to Italy in 1946, Huber produced phenomenal graphics. Bright, pure hues were combined with photographs in intense, complex visual organizations (Fig. **18–7**). Huber took advantage of the

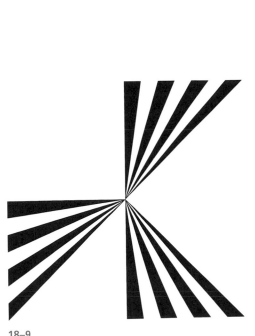

18–9

18–10

18–11

transparency of printing inks by layering shapes, typography, and images to create a complex web of graphic information (Fig. **18–8**). Sometimes Huber's designs seem pushed to the edge of chaos, but through balance and alignment he maintained order in the midst of complexity.

Functional graphics for science

German-born Anton Stankowski (1906–98) worked from 1929 until 1937 as a graphic designer in Zurich, where he enjoyed close contact with many of the leading artists and designers of Switzerland, including Bill, Matter, and Richard P. Lohse (1902–88). During his Zurich period, Stankowski was particularly innovative in photography, photomontage, and darkroom manipulation of images. Visual pattern and form were explored in his close-up photographs of common objects, whose texture and detail were transformed into abstract images.

In 1937 Stankowski moved to Stuttgart, Germany, where he painted and designed for more than five decades. A dialogue is evident between Stankowski's painting and his design. Ideas about color and form from his paintings often find their way into his graphic designs; conversely, wide-ranging form experimentation in search of design solutions seems to have provided shapes and compositional ideas for his fine art.

World War II and military service, including a period as a prisoner of war after his capture by the Russians, interrupted his career. After the war, his work started to crystallize into what was to become his major contribution to graphic design: the creation of visual forms to communicate invisible processes and physical forces (Figs. **18–9**, **18–10**, and **18–11**).

18–4. Max Bill, book cover, 1942. Mathematical precision is achieved by the alignment of type down the center of the page, creating harmony and order in an asymmetrical layout.

18–5. Max Bill, exhibition poster, 1945. Diamond-shaped photographs form a wedge; some photographs are placed on the white ground to equalize the figure and ground.

18–6. Anthony Froshaug, cover for the *Quarterly Bulletin of the Hochschule für Gestaltung, Ulm,* 1958. The four-column grid system, use of only two type sizes, and graphic resonance of this format were widely influential.

18–7. Max Huber, yearbook cover, 1951. An informal balance of halftones printed in red, black, and blue combines with yellow rectangles to turn the space into an energy-charged field.

18–8. Max Huber, poster for automobile races, 1948. Speed and movement are expressed by typography racing back in perspective and arrows arcing forward, bringing depth to the printed page.

18–9. Anton Stankowski, trademark for Standard Elektrik Lorenz AG, 1953. Dynamic equilibrium is achieved by an asymmetrical construction in an implied square, signifying communications transmission and reception.

18–10. Anton Stankowski, calendar cover for Standard Elektrik Lorenz AG, 1957. A radial configuration symbolizes transmission and radiation using the client's radio and telephone products.

18–11. Anton Stankowski, image from a Viessmann calendar. Linear elements change color after passing through the central bar, representing heat and energy transfer in furnace boilers.

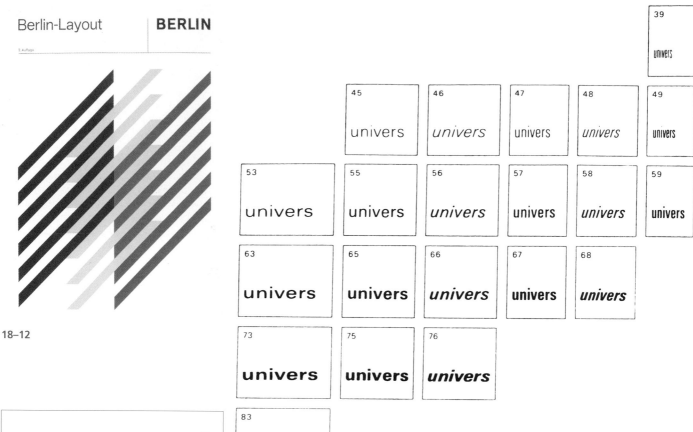

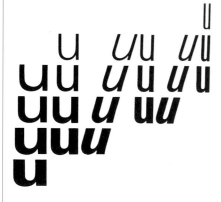

18–12

18–13

18–14

Helvetica
Helvetica Italic
Helvetica Medium
Helvetica Bold
Helvetica Bold Condensed

18–15

The abilities Stankowski brought to this problem were a strong mastery of constructivist design, an intellectual acumen for science and engineering, and a burning curiosity. Research and comprehension of the subject preceded his designs, for only after understanding the material to be presented can a designer invent forms that become symbols of complex scientific and engineering concepts. Stankowski tackled the unseen, ranging from electromagnetic energy to the internal workings of a computer, and transformed the concept underlying these forces into visual designs.

In 1968 the senate of Berlin commissioned Stankowski and his studio to develop a comprehensive design program for that city. Consistent design standards for architectural signage, street signs, and publications were developed. Instead of designing a trademark or unique typographic logo for use as the unifying visual element, Stankowski developed a tectonic element for consistent use on all material. This long horizontal line, with a short vertical line rising from it, became a symbol for the then-divided city of Berlin. The vertical line represented the Berlin Wall, which until 1989 separated the Soviet-dominated portion of the city from the rest of Berlin. The name *Berlin*, set in medium Akzidenz Grotesk, was always placed on the right side of the tectonic element (Fig. **18–12**).

New Swiss sans-serif typefaces

The emerging International Typographic Style was exemplified by several new sans-serif type families designed in the 1950s. The geometric sans-serif styles, mathematically constructed with drafting instruments during the 1920s and 1930s, were rejected in favor of more refined designs inspired by nineteenth-century Akzidenz Grotesk fonts (see Fig. 12–35). In 1954 a young Swiss designer working in Paris, Adrian Frutiger (b. 1928), completed a visually programmed family of twenty-one sans-serif fonts named Univers (Fig. **18–13**). The palette of typographic variations—limited to regular, italic, and bold in traditional typography—was expanded sevenfold. Numbers replaced conventional nomenclature. The normal or regular weight with the proper black-and-white relationships for book setting is called Univers 55, and the family ranges from Univers 39 (light/extra condensed) to Univers 83 (expanded/extrabold). Fonts to the left of Univers 55 are expanded; fonts to the right of Univers 55 are condensed. The stroke weights of fonts above Univers 55 are lighter, while stroke weights of fonts below Univers 55 are heavier. Because all twenty-one fonts have the same x-height and ascender and descender lengths, they form a uniform whole that can be used together with complete harmony (Fig. **18–14**). The size and weight of the capitals are close to the size and weight of the lowercase characters; therefore, the texture and tone of a Univers text setting is more uniform than that of most earlier typefaces, especially in multilingual publications. Frutiger labored for three years on Univers. To produce the Univers family, the Deberny and Peignot foundry in Paris invested over 200,000 hours of machine engraving, retouching, and final hand-punching to create the 35,000 matrixes needed to produce all twenty-one fonts in the full range of sizes.

In the mid-1950s, Edouard Hoffman of the HAAS type foundry in Switzerland decided that the Akzidenz Grotesk fonts should be refined and upgraded. Hoffman collaborated with Max Miedinger (1910–1980), who executed the designs, and their new sans serif, with an even larger x-height than that of Univers, was released as Neue Haas Grotesk. When this design was produced in Germany by the now defunct D. Stempel AG in 1961, the face was named Helvetica (Fig. **18–15**), the traditional Latin name for Switzerland. Helvetica's well-defined forms and excellent rhythm of positive and negative shapes made it the most specified typeface internationally during the 1960s and 1970s. However, because Helvetica's various weights, italics, and widths were developed by different designers in several countries, the original Helvetica family lacked the cohesiveness of Univers. As digital typesetting became prevalent in the 1980s, versions of the Helvetica family with more systemic compatibility were developed, including Linotype's 1983 Neue Helvetica with eight weights, each with extended, condensed, and italic versions.

18–12. Anton Stankowski, cover for *Berlin-Layout,* 1971. The cover design derives from a Stankowski painting.

18–13. Adrian Frutiger, schematic diagram of the twenty-one Univers fonts, 1954. Frutiger systematically altered the forms of fonts located on this chart above, below, and to the left or right of Univers 55.

18–14. Bruno Pläffli of Atelier Frutiger, composition with the letter *u,* c. 1960. All twenty-one variations of Univers can be used together to achieve dynamic contrasts of weight, tone, width, and direction.

18–15. Edouard Hoffman and Max Miedinger, Helvetica typeface, 1961. The basic version of Helvetica released by the Stempel foundry in 1961 is shown, along with some of the variations developed later.

A master of classical typography

While German and Swiss designers were forging the International Typographic Style, a major German typeface designer evolved from the traditions of calligraphy and Renaissance typography. A tremendous admiration for Rudolf Koch and Edward Johnston proved the catalyst that launched the career of Hermann Zapf (b. 1918). A native of Nuremberg, Germany, Zapf entered the graphic arts as an apprentice photo retoucher at age sixteen. A year later he started his study of calligraphy after acquiring a copy of Koch's *Das Schreiben als Kunstfertigkeit* (Writing as Art), a manual on the subject. Four years of disciplined self-education followed, and at age twenty-one Zapf's first typographic involvement began when he entered Koch's printing firm. Later that year Zapf became a freelance book and typographic designer, and at age twenty-two the first of his more than fifty typefaces was designed and cut for the Stempel foundry. Zapf developed an extraordinary sensitivity to letterforms in his activities as a calligrapher, typeface designer, typographer, and graphic designer; all of these activities contributed to his view of typeface design as "one of the most visible visual expressions of an age."

Zapf's triumvirate of typefaces designed during the late 1940s and the 1950s are widely regarded as major type designs (Fig. **18–16**): Palatino (released in 1950) is a roman style with broad letters, strong serifs, and elegant proportions somewhat reminiscent of Venetian faces; Melior (1952) is a modern style that departs from earlier models through its vertical stress and squared forms; and Optima (1958) is a thick-and-thin sans serif with tapered strokes. While Zapf's typeface designs are based on a deep understanding of the past, they are original inventions designed with a full understanding of twentieth-century technologies. To the complex and technically demanding craft of typeface design Zapf brought the

Palatino
Palatino Italic
Palatino Semibold
Palatino Bold

Melior
Melior Italic
Melior Semibold
Melior Bold Condensed

Optima
Optima Italic
Optima Semi Bold

18–16

18–16. Hermann Zapf, typefaces. Palatino, 1950; Melior, 1952; and Optima, 1958. These alphabets have a harmony and elegance seldom achieved in typeface design.

18–17. Hermann Zapf, page from *Manuale Typographicum*, 1968. Parandowski's quotation about the power of the printed word to "govern time and space" inspired this graphic field of tension radiating from the central cluster.

18–18. Hermann Zapf, page from *Manuale Typographicum*, 1968. Using his Michelangelo typeface, Zapf organized this page with classical symmetry and exquisite intervals between letters. The subtle shadow relief of the ruled lines suggests an inscriptionlike quality.

18–19. Emil Ruder, book jacket for an anthology of Dada poetry, reproduced in *Typography: A Manual of Design*, 1967. The contrast created by combining different fonts becomes a graphic metaphor for the randomness of the Dadaists.

18–20. Armin Hofmann, logotype for the Basel Civic Theater, 1954. This hand-lettered logotype anticipates the tight spacing and capital ligatures of phototypography. The control of spatial intervals between letterforms is magnificent.

18–17

18–18

18–19   18–20

spiritual awareness of a poet capable of inventing new forms to express the current century and to preserve it for posterity.

In the area of book design, Zapf's two editions of *Manuale Typographicum,* published in 1954 and 1968, are outstanding contributions to the art of the book (Figs. **18–17** and **18–18**). Encompassing eighteen languages and more than a hundred typefaces, these two volumes consist of quotations about the art of typography, with a full-page typographic interpretation for each quotation. Zapf, like Eric Gill, combines a great love and understanding of the classical traditions of typography with a twentieth-century attitude toward space and scale.

Design in Basel and Zurich

The further development of the International Typographic Style occurred in two cities, Basel and Zurich, located 70 kilometers (about 50 miles) apart in northern Switzerland. Fifteen-year-old Emil Ruder (1914–70) began a four-year compositor's apprenticeship in 1929 and attended the Zurich School of Arts and Crafts when he was in his late twenties. In 1947 Ruder joined the faculty of the Allgemeine Gewerbeschule (Basel School of Design) as the typography instructor and called upon his students to strike the correct balance between form and function. He taught that type loses its purpose when it loses its communicative meaning; therefore, legibility and readability are dominant concerns. His classroom projects developed sensitivity to negative or unprinted spaces, including the spaces between and inside letterforms. Ruder advocated systematic overall design and the use of a grid structure to bring all elements— typography, photography, illustration, diagrams, and charts— into harmony with each other while allowing for design variety. Problems of unifying type and image were addressed.

More than any other designer, Ruder realized the implications of Univers and the creative potential unleashed by the unity of proportion, because the consistent baseline and x-height allowed the mixing of all twenty-one typefaces. Ruder

and his students exhaustively explored the contrasts, textures, and scale possibilities of the new face in both commissioned and experimental work (Fig. **18–19**). His methodology of typographic design and education was presented in his 1967 book *Typography: A Manual of Design*, which had a world-wide influence.

In 1947 Armin Hofmann (b. 1920) began teaching graphic design at the Basel School of Design, after completing his education in Zurich and working as a staff designer for several studios. Together with Emil Ruder, he developed an educational model linked to the elementary design principles of the *Vorkurs* established in 1908. This curriculum was the decisive one for the 1950s and was widely used in the pharmaceutical industry by former students such as Karl Gerstner (b. 1930), the founder of the GGK agency. Also in 1947, Hofmann opened a design studio in collaboration with his wife, Dorothea. Hofmann applied deep aesthetic values and understanding of form to both teaching and designing. As time passed, he evolved a design philosophy based on the elemental graphic-form language of point, line, and plane, replacing traditional pictorial ideas with a modernist aesthetic. In his work and in his teaching, Hofmann continues to seek a dynamic harmony, where all the parts of a design are unified. He sees the relationship of contrasting elements as the means of invigorating visual design. These contrasts include light to dark, curved lines to straight lines, form to counterform, soft to hard, and dynamic to static, with resolution achieved when the designer brings the total into an absolute harmony.

Hofmann works in diverse areas, designing posters, advertisements, and logos, as well as other materials (Figs. **18–20** through **18–23**). His environmental graphics, which take the form of letterforms or abstract shapes based on letterforms, are often incised into molded concrete (Fig. **18–24**). In 1965 Hofmann published *Graphic Design Manual*, a book that presents his application of elemental design principles to graphic design.

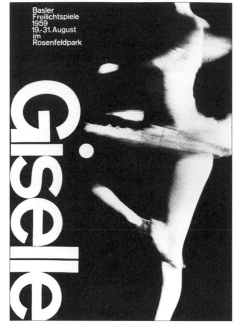

18–21

18–22

18–24

18–23

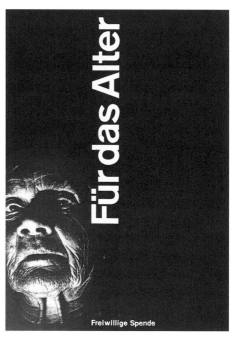

18–25

Zurich designers, including Carlo L. Vivarelli (1919–86), were also forging the new movement in the late 1940s. Vivarelli's "For the Elderly" poster, conceived to spread awareness of the elderly and their problems, used the angle of illumination on the face for dramatic impact (Fig. **18–25**). Swiss design began to coalesce into a unified international movement when the journal *New Graphic Design* began publication in 1959 (Figs. **18–26**, **18–27**, and **18–28**). The editors were Vivarelli and three other Zurich designers who played a major role in the evolution of the International Typographic Style: Lohse, Josef Müller-Brockmann (1914–96), and Hans Neuburg (1904–83). This trilingual periodical presented the philosophy and accomplish-

ments of the Swiss movement to an international audience. Its format and typography were a living expression of the order and refinement achieved by Swiss designers.

Emerging as a leading theorist and practitioner of the movement, Müller-Brockmann sought an absolute and universal form of graphic expression through objective and impersonal presentation, communicating to the audience without the interference of the designer's subjective feelings or propagandistic techniques of persuasion. A measure of his success can be gauged by observing the visual power and impact of his work. Designs made by Müller-Brockmann in the 1950s are as current and vital as they were a half-century ago and communicate

18–26   18–27

their message with intensity and clarity (Fig. **18–29**). His photographic posters treat the image as an objective symbol, with neutral photographs gaining impact through scale (Fig. **18–30**) and camera angle (Fig. **18–31**). In his celebrated concert posters, the language of constructivism creates a visual counterpart to the structural harmony of the music to be performed (Fig. **18–32**).

His exhibition poster "Der Film" (Fig. **18–33**) demonstrates the universal design harmony achieved by mathematical spatial division. The proportions are close to the three-to-five ratio of the golden mean, considered the most beautifully proportioned rectangle by the ancient Greeks. The space is divided into fifteen rectangular modules, with three modules across the horizontal dimension and five down the vertical dimension. The top nine modules approximate a square, the title fills three units, and three are below the title. *Film* occupies two units, and the secondary typographic information aligns with the front edge of the *F* in *Film*. This design organization grew out of functional communication needs. The title projects clearly at great distances against the field of black, and the overlapping of *Film* in front of *der* is a typographic equivalent to the cinematic techniques of overlapping images and dissolving from one image to another. The graphic power of this poster's elemental simplicity successfully combines effective communication, expression of the content, and visual harmony.

As with Müller-Brockmann's music posters, geometric forms become metaphorical in a poster for an exhibition of lamps (Fig. **18–34**). In a 1980 poster for an exhibition of his own he revealed the nature of the grid structures underlying his work (Fig. **18–35**). Through his designs, writing, and teaching, Müller-Brockmann became the era's most influential

18–21. Armin Hofmann, poster for the Basel theater production of *Giselle,* 1959. An organic, kinetic, and soft photographic image contrasts intensely with geometric, static, and hard-edged typographic shapes.

18–22. Armin Hofmann, trademark for the Swiss National Exhibition, Expo 1964. An *E* for Exhibition links with the Swiss cross. The open bottom permits the white space of the page to flow into the symbol.

18–23. Armin Hofmann, poster for Herman Miller furniture, 1962. Shapes and silhouettes of Herman Miller chairs cascade through space, anchored to the format and the type by the red logo at the top center.

18–24. Armin Hofmann, exterior sculpture for the Disentis, Switzerland, high school, 1975. The altered direction of the boards of the molds used to cast the concrete relief produces a vigorous textural contrast.

18–25. Carlo L. Vivarelli (designer) and Werner Bischof (photographer), "Für das Alter" (For the Elderly) poster, 1949. The contrasting juxtaposition of an organic, human, and textured photograph with sharp geometric typography intensifies the meaning of both.

18–26. Carlo L. Vivarelli, cover for *New Graphic Design* 2,1959. The mathematical structure of the organizational grid signifies the scientific and functional design philosophy of the Swiss movement.

18–27. Hans Neuburg, pages from *New Graphic Design* 7,1960. Asymmetrical balance, white space, and rigorous adherence to a four-column grid characterized this publication.

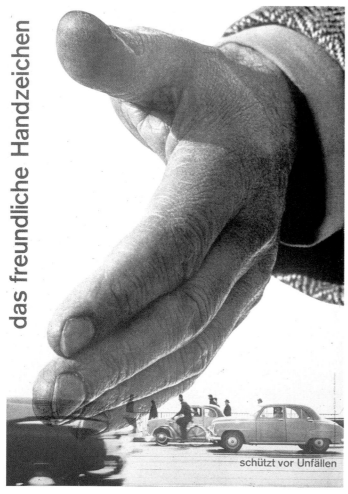

18–28

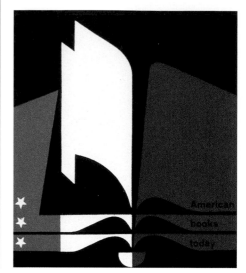

18–29

18–30

18–31

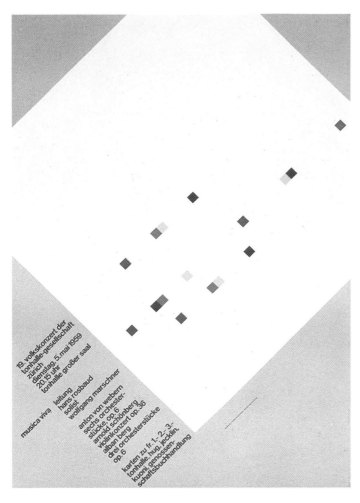

18–32

18–33

Swiss designer as the national movement he helped create grew beyond the country's borders.

In Switzerland, a country with outstanding design schools, such self-educated graphic designers as Siegfried Odermatt (b. 1926) are a rarity. Originally Odermatt planned to become a photographer, but after working in photographic studios for several years, he turned to design and typography. After a period of employment in several advertising agencies, Odermatt opened his own studio in 1950. Working for corporate clients in the areas of trademark development, informational graphics, advertising, and packaging, Odermatt played an important role in applying the International Typographic Style to the communications of business and industry. He combined succinct, efficient presentation of information with a dynamic visual quality, using straightforward photography with drama and impact. Ordinary images were turned into convincing and engaging photographs through the careful use of cropping, scale, and lighting, with attention to shape and texture as qualities that cause an image to emerge from the page (Figs. **18–36**, **18–37**, and **18–38**). Odermatt seeks

18–28. Hans Neuburg, pages from *New Graphic Design* 13, 1962. Trademark design competition entries are organized on a grid; spatial intervals create rhythm and movement.

18–29. Josef Müller-Brockmann, *American Books Today* catalog cover, 1953. Shapes signify books, while color signifies the country of their origin.

18–30. Josef Müller-Brockmann, Swiss Auto Club poster, 1954. Photography amplifies the text, "The friendly hand sign protects against accidents."

18–31. Josef Müller-Brockmann, public awareness poster, 1960. Red type declares "less noise," while the photograph graphically depicts the discomfort noise causes.

18–32. Josef Müller-Brockmann, "Musica Viva" concert poster, 1959. Colored squares march in musical rhythm on the tilted white square. Typography and shapes align in harmonious juxtaposition.

18–33. Josef Müller-Brockmann, "Der Film" exhibition poster, 1960. Against a black field, the word *Film* is white, the word *der* is gray, and the other typography is red.

18–34

18–36

18–35

18–34. Josef Müller-Brockmann, poster for an exhibition of lamps, 1975. Modulated, glowing multicolor disks signify the radiant energy of lighting fixtures.

18–35. Josef Müller-Brockmann, exhibition poster, 1980. The grid, always underlying Müller-Brockmann's designs, becomes visible as a major element in this poster.

18–36. Siegfried Odermatt, advertisement for Apotheke Sammet over-the-counter medicine, 1957. Close-up photography makes ordinary subjects arresting. The trademark is created from the firm's initials.

18–37. Siegfried Odermatt, cover for *Schelling Bulletin*, no. 4, 1963. This folder for a paperboard and packaging manufacturer uses an unexpected photographic view of an ordinary object.

18–38. Siegfried Odermatt, inside pages for *Schelling Bulletin*, no. 4, 1963. A four-column grid unifies typography with product photography.

originality through the idea, not through visual style—in his work, graphic design is always seen as an instrument of communication.

Much of Odermatt's work is purely typographic, and he believes a one-color typographic design can achieve the visual

impact and power of full-color graphics through strength of concept and orchestration of visual form, space, shape, and tone. By his fresh and original arrangements of graphic elements, Odermatt demonstrates the infinite possibilities for dividing and organizing space on the printed page. There is

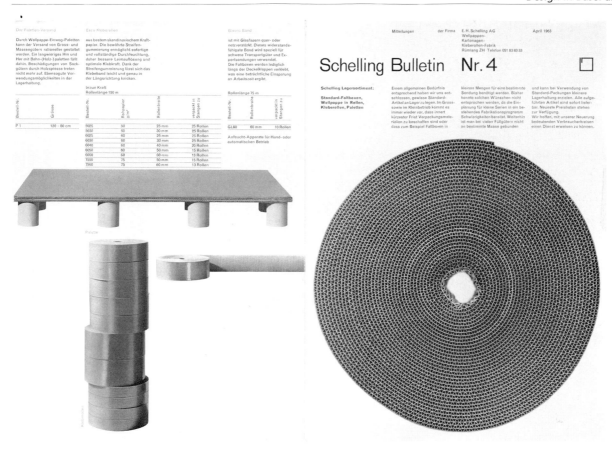

18–37

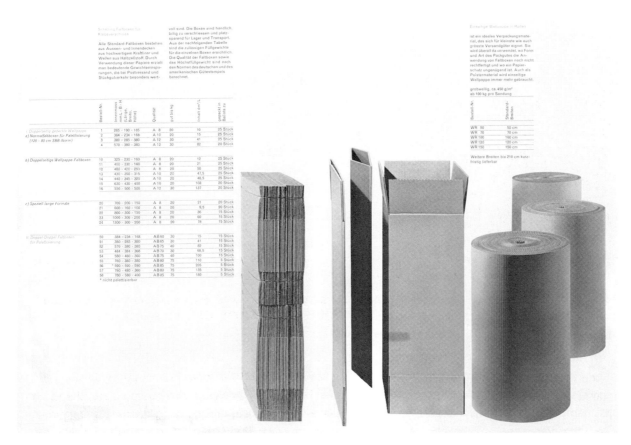

18–38

18–39   18–40   18–41

also an element of the playful and the uninhibited in his work, a feature that is unusual for Swiss design of this period. Rosmarie Tissi (b. 1937), who joined his studio in the early 1960s, is also known for her playful work (Fig. **18–39**). In 1968 she became an equal partner with Odermatt in the studio Odermatt & Tissi. This studio loosened the boundaries of the International Typographic Style and introduced elements of chance, the development of surprising and inventive forms, and intuitive visual organization into the vocabulary of graphic design. This phase of the studio's development marked the beginning of a break with the traditions of Swiss design and will be discussed further in chapter 23.

During the post–World War II era the spirit of internationalism grew. Increased trade enabled multinational corporations to operate in more than a hundred different countries. The speed and pace of communications were turning the world into a global village. There was an increasing need for communicative clarity, for multilingual formats, and for elementary pictographs and glyphs to enable people from around the world to comprehend signs and information. The new graphic design developed in Switzerland helped fulfill these needs, and its fundamental concepts and methodology spread throughout the world.

The international typographic style in America

The Swiss movement had a major impact on postwar American design. Its influence was first felt in the late 1940s and 50s, and became especially evident during the 1960s and 1970s. A self-taught graphic designer who embraced the potential of European modernism, Rudolph DeHarak (b. 1924) began his career in Los Angeles in 1946. Four years later he moved to New York, where he formed his own design studio in 1952.

DeHarak's evolution has been a continuing quest for communicative clarity and visual order, which are the qualities he deems vital to effective graphic design. He recognized these qualities in Swiss design during the late 1950s and adapted attributes of the movement such as grid structures and asymmetrical balance. Responding to the legibility and formal perfection of Akzidenz Grotesk before it was available in the United States, DeHarak obtained specimen sheets from European foundries so that he could assemble headlines for his designs, which combine purity of form with elemental signs and images. A series of album covers for Westminster Records (Fig. **18–40** and **18–41**) evoke conceptual images of the music's structure.

During the early 1960s DeHarak initiated a series of over 350 book jackets for McGraw-Hill Publishers using a uniform typographic system and grid (Fig. **18–42**). Each book's subject was implied and articulated through visual configurations ranging from elemental pictographs to abstract geometric

18–39. Rosmarie Tissi, Univac advertisement, 1965. A dynamic, powerful image is created by the careful cropping and placement of two telephone receivers.

18–40. Rudolph DeHarak, cover for the album *Sounds of the Alps,* c. 1961. Three vigorous brushstrokes signify sound waves and Switzerland's mountainous terrain.

18–41. Rudolph DeHarak, cover for the album *Vivaldi Gloria,* early 1960s. Squares of color become a twentieth-century designer's emotive response to eighteenth-century music.

18–42. Rudolph DeHarak, book jackets for McGraw-Hill Publishers, early 1960s. Each cover conforms to a consistent format, yet the subjects are interpreted through a remarkable variety of symbolic forms and images.

Conflict and Creativity

Control of the Mind, Part 2
edited by
Seymour M. Farber
and
Roger H.L. Wilson

$2.95

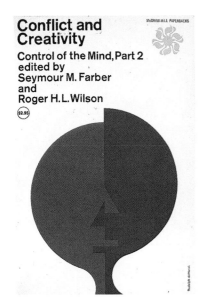

Computers and People
John A. Postley

How the new field of data processing
serves modern business

$2.45

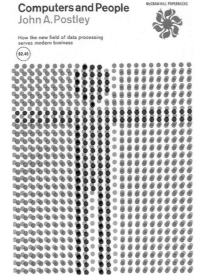

Man and Civilization
The Family's Search for Survival
edited by
Seymour M. Farber
Piero Mustacchi
Roger H.L. Wilson

$3.25

Table for the
Solution of
Cubic Equations
Herbert E. Salzer
Charles H. Richards
Isabelle Arsham

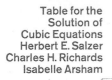

Monsieur Teste
Paul Valéry

Translated and with a note
on Valéry by Jackson Mathews

$1.65

Personality
and Psychotherapy
An Analysis in Terms of
Learning, Thinking, and Culture

John Dollard
Neal E. Miller

$3.25

Units, Dimensions,
and
Dimensionless Numbers

D.C. Ipsen

$2.65

**The Teaching
of Contempt**
Christian Roots
of Anti-Semitism
Jules Isaac

$2.15

**The Siege
of Leningrad**
Leon Goure
Foreword by Merle Fainsod

$2.95

18–42

18–43

18–44

18–45

18–43. Jacqueline S. Casey, announcement for the MIT Ocean Engineering program, 1967. Typography sits above an X-ray of a chambered nautilus shell superimposed on a wavelike repetition of fluid blue shapes.

18–44. Ralph Coburn, poster for the MIT jazz band, 1972. A staccato repetition of the letterforms of the word *jazz* establishes musical sequences and animates the space.

18–45. Jacqueline C. Casey, poster for an MIT open house, 1974. Stencil letterforms announce the open house, and the open *O* does double duty as a concrete symbol of the opening of the campus to visitors.

18–46. Dietmar Winkler, poster for a computer programming course, 1969. The term *COBAL* emerges from a kinetic construction of modular letters.

18–47. Arnold Saks, "Inflatable Sculpture" poster for the Jewish Museum, 1968. A sequence of bars bending upward signifies the action of energy upon pliable materials and graphically conveys the essence of the subject.

structures. This series of paperback books covered academic disciplines including history, psychology, sociology, management, and mathematics. DeHarak's approach appropriately expressed the conceptual content of each volume. The nature of book-jacket design in the United States was expanded and redefined by DeHarak's extensive production.

The International Typographic Style was rapidly embraced in corporate and institutional graphics during the 1960s and remained a prominent aspect of American design for more than two decades. A noteworthy example was found in the graphic-design office at the Massachusetts Institute of Technology (MIT), where a sustained level of quality and imagination was achieved. In the early 1950s MIT established a graphic-design program enabling all members of the university community to benefit from free, professional design assistance on their publications and publicity material, an early recognition of the cultural and communicative value of design by an American university. MIT based its graphic-design program on a commitment to the grid and sans-serif typography. The staff was innovative in the use of designed letterforms and manipulated words as vehicles to express content. This approach evolved in the work of Jacqueline S. Casey (1927–91), director

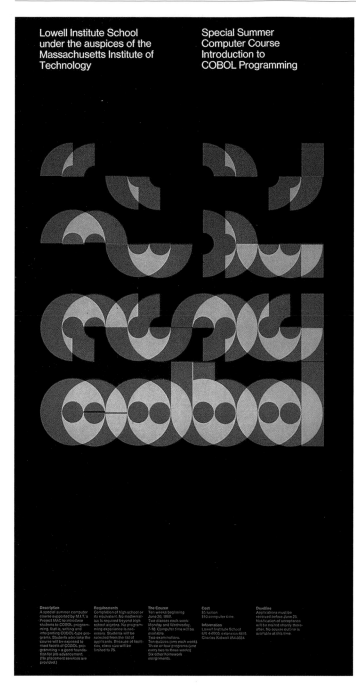

18–46

18–47

of the Design Services Office; Ralph Coburn (b. 1923); and Dietmar Winkler (b. 1938), a German-trained designer who worked with Casey and Coburn from 1966 until 1971.

The Design Services Office produces publications and posters (Fig. **18–43**) announcing concerts, speakers, seminars, exhibitions, and courses on the university campus. These frequently use solid-color backgrounds. Many of their solutions are purely typographic, originally created on a drafting table for economical line reproduction. In a sense, letterforms are used as illustrations, for the design and arrangement of the letters in key words frequently become the dominant image (Figs. **18–44** and **18–45**). The use of graphic form to express technical and scientific information is demonstrated by Dietmar Winkler's poster for a computer-programming course (Fig. **18–46**).

The rapid spread of the International Typographic Style resulted from the harmony and order of its methodology. The ability of elemental forms to express complex ideas with clarity and directness is seen in the "Inflatable Sculpture" exhibition poster (Fig. **18–47**) by Arnold Saks (b. 1931).

The design movement that began in Switzerland and Germany, then outgrew its native boundaries to become truly international, had practitioners in many nations around the globe. This approach was of special value in countries such as Canada and Switzerland, where bilingual or trilingual communications are the norm. It was particularly useful when a diverse body of informational materials ranging from signage to publicity needed to be unified into a coherent body. A growing awareness of design as a logical tool for large organizations caused corporate design and visual-identification systems to expand after World War II. During the mid-1960s the development of corporate design and the International Typographic Style were linked into one movement. This will be discussed in chapter 20.

The New York School

19

19–1

As previously mentioned, the first wave of modern design in America was imported by talented European immigrants seeking to escape the political climate of totalitarianism. These individuals brought Americans a firsthand introduction to the European avant-garde. The 1940s saw steps toward an original American approach to modernist design. While borrowing freely from the work of European designers, Americans added new forms and concepts. European design was often theoretical and highly structured; American design was pragmatic, intuitive, and less formal in its approach to organizing space. Just as Paris had been receptive to new ideas and images during the late nineteenth and early twentieth centuries, New York City assumed that role during the middle of the twentieth century. These cultural incubators nurtured creativity, and the prevailing climate attracted individuals of great talent and enabled them to realize their potential.

Despite the European underpinnings, unique aspects of American culture and society engendered an original approach to modern design. The United States is an egalitarian society with capitalistic values, limited artistic traditions before World War II, and a diverse ethnic heritage. Emphasis was placed on the expression of ideas and an open, direct presentation of information. In this highly competitive society, novelty of technique and originality of concept were much prized, and designers sought simultaneously to solve communications problems and satisfy a need for personal expression. This phase of American graphic design began with strong European roots during

the 1940s, gained international prominence in the 1950s, and continued into the twenty-first century.

Pioneers of the New York school

More than any other American designer, Paul Rand (1914–96) initiated this American approach to modern design. When he was twenty-three years old, Rand began the first phase of his design career as a promotional and editorial designer for the magazines *Apparel Arts, Esquire, Ken, Coronet*, and *Glass Packer*. His magazine covers broke with the traditions of American publication design. A thorough knowledge of the modern movement, particularly the works of Klee, Kandinsky, and the cubists, led Rand to the understanding that freely invented shapes could have a self-contained life, both symbolic and expressive, as a visual-communications tool. His ability to manipulate visual form (shape, color, space, line, value) and skillful analysis of communications content, reducing it to a symbolic essence without making it sterile or dull, allowed Rand to become widely influential while still in his twenties. The playful, visually dynamic, and unexpected often found their way into his work. A *Direction* magazine cover (Fig. **19–1**) shows the important role of visual and symbolic contrast in Rand's designs. The handwritten Christmas tag on a crisp rectangle contrasts sharply with the mechanical stencil lettering of the logo on a torn-edged collage element; a Christmas package wrapped with barbed wire instead of ribbon was a grim reminder of the spread of global war. Rand seized upon collage and montage as means to bring con-

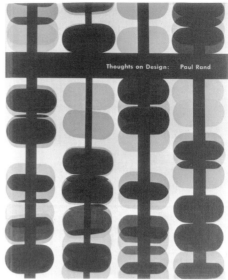

19–2

19–3

19–4

cepts, images, textures, and even objects into a cohesive whole (Fig. **19–2**).

From 1941 until 1954 Paul Rand applied his design approach at the Weintraub advertising agency. His collaborations with copywriter Bill Bernbach (1911–82) became a prototype for the now ubiquitous art/copy team working closely together to create a synergistic visual-verbal integration. Campaigns they created for clients, including Ohrbach's department store, featured entertaining puns and wordplay supported by Rand's whimsical integration of photography, drawing, and logo (Fig. **19–3**). The image visually reinforces the headline. After leaving the agency, Rand became an independent designer with increasing emphasis on trademark and corporate design. *Thoughts on Design*, his 1946 book (Fig. **19–4**), illustrated with over eighty examples of his work, inspired a generation of designers.

Rand understood the value of ordinary, universally understood signs and symbols as tools for translating ideas into visual communications (Figs. **19–5** and **19–6**). To engage the audience successfully and communicate memorably, he knew that the designer needed to alter and juxtapose signs and symbols. A reinterpretation of the message was sometimes necessary to make the ordinary into something extraordinary. Sensual visual contrasts marked his work. He played red against green, organic shape against geometric type, photographic tone against flat color, cut or torn edges against sharp forms, and the textural pattern of type against white. In addition, Rand took risks by exploring unproven ideas. In his poster design for the American Institute of Graphic Arts, design becomes play and the futurist concept of simultaneity is evoked.

19–1. Paul Rand, cover for *Direction* magazine, 1940. The red dots are symbolically ambiguous, becoming holiday decorations or blood drops.

19–2. Paul Rand, *Jazzways* yearbook cover, 1946. Collage technique, elemental symbolic forms, and dynamic composition characterized Rand's work in the late 1930s and 1940s.

19–3. Paul Rand, Ohrbach's advertisement, 1946. A combination of elements—logotype, photograph, decorative drawing, and type—are playfully unified.

19–4. Paul Rand, cover for *Thoughts on Design,* 1946. A photogram, with several exposures of an abacus placed on photographic paper in the darkroom, becomes a metaphor of the design process—moving elements around to compose space—and provides a visual record of the process.

For all his visual inventiveness, Rand defined design as the integration of form and function for effective communication. The cultural role of the designer was to upgrade rather than serve the least common denominator of public taste. During the early period of Rand's career, he made forays into the vocabulary of modern art but never parted from an immediate accessibility of image (Fig. **19–7**).

During a design career in a life cut short by illness, Alvin Lustig (1915–55) incorporated his subjective vision and private symbols into graphic design. Born in Colorado, Lustig alternated between the East and West Coasts and between architecture, graphic design, and interior design. At age twenty-one he began a graphic design and printing business in the rear of a Los Angeles drugstore. On projects for the Ward

19–6

19–5

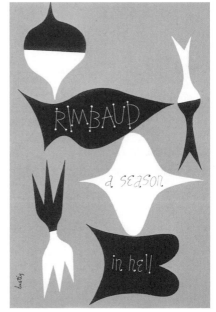

19–7

19–8

19–9

Ritchie Press, Lustig created abstract geometric designs using type rules and ornaments.

Sensing that Lustig's work was created by an "artist who might possess a touch of genius," publisher James Laughton of New Directions in New York began to give him book and jacket design commissions in 1940 (Figs. **19–8**, **19–9**, and **19–10**). As New Directions published books of outstanding literary quality, Lustig's design methodology—searching for symbols to capture the essence of the contents and treating form and content as one—received a positive response from its literary audience. For *27 Wagons Full of Cotton* (Fig. **19–11**), a delicate magnolia flower is brutally nailed to rough siding; these contradictory photographic symbols represent the violence and hatred behind the civilized facade in human affairs. A comparable ex-

pression was achieved by Lustig's designs for classical music recordings (Fig. **19–12**). Believing in the importance of painting for design and design education, he considered the artist's pure research into private symbols the wellspring for the public symbols created by the designer (Fig. **19–13**).

In 1945 Lustig became the visual design research director of *Look* magazine, a position he held until 1946. By 1950 he was becoming increasingly involved in design education, and in 1951 he was asked by Joseph Albers to help develop a graduate graphic design program at Yale University. However, his eyesight had begun to fail, and he was totally blind by the autumn of 1954. In the face of this overwhelming tragedy for an artist, Lustig continued to teach and design until his death more than a year later.

19–10   19–11   19–12

In 1940, twenty-four-year-old Alex Steinweiss (b. 1916) was named art director of Columbia Records. The modern design sensibilities of the 1940s were applied to record-album design as Steinweiss searched for visual forms and shapes to express music (Fig. **19–14**). Often Steinweiss approached space informally; elements were placed on the field with a casual balance sometimes bordering on a random scattering of forms.

Bradbury Thompson (1911–95) emerged as one of the most influential graphic designers in postwar America. After graduation from Washburn College in his hometown of Topeka, Kansas, in 1934, Thompson worked for printing firms there for several years before moving to New York. His designs for *Westvaco Inspirations*, four-color publications demonstrating printing papers, continued from 1939 until 1961, making a significant impact. A thorough knowledge of printing and typesetting, combined with an adventurous spirit of experimentation, allowed him to expand the range of design possibilities. *Westvaco Inspirations* used letterpress plates of art and illustration borrowed from advertising agencies and museums. With a limited budget for new plates and artwork, Thompson used the typecase and print shop as his "canvas, easel, and second studio." He discovered and explored the potential of eighteenth- and nineteenth-century engravings as design resources (Fig. **19–15**). Large, bold organic and geometric shapes were used to bring graphic and symbolic power to the page. Letterforms and patterns, such as the details from halftone reproductions in Figure **19-15,**

19–5. Paul Rand, poster for the American Institute of Graphic Art, 1968. A red "A. I. G. A." plays hide-and-seek against the green background, as a pictographic clown face does the same with an organic abstraction.

19–6. Paul Rand, poster for the film *No Way Out,* 1950. Rand's integration of photography, typography, signs, graphic shapes, and the surrounding white space stands in marked contrast to typical film posters.

19–7. Paul Rand, monograph cover, 1953. An exuberance of shape and whimsical images are recurring themes in Rand's advertisements and children's books.

19–8. Alvin Lustig, cover for Arthur Rimbaud's *A Season in Hell,* 1945. Sharp black-and-white biomorphic figures on a deep-red field suggest the French poet's spiritual descent into hell and his failures in love and art.

19–9. Alvin Lustig, cover for Federico Garcia Lorca's *3 Tragedies,* 1949. In this montage of five photographic images, the author's name and title become objects photographed in the world.

19–10. Alvin Lustig, cover for Tennessee Williams's *Camino Real,* 1952. The typographic title contrasts crisply with the graffiti-marred wall on which it is posted.

19–11. Alvin Lustig, cover for Tennessee Williams's *27 Wagons Full of Cotton,* 1949. Lustig understood the frail human spirit and brutal environmental forces articulated in Williams's plays.

19–12. Alvin Lustig, album cover for Vivaldi's *Gloria,* 1951. Moving like music notes along the median line, the abstracted letters forming the Italian composer's name echo the background triangular shapes in a composition of warm colors.

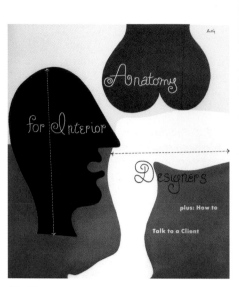

19–13

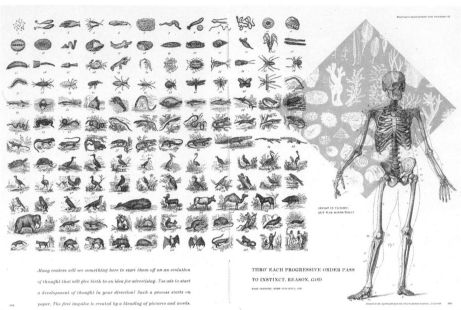

19–15

19–16

19–14

were often enlarged and used as design elements or to create visual patterns and movements. Four-color process plates were taken apart and used to create designs (Fig. **19–16**) and often overprinted to create new colors. In sum, Thompson achieved a rare mastery of complex organization, form, and visual flow. For *Westvaco Inspirations 210* (Fig. **19–17**), a photograph loaned for use as a printing specimen was the catalyst for Thompson's typographic invention. Typography gained expression through scale and color (Fig. **19–18**).

During the 1960s and 1970s, Thompson turned increasingly to a classical approach to book and editorial format design. Readability, formal harmony, and a sensitive use of Old Style typefaces marked his work for periodicals such as *Smithsonian* and *ARTnews*, United States postage stamps, and a steady flow of books, including the monumental Washburn College Bible.

The sensibilities of the New York School were carried to Los Angeles by Saul Bass (1919–96). He moved from New York to

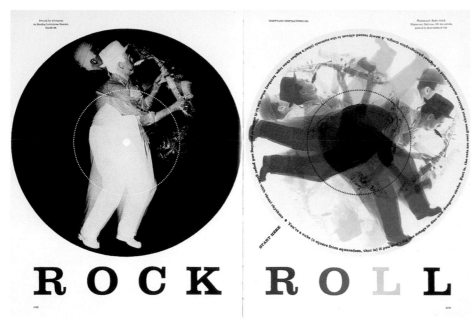

19–17

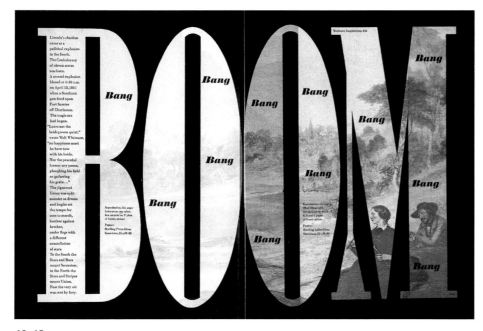

19–18

19–13. Alvin Lustig, cover for *Anatomy for Interior Designers,* 1948, Image courtesy of R. Roger Remington, Special Collections, Wallace Library, Rochester Institute of Technology.

19–14. Alex Steinweiss, album cover for Beethoven's *Symphony No. 5,* 1949. This collage of diverse elements typifies Steinweiss's album covers.

19–15. Bradbury Thompson, pages from *Westvaco Inspirations* 151, 1945. The vast storehouse of printed images now in the public domain was deftly probed and became part of the modern design vocabulary.

19–16. Bradbury Thompson, pages from *Westvaco Inspirations* 186, 1951. This spirited collage opens an issue called "Enlarging upon Printing," exploring such possibilities as enlarging halftone dots.

19–17. Bradbury Thompson, pages from *Westvaco Inspirations* 210, 1958. A multiple-exposure photograph of a saxophone player is reversed from a black circle on the left and overprinted in primary colors on the right.

19–18. Bradbury Thompson, pages from *Westvaco Inspirations* 216, 1961. Complex typography interpreted the American Civil War; combinations of four-color process printing plates appear behind the large letters.

California in 1950, and he opened a studio there two years later. Paul Rand's use of shape and asymmetrical balance during the 1940s was an important inspiration for Bass, but while Rand's carefully orchestrated compositions used complex contrasts of shape, color, and texture, Bass frequently reduced his designs to a single dominant image.

Bass had a remarkable ability to express the nucleus of a design with images that become glyphs, or elemental pictorial signs that exert great graphic power (Fig. **19–19**). Although

Bass reduced messages to simple pictographic images, his work is not simply the elemental graphics of constructivism. Irregular forms are cut from paper with scissors or drawn with a brush. Freely drawn, decorative letterforms are often combined with typography or handwriting. There is a robust energy about his forms and an almost casual quality about their execution. While images are simplified to a minimal statement, they lack the exactitude of measurement or construction that could make them rigid.

19–19

19–20

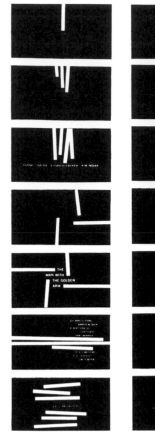

19–21

19–22

19–23

19–24

19–19. Saul Bass, billboard for Pabco Paints, early 1950s. The process of painting is reduced to a multicolored stripe, while happy customers are articulated by three simple marks.

19–20. Saul Bass, logo for *The Man with the Golden Arm,* 1955. This consistent and memorable visual identifier was flexible enough for uses ranging from minute newspaper advertisements to large-scale posters.

19–21. Saul Bass, film titles for *The Man with the Golden Arm,* 1955. Abstract graphic elements create a spare, gaunt intensity reflecting the character of the film. Graphic design for film was revolutionized.

19–22. Saul Bass, poster for *Exodus,* 1960. The struggle of Israel's birth is expressed by two levels of reality: the two-dimensional logo and the photographically frozen moment when this image is engulfed in flames.

19–23. George Tscherny, dance program cover, 1958. Two pieces of cut paper capture the renowned modern dancer Martha Graham in one of her classic poses.

19–24. George Tscherny, exhibition catalogue cover, 1961. José de Rivera is a constructivist sculptor whose parabolic curves twist and bend in space. Tscherny expressed this by photographing bent and twisted type.

Motion pictures had long used traditional portraits of actors and actresses in promoting films and mediocre and garish typography for film titles. Then producer/director Otto Preminger commissioned Bass to create unified graphic materials for his films, including logos, theater posters, advertising, and animated film titles. The first comprehensive design program unifying both print and media graphics for a film was the 1955 design program for Preminger's *The Man with the Golden Arm.* Bass's symbol for this film about drug addiction is a thick pictographic arm thrusting downward into a rectangle composed of slablike bars and bracketed with the film title (Fig. **19–20**). The titles for this motion picture were equally innovative (Fig. **19–21**). Accompanied by staccato jazz music, a single white bar thrusts down onto the screen, followed by three more; when all four reach the center of the screen, typography appears, listing the featured performers. All of these elements, except one bar, retained for continuity, fade. Then, four bars sweep in from the top, bottom, and sides to frame the film-title typography, which suddenly appears. This kinetic sequence of animated bars and typography continues in perfect synchronization to the throbbing wail of jazz music through the credits. Finally, the bars thrust into the space and transform into the pictographic arm of the logo. From this beginning, Bass became the acknowledged master of the film title. He pioneered an organic process of forms that appear, disintegrate, reform, and transform in time and space. This combination, recombination, and synthesis of form was carried over into the area of printed graphics.

A typical Bass motion picture design program can be seen in the 1960 graphics for *Exodus.* Bass created a pictograph of arms reaching upward and struggling for a rifle, conveying the violence and strife connected with the birth of the nation of Israel. This mark was used in a comprehensive publicity program, including newspaper, magazine, and trade advertisement posters (Fig. **19–22**) and film titles, and even stationery, shipping labels, and other routine printed matter. Each individual item was approached as a unique communications problem. The simplicity and directness of Bass's work enables the viewer to interpret the content immediately.

In addition to his film graphics, Bass created numerous corporate-identity programs. He also directed a number of films, ranging from the outstanding short film *Why Man Creates,* which used a kaleidoscope of film techniques probing the nature of human creativity and expression, to a feature-length motion picture.

George Tscherny (b. 1924), a native of Budapest, Hungary, immigrated to the United States as a child and received his visual education there. Tscherny headed the graphic-design department for the New York design firm George Nelson & Associates before opening his own design office in 1956. Tscherny has functioned as an independent designer, which is unusual in a profession where partnerships, large staffs, and staff positions are the norm. An intuitive and sensitive designer, Tscherny possesses an ability to seize the essence of the subject and express it in stunningly simple terms. The results are elegant, to the point, and disarmingly simple. Tscherny's vocabulary of techniques for solving design problems includes type, photography, simple calligraphic brush drawing, and bold, simple shapes cut from colored papers. Regardless of technique, his process of reducing complex content to an elemental graphic symbol expressing the underlying order or basic form of the subject is constant (Figs. **19–23** and **19–24**).

The New York firm of Brownjohn, Chermayeff, and Geismar, founded by three youthful designers in 1957, did important work. Their decision to call their firm a design office instead of an art studio reflected their attitudes toward design and the design process. Robert Brownjohn (1925–70) had studied painting and design under Moholy-Nagy and architecture under the distinguished architect-teacher Serge Chermayeff. Ivan Chermayeff (b. 1932), son of Serge Chermayeff, had worked as an assistant to Alvin Lustig and as a record-album designer; his close friend from the graduate graphic design program at Yale University, Thomas H. Geismar (b. 1931), had served two years with the United States Army as an exhibition designer and then freelanced. The initial contribution of these three to American graphic design sprang

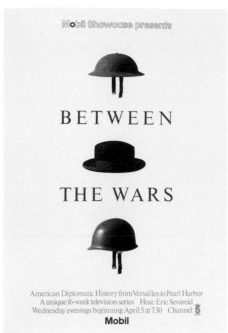

19–25

19–26

19–27

from a strong aesthetic background and an understanding of the major ideas of European modern art, which had been reinforced by their contacts with the elder Chermayeff, Moholy-Nagy, and Lustig. A communicative immediacy, a strong sense of form, and a vitality and freshness characterized their work in the early months of the partnership. Images and symbols were combined with a surreal sense of dislocation to convey the essence of the subject on book jackets and posters (Figs. **19–25** and **19–26**). Typographic solutions, such as the record-album cover for Manchito and his orchestra (Fig. **19–27**), used color repetition and unusual letterforms to express the subject matter. A fine sense of both typographic and art history, developed as a result of the principals' wide-ranging educational backgrounds, enabled them to solve problems through inventive and symbolic manipulation of forms and imagery. Solutions grew out of the needs of the client and the limitations of the problem at hand.

In 1960 Brownjohn left the partnership and moved to England, where he made significant contributions to British graphic design, especially in the area of film titles. Particularly inventive was his title design for the motion picture *Goldfinger*. Brownjohn's typographic designs for the credits were 35mm color slides projected upon a moving human body filmed in real time. This integration of two-dimensional graphics with figurative cinematography inspired numerous other experimental titling efforts. Meanwhile the firm, renamed Chermayeff & Geismar Associates, played a major role in the development of postwar corporate identity, discussed in the next chapter.

Graphic design education at Yale University School of Art

In 1950 Josef Albers was appointed director of the art school at Yale Univeristy. During the same year he invited Alvin Eisenman (b. 1921) to direct the graphic design program, providing the genesis of the first such program to be supported by a major university. In addition to teaching, Eisenman was appointed typographer and successor to Carl Purington Rollins at the Yale University Press. According to John T. Hill, a Yale colleague, "Both Albers and Eisenman shared a passion for type and typography. From his teaching at the Bauhaus, Albers brought exercises which examined letters and typography as formal elements devoid of their literal function. Eisenman brought a rigorous study of classic type design and the traditions of fine book design and printing." (Figs. **19–28** and **19–29**) Eisenman was joined in 1951 by Alvin Lustig, who remained on the faculty until 1955, when his life was cut short by a progressive illness at the age of 40.

As a result of Eisenman's vision, for over half a century many leading graphic designers, photographers, printmakers and other innovators in the visual arts have taught in the Yale graphic design program. The program has contributed to the advancement of professional instruction in graphic design and design education internationally, as many of its alumni have become prominent designers and educators around the world. In addition to Eiseman and Lustig, the faculty has included Norman Ives, Paul Rand, Herbert Matter, Bradbury Thompson, Armin Hofman, Alexy Brodovitch, Walken Evans, John T. Hill, Inge Druckery, Dan Friedman, Philip Burton,

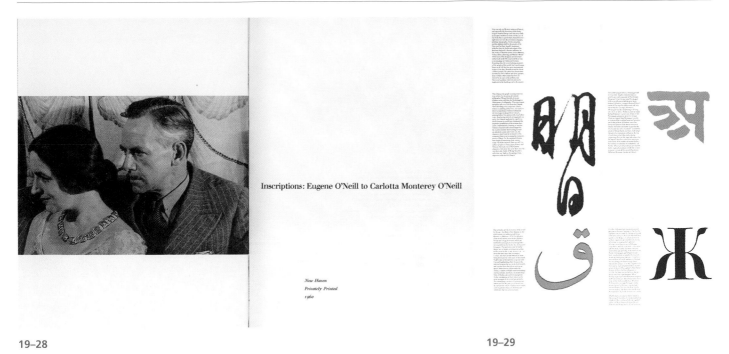

Inscriptions: Eugene O'Neill to Carlotta Monterey O'Neill

New Haven
Privately Printed
1960

19–28

19–29

19–25. Thomas H. Geismar, cover for *Common Sense and Nuclear Warfare*, c. 1958. The atomic blast became a visual metaphor for the human brain, graphically echoing the title.

19–26. Ivan Chermayeff, *Between the Wars*, 1977. The interwar years are represented by Churchill's hat between two helmets.

19–27. Robert Brownjohn, album cover for Machito and His Orchestra, 1959. A pattern of abstract shapes is formed by repeating the bottom portions of letters fragmented by a stencil-lettering effect.

19–28. Alvin Eisenman, the title spread for *Inscriptions: Eugene O'Neill to Carlotta Monterey O'Neill*, 1960.

19–29. Alvin Eisenman, "Homage to the Book" folder, 1968.

Douglas Scott, Christopher Pullman, and Sheila de Bretteville, the current director. The list of visting lecturers also reads like Who's Who of twentieth-century graphic design. It includes luminaries such as Lester Beall, Otl Aicher, Raymond Savignac, Dieter Rot, Peter Brattinga, Robert Frank, Ken Hiebert, Anton Stankowski, George Tscherny, April Greiman, Wolfgang Weingart, Rudi De Harak, Bob Gill, Shigeo Fukuda, Steven Heller, Jan Tschichold, Stefan Geissbuhler, Adrian Frutiger, Greer Allen, Matthew Carter, and Malcom Grear.

In the first class after Albers's restructuring, Norman Ives (1923–1978) received his MFA in graphic design in 1952. While an undergraduate at Wesleyan, he had developed a love for literature and the classics that became a part of his overall vision. In his early paintings one senses overtones of Arp and Klee and in his typographic work the playful approach and expressive use of letters found in the work of Apollinaire, Sandberg, and Werkman.

After graduation, Eisenman asked Ives to join his newly assembled faculty. Ives immediately proved to be a naturally gifted teacher and was admired for his succinctness, dearth of rhetoric, and insightful criticism and generosity.

Ives began making collages in the late 1950s, initially using triangular shapes of the same size cut from letters and words on posters and broadsides. These were then glued to grids drawn on boards. Although they retained their colors and forms, they were detached from their original sources, an aspect that distinguished them from the scraps used by Schwitters, who preserved much of the identity of his materials (Figs. **19–30**).

An editorial design revolution

During the 1940s, only a few American magazines were well designed. Three of them were *Fortune*, a business magazine whose art directors included Burtin and Leo Lionni (1910–99); *Vogue*, where Alexander Liberman (1912–99) (see chapter 17) replaced Dr. Agha as art director in 1943; and especially *Harper's Bazaar*, where Brodovitch continued as art director until his retirement in 1958. One of Dr. Agha's assistants at *Vogue* during the 1930s, Cipe Pineles (1910–91), made a major contribution to editorial design during the 1940s and 1950s, first as art director at *Glamour* and then at *Seventeen, Charm,* and *Mademoiselle*. Pineles often commissioned illustrations from painters, resulting in editorial pages that broke with conventional imagery (Fig. **19–31**). Pineles became the first woman admitted to membership in the New York Art Director's Club, breaking the bastion of the male-dominated professional design societies.

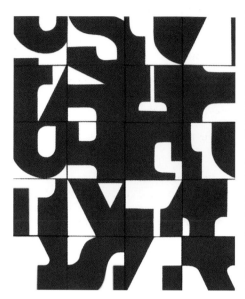

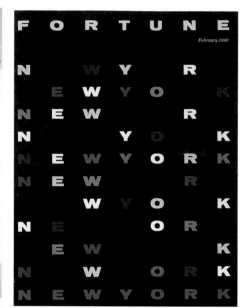

19–30   19–31   19–32

Born in the Netherlands, Leo Lionni (1910–99) studied economics in Italy from 1931 until 35. While in Italy, he became acquainted with the futurist artist Marinetti, who encouraged him to paint. Lionni's career as a graphic designer began when he worked as a designer and art director for Motta, an Italian food distributor. In 1939 he moved to the United States, where he was hired as art director at the pioneering Philadelphia advertising agency N. W. Ayer, whose clients included the Container Corporation of America. He also contributed to the war effort with designs such as his 1941 poster "Keep 'em Rolling," where three tanks and the image of a welder are integrated with an American flag. In 1949 he became art director at *Fortune* magazine, where he remained until his retirement in 1961 (Fig. **19–32**). While there he gave the magazine a unique identity, largely through his innovative use of photography. In addition, he served as Olivetti's design director in America and was coeditor of *Print* magazine from 1955 until 1959.

Over the course of the 1950s a revolution in editorial design occurred, spurred in part by the design classes Brodovitch taught first at his home and then at the New School for Social Research in New York. The seeds for an expansive, design-oriented period of editorial graphics were sown in these classes. One of his students, Otto Storch (1913–1999), later wrote, "Brodovitch would dump photostats, type proofs, colored pieces of paper, and someone's shoe lace, if it became untied, on a long table together with rubber cement. He would fold his arms and with a sad expression challenge us to do something brilliant." Brodovitch's students learned to examine each problem thoroughly, develop a solution from the resulting understanding, and then search for a brilliant visual presentation. His impact on the generation of

editorial designers and photographers who came into their own during the 1950s was phenomenal, and he helped editorial design experience one of its greatest eras.

Storch, working as an art director at the Dell publishing house, was unhappy with the subject matter in his assignments. Keenly interested in Brodovitch's design of *Harper's Bazaar,* Storch joined the art directors, photographers, fashion and general illustrators, and packaging, set, and typographic designers who gathered to learn from the master. After class one evening in 1946, Brodovitch reviewed Storch's portfolio and advised him to quit his job because he showed potential but his position did not. A seven-year period of freelancing followed, and then Storch joined the McCall's Corporation as assistant art director for *Better Living* magazine. In 1953 he was named art director of *McCall's* magazine. When this major women's publication developed circulation problems in the late 1950s, a new editor named Herbert Mayes was brought in to revitalize the magazine. Mayes gave Storch a free hand to upgrade the graphics in 1958, and an astounding visual approach developed. Typography was unified with photography as the type was designed to lock tightly into the photographic image (Fig. **19–33**). Headlines often became parts of illustrations. Type warped and bent, or became the illustration, as in Figure **19–34**, where it takes on the shape of a mattress.

Scale was explored in this large-format publication, whose 27 by 34.5–centimeter (10⅝ by 13½–inch) pages provided abundant space for design. Small objects became large graphics. Subjects such as a beautiful ear of fresh summer corn (Fig. **19–35**) were presented as full double-page layouts. Storch and the photographers who worked with him went to great lengths to produce unexpected and poetic photographic

19–33

19–34

19–30. Norman Ives, *Ionic-Reconstruction,* acrylic and dry pigment on canvas, 1965. Ives produced painted versions of his collages, as in this construction comprised of 20 separate canvases.

19–31. Cipe Pineles, cover for *Seventeen,* 1949. Stripe patterns and a mirror-image reflection achieve a graphic vitality.

19–32. Leo Lionni, *Fortune* magazine cover, 1943.

19–33. Otto Storch (art director) and Paul Dome (photographer), pages from *McCall's,* 1961. Introductory pages for a frozen-foods feature unify typography and photography into a cohesive structure.

19–34. Otto Storch (art director) and Dan Wynn (photographer), pages from *McCall's,* 1961. Typography bends with the elasticity of a soft mattress under the weight of the sleeping woman.

essays. Foods and fashions were often shot on location instead of in the studio.

Storch ranks among the major innovators of the period. His philosophy that idea, copy, art, and typography should be inseparable in editorial design (Fig. **19–36**) influenced both editorial and advertising graphics. Success made the management at *McCall's* more conservative, and opposition to Storch's creative layouts began to build. After nearly fifteen years as art director of *McCall's,* he resigned to concentrate on editorial and advertising photography.

After gaining experience in studios and an advertising agency, Vienna-born Henry Wolf (1925–2005) became art director of *Esquire* in 1953. Wolf also studied under Brodovitch, and he redesigned *Esquire*'s format, placing greater emphasis on the use of white space and large photographs. When Brodovitch retired in 1958, Wolf replaced him as art director of *Harper's Bazaar.* Wolf experimented with typography, making it large enough to fill the page on one spread and then using small headlines on other pages. Wolf's vision of the magazine cover was a simple image conveying a visual idea. His "Americanization of Paris" cover (Fig. **19–37**) inspired letters asking where instant wine could be purchased. The sophistication and inventiveness of the photography commissioned by *Harper's Bazaar* during his tenure were monumental achievements (Figs. **19–38** and **19–39**).

19–35

19–37

19–36

19–38

In 1961 Wolf left *Harper's Bazaar* to design the new magazine *Show* (Fig. **19–40**), a short-lived periodical that explored new design territory as a result of Wolf's imaginative art direction. He then turned his attention toward advertising and photography.

In the late 1960s, broad factors at work in America ended the era of large pages, huge photographs, and design as a significant component of content. Television eroded magazines' advertising revenue and supplanted their traditional role of providing popular entertainment. At the same time, public concerns about the Vietnam War, environmental problems, the rights of minorities and women, and a host of other issues produced a

need for different magazines. The public demanded higher information content, and skyrocketing postal rates, paper shortages, and escalating paper and printing costs shrank the large-format periodicals. *Esquire*, for example, went from 25.5 by 33.4 centimeters (10 by 13 inches) to a typical format size of about 21by 27.5 centimeters (8 by 11 inches). Major weeklies including *Life*, *Look*, and the *Saturday Evening Post* ceased publication.

Editorial design after the decline
Many predicted the death of the magazine as a communications form during the 1960s; however, a new, smaller-format breed of periodicals emerged and thrived by addressing the in-

19–39　　　　　**19–40**

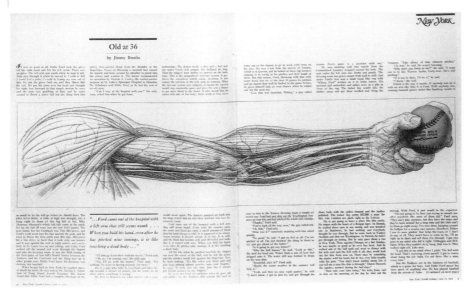

19–41

19–35. Otto Storch (art director and photographer), pages from *McCall's,* 1965. The soft beauty of an ear of corn fills the pages. A photograph of a roadside market's handmade sign serves as the title.

19–36. Otto Storch (art director) and Allen Arbus (photographer), pages from *McCall's,* 1959. Typography tumbles from a heel and hand of moving models. Contrasting colors and values create a dynamic visual impact.

19–37. Henry Wolf, cover for *Esquire,* 1958. "The Americanization of Paris" is signified by a packet of "instant red wine," satirizing the creeping spread of American technology, customs, and conveniences.

19–38. Henry Wolf, cover for *Harper's Bazaar,* 1959. This refracted image typifies Wolf's imaginative visual solutions for ordinary design problems. As a subtle detail, the logo is refracted as well.

19–39. Henry Wolf, cover for *Harper's Bazaar,* 1959. Colors on a peacock feather are echoed by the eye makeup in an arresting juxtaposition.

19–40. Henry Wolf, cover for *Show,* 1963. On this Valentine's Day cover, an X-ray machine locates the model's graphic red heart.

19–41. Peter Palazzo (art director), pages for *New York,* 1965. A transparent anatomical drawing of an arm combines with a photograph of a baseball to express the arm problems of a major-league pitcher.

terests of specialized audiences. Advertisers who wished to reach these audiences bought space. The new editorial climate, with more emphasis on content, longer text, and less opportunity for lavish visual treatment, necessitated a new approach to editorial design. Layout became more controlled, and the use of a standard typographic format and grid became the norm.

A harbinger for the future evolution of the magazine as a graphic communications form can be found in the work of Peter Palazzo (1926–2005), design editor of the *New York Herald Tribune* from 1962 until 1965. Palazzo received considerable acclaim for his overall typographic design of this newspaper, the editorial design approach of the *Book Week Supplement* and

New York magazine, and the conceptual power of many of the images he commissioned. In the weekly *New York* magazine section, Palazzo established a three-column grid and a consistent size and style for article titles, which were always bracketed by a thick ruled line above and a thin rule below (Fig. **19–41**). The total effect was somewhere between the newspaper (with its dominant masses of text) and the magazine design of the period (with engaging visuals and ample white space). His cover designs used simple, direct symbolic images to make editorial comments on important issues (Fig. **19–42**). After the *New York Herald Tribune* ceased publication in April 1967, the New York supplement continued as an independent city magazine.

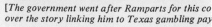

[*The government went after Ramparts for this co*
over the story linking him to Texas gambling pay

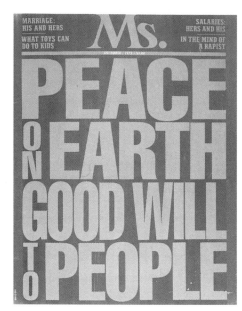

19–42   19–43   19–44

During the late 1960s American graphic design slowly started to become a national profession. New photographic typesetting and printing technology permitted excellent work to be produced in smaller cities; professional educational programs developed around the country. Two national design magazines—*Print*, published in New York from 1940, and *Communication Arts*, launched in the San Francisco area in 1959—communicated to an increasingly nationwide design community and played a major role in defining the profession and its standards.

A new breed of editorial art directors who were as much editors as designers emerged in some cities, including Atlanta and San Francisco. They helped shape the editorial viewpoints and philosophies of their publications. One prototype for this new editorial designer is Dugald Stermer (b. 1936), who left a studio job in Texas in 1965 to return to his native California and become art director of *Ramparts* magazine. Public opposition to the Vietnam War and concern about a host of other social and environmental issues were exploding, and *Ramparts* became the journal of record for the movement. Stermer developed a format using Times Roman typography with capital initials, two columns of text on the page, and centered titles and headings. The dignity and readability of classical, traditional typography thus packaged the most radical periodical of the era. Stermer made a major contribution in the use of images, often placing full-page illustrations or photographs on covers and at the beginnings of articles. Stermer and editors Warren Hinkle, Robert Scheer, and Sol Stern came perilously close to being indicted for conspiracy as a result of the

December 1967 cover design (Fig. **19–43**). At a time when many young Americans were burning their Selective Service registration cards as a matter of conscience, this cover depicted four hands holding burning facsimile draft cards of Stermer and the three editors. Convincing arguments by attorney Edward Bennet Williams persuaded the grand jury not to indict the four.

In contrast to the consistent format adopted by Stermer, the design of *Ms.* magazine by Bea Feitler (1938–82) depended heavily on diversifying typographic style and scale to bring vitality and expression to this journal of the women's movement. Social conventions and standard design thinking were challenged by the *Ms.* 1972 Christmas cover (Fig. **19–44**). The traditional holiday greeting, normally expressing "good will to men," is directed toward "people." Feitler had an original approach to typography and design that depended not on consistency of style but on a finely tuned ability to make appropriate choices uninhibited by current fashion or standard typographic practice. In a single issue of *Ms.* magazine her graphic range included fifteenth-century Garamonds with ornamental initials, simple geometric sans-serif types, and novelty and illustrated letterforms. After her tenure at *Ms.*, Feitler became active as a freelance designer of periodicals and books.

A number of currents—the conceptual approach to cover design, the role of art director expanding into editorial deliberations, as illustrated by Stermer, and the growing taste for nostalgia, ephemera, and popular culture partly inspired by 1960s pop art—dovetailed in the work of Mike Salisbury (b. 1941),

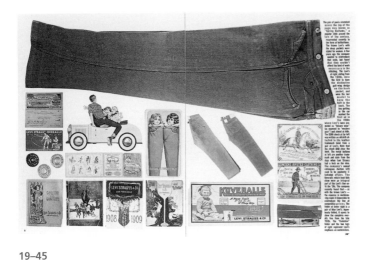

19–45

19–46

who became the art director of *West*, the Sunday supplement of the *Los Angeles Times*, in 1967. For five years, until the newspaper terminated it because its advertising revenue failed to meet production costs, Salisbury made *West* a vital expression of California culture. The visual delights of vernacular artifacts, ranging from orange-crate labels to blue jeans advertising (Fig. **19–45**) to customized cars, were featured in editorial spreads researched by Salisbury and designed with a combination of randomness and order in original layouts that intensified the pages of the publication.

In 1974 Salisbury redesigned the entire format of *Rolling Stone*, a rock-and-roll newspaper repositioned as a tabloid magazine (Fig. **19–46**). The element of surprise became Salisbury's primary design tool for giving *Rolling Stone* visual energy. Typography was used differently for each article in an issue, and the range of illustrations and photographic approaches knew no bounds. In addition to redefining *Rolling Stone*'s format, Salisbury established an uninhibited, freewheeling design approach that influenced the layout of many popular, specialized, and regional periodicals for a decade. He also worked as a consultant designer or art director for *Oui*, *City*, and *New West*.

The new advertising

The 1940s were a lackluster decade for advertising. Repetition of hyperbolic slogans, movie-star testimonials, and exaggerated claims were mainstays of the decade, punctuated by occasional design excellence. On 1 June 1949 a new advertising agency, Doyle Dane Bernbach, opened its doors at 350 Madison Avenue in New York City with a staff of thirteen and less than half a million dollars in client accounts. Copywriter Bill Bernbach was the partner with responsibility for the creative area, and his initial staff consisted of art director Bob Gage (1919–2000) and copywriter Phyllis Robinson (b. 1921).

19–42. Peter Palazzo (art director), cover for *New York*, 1965. For a special issue on women's issues and their desire for greater freedom and equality, Palazzo applied eye shadow and mascara to the Statue of Liberty.

19–43. Dugald Stermer (art director), cover for *Ramparts*, 1967. Because the editors' names are clearly visible on the burning draft cards, this graphic depiction of civil disobedience takes on the quality of a self-documented crime.

19–44. Bea Feitler (art director), cover for *Ms.* magazine, 1972. The lime-green typography against a fluorescent pink background projected joyously from newsstands.

19–45. Mike Salisbury, pages from *West*, late 1960s. Here the art director became a visual historian, researching and selecting old Levi's advertisements and products for a pictorial essay.

19–46. Mike Salisbury, pages from *Rolling Stone*, 1974. Diverse typefaces are contained in plaques and boxes. Full, two-page photographs produce a lively graphic pacing.

Doyle Dane Bernbach "took the exclamation mark out of advertising" and made it talk intelligently to consumers. The company's first client was a budget department store badly in need of a fresh image (Fig. **19–47**). In contrast to the crowded space and multiple messages of much advertising of the period, Doyle Dane Bernbach used white space effectively to focus the reader's attention toward the headline and image on crowded newspaper pages (Fig. **19–48**).

For each campaign they developed a strategy surrounding important advantages, distinguishing characteristics, or superior features of the product. In order to break through to consumers bombarded by perpetual commercial messages, Bernbach sought an imaginative package for this information. His major contribution was combining words and images in a new way. Traditionally, a copywriter's headline and body copy were

19–47

19–48

19–49

It's ugly, but it gets you there.

19–50

19–51

19–52

sent to the art director, who then made a layout. In the Bernbach approach, a synergistic relationship between visual and verbal components was established. Paul Rand had developed a bellwether approach to advertising in the 1940s, integrating words and phrases in a freer organization, using visual metaphors and puns seldom seen in advertising. Now Bernbach and his colleagues removed the boundaries separating verbal and visual communications and evolved visual/verbal

syntax: word and image fused into a conceptual expression of an idea so that they become completely interdependent (Fig. **19–49**). In the Volkswagen campaign, "strange little cars with their beetle shapes" were marketed to a public used to luxury and high horsepower as status symbols. The recognition value of Volkswagen advertising was demonstrated by an ad appearing immediately after the first lunar landing (Fig. **19–50**), which gained impact from its continuity with earlier ads.

19–47. Bob Gage (art director), Bill Bernbach, and Judy Protas (writers), Ohrbach's advertisement, 1958. A "catty lady" learns how a friend dresses so well on an ordinary income: she buys high fashions for low price.

19–48. Charlie Piccirillo (art director) and Judy Protas (writer), back-to-school advertisement of Ohrbach's, 1962. Seasonal clichés yield to a direct presentation of the joys and sorrows of everyday life.

19–49. Helmut Krone (art director) and Julian Koenig (writer), Volkswagen advertisement, 1960. An economy car is made lovable as conventional exaggerated claims and superlatives yield to straightforward facts.

19–50. Jim Brown (art director) and Larry Levenson (writer), Volkswagen advertisement, 1969. Linking the car to a space vehicle reinforced the concept of a homely but well-engineered, reliable machine.

19–51. Bill Taupin (art director) and Judy Protas (writer), subway poster, c. 1965. Mass communication stereotypes were replaced by more realistic images of people, and taboos against representing ethnic minorities were broken.

19–52. Bert Steinhauser (art director) and Chuck Kollewe (writer), political-action advertisement, 1967. Startling words and a vivid picture challenged readers to write Congress about a rat-extermination bill.

This approach to advertising led to a new working relationship, as writers and art directors worked as "creative teams." In addition to Gage, Bill Taubin, Helmut Krone (1925–96), Len Sirowitz (b. 1932), and Bert Steinhauser rank among the art directors who produced outstanding creative work in collaboration with Doyle Dane Bernbach copywriters. Because concept was dominant, the design of many Doyle Dane Bernbach advertisements was reduced to the basic elements necessary to convey the message: a large, arresting visual image, a concise headline of bold weight, and body copy that stakes its claim with factual and often entertaining writing instead of puffery and meaningless superlatives. Often the visual organization was simple and symmetrical, for design arrangements were not allowed to distract from the straightforward presentation of an idea. Advertising stereotypes were replaced by real people from America's pluralistic society (Fig. **19–51**). The potency of this approach was demonstrated when a public-service ad influenced congressional action (Fig. **19–52**) and Steinhauser, the art director, received a letter of thanks from President Lyndon B. Johnson after the bill was passed.

Doyle Dane Bernbach became a training ground for what was eventually called "the new advertising." Many writers and art directors who developed there participated in spin-off

agencies as the boutique agency, a small shop with emphasis on creativity rather than on full marketing services, challenged the dominance of the monolithic multimillion-dollar agencies during the flowering of advertising creativity in the 1960s. The notion of the advertising superstar was fed by a proliferation of awards, competitions, professional periodicals, and annuals. By the 1980s Doyle Dane Bernbach had evolved into a more traditional large advertising agency.

Regular television broadcasting started in 1941, and immediately after World War II it began its spectacular growth as an advertising medium. By the early 1960s television was the second largest medium (after newspapers) in total advertising revenue and the largest medium in major national advertising budgets. Print art directors began to turn toward the design of television commercials. This ubiquitous communication form expanded public understanding of cinematic form by adopting techniques from experimental film; at their worst, television's commercials became a blight on the public consciousness.

The "new advertising" developed at the same time as the "new journalism," and a spate of comparisons was inevitable. The journalistic approach of writers like Tom Wolfe (b. 1931) replaced traditional objectivity with subjective responses as a component of reportage. The journalist experienced a story as a participant rather than as a dispassionate observer. By contrast, although the new advertising continued the essential orientation toward persuasive selling techniques and subjective emotional appeals, its methods were more honest, literate, and tasteful. In the 1970s advertising became increasingly involved in positioning products and services against their competitors, and the general level of print advertising creativity declined.

American typographic expressionism

A playful direction taken by New York graphic designers in the 1950s and 1960s involved figurative typography. This took many forms—letterforms became objects; objects became letterforms. Gene Federico (1919–1999) was one of the first graphic designers to delight in using letterforms as images (Fig. **19–53**). Another approach to figurative typography used the visual properties of the words themselves, or their organization in the space, to express an idea. Don Egensteiner's "Tonnage" advertisement (Fig. **19-54**) is an example of the visual organization of type taking on connotative meaning. Typography was sometimes scratched, torn, bent, or vibrated to express a concept or introduce the unexpected to the printed page.

Another typographic trend that began slowly in the 1950s was a reexamination of nineteenth-century decorative and novelty typefaces that had been rejected for many decades under the influence of the modern movement. This revival of interest was inspired by Robert M. Jones, art director of RCA Victor Records, who established the private Glad Hand Press in 1953.

19–53

19–55

19–56

19–57

19–58

19–59

19–54

Jones had a fondness for colonial and nineteenth-century printing, and exercised this interest in hundreds of pieces of graphic ephemera produced at the press. In addition, he often set typography for his record-album designs using wood type.

Phototypography, the setting of type by exposing negatives of alphabet characters to photographic paper, was attempted as early as 1893, with limited results. During the 1920s inventors in England and America moved closer to success. The year

1925 saw the quiet dawning of a new era of typography with the public announcement of the Thothmic photographic composing machine, invented by E. K. Hunter and J. R. C. August of London. A keyboard produced a punched tape to control a long, opaque master film with transparent letterforms. As a given letter moved in position in front of a lens, it was exposed to photographic paper by a beam of light. The Thothmic was a harbinger of the graphic revolution that came a half-century later.

19–53. Gene Federico (art director), advertisement for *Woman's Day*, 1953. In this double-page advertisement from the *New Yorker* magazine, the perfectly round Futura *O*s form bicycle wheels.

19–54. Don Egensteiner (art director), advertisement for Young and Rubicam Advertising, 1960. The heavy, one-word headline crashes into the body copy to accomplish a major objective: grabbing attention.

19–55. John Alcorn, cover for a phototype specimen booklet, 1964. The symmetrical mixture of decorative fonts approximates the nineteenth-century wood-type poster, but the spacing and use of color were current.

19–56. Herb Lubalin, typogram from a Stettler typeface announcement poster, 1965. Marriage, "the most licentious of human institutions," becomes an illustration through the joined *R*s.

19–57. Herb Lubalin (designer) and Tom Carnase (letterer), proposed magazine logo, 1967. The ampersand enfolds and protects the "child" in a visual metaphor for motherly love.

19–58. Herb Lubalin, proposed New York City logo, 1966. Isometric perspective creates a dynamic tension between two- and three-dimensionality while implying the city's high-rise architecture.

19–59. Herb Lubalin, Ice Capades logo, 1967.

Commercially viable photographic display typesetting in the United States began when the Photolettering firm was established in New York in 1936. It was headed by Edward Rondthaler (b. 1905), who had been instrumental in perfecting the Rutherford Photolettering Machine, which sets type by exposing film negatives of type characters onto photopaper. Although phototypography had the potential to replace the rigid quality of metal type with a dynamic new flexibility, for over two decades it was used only as an alternative method of setting type, with some production advantages and some disadvantages. A major advantage of phototype was a radical reduction in the cost of introducing new typestyles. The large-scale expansion of phototype during the 1960s was accompanied by new designs and reissues of old designs. A specimen book (Fig. **19–55**) designed by John Alcorn (1935–92) introduced Morgan Press nineteenth-century typefaces as phototype from Headliners Process Lettering. This was one of many phototype collections making Victorian faces widely available. Graphic designers rethought the value of supposedly outmoded forms and incorporated them in their work.

Someone was needed to define the aesthetic potential of phototypography by understanding its new flexibility and exploring its possibilities for graphic expression. Herb Lubalin (1918–81), a total generalist whose achievements include advertising and editorial design, trademark and typeface design, posters, and packaging, was hailed as the typographic genius of his time. Major thrusts of American graphic design—including the visual/verbal concept orientation of Doyle Dane Bernbach and the trends toward figurative and more structured typography—came together in Lubalin's work. Space and surface became his primary visual considerations. He abandoned traditional typographic rules and practice and looked at alphabet characters as both visual form and message communication.

Discontented with the rigid limitations of metal type in the 1950s, Lubalin would cut apart his type proofs with a razor blade and reassemble them. In his hands, type was compressed until letters joined into ligatures, and enlarged to unexpected sizes; letterforms were joined, overlapped, and enlarged; capital *O*s became receptacles for images. Words and letters could become images; an image could become a word or a letter. This typographic play engages the reader and requires participation. Lubalin practiced design not as an art form or craft created in a vacuum but as a means of giving visual form to a concept or a message. In his most innovative work, concept and visual form are yoked into a oneness called a *typogram,* meaning a brief, visual typographic poem. Lubalin's wit and strong message orientation enabled him to transform words into ideographic typograms about the subject (Figs. **19–56** through **19–59**).

In 1960, most display typography was the hand-set, metal type of Gutenberg's day, but this five-hundred-year-old craft was being rendered obsolete by phototype. By the end of the decade, metal type was virtually a thing of the past. More than any other graphic designer, Lubalin explored the creative potential of phototypography to see how the fixed relationships of letterforms marching on square blocks of metal could be exploded by phototype's dynamic and elastic qualities. In phototype systems, letterspacing could be compressed to extinction and forms could overlap. A greater range of type sizes was available; type could be set to any size required by the layout or enlarged to huge sizes without losing sharpness. Special lenses could be used to expand, condense, italicize, backslant, or outline letterforms. Lubalin incorporated these possibilities into his work not just as technical or design ends in themselves but as potent means of intensifying the printed image and expressing content.

During the metal-type era, hundreds of thousands of dollars had to be invested in the deployment of a single new typeface. Matrixes had to be manufactured for every size of hand-set and hot-metal keyboard type, then each typesetting firm had to purchase a large stock of metal type in each size and variation of roman, bold, italic, and so on to meet client requests. Phototypography reduced this process to the relatively inexpensive creation of simple film fonts, and a proliferation of typeface designs to rival the Victorian era began. Visual Graphics

19–60

19–61

19–63

19–62

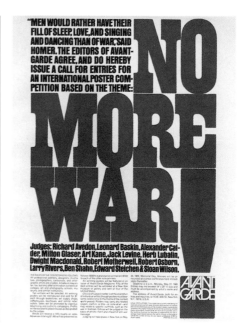

19–66

Corporation, manufacturer of the Phototypositor display typesetting machine, which enabled design studios and printing firms around the world to set excellent photodisplay type, sponsored a National Typeface Design Competition in 1965. Lubalin's posters demonstrating the dozen winning designs spurred the awareness of phototypography and its design potential (Fig. **19–60**). When his detractors said his typography suffered from a decline in legibility due to tight spacing and overlapping forms, Lubalin responded, "Sometimes you have to compromise legibility to achieve impact." Lubalin's attentiveness to detail and typographic experimentation raised other designers' typographic sensitivities, inspiring them to try new things.

Lubalin also made significant contributions to editorial design during the 1960s. A host of editorial redesigns, including two for the ill-fated *Saturday Evening Post*, accompanied his collaboration with publisher Ralph Ginzburg (b. 1929) on a series of magazines. A hardbound quarterly journal called *Eros*, launched in 1962 with a massive direct-mail campaign, was billed as the magazine of love. Its ninety-six-page advertisement-free format allowed Lubalin to explore scale, white space, and visual flow. In a photographic essay about President John F. Kennedy (Figs. **19–61** and **19–62**), scale changes ranging from a double-page bleed photograph to pages jammed with eight or nine photographs established a lively pace. After pondering

"She was one of the most unappreciated people in the world."
Joshua Logan, director.

19–64

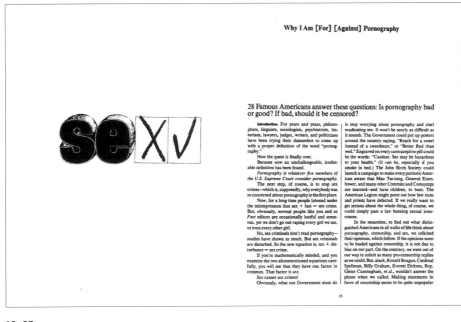

Why I Am [For] [Against] Pornography

28 Famous Americans answer these questions: Is pornography bad or good? If bad, should it be censored?

Introduction. For years and years, philosophers, linguists, sociologists, psychiatrists, historians, lawyers, judges, writers, and politicians have been trying their damnedest to come up with a proper definition of the word "pornography."

Now the quest is finally over.

Because now an unchallengeable, irrefutable definition has been found.

Pornography is whatever five members of the U.S. Supreme Court consider pornography.

The next step, of course, is to stop sex crimes—which is, supposedly, why everybody was so concerned about pornography in the first place.

Now, for a long time people labored under the misimpression that sex + lust = sex crime. But, obviously, normal people like you and us *Fact* editors are occasionally lustful and sensuous, yet we don't go out raping every girl we see, or even every other girl.

No, sex criminals don't read pornography—studies have shown as much. But sex criminals *are* disturbed. So the new equation is, sex + disturbance = sex crime.

If you're mathematically minded, and you examine the two aforementioned equations carefully, you will see that they have one factor in common. That factor is *sex.*

Sex causes sex crimes!

Obviously, what our Government must do is stop worrying about pornography and start eradicating sex. It won't be nearly as difficult as it sounds. The Government could put up posters around the country saying, "Reach for a sweet instead of a sweetheart," or "Better Red than wed." Engraved on every contraceptive pill could be the words: "Caution: Sex may be hazardous to your health." (It *can* be, especially if you smoke in bed.) The John Birch Society could launch a campaign to make every patriotic American aware that Mao Tse-tung, General Eisenhower, and many other Commies and Comsymps are married—and have children, to boot. The American Legion might point out how few nuns and priests have defected. If we really want to get serious about the whole thing, of course, we could simply pass a law banning sexual intercourse.

In the meantime, to find out what distinguished Americans in all walks of life think about pornography, censorship, and sex, we solicited their opinions, which follow. If the opinions seem to be loaded against censorship, it is not due to bias on our part. On the contrary, we went out of our way to solicit as many pro-censorship replies as we could. But, alack, Ronald Reagan, Cardinal Spellman, Billy Graham, Everett Dirksen, Rep. Glenn Cunningham, et al., wouldn't answer the phone when we called. Making statements in favor of censorship seems to be quite unpopular

15

19–65

over photographic contact sheets, Lubalin designed layouts of remarkable vitality (Figs. **19–63** and **19–64**). Believing that typeface selection should express content and be governed by the visual configuration of the words, Lubalin used a variety of display types in *Eros,* including giant condensed sans serifs, novelty faces, and delicate Old Style romans. Although the visual and written content of *Eros* was tame in comparison to the explicit material permitted a decade later, Ginzburg was convicted of sending obscene material through the mail and after exhausting all appeals was imprisoned for eight months in 1972.

In 1967 Ginzburg launched *Fact* magazine, which featured editorial exposés of hallowed institutions and sacred cows.

Lubalin's graphic treatment on a frugal production budget presaged the restrained economics of inflationary 1970s publishing. Lacking funds to hire ten different illustrators or photographers for each issue, Lubalin commissioned one illustrator to illustrate every article in an issue for a flat fee. Design economy was achieved by a standardized format using Times Roman Bold titles and Times New Roman subtitles (Fig. **19–65**).

Ginzburg and Lubalin closed out the decade with the square format *Avant Garde,* a lavishly visual periodical that published visual essays, fiction, and reportage. Born amidst the social upheavals of civil rights, women's liberation, the sexual revolution, and antiwar protest (Fig. **19–66**), this magazine became one of

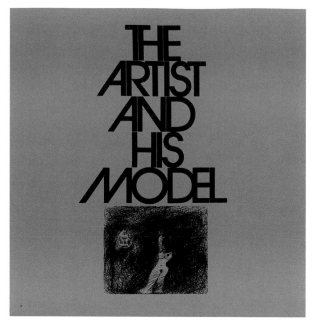

19–67

19–68

Lubalin's most innovative achievements. Although his layouts have a strong underlying geometric structure, this is not the classical geometry of the Basel and Zurich designers. Instead, it is the exuberant and optimistic order of the expansive American character, unencumbered by a sense of tradition or any thought of limitations that cannot be overcome. The logotype for *Avant Garde*, with tightly integrated capital ligatures, was developed into a family of geometric sans-serif typefaces bearing the same name (Fig. **19–67**). By 1970 typeface design began to occupy more of Lubalin's time. He saw the designer's task as projecting a message from a surface using three interdependent means of expression: photography, illustration, and letterforms.

As phototype facilitated production of new typefaces, design piracy became a pressing issue. Original typeface designs requiring hundreds of hours of work could now be photocopied by unscrupulous operators who produced instant film fonts but did not compensate the designers. To enable designers to be adequately compensated for their work while licensing and producing master fonts available to all manufacturers, Lubalin, phototypography pioneer Rondthaler, and

typographer Aaron Burns (1922–91) established the International Typeface Corporation (ITC) in 1970. Thirty-four fully developed type families and about sixty additional display faces were developed and licensed during ITC's first decade. Following the examples of Univers and Helvetica, ITC fonts had large x-heights and short ascenders and descenders; these became the prevailing characteristics of fonts designed during the 1970s and early the 1980s. With Lubalin as design director, ITC began a journal, *U&lc*, to publicize and demonstrate its typefaces. The complex, dynamic style of this tabloid-size publication and the popularity of ITC typefaces had a major impact on typographic design of the 1970s (Figs. **19–68**, **19–69**, and **19–70**).

From the time that Lubalin left his position as vice president and creative director of the Sudler and Hennessey advertising agency in 1964, he formed partnerships and associations with a number of associates, including graphic designers Ernie Smith and Alan Peckolick (b. 1940) and lettering artists Tony DiSpigna (b. 1943) and Tom Carnase (b. 1939). Their works share visual similarities with Lubalin's oeuvre while achieving original solutions to a diverse range of problems.

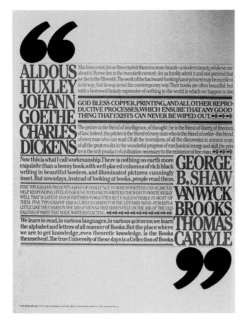

19–69   19–70   19–71

George Lois

Among the young art directors and copywriters who passed through Doyle Dane Bernbach during the late 1950s, George Lois (b. 1931) became the *enfant terrible* of American mass communications. Lois's energetic efforts to sell his work, including such legendary tactics as climbing out on the third-floor ledge of the A. Goodman & Company president's office demanding that his poster proposal be approved (Fig. **19–71**), combined with a tendency to push concepts to the very limit of propriety, earned him this reputation. Lois adopted the Bernbach philosophy that fully integrated visual/verbal concepts were vital to successful message conveyance. He wrote that an art director must treat words "with the same reverence that he accords graphics, because the verbal and visual elements of modern communication are as indivisible as words and music in a song." His designs are deceptively simple and direct (Figs. **19–72** and **19–73**). Backgrounds are usually removed to enable the content-bearing verbal and pictorial images to interact unhampered, a technique he learned at Bernbach, his third agency. At age twenty-eight Lois left Bernbach to cofound Papert, Koenig and Lois, which grew to $40 million per year in billing in seven short years. On several subsequent occasions, Lois left an agency partnership to form yet another advertising agency.

In 1962 *Esquire* magazine was in serious trouble. If any two consecutive issues lost money on newsstand sales, it would have to fold. After being *the* man's magazine in America, *Esquire* was losing its younger audience to *Playboy*, founded by former *Esquire* staff member Hugh Hefner in 1960. *Esquire* editor Harold Hayes asked Lois to develop effective cover designs for the literate but nearly bankrupt maga-

19–67. Herb Lubalin (designer) and Pablo Picasso (lithographer), section opener for an issue of *Avant Garde* (1969). The magazine's title logo spawned a typeface filled with unusual capital ligatures, here used in an issue about Picasso.

19–68. Herb Lubalin, cover for *U&lc,* 1974. Fifty-nine typographic elements, seven illustrations, and sixteen rules—a total of eighty-two separate elements—are integrated into an information-filled page.

19–69. Herb Lubalin, type specimen page from *U&lc,* 1978. A tight square of typography is bracketed by huge quotation marks in the generous margins.

19–70. Herb Lubalin, type specimen page from *U&lc,* 1978. An informal layout gains cohesiveness from the large words pinwheeling around an implied central axis.

19–71. George Lois, subway advertisement poster for Goodman's Matzos, 1960. The large-scale cracker anticipates the 1960s pop-art fascination with blown-up everyday objects.

zine. Lois believed design—a harmony of elements—had no place on a magazine cover. Instead, he opted for the cover as a statement capable of capturing the reader with a spirited comment on a major article. An ability to stay closely in touch with one's times is a vital requirement for someone in visual communications, and many of Lois's most innovative concepts grew from his ability to understand and respond to the people and events of his era. Over the next decade, Lois designed over ninety-two *Esquire* covers in collaboration with photographer Carl Fischer (b. 1924). These covers helped recapture the magazine's audience, and by 1967 *Esquire* was turning a three-million-dollar profit.

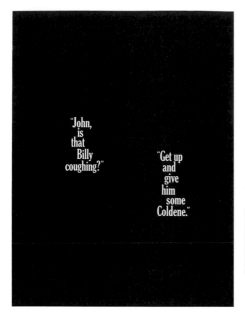

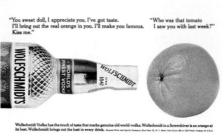

19–72

19–73

19–74

19–75

19–72. George Lois, advertisement for Coldene, 1961. Unlike the coarse hard-sell advertising of most medications this ad shows a simple black page with twelve words suggesting a midnight exchange between concerned parents.

19–73. George Lois, advertisement for Wolfschmidt's, 1962. Blatant symbolism combines with outrageous humor. This ad campaign has continuity, for the preceding ad featured the loquacious bottle talking to a tomato.

19–74. George Lois (designer) and Carl Fischer (photographer), *Esquire* cover, April 1968. Muhammad Ali posed as Saint Sebastian, who was condemned by Roman Emperor Diocletian and shot by archers.

19–75. George Lois (designer) and Carl Fischer (photographer), *Esquire* cover, May 1968. This composite photograph of candidate Richard M. Nixon being made up for a television appearance is typical of Lois's audacity.

Lois thought Fischer was one of the few photographers who understood ideas. Their collaborative efforts created covers that challenged, shocked, and often provoked their audience. Unexpected combinations of images and photographic montage techniques served to intensify an event or make a satirical statement.

Lois's skill in persuading people to participate in photographs resulted in powerful images. He persuaded boxer Muhammad Ali, who had been stripped of his world heavyweight championship title because as a conscientious objector he refused military service, to pose as a famous religious martyr (Fig. **19–74**). As Richard Nixon mounted his second presidential campaign in 1968, Lois combined a stock photograph of the candidate with Fischer's photograph of four hands

applying makeup (Fig. **19–75**). This concept grew out of Lois's recollection of the 1960 presidential campaign, when Nixon lost the race to John F. Kennedy partly because Nixon's "five o'clock shadow made him look evil." After the cover ran, Lois received a call from one of Nixon's staffers, who berated Lois because the lipstick attacked Nixon's masculinity.

The New York School was born from an excitement about European modernism and fueled by economic and technological expansion; it became a dominant force in graphic design from the 1940s until the 1970s. Many of its practitioners, young revolutionaries who altered the course of American visual communications in the 1940s and 1950s, continued to design in the 1990s.

Corporate Identity and Visual Systems

20

The technological advances made during World War II were immense. After the war, productive capacity turned toward consumer goods, and many believed that the outlook for the capitalist economic structure could be unending economic expansion and prosperity. With this bright view of the future in mind, "Good design is good business" became a rallying cry in the graphic-design community during the 1950s. Prosperity and technological development appeared closely linked to the era's increasingly important corporations, and the more perceptive corporate leaders comprehended the need to develop a corporate image and identity for diverse audiences. Design was seen as a major way to shape a reputation for quality and reliability.

Visual marks had been used for identification for centuries. In medieval times, proprietary marks were compulsory and enabled the guilds to control trade. By the 1700s virtually every trader and dealer had a trademark or stamp. The industrial revolution, with its mass manufacturing and marketing, increased the value and importance of trademarks for visual identification. But the visual identification systems that began during the 1950s went far beyond trademarks or symbols. The national and multinational scope of many corporations made it difficult for them to maintain a cohesive image, but by unifying all communications from a given organization into a consistent design system, such an image could be projected, and the design system enlisted to help accomplish specific corporate goals.

Pintori at Olivetti

The first phase in the development of postwar visual identification resulted from pioneering efforts by strong individual designers who put their personal imprint on a client's designed image. This was the case with Behrens at AEG (see chapter 12) and with the Olivetti Corporation, an Italian typewriter and business machines company whose dual commitment to humanist ideals and technological progress dated from its 1908 founding by Camillo Olivetti. Adriano Olivetti (1901–70), son of the founder, became president in 1938. He had a keen sense of the contribution that graphic, product, and architectural design could make to an organization. In 1936 he hired twenty-four-year-old Giovanni Pintori (1912–1998) to join the publicity department. For a thirty-one-year period, Pintori put his personal stamp on Olivetti's graphic images. The logotype he designed for Olivetti in 1947 consisted of the name in lowercase sans-serif letters, slightly letterspaced. Identity was achieved not through a systematic design program but through the general visual appearance of promotional graphics.

In a one of Pintori's more celebrated posters (Fig. **20–1**) Olivetti's mission is subtly implied by a collage created solely from numbers and the company logo. Pintori's ability to generate graphic metaphors for technological processes is shown in a 1956 poster for the Olivetti Elettrosumma 22 (Fig. **20–2**). There is a casual and almost relaxed quality to Pintori's organization of space. Even his most complex designs have a feeling of simplicity, because he is able to combine small elements into unified structures through a repetition of size and visual rhythms. This complexity of form was well suited to Olivetti's publicity needs during the 1940s and 1950s, for the firm sought a high-technology image to promote advanced industrial design and engineering. Pintori was particularly adept at using simplified graphic shapes to visualize mechanisms and processes (Fig. **20–3**). His abstract configurations suggest the function or purpose of the product being advertised. Olivetti received international recognition for its commitment to design excellence.

Design at CBS

The Columbia Broadcasting System (CBS) of New York City moved to the forefront of corporate identity design as a result of two vital assets: CBS president Frank Stanton (b. 1908), who understood art and design and their potential in corporate affairs, and William Golden (1911–59), CBS art director for almost two decades. Golden brought uncompromising visual standards and keen insight into the communications process. The effectiveness of the CBS corporate identity did not depend on a regimented design program or application of specific graphic elements, such as a single corporate typeface,

20–1

Olivetti Elettrosumma 22

20–2

olivetti
82 Diaspron

20–3

20–4

20–5

to all corporate communications. Rather, the quality and intelligence of each successive design solution enabled CBS to establish an ongoing and successful corporate identity.

Golden designed one of the most successful trademarks of the twentieth century for CBS (Fig. **20–4**). When the pictographic CBS eye first appeared as an on-air logo on 16 November 1951, it was superimposed over a cloud-filled sky and projected an almost surreal sense of an eye in the sky. After one year, Golden suggested to Frank Stanton that they might abandon the eye and seek another logo. Stanton reminded Golden of the old advertising adage, "Just when you're beginning to

get bored with what you have done is probably the time it is beginning to be noticed by your audience." The eye remained. In applying this trademark to the corporation's printed material, from shipping labels to press releases, care and concern were used in even the most modest graphic designs. Dogmatic consistency in how the CBS trademark was used was not considered necessary. It was used in print with a variety of different company signatures, and Golden and his staff avoided forcing it where it did not belong. Even in printed advertising, it was sometimes omitted if it conflicted with the rest of the design. The effectiveness of the CBS symbol demonstrated to the

20–6

20–1. Giovanni Pintori, Olivetti poster, 1949. Olivetti's products are suggested by a melange of numbers.

20–2. Giovanni Pintori, poster for the Olivetti Elettrosumma 22, 1956. An informal structure of cubes and numerals suggests the mathematical building process that takes place when this calculating machine is used.

20–3. Giovanni Pintori, poster for the Olivetti 82 Diaspron, c. 1958. A schematic diagram depicting a typewriter key's mechanical action combines with a photograph to communicate two levels of information.

20–4. William Golden, CBS Television trademark, 1951. Two circles and two arcs form a pictographic eye. Translucent and hovering in the sky, it symbolizes the awesome power of projected video images.

20–5. William Golden (designer) and Ben Shahn (illustrator), trade ad for CBS Television, 1957. Textured shopping carts and text type unify into a horizontal band. This tonal complexity contrasts with a bold headline in the white space above and the staccato repetition of the black wheels below.

20–6. Georg Olden, television title for I've Got A Secret, 1950s. The zippered mouth becomes an immediate and unequivocal symbolic statement.

larger management community that a contemporary graphic mark could compete successfully with more traditional illustrative or alphabetic trademarks.

A corporate philosophy and approach to advertising emerged in the late 1940s and early 1950s. Advertising was created not by an outside agency but by internal staff; this permitted CBS to maintain a unified approach to advertising and other graphics. Fine artists including Feliks Topolski, René Bouche, and Ben Shahn were commissioned to create illustrations for CBS advertisements. The climate of creative freedom encouraged them to accept these commissions and resulted in a high level of artistry

compared to typical newspaper and trade publication advertisements of the period. A classic example of this approach is "The Big Push" (Fig. 20–5), which appeared in business and advertising trade publications during a booming economy. The text says Americans will purchase more than in any other summer in history and recommends television advertising during this big summer sales push. Shahn's drawing adds an ambience of quality and distinction to the commercial message.

In a 1959 lecture at a design conference, Golden called upon designers to have a sense of responsibility and a rational understanding of the function of their work. He declared the word design a verb "in the sense that we design something to be communicated to someone," and added that the designer's primary function is ensuring that the message is accurately and adequately communicated.

Stanton's recognition of the importance of design helped designers gain executive and administrative authority. In 1951 Golden was named creative director in charge of advertising and sales promotion for the CBS Television Network.

In 1945 CBS hired Georg Olden (1920–75) to establish a graphics department to design on-air visuals for its new television division. Television was a fledgling medium poised to grow rapidly in the next few years. Only about ten thousand television sets were in use when wartime restrictions on their manufacture were lifted in 1946; this number grew rapidly to a million sets in 1949 and soared past the fifty-million mark when Olden left CBS to become television group art director at BBDO Advertising in 1960. During his fifteen-year tenure at CBS, Olden played a major role in defining the early development of television broadcast graphics.

Olden realized the limitations of early black-and-white television. The medium was incapable of differentiating between subtle color and tonal contrasts, and television sets often markedly cropped the edges of the signal. Two-dimensional titles were only on the air for a few seconds, requiring rapid viewer comprehension. To overcome these problems, he designed on-air graphics from the center out, using simple symbolic imagery with strong silhouettes and linear properties. Emphasis was placed on concepts that quickly captured the essence of each program using the connotative power of simple signs, symbols, and images (Fig. 20–6).

Olden, the grandson of a slave from a northern Kentucky plantation who escaped to the north as the Civil War broke out and eventually joined the Union army, was the first African American to achieve prominence as a graphic designer. He accomplished this in the era before the civil-rights movement, when very few blacks held professional positions in America. Another African American to achieve early prominence in graphic design, Reynolds Ruffins (b. 1930), was a founding partner in Push Pin Studios (see Fig. 21–17).

20–7

20–8

20–9

20–10

The United States Postal Service commissioned Olden to design the postage stamp for the hundredth anniversary of the Emancipation Proclamation (Fig. **20–7**), making him the first African-American designer to be accorded the honor of designing a United States postage stamp. This stamp design possesses the economy and directness of his television graphics.

Lou Dorfsman (b. 1918) became art director for CBS Radio in 1946. He combined conceptual clarity with a straightforward and provocative visual presentation (Fig. **20–8**). Typography and image were arranged in well-ordered relationships using blank space as a design element. In 1954 he was named director of advertising and promotion for the CBS Radio Network. As art director of the CBS Radio Network during the 1950s, Dorfsman forged a design approach combining a pragmatic sense of effective communication with imaginative problem solving. He did not advocate continuity in typefaces, spatial layouts, or imagery; rather, the high quality of his solutions to communications problems during his four decades with CBS enabled him to project an exemplary image for the corporation.

After Golden's sudden death at age forty-eight, Dorfsman became the creative director of CBS Television (Figs. **20–9** and

20–10). He was named director of design for the entire CBS Corporation in 1964 and vice president in 1968, in keeping with Stanton's philosophy that design is a vital area that should be managed by professionals.

When architect Eero Saarinen (1910–61) designed a new CBS headquarters building in 1966, Dorfsman designed all aspects of the typographic information, right down to the numerals on the wall clocks and elevator buttons, exit signs, and elevator-inspection certificates. Dorfsman also applied his graphic design sense to film, computer animation in the production of promotional spots, informational materials, and network title sequences.

The CBS approach to corporate image and design was not dependent on a system or style but rather on the management policy toward design and the creative abilities of its design personnel. The strength of this approach is a varying and dynamic corporate design that can shift with company needs and evolving sensibilities; the potential danger is the lack of a fallback position if management or design authority moves into less astute hands. CBS's era of design leadership lasted until the late 1980s. After new owners purchased the company, its philosophy on design changed and Dorfsman resigned.

20–12

20–11

20–7. Georg Olden, stamp for the centenary of the Emancipation Proclamation, 1963. Olden reduced a complex subject, slavery's end, to its most elemental expression.

20–8. Lou Dorfsman (designer) and Andy Warhol (illustrator), program ad for CBS Radio, 1951. The open, direct presentation is typical of Dorfsman's work.

20–9. Lou Dorfsman (designer) and Edward Sorel (illustrator), ad for CBS Reports, 1964. To overcome the graphic jungle of the American newspaper, Dorfsman's program ads were simple, arresting, and distinctive.

20–10. Lou Dorfsman, advertisement for a program series, 1968. The combination of images carried tremendous shock value, gaining viewers for important news programs.

20–11. Herbert Matter, New York, New Haven, and Hartford Railroad trademark, 1954. The mathematical harmony of parts demonstrates how alphabetic forms can be unified into a unique gestalt.

20–12. Herbert Matter, New York, New Haven, and Hartford Railroad trademark, 1954. Matter's trademark proved to be very adaptable when applied to heavy railroad equipment.

The New Haven Railroad design program

A short-lived but highly visible effort at corporate identity occurred in 1954, when Patrick McGinnis, president of the New York, New Haven, and Hartford Railroad, launched a corporate design program. The New Haven Railroad was in the midst of a technological updating, with new engines, cars, and signal systems. McGinnis believed a contemporary logo and design program replacing the old logotype and olive-green and Tuscan-red color scheme would enable the firm to project a modern and progressive image to industry and passengers. Herbert Matter was commissioned to design the new trademark. He developed a geometric capital *N* above an *H* and a red, black, and white color scheme (Figs. **20–11** and **20–12**). The traditional industrial feeling of slab-serif type, long associated with the railroad industry, was updated for a more modern look, based on the mathematical harmony of parts.

Marcel Breuer was commissioned to design the interiors and exteriors of the new trains. Using Matter's color scheme and logo, Breuer designed a passenger train that looked like a Russian constructivist painting roaring along the New Haven's

1,700 miles of track. The dingy gray and earth tones previously used for freight cars were replaced by solid red or black. Plans called for implementation of a comprehensive corporate-identity program encompassing everything from stations to matchbooks, but the commuter railroad developed financial problems and suffered from a consumer uprising against its late trains, poor scheduling, and rising fares. On 20 January 1956, McGinnis resigned as president, and the corporate-identity program came to an abrupt halt. However, the new management continued to apply the logo and color scheme whenever possible. Printed pieces designed by Matter offered a degree of guidance, and the strength of the logo and color scheme provided some semblance of continuity.

Norman Ives is one of the long neglected masters of corporate image design. His carefully constructed logos clearly reflect the teachings of one of his principal mentors, Josef Albers (Fig. **20–13**). In 1960 Ives described the designer's mission in logo design:

A symbol is an image of a company, an institution or on idea that should convey with a clear statement or

20–13

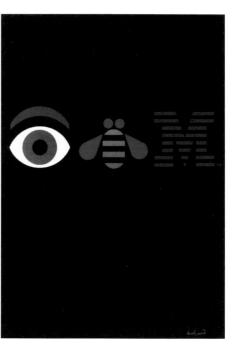

20–14

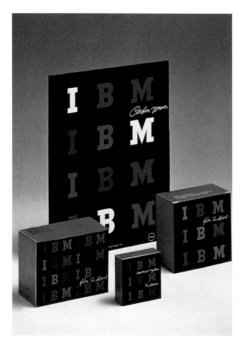

20–15

20–16

20–17

by suggestion, the activity it represents….The symbol, besides being memorable and legible, must be designed so that it can be used in many sizes and situations without losing its identity. The designer must distort, unify, and create a new form for the letter, so that it is unique, and yet has the necessary attributes of the letter for recognition. There is no part of a symbol that can be eliminated without destroying the image it creates. It is a true gestalt, in which the psychological effect of the total image is greater than the sum of its parts would indicate.

Corporate identification comes of age

While World War II left most industrial countries devastated, the manufacturing capacity of the United States escaped undamaged. An era of unprecedented industrial expansion

began, with large corporations playing an important role in developing and marketing products and services. During the 1950s and 1960s many American designers—including Rand, Beall, Bass, and design firms such as Lippincott & Margules and Chermayeff & Geismar—embraced corporate visual identification as a major design activity.

After playing a pivotal role in the evolution of American graphic and advertising design during the 1940s and early 1950s, Rand became more involved in trademark design and visual identification systems in the mid-1950s. Rand realized that to be functional over a long period of time, a trademark should be reduced to elementary shapes that are universal, visually unique, and stylistically timeless.

Rand's trademark for International Business Machines (Fig. **20–14**) was developed from an infrequently used typeface

20–13. Norman Ives, trademark for Eastern Press, New Haven, Connecticut, 1958. The influence of Joseph Albers is definitely evident in this logo.

20–14. Paul Rand, IBM trademark, 1956. The original design is shown with outline versions and the eight- and thirteen-stripe versions currently used.

20–15. Paul Rand, IBM package designs, late 1950s. A strong corporate identification was achieved through a repeating pattern of blue, green, and magenta capital letters on black package fronts, white handwritten product names, and blue package tops and sides.

20–16. Paul Rand, IBM package design, 1975. After two decades the original packaging design program was replaced by an updated design using the eight-stripe logo.

20–17. Paul Rand, "Eye Bee M" poster, 1981. Using the rebus principle, Rand designed this poster for the presentation of the Golden Circle award, an in-house IBM occasion. Although Rand eventually prevailed, it was temporarily banned, as it was felt that it would encourage IBM staff designers to take liberties with the IBM logo.

called City Medium, designed by Georg Trump in 1930. This geometric slab-serif typeface was designed along lines similar to Futura. Redesigned into the IBM corporate logo, it was transformed into a powerful and unique alphabet image, for the slab serifs and square negative spaces in the *B* lent the trademark unity and distinction. In the 1970s Rand updated the logo by introducing stripes to unify the three letterforms and evoke scan lines on video terminals. Package designs by Rand show the application of the logo in the 1950s (Fig. 20–15) and after its redesign in the 1970s (Fig. 20–16). Rand's 1981 "Eye Bee M" poster (Fig. 20–17) demonstrates that he was prepared to divert from the original logo when a design concept called for it.

Eliot Noyes (1910–77), IBM's consulting design director during the late 1950s, wrote that the IBM design program sought "to express the extremely advanced and up-to-date nature of its products. To this end we are not looking for a theme but for a consistency of design quality which will in effect become a kind of theme, but a very flexible one." The IBM design program was flexible enough to avoid stifling the creativity of designers working within the guidelines of the program. The model developed by IBM, with design consultants such as Rand and internal staff design departments whose managers have the authority to maintain the corporate visual identity, produced an evolving design program of consistently high quality.

After a 1959 study of the "public faces" of the Westinghouse Corporation, a decision was made to redesign its "Circle-W" trademark. Rand was commissioned to symbolically incor-

porate the nature of the company's business in a new mark that would be simple, memorable, and distinct (Fig. 20–18). General graphic forms, rather than specific signs or symbols, suggest Westinghouse products by evoking wires and plugs, electronic diagrams and circuitry, and molecular structures. Rand, who also developed a typeface for Westinghouse, applied these new elements to packaging, signage, and advertising.

Rand's 1965 redesign of the trademark for the American Broadcasting Company (Fig. 20–19) reduced the information to its essence while achieving a memorable and unique image. The NeXT computer logo (Fig. 20–20) was designed in 1986 after IBM agreed to loan its longtime design consultant to a competitive computer company. The black box at a twenty-eight-degree angle signified the NeXT computer, which itself looked like a black box.

The annual report to stockholders, a legal publication required by federal law, evolved from a dry financial report into a major communications instrument during the postwar period. Landmarks in this evolution include the IBM annual reports designed by Rand during the late 1950s. The 1958 IBM annual report (Fig. 20–21) established a standard for corporate literature. Imagery included close-up photography of electronic components that almost became abstract patterns, and simple dramatic photographs of products and people.

Beall helped launch the modern movement in American design during the late 1920s and early 1930s. During the last two decades of his career, he created pioneering corporate-identity programs for many corporations, including Martin Marietta, Connecticut General Life Insurance, and International Paper Company. He also contributed to the development of the corporate-identity manual, a firm's book of guidelines and standards for implementing its program. Beall's manuals specifically prescribed the permissible uses and forbidden abuses of the trademark. If a plant manager in a small town retained a sign painter to paint the trademark and name on a sign, for example, the corporate design manual specified their exact proportions and placement. In discussing his mark for International Paper Company, one of the largest paper manufacturers in the world, Beall wrote,

> Our assignment was to provide management with a strong mark that could be readily adapted to an immense variety of applications. This ranged from its bold use on the barks of trees to its intricate involvement in repeat patterns, carton designs, labels, and trucks. In addition to its functional strength, the new mark is a powerful force in stimulating and integrating divisional and corporate identity with positive psychological effects on human relations. (Figs. 20–22 and 20–23)

The International Paper Company trademark was initially controversial: The letters *I* and *P* are distorted to make a tree

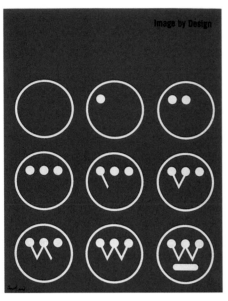

20–18

20–19

20–20

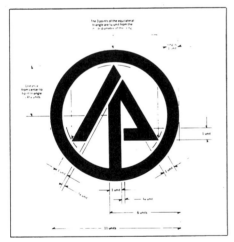

20–22

20–23

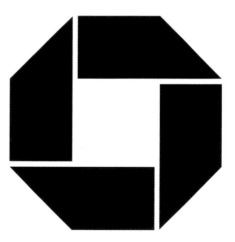

20–24

symbol, and critics questioned whether letterforms should be altered to this extreme. The continuing viability of this mark since its inception indicates that Beall's critics were overly cautious.

Chermayeff & Geismar Associates moved to the forefront of the corporate-identity movement in 1960 with a comprehensive visual image program for the Chase Manhattan Bank of New York. Chase Manhattan's new logo was composed of four geometric wedges rotating around a central square to form an external octagon (Fig. **20–24**). It was an abstract form unto itself, free from alphabetic, pictographic, or figurative connotations. Although it had overtones of security or protection because four elements confined the square, it proved a completely abstract form could successfully function as a large organization's visual identifier.

A distinctive sans-serif typeface was designed for use with the logo. The selection of an expanded letter grew out of the firm's study of the bank's design and communications needs. Urban signage, for instance, is often seen by pedestrians at extreme angles, but an extended letterform retains its character recognition even when viewed under these conditions. The uncommon presence of the expanded sans-serif type in this design system launched a fashion for this kind of letterform during the first half of the 1960s. Consistency and uniformity in the application of both logo and letterform enabled redundancy, in a sense, to become a third identifying element.

The Chase Manhattan Bank corporate identification system became a prototype for the genre. Other financial institutions seriously evaluated their corporate image and the need for an

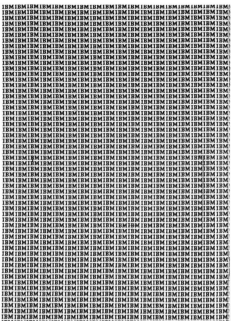

20–21

20–18. Paul Rand, Westinghouse trademark, 1960. This mark is shown as it might be constructed in an animated film sequence.

20–19. Paul Rand, American Broadcasting Company trademark, 1965. The continuing legacy of the Bauhaus and Herbert Bayer's universal alphabet informs this trademark, in which each letterform is reduced to its most elemental configuration.

20–20. Paul Rand, NeXT trademark, 1986. The four-letter name is separated into two lines to startle the viewer by giving a common word an uncommon image.

20–21. Paul Rand, IBM annual report, 1958. Advanced technology and organizational efficiency were expressed through design.

20–22. Lester Beall, International Paper Company trademark, 1960. Initials, tree, and upward arrow combine in a mark whose fundamental simplicity—an isometric triangle in a circle—assures a timeless harmony.

20–23. Lester Beall, International Paper Company trademark, 1960. For a forest products company, stenciling trees is one of numerous applications that must be considered.

20–24. Chermayeff & Geismar Associates, Chase Manhattan Bank corporate identity program, 1960. Consistent use of the mark, color, and typeface built recognition value through visual redundancy.

20–25

20–27

20–26

20–29

20–30

20–25. Chermayeff & Geismar Associates, Mobil Oil trademark, 1964.

20–26. Chermayeff & Geismar Associates, trademarks for (left to right, top row to bottom) the American Film Institute, 1964; Time Warner, 1990; the American Revolution Bicentennial, 1971; Screen Gems, 1966; Burlington Industries, 1965; the National Broadcasting Company, 1986; Rockefeller Center, 1985; and the National Aquarium in Baltimore, 1979.

20–27. Saul Bass & Associates, trademark for Minolta, 1980.

20–28. Saul Bass & Associates, AT&T computer graphics animation identification tag, 1984. A spinning globe gathers electronic bits of information, then transforms into the AT&T trademark.

20–29. Muriel Cooper, MIT Press logo, 1963. Vertical lines imply books and can be read as *mitp.*

20–30. Muriel Cooper, *Bauhaus,* book by Hans Wingler, 1969.

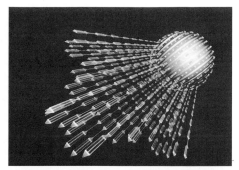
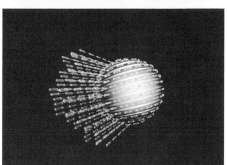

20–28

effective visual identifier. The recognition value gained by the Chase Manhattan mark indicated that a successful logo could, in effect, become an additional character in the inventory of symbolic forms carried in each person's mind. Tom Geismar observed that a symbol must be memorable and have "some barb to it that will make it stick in your mind." At the same time it must be "attractive, pleasant, and appropriate. The challenge is to combine all those things into something simple."

One of Chermayeff & Geismar's most far-reaching corporate design programs was for Mobil Oil, a multinational corporation operating in more than a hundred countries. Executed in an elemental geometric sans-serif typeface, the Mobil Oil trademark is the ultimate in simplicity (Fig. **20–25**). The name *Mobil* is executed in five vertical strokes, the diagonals of the *M,* and two circles. The name became the trademark, with the round, red *O* separating it from the visual presentation of other words.

Chermayeff & Geismar has produced more than one hundred corporate design programs, including the trademarks illustrated in Figure **20–26**. The firm continues to accept a steady stream of smaller projects, such as posters, requiring immediate, innovative solutions. Rather than maintaining design consistency from project to project, the company allows each solution to evolve from its problem.

Bass's mastery of elemental form can be seen in the iconic and widely imitated trademarks produced by his firm Saul Bass & Associates, later renamed Saul Bass/Herb Yeager & Associates. Bass believed a trademark must be readily understood yet possess elements of metaphor and ambiguity that will attract

the viewer again and again. Many Bass trademarks, such as the mark for Minolta, became important cultural icons (Fig. **20–27**). Within two years after Bass redesigned the Bell Telephone System bell trademark, public recognition of the symbol rose from 71 to more than 90 percent. After the AT&T long-distance telephone network was split from the local Bell system telephone companies in 1984, Bass designed a new mark to reposition the firm as "a global communications company" rather than "the national telephone system," with information bits circling the globe. This concept was expressed by making computer-graphics animation the identification tag for AT&T television commercials (Fig. **20–28**).

Muriel Cooper (1925–94) had two careers—the first as a print designer for MIT publications and books, and the second as founder and director of the VLW, Visible Language Workshop. From her student years at Massachusetts College of Art, she was fascinated with animation and pushing the border between the static medium of print and the x, y, z axis of the computer screen. In 1963 she designed the MIT Press logo, a series of vertical lines suggesting half a dozen books on a shelf, and spelling out a gestalt *M I T* (Fig. **20–29**).

Cooper designed more than 500 books, including the seminal 1969 *Bauhaus*, by Hans Wingler, perhaps her best known design (Fig. **20–30**). This was the first complete Bauhaus book in English. After the enthusiastic reception of the first authoritative text of its kind in English, Cooper made a film version of the thick *Bauhaus,* a speed-reading version of what one design historian has dubbed the King James Version. It was Cooper's pursuit of dynamic media that led to the 1978

20–31

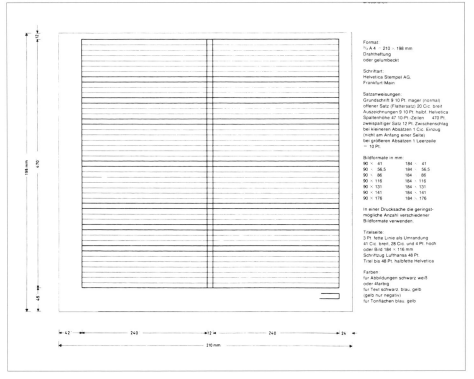

20–32

20–33

20–31. Otl Aicher in collaboration with Tomás Gonda, Fritz Querengässer, and Nick Roericht, pages from the Lufthansa identity manual, 1962. All typographic details were rigorously specified.

20–32. Otl Aicher in collaboration with Tomás Gonda, Fritz Querengässer, and Nick Roericht, page from the Lufthansa identity manual, 1962. The supercargo double trademark gains unity through consistent line weight.

20–33. Otl Aicher in collaboration with Tomás Gonda, Fritz Querengässer, and Nick Roericht, page from the Lufthansa identity manual, 1962. Carefully constructed grid formats regulated all publication formats.

20–34. Otl Aicher in collaboration with Tomás Gonda, Fritz Querengässer, and Nick Roericht, aircraft identification from the Lufthansa identity manual, 1962. Color and insignia are standardized.

20–35. Ralph Eckerstrom, trademark for Container Corporation of America, 1957. A flat image becomes an isometric optical illusion, signifying packaging while provoking visual interest.

founding of the VLW at MIT, which she said was an attempt to recreate the atmosphere of Paris in the 1920s. In the VLW, where workstations were in the open, Cooper encouraged her interdisciplinary graduate students to formulate good questions rather than pat answers.

While most graphic designers were limited to off-the-shelf software, Cooper's work was accelerated by powerful beta site computers at MIT that allowed her to create almost anything she could imagine. She was the first graphic designer to employ such new electronic media as 3-D text, which allowed vast amounts of complex data to be read in context, the top layer sharp, the layers below successively lighter. In this way

she was able to combine the traditional x-y axis of the flat screen with the z axis of depth, but she did not stop there. Trusting her designer's eye, she pushed her programmers for additional tools—color, transparency, and eventually type that could pulse and move. Her goal, until her untimely death in 1994, was to move graphic design from form to content; to be able to create clear, compelling communication that could be plucked and digested from an ocean of print and the electronic sea of the World Wide Web. Cooper was also a founding member of the MIT Media Lab (1985), perhaps the most advanced new graduate research program on new media in the world.

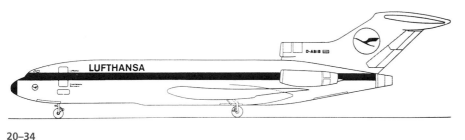

20–34

20–35

Programmed visual identification systems

During the 1960s, the impetus of the International Typographic Style and the visual-identity movement joined with the development of highly systematic design programs to combine complex and diverse parts into a unified whole. The 1962 Lufthansa German Airlines identification system was conceived and produced at the Ulm Institute of Design. The principles of the International Typographic Style were extended into a design program addressing all visual-communication and product-design needs of a large corporation. This program was designed by Otl Aicher in collaboration with Tomás Gonda (1926–88), Fritz Querengässer, and Nick Roericht. Aicher believed a large organization could achieve a uniform, and thus significant, corporate image by systematically controlling the use of constant elements. A flying crane trademark used since the 1930s was retained but enclosed in a circle and subordinated to the name *Lufthansa* in a consistent letterspacing arrangement (Fig. **20–31**). The air-freight service combined the crane icon with an isometric package and bold lines to create an arrow configuration (Fig. **20–32**).

Paper formats were standardized, making the production of printed matter more economical. Grid systems (Fig. **20–33**) and detailed typographic specifications were worked out to take into account every visual communications need from food service packaging to timetables and aircraft identification. A blue-and-yellow color scheme was applied throughout. Uniforms, packaging, the character of photographs to be used in ads and posters, and aircraft interiors and exteriors (Fig. **20–34**) were all addressed by this extensive system. The Lufthansa corporate-identity program became an international prototype for the closed identity system, with every detail and specification addressed for absolute uniformity.

The Container Corporation of America (CCA) became an early advocate of systematic corporate identity in the 1960s. A new corporate logo (Fig. **20–35**) was created by design director Ralph Eckerstrom (c. 1920–96) and his staff. The corporate initials were packaged in a rectangle with two corners shaved at a forty-five-degree angle to imply an isometric box. Eckerstrom stated the requirements of a corporate identification program: "As a function of management, design must be an integrated part of overall company operation and directly related to the company's business and sales activities. It must have continuity as a creative force. It must reflect total corporate character. Unless it meets these requirements, the company image it seeks to create will never coalesce into a unified whole, but will remain a mosaic of unrelated fragments."

The "Great Ideas of Western Man" advertising campaign had varied widely in its typographic approaches during the 1950s; now it entered a two-decade period of typographic continuity. In 1964 CCA established the Center for Advanced Research in Design, an independent design studio that worked on advanced and experimental projects and received commissions from other organizations. The center developed a comprehensive visual identification system for Atlantic Richfield, a major petroleum products company whose name later changed to Arco. CCA was purchased by Mobil Oil in 1976, then sold to the Jefferson Smurfit company in 1986. Decentralized and lacking an autonomous identity, CCA's era as a design patron drifted to a close.

Unimark, an international design firm that grew to 402 employees in 48 design offices around the world, was founded in Chicago in 1965 by a group of partners including Ralph Eckerstrom, James K. Fogleman, and Massimo Vignelli (b. 1931). Unimark rejected individualistic design and believed that design could be a system, a basic structure set up so that other people could implement it effectively. The basic tool for this effort was the grid, standardizing all graphic communications for dozens of large Unimark clients, including Alcoa, Ford Motor Company, JCPenney, Memorex, Panasonic, Steelcase, and Xerox. Helvetica was the preferred typeface for all Unimark visual identity systems, as it was considered the most legible type family. Objectivity was Unimark's goal as it spread a generic conformity across the face of multinational corporate communications. The design programs it created

20–36

were rational and so rigorously systematized that they became virtually foolproof as long as the standards were maintained.

The graphic excellence of Unimark design programs can be seen in the Knoll program (Fig. **20–36**), directed by Massimo Vignelli, who was Unimark's director of design and head of the New York office. This program set the standard for furniture-industry graphics for years to come. But Unimark's far-flung design empire—with offices in major North American cities, England, Australia, Italy, and South Africa—proved vulnerable to the effects of recession in the early 1970s, and a retrenchment process began.

The Unimark philosophy continued as its founders and the legion of designers they trained continued to implement its ideals. When the New York office closed, Vignelli Associates was founded by Massimo and Leila Vignelli in 1971. Their typographic range expanded beyond Helvetica to include such classical faces as Bodoni, Century, Garamond, and Times Roman, but the rational order of grid systems and emphasis on lucid and objective communication remained a constant. Vignelli continues to put his imprint on the evolution of information design.

The Federal Design Improvement Program

In May 1974 the United States government initiated the Federal Design Improvement Program in response to a growing awareness that design could be an effective tool for achieving objectives. This initiative was coordinated by the Architectural and Environmental Arts Program (later renamed the Design Arts Program) of the National Endowment for the Arts. All aspects of federal design, including architecture, interior space planning, landscaping, and graphic design, were upgraded under the program. The Graphics Improvement Program, under the direction of Jerome Perlmutter, set out to improve the quality of visual communications and the ability of government agencies to communicate effectively to citizens.

The prototype federal graphic standards system was designed by John Massey for the Department of Labor. Problems identified by this case study included outmoded, unresponsive, and impersonal images, a lack of uniform and effective communications policies, and insufficient image continuity. Massey's goals for the new design program were "uniformity of identification; a standard of quality; a more systematic and economic template for publication design; a closer

20–37

20–38

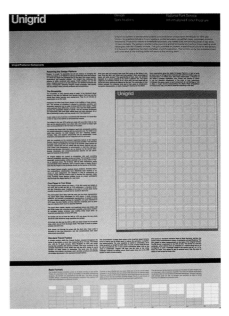

20–39

relationship between graphic design (as a means) and program development (as an end) so that the proposed graphics system will become an effective tool in assisting the department to achieve program objectives."

A graphic standards manual established a cohesive system for visual identification and publication formats. Standards for format sizes, typography, grid systems, paper specifications, and colors realized tremendous economies in material and time. These standards, however, were carefully structured so that the creativity and responsiveness to each communications project would not be seriously hampered. With the mechanics of the printing and format predetermined, Department of Labor staff designers were able to devote their time to the creative aspects of the problem at hand.

The Department of Labor communications mark (Fig. 20–37) is composed of two interlocking *L*s that form a diamond configuration around a star. A set of publication format sizes provided economy of production and minimized paper waste, while a series of grid systems and uniform typographic specifications ensured consistency (Fig. 20–38). Routine printed materials, including stationery, envelopes, and forms, were given standardized formats.

Over forty federal departments and agencies initiated visual identification programs, and many of the leading designers in America were called upon to develop them. One of the most successful is the Unigrid system, developed in 1977 for the United States National Park Service by Vignelli Associates in collaboration with the Park Service Division of Publications, headed by Vincent Gleason.

20–36. Massimo Vignelli and the Unimark New York office staff, Knoll Graphics, 1966–1970s. Knoll is renowned for furniture design, so the graphic program signified a strong design orientation.

20–37. John Massey, trademark for the U.S. Department of Labor, 1974. Stripes on the *L* forms suggest the American flag's stars and stripes.

20–38. John Massey, typographic cover format from the U.S. Department of Labor graphic standards manual, 1974. Standardized formats bring economy and efficiency to the design process.

20–39. Massimo Vignelli (consulting designer), Vincent Gleason (art director), and Dennis McLaughlin (graphic designer), Unigrid system for the National Park Service, 1977. Design specifications for the Unigrid system and standard formats are presented on a large broadside.

The Unigrid (Figs. 20–39 and 20–40) unified the hundreds of informational folders used at about 350 national park locations. It is based on simple basic elements: ten format sizes, all derived from the Unigrid; broadside or full-sheet presentation of the folders, instead of layouts structured on folded panels; black title bands with park names serving as logotypes; horizontal organization of illustrations, maps, and text; standardized typographic specifications; and a master grid coordinating design in the studio with production at the printing plant. Typography is restricted to Helvetica and Times Roman in a limited number of sizes and weights.

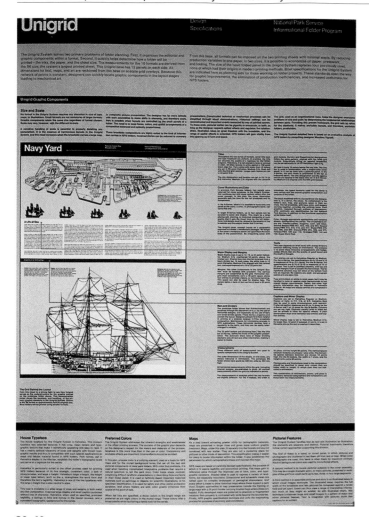

20–40

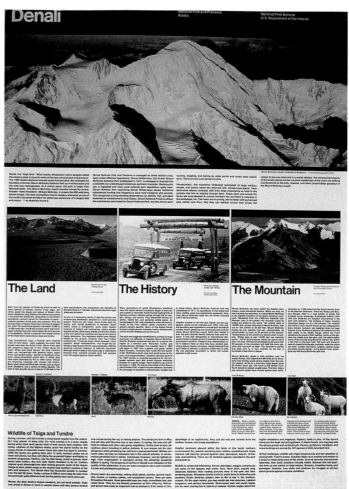

20–41

The standardized format of the Unigrid enables the Park Service publications staff to focus on achieving excellence in the development and presentation of pictorial and typographic information (Fig. **20–41**). The program proved so successful that a format was also developed for the Park Service's series of 150 handbooks.

To attract outstanding architects and designers to government service, traditional civil service procedures were supplemented by portfolio reviews conducted by professionals. Designers were recruited by a publicity campaign with the theme "Excellence attracts excellence." However, by 1980 momentum for federal design excellence became a casualty of tax cuts and huge federal deficits. Many established design programs for such agencies as the Park Service were maintained, while others sank back toward mediocrity.

Transportation signage symbols

Major international events, large airports, and other transportation facilities handling international travelers have commissioned graphic designers to create pictographic signage programs to communicate important information and direc-

tions quickly and simply. The development of these sign-and-symbol systems involved considerable time and expense, and near duplication of effort often occurred. In 1974 the United States Department of Transportation commissioned the American Institute of Graphic Arts (AIGA), the nation's oldest professional graphic design organization, to create a master set of thirty-four passenger and pedestrian-oriented symbols for use in transportation facilities. The goal was a consistent and interrelated group of symbols for worldwide transportation facilities meant to bridge language barriers and simplify basic messages.

The first step was the compilation and inventory of symbol systems developed for individual transportation facilities and international events (Fig. **20–42**). A committee of five prominent graphic designers, headed by Thomas H. Geismar, acted as evaluators and advisers on the project. The Department of Transportation provided the AIGA with a list of message areas. Prior solutions to the thirty-four subject areas were evaluated by each member of the advisory committee, and a summary recommendation was prepared to guide the design of the symbol system. Some existing symbols were retained, while in

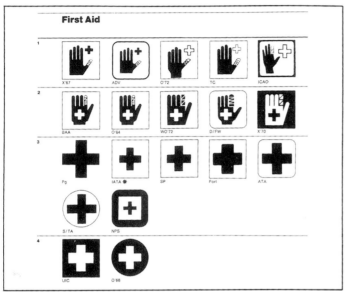

20–42

20–43

other categories totally new glyphs were developed with clarity of image their overriding goal. The final set of symbols (Fig. **20–43**) was designed and drawn by Roger Cook (b. 1930) and Don Shanosky (b. 1937) of Cook and Shanosky Associates in Princeton, New Jersey. These signs combined overall harmony with a visual consistency of line, shape, weight, and form. This effort represented an important first step toward the goal of unified and effective graphic communications transcending cultural and language barriers in a shrinking world. A 288-page book published by the Department of Transportation provided invaluable information about the design and evaluation process used to arrive at the system.

Design systems for the Olympic Games

By the late 1960s the concept of comprehensive design systems had become a reality. Planners realized that comprehensive planning for large organizations and events was not only functional and desirable but necessary. This was particularly true in the case of international events, including world's fairs and Olympic Games, where an international and multilingual audience had to be directed and informed. Among many out-

20–40. Massimo Vignelli (consulting designer), Vincent Gleason (art director), and Dennis McLaughlin (graphic designer), Unigrid system for the National Park Service, 1977. The reverse side of Figure 20–39 demonstrates and specifies all graphic components on a sample broadside.

20–41. National Park Service publication staff, including Vincent Gleason (chief), and designers Melissa Cronyn, Nicholas Kirilloff, Dennis McLaughlin, Linda Meyers, Phillip Musselwhite, and Mitchell Zetlin, publication created with the Unigrid, 1977–90.

20–42. Various artists/designers, nineteen first aid symbols from various systems throughout the world. Semantic, syntactic, and pragmatic values of existing programs were evaluated.

20–43. Roger Cook and Don Shanosky, signage symbol system for the U.S. Department of Transportation, 1974. This poster introduced the thirty-four symbols to a wide audience.

standing efforts, the design programs for the 1968 Mexico City Nineteenth Olympiad, the 1972 Munich Twentieth Olympiad, and the 1984 Los Angeles Twenty-Third Olympiad were milestones in the evolution of graphic systems.

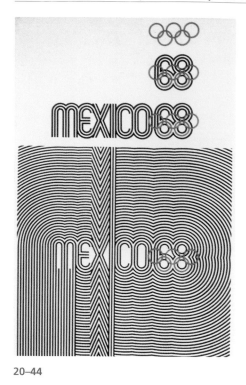

20–44

20–45

20–46

20–47

20–48

A theme—"The young of the world united in friendship through understanding"—was adopted by the organizing committee of the Nineteenth Olympiad, chaired by Mexican architect Pedro Ramirez Vazquez. Realizing that an effective information system encompassing environmental directions, visual identification, and publicity was needed, Vazquez assembled an international design team, with American Lance Wyman (b. 1937) as director of graphic design and British industrial designer Peter Murdoch (b. 1940) as director of special products.

Because the Nineteenth Olympiad took place in and around Mexico City itself, rather than in a special location built for the purpose, the design system had to be deployed throughout one of the world's largest cities. Traffic control, urban logistics, and a multilingual audience compounded the challenge. Wyman's initial analysis of the problem determined that the solution should reflect the cultural heritage of Mexico. An exhaustive study of ancient Aztec artifacts and Mexican folk art led him to employ two design ideas: the use

20–44. Lance Wyman, logo for the Nineteenth Olympiad, 1966. This sequence shows the development of the logo and how it was extended into a dynamic animated film.

20–45. Lance Wyman, alphabet for the Nineteenth Olympiad, 1967. Composed of five bands or ribbons, the alphabet echoes design motifs from early Mexican folk arts.

20–46. Lance Wyman, Eduardo Terrazas, and Manuel Villazon, sports symbols for the Nineteenth Olympiad, 1967. Sports equipment pictographs permitted immediate identification by an international audience.

20–47. Lance Wyman and Eduardo Terrazas, cultural symbols for the Nineteenth Olympiad, 1967. The cultural events expressed as pictographs are a Youth Reception, Film Festival, Youth Camp, World Art Exhibition, Music and Performing Arts Festival, Sculptors' Conference, Poets' Reunion, Children's Art Festival, Folklore Festival, Ballet, Folk Arts Festival, Olympic Flame, Stamp Exhibit, Olympiad History Exhibition, Nuclear Energy Exhibition, Space Research Exhibition, Human Genetics and Biology, Olympiad Facilities Exhibition, Advertising in Service of Peace, and Films of Olympiad Games.

20–48. Lance Wyman, Mexican Olympiad postage stamps, 1967–68. Silhouetted athletes are printed over brilliant color backgrounds. The images were designed to flow from stamp to stamp in a continuous design.

of repeated multiple lines to form patterns and the use of bright, pure hues. Throughout the country, arts and crafts, adobe homes, paper flowers, marketplaces, and clothing sang with joyous, pure color, and this exuberant color spirit figured prominently in Wyman's planning.

Designing a logotype for the Olympiad (Fig. **20–44**) formed a basis for the further evolution of the design program. The five rings of the Olympiad symbol were overlapped and merged with the numeral 68 and then combined with the word Mexico. The repeated-stripe pattern observed in traditional Mexican art was used to form the letters. Following development of the logotype, Wyman extended it into a display typeface (Fig. **20–45**) that could be applied to a range of graphics, from tickets to billboards and from uniform patches to giant color-coded balloons hovering over the arenas. The system encompassed pictographic symbols for athletic (Fig. **20–46**) and cultural (Fig. **20–47**) events, formats for the Department of Publications, site identification, directional signs for implementation by the Department of Urban Design throughout the city, informational posters, maps, postage stamps (Fig. **20–48**), film titles, and television spots.

For the exterior environmental signage, Wyman and Murdoch collaborated on the development of a complete system of modular functional components with interchangeable parts (Fig. **20–49**). These combined directional and identifica-

tion signage with pictures of objects such as mailboxes, telephones, and water fountains. This design system was so effective that the *New York Times* proclaimed, "You can be illiterate in all languages and still navigate the surroundings successfully, so long as you are not color-blind."

Wyman's goal was to create a completely unified design system easily understood by people of all language backgrounds and flexible enough to meet a vast range of applications. Measured in terms of graphic originality, innovative functional application, and its value to thousands of visitors to the Mexican Olympiad, the graphic design system developed by Wyman and his associates in Mexico was one of the most successful in the evolution of visual identification. After completing the two-year Olympiad project, Wyman returned to New York City and reestablished his design firm, where the expertise gained on the Mexican project has been applied to comprehensive design programs for shopping plazas and zoos.

For the 1972 Twentieth Olympiad in Munich, Germany, Otl Aicher directed a design team in the development and implementation of a more formal and systematized design program. An identification manual (Fig. **20–50**) established standards for use of the event's symbol, a radiant sunburst/spiral configuration centered beneath the Olympic rings and bracketed by two vertical lines. Univers was selected as the typeface, and a system of publication grids was established. The color palette consisted of a partial spectrum composed of two blues, two greens, yellow, orange, and three neutral tones (black, white, and a middle-valued gray). Excluding one segment of the spectrum in this way created harmony and projected a festive air.

An extensive series of pictographs was drawn on a modular square grid divided by horizontal, vertical, and diagonal lines (Fig. **20–51**). For each Olympic sport a pictograph was designed (Fig. **20–52**) that emphasized the motion of the athletes and their equipment. Immediate identification was achieved in spite of language barriers. These pictographs were widely used in printed graphics (Fig. **20–53**) and identification signs. The geometry of the pictographs served as a counterpoint to another level of imagery: high-contrast photographs of athletes used on publications (Fig. **20–54**) and a series of twenty-two commemorative posters depicting major Olympic sports. These used the modified-spectrum palette of four cool and two warm colors. The track-events poster (Fig. **20–55**), for example, defines the track and runners in the lighter green and two shades of blue against a dark-green field.

The 1984 Los Angeles Twenty-Third Olympiad saw a sprawling city transformed into a joyous environment of color and shape that unified twenty-eight athletic sites, forty-two cultural locations, and three Olympic Villages for housing athletes. Hundreds of designers and architects working for more

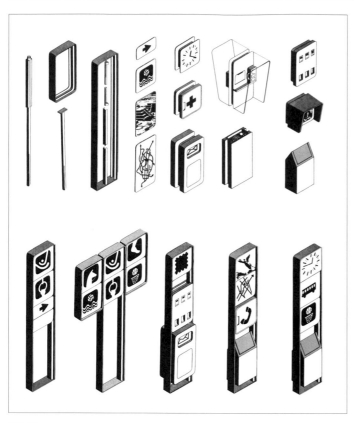

20–49

20–49. Peter Murdoch, preliminary studies for the Mexican Olympiad signage and facilities, 1968. Modular components were assembled into units throughout the city.

20–50. Otl Aicher and his staff, Munich Olympiad graphics standards manual pages, c. 1970. Every detail of the graphics program was determined.

20–51. Otl Aicher, grid for the Munich Olympiad pictographs, c. 1972. The complexity of the grid permitted an infinite range of permutations.

20–52. Otl Aicher and his staff, sports pictographs for the Munich Olympiad, c. 1970.

20–53. Otl Aicher and his staff, informational graphics for the Munich Olympiad, 1972. Pictographs function as signifiers and illustrations.

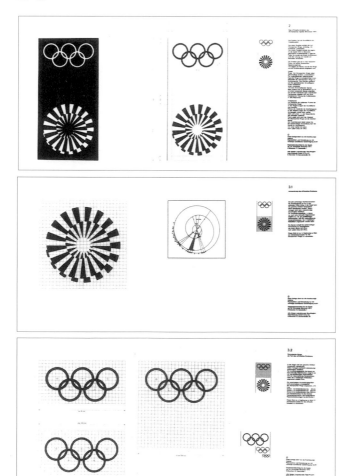

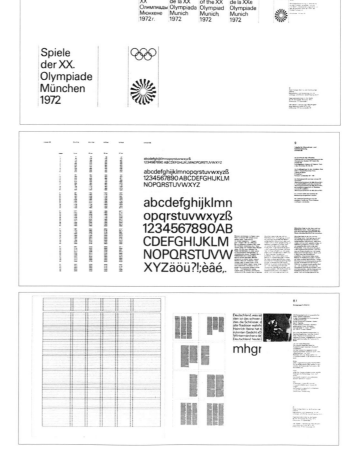

20–50

20–51

20–52

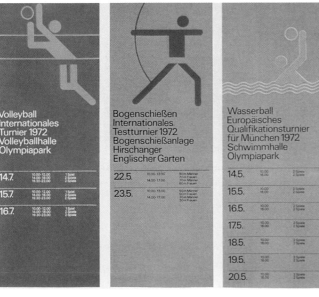

20–53

than sixty design firms were involved. Continuing the practice of combining a symbol specifically designed for this edition of the Olympics with the traditional linked rings, the Los Angeles Olympic Organizing Committee selected a dynamic star-in-motion configuration (Fig. **20–56**) in a 1980 competition among leading Los Angeles design firms.

Lacking the huge government subsidies of many earlier Olympic games, the organizing committee decided to use twenty-six existing athletic facilities, adding only one new swimming pool and a cycling track. The design problem was well defined: how to temporarily transform these far-flung facilities to create a unified celebratory feeling, express the international character of the games, and invent a designed environment that would work effectively both on site and for the global television audience. For help in addressing these challenges, the organizing committee called on two design firms to spearhead the effort. An architectural firm, the Jerde Partnership, directed by Jon Jerde (b. 1940) and David Meckel, collaborated with an environmental and graphic design firm, Sussman/Prejza & Co., headed by Deborah Sussman (b. 1931) and Paul Prejza, in planning the visual vocabulary—architecture, color, graphics, and signage—for this massive event.

A "parts kit" was assembled to provide a uniform idiom for designing components and environments. Forms were simple and basic. Sonotube columns, normally used as molds for casting concrete columns but used here as columns themselves, were decorated with colorful painted stripes. The sonotubes were lined up to make colonnades, combined with rented tents to make colorful pavilions, or topped with flat graphic pediments echoing the forms of earlier Olympiads. A poster-size design guide (Fig. **20–57**) was produced to provide all participants with consistent parameters for using the parts kit. Gateways and monumental towers were built from aqua-and-magenta scaffolding and punctuated with ornaments and banners.

Sussman selected a bright, vibrant palette with hot magenta as the basic color. Its primary supporting palette consisted of vivid aqua, chrome yellow, and vermilion. A secondary palette included yellow, green, lavender, and light blue, with violet, blue, and pink accents. Graphic forms were derived from the stars and stripes of the American flag combined with the stripes of the star-in-motion logo. These elements were freely pulled apart, recreated in the dazzling color palette, and combined in a layering of stripes—light against dark, thick against thin, and warm against cool. The program was infinitely adaptable, while adherence to the color palette, stripe-and-star motif, and approach to spatial organization permitted diverse materials (Fig. **20–58**) to evoke the Los Angeles Olympics.

These graphic themes were used extensively on entryways and sports arenas, providing a dynamic backdrop for events

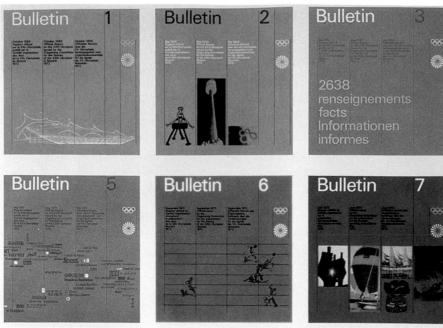

20–54

20–55

20–58

20–54. Otl Aicher and his staff, covers for the *Munich Olympiad Bulletin,* 1971. An inventive variety is achieved with a consistent format. In number six, the grid becomes part of the illustration.

20–55. Otl Aicher and his staff, poster for the Munich Olympiad, 1972. Each poster had a wide expanse of one dominant color as a ground for a posterized photograph of athletic competition.

20–56. Jim Berté (designer) and Robert Miles Runyan (art director), symbol for the games of the Los Angeles Olympiad, 1980. The "star in-motion" is generated by three weights of horizontal lines.

20–57. Debra Valencia (designer) and Deborah Sussman (art director), design guide for the Los Angeles Olympiad, 1983. The design parameters allow diversity within a fixed range of possibilities.

20–58. Deborah Sussman, *Design Quarterly* cover, 1985. This periodical cover captures the graphic resonance created for the Los Angeles Olympiad.

20–59. The Jerde Partnership, Sussman/Prejza & Co., and Daniel Benjamin, entrance to the Los Angeles Olympiad swimming competition venue, 1984.

20–60. Sussman/Prejza & Co., identification signage for the Los Angeles Olympiad, 1984. Color and decorative shapes transformed information graphics into a part of the celebration.

telecast around the globe to millions of viewers. Each sports arena was transformed with its own color combinations and visual motifs developed from the design guidelines. Entryways to the sporting events became festive colonnades (Fig. 20–59).

The informational signage system (Fig. 20–60) was consistent yet flexible. Staff uniforms, street banners, and food packaging extended the graphic theme to all aspects of the event. Scores of designers and design firms produced Olympic graphics and environments conforming to the design guide developed by the principal design firms. In a sense, graphics helped restore the Olympics as an international celebration after terrorist activities (1972) and political boycotts (1980, 1984) had tainted the games.

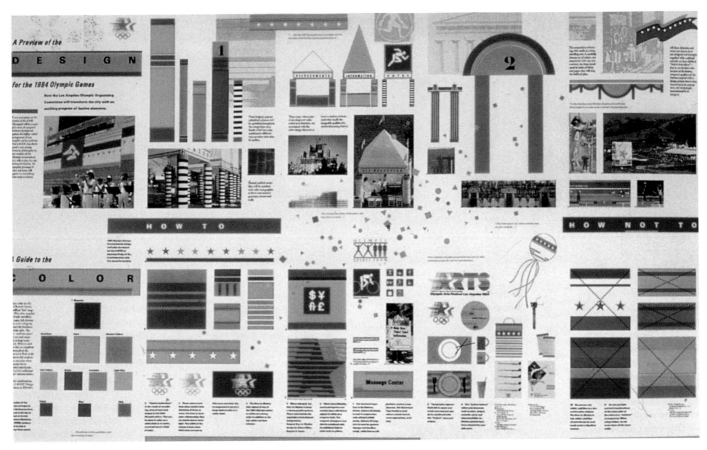

20–57

20–59

20–56

20–60

20–61

20–62

The Music Television logo

Music Television (MTV) first went on the air in 1981. Media visionary Bob Pittman initiated the idea of a round-the-clock music television station at a time when music videos had not yet reached full flower as a creative medium and only eighteen million American households subscribed to cable television. The fledgling network commissioned a logo design from Manhattan Design, a New York City studio noted for its independent, risk-taking experimentation, especially for music-industry clients. Partners Pat Gorman (b. 1947), Frank Olinsky (b. 1950), and Patti Rogoff (b. 1945) all had fine-arts backgrounds; in addition, each had a bold, iconoclastic approach gained from an interest in comic-book art. Olinsky's father was an animator and illustrator, while Gorman's father was an actor. Gorman spent hours growing up in studios, playing with equipment, so television became her native language.

During the design process, Gorman felt Olinsky's sketch of a bold, three-dimensional sans-serif *M* needed further development, so she scrawled a large, graffiti-like *tv* on its face, creating a memorable and influential trademark (Fig. **20–61**).

A moment of insight occurred when the designers realized the logo, with the broad flat surface of the *M* and the vigorous *tv*, could through infinite variations of color, decoration,

material, dimensionality, viewing angle, and motion (Figs. **20–62**, **20–63**, and **20–64**). The logo could assume different personalities, participate in animated events, and be demolished. The concept of a logo with a constantly changing persona runs contrary to the widely held belief that trademarks and visual identifiers should be absolutely fixed and used in a consistent manner. Once this concept was decided upon, Manhattan Design produced hundreds of sketches to show possible variations.

During the network's early years, the MTV logo appeared as a ten-second network identification spot at the top of each hour. Manhattan Design, MTV internal staff, and several animation studios storyboarded an unending stream of ten-second identification spots and quick station tags. The constant creation of new identification sequences led to an ongoing collaboration involving animation, illustration, photography, and direct manipulation of the video medium.

Gorman observed that the MTV logo "changed the *face*, the *idea*, and the *speed* of graphic design"; it played a major role in redefining visual identity in the electronic age. During the 1980s print graphics began to reflect the influence of television in the use of color, texture, decorative graphic elements, and sequence.

20–63

20–64

The MTV logo was a harbinger of the world of motion graphics that would soon open up as cable television, video games, and computer graphics expanded the variety and range of kinetic graphic messages. On 8 September 1996, the *New York Times* observed, "The move of information from the printed page to other media has changed the nature of graphic identity. The MTV logo, which emerges from an unexpected metamorphosis, is probably the ultimate in animated identity." By 1995 MTV was reaching more than 250 million homes in 58 countries, and this logo's worldwide recognition factor was second only to that of Coca-Cola.

In the last half of the twentieth century, visual identity gained increased importance as the world entered the information age. Complex international events, large governmental entities, and multinational corporations required complex design systems developed by graphic designers to manage information flow and visual identity. While accomplishing these pragmatic goals, design systems can also create a spirit or resonance, helping to express and define the very nature of the large organization or event. The identity of a large organization can be created or redefined by design.

20–61. Manhattan Design, MTV logo, 1981.

20–62. Pat Gorman and Frank Olinsky of Manhattan Design (design) and Broadcast Arts (fabrication), MTV "taxi" logo, 1981. As a dimensional object, the logo appears in limitless guises and environments.

20–63. Pat Gorman and Frank Olinsky of Manhattan Design, MTV "Colorforms" logo, 1985. Random patterns of geometric shapes convey a playful resonance.

20–64. Pat Gorman and Frank Olinsky of Manhattan Design, MTV "puzzle" logo, 1985. The logo is assembled, dismantled, melted, and shattered without losing its ability to verify identity.

The Conceptual Image

21

Sensing that traditional narrative illustration did not address the needs of the times, post–World War I graphic designers reinvented the communicative image to express the age of the machine and advanced visual ideas. In a similar quest for new imagery, the decades after World War II saw the development of the conceptual image in graphic design. Images conveyed not merely narrative information but ideas and concepts. Mental content joined perceived content as motif. The illustrator interpreting a writer's text yielded to the graphic imagist making a statement. A new breed of image-maker was concerned with the total design of the space and the integration of word and image. In the exploding information culture of the second half of the twentieth century, the entire history of visual arts was available to the graphic artist as a library of potential forms and images. In particular, inspiration was gained from the advances of twentieth-century art movements: the spatial configurations of cubism; the juxtapositions, dislocations, and scale changes of surrealism; the pure color loosened from natural reference by expressionism and fauvism; and the recycling of mass-media images by pop art. Graphic artists had greater opportunity for self-expression, created more personal images, and pioneered individual styles and techniques. The traditional boundaries between the fine arts and public visual communications became blurred.

The creation of conceptual images became a significant design approach in Poland, the United States, Germany, and even Cuba. It also cropped up around the world in the work of individuals whose search for relevant and effective images in the post–World War II era led them toward the conceptual image. In the most original work of the Italian graphic designer Armando Testa (1917–92), for example, metaphysical combinations were used to convey elemental truths about the subject. Testa was an abstract painter until after the war, when he established a graphic design studio in his native Turin. His 1950s publicity campaigns for Pirelli tires had an international impact on graphic design thinking (Fig. **21–1**). Testa borrowed the vocabulary of surrealism by combining the image of a tire with immediately recognizable symbols. In his posters and advertisements, the image is the primary means of communication, and he reduces the verbal content to a few words or just the product name. Testa effectively used more subtle contradictions, such as images made of artificial materials (Fig. **21–2**), as a means of injecting unexpected elements into graphic design.

The Polish poster

The violence of World War II swept over Europe on 1 September 1939 with Hitler's lightning invasion of Poland from the north, south, and west without a declaration of war. Seventeen days later, Soviet troops invaded Poland from the east, and a six-year period of devastation followed. Poland emerged from the war with enormous population losses, its industry devastated, and its agriculture in ruins. The capital city of Warsaw was almost completely eradicated. Printing and graphic design, like so many aspects of Polish society and culture, virtually ceased to exist. It is a monumental tribute to the resilience of the human spirit that an internationally renowned Polish school of poster art emerged from this devastation.

In the communist society established in Poland after the war, the clients were state-controlled institutions and industry. Graphic designers joined filmmakers, writers, and fine artists in the Polish Union of Artists, which established standards and set fees. Entry into the union came after completion of the educational program at either the Warsaw or the Krakow Academy of Art. Entry standards for these schools were rigorous, and the number of graduates was carefully controlled to equal the need for design.

The first Polish poster artist to emerge after the war was Tadeusz Trepkowski (1914–56). In the first decade after the devastation, Trepkowski expressed the tragic memories and aspirations for the future that were deeply fixed in the national psyche. His approach involved reducing the imagery and words until the content was distilled into its simplest statement. In his famous 1953 antiwar poster (Fig. **21–3**), Trepkowski used a few simple shapes to symbolize a devastated city, superimposed on a silhouette of a falling bomb.

Henryk Tomaszewski (1914–2005) became the spiritual head of Polish graphic design after Trepkowski's early death

21–1   21–2   21–3

and became an important impetus for the movement from his position as professor at the Warsaw Academy of Fine Arts. The poster became a source of great national pride in Poland; its role in the cultural life of the nation is unique. Electronic broadcasting lacked the frequency and diversity of Western media, and the din of economic competition was less pronounced in a communist country. Therefore, posters for cultural events, the circus, movies, and politics served as important communications. In 1964 the Warsaw International Poster Biennial began, and Muzeum Plakatu—a museum devoted exclusively to the art of the poster—was established in Wilanow, near Warsaw.

The Polish poster began to receive international attention during the 1950s. Tomaszewski led the trend toward developing an aesthetically pleasing approach, escaping from the somber world of tragedy and remembrance into a bright, decorative world of color and shape (Fig. **21–4** and Fig. **21–5**). In an almost casual collage approach, designs were created from torn and cut pieces of colored paper, then printed by the silkscreen process. Typical of this style is the film poster for *Rzeczpospolita Babska* (Fig. **21–6**) by Jerzy Flisak (b. 1930). The symbolic female figure has a pink, doll-like head with round, rouged cheeks and a heart-shaped mouth. The circus poster has flourished as a lighthearted expression of the magic and charm of this traditional entertainment since 1962, when concern about mediocre circus publicity inspired a juried program to select a dozen circus posters per year for publication by the Graphic Arts Publishers in Warsaw. The word *cyrk*

21–1. Armando Testa, poster for Pirelli, 1954. The strength of a bull elephant is bestowed on the tire by the surrealist technique of image combination.

21–2. Armando Testa, rubber and plastics exhibition poster, 1972. A hand made of synthetic materials holds a plastic ball in a distinctive and appropriate image for this trade exhibition.

21–3. Tadeusz Trepkowski, antiwar poster, 1953. A passionate statement is reduced to just one word, *No!*

(circus) is the only type or lettering on each poster (Fig. **21–7**). Printed strips with typographic information giving full particulars for the specific engagement were pasted under the poster image on kiosks and walls.

The next major trend in Polish posters started to evolve during the 1960s and reached a crescendo in the 1970s. This was a tendency toward the metaphysical and surrealism, as a darker, more somber side of the national character was addressed. It has been speculated that this represented either a subtle reaction to the social constraints of the dictatorial regime or a despair and yearning for the autonomy that has so often been denied the Polish nation during its history. One of the first graphic designers to incorporate this new metaphysical sensitivity into his work was Franciszek Starowiejski (b. 1930). In his 1962 poster for the Warsaw Drama Theater, a serpent hovers in space, coiling around two circles that

21–4

21–5

21–6

21–7

21–8

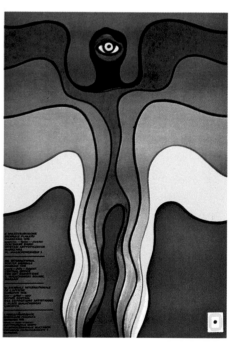

21–9

become shaking hands (Fig. **21–8**). This enigmatic image was a harbinger of things to come in Starowiejski's work, which sometimes tends toward the slime-and-gore school of graphics, and in the work of a number of other Polish graphic designers. Jan Lenica (b. 1928–2001) pushed the collage style toward a more menacing and surreal communication in posters and experimental animated films. Then, during the mid-1960s, he began using flowing, stylized contour lines that weave through the space and divide it into colored zones that form an image (Fig. **21–9** and **21–10**).

Lenica and Starowiejski were joined in their break from the mainstream by several others of the emerging generation who realized that the Polish poster was in danger of fossilizing into an academic national style. This potential pitfall has been

21–10

21–11

21–12

avoided, as designers including Waldemar Swierzy (b. 1931) have arrived at unique personal visions. Approaching graphic design from a painterly viewpoint, Swierzy draws on folk art and twentieth-century fine art for inspiration (Fig. **21–11**). This prolific artist has created more than a thousand posters in a wide variety of media. He often incorporates acrylics, crayon, pencil, and watercolor into designs. In his famous poster for the American rock musician Jimi Hendrix (Fig. **21–12**), Swierzy animated the large portrait with swirling energetic gestures. The spontaneous quality of much of his work is deceptive, for Swierzy sometimes devotes three weeks to a poster and might even execute a poster five or more times before being satisfied with the results.

An exiled Polish poster artist, Roman Cieslewicz (1930–96) lived in Paris from the 1960s on. Closely associated with the Polish avant-garde theater, Cieslewicz took the poster, a public art form, and transformed it into a metaphysical medium to express profound ideas that would be difficult to articulate verbally (Fig. **21–13**). Cieslewicz's techniques include enlarging collage, montage, and halftone images to a scale that turns the dots into texture, setting up an interplay between two levels of information: the image and the dots that create it (Fig. **21–14**).

In 1980 shortages of food, electricity, and housing led to strikes and the formation of the illegal Solidarity labor union, whose logo (Fig. **21–15**), designed by Jerzy Janiszewski, became an international symbol of struggle against oppression. As a result of government censorship during Poland's social unrest, the country's posters frequently addressed issues ranging

21–4. Henry K. Tomaszewski, football poster for the Olympic Games in London, 1948

21–5. Henry K. Tomaszewski, poster for the play *Marie and Napoleon,* 1964. Tomaszewski led Polish graphic design toward colorful and artistic expression.

21–6. Jerzy Flisak, cinema poster for *Rzeczpospolita Babska,* undated. Bright colors and informal shapes convey the delightful resonance of the 1950s Polish poster.

21–7. Roman Cieslewicz, circus poster, 1962. Collage elements superimpose the word Cyrk and a clown on a high-contrast photograph of an elephant.

21–8. Franciszek Starowiejski, Warsaw Drama Theater poster, 1962. The cube drawn in perspective transforms the flat page into deep space, forcing the strange complex above it to float.

21–9. Jan Lenica, Warsaw Poster Biennale poster, 1976. Meandering arabesques metamorphose into a winged being.

21–10. Jan Lenica, poster for Alban Berg's *Wozzeck,* 1964. As with many of Lenica's posters, the spirit of art nouveau is evident.

21–11. Waldemar Swierzy, *Ulica Hanby* poster, 1959. The painterly lettering becomes an extension of the lipstick.

21–12. Waldemar Swierzy, Jimi Hendrix poster, 1974. The electric vitality of gestural strokes on the cobalt blue portrait suggests the vigorous energy of hard rock music.

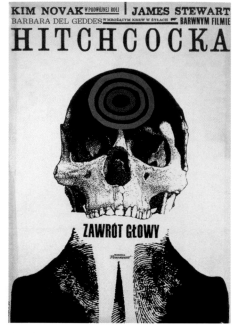

21–13   21–14   21–16

21–15

21–13. Roman Cieslewicz, poster for *Vertigo,* 1963. A target on the forehead of a skull, also alluding to the film's title, is combined with a fingerprint in this enigmatic interpretation of the Polish version of Hitchcock's film.

21–14. Roman Cieslewicz, Krackow Temporary Theater poster, 1974. With this surreal image, the viewer may try to complete the portrait by seeking an image in the clouds, but the effort will prove fruitless.

21–15. Jerzy Janiszewski, Solidarity logo, c. 1980. Crude letterforms evoke street graffiti, and the crowded letters are a metaphor for people standing solidly together in the street.

21–16. Marian Nowinski, political poster, 1979. A book bearing the name of Chilean poet Pablo Neruda, whose works were banned and burned by the Pinochet regime, is closed by large metal spikes.

21–17. Reynolds Ruffins, illustration for *Amtrak Express* magazine, 1983. Decorative color and abstracted forms typify Ruffins's work over a half century.

21–18. Milton Glaser, record album cover for *The Sound of Harlem,* 1964. In this early example of Glaser's contour line and flat color period, the figures are weightless shapes flowing in musical rhythm.

beyond its boundaries rather than internal political struggles such as the banning of Solidarity. An international issue is the subject of a poster by Marian Nowinski (b. 1944) eloquently (Fig. **21–16**) lamenting censorship and the suppression of Chilean poet Pablo Neruda. For many viewers it also expresses solidarity with the Chilean struggle for democracy and independence. Powerful images such as this transcend their immediate subject matter to become universal statements about censorship and the suppression of ideas everywhere.

The legalization of Solidarity and its overwhelming victory in the May 1989 elections ended one-party communist rule and marked the beginning of a new era in Polish history. For half a century, the Polish poster developed as a result of a conscious decision by the government to sanction and support poster art as a major form of expression and communication. The posters were creative statements trafficking in ideas rather than commodities. Despite political changes, a tradition of excellence bolstered by strong design education may ensure a continuing poster art form in Poland. Inventiveness is already being demonstrated by younger graphic designers entering the profession.

American conceptual images

During the 1950s the golden age of American illustration was drawing to a close. For over fifty years narrative illustration had ruled American graphic design, but improvements in paper, printing, and photography caused the illustrator's edge over the photographer to recede rapidly. Traditionally, illustrators had exaggerated value contrasts, intensified color, and

21–17

21–18

made edges and details sharper than life to create more convincing images than photography. But now, improvements in materials and processes enabled photography to expand its range of lighting conditions and image fidelity. The death of illustration was somberly predicted as photography made rapid inroads into the profession's traditional market. But as photography stole illustration's traditional function, a new approach to illustration emerged.

This more conceptual approach to illustration began with a group of young New York graphic artists. Art students Seymour Chwast (b. 1931), Milton Glaser (b. 1929), Reynolds Ruffins (b. 1930), and Edward Sorel (b. 1929) banded together and shared a loft studio. On graduation from Cooper Union in 1951, Glaser received a Fulbright scholarship to study etching under Giorgio Morandi in Italy, and the other three friends found employment in New York advertising and publishing. Freelance assignments were solicited through a joint publication called the *Push Pin Almanack*. Published bimonthly, it featured interesting editorial material from old almanacs illustrated by the group. When Glaser returned from Europe in August 1954, the Push Pin Studio was formed. Ruffins left the studio after a time and became a prominent decorative and children's book illustrator (Fig. **21–17**). In 1958 Sorel started freelancing, and he later emerged as one of the major political satirists of his generation. Glaser and Chwast continued their partnership for two decades; then Glaser left to pursue a wide range of interests, including magazine, corporate, and environmental design. Chwast remains as director of the renamed Pushpin Group. The *Push Pin Almanack* became the *Push Pin*

Graphic, and this experimental magazine provided a forum for presenting new ideas, imagery, and techniques.

Push Pin Studio artists' philosophies and personal visions attained global influence. Graphic design has often been fragmented into separate tasks of image making and layout or design. Like turn-of-the-century graphic designers Mucha and Bradley, Glaser and Chwast united these components into a total communication conveying the individual vision of the creator, who was also involved in the total conception and design of the printed page. Using art and graphic history from Renaissance paintings to comic books as a data bank of form, images, and visual ideas, Push Pin artists freely paraphrased and incorporated a multiplicity of ideas into their work, often reshaping these eclectic sources into new and unexpected forms.

Glaser's singular genius is hard to categorize, for over the course of several decades he "reinvented himself as a creative force" by exploring new graphic techniques and motifs. During the 1960s he created images using flat shapes formed by thin, black-ink contour lines, adding color by applying adhesive color films (Fig. **21–18**). This almost schematic drawing style echoed the simple iconography of comic books, the flowing curvilinear drawing of Persian and art nouveau arabesques, the flat color of Japanese prints and Matisse cutouts, and the dynamic of contemporary pop art. As with other graphic designers whose work captured and expressed the sensibilities of their times, Glaser was widely imitated. Only his ability to maintain a steady stream of innovative conceptual solutions, along with his restless exploration of different techniques, prevented him from being consumed by his followers.

21–19

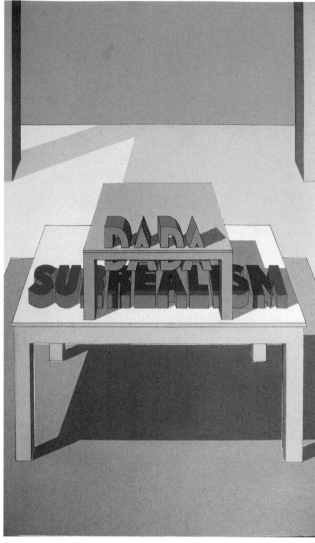

21–20

While the images described above are formed by the edge, another approach developed by Glaser evolved from the mass. Inspired in the late 1950s by oriental calligraphic brush drawing and Picasso aquatints, Glaser began making gestured silhouette wash drawings that tease by only suggesting the subject, requiring the viewer to fill in the details from his or her own imagination.

Glaser's concert posters and record-album designs manifest a singular ability to combine his personal vision with the essence of the content. Glaser's 1967 image of the popular folk-rock singer Bob Dylan (Fig. **21–19**) is presented as a black silhouette with brightly colored hair patterns inspired by art nouveau sources. Nearly six million copies of the poster were produced for inclusion in a best-selling record album. As did Flagg's Uncle Sam poster, it became a graphic icon in the collective American experience. A photographer told Glaser about being on assignment on the Amazon River and seeing the Dylan poster in a hut at a remote Indian village.

In a rejected poster design for the Museum of Modern Art's Dada and surrealism exhibition, the words themselves take on a metaphysical afterlife as objects (Fig. **21–20**). "Dada" is impaled through the tabletop to hover over its wayward offspring, "surrealism." Like the art movements it represents, this design defies rational interpretation. Glaser often assimilates spatial devices and imagery from surrealism to express complex concepts (Fig. **21–21**).

During the 1980s and 1990s Glaser became increasingly interested in illusions and dimensionality. His drawings from this time are presented as dimensional objects in ways that intensify their meaning (Fig. **21–22**). For Glaser, geometric forms, words, and numbers are not merely abstract signs but tangible entities with an object-life that allows them to be interpreted as motifs, just as figures and inanimate objects are interpreted by an artist. In very personal works, the dialogue between perceptual and conceptual iconography is explored (Fig. **21–23**).

21–21

21–22

21–23

Chwast's vision is very personal, yet communicates on a universal level. He frequently uses the technique of line drawings overlaid with adhesive color films and experiments with a large variety of media and substrata. Echoes of children's art, primitive art, folk art, expressionist woodcuts, and comic books appear in his imaginative reinventions of the world. Chwast's color is frontal and intense. In contrast to Glaser's spatial depth, in Chwast's work, an absolute flatness is usually maintained. Chwast's innocent vision, love of Victorian and figurative letterforms, and ability to integrate figurative and alphabetic information has enabled him to produce unexpected design solutions. His album cover for *The Threepenny Opera* (Fig. **21–24**) demonstrates his ability to synthesize diverse resources—-the German expressionist woodcut, surreal spatial dislocations, and dynamic color found in primitive art—into an appropriate expression of the subject. In his 1965 moving announcement for Elektra Productions (Fig. **21–25**), each letter in the word lumbers across the space, endowed with its own form of transportation. From antiwar protest (Fig. **21–26**) to food packaging and magazine covers, Chwast has reformulated earlier art and graphics to express new concepts in new contexts.

Both Chwast and Glaser developed a number of novelty display typefaces. Often these began as lettering for assignments, then were developed into full alphabets. Figure **21–27** shows the logo Chwast developed for Artone Ink; the graded version of Blimp, based on old woodtypes; a geometric face inspired by the logo Glaser designed for a film studio; a typeface based on lettering first developed for a *Mademoiselle* poster; and the

21–19. Milton Glaser, Bob Dylan poster, 1967. Transcending subject and function, this image became a symbolic crystallization of its time.

21–20. Milton Glaser, Dada and Surrealism exhibition poster, 1968. The smaller table isolates the word *real* within the longer word *surrealism*.

21–21. Milton Glaser, Poppy Records poster, 1968. A poppy blooming from a granite cube symbolizes a new, independent company breaking through the monolithic conventions of the recording industry.

21–22. Milton Glaser, "Bach Variations" poster, 1985. A variety of drawing approaches signifies the diversity of Bach's musical oeuvre.

21–23. Milton Glaser, "Art Is" poster, 1996. Visual and verbal meanings are explored by manifesting a hat as a photograph, a shadow, a word, a pictograph, and a written definition.

Buffalo typeface, originally devised for a French product named Buffalo Gum, which was never produced.

The term *Push Pin style* became widely used for the studio's work and influence, which spread around the world. The studio hired other designers and illustrators in addition to Glaser and Chwast, and a number of these younger individuals, who worked for the studio and then moved on to freelance or to other positions, extended the boundaries of the Push Pin aesthetic. The Push Pin approach is less a set of visual conventions, or a unity of visual techniques or images, than it is an attitude

21–24

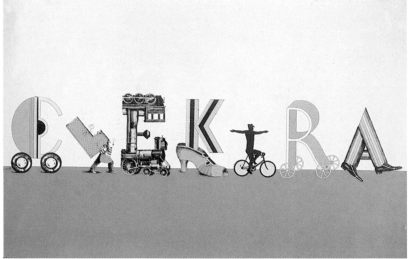

21–25

End Bad Breath.

21–26

21–27

21–28

about visual communications, an openness about trying new forms and techniques as well as reinterpreting work from earlier periods, and an ability to integrate word and image into a conceptual and decorative whole.

An influential young graphic designer in the late 1960s and early 1970s, Barry Zaid (b. 1939), joined Push Pin for a few years during this period. A Canadian who majored first in architecture and then in English during college before becoming a self-taught graphic designer and illustrator, Zaid worked in Toronto and then London before joining Push Pin Studio. As a graphic archeologist basing his work on

a thorough study of the graphic vernacular of bygone eras, Zaid became an important force in the revivalism and historicism that were prevalent in graphic design during this period. He was particularly prominent in the revival of 1920s art deco decorative geometric forms (Figs. **21–28** and **21–29**), including the cover of the 1970 book *Art Deco* by English art historian Bevis Hillier. Zaid's historicism did not merely mimic nostalgic forms, for his spatial organization, scale, and color were of his own time.

Among the other illustrators and designers who passed through Push Pin Studio, James McMullan (b. 1934) revived

21–29

watercolor, a medium that had declined from a position second only to oil paint for fine art and illustration, and restored it as a means of graphic expression. McMullan achieved prominence during the 1960s with energetic ink-line and watercolor illustrations that often combined multiple images with significant changes in spatial depth and image size and scale. Moving into the 1970s, McMullan's watercolor technique became increasingly masterly, and he developed a photo-documentary approach emphasizing sharp detail and realism. At the same time, however, a concern for total design asserted itself, and McMullan began to make fluid lettering an important part of his images. In his 1977 poster for Eugene O'Neill's play *Anna Christie* (Fig. **21–30**), the intimate portrayal of a figure sitting in an interior is superimposed on an ocean scene. The dual image combines to communicate the locale of the play while creating an engaging spatial interplay.

Another Push Pin alumnus who moved toward a total design approach is Paul Davis (b. 1938), who first appeared in the *Push Pin Graphic* with a series of primitive figures painted on rough wood panels with superimposed targets. From this beginning Davis moved toward a painting style of minute detail that drew inspiration from primitive colonial American art. He evolved into a master of meticulous naturalism; the solid shapes of his forms project a convincing weight and volume. Like McMullan, Davis often became involved in a painterly integration of image and words. His work demonstrates enormous inventiveness in relating sensitive portraits to environmental backgrounds and expressive lettering (Fig. **21–31**).

The Push Pin school of graphic illustration and design presented an alternative to the narrative illustration of the past, the mathematical and objective typographic and photographic orientation of the International Typographic Style, and the formal concerns of the New York School. Warm, friendly, and accessible, Push Pin designs project vitality with lush color and unashamed allusions to other art. Although not formally associated with the Push Pin Studio, graphic designer Richard Hess (1934–91) turned to illustration and developed a painting technique closely related to the work of Paul Davis. Hess had a stronger inclination toward surrealism than Davis and was inspired by René Magritte's spatial illusions. An understanding of the folklore and imagery of nineteenth-century America enabled Hess to produce a number of images that thoroughly captured the essence of this earlier period (Fig. **21–32**).

21–30

21–31

The Push Pin group did not maintain a monopoly on the conceptual image in America, for a number of autonomous designers forged individual approaches to communications problem solving while combining the traditional conceptualization and layout role of the graphic designer with the image-making role of the illustrator. One such person, Arnold Varga (1926–94), practically reinvented the retail newspaper advertisement. Varga entered the field in 1946. Beginning in the mid-1950s, his newspaper advertisements for two Pittsburgh department stores, Joseph P. Horne & Co. and Cox's, turned this usually pedestrian form of visual design into memorable image-building communications. Many of Varga's ads used carefully integrated white space and headlines with large, simple illustrations to break through the monotonous gray of the newspaper page. A multiple-image picture-and-caption approach, such as the gourmet shop advertisement for Joseph P. Horne (Fig. **21–33**), achieved notable public response—people actually offered to buy this advertisement to hang on their walls!

21–32

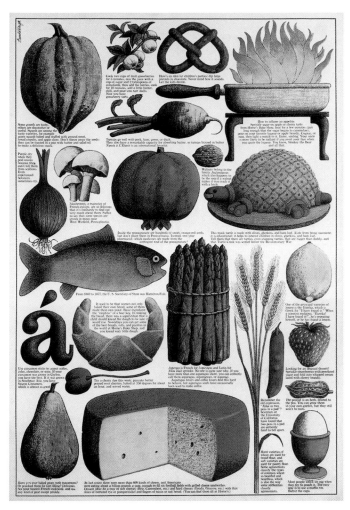

21–33

21–34

Conceptual image making is not the exclusive province of the illustrator. Designers such as Paul Rand, Lou Danziger, Herbert Leupin, and Raymond Savignac incorporated the technique of creating a central image to communicate visual ideas by combining two symbols together to create a "fused image." This was a means of combining form and content to create memorable images for book covers, posters, and advertisements.

Paul Rand's cover design for *Modern Art in Your Life* (Fig. **21–34**) uses a common household place setting and artists'

21–30. James McMullan, *Anna Christie* poster, 1977. McMullan often calls attention to the physical properties of the medium; the red background changes into painterly strokes, then becomes lettering.

21–31. Paul Davis, poster for *For Colored Girls,* 1976. The urban environment is evoked by a graffiti-like title and subway-mosaic theater identification.

21–32. Henrietta Condak (art director) and Richard Hess (illustrator), album cover for *Charles Ives: The 100th Anniversary,* 1974. A complex Victorian poster format frames many images from the composer's time.

21–33. Arnold Varga, newspaper advertisement for Joseph P. Horne, c. 1966. The joys of food and cooking are conveyed. (Reproduced from a proof not showing the Horne logo and text at the bottom of the page.)

21–34, Paul Rand, *Modern Art in Your Life* cover design, 1949. With this MoMA publication Rand makes modern art seem as accessible as a daily meal. As Steven Heller aptly stated in his superb biography of Rand, published in 1999, "Rand's jackets and covers were both mini canvases and mini posters. He composed the limited image area for maximum impact."

21–35

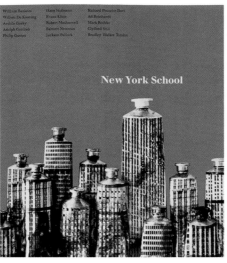

21–36

21–37

21–38

21–39

21–40

tools as a visual metaphor to communicate with wit and reinforce the content of the title. Lou Danziger uses the American flag and an artist's paint brush (Fig. **21–35**) to create a memorable image for American painting at the Metropolitan Museum of Art. Paint tubes turn into skyscrapers (Fig. **21–36**), becoming a cover for *The New York School: The First Generation*. Herbert Leupin's poster advertisement for the *Tribune de Lausanne* (Fig. **21–37**) combines the newspaper with the coffee pot to suggest timely news every morning. The French poster artist Raymond Savignac (b. 1907–2002)

creates a humorous advertising poster for Gitanes by using cigarettes as confetti and alternating both shape and color (Fig. **23–38**) to help communicate the idea of night and day.

Designers and art directors call on the entire range of image-making possibilities to convey concepts and ideas. This is particularly true of graphic designers working in the music recording industry. Art and music share a common idiom of expression and experience. The same words (rhythm, texture, tone, color, and resonance) are used to convey the perceptual and spiritual dimensions of both visual and auditory experiences.

21–41

21–42

21–35. Lou Danziger, "American Paintings from the Metropolitan Museum of Art" poster, 1966.

21–36. Lou Danziger, "New York School, The First Generation" poster, 1966.

21–37. Herbert Leupin, poster for *Tribune de Lausanne*, 1955.

21–38. Raymond Savignac, poster for Gitanes, 1954.

21–39. John Berg, record album cover for the *William Tell Overture*, 1963. In "the new advertising," complex visual organization was replaced by the simple presentation of a concept.

21–40. John Berg (art director) and Virginia Team (designer), record album cover for the Byrds' *Byrdmaniax*, 1971. An enigmatic image transcends normal portraiture as masklike faces emerge from an oily fluid.

21–41. Woody Pirtle, logo for Mr. and Mrs. Aubrey Hair, 1975. In this graphic pun, the comb relates to the client's name, which is spelled by the comb's teeth.

21–42. Woody Pirtle, poster for Knoll furniture, 1982. A hot pepper becomes a red and green chair, signifying the availability of Knoll's "hot" furniture in Texas.

The design staff of CBS Records operated at the forefront of the graphic interpretation of music. Conceptual image making emerged as a significant direction in album design during the early 1960s, after Bob Cato (1923–1999) became head of the creative services department and hired John Berg (b. 1932), who served as art director at CBS's Columbia Records until 1984. Photographs of musicians performing and portraits of composers yielded to more symbolic and conceptual images, as in Berg's New York Philharmonic *William Tell Overture* album (Fig. **21–39**). For two decades Berg and his staff wrested the maximum potential from the large 961-square-centimeter (150-square-inch) format of vinyl long-play records that preceded compact-disk technology. The art director became a conceptualizer and collaborator, working with illustrators and photographers to realize imaginative expressions for the spectrum of musical experience. The fantastic,

the real, and the surreal joined the classical and outrageous in Columbia Records' graphic repertoire (Fig. **21–40**).

Illustrative, conceptual images and the influence of Push Pin Studios often mingled with Wild West, Mexican, and Native American motifs and colors in a regional school of graphic design that emerged in Texas during the 1970s and became a major force in the 1980s. A high level of aesthetic awareness, an open friendliness, and a strong sense of humor characterize graphic design from the Lone Star State. Intuitive approaches to problem solving combine with a pragmatic emphasis on content. Texas designers acknowledge the importance of Stan Richards (b. 1932), head of the Richards Group in Dallas, as a catalytic figure in the emergence of their state as a major design center. The work of Woody Pirtle (b. 1943), one of many major Texas designers who worked for Richards during their formative years, epitomizes the originality of Texas graphics. His logo for Mr. and Mrs. Aubrey Hair (Fig. **21–41**) evidences an unexpected wit, while his Knoll "hot seat" poster (Fig. **21–42**) ironically combines the clean Helvetica type and generous white space of modernism with regional iconography. In 1988 Pirtle moved on to join the Manhattan office of the British design studio Pentagram.

The 1980s saw graphic design in the United States become a truly national profession. Outstanding practitioners emerged all around the country, often far from the traditional centers. *Print* magazine, the American graphic design periodical founded in 1940, instituted a regional design annual in 1981 to reflect the emerging national scope of the discipline.

21–43

21–44

21–45

The poster mania

In contrast to postwar Polish posters, which were patronized by government agencies as a national cultural form, the poster craze in the United States during the 1960s was a grassroots affair fostered by a climate of social activism. The civil rights movement, the public protest against the Vietnam War, the early stirrings of the women's liberation movement, and a search for alternative lifestyles figured into the social upheavals of the decade. Posters of the period were hung on apartment walls more frequently than they were posted in the streets. These posters made statements about social viewpoints rather than spreading commercial messages. The first wave of poster culture emerged from the late1960s hippie subculture centered in the Haight-Ashbury section of San Francisco. Because the media and general public related these posters to antiestablishment values, rock music, and psychedelic drugs, they were called *psychedelic posters* (Fig. **21–43**).

The graphics movement that expressed this cultural climate drew from a number of resources: the flowing, sinuous curves of art nouveau, the intense optical color vibration associated with the brief op-art movement popularized by a Museum of Modern Art exhibition, and the recycling of images from popular culture or by manipulation (such as reducing continuous-tone images to high-contrast black and white) that was prevalent in pop art.

Many of the initial artists in this movement were largely self-taught, and their primary clients were rock-and-roll concert and dance promoters. Dances in the 1960s were intense perceptual experiences of loud music and light shows that dissolved the environment into throbbing fields of projected color and bursting strobes. This experience was paralleled graphically in posters using swirling forms and lettering warped and bent to the edge of illegibility, frequently printed in close-valued complementary colors. A Grateful Dead poster (Fig. **21–44**) designed by Robert Wesley "Wes" Wilson (b. 1937) contains swirling lines and letterforms, which are variants of Alfred Roller's art nouveau. Wilson was the innovator of the psychedelic-poster style and created many of its stronger images. According to newspaper reports, respectable and intelligent businessmen were unable to comprehend the lettering on these posters, yet they communicated well enough to fill auditoriums with a younger generation who deciphered, rather than read, the message. Other prominent members of this brief movement included Kelly/Mouse Studios and Victor Moscoso (b. 1936), the only major artist of the movement with formal art training (Figs. **21–45** and **21–46**).

Some aspects of the psychedelic-poster movement were used in the exceedingly popular art of New York designer Peter Max (b. 1937). In his series of posters during the late 1960s, the art nouveau aspects of psychedelic art were combined with more accessible images and softer colors. One of his most famous images, the 1970 "Love" graphic (Fig. **21–47**), combined the fluid organic line of art nouveau with the bold, hard contour of the comic book and pop art. In his finest work, Max ex-

21–46

21–47

21–48

perimented with images and printing techniques. His posters and merchandise, from mugs and T-shirts to clocks, offered a more palatable version of psychedelic art and found a mass audience among young people across America. After the poster mania reached its peak in the early 1970s, American poster art of inventive quality retreated to the university campus, one of the few surviving pedestrian environments in America. Because universities sponsor a large number of events, the campus is an ideal poster-communications environment.

David Lance Goines (b. 1945) proves that even in the late twentieth-century era of overspecialization, it is possible for individual artists and craftsmen to define a personal direction and operate as independent creative forces with total control over their work. A native of Oregon, Goines had an early interest in calligraphy that blossomed into serious study at the University of California at Berkeley. He was expelled from the university at age nineteen for his participation in the free-speech movement and learned graphic arts as an apprentice pressman at the radical Berkeley Free Press, where he wrote, printed, and bound a book on calligraphy. When the Berkeley Free Press failed in 1971, Goines acquired it, renamed it the Saint Hieronymous Press, and continued to print and publish books while developing his poster style. Offset lithography and graphic design are unified in Goines's work, becoming a medium for personal expression and public communications. He designs, illustrates, and hand-letters posters, makes the negatives and plates, and then operates the press to print the

21–43. Wes Wilson, concert poster for The Association, 1966. Lettering becomes an image, signifying a cultural and generational shift in values.

21–44. Wes Wilson, concert poster for the Grateful Dead, Junior Wells Chicago Blues Band, and The Doors, 1966. Hand-drawn line art is printed in intensely vibrating colors.

21–45. Victor Moscoso, poster for the Chambers Brothers, 1967. The vibrant contrasting colors and Vienna Secession lettering inside of the sunglasses implies the drug culture of the period.

21–46. Victor Moscoso, Miller Blues Band concert poster, 1967. The shimmering nude female figure in the center of the poster reflects the uninhibitedness of the 1960s.

21–47. Peter Max, "Love" poster, 1970. Max's split fountain printing resulted in colors lyrically dissolving into one another.

21–48. David Lance Goines, classical film screening poster, 1973. The directness of image and composition gains graphic distinction from a poetic sense of color and sensitive drawing.

edition. This thoughtful and scholarly designer has evolved a highly personal style that integrates diverse sources of inspiration. Symmetrical composition, simplified line drawing, quiet planes of flat color, and subtle stripes rimming the contours of his forms are characteristics of his poster designs (Fig. 21–48).

During the 1980s, a conservative decade characterized by economic disparity between rich and poor, environmental

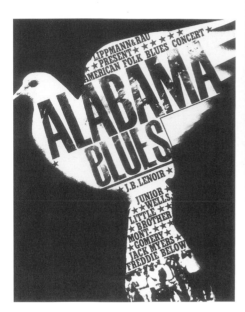

21–49   21–50   21–51

indifference, and limited social activism, many American posters were produced as decorative objects. Limited-edition images of photographs or paintings became posters rather than reproductions because the artist's name and often a title—frequently letterspaced in elegant, all-capital type—were added. These were sold in specialty shops and department stores. Typical subjects included flowers, high-performance sports cars, and fruit presented against simple backgrounds with exquisite composition and lighting.

European visual poets

Poetry was once defined as bringing together unlike things to create a new experience or evoke an unexpected emotional response. In Europe, beginning in the 1960s and continuing into the 1990s, there emerged a poetic approach to graphic design based on imagery and its manipulation through collage, montage, and both photographic and photomechanical techniques. The graphic poets stretched time and typography, merged and floated objects, and fractured and fragmented images in a sometimes disturbing but always engaging manner. The conservative, traditional, and expected were rejected by these graphic designers, who defined the design process not as form arrangements or construction but as the invention of unexpected images to convey ideas or feelings. A receptive audience and client list developed for their book and album covers, magazine designs, and posters for concerts, television, and radio.

A German master of this movement is Gunther Kieser (b. 1930), who began his freelance career in 1952. This brilliant imagist has consistently demonstrated an ability to invent unexpected visual content to solve communications problems. Kieser brings together images or ideas to create a new vitality, new arrangement, or synthesis of disparate objects. His Alabama Blues poster combines two photographs, a dove and a civil-rights demonstration, with typography inspired by nineteenth-century wood type (Fig. **21–49**); these diverse elements act in concert to make a potent statement. Kieser's poetic visual statements always have a rational basis that links expressive forms to communicative content. It is this ability that separates him from design practitioners who use fantasy or surrealism as ends rather than means.

In the late 1970s and early 1980s Kieser began to construct fictitious objects that are convincingly real. Viewers stop in their tracks to study the huge posters bearing color photographs of Kieser's private visions to determine if they are having delusions. In a poster for the 1978 Frankfurt Jazz Festival (Fig. **21–50**), Kieser and his photographer almost convince us that a moss-covered tree stump can grow in the shape of a trumpet.

Launched in Munich in 1959, the German periodical *Twen*, whose name—derived by chopping the last two letters from the English word *twenty*—signified the age group of sophisticated young adults to whom the magazine was addressed, featured excellent photography used in dynamic layouts by art director Willy Fleckhouse (1925–1983). With a genius for

21–52

21–53

cropping images and using typography and white space in unexpected ways, Fleckhouse made the bold, uninhibited pages of *Twen* a milestone in editorial design. While the Brodovitch tradition was undoubtedly a resource for Fleckhouse, the dynamic of scale, space, and poetic images in *Twen* made a provocative and original statement (Figs. **21–51** and **21–52**).

One of the most innovative image makers in late-twentieth-century design is Gunter Rambow (b. 1938) of Frankfurt, Germany, who often collaborated with Gerhard Lienemeyer (b. 1936) and Michael van de Sand (b. 1945). In Rambow's designs, the medium of photography is manipulated, massaged, montaged, and airbrushed to convert the ordinary into the extraordinary. Everyday images are combined or dislocated, then printed as straightforward, documentary black-and-white images in an original metaphysical statement of poetry and profundity. In a series of posters commissioned by the Frankfurt book publisher S. Fischer-Verlag for annual distribution beginning in 1976 (Fig. **21–53**), the book is used as a symbolic object, altered and transformed to make a statement about itself as a communication form. The book as a means of communicating with vast numbers of people is symbolized by a huge book emerging from a crowd scene: the book as a door or window opening on a world of new knowledge is symbolized by turning the cover of a book into a door one year and a window the next (Fig. **21–54**). These metaphysical and symbolic advertisements carry no verbal informa-

21–49. Gunther Kieser, Alabama Blues concert poster, 1966. A concert announcement becomes a potent symbol of the longing for freedom and justice contained in the music.

21–50. Gunther Kieser (designer) and Hartmann (photographer), Frankfurt Jazz Festival poster, 1978. Symbolic fabrications are disseminated through photographs of sculpted objects.

21–51. Willy Fleckhouse (art director), cover for *Twen*, 1970. Graphic communications often become political symbols in the struggle between alternative value systems and generations.

21–52. Willy Fleckhouse (art director), pages from *Twen*, 1970. Sensitive cropping, a full-page photographic symbol, and white space create a dynamic and expansive layout.

21–53. Gunter Rambow (designer/photographer) and Michael van de Sand (photographer), S. Fischer Verlag poster, 1976. The portability of the book is conveyed in memorable fashion.

tion except the logo and name of the client, giving the audience of editors and publishers memorable and thought-provoking visual phenomena rather than a sales message.

Rambow often imbues straightforward photographs with a sense of magic or mystery (Fig. **21–55**), and he uses collage and montage as a means of creating a new graphic reality. Images are often altered or combined and then rephotographed. In the 1980 poster for the play *Die Hamletmaschine* (Fig. **21–56**), a photograph of a wall was placed under a photograph of a man

21–54

21–55

21–56

21–57

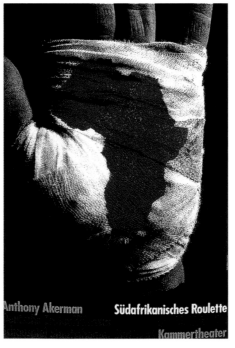

21–58

21–59

standing in front of this wall, then part of the top photograph was torn away. The final rephotographed image presents the viewer with a perplexing impossibility. This image seems to be capable of self-destruction—a figure appears to possess the existential ability to negate itself (Fig. **21–57**). The iconic power of Rambow's images can be seen in the *Südafrikanisches Roulette*

theater poster (Fig. **21–58**), designed by Rambow and photographed by Rambow and Van de Sand.

During the 1960s literary and graphic design communities throughout the world were astounded and delighted by the experimental typography of French designer Robert Massin (b. 1925), who designed editions of poetry and plays for the Paris

21–60

21–61

21–62

21–54. Gunter Rambow (designer/photographer) and Michael van de Sand (photographer), S. Fischer–Verlag poster, 1980. The book and the concept of reading as a window on the world gain intensity from the luminous sunlight streaming from this volume.

21–55. Gunter Rambow (designer/photographer), Gunter Rambow and Gerhard Lienemeyer (typographers), poster for the play *Antigone,* 1978. Pathos and isolation are conveyed by the burning chair photographed from a low vantage point at dusk.

21–56. Gunter Rambow, poster for the play *Die Hamletmaschine,* 1980. A chilling sense of anonymity is produced by this self-inflicted act of vandalism.

21–57. Gunter Rambow, poster for *Othello,* 1978. The pathos of the play is expressed by an image within an image: a tattered poster hanging on a wire fence in front a bleak apartment complex.

21–58. Gunter Rambow (designer/photographer) and Michael van de Sand (photographer), theater poster for *Südafrikanisches Roulette* (South African Roulette), 1988. A bandaged hand with a bloodstain shaped like Africa conveys the pathos of suffering and revolution.

21–59 through **21–62.** Robert Massin (designer) and Henry Cohen (photographer), cover and double-page spreads from Eugene Ionesco's *La cantatrice chauve,* 1964. The pictorial directness of the comic book is combined with the expressive typography of futurist poetry.

Dadaist typography, but his intensification of both narrative literary content and visual form into a cohesive unity expressing the author's meaning is unique.

Massin's designs for Eugene Ionesco's plays combine the pictorial conventions of the comic book with the sequencing and visual flow of the cinema. The drama of *La cantatrice chauve* (*The Bald Soprano*) is enacted through Henry Cohen's high-contrast photographs (Fig. **21–59**). Each character is assigned a typeface for his or her speaking voice (Fig. **21–60**) and is identified not by name but by a small photographic portrait. By printing typography via letterpress onto sheets of rubber and then manipulating and photographing it, Massin created unprecedented figurative typography (Fig. **21–61**), while a major argument in the play provided him with the opportunity to generate an explosive typographic event (Fig. **21–62**). Visual vitality, tension, and confusion appropriate to the play are graphically conveyed. In his design for Ionesco's *Délire à deux* (*Frenzy for Two*), words become the expressionistic image (Fig. **21–63**). Massin's manipulations of typography anticipated the elastic spatial possibilities inherent in bitmapped computer graphics of the 1980s. His many years of research into letterforms and their history led to the important 1970 book *Letter and Image*, which explores the pictorial and graphic properties of alphabet design through the ages.

publisher Editions Gallimard. As a young man, Massin apprenticed in sculpture, engraving, and letter-cutting under his father. He did not seek formal design training but learned graphic design under typographic designer Pierre Faucheux. In its dynamic configurations and use of letterforms as concrete visual form, Massin's work has affinities with futurist and

21–63

21–64

During the May 1968 student revolts in Paris, the streets were filled with posters and placards, mostly handmade by amateurs. Three young graphic designers, Pierre Bernard (b. 1942), François Miehe (b. 1942), and Gerard Paris-Clavel (b. 1943), were deeply involved in the radical politics of the day. Bernard and Paris-Clavel had each spent a year in Poland studying under Henryk Tomaszewski, who stressed an attitude of being both artist and citizen. His teaching advocated an intellectual rigor and clear personal conviction about the world. These three young designers believed publicity and design were directed toward creating artificial demands in order to maximize profits, so they joined forces to turn their graphic design toward political, social, and cultural rather than commercial ends. Seeking to address real human needs, they formed the Grapus studio in 1970 to realize this mission. Grapus was a collective; intensive dialogue took place about the meaning and means of every project. The starting point of Grapus's problem solving was a thorough analysis and lengthy discussion about content and message. The most significant aspects of the problem and the kernel of the message were determined, and then a graphic expression of the essence of the content was sought. (In those days, French left-wing radicals were called *crapules staliniennes* [Stalinist scum]. This phrase was melded with the word graphic to produce the group's name.)

Grapus favored universal symbols with readily understood meanings: hands, wings, sun, moon, earth, fireworks, blood, and flags. Typographic refinement and technical polish yielded to handwritten headlines and scrawled graffiti, creating a raw vitality and energy. Often a palette of primary colors was used for its intense graphic power.

21–63. Robert Massin, pages from Eugene Ionesco's *Délire à deux*, 1966. The words leap and run and overlap and smear into ink blots in a calligraphic homage to the nonrepresentational, surreal ideas of Ionesco, a master of the theater of the absurd.

21–64. Grapus, exhibition poster, 1982. A layering of emotionally charged graphic symbols contradict each other and unsettle viewers.

Grapus was motivated by the dual goals of achieving social and political change while striving to realize creative artistic impulses. A 1982 poster (Fig. 21–64) for an exhibition of Grapus graphics features a central figure holding a dimensional arrow with cutout letters. Bounding into the space on a jack-in-the-box spring, it layers an arresting group of cultural icons: the ubiquitous yellow smile face, Mickey Mouse ears, and Hitler's hair and mustache. Its eyes are the communist and French tricolor indicia, and a small television antenna sprouts from the top of its head. Grapus spawned many imitators. The shocking verve of its statements, especially the dynamic informality of its spatial organization and casual, graffiti-like lettering, was copied by fashionable advertising.

The third-world poster

From the end of World War II until the dismantling of the Iron Curtain in 1989, the industrialized nations formed two groups: the capitalist democracies of Western Europe, North America, and Japan, and the communist block led by the Soviet Union. The emerging nations of Latin America, Asia, and Africa have been called the third world. In social and political struggles, ideas are weapons, and the poster is a major vehicle for spreading them. The medium is effective because access to newspapers, radio, and television is often limited in these countries, where the poster is sometimes used with the intensity and frequency of European posters during World War I.

In this context, posters become vehicles for challenging authority and expressing dissent untouched by the traditional censorship of government, business, and newspapers. Some are spontaneous expressions, crude folk art created by unskilled hands, while others are created by accomplished artists. In both cases, the artists/advocates who create such posters have an agenda and seek to alter viewers' perspectives.

Third-world posters address two constituencies: In their native lands, they tackle political and social issues, motivating people toward one side of a political or social struggle; a secondary audience exists in the industrial democracies, where

distributors such as Liberation Graphics in Alexandria, Virginia, make posters available to Westerners who feel strongly about international issues.

Cuba became a major center for poster design after the revolutionary force led by Fidel Castro defeated the regime of President Fulgenico Batista on New Year's Day in 1959. Over the next two years, Cuba's Marxist course led to a complete breakdown in diplomatic ties with the United States and a close association with the Soviet bloc. The creative arts had been virtually ignored under Batista, but three meetings in June 1961 enabled artists and writers to meet with the Castro regime to forge a mutual understanding. At the final meeting, on 30 June, Castro delivered his lengthy address "Words to the Intellectuals," defining his policy toward the creative arts. Castro assured artists and writers "that freedom of form must be respected," but freedom of content was seen as a more subtle and complex matter. He said artists and intellectuals "can find within the Revolution a place to work and create, a place where their creative spirit, even though they are not revolutionary writers and artists, has the opportunity and freedom to be expressed. This means: within the Revolution, everything; against the Revolution, nothing." Each person could "express freely the ideas he wants to express," but "we will always evaluate his creation from the Revolutionary point of view." Castro defined "the good, the useful, and the beautiful" as whatever is "noble, useful, and beautiful" for "the great majority of the people—that is, the oppressed and exploited classes." Popular art forms—cinema and theater, posters and leaflets, songs and poetry—and propaganda media were encouraged. Traditional painting and sculpture were seen as relatively inefficient in reaching large audiences with the revolutionary message.

Artists and writers admitted to the union for creative workers receive salaries, work space, and materials. Graphic designers work for a variety of government agencies with specific missions. Leading Cuban graphic designers include Raul Martinez, a painter who creates illustrative designs (Fig. 21–65), and New York-educated Felix Beltran (b. 1938). Beltran served as art director for the Commission for Revolutionary Action (COR), which creates internal ideological propaganda and maintains public consciousness of the revolution by promoting commemorative days (Fig. 21–66) and past leaders.

Bureaus and institutes have responsibility for motion pictures, musical and theatrical events, publishing, and exhibition programs, and use graphics to promote these cultural events. Emphasis is on outreach—unlike in many countries, where cultural programs are only available to the urban population, in Cuba a serious attempt is made to reach the rural areas. Film posters are lively and happy affairs printed in an uninhibited palette of bright silk-screened colors.

21–65

21–66

21–67

Posters and leaflets for export throughout the third world are produced by the Organization of Solidarity with Asia, Africa, and Latin America (OSPAAAL) to support revolutionary activity and build public consciousness for ideological viewpoints. OSPAAAL posters are printed via offset and use elemental symbolic images readily comprehended by people of diverse nationalities, languages, and cultural backgrounds. The Castro government sees itself as being involved in an ideological war against "Yankee imperialism" for the hearts and minds of people in the emerging third-world countries. The eye of the beholder is tantalized while revolutionary consciousness is formed through repeated exposure. The international distribution of OSPAAAL graphics is evidenced by the presence of Arabic, English, French, and Spanish typography on each poster.

Lacking artistic traditions, Cuban graphic designers have assimilated a variety of resources. American sources—including pop art, the psychedelic poster, and Push Pin Studio—and the Polish poster are important inspirations. The "heroic worker" school of romanticized realism prevalent in the former Soviet Union and in China is avoided. The icon, ideograph, and telegraphic message are far more effective in developing nations. Myth and reality have been unified in a powerful graphic symbol based on the image of Ernesto ("Che") Guevara. A leader of the Cuban revolution, Guevara left Cuba in the mid-1960s to lead guerrillas in the South American country of Bolivia, and on 9 October 1967 he was killed in a gun battle in the jungle village of Higuera. Graphic designers have converted Che's image, one of the most repro-

21–65. Raul Martinez, poster honoring the Cuban people, c. 1970. Leaders and workers are cheerfully depicted in a comic book drawing style and bright, intense color.

21–66. Artist not identified, poster for COR, 1967. Clouds part to reveal an orange sun, symbolizing the ill-fated 26 July 1953 assault on the Santiago army barracks, which launched the Cuban revolution.

21–67. Elena Serrano, "Day of the Heroic Guerrilla" poster, 1968. An iconographic image of Che Guevara transforms into a map of South America in a radiating image signifying revolutionary victory.

duced of the late twentieth century, into a symbolic icon (Fig. 21–67) representing struggle against oppression throughout the third world. Drawn in light-and-shadow planes like high-contrast photography, the fallen guerrilla wears a beard and a beret with a star; his head tilts slightly upward. A specific person, Ernesto Guevara, was converted into the mythic hero or savior who sacrificed his life so others might live.

The importance of conceptual images in the second half of the twentieth century developed in response to many factors, and ideas and forms from modern art have filtered into popular cultures. By usurping graphic art's documentary function, photography and video have repositioned graphic illustration toward a more expressive and symbolic role. The complexity of the political, social, and cultural ideas and emotions graphic artists need to communicate can frequently be presented more effectively by iconic and symbolic rather than narrative images.

National Visions within a Global Dialogue

22

In 1966 the German graphic designer Olaf Leu wrote that German design no longer had any national attributes. Observing that while some might favor this development, Leu acknowledged that others regretted it. At that time the purist geometry of the International Typographic Style and the unbridled freedom of American design coexisted as important influences on German design as well as on design activity around the globe. A period of international dialogue had begun. Just as events in Southeast Asia and the Middle East directly affect Europe, the Americas, and Japan, conceptual innovation and visual invention spread rapidly. An international culture embracing the fine arts, performing arts, and design spans national boundaries, extending from traditional centers to every corner of the globe. This has been spurred by graphic arts technology, which makes professional typography and printing possible in small cities and developing countries, and by the swift growth of graphic design education.

During the 1980s and 1990s the rapid development of electronic and computer technology began to change the processes and appearance of design. Overnight express mail, fax machines, the Internet, global televisual communications such as the continuous Cable News Network (CNN), and direct-dial international long-distance telephone service all served to further shrink the human community into Marshall McLuhan's "global village." The advanced technology of the late twentieth century created a cultural milieu of simultaneity—ancient and modern cultures, Eastern and Western thought, handicraft and industrial production—until past, present, and future blur into a continuum of information and visual form. This complex world of cultural and visual diversity created an environment where a vast global dialogue coexists with national visions, resulting in an explosive and pluralistic era for graphic design. The many countries where designers have developed a unique national posture for design include the United Kingdom, Japan, and the Netherlands.

Postwar graphic design in the United Kingdom

The historical influence of the United Kingdom, a constitutional democracy uniting England, Northern Ireland, Scotland, and Wales, has transcended its size. Under Queen Elizabeth I (1533–1603) England became a major naval power and started its vast colonial empire, spreading English social customs and language around the globe. This international influence continues today.

In post–World War II England, graphic design was characterized by an international culture that embraced the fine and performing arts and the spread of English social customs and language around the world. Both the purist modernism of Switzerland and the graphic expressionism of New York were assimilated, but the pitfall of becoming a colony to these pervasive influences was successfully avoided by outstanding English designers who made significant contributions to the international dialogue. After the trauma of the war, Herbert Spencer (1922–2002) became an important voice in renewing British graphic design through his writing, teaching, and graphic design practice. Spencer's understanding of modern art and design was translated into a rare typographic sensitivity and structural vitality. As editor and designer of the journal *Typographica* and author of an influential 1969 book that informed the postwar generation about the accomplishments of earlier twentieth-century designers, *Pioneers of Modern Typography*, Spencer helped encourage the worldwide dialogue.

A design partnership that formed in 1962 became an early locus of British design. Alan Fletcher (b. 1931), Colin Forbes (b. 1928), and Bob Gill (b. 1931) launched a studio that carried their names. In 1965, after Gill left the partnership and architect Theo Crosby (1925–94) joined the firm, the name was changed to Crosby, Fletcher, Forbes. Exhibition design, historic conservation, and industrial design were added to the firm's activities. As additional partners were added, the name of the studio was changed to Pentagram. (Continued growth made even this five-pronged name obsolete, for Pentagram had seventeen partners and 148 employees in its London, Austin [Texas], Hong Kong, New York, and San Francisco offices by 1996. This discussion is about Pentagram's formative years in London.)

22–1

22–2

22–3

22–4

Intelligence and a talent for developing design solutions suited to the needs of the problem were the hallmarks of Pentagram design. Asked to design a cover for a magazine containing an article about their work, the designers mailed a parcel from London to Zurich with a request for its return unopened. A color photograph documenting its journey through the postal system became the cover design (Fig. **22–1**). Thorough evaluation of the communications problem and the specific nature of the environmental conditions under which the design was to appear combined with British wit and a willingness to try the unexpected. This, perhaps, summarizes the essence of the Pentagram approach to graphic design.

In the best English tradition, Pentagram's partners combined a sense of the contemporary (Fig. **22–2** and **22–3**) with a strong understanding of history (Fig. **22–4**). The firm's design solutions range from clean geometric forms in corporate identity systems to a warm historicism in packaging design and graphics for smaller clients. Conceptual, visual, and often imbued with expressive humor, the attitudes this studio brought to graphic design enabled Britain to establish an international presence in the field just as it did at the turn of the century and in the years after World War I. Pentagram's expansion into other countries is a testament to the organizational skills and creativity of the original partners.

The rise of Japanese design

Japan, an island nation off the east coast of Asia, has over 125 million people and a population density of about 860 persons per square mile. Eighty percent of the island consists of rugged, uninhabitable mountains, and both food and fuel have to be imported. Japan retained an isolated and feudal society until the middle of the nineteenth century. Japan's rapid industrial development throughout the course of the twentieth century, particularly during the decades after World War II, is a major testament to the will and energy of the Japanese people. During the postwar period technological leadership and an awareness of Western social patterns and lifestyles raised philosophic issues for Japanese graphic designers as they sought to maintain national traditions while incorporating international influences. The tree-planting poster (Fig. **22–5**) by Ryuichi Yamashiro (b. 1920) demonstrates just how successfully this could be accomplished, as Eastern calligraphy and spatial concerns unite with a Western communications concept.

European constructivism is a major resource for the Japanese design movement. However, the systematic organization and strong theoretical foundation of constructivism is tempered by a traditional Japanese inclination toward intuitive problem-solving activity and a heritage of simplified emblematic form. In the same way, Japanese designers are more prone to central placement and the organization of space around a median axis, reflecting the compositional traditions of many Japanese arts and crafts rather than the relational asymmetrical balance of European constructivism. An important inspiration for the Japanese graphic designer is the traditional family symbol or crest, the *mon* (Fig. **22–6**), in use for a thousand years. This simplified design of flowers, birds, animals, plants, or household objects contained in a circle was applied to belongings and clothing.

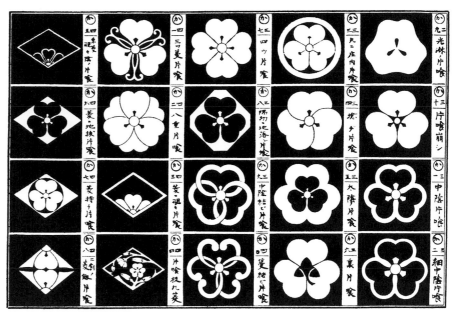

22–5   22–6

Yusaku Kamekura (1915–97) was apprenticed to an architect and then worked as art director for several Japanese cultural magazines from 1937 until 1948. During the postwar recovery period Kamekura emerged as an influential design leader who earned the reverential name "Boss" in Japanese design circles. Under his leadership, Japanese graphic designers dispelled the widely held belief that visual communications must be hand-drawn, and the notion of applied arts' inferiority to fine art faded as Japanese designers established their professional status.

Kamekura charted the course of this new Japanese movement through the vitality and strength of his creative work, his leadership in founding the Japan Advertising Art Club to bring professionalism and focus to the new discipline, and the establishment, in 1960, of the Japan Design Center. As managing director of this organization, Kamekura brought leading graphic designers together with industry.

Technical discipline, a thorough understanding of printing techniques, and careful construction of the visual elements characterize Kamekura's work (Figs. **22–7** and **22–8**). When global attention focused on Japan for the 1964 Olympics, the logo and posters he created for these events received international acclaim and established Japan as a center of creative design (Figs. **22–9** and **22–10**). Kamekura's works are conspicuously modern yet often evoke the poetic traditions of Japanese art. The emblematic simplicity of his constructivist geometry and international style–inspired typography (Figs. **22–11** and **22–12**) is the result of an extraordinary complexity where all parts are unified into an expressive whole.

22–1. Alan Fletcher, Colin Forbes, and Bob Gill, cover for *Graphis,* 1965. The record of a parcel's international journey carrying Pentagram work to the magazine also became the package carrying *Graphis* to its readers.

22–2. Colin Forbes, symbol for the Zinc Development Association Die Casting Conference, 1966. Pentagram solutions seem to appear magically from the content. The opportunity to render the year in male and female components of a die-casting mold occurs only once each decade.

22–3. Alan Fletcher, Victoria and Albert Museum logo, 1990. In 1996 Fletcher discussed the V&A logo in *"Beware Wet Paint": Designs by Alan Fletcher:* "The already classic symbol for the Victoria & Albert Museum (designed in 1989) is in a typeface originally designed by Giambattista Bodoni. The problem centered on endowing the three characters with a single personality. The solution was to divide and remove half of one letter, and add and insert an ampersand to reinstate the missing crossbar."

22–4. Alan Fletcher and Georg Staehelin, logo for an exclusive boutique, 1968. Ornamented initials from five different Renaissance designs provide an unexpected graphic expression of the name.

22–5. Ryuichi Yamashiro, poster for a tree-planting campaign, 1961. The Japanese characters for *tree*, *grove*, and *forest* are repeated to form a forest.

22–6. Japanese traditional crests and much postwar Japanese graphic design share direct frontal presentation of simplified images, symmetrical composition, and a refined use of line and space.

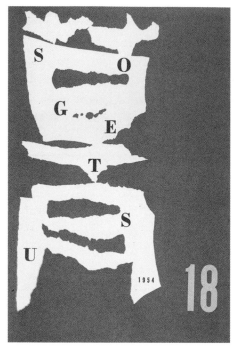

22–7

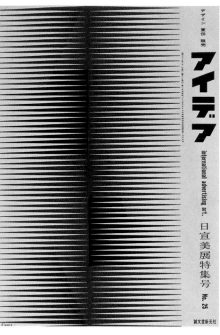

22–8

22–9

22–10

22–11

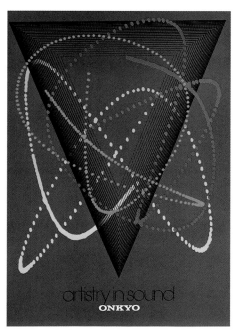

22–12

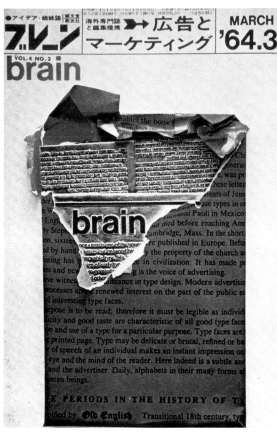

22–13

An imaginative approach to photographic design was developed by Masuda Tadashi (b. 1922). His growing involvement in the use of photographic illustration to solve graphic design problems, combined with his interest in collaborative and team design, culminated in the establishment of the Masuda Tadashi Design Institute in 1958. Many art directors and graphic designers view photographers and illustrators as subcontractors on call to give form to the designer's concepts. In Tadashi's collaborative team approach, unexpected solutions and new ways of seeing things emerged. Type placement on, above, or below the photograph is usually done with great sensitivity. A favored layout approach uses a structure of fine, ruled lines as a vessel to contain the typographic information. Color is used very effectively: Bright colored backgrounds are sometimes juxtaposed with objects of contrasting hue, and a uniform color cast is often used to unify an image. Focal points such as the rich blue paper wrapping the printing plates on a *Brain* cover (Fig. **22–13**) are examples of the technique of using one intense color in an otherwise muted photograph.

As Japanese design evolved, the constructivist impulse was extended by original thinkers who combined personal visions with the universal harmony of geometric form. Kazumasa Nagai (b. 1929), a sculpture major at the Tokyo University of Fine Arts and Music, turned to graphic design after graduating in 1951. His oeuvre might be considered ongoing research into linear form and the properties of line as a graphic medium for spatial modulation. His explorations of the nature of line through fine-art drawings and prints are the wellspring for his posters, abstract trademarks, and advertisements. The technical perfection of his designs and their printed production is formidable. His poster for a Paris exhibition of works by twelve Japanese graphic designers, Tradition et nouvelles techniques (Traditional and New Techniques, Fig. **22–14**), creates a universe of geometric forms evoking planets and energy forces moving in space.

While Nagai bases his designs on line, Ikko Tanaka (1930–2002) uses plane and shape as the nucleus for his work. Over the course of the 1950s Tanaka assimilated many of the Bauhaus design traditions, then opened Tanaka Design Studio in 1963. A pluralistic designer, he has explored many directions. Two underlying visual concepts in much of his work are grid structure and vibrant planes of color that explore warm/cool contrast, close-valued color, and analogous color ranges. Traditional Japanese motifs, including landscape (Fig. **22–15**), Kanze Noh theater, calligraphy, masks, and woodblock prints, are reinvented in a modernist design idiom. In some of his most original works, color planes are arranged on a grid to signify abstracted and expressive portraits, as seen in his "Nihon Buyo" poster for the Asian Performing Arts

22–7. Yusaku Kamekura, booklet cover, 1954. Torn paper Japanese characters and Bodoni letterforms spell the same word, typifying Kamekura's synthesis of Asian and occidental forms.

22–8. Yusaku Kamekura, magazine cover, 1957. Sharp wedges create kinetic rhythms. The exact registration of colors evidences the disciplined skill of Japanese printers.

22–9. Yusaku Kamekura, Tokyo Olympics logo and poster, 1964. Three simple symbols—the red sun of the Japanese flag, the Olympic rings, and the words *Tokyo 1964*—combine into an immediate and compelling message.

22–10. Yusaku Kamekura (designer) and Osamu Hayasaki (photographer), Tokyo Olympics poster, 1964. A meticulously planned and lit photograph becomes an emblematic expression of the footrace.

22–11. Yusaku Kamekura, poster of the Osaka World Exposition, 1970. The imagination of Japanese designers is constantly tested as they invent new sun images as part of the heritage of the land of the rising sun.

22–12. Yusaku Kamekura, poster for a stereo manufacturer, 1980. Technical perfection in stereo sound is signified by bright traceries darting around a black linear triangle.

22–13. Masuda Tadashi (designer) and Doki Mitsuo (photographer), cover for *Brain* magazine, 1964. To illustrate an article on typography, metal printing plates are wrapped in typographic printed proofs that are torn to reveal their contents.

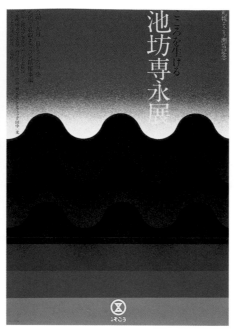

22–14

22–15

22–16

22–17

22–14. Kazumasa Nagai, exhibition poster, 1984. An imaginary universe is created from colorful linear elements.

22–15. Ikko Tanaka, poster for Senei Ikenobo's flower arrangement, 1974. The mountains and waves of traditional woodblock prints are evoked by a rhythmic sequence of blue and blue green bands under a graduated tan sky.

22–16. Ikko Tanaka, *Nihon Buyo* poster, 1981. A traditional Japanese theatrical character is reinvented using the aesthetic forms of a later age.

22–17. Takenobu Igarashi, trademark for Parco Part 3 department store, 1981. Letters assembled of geometric segments can be presented as a relief or as three-dimensional environmental signage.

22–18. Takenobu Igarashi, poster for Expo '85, 1982. An international housing exposition is signified by exploded structural forms.

22–19. Takenobu Igarashi, poster calendar, 1990. Each of the 6,226 numbers designed in the ten-year project is different from all others.

22–18   22–19

Institute (Fig. **22–16**). These visages have remarkable individual character and personality.

Takenobu Igarashi (b. 1944) has created a paradigm for the blending of Eastern and Western ideas. After graduating from Tama University in 1968, Igarashi earned a graduate degree from the University of California, Los Angeles. Upon returning to Japan he found design firms and corporations unreceptive to a designer who had spent time abroad, so he opened his own design office in 1970. Much of Igarashi Studio's work is in trademark, corporate identity, environmental, and product design. By 1976 Igarashi's experiments with alphabets drawn on isometric grids were attracting clients and international recognition. The isometric alphabets have evolved into three-dimensional alphabetic sculptures that Igarashi calls *architectural alphabets*. These have been applied to signage as part of visual identity programs (Fig. **22–17**). Igarashi achieves unexpected variety in his isometric alphabets. The dynamic letters of his Expo '85 poster (Fig. **22–18**) become a metaphor for the materials and processes of the built environment. In 1983 Igarashi began the ten-year project of designing the Igarashi Poster Calendar, starting with five years for the Museum of Modern Art in New York and then continuing with five more for the Alphabet Gallery in Tokyo. As shown in the 1990 calendar (Fig. **22–19**), each month has a different design theme and each number is a unique drawing.

Igarashi says 95 percent of his designs are based on a grid system. His work is composed from elemental forms: the dot, the smallest component of perception; lines, which define positions and create boundaries between planes; grids, whose *x* and *y* axes bring mathematical order to his work;

surfaces, which can be visual and tactile; flat or dimensional planes; and the basic geometric forms of circle, triangle, and square. Igarashi's best works achieve *boundlessness* (Fig. **22–20**), an expansive power created by color, texture, and ambiguity.

The work of Tadanori Yokoo (b. 1936) replaces the order and logic of constructivism with the restless vitality of Dada and a fascination with mass media, popular art, and comic books. During the mid-1960s Yokoo used the comic-book technique of black line drawing as a vessel to contain flat areas of photomechanical color. Photographic elements were often collaged into the designs, and traditional Japanese images were translated into the pop art idiom (Fig. **22–21**). During the late 1960s and into the 1970s Yokoo's design vocabulary and range of art and printing techniques became increasingly uninhibited. The "Sixth International Biennial Exhibition of Prints in Tokyo" poster (Fig. **22–22**) combines a variety of techniques: a halftone group portrait in pink; a sky with an airbrushed brown band across the top and a red one at the horizon; calligraphic writing on vertical bands, as found in earlier Asian art; and a monumental montage figure towering over a lighthouse on a bank across water. During the 1970s and 1980s Yokoo's work often moved toward unexpected and even mystical images (Fig. **22–23**). Yokoo expresses the passions and curiosity of a Japanese generation that grew up with American popular culture and electronic media—television, movies, radio, and records. Accordingly, shifting values and a rejection of tradition have found symbolic expression in Yokoo's uninhibited graphics, causing him to gain a cult reputation.

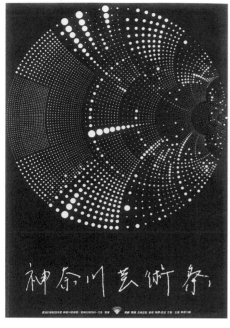

22–20

22–21

22–22

22–23

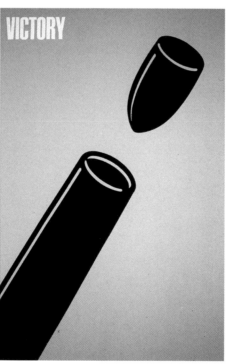

22–24

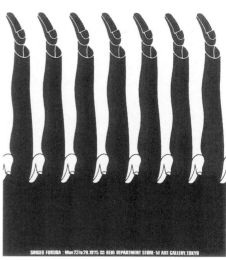

22–25

Designs by Shigeo Fukuda (b. 1932) are disarmingly simple, as readable and immediate as a one-panel cartoon, yet they engage the viewer with their unexpected violations of spatial logic and universal order. Fukuda achieved early renown for his unconventional views of the world; these form the core of his work. His disarming directness is seen in "Victory 1945," awarded first prize in an international competition for a poster commemorating the thirtieth anniversary of the end of World War II (Fig. **22–24**). In other works he expresses a non-

verbal concept or presents an inexplicable visual phenomenon (Fig. **22–25**). His images are a construct of memory and association rather than a direct impression of the senses.

Playfulness and humor are abundant in Fukuda's work. The enigma and contradictions of Dada and surrealism are reinvented not with high-minded seriousness but with a joyful affection for everyday life (Fig. **22–26**). Given his humor and simplified drawing, one might ask what separates Fukuda's work from ordinary comics. Intentional ambiguity and purposeful-

22–26

22–27

ness pervade his work, giving it a life beyond the ephemeral or disposable. With the simplest of means, a complex idea is projected with disarming clarity and unexpected imagery.

The Japanese understand nonverbal communication, in part because Zen Buddhism teaches the use of all five senses in receiving communication, and even states, "silence is communication." In this tradition Koichi Sato (b. 1944) brings delicate color motifs and metaphysical forms to his quietly poetic designs. Sato graduated from Tokyo University of Art and Music in 1968 and opened his own studio two years later. His painting of a white tray—which he tilted so the blue-colored water filling it graduated toward one end —became an important inspiration for his evolution. His first use of gradation in graphic design is in a 1974 concert poster (Fig. **22–27**).

Sato thinks in opposites: traditional/futuristic; organic/mechanical; East/West; light/dark. He writes haiku poetry, and his graphic designs share the multiple levels of meaning and expression of deep emotion found in this traditional form. Many of his works are glowing fields of color dispersed with Japanese calligraphy (Fig. **22–28**). Auras and glowing luminosity are found in his work, bringing a metaphysical poetics to the printed page (Fig. **22–29**).

The postwar miracle of Japan, which rose from the ashes of defeat to become a leader in technology and manufacturing, is paralleled by its emergence as a major center for graphic creativity. The finest contemporary Japanese graphic design has a strong emphasis on the aesthetic dimension, not at the expense of communicating the client's message but as a means of reinforcing and extending it.

22–20. Takenobu Igarashi, poster for the Kanagawa Art Festival, 1984. A universe composed of dots evokes infinite time and space.

22–21. Tadanori Yokoo, poster for Koshimaki Osen, 1966. East and West meet in a virtual catalogue of images and techniques.

22–22. Tadanori Yokoo, poster for printmaking exhibition, 1968. As Yokoo began to open his densely packed spaces and expand his range of printing techniques, he moved from pop art to personal statement.

22–23. Tadanori Yokoo, exhibition poster, 1973. A Persian manuscript border frames an enigmatic black rectangle, where two plates of food hover inexplicably.

22–24. Shigeo Fukuda, "Victory 1945" poster, 1975. The simple act of turning the shell back toward the gun signifies the folly of war.

22–25. Shigeo Fukuda, exhibition poster for Keio department store, 1975. "Impossible" optical illusions are typical of Fukuda's work.

22–26. Shigeo Fukuda, teacups, 1975. Fukuda's visual puns and illusions are expressed three-dimensionally in toys, products, environments, and sculpture.

22–27. Koichi Sato, "New Music Media" poster for the May Corporation, 1974. A black fish, glowing pale green water, and a black box with shading around the edges emit a quiet poetry.

22–28   22–29   22–30

Design in the Netherlands

World War II and the German occupation completely disrupted Dutch society; transportation and communication came to a virtual halt and grave shortages developed. The postwar years were a time for rebuilding the economy, and working to restore prewar cultural and social life. As Dutch design evolved, two strong currents became evident: a pragmatic constructivism whose inspiration derived from Dutch traditions from the first half of the century, including the de Stijl movement, Piet Zwart, and Paul Schuitema as well as postwar influences from Switzerland; and a vigorous expressionism, with jolting images and spontaneous spatial syntax. This duality is not surprising, for the Dutch are known as a thrifty people who favor order and structure; they are also broad-minded and tolerant of diverse political, religious, and artistic ideas. Perhaps the former stems from the cooperative spirit of a densely populated small country, much of which lies below sea level and must be protected by 1,500 miles of dikes, while the latter stems in part from Holland's traditional role as a seafaring nation, with international influences flowing through its ports. Exposure to diverse ideas and cultures spurred an attitude of tolerance. From the 1500s, Dutch printers were free to print material banned in other countries, while scientists and philosophers whose radical theories made life uncomfortable for them elsewhere sought refuge in Holland. Dutch citizens prize their individuality and free expression and extend this freedom to others, creating a social climate that encourages innovation.

A strong impetus toward functional design began in January 1963. A group including graphic designer Wim Crouwel (b. 1928), product designer Frisco Kramer, and graphic and architectural designer Benno Wissing (b. 1923) joined forces in Amsterdam to form a large, multidisciplinary design firm, Total Design (TD). Before TD, the Netherlands had no comprehensive firms capable of large-scale projects; these were being assigned to designers in other countries. TD offered extensive design programs for business, industry, and government. Its intention was to conceive and implement "ideas on design in all fields, in order whenever possible to achieve a unity of thought, or 'total design' in these fields." Crouwel played an important role in establishing TD's philosophy and direction. During the early 1950s he had been in direct contact with Swiss designers forging the International Typographic Style. However, Crouwel's design philosophy was less emphatic about universal form and standardized formats; he emphasized the designer as an objective problem solver who finds solutions through research and analysis, simplifying the message and the means for conveying it to an audience. He believed the flood of typographic messages in contemporary society demanded clarity and simplicity. Crouwel achieved a remarkable minimalism imbued with an aesthetic spirit (Fig. **22–30**).

TD sought a "total image" for clients through integrated graphics, architecture, and products. During the 1960s and 1970s the firm played a dominant role in Dutch design, initiating a purifying process through programs with limited typeface choices, standardized formats for paper and typography, and

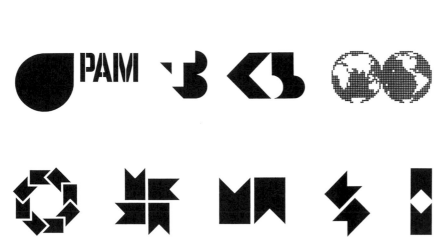

22–31

22–32

22–33

22–28. Koichi Sato, "Eclipse Music '84" concert poster for Map Company, Ltd., 1984. The red ground turns yellow and blue calligraphy into a kinetic expression of the surging energy of the music.

22–29. Koichi Sato, image poster for the Yuny supermarket, 1985. A metaphysical event in a subtle palette of blues creates a poetic image for the client.

22–30. Wim Crouwel, postage stamps for the PTT, 1976. Absolute simplicity gains expression through color gradation.

22–31. Total Design, trademarks for (top row) PAM petroleum company (1964); Thijssen Bornemisza (1971); Kunst an Bedrijf Foundation (1978); Hat Spectrum publishing company (1971); and (bottom row) Furness Holding (1969) and its subsidiaries Furness road transport division (1969), harbor division (1969), trade division (1972), and insurance company (1969).

22–32. Wim Crouwel, poster for Amsterdam's Stedelijk Museum design exhibition Vormgevers (Designers), 1966. The matrix governing the design of the poster and lettering is revealed as a design element.

22–33. Benno Wissing, poster for the exhibition Plannenmaken: 25 jaar bond van Nederlandse stedebouwkundigen (Plan Making: Alliance of Dutch Urban Development, 25 Years), 1961. A dynamic image is created with simple forms and overlapping primary colors contrasting with the texture of the photograph.

consistent schema for layouts. Projects included visual-identity programs (Fig. 22–31), museum exhibitions with related graphics (Figs. 22–32 and 22–33), book design, signage, and environments. TD used a team approach, with each team headed by a senior designer who established its direction.

Kramer left TD in 1967 and Wissing departed in 1972. Crouwel remained as a guiding force until 1981, when he became a full-time professor but continued as an adviser to TD. The firm became an important training ground for young designers, who gained experience there and then left to launch new firms. TD, now Total Identity, continues as a major force in European design, with offices in six cities and over fifty professionals on staff.

Another thrust toward modern design came from Pieter Brattinga (b. 1931), who learned all aspects of printing by working at his father's printing firm, De Jong & Co., at Hilversum, near Amsterdam. During the 1950s Brattinga functioned as a mediator between designers and printers. From 1954 until 1973, he curated exhibitions held in a small gallery at the printing firm, which introduced advanced art and graphic design to a wider audience. His posters for these exhibitions (Fig. **22–34**) were designed on a grid of fifteen square modules, with one or more always appearing as an element in the design. Brattinga edited a square-format journal, *Kwadraatblad* (Quadrate), published by De Jong & Co. to demonstrate its printing capabilities while providing leading artists and designers an opportunity to explore the limits of the print medium. Often controversial, these publications showed clients and designers an extended range of possibilities. Brattinga also designed posters and publications for the Kröller-Müller Museum in Otterlo.

In addition to major corporations, Dutch cultural institutions and government agencies are major patrons of graphic design. Each government agency has a visual-identity program, called a house style in the Netherlands, and consciously tries to communicate effectively with citizens. Cities have commissioned visual-identity programs; postage stamps and currency have achieved distinction in design. The Netherlands Postal and Telecommunications Service (PTT) emphasized the importance of design as early as 1919, when Jean François van Royen (1878–1942) became general secretary of the PTT board. He believed his government agency shouldered responsibility for aesthetic excellence in all areas, from telephone booths and buildings to postage stamps. He continually struggled to overcome obstacles to good design.

In 1942 Van Royen died in a concentration camp. After the war PTT established its Aesthetic Design Department, headed by an aesthetic adviser whose office commissioned all designs produced by PTT. This department functioned as an intermediary between PTT, the public, and artists and designers who received commissions. For two decades after the war decorative and pictorial approaches prevailed, but from around 1966 the Aesthetic Design Department moved in more contemporary and adventurous directions. In 1976 R. D. E. Oxenaar (b. 1929) was appointed aesthetic adviser; under his leadership, PTT design moved onto an extraordinary plane. Oxenaar embraced a philosophy of autonomous expression coupled with utilitarian needs. This enabled PTT to achieve visual innovation while meeting the requirements of the agency and its audiences. Netherlands postage stamps have been unusually

adventurous in their design, with a wide range of approaches from classical modernism to expressionism (see Figs. 22–30, 22–47, and 22–50). Young designers have received stamp design commissions early in their careers.

PTT implemented its first comprehensive visual-identity system in 1981. Two design firms, Total Design and Studio Dumbar, were commissioned to collaborate on this extensive and far-reaching project. Rigorous graphic standards were established, but certain items—including postage stamps created by diverse artists, unique publications including annual reports, and interiors of post offices in historical buildings—were exempt from the design system.

On 1 January 1989, the PTT was privatized and faced new competition in many of its services. The Aesthetic Design Department was renamed the Corporate Policy Unit for Art and Design; it continues to procure art for PTT facilities and commission product and graphic designs. The PTT believed the existing identity system was effective, but changes were necessary to signify the shift from government agency to private corporation. Studio Dumbar (discussed below) received the commission to revise the identity system (Fig. **22–35**). Prominent use of the sans-serif PTT initials continued, with more vibrant colors and geometric elements (squares, dots, and lines) used to intensify and energize PTT graphics, products, and environments. Bright hues become identifiers, with red used for the postal service and intense green for the telephone service. Telephone booths, which need to be located quickly in emergencies, form bright, green oases in urban environments regardless of season or time of day.

In 1965 the Nederlandsche Bank selected R. D. E. Oxenaar to design Dutch paper currency. He was disappointed with his first design, a green five-guilder note, and agreed to design additional currency only if he could be involved in every step from the beginning to final production. His design process addressed production requirements, safeguards against counterfeiting, and ease of use. A major advance occurred in 1978, when a new hundred-guilder note was needed and Oxenaar was given the freedom to select the subject. He rejected traditional symbols of authority such as engraved portraits of venerated figures and national emblems. His new design featured a snipe, a long-billed brown bird found in marshy areas. The public responded positively to this bank note, so Nederlandse Bank permitted Oxenaar to select additional currency subjects (Fig. **22–36**), including a sunflower and a lighthouse. Each note had a dominant color and large sans-serif numbers for the denomination. Composition and color were used to achieve an energy and expressiveness unprecedented in currency design. Oxenaar's work confirms a great truth: The personal and subjective interests of the artist can be realized while fulfilling the needs of public communication.

Just as the 1960s saw a strong impetus toward functional corporate design in the Netherlands with the founding of Total Design, it also saw the emergence of the Provo youth movement, which emphasized individual freedom and rejected social conformity. The prevailing climate provided fertile ground for a new expressionism in graphic design; this tendency in Dutch design increased dramatically during the 1970s and 1980s. Dutch art and design has a long tradition of emphasis on traditional values of harmony, unity, and order. Late twentieth-century designers including Anthon Beeke (b. 1940) and the groups Studio Dumbar, Hard Werken, and Wild Plakken pushed beyond these traditional values in their quest for individual meaning and subjective expression.

Anthon Beeke participated in Fluxus, a 1960s neo-Dada movement exploring conceptual and performance art, happenings, experimental poetry, and language art. This exposure

22–34. Pieter Brattinga, poster for exhibition De man achter due vormgeving van de PTT (The Man Behind the Design for the Dutch Post Service), 1960. A vibrant translucency, achieved by overprinting gray and blue on a halftone photograph, expresses the subject.

22–35. Studio Dumbar, PTT corporate identity system, 1989. Architectural identification, vehicles, and signage were produced from guidelines in the identity manual, shown at right.

22–34

22–35

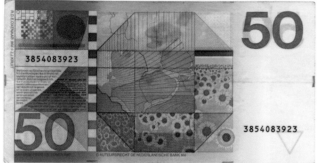

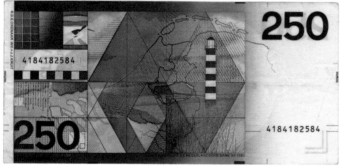

22–36

22–37

helped Beeke seek unconventional solutions to visual-communications assignments; he emerged as a provocateur pushing for maximum freedom of expression and thought. His posters (Fig. **22–37**) often use photographic depictions of the human figure. These are often embellished with objects, fragmented, distorted, or altered to create jolting ambiguities, unexpected perceptual experiences, and shocking messages. Many of his works have erotic overtones. His typographic oeuvre is unrestrained. The visual style of tabloid journalism, handwritten titles jotted onto photographs, or even eloquent classical

typography might be used and, on occasion, combined. Beeke and those inspired by his example define design not as a quest for ideal form or beauty but as a search for underlying truth. This search is undertaken from a philosophical vantage point acknowledging dark undercurrents running beneath the surface, and a belief that design should not avoid the true nature of the human condition by glossing over reality (Figs. **22–38** and **22–39**).

Like H. N. Werkman, Ghislain (Gielijn) Daphnis Escher (b. 1945) is a designer who cannot be placed in any category.

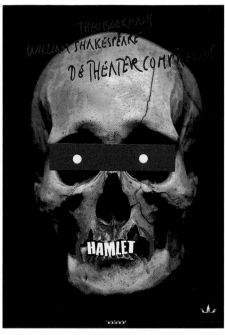

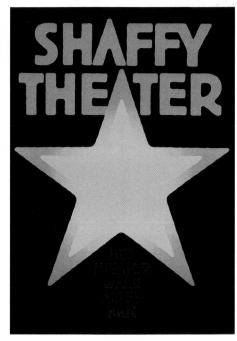

22–38   22–39   22–40

Through their simplicity and flat surfaces of color his posters stand out from the urban surroundings where they hang, and through their quiet dignity they attract attention on crowded streets. His posters are uncompromising aesthetic statements, far removed from the mainstream of modern graphic design. With their anecdotal appeal they subtly reach the essence of the subject at hand (Figs. **22–40**, **22–41**, and **22–42**).

Gert Dumbar (b. 1940) founded Studio Dumbar in 1977. First located in The Hague and now in Rotterdam, this studio has a comprehensive range, designing everything from experimental graphics for cultural clients to corporate identity programs (see Fig. 22–35) and literature. Dumbar rejects what he calls "dehumanized forms" and advocates graphic design with "stylistic durability to survive beyond its time." As a design student at London's Royal College of Art in the early 1960s, Dumbar developed a technique he called *staged photography*, consisting of still lifes and environments incorporating found material and papier-mâché figures and objects sculpted or assembled for the project (Fig. **22–43**). These were photographed, often by Lex van Pieterson (b. 1946), in front of collage backgrounds that became part of the overall composition. Illustration, photography, typography, and sculpture were integrated into a lively visual syntax. Fragmented, sometimes complex to the edge of chaos, and layered with complex typography, many Dumbar projects caused consternation among advocates of a more ordered aesthetic. But by the late 1980s many European designers were mimicking Studio Dumbar's approach, causing Gert Dumbar to place a moratorium on these techniques within his firm.

22–36. R.E.D. Oxenaar with J. J. Kruit, designs for Netherlands currency: 50 guilder, 1982, and 250 guilder, 1986. A rare aesthetic attainment and functional practicality enabled currency to contribute to a sense of national identity.

22–37. Anthon Beeke (designer and photographer), theater poster for *Leonce en Lena* (Leonce and Lena), 1979. The image becomes a covert allusion to something not directly stated, disconcerting in its ambiguity.

22–38. Anthon Beeke (designer and photographer), poster for *Een meeuw* (The Seagull), 2003. The face of a woman encircled by a wreath of feathers at first appears to be the center of a flower. However, the carnival atmosphere quickly turns cynical as the face takes on the appearance of a blood-spattered specter.

22–39. Anthon Beeke (designer and photographer), poster for *Hamlet,* 2002. The skull image for Hamlet at first appears to be an ordinary interpretation of the subject, but another element is introduced as the eyes are bluntly covered with a red rectangle. Even without eyes, the skull stares at us through two white dots. Its teeth spell *HAMLET* and seem to be emitting caustic laughter.

22–40. Ghislain (Gielijn) Daphnis Escher, poster for the Shaffy Theater, 1974. Instead of promoting a play, this poster promotes the theater itself.

Dumbar values the role of humor and impulse in design and believes an element of fun and play should permeate visual communications whenever appropriate. Studio Dumbar makes a conscious effort to produce innovative and provocative graphics (Fig. **22–44**); the goal is to achieve the level of freedom and diverse techniques usually associated with fine

22–41

22–42

22–43

22–44

22–45

arts while successfully meeting client objectives. Dumbar says, "We follow our fingertips," meaning the intuitive sense of the designer should lead the project.

Teamwork and dialogue are important in the studio's process. Dumbar is generous in recognizing the accomplishments of his staff and encourages individual approaches. The structure of the studio is unique: there is almost no overhead or bureaucracy; designers are free to express themselves in their work. The rectangle printing format is often challenged

by producing posters in die-cut shapes whose configuration is determined by the imagery. The role of enlightened clients is acknowledged by Dumbar, who says he hopes there is never a monument to Dutch designers but one to Dutch clients!

In 1978 a group of Rotterdam designers launched a new monthly magazine (Fig. **22–45**) titled *Hard werken* (Hard Working); two years later they formed Hard Werken Design, which was more an informal association than a structured business. The group included Henk Elenga (b. 1947, who later

22–46

22–47

opened Hard Werken L.A. Desk in Los Angeles), Gerard Hadders (b. 1954), Tom van der Haspel (b. 1953), Helen Howard, and Rick Vermeulen (b. 1950). Joining in a reaction to formalism and modernism, Hard Werken developed a relaxed, anything-goes attitude. Rejecting all styles and theories, its members sought solutions from their subjective interpretation of the problem (Fig. **22–46**). Their openness to any conceivable typographic or image possibility resulted in surprising and original results. Hard Werken emphasized not just the message content but also the methods and materials used to convey it to an audience (Fig. **22–47**). Formal precepts governing design were suspended. Unlike the collaborative atmosphere at Studio Dumbar, Hard Werken was initially a collective of autonomous designers who could decide whether others could participate on projects.

Hard Werken embraced the contemporary art scene and rejected design refinement; its work could be raw and offensive. It adhered to no fixed political or aesthetic position but embraced creative anarchy. Rejecting boundaries, Hard Werken designed audiovisual presentations, exhibitions, furniture, interior designs, lamps, and theater sets. By 1990, the group had evolved into a more structured company. Then, in 1994, it merged with the Ten Cate Bergmans design office to form a large communications firm named Inízio.

Hard Werken embraced a cultural agenda; by contrast, the collaborative group Wild Plakken, formed by Frank Beekers (b. 1952), Lies Ros (b. 1952), and Rob Schröder (b. 1950) in 1977, had a definite social and political mission: They created designs for clients actively working for meaningful social or

22–41. Ghislain (Gielijn) Daphnis Escher, "Dueten" (Duets) poster, 1997. Both title and subject are adroitly suggested through typography.

22–42. Ghislain (Gielijn) Daphnis Escher, poster for the exhibition Sandberg nu: Hommage aan Sandberg (Sandberg Now: Homage to Sandberg), 2004. The name *Sandberg*, which might be roughly translated as "sand mountain," is represented by a mound of sand.

22–43. Gert Dumbar (designer), Lex van Pieterson (photographer), and Tel design (studio), poster for the Mondrian collection at the Haags Gerneentemuseum, 1971. Dumbar's sculptural fantasy caused great consternation among those who failed to understand it as a perceptive homage to Mondrian's creative process.

22–44. Studio Dumbar, poster for Holland Dance Festival, 1995. In this poster series, graphic forms reflect the dancers' movements.

22–45. Hard Werken Design, covers for *Hard werken* magazine no. 1, 1979, and no. 10, 1982. Experimentation with images, printing techniques, and materials characterized early Hard Werken designs.

22–46. Hard Werken Design, souvenir stamp sheet for the PTT, 1988. The self-referential attributes of modern painting and literature are applied to postage stamps.

22–47. Hard Werken Design, film festival poster, 1989. Neon was but one of many materials used over the years to fabricate this logo.

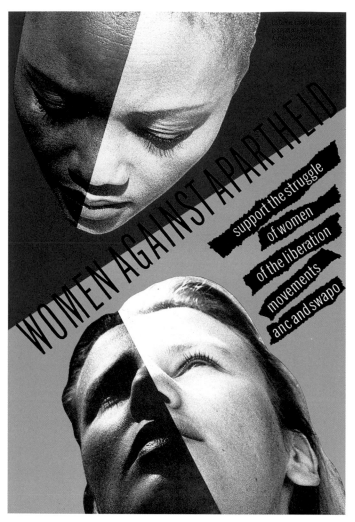

22–48

22–49

political change. The designers closely collaborated on each project. The name *Wild Plakken* can be translated as "Wild Pasting" or "Unauthorized Bill-Posting." The name was thrust upon the studio in the early 1980s because it illegally pasted posters in the center of Amsterdam; Schröder was jailed several times for illegal posting. Wild Plakken accepted or rejected commissions based on the client's ideological viewpoint; the group believed a designer should match his or her beliefs to the content of his or her graphic designs. Their work addressed such issues as racism (Fig. **22–48**), the environment, abortion, women's rights, and gay rights. Clients included trade unions, left-wing political parties, women's rights organizations, museums, and performing-arts groups.

In their formative years Wild Plakken used clear, straightforward images that might be called *closed texts* because viewers could only interpret them in one specific, carefully controlled way. As their work evolved, Wild Plakken offered viewers what might be called *open texts*, giving viewers greater freedom for imaginative interpretation (Figs. **22–49** and **22–50**) by introduc-

ing surrealist imagery, photomontages using torn and fragmented images, and brightly colored shapes. Their work projects a raw power when juxtaposed against the refined photography of conventional print advertising.

Wild Plakken did virtually all of its own photography, because the designers then felt free to experiment in the darkroom or cut, tear, and combine the images unencumbered by the need to maintain the integrity of another photographer's work. Wild Plakken designers believed the way a design looks should be determined by the nature and content of the subject. They thought designers risk becoming superficial or mere reflectors of fashionable trends if they are not deeply committed to the design process, clients, and content. After eleven years of close collaboration, Beekers left Wild Plakken to launch his own studio.

The creativity and vitality of Studio Dumbar, Hard Werken, and Wild Plakken inspired a generation of Dutch designers, and their collective oeuvre ignited efforts by visual communicators in other countries to push the limits of the printed page.

22–50

Life in the late twentieth century was characterized by a global economy and instantaneous communications. As the human community becomes progressively more international, national and regional cultural traditions continue to inform design activities in many countries. Rapid economic growth and industrialization of developing countries have been accompanied by growing professionalism in graphic design. In the Middle East, Latin America, Asia, and parts of Africa, many designers are combining advanced technology and international design directions with their traditional culture and contemporary vernacular forms. As colonial influences decline, artists and designers have worked to develop a cultural identity, reexamine the role of art and design in an evolving society, and preserve traditions while addressing contemporary issues.

Unfortunately, limitations of space prevent inclusion of a survey of these emerging design directions in this edition. For the twenty-first century one anticipates a growing international cross-fertilization combined with homage to local traditions and individual expression in graphic design.

22–48. Wild Plakken, poster for the antiapartheid movement of the Netherlands, 1984. The multiracial unity of all women is signified by photographs split into dark and light skin color.

22–49. Wild Plakken, informational folder cover, 1988. The cover for this folder, used in Berlin to disseminate information about Dutch culture, reads, "Where Not Only Tulips Bloom."

22–50. Wild Plakken, postage stamps for the PTT: children and traffic, 1985; Dutch trade unions, 1989; and elderly people and mobility, 1995. Color, type, and image are orchestrated into dynamic stamps.

Postmodern Design

23

By the 1970s, many believed the modern era was drawing to a close in art, design, politics, and literature. The cultural norms of Western society were scrutinized, and the authority of traditional institutions was questioned. Pluralism emerged as people began to dispute the underlying tenets of modernism. The continuing quest for equality by women and minorities contributed to a growing climate of cultural diversity, as did immigration, international travel, and global communications. Accepted viewpoints were challenged by those who sought to remedy bias and distortion in the historical record. The social, economic, and environmental awareness of the period caused many to believe the modern aesthetic was no longer relevant in an emerging postindustrial society. People in many fields embraced the term *postmodernism* to express a climate of cultural change. These included architects, economists, feminists, and even theologians. Maddeningly vague and overused, *postmodernism* became a byword in the last quarter of the twentieth century.

In design, postmodernism designated the work of architects and designers who were breaking with the international style so prevalent since the Bauhaus. Postmodernism sent shock waves through the design establishment as it challenged the order and clarity of modern design, particularly corporate design. (Some observers reject the term *postmodern*, arguing that it is merely a continuation of the modern movement. *Late modernism* and *mannerism* are proffered as alternative terms for late twentieth-century design.) Design forms and terminology have political and social meaning,

expressing attitudes and values of their time; postmodernism gained a strong foothold among the generation of designers who emerged in the 1970s. Perhaps the international style had been so thoroughly refined, explored, and accepted that a backlash was inevitable. Historical references, decoration, and the vernacular were disdained by modernists, while postmodern designers drew upon these resources to expand the range of design possibilities.

As the social activism of the late 1960s gave way to more self-absorbed, personal involvement during the 1970s, media pundits spoke of the "Me Generation" to convey the spirit of the decade. The intuitive and playful aspects of postmodern design reflect personal involvement. Postmodern designers place a form in space because it "feels" right rather than to fulfill a rational communicative need. As radically different as a psychedelic poster and a visual-identity manual might be, both are corporate design, for or relating to a unified body of people with common values. On the other hand, postmodernist design is often subjective and even eccentric; the designer becomes an artist performing before an audience with the bravura of a street musician, and the audience either responds or passes on.

The umbrella term *postmodernism* does not tell the whole story, because while architecture may fit rather neatly into historical categories (Victorian, art nouveau, modern, and postmodern), graphic design is far too pluralistic and diverse to fit such a simplistic system. Just three examples of graphic-design expressions having no parallel in architecture are World War I posters, the work of the Push Pin group, and the psychedelic poster. Graphic design, rapidly changing and ephemeral, was never dominated by the international style the way architecture was. Postmodern graphic design can be loosely categorized as moving in several major directions: the early extensions of the International Typographic Style by Swiss designers who broke with the dicta of the movement; new-wave typography, which began in Basel, Switzerland, through the teaching and research of Wolfgang Weingart (b. 1941); the exuberant mannerism of the early 1980s, with significant contributions from the Memphis group in Milan, Italy, and from San Francisco designers; retro, the eclectic revivals and eccentric reinventions of earlier models, particularly European vernacular and modern design from the decades between the world wars; and the electronic revolution spawned by the Macintosh computer in the late 1980s, which drew upon all of the earlier thrusts.

Precursors to postmodern design

During the 1960s, *supermannerism* and *supergraphics* were words coined to describe breaks with modern design. As were many art history labels, *supermannerism* was first used as a disparaging term. *Mannerism* was first used as a label for the

23-1. Robert Venturi, competition model for the Football Hall of Fame, 1967. A vast, kinetic electronic graphics display dominates the building, as information replaces structure as the dominant "subject" of architecture. (Photograph by George Pohl).

23-1

stylish art of the 1500s, which broke with the natural and harmonious beauty of the High Renaissance. Mannerism departed from the norm by taking liberties with the classical vocabulary of form; the term *supermannerism* was first used by advocates of the purist modern movement to describe work by young architects whose expanded formal range embraced the pop-art notion of changing scale and context. Zigzag diagonals were added to the horizontal and vertical structures of modern architecture. An architecture of inclusion replaced the machine aesthetic and simple geometric forms of the international style.

In the late 1960s the application of graphic design to architecture in large-scale environmental graphics extended the formal concepts of *art concret* and the International Typographic Style. *Supergraphics* became the popular name for bold geometric shapes of bright color, giant Helvetica letterforms, and huge pictographs warping walls, bending corners, and flowing from the floor to the wall and across the ceiling, expanding or contracting space in scale changes relative to the architecture. Psychological as well as decorative values were addressed as designers created forms to enliven dismal institutional architecture, reverse or shorten the perspective of endless hallways, and bring vitality and color to the built environment.

Philadelphia-born Robert Venturi (b. 1925) is the most controversial and original architect branded with the supermannerist label. When Venturi looked at the vulgar and disdained urban landscape of billboards, electric signs, and pedestrian buildings he saw a vitality and functional purpose and urged designers to learn from the hyperbolic glitter of places such as

Las Vegas. Venturi saw the building not as sculptured form but as a component of the larger urban traffic/communication/interior/exterior environmental system. Uncommon uses and juxtaposition of materials, graphic elements from the commercial roadside strip, billboards, and environmental-scale lettering were freely added to his architectural vocabulary. Venturi sees graphic communications and new technologies as important tools for architecture; his proposal for the Football Hall of Fame (Fig. 23–1) featured a giant illuminated sign that would have been visible for miles on the approaching interstate highway.

Supermannerist architect Charles W. Moore (1923–93) designed a large condominium project at Gualala, California, in the mid-1960s. He called on graphic designer Barbara Stauffacher Solomon (b. 1932) to bring the walls and ceilings of this large architectural project to life through the application of color and shape (Fig. 23–2). Solomon, a San Francisco native and painter who had studied graphic design at the Basel School of Design during the late 1950s, used a pallet of pure hue and elementary shape in compositions that transformed the totality of the space. In 1970 the American Institute of Architects presented its medal to Solomon for "bold, fresh, and exciting designs clearly illustrating the importance of rational but vigorous graphics in bringing order to the urban scene."

Both the name *supergraphics* and the idea caught the public's fancy; by 1970 supergraphics were being used in corporate identification systems, interior design for shops and boutiques, and to brighten factory and school environments, bringing about greater graphic-design involvement in environmental design.

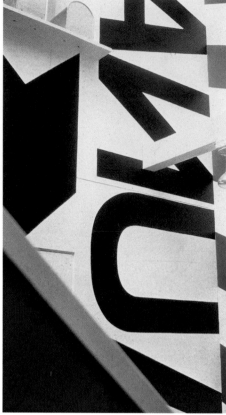

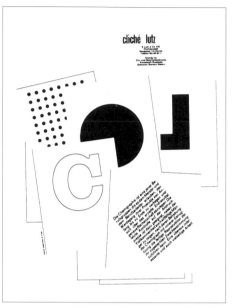

23–2

23–3

Early Swiss postmodern design

Tendencies toward postmodern graphic design first emerged from individuals working within the dicta of the International Typographic Style. The main thrust of this movement was toward neutral and objective typography; the playful, unexpected, and disorganized were rarely allowed to encroach upon its cool clarity and scientific objectivity. One of the earliest indications that a younger generation of graphic designers was starting to enlarge its range of possibilities in the 1960s was the 1964 advertisement (Fig. **23–3**) for the printer E. Lutz & Company by Rosmarie Tissi. Different kinds of copy printed by the client—headlines, text, halftones, and solids—are illustrated by elemental symbols. Rather than align these images in boxes ordered on a grid, the five images appear to have been intuitively and randomly placed. The ruled lines forming the edges of the squares on which these images rest have lost-and-found edges to engage the viewer, who must fill in the missing lines.

In 1966 Siegfried Odermatt designed a trademark for the Union Safe Company that is the antithesis of Swiss design, for the letterforms in the word *Union* are jammed together to form a compact unit suggesting the sturdy strength of the product, sacrificing legibility in the process. In full-page newspaper advertisements for Union (Figs. **23–4**), placed during

prestigious banking conferences, Odermatt treated this logo as pure form to be manipulated visually, creating a plastic dynamic on the newspaper page. Odermatt and Tissi have always used strong graphic impact, a playful sense of form, and unexpected manipulation of space in seeking logical and effective solutions to design problems.

When Odermatt and Tissi turned to typeface design, their originality of form produced unexpected letterforms, as can be seen in Tissi's advertisement for Englersatz AG (Fig. **23–5**), which features her typefaces. A presentation folder designed by Tissi for the printing firm Anton Schöb (Fig. **23–6**) achieves typographic vitality by overlapping and combining letterforms. Placing text typography on geometric shapes whose configuration is generated by the line lengths of the text is a technique Odermatt and Tissi frequently used during the 1980s.

Another Swiss designer with a strong interest in complexity of form is Steff Geissbuhler (b. 1942), who joined the Geigy pharmaceutical company in the mid-1960s. In a capabilities brochure for the publicity department (Fig. **23–7**), his swirling typographic configuration becomes a circular tunnel moving back into space. He moved to Philadelphia and established an independent design practice before becoming a partner at Chermayeff & Geismar Associates. While at Chermayeff & Geismar he created corporate identity programs for Merck, Time Warner,

23–4

23–5

23–6

NBC, Telemundo, Union Pacific Corporation, Toledo Museum of Art, Crane & Co., and the May Department Stores Companies, among others. Complexity of form is never used as an end in itself; the dynamic of multiple components forming a whole grows from the fundamental content of the design problem at hand (Figs. 23–8). Careful structural control enables Geissbuhler to organize vast numbers of elements into a cohesive whole.

Other Swiss designers were interested in using typography as a means of bending the traditions of modernism to experiment and express their ideas for communication with the viewer. Bruno Monguzzi (b. 1941) is an extraordinary designer, typographer and teacher. After study in Geneva and London he began his career at Studio Boggeri in Milan in 1961. His typographic solutions express the subject matter through an innovative bond of form and function. In his poster for the exhibition Anwesenheit bei Abwesenheit [Presence in Absence]: The Photograms in 20th Century Art (Fig. 23–9), his idea was to represent the process of light directly sensitizing the emulsion of photographic paper. For this he created a photogram of a hand holding a perfect circular form against a rounded rectangle revealing a grided background. The result is strong, visually and conceptually, evoking the ideas of surrealism and constructivism while integrating type and image to create an arresting poster.

23–2. Barbara Stauffacher Solomon, supergraphics for Sea Ranch, 1966. Vibrant primary colors, sans-serif letters, arcs, and slashing diagonals form a strong counterpoint to the architectural structure and the brilliant sunlight.

23–3. Rosmarie Tissi, advertisement for E. Lutz & Company, 1964. The space comes to life through subtle shifts and angles that throw the page into a state of suspended animation.

23–4. Siegfried Odermatt, advertisement for Union wall safes, 1968. Overlapping and cropping the logo, printed in black and blue-gray, brings the vitality and impact of pure form to the newspaper page.

23–5. Rosmarie Tissi, advertisement for Englersatz AG, printers, 1980. The whimsical geometric shapes of Tissi's typefaces engage the viewer with their texture and dimensionality.

23–6. Rosmarie Tissi, direct mail folder for Anton Schöb printers, 1981. Dynamic color and shape create an expressive backdrop for the message.

Odermatt, Tissi, Geissbuhler, and others working in the 1960s did not rebel against the International Typographic Style; rather, they expanded its parameters. In the 1970s, this development was followed by a revolt, as practitioners and teachers schooled in the International Typographic Style sought to reinvent typographic design. These new directions were quickly labeled *new-wave typography*.

23–7

23–8

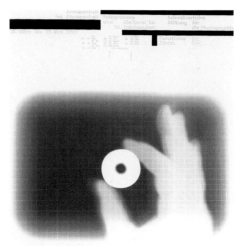

23–9

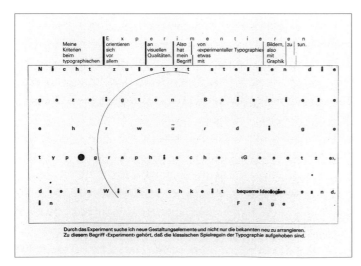

Hausanschlußkästen aus Isolierstoff	**BEG** ■	**Berliner Elektrizitäts-Gesellschaft**	
Hausanschlußsicherungen		1000 Berlin	
Berührungsschutz für den Netzanschluß		Postfach 437	
Steuerleitungsklemmen		Fernruf	59 67 21
Endverschlußrichter			
	BEG ■		

23–10

23–11

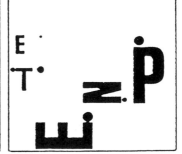

23–12

23–13

23–7. Steff Geissbuhler, Geigy brochure cover, 1965. Legibility is sacrificed in favor of dynamic visual organization.

23–8. Steff Geissbuhler, Blazer financial services poster, 1974. A kinetic repetition of forms moving across the space suggests travel while connoting categories of service. This is one of five posters used as decorative wall displays.

23–9. Bruno Monguzzi, poster for the exhibition Anwesenheit bei Abwesenheit [Presence in Absence]: The Photograms in 20th Century Art, 1990.

23–10. Wolfgang Weingart, part of a German typesetter's examination, 1963. The strong influence of Swiss typography is evident.

23–11. Wolfgang Weingart, experimental text setting, 1969. Traditional word spacing and letterspacing concepts dating from medieval times were called into question.

23–12. Wolfgang Weingart, typographic experiments, 1971. A form-and-space exploration relates bullets to letterforms. Four German words explore inverted lowercase *m* forms to make a *B* and an *a*, while colons and apostrophes combine to form accented *u* letterforms.

23–13. Wolfgang Weingart, announcement from *Typografische Monatsblätter* magazine, 1974. This early layered collage, with overlapping images and complex dropouts, uses numbers and arrows rather than left-to-right and top-to-bottom sequencing to direct the reader through the page.

New-wave typography

Just as Herbert Bayer, Jan Tschichold, and others employed a new approach to typographic design in the 1920s, some forty years later, opposition to the cool formalism of the modernist tradition emerged first in Switzerland, then spread around the world. In 1964 young Wolfgang Weingart, who had already completed a three-year apprenticeship in typography (Fig. **23–10**) and studied art, arrived in Basel from southeastern Germany to study with Emil Ruder. Weingart joined Armin Hofmann on the faculty of the Basel School in 1968. As a student, Weingart had worked under the influence of Ruder and Hofmann; when he began to teach, however, he taught type differently from his mentors. Weingart began to question the typography of absolute order and cleanness. He wondered if perhaps the international style had become so refined and prevalent throughout the world that it had reached an anemic phase. Rejecting the right angle as an exclusive organizing principle, Weingart achieved a joyous and intuitive design with a richness of visual effects. Ideology and rules collapsed in the face of his boundless energy. Drawing on broad technical knowledge and a willingness to explore the untried, he turned up the intensity of the page.

From 1968 until 1974 Weingart worked with lead type and letterpress systems (Figs. **23–11** and **23–12**). In his teaching and personal projects he sought to breathe a new spirit into the typography of order and neatness by questioning the premises, rules, and surface appearances that were hardening the innovations of the Swiss masters into an academic style. Time-honored traditions of typography and visual-language systems were rethought. To emphasize an important word in a headline, Weingart often made it white on a chunky, black rectangle. Wide letterspacing, discarded in the fetish for tight type in the revolution from metal to photographic typographic

systems in the 1960s, was explored. In response to a request to identify the kinds of typography he designed, Weingart listed "sunshine type, bunny type, ant type, five-minute type, typewriter type," and "for-the-people type." The humor and expressive metaphors Weingart used to define his work find close parallels in his typographic invention.

But by the mid-1970s Weingart set off in a new direction when he turned his attention toward offset printing and film systems. He used the printer's camera to alter images and explored the unique properties of the film image. Weingart began to move away from purely typographic design and embraced collage as a medium for visual communication (Fig. **23–13**). A new technique—the sandwiching or layering of images and type that have been photographed as film positives—enabled him to overlap complex visual information (Fig. **23–14**), juxtapose textures with images, and unify typography with pictorial images in unprecedented ways. He took particular delight in the graphic qualities of enlarged halftone dots (Fig. **23–15**) and the moiré patterns produced when these dot patterns are overlapped and then shifted against each other. His design process involved multiple film positives and masks that were stacked, arranged, then exposed with careful registration to produce one negative, which went to

23–14

23–15

23–16

the printer. In color work such as the Kunstkredit exhibition poster (Fig. **23–16**), the process was extended to allow the interaction of two colors, using overprinting to build dimensional layers of illusionistic forms.

Weingart advocates the "Gutenberg approach" to graphic communications: Designers, like the early typographic printers, should strive to stay involved in all aspects of the process (including concept, typesetting, prepress production, and printing) to ensure the realization of their vision. By the time homogenized versions of Weingart's innovations were assimilated into the mainstream of graphic design, he had moved on to new explorations.

In October 1972 Weingart traveled to America and delivered presentations at eight prominent design schools. His new design sensibility fell on fertile soil. Young designers who spent time at Basel afterwards came to the United States to teach and practice. These included Dan Friedman (1945–95), April Greiman (b. 1948), and Willi Kunz (b. 1943). A new typographic vocabulary began to filter into an American design profession restless with the redundancy of sans-serif and grid-based corporate systems. Weingart and others who pioneered the typographic new wave strongly rejected the notion of style and saw their work as an attempt to expand the parameters of typographic communication, yet their work was so widely imitated, especially in design education, that it gave rise to a prevailing typographic approach in the late 1970s and 1980s. Specific design ideas explored by Weingart and his students in the late 1960s and early 1970s and adopted a decade later include letterspaced sans-serif type; bold stair-step rules; ruled lines

punctuating and energizing space; diagonal type; the introduction of italic type and/or weight changes within words; and type reversed from a series of bars.

Dan Friedman, an American who studied at the Ulm Institute of Design in 1967 and 1968 and at the Basel School of Design from 1968 to 1970, rethought the nature of typographic forms and how they could operate in space; he called his *Typografische Monatsblätter* (Fig. **23–17**) magazine cover a visual manifesto for a more inclusive typography. After returning to the United States he taught courses at Yale University and the Philadelphia College of Art in 1970 and 1971. At a time when letterpress typography was collapsing but the new photographic and computer-generated processes were still evolving, Friedman addressed the problem of teaching the basics of a new typography through syntactic and semantic investigations, using such ordinary copy as a daily weather report (Fig. **23–18**). After exploring principles of rhythm, harmony, and proportion, students were given a neutral message in 30-point Univers 55 and 65. A sequence of design operations ranging from simple to complex was conducted, varying the effects of the message through changes in position; weight and scale; slant (roman to italic); line-, word-, and letterspacing; clustering; symbolic gesture; and pictorial confrontation. Another concern was the evaluation of legibility and readability, for Friedman believed "that legibility (a quality of efficient, clear, and simple reading) is often in conflict with readability (a quality that promotes interest, pleasure, and challenge in reading)." He urged his students to make their work both functional and aesthetically unconventional. Exploration of the spatial intervals between

23–17

23–14. Wolfgang Weingart, exhibition poster, 1977. A kaleido-scope of shifting images and forms calls experiences of the museum and its art into play.

23–15. Wolfgang Weingart, exhibition poster, 1982. Moiré patterns are created by layered film positives.

23–16. Wolfgang Weingart, exhibition poster, 1982. Modulated patterns of overlapping colored dots warp and modulate the space.

23–17. Dan Friedman, *Typografische Monatsblätter* magazine cover, 1971. Letterforms become kinetic objects moving in time and urban space.

23–18. Dan Friedman (instructor) and Rosalie Hanson (student), typographic permutations, 1970. Friedman's students explored contrasts: functional/unconventional; legible/readable; simple/complex; orderly/disorderly; legible/unpredictable; static/dynamic; banal/original.

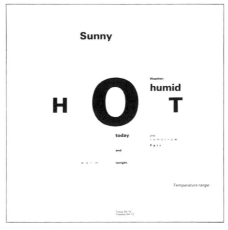

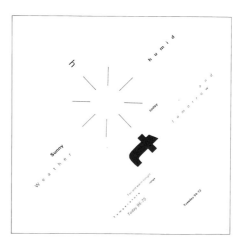

23–18

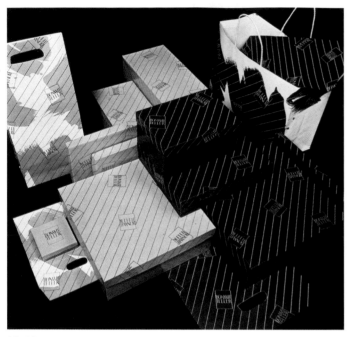

23–19

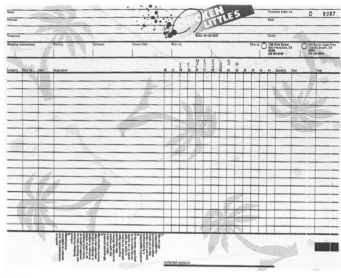

23–20

23–21

23–22

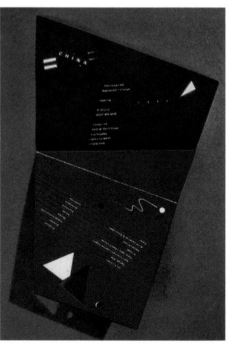

23–23

letters, lines, and words gave some works by Friedman and his students a deconstructed quality—that is, the syntactic structure has been pulled apart. But even in the most random solutions, an underlying structure is evident. The 1973 publication of this work in the journal *Visible Language* had a widespread influence on typographic education in the United States and other countries.

Friedman's graphic design, furniture, and sculptural works were paradigms of the emerging postmodern currents. His formal background at Ulm and typographic experimentation at Basel were synthesized as he played formal structure against spontaneous and expressive forms (Figs. **23–19** and **23–20**). Texture, surface, and spatial layering were explored in his work; organic and geometric forms were contrasted.

23–19. Dan Friedman (in association with Anspach Grossman Portugal, Inc.), Bonwit Teller gift packaging proposal, 1977. Spontaneous hand-drawn forms are layered with mechanical linear patterns and typography.

23–20. Dan Friedman, order form for Chicken Little's, 1978. Rational clarity is juxtaposed with a loose, decorative spontaneity.

23–21. April Greiman, masthead for *Luxe,* 1978. The step rule, mixture of letterspaced and italic type, and isolation of each letter as an independent form reflect Greiman's Basel heritage.

23–22. April Greiman, China Club advertisement, 1980. Overlapping forms and movements in and out of space animate the flat typographic page.

23–23. April Greiman, China Club invitation, 1980. The space is energized by gestural and geometric forms moving in counterpoint to the typographic structure.

Friedman believed that forms could be amusing to look at and provocative, and he freely injected these properties into his designs. As his work progressed, he rejected the term *postmodernism* in favor of *radical modernism,* which he defined as a reaffirmation of the idealism of modernism altered to accommodate the radical cultural and social changes occurring in the late twentieth century.

On the West Coast, April Greiman established a studio in Los Angeles after studying with Weingart and Hofmann in Basel during the early 1970s. Weingart observed, "April Greiman took the ideas developed at Basel in a new direction, particularly in her use of color and photography. All things are possible in America!" While Greiman draws from Basel design, using forms such as the step-rule at the bottom of the Luxe logotype (Fig. **23–21**), which was inspired by the pattern of the stairways in ruins at an archaeological site visited by Weingart during his travels, she evolved a new attitude toward space. Typographic design has usually been the most two-dimensional of all the visual disciplines, but Greiman achieves a sense of depth in her typographic pages. Overlapping forms, diagonal lines that imply perspective or reverse perspective, gestured strokes that move back in space, overlap, or move behind geometric elements, and floating forms that cast shadows are the means she uses to make forms move forward and backward from the surface of the printed page. Greiman's typographic space operates with the same governing principle defined by El Lissitzky in his PROUN paintings but never applied to his typography (Figs. **23–22** and **23–23**).

Strong tactile qualities are found in Greiman's work, as textures resulting from enlarged four-color process screens and repetitive patterns of dots or ruled lines contrast with flat shapes of color or tone. The intuitive dispersal of numerous

elements could collapse into chaos, but a point-counterpoint organization maintains order by pulling the eye into the page through dominant elements that quickly lead to others as the viewer moves through the page's richness of form.

In collaboration with the photographer Jayme Odgers (b. 1939), Greiman moved graphic design and photographic illustration into a new realm of dynamic space (Fig. **23–24**). Graphic elements become part of the real space of photographs. Odgers's wide-angle photographs with extreme depth of field have objects thrusting into the picture space from the peripheral edges.

Swiss-born Willi Kunz played a role in introducing the new typography developed at Basel in the United States. After apprenticing as a typesetter, Kunz completed his postgraduate studies at the Zurich School of Arts and Crafts. He moved to New York City in 1970 and worked there as a graphic designer until 1973, when he accepted a one-year appointment to teach typography at the Basel School of Design as Weingart's sabbatical-leave replacement. Inspired by the research of Weingart and his students, and with the type shop at his disposal, Kunz began a series of typographic interpretations of writings by Canadian philosopher Marshall McLuhan. These were handprinted and published under the title *12 T y p o graphical Interpretations* (Fig. **23–25**). McLuhan's thoughts on communications and printing were visualized and intensified by contrasting type weights, sometimes within the same word; geometric stair-step forms; unorthodox letter-, word-, and linespacing; lines and bars used as visual punctuation and spatial elements; and textual areas introduced into the spatial field.

After Kunz returned to New York and established his design office, his exhibition poster for photographer Fredrich Cantor (Fig. **23–26**) was hailed by *Print* magazine as a "quintessential example of PostModern design." The contrasting sizes of the photographs, the mixed weight of the typography, the diagonal letterspaced type, and the stepped pattern of dots covering part of the space all heralded the arrival of a new typographic syntax.

Kunz does not construct his work on a predetermined grid; rather, he starts the visual composition and permits structure and alignments to grow through the design process. He builds his typographic constellations with concern for the essential message, the structure unfolding in response to the information to be conveyed. He might be called an information architect who uses visual hierarchy and syntax to bring order and clarity to messages, as seen in a lecture series and exhibition schedule announcement (Fig. **23–27**). Kunz's working method is not unlike the process used by Piet Zwart in that he believes design must be resolved by working with the actual typographic materials and generally does not spend a large amount of time working on preliminary sketches. After the

23–24

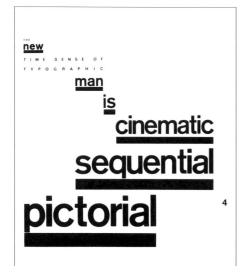

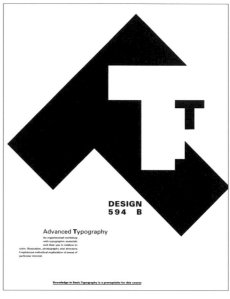

23–27

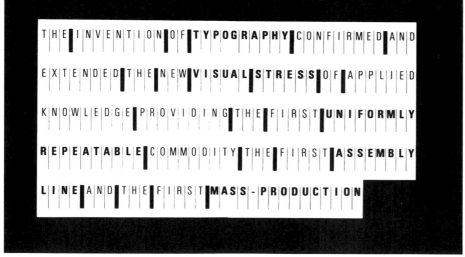

23–25

23–24. April Greiman (design and typography) and Jayme Odgers (art direction, photography, and design), poster for California Institute of the Arts, 1979. The printed surface is redefined as a continuum of time and space.

23–25. Willi Kunz, pages from *12 T y p o graphical Interpretations,* 1975. Marshall McLuhan noted that Kunz understood "the resonant interval in structuring designs."

23–26. Willi Kunz, photography exhibition poster, 1978. A dynamic equilibrium between diverse parts is achieved.

23–27. Willi Kunz, Typographic Workshop poster, 1974.

23–28. Kenneth Hiebert, exhibition and symposium poster, 1979. A formal grid structure is implied, but a playful intuitive process of form exploration led Hiebert to unexpected relationships.

23–26

23–28

basic ideas are formed, he has actual type material set, then develops the final solution from a careful probing of the organizational possibilities of the project.

As new-wave typography spread, many designers working in the International Typographic Style began to test their precepts against the exploratory design attitudes that were emerging. Dada photomontage techniques were used; grids were established, then violated; functional elements of 1920s new typography were used as decorative elements; and designers began to define the overall space as a field of tension, much as Zwart had done half a century earlier. Moreover, intuition and play reentered the design process. This can be seen in the work of designer and educator Kenneth Hiebert (b. 1930), who retained the harmonious balance achieved through experience with grid systems but, in designs such as his 1979 art/design/play poster for a Paul Rand exhibition (Fig. **23–28**), introduced texture, a small dot pattern, and a wider typeface range, and shifted forms on the grid.

A very early application of the architectural term *postmodern* to graphic design, was the title of a 1977 Chicago exhibition curated by Bill Bonnell: Postmodern Typography: Recent American Developments. Ironically, the exhibition included works by Steff Geissbuhler, April Greiman, Dan Friedman, and Willi Kunz—all of whom had come to America after work or study in Switzerland.

The Memphis and San Francisco schools

A new movement in postmodern design swept into international prominence as the 1970s closed and the 1980s began. This work was pluralistic, eclectic, and hedonistic. Designers were deeply enamored of texture, pattern, surface, color, and a playful geometry. Innovation occurred in many cities and countries around the globe, with important contributions from diverse groups, including architects and product designers in Milan, Italy, and graphic designers in San Francisco, California.

An important inspiration for all areas of design emerged in 1981, when global attention was concentrated on an exhibition of the Italian design group Memphis, led by eminent Italian architectural and product designer Ettore Sottsass (b. 1917). The group chose the name *Memphis* to reflect the inspiration they drew from both contemporary popular culture and the artifacts and ornaments of ancient cultures. Function became secondary to surface pattern and texture, color, and fantastic forms in their lamps, sofas, and cabinets. The Memphis sensibility embraces exaggerated geometric forms in bright (even garish) colors, bold geometric and organic patterns, often printed on plastic laminates, and allusions to earlier cultures, such as the use of marble and granite for table and chair legs evocative of columns in Greco-Roman architecture. In Memphis designs, form no longer follows function—it becomes the reason for the design to exist. Christoph Radl

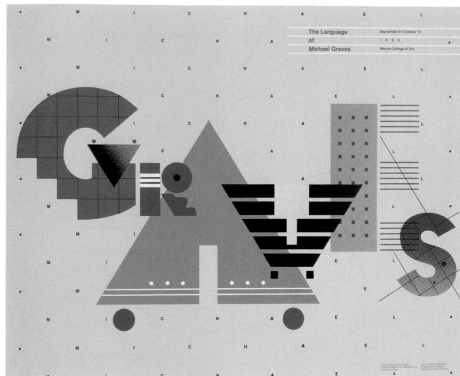

23–29

23–30

(Fig. **23–29**) headed the Memphis graphic design section. The experimental attitude, fascination with tactile and decorative color pattern, and exuberant geometry had a direct influence on postmodern design throughout the world. Memphis exploded on the scene just as the prosperous 1980s began and helped set the stage for an extravagantly decorative period of design.

Postmodernist architect Michael Graves (b. 1934) became another source of design inspiration. Graves became known in the 1960s for private houses designed in the minimalist tradition of orthodox modernism influenced by Le Corbusier. In the late 1970s he rebelled against the modernist tradition and expanded his range of architectural forms. Classical colonnades and loggias were revived and combined with visual elements inspired by cubist paintings. Graves's geometry is not the cool purism of Mies van der Rohe; it is an energetic, high-spirited geometry of decorative surfaces and tactile repetitive patterns. His visual motifs are expressed in a poster designed by Philadelphia graphic designer William Longhauser (b. 1947) for an exhibition of Graves's works (Fig. **23–30**). In this poster, which became an influential postmodern design in itself, a background pattern of repetitive dots is produced by the letters *M I C H A E L* letterspaced on a grid.

The design community and art schools in San Francisco were strongly influenced by the international style. This direction was punctuated by the flowering of the psychedelic poster in the late 1960s, proving to Bay Area graphic designers that tremendous potential existed for innovative form and color. In the early 1980s, San Francisco postmodern design emerged quickly, earning the city a reputation as a major center for creative design. Michael Vanderbyl (b. 1947), Michael Manwaring (b. 1942), and Michael Cronin (b. 1951) figured prominently in the evolution of the medium. An ongoing dialogue between these and other San Francisco designers enabled them to learn from each other as they forged the Bay Area postmodern movement. The range of graphic possibilities they expored together conveyed a cheerful optimism, a warm sense of humor, and an unbridled attitude about form and space. Freely drawn gestures, a sunny palette of pastel hues, and intuitive composition are often found in their work. Grays were often used with tints of lavender, turquoise, and peach.

Vanderbyl's poster for California Public Radio (Fig. **23–31**) is an important harbinger of the emerging school. The palette, repetition of ruled lines, and overall pattern of radio waves on the background foretell the new directions. Forms such as the lines and gestures signifying radio waves are carefully selected for their symbolic meaning; they also play strong decorative and structural roles. Vanderbyl paid homage to the exuberant furniture and textile designs of Memphis in a promotional mailer for Simpson Paper Company (Fig. **23–32**), and aimed his wit at postmodern architecture in a poster series that used graphic images to make editorial comments about

23–31

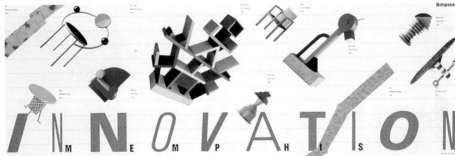

23–32

aspects of the movement (Fig. **23–33**). This series evidences the emergence of a self-referential attitude within design disciplines. In graphics for products ranging from woolen knit caps to office furniture (Fig. **23–34**) Vanderbyl combines a casual postmodern vitality with a typographic clarity echoing his background in the ordered typography of the International Typographic Style. The Hickory Business Furniture catalogue cover is part of a systematic design program combining informational graphics with vibrant visual expression.

In Bay Area designs, elements are given symbolic roles and become part of the content. A lyrical resonance permeates the color, form, and texture in Michael Manwaring's graphic and environmental designs. In his series of posters for Santa Cruz clothing (Fig. **23–35**), graphic forms and color serve the function of a traditional headline, linking lifestyle values to consumer products. In Manwaring's brochure cover for Barr Exhibits (Fig. **23–36**), the juxtaposition of a dimensional exhibition in the shape of the letter *B* against a grid pattern of small squares denoting floor plans and structural elements conveys the essence of the client's activity.

Although the San Francisco designers share a set of gestures, shapes, palettes, and intuitive spatial arrangements, personal attitudes are evident in their work. Michael Cronin often builds his compositions with shapes that become symbolic vessels or containers for color. His Beethoven Festival poster (Fig. **23–37**), designed with Shannon Terry, uses the repetition of diagonal and curved forms to bring order and harmony to the composition. Three treatments of display typography are unified by their structural relationship to the edges of the rectangle and the green architectural elements.

The ornamental and mannerist postmodern design styles spawned by diverse international sources, including Memphis, Michael Graves, and San Francisco designers, became a dominant design direction during the 1980s. In a decade when economic expansion and materialism were fueled by abundant energy supplies and heavily leveraged debt, architects around the world decorated facades with arches, pediments, and colonnades, then embellished them with marble, chrome, and pastel colors. Graphic designers used lush palettes and ornamented their work with gestures, textures, and decorative geometric elements. Surface and style often became ends in themselves.

23–29. Christoph Radl and Valentina Grego, Memphis logo designs, early 1980s. The Memphis vocabulary of form and pattern is given typographic expression in this series of logo designs.

23–30. William Longhauser, poster for a Michael Graves exhibition, 1983. Letterforms retain their legibility while being transformed into decorative geometric forms evoking a postmodern architectural landscape.

23–31. Michael Vanderbyl, California Public Radio poster, 1979. A rectangle negates the eye while triangles over the ear and flaring away from the mouth signify the auditory, nonvisual medium of radio.

23–32. Michael Vanderbyl, promotional mailer for Simpson Paper Company, 1985. Diagonal placement, textured letterforms, and mixed fonts echo the uninhibited vigor of the Italian design studio Memphis.

23–33

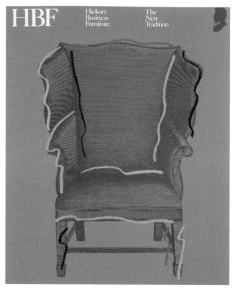

23–34

23–35

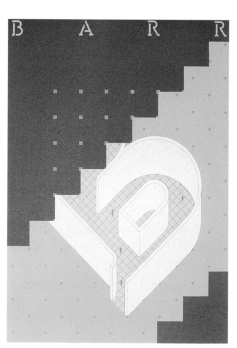

23–36

23–37

23–38

23–33. Michael Vanderbyl, postmodern architecture poster, 1984. An "innovative" postmodern building sticks out its tongue at an "obsolete" modern building, the stereotypical and oft criticized "boring glass box."

23–34. Michael Vanderbyl, cover for an HBF business furniture catalogue, 1985. Gestures and other elements of art are used as decorative elements.

23–35. Michael Manwaring, retail display poster for Santa Cruz, 1984. Diagonal torn-edged collage elements and rubber stamps convey a lively informality.

23–36. Michael Manwaring, brochure cover for Barr Exhibits, 1984. Postmodern design delights in pastel shades and repeated patterns. The viewer participates in the design by deciphering the half-hidden, dimensional *B*.

23–37. Michael Cronin and Shannon Terry, Beethoven Festival poster, 1983. Beethoven's passion is signaled by the corresponding forms of flame and hair.

23–38. Paula Scher, poster for CBS records, 1979. The synthesis of contradictory sources of inspiration, in this case Russian constructivism and nineteenth-century wood-type posters, is often a springboard to innovation.

Retro and vernacular design

During the 1980s graphic designers gained a growing understanding and appreciation of their history. A movement based on historical revival first emerged in New York and spread rapidly throughout the world. Called *retro* by some designers, it was based on an uninhibited eclectic interest in modernist European design from the first half of the century, a flagrant disregard for the rules of proper typography, and a fascination with eccentric and mannered typefaces designed and widely used during the 1920s and 1930s, then more or less forgotten after World War II. The prefix *retro* suggests the term *retrograde*, implying "backward-looking" and "contrary to the usual." Retro may be considered an aspect of postmodernism because of its interest in historical revivals, yet it paraphrases modern design from the decades between the wars rather than the Greco-Roman and Renaissance motifs employed by many architects. The term *vernacular design* refers to artistic and technical expression broadly characteristic of a locale or historical period; it closely relates to retro design. Vernacular design is the paraphrasing of earlier commonplace graphic forms, such as baseball cards, matchbook covers, and unskilled commercial illustrations and printing from past decades.

The New York approach to retro began with a small number of designers, including Paula Scher (b. 1948), Louise Fili (b. 1951), and Carin Goldberg (b. 1953). They rediscovered earlier twentieth-century graphics, ranging from the turn-of-the-century Vienna Secession to modernist but decorative

European typefaces popular during the two decades between the world wars. Their approach to space, color, and texture is often personal and original. Unorthodox attitudes about the accepted rules and regulations of design and typography permit them to take risks and experiment by exuberantly mixing fonts, using extreme letterspacing, and printing type in subtle color-on-color combinations. They are, however, typographic precisionists seeking a sublime level of visual organization. In many of their designs, typography does not play a role secondary to illustration and photography but moves to center stage to become figurative, animated, and expressive. The self-consciously eclectic aspects of retro continue a trait of New York design: Scher credits Seymour Chwast of Push Pin Studios and his use of Victorian, art nouveau, and art deco forms as an important inspiration; Fili worked with the late Herb Lubalin, who often called upon the extravagance of Victorian and art nouveau typographic themes. Scher and Fili moved New York's tradition of historicism forward into the 1920s and 1930s.

Paula Scher, an outspoken designer with an ironic sense of humor, worked for CBS Records during the 1970s, when music graphics were characterized by generous budgets, elaborate photography and illustrations, and opportunities to experiment. The highly successful recording industry crashed in 1978 as inflation, skyrocketing production costs, and slumping sales took a powerful toll. By 1979 tight budgets often forced Scher to develop typographic solutions based on imagination, art- and design-history sources, and her fascination with obscure and little-used typefaces. Art deco, Russian constructivism, and outmoded typefaces were incorporated into her work.

Russian constructivism provided important typographic inspiration (Fig. **23–38**). Scher did not copy the earlier constructivist style but used its vocabulary of forms and form relationships, reinventing and combining them in unexpected ways. Her use of color and space are different; the floating weightlessness of Russian constructivism is replaced by a dense packing of forms in space with the weight and vigor of old wood-type posters. After Scher formed the Koppel and Scher studio in partnership with Terry Koppel (b. 1950) in 1984, their "Great Beginnings" booklet (Fig. **23–39**) announced their new partnership with period typographic interpretations of the first paragraphs of great novels. Retro designs became a national phenomenon in 1985 after Scher designed the first of two folios for a paper manufacturer, presenting twenty-two complete fonts of "an eclectic collection of eccentric and decorative type," including such anomalies as the 1911 decorative script Phyllis, the playful 1925 Greco Rosart (renamed Greco Deco by Scher), and the quirky, thick-and-thin sans-serif Trio. Designers suddenly had access to

23–39. Paula Scher, "Great Beginnings" spread for Koppel & Scher promotional booklet, 1984. Typographic ideas paraphrasing Russian constructivism, futurism, and Dada are freely combined and reinvented.

23–40. Paula Scher, Swatch Watch poster, 1985. A famous Herbert Matter poster from the 1930s (see Fig. 16–62) is unabashedly parodied for Swatch, the Swiss watch manufacturer.

23–41. Louise Fili, book cover for *The Lover,* 1985. A delicately vignetted photograph is used with lettering that seems to cast soft shadows.

23–42. Carin Goldberg (designer) and Frank Metz (art director), book cover for *The Sonnets of Orpheus,* 1987. Design motifs and sans-serif lettering constrained by black rectangles were inspired by the Vienna Workshops.

23–43. Carin Goldberg (designer) and Gene Greif (illustrator), book cover for *When Water Comes Together with Other Water,* 1987. Wavy ornaments signifying water were added to the Eagle typeface.

complete fonts of eccentric 1920s and 1930s typefaces whose availability had vanished with hand-set metal type. The close paraphrasing of resources has been a controversial aspect of some retro designs (Fig. **23–40**).

Retro thrived in book-jacket design. The work of Louise Fili, who developed a deep love of typography while working in her college's type shop, is highly personal and intuitive. After working for Herb Lubalin and art directing Pantheon Books from 1978 to 1989, she launched her own studio. Her early work evidenced Lubalin's influence, then grew in power and originality from this starting point. Fili routinely vacationed in Europe each summer after the annual crunch of producing cover designs for Pantheon's huge fall list, and her travels inspired the development of an original approach to American book-jacket design. Eccentric letterforms on signs at little Italian seashore resorts built between the world wars fascinated her, as did graphics from the same era found in French and Italian flea markets and used-book stalls. These vernacular graphics incorporated textured backgrounds, silhouetted photographs, and modernistic sans-serif typefaces with decorative elements or exaggerated proportions. After World War II, design sensibilities shifted, and these typestyles and techniques fell into disuse. When typography converted from metal to photographic methods in the 1960s and 1970s, the outmoded faces were not converted to the new processes. Fili responded to them with fresh eyes and began to introduce them into her work.

Fili's work is elegant and refined, possessing great subtlety and even softness. Seeking the right graphic resonance for each book, she searches for the appropriate typeface, color scheme, and imagery by producing volumes of tissue layouts. Although the death of hand-set metal typography made many old faces unavailable, Fili works around this problem and uses now-forgotten faces—such as Iris, a condensed sans serif with thin horizontal strokes, and Electra Seminegra, a bold geometric sans-serif face with inverted triangles for the crossbar of the capital A—by restoring letterforms from old printed specimens and commissioning handlettering of the missing letters or even an entire title. In Fili's book covers, color and imagery resonate with the essence and spirit of the literature, almost as though she has developed a sixth sense for interpreting the author's work (Fig. **23–41**).

Carin Goldberg developed a fine-tuned reverence for type as an assistant to Lou Dorfsman at CBS in the 1970s, where every type proof entering the offices was hand-altered and improved. She then worked at CBS Records under Paula Scher, whose curiosity, reverence for design history, and attitude toward her work became vital influences. When Goldberg opened a design office she focused on book jackets because her primary interest was in single-surface, posterlike areas. She describes her work as being 90 percent intuition and acknowledges the influence of early modernist designers, especially Cassandre. Goldberg's early experience as a painter informs her attitude toward space, as does an architectural orientation inspired by classes she shared with architecture students in school and by the location of her studio adjacent to her husband's architectural office. She says she "paints with her T-square"—functioning as a typographic precisionist with a painterly orientation. This explains the personal attitude that underlies her work, transcending her myriad and eclectic sources (Figs. **23–42** and **23–43**).

Lorraine Louie (b. 1955) and Daniel Pelavin (b. 1948) embraced the general resonance of the retro approach. Shape, spatial composition, and color are primary vehicles in Louie's work. A series for the literary journal *The Quarterly* (Fig. **23–44**) uses a large *Q* as a sign for the publication. Colorful geometric shapes balanced within the space energize each issue. Pelavin dates his affinities for 1930s and 1940s work to pre–World War II "late moderne" architecture and furniture from his college days in Michigan. High school industrial arts and drafting classes helped him develop formidable lettering skills. Pelavin draws inspiration from Gustav Klimt, the Vienna Workshops (Fig. **23–45**), and streamlined art deco forms. He combines a reductive abstraction with precise mechanistic forms (Fig. **23–46**).

When Scher and Fili created their first designs in what later became known as the retro idiom, many veteran designers, raised on formal purity and typographic refinement, were appalled to see the return of these exiled letterforms and

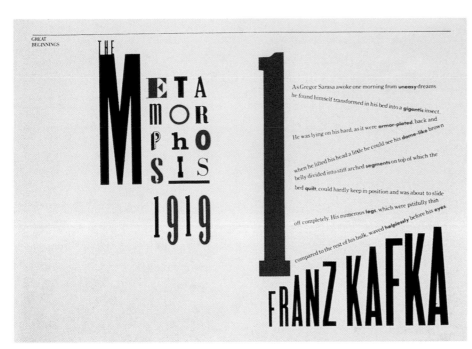

23–39

23–40

23–41

23–42

23–43

23–44

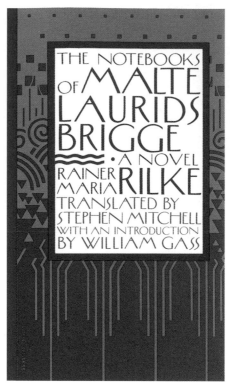

23–45

23–46

eccentric spatial organizations. But retro, like new-wave typography in the late 1970s and early 1980s, refused to go away, and more and more designers and clients responded to its energy and fresh approach. It crept into the design vocabulary as designers dared to use such eccentric typefaces as Empire, Bernhard Fashion, and Huxley. Precise spacing, scale relationships, and color combinations give the best retro designs their remarkable vitality.

Other original voices explored reinvention of historical models quite differently from the New York designers. At the Duffy Design Group in Minneapolis, Minnesota, Joe Duffy (b. 1949) and Charles S. Anderson (b. 1958) designed nostalgic revivals of vernacular and modernistic graphic arts from the first half of the century. Historical graphic resources as diverse as Aztec ornaments and Ouija boards were plumbed for their form and color. Anderson recalls growing up in the small town of Boone, Iowa, and being impressed by old graphics from the 1940s that had never been thrown away. The walls of an old print shop in town were covered with graphics from an earlier decade, and a retired artist who had created ubiquitous clip art as a newspaper illustrator made an indelible impression on the designer. Inspiration came from humble, coarsely printed spot drawings on old matchbook covers and newspaper ads (Fig. **23–47**); the warmth of traditional typefaces and nineteenth-century woodcuts applied to grocery-store packaging (Fig. **23–48**); and decorative emblematic labels (Fig. **23–49**) and trademarks recalling

postage stamps, official seals, and pictorial trademarks of an earlier time. The power of graphic design was demonstrated by the Classico spaghetti sauce labels, when sales of this product, packaged in old-style mason jars with ornately illustrated and designed labels, soared to $92 million within two years in spite of a limited advertising budget.

In 1989 Anderson left the Duffy Design Group and opened the Charles S. Anderson Design Company. He declared his intent to give images or messages "a tangible and inherent artistic value. We see a new modernism evolving. One not based on sterile minimalism and an absence of humanity, but one that is rich in cultural vocabulary and personal expression." The firm's work reflects a genuine enchantment with textural properties, as enlarged details from cheap printing, such as comic books, and overall patterns based on spot illustrations find their way into designs. A subsidiary company, the CSA Archive, was formed to manufacture publications and other products. These ranged from a set of watches with whimsical illustrated faces (Fig. **23–50**) to a massive collection of historical and original line illustrations (Fig. **23–51**).

In London one of the more original visions of the 1980s emerged as Neville Brody designed graphics and album covers for rock music and art-directed English magazines, including *The Face* and *Arena*. Although Brody has been influenced by the geometric forms of the Russian constructivist artists, especially Rodchenko, and by Dada's experimental attitudes and

23–47

23–48

23–49

23–44. Lorraine Louie (designer) and Susan Mitchell (art director), cover for *The Quarterly*, 1987. For this series Louie invented a vast inventory of colorful shapes organized with an unerring sense of balance.

23–45. Daniel Pelavin (designer) and Judith Loeser (art director), book cover for *The Notebooks of Malte Laurids Brigge*, 1985. The lettering was inspired by a Gustav Klimt poster (see Fig. 12–9).

23–46. Daniel Pelavin (designer), book cover for *Hoover's Guide to the Top Southern California Companies*, 1996. A tightly composed linear structure presents symbolic iconography with planes of color evoking the feeling of cloisonné.

23–47. Charles S. Anderson, *Marine Midland Auto Financing Division* trademark, 1985. The nostalgic automobile and the line technique used to draw it evoke newspaper spot illustrations of the 1930s and 1940s.

23–48. Charles S. Anderson (designer and illustrator) and Lynn Schulte (illustrator), label designs for Classico pasta sauce, 1985. Duffy Design Group countered the garish color and strident typography of many mass-marketed grocery packages with subtle color and elegant typography.

23–49. Joe Duffy and Charles S. Anderson, identity program for various lines of Chaps/Ralph Lauren clothing, 1987.

rejection of the canons of the ruling establishment, it would misrepresent his philosophy and values to label him a retro designer reinventing past styles. As an art student in the late 1970s, Brody wondered if "within mass communications, the human had been lost completely." Confronting the decision between pursuing fine art or graphic design, Brody thought, "Why can't you take a painterly approach within the printed medium? I wanted to make people more aware rather than less aware, and with the design that I had started to do, I followed the idea of design to reveal, not to conceal." Brody's work evolved from an effort to discover an intuitive yet logical approach to design, expressing a personal vision that could have meaning to his audience.

Brody has stated that he never learned the rules of correct typography, which left him free to invent working methods and spatial configurations. His typographic configurations project an absolute emblematic authority that evokes heraldry and military emblems (Fig. **23–52**). He designed a series of geometric sans-serif typefaces for *The Face*, bringing a strong graphic image to the magazine. Headlines became objects, with each carefully crafted to express content. Brody viewed the magazine as a multidimensional object existing in time and space and maintaining continuity from issue to issue. This continuity was explored when graphic elements such as the contents page logo were deconstructed into abstract glyphs over several months (Fig. **23–53**). Brody's ability to load a lay-

700. Proposed cover for Parliament, *The Bomb*, Mamograms Records, 1985.

23–52

23–50

23–51

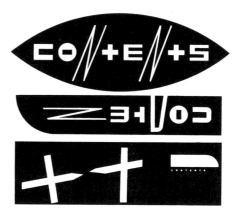

23–53

out with levels of meaning is seen in the opening spread of an interview with Andy Warhol (Fig. **23–54**): The repeated photograph echoes Warhol's use of repeated images; the large *W* is actually the *M* from a feature on the popular singer Madonna from the month before, turned upside down and bringing a small portion of a photograph and part of a head-line with it, paraphrasing Warhol's use of existing graphic material. The oval within a circle and the cross above it refer to the sexuality of Warhol's life and work.

Seldom have a designer's hard-won accomplishments been plagiarized as Brody's distinctive work was in the late 1980s. As clones of his typefaces and emblematic logo designs appeared all around the world, Brody designed a new quarterly magazine, *Arena*, using the clean, informational attributes of Helvetica type in dynamic ways. Large scale, strong value contrasts, and clear, simple layouts characterize his art direction of this publication.

The major thrust of postmodern graphic design is a spirit of liberation, a freedom to be intuitive and personal, and to go against the modern design so dominant through much of the twentieth century. Designers felt free to respond positively to vernacular and historic forms, and to incorporate these into their work. An atmosphere of inclusion and expanding possi-bilities enabled many designers to experiment with highly per-sonal, even eccentric, ideas. This is seen clearly in the work of Paula Scher, whose unfolding repertoire moves in several new directions, including lettering and images casually hand-painted on coarse paper. The result has been posters (Fig. **23–55**) and book jackets whose words and pictures are uni-fied through a common technique and surface; these designs project an unrefined, handmade character in counterpoint to the precision of computer-aided design. From the mid-1980s onward, designers became increasingly fascinated with the potential of computer-assisted design, not only as an efficient production tool but also as a potent catalyst for innovation. The unfolding strands of postmodern design became inter-twined with electronic capabilities.

23–54

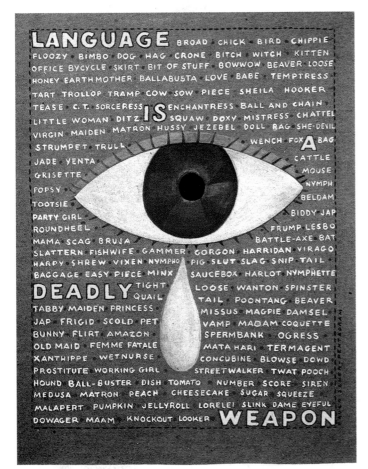

23–55

23–50. Charles S. Anderson Design Co., watches and their packages, 1992. Within the expanding possibilities of postindustrial society, a design firm becomes creator, packager, and marketer of manufactured goods.

23–51. Charles S. Anderson Design Co., cover for *CSA Archive Catalog of Stock Art*, 1995. The heaviness of bold black type and illustration are tempered by an underlay of abstract shapes in three warm colors.

23–52. Neville Brody, record album cover design for Parliament, 1985. Hand-lettered words are executed with a mechanistic and mathematical perfection.

23–53. Neville Brody, contents page logos from *The Face*, nos. 49, 52, and 55, 1984. Over eight or nine issues, the word *contents* was deconstructed from a readable word into abstract marks as Brody investigated an organic process of change and the role of visual coding in the editorial environment.

23–54. Neville Brody, editorial pages for *The Face*, no. 59, March 1985. Type and image become objects composed against each other to achieve a dynamic whole.

23–55. Paula Scher, "Language is a Deadly Weapon" graphic for MTV's "Free Your Mind" campaign, 1994. Derogatory terms for women are presented to increase sensitivity to the effect of slang upon others.

The Digital Revolution and Beyond

24

During the last quarter of the twentieth century, electronic and computer technology advanced at an extraordinary pace, transforming many areas of human activity. Graphic design was irrevocably changed by digital-computer hardware and software and the explosive growth of the Internet. The Industrial Revolution had fragmented the process of creating and printing graphic communications into a series of specialized steps. After phototype became prevalent during the 1960s, skilled specialists included graphic designers, who created page layouts; typesetters, who operated text and display typesetting equipment; production artists, who pasted all of the elements into position on boards; camera operators, who made photographic negatives of the pasteups, art, and photographs; strippers, who assembled these negatives together; platemakers, who prepared the printing plates; and press operators, who ran the printing presses. By the 1990s digital technology enabled one person operating a desktop computer to control most—or even all—of these functions. New photo-optical printing machines used computer-controlled lasers to photosensitize printing drums, making short-run and even individualized full-color press sheets possible.

In spite of strong initial resistance by many designers, the new technology improved rapidly, inviting widespread acceptance. Computer users were empowered by greater control over the design and production process. Digital technology and advanced software also expanded the creative potential of graphic design by making possible an unprecedented manipulation of color, form, space, and imagery.

The growth of cable and satellite television in the last quarter of the century expanded the number of broadcast channels, inspired creative and technical advances in broadcast and motion graphics, and paved the way for consumers to embrace the power and flexibility of the Internet. The rapid development of the Internet and the World Wide Web during the 1990s transformed the way people communicate and access information, generating a revolution surpassing even Gutenberg in its magnitude. By the early twenty-first century, many people had become dependent on the Internet for access to both information and entertainment, a phenomenon that has affected all aspects of society and culture. Technology has transformed the era of corporate communications for mass audiences into a period of decentralized media offering near limitless options for individuals. Computer graphics experimentation churned through modern and postmodern design ideas, retro revivals, eccentric work, and explored electronic techniques to create a period of pluralism and diversity in design.

The origins of computer-aided graphic design

The digital revolution came to the desktop of individual graphic designers as a result of affordable yet powerful hardware and software initiated primarily by three companies during the 1980s: Apple Computer developed the Macintosh computer; Adobe Systems invented the PostScript programming language underlying page-layout software and electronically generated typography; and Aldus created PageMaker, an early software application using PostScript to design pages on the computer screen.

Apple Computer's 1984 introduction of the first-generation Macintosh computer, based on technology pioneered in its Lisa computer, foretold a graphic revolution. The Macintosh displayed bitmapped graphics; that is, its screen presented information as dots called pixels, with 72 dots per inch (dpi) on a black-and-white screen. Its interface with the user was achieved via a desktop device, called a mouse, whose movement controlled a pointer on the screen. By placing the pointer on an on-screen icon (Fig. **24–1**) and clicking a button on the mouse, the user was able to control the computer intuitively, and so to focus on creative work rather than machine operation or computer programming.

The first mouse, a small wooden box on steel wheels, was invented by scientist Douglas C. Engelbart (b. 1925) in the 1960s at the federal government's Augmentation Research Center. It was called an "*x-y* position indicator for a display system" in the patent. A colleague dubbed Engelbart's little position-indicator device "the mouse," and the name stuck. The mouse made computers accessible through intuitive processes rather than tedious mathematical coding and

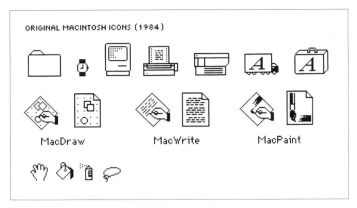

24–1

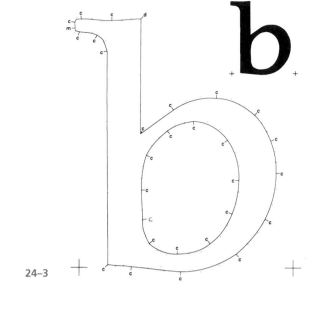

24–3

24–1. Susan Kare (graphic designer) and Bill Adkinson (computer programmer), icons for the 128K Macintosh computer, 1984. The pictograph is the symbolic medium permitting a new interface between man and machine.

24–2. Susan Kare, screen fonts for the Macintosh computer, 1984. The low-resolution dot pattern dictates the letterform design and jagged edges.

24–3. Sumner Stone, digitized data for Stone Medium *b*, 1985. The outline Bézier curves and filled laser-printed output are shown.

empowered thousands of people, from accountants and writers to artists and designers, to use computers.

Engelbart has been lauded as a visionary whose early innovations humanized computers by making their technology more accessible. Decades ago his research foreshadowed electronic mail systems, icon- and window-based computer operating systems, the Internet, networking software allowing several users to work on a document at the same time, and videoconferencing.

Apple released software applications for word processing, drawing, and painting. Early bitmapped fonts (Fig. **24–2**) were designed by Susan Kare (b. 1954), then of the Apple Computer design department. Letterform design was controlled by the matrix of dots in these early fonts.

Adobe Systems' PostScript page description language enabled printers to output text, images, and graphic elements, and determine their placement on the page. PostScript fonts are not simply made up of bitmapped dots; rather, they are stored as graphical commands and data. Type characters are generated as outlines that are then filled in as solid forms.

The curved lines of the characters are formed of Bézier splines. Named after the French mathematician Pierre Bézier (1910–1999), who invented them, these are mathematically generated nonuniform curves (in contrast to curves with uniform curvature, called arcs) defined by four control points. Bézier curves can create complex shapes with smooth endpoints, making them particularly useful for creating letterforms (Fig. **24–3**) and computer graphics.

In 1985 Apple Computer introduced its first laser printer, whose 300-dpi output of PostScript fonts enabled its typographic proofs to more closely duplicate typesetting. A controversy about resolution quality ended after the arrival of 600-dpi laser printers and high-resolution image-setters such as the Linotron, capable of either 1,270- or 2,540-dpi output.

Page-layout programs made possible by PostScript permitted the design of complete pages on the screen. In 1984 a thirty-six-year-old former newspaper editor named Paul Brainerd formed a company called Aldus (after the fifteenth-century printer Aldus Manutius) to develop software enabling newspapers to produce advertisements more efficiently. In July 1985

Aldus introduced PageMaker software for the Macintosh computer. PageMaker could alter type size, choice of font, and column dimensions. It integrated text type with other elements, such as scans of pictures, ruled lines, headlines, and borders. A desktop metaphor enabled the user to create elements on the computer screen, then position these on the page in a manner similar to the traditional way elements are prepared and pasted into position for offset printing. Brainerd coined the term *desktop publishing* for this new method.

Desktop publishing saved significant amounts of time and money in preparing pages for printing. Procedures including layout, typesetting, making position photostats, and pasting elements into position were all combined into a seamless electronic process. A comparison can be made to George Eastman's invention of the Kodak camera. Just as photography was wrested from the exclusive use of specialists and made available to the general public in the 1880s, typography left the exclusive domain of professionals and became accessible to a larger sphere of people in the 1980s.

Earlier digital hardware included digital typesetting systems, powerful electronic image processors such as Scitex systems, which electronically scanned images and permitted extensive editing, and Quantel Video and Graphic Paintboxes, which permitted precise color control and allowed images to be overlapped, combined, and altered. The LightSpeed system was a sophisticated early page-layout machine. All of these systems were very expensive and rarely available to designers for experimentation; the profound significance of Macintosh computers and software stems from their broad accessibility to individual graphic designers and laypersons.

By 1990 the color-capable Macintosh II computer and improved software had spurred a technological and creative revolution in graphic design as radical as the fifteenth-century shift from hand-lettered manuscript books to Gutenberg's movable type. An unprecedented expansion of design education and professional activity produced a larger field with vast numbers of trained practitioners. The number of individual designers and firms producing fine work rose exponentially. On the other hand, digital technology also enabled untrained and marginally trained practitioners to enter the field.

Pioneers of digital graphic design

By providing designers with new processes and capabilities, new technology often enabled them to create unprecedented images and forms. While many designers rejected and decried digital technology during its infancy and called designers who did explore it "the new primitives," others embraced it as an innovative tool capable of expanding the scope of design possibilities and the very nature of the design process. Using a computer as a design tool enabled one to make and correct mistakes. Color, texture, images, and typography could be stretched, bent, made transparent, layered, and combined in unprecedented ways.

Early pioneers who embraced the new technology and explored its creative potential included Los Angeles designer April Greiman, *Emigre* magazine designer/editor Rudy Vanderlans (b. 1955), and typeface designer Zuzana Licko (b. 1961).

April Greiman explored the visual properties of bitmapped fonts, the layering and overlapping of computer-screen information, the synthesis of video and print, and the tactile patterns and shapes made possible by the new technology. In her first graphic design using Macintosh output (Fig. **24–4**), bitmapped type and computer-generated textures were photostatted to a large size and pasted up through conventional typesetting.

When asked to design an issue of *Design Quarterly* magazine for the Walker Art Center in Minneapolis, Greiman created a single-sheet magazine (Fig. **24–5**) with a 61 cm by 183 cm (2 by 6 feet) digital collage executed entirely on the Macintosh computer. She explored capturing images from video and digitizing them, layering images in space, and integrating words and pictures into a single computer file.

As computers and their software became more powerful, a new spatial elasticity became possible in typography and imagery. In 1988 Greiman expressed an obligation to "take on the challenge of continuing forward toward a new landscape of communications. To use these tools to imitate what we already know and think is a pity." In addition to using the new technology to make decisions about type and layout, she said, "I think there has to be another layer applied here. And that's about ideas."

In 1984 Rudy Vanderlans began to edit, design, and publish a magazine called *Emigre*. Joining him were two Dutch friends whom he had known at the Royal Academy of Fine Arts at The Hague and who were at that time also living in San Francisco. They originally intended to present their unpublished works along with creative works by others. The journal's name was selected because its founders believed exposure to various cultures, and living in different cultural environments, had a significant impact on creative work. Vanderlans used typewriter type and copier images in the first issue, then used low-resolution Macintosh type for early subsequent issues. A magazine with a printing run of seven thousand copies became a lightning rod for experimentation, outraging many design professionals while captivating those who embraced the potential of computer technology to redefine graphic design. *Emigre*'s experimental approach helped define and demonstrate the capabilities of the new technology, both in its editorial design (Figs. **24–6** and **24–7**) and by presenting work and interviews with designers from around the world whose work was too experimental for other design publications.

In 1987 Vanderlans left his newspaper design job and formed a partnership, Emigre Graphics, with designer Zuzana Licko, whose educational background included computer-programming courses. Dissatisfied with the limited fonts available for the early Macintosh, Licko used a public-domain character-generation software called FontEditor to create digital typefaces. Her first fonts were designed for low-resolution

24–4

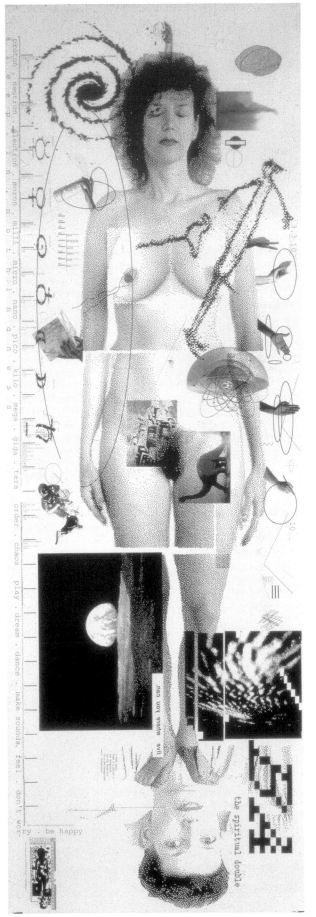

24–5

24–4. April Greiman, poster for the Los Angeles Institute of Contemporary Art, 1986. Computer output, printed as layers of lavender, blue-gray, red-orange, and tan, overlap and combine into an even fuller palette of color.

24–5. April Greiman, graphic imagery for *Design Quarterly*, no. 133, 1987. This poster composed of digitized images was output by a low-resolution printer.

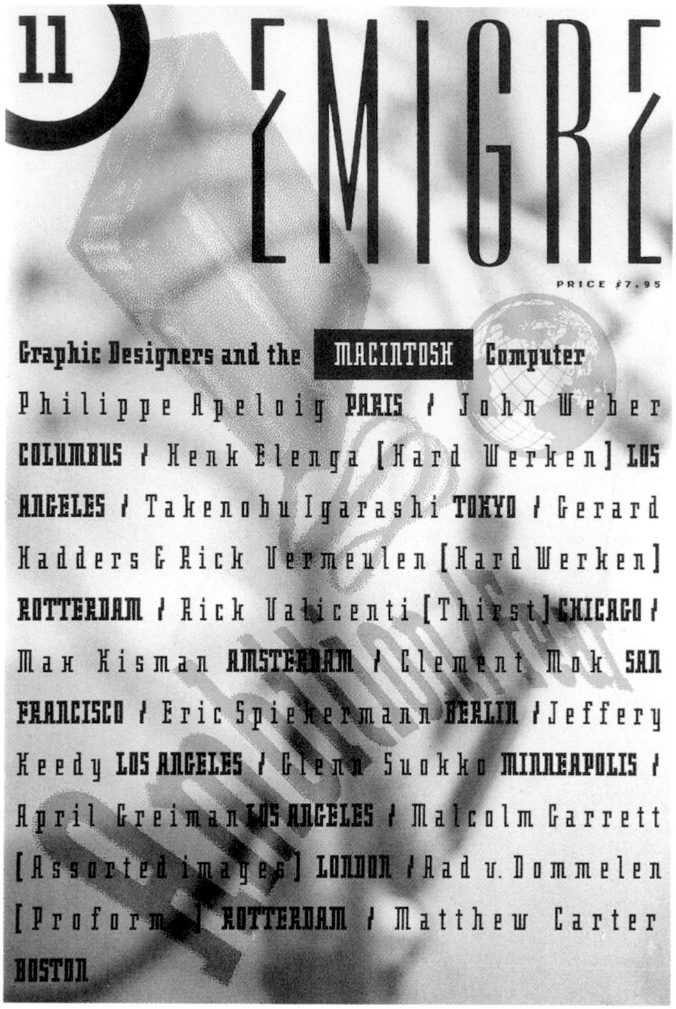

24–6

24–7

technology (Fig. **24–8**), then converted to companion high-resolution versions later as font-design software and printer resolution improved. Licko recalls how the unpleasant experience of a college calligraphy class, where she had been forced to write with her right hand even though she was left-handed, contributed to her original approaches to font design; she had rejected calligraphy, the traditional basis for conventional fonts.

Many art school and university design-education programs became important centers for redefining graphic design through theoretical discourse and experimentation with computer technology. The design department at Michigan's Cranbrook Academy of Art, where graphic designer Katherine McCoy (b. 1945) cochaired the design department with her husband, product designer Michael McCoy, from 1971 until 1995, became a magnet for people interested in pushing the boundaries of design. Then a small graduate school with 150 students in nine departments, Cranbrook has long emphasized experimentation while rejecting a uniform philosophy or methodology. The faculty believed students should find their

own directions while interacting with others engaged in similar searches. McCoy likened Cranbrook to "a tribal community, intense and immersive," where she functioned as "a parade director and referee."

During McCoy's twenty-four years at Cranbrook, the program evolved from a rational, systematic approach to design problem solving influenced by the International Typographic Style, through an approach that questioned the expressive limits of this style, into one where complexity and layering, vernacular and premodern forms, and the validity of normative rules and conventions were explored. McCoy's poster (Fig. **24–9**) challenged norms of college recruiting materials and demonstrated a complexity of form and meaning. Breaking away from prevailing notions of simple, reductive communications, McCoy overlaid different levels of visual and verbal messages, requiring her audience to decipher them.

Edward Fella (b. 1939), a Detroit graphic designer with whom McCoy worked at the Designers & Partners studio before her appointment at Cranbrook, was a major inspiration

We Read Best What We Read Most (Oakland 8)

We Read Best What We Read Most (Emperor 14)

We Read Best What We Read Most (Modula)

We Read Best What We Read Most (Emigre 14)

We Read Best What We Read Most (Matrix)

24–8

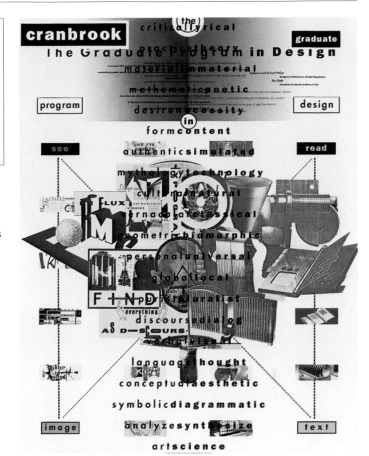

24–9

24–6. Rudy VanderLans, cover for *Emigre, no.* 11, 1989. Three levels of visual information are layered in dimensional space.

24–7. Glenn A. Suokko (designer) and Emigre Graphics, cover for *Emigre,* no. 10, 1989. Traditional typographic syntax yielded to an experiment in unconventional information sequencing for a special issue about a graphic design exchange between Cranbrook and Dutch designers.

24–8. Zuzana Licko, digital typefaces, late 1980s. Oakland, Emperor, and Emigre were originally designed as bitmapped fonts for 72-dpi resolution. Modula and Matrix are higher-resolution versions of the latter two fonts.

24–9. Katherine McCoy, Cranbrook recruiting poster, 1989. A photographic collage of student projects is layered with a listing of polemic oppositions and a communications-theory diagram.

24–10. Edward Fella, mailer for Detroit Focus Gallery, 1987. The "transparent" typography of mass communications yields to a typography that references its form, history, and production processes.

within the program. After serving as a frequent Cranbrook guest critic for many years, Fella attended the academy's graduate program from 1985 to 1987, then accepted a California teaching position. With roots in American vernacular design and early modernist typography, Fella's experimental work became a major influence on a generation of designers. From 1983 until 1991, Fella contributed graphics to the Detroit Focus Gallery and produced flyers (Fig. **24–10**) whose typography and lettering challenged the reader in the same way advanced art in the gallery challenged the viewer. He explored entropy, the disintegration of form from repeated copying, and an unbounded range of techniques, from found typography, scribbles, and brush writing to typesetting, rubdown letters, public-domain clip art, and stencils. Echoing futurism, Fella investigated the aesthetic potential of invented letterforms, irregular spatial intervals, eccentric characters, personal glyphs, and vernacular imagery. He combined these materials with great compositional skill (Fig. **24–11**) and often attached asides, notes, and addenda to the primary message. Fella

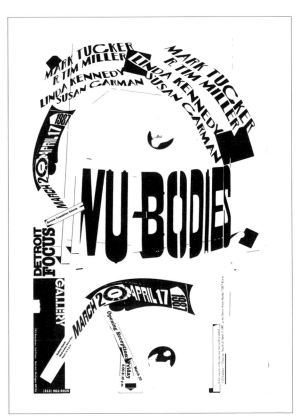

24–10

24–11

24–12

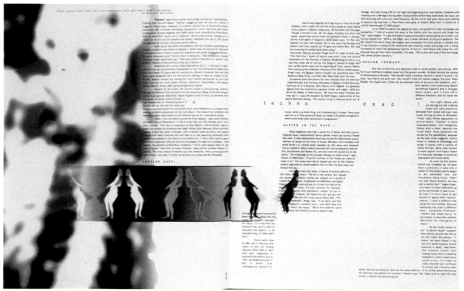

24–13

24–11. Edward Fella, announcement for a lecture, 1995. A medley of personal and eccentric letterforms is composed with connective logic and visual whimsy.

24–12. David Carson (art director) and Pat Blashill (photographer), "Hanging at Carmine Street," *Beach Culture,* 1991. Responding to the title of an editorial feature on a public swimming pool, Carson was inspired to "hang some type."

24–13. David Carson (art director) and John Ritter (photographer), "Is Techno Dead," *Ray Gun,* 1994. Text type and spatial intervals join with computer-manipulated photographs in a rhythmic melody of white and dark shapes.

24–14. David Carson (art director) and Chris Cuffaro (photographer), "Morrissey: The Loneliest Monk," *Ray Gun,* 1994. The unusual photographic cropping and de-constructed headline convey the musician's romanticism and mystery.

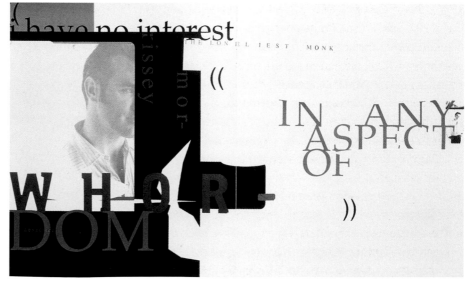

24–14

wryly observed, "Deconstruction is a way of exposing the glue that holds together western culture."

By the mid-1990s, the complexity of form, theoretical concerns, and computer manipulations found in the work of early pioneers made their way into the mainstream of graphic communications.

Revitalizing magazine design

During the early 1990s accelerating progress in computers, software, and output devices enabled graphic designers to achieve results virtually identical to those of conventional working methods, for the promise of seamless on-screen color graphics had been fulfilled. Designers explored the unprecedented possibilities of computers and graphics software while at the same interest in handmade and expressionist lettering and images was renewed.

QuarkXPress, another page-design application, enabled designers to place elements on a page in increments of one hundred-thousandth of an inch and to kern type in intervals of one twenty-thousandth of an em (a horizontal measurement equivalent to the width of the letter *m*). Adobe Photoshop, an application initially developed for electronic photographic retouching, enabled unprecedented image manipulation and creation.

New developments migrated from personal exploration and design education to the mainstream as editorial designers for specialized magazines applied computer experimentation to their pages. David Carson (b. 1956), a former professional surfer and schoolteacher, turned to editorial design in the 1980s. Carson eschewed grid formats, information hierarchy, and consistent layout or typographic patterns; instead, he chose to explore the expressive possibilities of each subject (Fig. **24–12**) and each page or spread, rejecting conventional notions of typographic syntax and imagery. As art director and designer for *Transworld Skateboarding* (1983–87), *Musician* (1988), *Beach Culture* (1989–91), *Surfer* (1991–92), and *Ray Gun* (1992–96), Carson flouted design conventions. His revolutionary layouts included page numbers set in large display type, and normally diminutive picture captions enlarged into prominent design elements. Carson often letterspaced his article titles erratically across images or arranged them in expressive rather than normative sequences. He also required his reader to decipher his message by slicing away parts of letters. Carson's text type often challenged the fundamental criteria for legibility. He explored reverse leading, extreme forced justification, text columns jammed together with no gutter, text columns the width of a page (and, on at least one occasion, a double-page spread), text with minimal value contrast between type and the image or color underneath, and text columns set in curved or irregular shapes (Fig. **24–13**). White display type placed over text covered some of the words, but

the text could still be understood. Writing and subject matter receive Carson's careful attention, for his designs emerge from the meaning of the words, or comment on the subject, as he seeks to bring the layout into harmony.

Unconventional treatment of images included "unnatural" cropping to express content. Although he was viewed as the epitome of the computer revolution, *Ray Gun* 14 (Fig. **24–14**) was the first magazine Carson sent to the printer as electronic files. Before that he had generated elements by computer, then prepared camera-ready art on boards.

Carson became quite controversial during the early 1990s. He inspired young designers while angering others who believed he was crossing the line between order and chaos. Carson's typography was decried and denounced, but as he and others pushed their work to the edge of illegibility, designers discovered many readers were more resilient than they had assumed, and noted that messages were often read under less than ideal circumstances. Film and video techniques informed Carson's magazine designs, for the hierarchical and regularized structure of page design yielded in his work to a shifting, kinetic spatial environment where type and image overlap, fade, and blur. Disparate visual and verbal elements jostle and collide in space the way sound and image bump and shove in film and video. Carson consciously made his pages cinematic by letting articles and headlines flow from spread to spread and by wrapping pictures around the edge of the page onto the other side.

During Carson's tenure as art director of *Ray Gun* magazine he provided a rare open forum for major illustrators and photographers while introducing new artists and turning a half-dozen pages over to readers to display their illustrations for song lyrics. This populist gesture recurred as *zines*, self-published personal magazines using desktop-publishing software and cheap printing or copier reproduction, began appearing in magazine racks. Carson left Ray Gun in 1996 and applied his approach to print and other media communications for mass-media advertisers such as Coca-Cola and Nike. He believes one should not mistake legibility for communication, because while many highly legible traditional printed messages offer little visual appeal to readers, more expressionist designs can attract and engage them.

After art-directing *Texas Monthly* and *Regardie's*, Fred Woodward (b. 1953) became art director of the semimonthly rock-and-roll magazine *Rolling Stone* in 1987; Gail Anderson (b. 1962) became deputy art director later that year. As intuitive designers, Woodward and Anderson tried to match typefaces and images to the content. *Rolling Stone*'s tradition of editorial and graphic excellence (see Fig. 19–46) dated to its 1967 inception, so pressure to compete with this legacy prevailed. A turning point occurred when Woodward reinstated

24–15

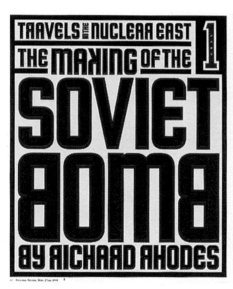  

24–16   24–17

the Oxford rules (one name used for multiple-line thick-and-thin borders) found in the magazine's earlier periods. He felt these borders gave him great license, almost as though anything he put within them would look like *Rolling Stone*.

The magazine had a Phototypositor and hundreds of typefaces; Woodward added to this stock and made audacious typography a hallmark of his work. A breakthrough design (Fig. **24–15**) used large-scale type and a full-page photograph to make a strong visual statement about singer Sinead O'Connor. This layout changed the look and feel of *Rolling Stone*, for Woodward felt challenged to build on it. Text pages were punctuated by expansive double-page opening spreads juxtaposing full-page portraits opposite title pages dominated by display type; frequently these had little or no

text. Content was expressed through unexpected selection, scale, and placement of type.

Although the magazine converted to Macintosh computers in the early 1990s, Woodward sought a handmade look. *Rolling Stone* used a wide range of fonts, freely exploiting not only digital manipulation but calligraphy, handlettering, found type, and graphic entropy achieved by running type through a copier many times. When Woodward said he preferred never to use a typeface more than once he was expressing an interest in dynamic change, and in creating a publication that constantly reinvented its design in response to content. Figure **24–16** demonstrates how the typeface, its treatment, the color palette, and the image all emerged from associations with the article topic.

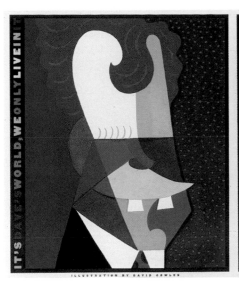

24–18

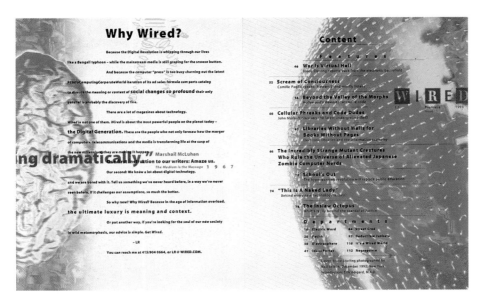

24–19

24–15. Fred Woodward (art director and designer) and Andrew Macpherson (photographer), "Sinead O'Connor…," *Rolling Stone*, 1990. This breakthrough layout used large-scale display type over two pages as a dynamic counterpoint to the photographic portrait.

24–16. Fred Woodward (art director), Gail Anderson (designer), and Matt Mahurin (photographer), "The Making of the Soviet Bomb," *Rolling Stone*, 1993. Blocky sans-serif letters evoke Russian constructivism, while reversed *B*s, *R*s, and a *K* connote the Cyrillic alphabet used in Russia.

24–17. Fred Woodward (art director) and Lee Bearson (designer), "Cyber Nation," *Rolling Stone*, 1994. Typeface selection, its computer manipulation, and the color palette all signify and express the article's content.

24–18. Fred Woodward (art director), Geraldine Hessler (designer), and David Cowles (illustrator), "Man of the Year: David Letterman," *Rolling Stone*, 1995. Visual cohesiveness between type and image is achieved, as both are constructed from broad flat shapes of interlocking color.

24–19. Erik Adigard/MAD (designer), John Plunkett, Barbara Kuhr, (art directors), *WIRED* magazine contents spread with publishing mission, premiere issue, March 1994. Publisher Louis Rossetto's manifesto of *WIRED*'s editorial mission was conveyed by the text of the opening paragraph of Marshall McLuhan's 1967 book, *The Medium is the Massage*.

Typography's new elasticity permitted outline letters in the title for an article about computers (Fig. **24–17**) to be extruded into perspective forms and combined with wireframe drawing for a kinetic three-dimensional effect. Display type on the box form was skewed into perspective, as was the text type that became the front plane of the box. Computer software allowed designers to control type interactively (Fig. **24–18**) by changing the scale, color, and overlapping of forms until a dynamic equilibrium was achieved. The software gave illustrators and photographers the latitude and openness to achieve their finest work.

In the mid-1990s, as the U.S. economy recovered from a devastating recession, a new cultural paradigm was emerging: personal computers and the Internet were launching the infor-mation age. The magazine that would give voice to and act as a virtual roadmap of the new "digital generation" was *WIRED*.

WIRED magazine's design team, John Plunkett (b. 1952) and Barbara Kuhr (b. 1954), principals of Plunkett + Kuhr located in Park City, Utah, envisioned a magazine that would do for the emerging information highway what *Rolling Stone* had done for rock and roll a generation earlier: define it, explain it, and make it indispensible to the magazine's readers.

Plunkett and Kuhr came to *WIRED,* a San Francisco publica-tion, via Paris, France, where they had met the magazine's fu-ture founding publisher, Louis Rossetto, in 1984. In 1991, Kuhr designed a color-xeroxed prototype for *WIRED,* and after much searching for funding by Rossetto and his partner Jane Metcalf, *WIRED* was born in 1994 (Fig. **24–19**). Plunkett imagined the design problem as that of finding a way to use the convention of ink on paper "to report on this emerging, fluid, non-linear, asynchronous, electronic world."

The pulse of the information age was presented in a decidedly nonlinear fashion, with florescent and PMS inks rarely, if ever, used in magazine publishing. "Electronic Word," an eight-page front-of-book section of news and products (Fig. **24–20**) was often cited as difficult to read but was, in fact, a layered design meant to emulate the emerging visual nervous system of the Internet, with its often overlapping and simultaneous information streams. The design was decidedly influenced by Quentin Fiori's 1967 design for Marshall McLuhan's *The Medium is the Message*. Feature article designs, clearly postmodern, used a wide range of edgy fonts in headlines (Fig. **24–21**). *WIRED*'s designers soon ordered their own text font, Wiredbaum, designed by Matthew Carter (see p. 500), and based on the modern serif font Walbaum.

There was no other magazine that looked like *WIRED*. The timing was perfect, following on the heels of the debut of the Internet, and *WIRED*'s machine-aesthetic design debut was an overnight sensation.

The digital type foundry

Early digital type-design systems such as the pre-PostScript Ikarus system, used in the 1980s by typesetting machinery manufacturers, were very expensive. When font-design software for desktop computers—for example, Fontographer—became available, it enabled designers to design and market original typefaces as electronic files on computer disks, with significant reductions in the high cost of designing and distributing fonts. A virtual explosion in the release of new typefaces occurred in the 1990s, as large type vendors were joined by independent type manufacturers.

Adobe Systems became a prolific and influential digital type foundry. An early type family developed for its PostScript page-description language was Stone (Fig. **24–22**), designed by Sumner Stone (b. 1945). Trained both as a calligrapher and as a mathematician, Stone was type director of Adobe Systems before opening his own type foundry in 1990. The Stone family has three versions—serif, sans-serif, and informal—that share basic letterform proportions and structure. Each version has three roman and three italic fonts, for a total of eighteen typefaces in the family. Reproduction quality on 300-dpi laser printers was a major consideration in its character designs.

In the past when designers developed a typeface for a proprietary system such as Linotype or Monotype, they took the specific nature of the typesetting equipment into account. Contemporary typeface designers create fonts for use on many output devices, including low- and high-resolution display screens, inkjet and high-resolution printers, and output

systems that do not yet exist. Moreover, the environment in which type is used has expanded dramatically, with people in many fields, not just designers and typesetters, making typographic decisions and creating typeset documents.

Carol Twombly (b. 1959) and Robert Slimbach (b. 1956) emerged as outstanding staff typeface designers at Adobe, creating original designs and respected digital adaptations of classical typefaces. Twombly's numerous typefaces include three masterful families (Fig. **24–23**) inspired by historical lettering. These were the first three display fonts in the Adobe Originals type program, a series of new designs created for digital technology. Charlemagne is freely based on the decorative capitals used as versals and titling in Carolingian-era illuminated manuscripts. Lithos was inspired by the monoline simplicity and even-textured economy of Greek stone inscriptions, but Twombly transformed these carved letters into a highly original family of five weights, with inventive characters and a distinctive appearance. After its release, Lithos was adopted for on-screen graphics by the MTV cable-television channel and became wildly popular. The time-honored inscription on Trajan's column (see Fig. 2–17) has inspired numerous fonts, including Twombly's version. Her font closely paraphrases the source, but the conversion from stone to a typeface required a less heavy *N*, a bolder *S*, and more prominent serifs.

A master calligrapher, Robert Slimbach seeks inspiration from classical typefaces as he designs text faces for digital technology. He also creates vibrant fonts based on calligraphy and hand-lettering (Fig. **24–24**). Extensive research and documentation combined with meticulous craft have resulted in typefaces with excellent fidelity to the originals. Slimbach's fonts are hailed for maintaining the spirit of the original while making adjustments and refinements appropriate to digital technology.

In 1992 Adobe released its first multiple-master typefaces. Two or more master designs combine to generate an extensive sequence of fonts. The master designs determine the range of fonts that can be generated through changes in a design axis. The design axis controlled *weight*, determined by stroke thickness and the resulting ratio of black form to white background; *width,* determined by making the letters wider (expanded) or narrower (condensed); *style*, in which visual attributes ranging from no serifs to large serifs, or wedge-shaped serifs to slab serifs, were altered; and *optical size*, involving subtle adjustments in proportion, weight, contrast between thick-and-thin elements, and spacing to optimize legibility and design. The optical size axis was an important consideration. During the phototype era, one set of master characters was drawn for use in all sizes, even though small text characters need sturdier serifs and heavier thin strokes than do large display type sizes. Myriad, a two-axis sans serif (Fig. **24–25**), was one of the first multiple master fonts.

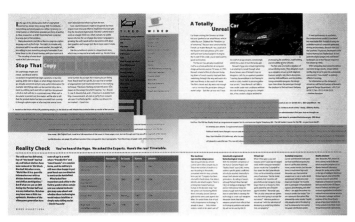

24–20

24–21

24–22

24–23

24–20. John Plunkett, Barbara Kuhr (designers and art directors), *WIRED* magazine, front-of-book spread. The "Electronic Word" section used layered form, with text often running over layers of images to express the multidimensional content of the Internet and "shape" the readers' experience, in the words of the designers. Car photograph: Renault, Ltd.

24–21. John Plunkett, Barbara Kuhr (designers and art directors), *WIRED* magazine feature spread. Photograph of David Byrne by Neil Selkirk. Postmodern text designs and florescent colors signaled a new paradigm for print communication about the new electronic media.

24–22. Sumner Stone, the Stone type family, 1987. This typographic arrangement by Min Wang shows the harmony of the serif, sans-serif, and informal versions.

24–23. Carol Twombly, typefaces Charlemagne, Lithos, and Trajan, 1989. The inscriptional spirit of the ancient world is translated into the digital realm.

24–24. Robert Slimbach, typefaces Adobe Garamond, 1989; Myriad (designed with Carol Twombly) and Minion, 1990; Caflisch script, 1993; Poetica, 1992; Adobe Jenson, 1996; and Cronos, 1997.

Adobe Garamond

Myriad

Minion

Caflisch Script

Poetica

Adobe Jenson

Cronos

24–24

24–25

Dead History

EXOCE+

Keedy Sans

Remedy

Suburban

Template Gothic

Totally Gothic

Filosofia

Mrs Eaves

24–26

Twombly and Slimbach executed the actual drawing and digitization over a two-year period.

Many cottage-industry type foundries vaulted into existence around the globe, owned and operated by independent designers and entrepreneurs who were empowered by the new technology to create and distribute their original typefaces. A rift arose between designers who believed the traditional values should be maintained and designers who advocated experimentation and even eccentricity. Quite often this split formed along generation lines. Young designers were not trying to expand the range within existing categories of typefaces (for example, the way Univers extended the range of sans-serif types, see Fig. 18–13) or create new decorative and novelty types (Fig. 11–32); rather, they sought to invent totally new kinds of typefaces. These fonts could not be evaluated against proven typographic traditions.

By 1990 Emigre Fonts began receiving many idiosyncratic and novel fonts from outside designers. Licko and Vanderlans recognized the inherent formal inventiveness and originality of many of these submissions and began to license and distribute the designs. Often these fonts proved extremely controversial (Fig. **24–26**) even as they were rapidly adopted and extensively used in major advertising campaigns and publication designs. Later in the decade Licko designed two significant revivals: Mrs Eaves is an exemplary interpretation of John Baskerville's eighteenth-century transitional fonts (see Figs. 8–12 and 8–13), and Filosofia captures the spirit of modern-style fonts (see Figs. 8–17 and 8–18) while actually resolving some of the legibility issues inherent in the eighteenth-century originals.

From 1955 until 1957, London-born Matthew Carter (b. 1937) learned to cut punches for metal type by hand at the type foundry of the Enschedé printing house in the Netherlands. For over forty years Carter designed scores of typefaces, as typographic technology evolved from metal type to phototype, then digital type. During an association with Linotype from 1965 to 1981, Carter's designs included the ubiquitous Bell Centennial (1978), created for early high-speed digital and cathode ray tube (CRT) technology. It was designed for outstanding legibility in telephone directories using small type on coarse newsprint. After cofounding and directing the type-design activities of the Bitstream digital foundry from 1981 to 1992, Carter formed Carter & Cone Type of Cambridge, Massachusetts.

Carter designs outstanding fonts based on earlier models (Fig. **24–27**). Galliard, issued in four weights with italics, is a masterful adaptation of a sixteenth-century design by Robert Granjon. Mantinia is a titling face inspired by painted and engraved capital letters by the Renaissance painter Andrea Mantegna. Sophia is an original display typeface inspired by hybrid alphabets of capitals, Greek letterforms, and uncials from sixth-century Constantinople; it contains ten joining characters that fuse with other letters to form ligatures. While there are many twentieth-century revivals of William Caslon's text types, his vigorous and somewhat eccentric display types had not been redesigned for digital typesetting until Carter released his Big Caslon CC.

Standardization and interchangeable parts became the norm of the Industrial Revolution; in typography this conform-

24–27

24–28

ity was realized through repetition of letterform parts and redundant layout formats. The digital revolution ushered in an era of individualization, flexibility, and customization.

Matthew Carter's typeface Walker (Fig. **24–28**), designed for the Minneapolis-based Walker Art Center, provides a stunning example of expanding typographic possibilities. Sturdy sans-serif capitals have a series of five add-on serifs called "snap-on (née Deputy) serifs" by Carter, that can be attached at will to the vertical strokes of each letter; further, these are available in a variety of widths. Carter also designed a series of ruled lines running over, under, or both under and over the letters, linking their forms into a dynamic unity. Of the basic letterforms, Carter said, "I think of them rather like store window mannequins with good bone structure on which to hang many different kinds of clothing." Ligatures and alternate characters complete a character set, permitting the Walker Art Center to modulate forms to suit the message at hand (Fig. **24–29**). The typeface, or rather its function through various permutations, becomes the corporate identity. Laurie Haycock Makela (b. 1956), Walker's design director from 1991 until 1996, and Matt Eller (b. 1968), a senior designer who became design director in 1996, used the Walker system to achieve a freedom of typographic expression appropriate to a center for art, design, and performance.

The digital type foundry decentralized and democratized the creation, distribution, and use of type fonts. The 1990s experienced increased access to typography and the proliferation of experimental and novelty typefaces. Excellent and mediocre versions of traditional typefaces were released, and the glut of

24–25. Robert Slimbach and Carol Twombly, Myriad, a two-axis multiple-master font, 1990. From left to right, the set width of the characters goes from condensed to extended; from top to bottom, the stroke weight becomes thicker.

24–26. Emigre fonts include P. Scott Makela, Dead History, 1990; Jonathan Barnbrook, Exocet, 1990; Jeffrey Keedy, Keedy Sans, 1989; Frank Heine, Remedy, 1991; Rudy VanderLans, Suburban, 1994; Barry Deck, Template Gothic, 1990; Zuzana Licko, Totally Gothic, 1990, Filosofia, 1997, and Mrs Eaves, 1996.

24–27. Matthew Carter, typeface designs: Galliard, 1978; Mantinia, 1993; Sophia, 1993; and Big Caslon CC, 1994.

24–28. Matthew Carter, Walker typeface, 1995. Snap-on serifs and other variables extend the formal range.

new designs included unprecedented innovations along with ill-conceived and poorly crafted fonts.

Digital imaging

The photograph lost its status as an undisputed documentation of visual reality, because electronic imaging software allowed seamless and undetectable image manipulation. The boundaries between photography, illustration, and fine art began to crumble along with those separating designer, illustrator, and photographer. However, access to early image-manipulation systems was very costly, and often designers

24–29

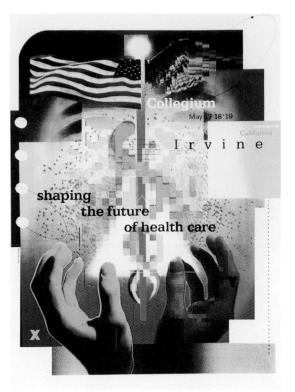

24–32

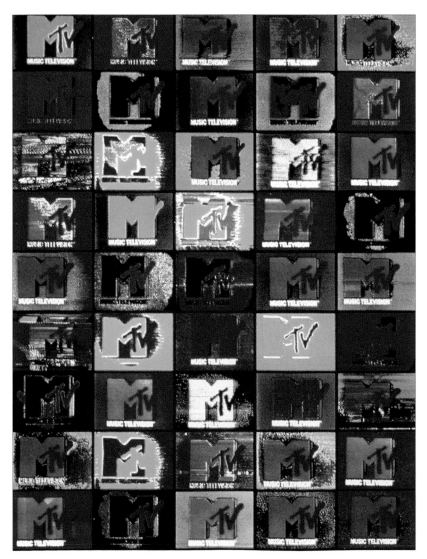

24–30

24–29. Laurie Haycock Makela and Matt Eller, Walker Art Center graphics, 1995–96. Early applications of the Walker typeface system explore only a small portion of its infinite range of possibilities.

24–30. Pat Gorman of Manhattan Design, MTV press kit cover, 1982. Randomly generated color combinations were selected and composed in a repeat pattern; visual elements convey the network's character in a nonverbal manner.

24–31. Woody Pirtle, digital illustration for Mead Paper Company, 1985. Original photographs, the wireframe construct of early high-end digital editing devices, and the printed image are shown.

24–32. April Greiman, "Shaping the Future of Health Care" poster, 1987. Color and composition transform easily comprehended symbolic images into a potent expression of future possibilities.

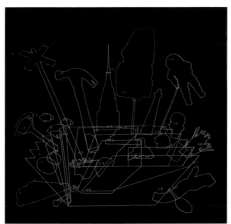

24–31

were denied hands-on access; they could only direct techni-cians rather than actually work on the system. Before the advent of the Macintosh computer, the creative potential of electronic technology was seldom explored, because artists and designers rarely had unfettered access to sophisticated technology; hourly rental fees for mainframe computers and video-editing facilities were often prohibitive. An MTV press kit cover (Fig. **24–30**) designed by Pat Gorman of Manhattan Design is a forerunner of the image invention made possible with digital computers.

Gorman created color variations of the MTV logo by exploring editing controls in a television studio. The studio engineer became so upset over her experimentation that he left her alone with the equipment, locking her in the studio so others would not observe her audacious behavior. Gorman called this design the "bad television" logo because it stands in stark contrast to broadcast television's focus on "correct" color fidelity. Widely reproduced, and making an appearance on the cover of *Billboard* magazine in 1983, this design illus-trated the creative potential of electronic image manipulation.

In an image for Mead Paper Company, designer Woody Pirtle created a surreal book whose pages open to allow objects and figures to float out into an expansive sky (Fig. **24–31**). Many photographs were digitized, silhouetted, and electronically combined into an electronic montage.

To create an advertisement for a health-care symposium (Fig. **24–32**), April Greiman "built" a poster by combining dig-itized images—photographs of a flag and an eagle, an X-ray, and a drawing of the medical profession's traditional caduceus

symbol—with color shapes and gradations and a video clip of hands shot live into the Paintbox program. A wide variety of effects, including mosaic, fading, outline, overlap, and increas-ing and decreasing levels of transparency, enable complex iconography to evolve as an integrated and organic whole.

These uncommon electronic montages from the 1980s were harbingers of the current revolution in image making, when thousands of designers, illustrators, and photographers use desktop computers with drawing, painting, and image-manipulation software to create imagery. The potent merger of video and print technology unleashed new graphic possibil-ities. Optical disks, video capture-and-edit capabilities, and interactive print- and time-based media expanded graphic-design activity further.

Interactive media, the Internet, and the World Wide Web

Hypertext is text on a computer screen containing pointers to other text, which are instantly available simply by placing a cursor on the key word or icon and clicking the mouse. Hypertext can be accessed in a nonlinear way. For example, by clicking on the name *Marco Polo* within a world-history text, a reader can get another page with a biography and portrait of Polo to open onto the computer screen. The Macintosh Hypercard software designed by computer programmer Bill Adkinson was an early application of the concept.

Interactive media, also called *hypermedia*, extends the hypertext concept to a combination of audio, visual, and cine-matic communications connected to form a coherent body of information. These materials are linked to permit viewer access in a nonlinear way, allowing each viewer to pursue information along a personally chosen path. Unlike books or films, which present information in linear sequences, interactive media has a nonlinear structure. Interactive media is usually created by teams of professionals, including audiovisual specialists, authors, computer programmers, content specialists, directors, graphic designers, image makers, and producers. Interactive media presentations are stored on DVDs and CD-ROMs or housed on Web sites, offering an ever increasing ability to store diverse media including animation, illustration, still photography, sound, text, and video.

VizAbility (Fig. **24–33**) was an exemplary interactive CD-ROM program that taught concepts relating to visual perception and helped users develop heightened visual awareness. The main screen became a contents page using the metaphor of an unfolded cube for the six chapters; clicking on an image took the user to a title page for that chapter (Figs. **24–34** and **24–35**). VizAbility was designed by MetaDesign San Francisco. An information-graphics firm with offices in Berlin, London, and San Francisco, MetaDesign is headed by German designer Erik Spiekermann (b. 1947), designer of the Meta type family and founder of the FontShop digital type foundry.

In contrast to printed communications that are finalized after they flow from the printing press, some interactive media programs are open-ended. Unlimited revisions are possible, and content can continually be added or modified. Seven basic structural methods are used, often in tandem, to bring order and cohesion to the viewer's experience: linear series, spatial zooms, parallel texts, overlays, hierarchies, matrices, and webs or networks. A *linear series* is a sequence of screens, much like the pages of a book or images in a slide show, which can be called up on the screen one after another. A *spatial zoom* lets the viewer acquire closer or more detailed data by clicking on a word to see its definition or by zooming in on a detail of a map or diagram. *Parallel texts* are modified versions of the same document. *Overlays* are different views of the same information—for example, a series of maps showing the Roman Empire at different stages of its history. *Hierarchies* are branching structures organized like a family tree; these permit one to select options that lead down the various branches. A *matrix* organizes data on a grid of interconnected pathways; these intersect at appropriate tangential points. Networks or *web structures* are constructed with links designed to guide the viewer through interconnected information.

Computer communications took a quantum leap forward with the development of the Internet, a vast network of linked computers. The Internet had its origins in the late 1960s, when scientists at the United States Department of

24–33

24–33. Bill Hill and Terry Irwin (creative directors) and Jeff Zwerner (designer), MetaDesign San Francisco (design firm), VizAbility Interactive CD-ROM, 1995. A coordinated design system unifies booklets, packaging, and screen design.

24–34 through 24–35. Bill Hill and Terry Irwin (creative directors) and Jeff Zwerner (designer), MetaDesign San Francisco (design firm), VizAbility Interactive CD-ROM screen designs, 1995. A consistent yet lively format design becomes an important aid to the user. Clicking on icons along the bottom of each screen lets users navigate through the program.

Defense Advanced Research Projects Agency (DARPA) established the ARPAnet computer network so they could transfer data between sites working on similar research projects. Supercomputer sites around the United States were connected by the National Science Foundation (NSF) into NSFNET in 1986; this totally replaced ARPAnet within two years. In 1991 the United States Congress passed legislation widening access to public schools, two-year colleges, and business organizations, generating a dramatic expansion of what was now called the Internet. By early 1997 over thirty million users in more than one hundred countries were linked into an electronic global community. In early 2005, there were over 800 million Internet users in the world, more than 200 million in the United States.

The now omnipresent *World Wide Web* provided a means to easily organize and access the vast and ever increasing content on the Internet, including text, images, sound, animation, and video. The Web was first developed in 1990 by physicist Tim Berners-Lee at the European Organization for Nuclear Research (CERN) in Geneva, Switzerland. Berners-Lee devel-

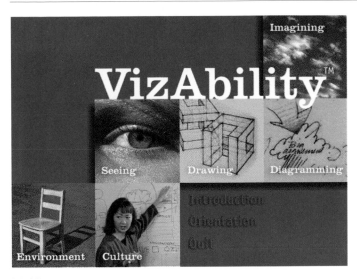

24–34

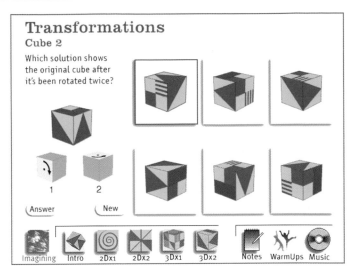

24–35

oped the three main building blocks of the Web, the Hypertext Transfer Protocol (HTTP), the Hypertext Markup Language (HTML), and a specification for the "address" of every file on the Web called the Uniform Resource Locator (URL). One navigates the Web via *hyperlinks*, which are highlighted or underlined words, phrases, icons, or images linking elements in one document to other documents existing anywhere on the Web. At first limited to the scientific community, the Web started to take off in 1993, with the development of the graphical Mosaic browser at the National Center for Supercomputing Applications (NCSA) by a team including Marc Andreessen. Leaving NCSA, Andreessen cofounded Netscape Communications to produce the first major commercial graphical browser in late 1994, Netscape Navigator, which caused the number of Web users to mushroom. Expansion of Web use continues at an incredible rate to this day, as the Web has become a ubiquitous tool of commerce, research, and expression for users and corporations around the world.

In the 1990s the phrase *information superhighway* was used to express the global access to enormous amounts of information provided by the Internet and the Web. In 1997 an estimated 150 million Web pages were online, and in 2005 there were over eight billion Web sites.

The Internet represents an unprecedented advance in human communications. Its explosive growth through the late 1990s opened new horizons for graphic design by professionals and individuals using computers and Internet access to produce Web sites. A previously inconceivable decentralization of media communications has occurred.

The early years of Web-page design posed significant constraints for graphic designers. A computer's screen size and typographic defaults often reconfigured the intended page

design until more sophisticated software downloaded fonts. Early in the Internet revolution, many feared a collapse of design standards due to the limitations of the HTML programming language and the widespread access to Web-page design by individuals without design training. Nevertheless, in the infancy of the medium, many designers, including Jessica Helfand (b. 1960), whose distinctive Web projects include the initial design for the Discovery Channel's site, demonstrated that graphic designers can create identity, aid navigation, and bring visual interest to Web sites. The Discovery Channel Web site became a paradigm of Web design. The title page (Fig. **24–36**) and secondary opening pages (Figs. **24–37** and **24–38**) use geometric zoning to create areas for titles, subtitles, and a sidebar of information. Images are used as signifiers to direct viewers as they navigate the site. Opening screens for editorial features (Figs. **24–39**, **24–40**, and **24–41**) use arresting images and understated typography, in contrast to the strident jumble of competing small elements on many Web sites.

In 1976 architect and designer Richard Saul Wurman (b. 1935) coined the term *information architecture* and predicted it would become a new profession of individuals who made complex information understandable. Twenty years later this term became widely used to denote a process of analyzing complex information and giving it structure and order, enabling audiences to glean its essence in an efficient and agreeable manner.

Clement Mok (b. 1958), an Apple Computer creative director who left to open Clement Mok Designs in 1987 (renamed Studio Archetype in 1996), emerged as an early advocate of the graphic designer's role in the rapidly changing world of interactive media. Mok realized that the digital revolution was merging commerce, technology, and design into a symbiotic whole (Fig. **24–42**). Mok believed design should be defined

24–36

24–37

24–38

24–39

24–40

24–41

24–42

24–43

24–36 through 24–41. Jessica Helfand (creative director), Melissa Tardiff (art director), Jessica Helfand Studio; Interactive Bureau (agency); John Lyle Sanford (Discovery Channel design director), Discovery Channel Web site, 1994–95. Three goals—effective visual identity, functional wayfinding through the Web site, and editorial presentation of broadcast programs—are achieved with clarity, cohesiveness, and a clear design aesthetic.

24–42. Clement Mok and Brian Forst (designers), Scott Peterson (photographer), and Studio Archetype (design studio), iQVC main categories screen for Internet shopping, 1995. Drawers and cubbyholes make this screen adaptable to new and seasonal promotions, just like a storefront.

24–43. Bob Aufuldish, fontBoy interactive catalogue Web site title page, 1995. The uninhibited aesthetic of the typefaces is conveyed.

24–44. Bob Aufuldish, fontBoy interactive catalogue Web site main holding page, 1995. The viewer has clicked on the floating g, bringing the typeface name and weights onto the screen.

24–45. Charles S. Anderson Design Co., Web page for CSA Archive, 1996. The tactile informality of a collage with found materials avoids the strident sameness of most Web sites.

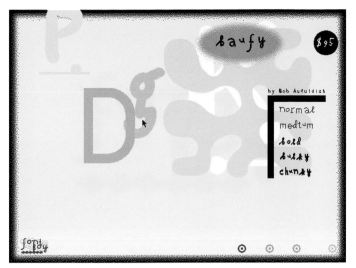

24–44

24–45

not as an isolated entity, such as packaging or graphics added on to the product or service, but as an integral part of an organization's overall vision and strategy.

Interactive media permits small firms and individuals to efficiently communicate with audiences and market products or services. This is demonstrated by the first fontBoy interactive type catalogue (Fig. **24–43**), designed by Bob Aufuldish (b. 1961). On the main holding screen, letterforms float randomly in space. When a viewer passes the cursor over a letterform, its movement stops and the font name appears (Fig. **24–44**); double-clicking on the letter opens another screen showing the entire font. Typefaces can be accessed from a menu page as well. This electronic typebook of "baroque modern" fonts by Aufuldish and Kathy Warinner (b. 1957) enables viewers to print bitmapped specimens, obtain ordering information, review future releases, and read brief biographies of the typeface designers. Aufuldish started a type foundry because he believed there was still room for experimentation and exploration in font design. He expressed interest in "a new typography waiting to happen—what I call baroque modernism for the new millennium—and I want to make and release type to inspire that new typography."

Whimsy pervaded fontBoy designs, in the form of funny sounds, unusual colors, and playful shapes that ranged from comical paraphrases of vernacular forms to abstract images inspired by modern painters such as Matisse and Miró. A sophisticated aesthetic parodied itself, in contrast to the restrained utilitarian focus of many interactive designs. Likewise, the Web site for the CSA Archive (Fig. **24–45**) demonstrates the ability to bring an inventive resonance to the Internet rather than let the medium drive the design approach and the message.

With access to personal computers now almost universal, the control of text and images has become the domain of any designer. As mentioned earlier, increasingly sophisticated programs enable designers to assume the roles previously performed by typesetting and production businesses. The crest of the graphic design profession was once largely dominated by a few individuals, while today the playing field is far more level. The widening of the design profession occurred not only through the creation of new computer software and the Internet, but also as a result of both the expansion and increased quality of design education.

The new conceptual poster

In spite of advances in technology print design continues to thrive in the Internet age. Some designers, such as Helmut Brade (b. 1937), remain faithful to the more traditional methods as well. A native of Halle, Germany, Brade works as a graphic and stage designer. Displaying wry humor, his colorful and highly illustrative posters effectively penetrate to the core of the subject depicted (Fig. **24–46**).

In addition to being a poster artist and textile designer, Gitte Kath (b. 1948) is scenographer and director at the Mill Theatre in Haderslev, Denmark. Except for a few posters for organizations such as Amnesty International, the Paralympics in Sydney, Australia, and the Umbrella Theatre in Copenhagen, Kath has created most of her posters for the Mill Theatre. Intensely meditative, the posters usually take several months to produce. Her design process involves collecting material, photographing it, and then introducing paint and text, the latter often her own handwriting or enlarged typewritten letters. Many of these visual elements reflect the transitory nature of life, and she has sometimes used a worn and discolored wall in her home as a

24–46

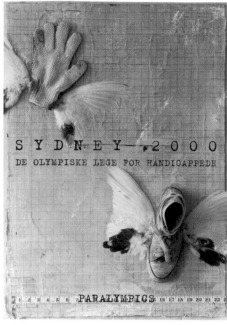

24–47

24–48

24–49

24–50

background for the photographed objects. Kath approaches her posters more as a painter than as a graphic designer—they relate both to traditional still-life painting and twentieth-century assemblage. Although imbued with a poetic resonance that alludes to the essence of her subjects, her uncompromising approach inevitably requires a dialogue with the viewer (Figs. **24–47** and **24–48**).

Having received her artistic training in Bulgaria, artist and designer Luba Lukova (b. 1960) has lived in the United States since 1981. Now working in New York, she has won numer-

ous awards, including the Grand Prix Savignac/World's Most Memorable Poster at the International Poster Salon, held in Paris in 2001. Employing radically contrasting images (Figs. **24–49** and **24–50**), her subtle and lucid statements often bluntly confront social and political issues such as war and environmental conservation.

Conceptualism, a common attribute of Japanese graphic design, is profusely present in the complex designs of Hideki Nakajima (b. 1961). Laden with ambiguities, his elegant posters consist of highly abstract minimalistic and direct images of color

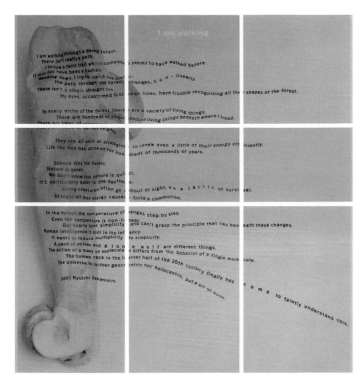

24–51

24–52

and light. His painterly and harmonious use of space is created by blending digital imagery, linear moiré patterns, flat planes of color and bold typography (Fig. **24–51**). In "I Am Walking," a large poster in nine sections, Nakajima subtly guides the reader through the text of a poem about walking in a forest.

Makoto Saito (b. 1952) is active as a design director, architecture designer, and graphic designer. Armed with a fecund imagination, he orchestrates an arcane symbolic content that follows no previous models. Serendipity plays a prominent role as he discovers his solutions during the creative process. His 1988 poster for Alpha Cubic Co., Ltd., consists of an intricately reconstructed face. With no text other than the name of the company, it proves to be both a quandary and source of intrigue for the onlooker (Fig. **24–52**). It is a mistake to read too much into Saito's pieces. He once stated: "Ten people looking at one of my posters can imagine ten different things." So far, Saito refuses to use a computer, saying "No matter how fast a computer can work, my imagination is much faster." (Fig. **24–53**). Saito's 1999 poster "Sunrise Sunset" is an elegant and touching tribute to the late Yusaku Kamekura.

Shin Matsunaga (b. 1940) presents commonplace objects as fresh, rich, and unexpected images. Using simple geometric elements he endows his images with vibrant color and a balance, warmth, and softness that seems almost spiritual. His 2002 poster for the JAGDA Member's Poster Exhibition uses the familiar rising sun theme as a central element (Fig. **24–54**).

The application of layers of ethereal light is a recurring design device in posters by the Tokyo graphic designer Mitsuo

24–46. Helmut Brade, poster for *Jedermann* (*Even the Rich Die*), by Hugo von Hofmannsthal, 2001. The contrast of the skull and jester's cap sardonically suggests the play's title.

24–47. Gitte Kath, poster for the Sydney 2000 Paralympics. This design was selected for the official Paralympic poster of the Danish Sports Organisation for the Disabled.

24–48. Gitte Kath, poster for *The Chalk Circle, or the Story of the Abandoned Doll,* a play for children and adults inspired by Bertolt Brecht's *The Chalk Circle.*

24–49. Luba Lukova, "Peace," poster, 2001. A medley of weapons is used to construct a dove.

24–50. Luba Lukova, "Water," poster, 2002. The message for water conservation is a barren lake bed that forms the body of a dead fish.

24–51. Hideki Nakajima, "I Am Walking," poster, 2001. This poster is a collaborative work with Ryuichi Sakamoto, a well-known Japanese musician and a winner of a Grammy award. Sakamoto wrote the poem for this poster, and Nakajima provided a typographic interpretation of the text.

24–52. Makoto Saito, poster for Alpha Cubic Co., Ltd., 1988.

24–53

24–54

24–55

24–56

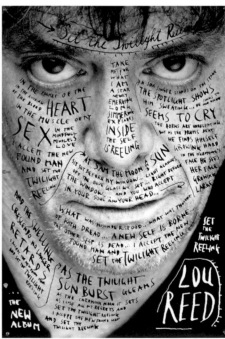

24–57

Katsui (b. 1931). As with Matsunaga, the familiar circular shape is used in his majestic 1998 poster, "En hommage à Yusaku Kamekura," a design fully worthy of its subject (Fig. **24–55**).

Jianping He (b. 1973) first studied art at the China Academy of Art at Hangzhou. After continuing his studies at the Berlin University of Arts he remained in Berlin, where he opened Hesign Studio. With their remarkable blend of type and photography, his posters retain the majesty and serenity of traditional Chinese landscape painting (Fig. **24–56**).

Born in Austria, Stefan Sagmeister (b. 1962) received his first diploma in graphic design from the University of Applied Arts in Vienna, and while on a Fulbright scholarship he earned

24–58

24–59

24–60

a master's from Pratt Institute in New York. After first working in New York and later as creative director for the Hong Kong office of the Leo Burnett advertising agency, he returned to New York in 1993 to found Sagmeister, Inc. He has designed graphics and packaging for the Rolling Stones, David Byrne, Lou Reed, Aerosmith, and Pat Metheny, among other clients. Sagmeister's graphic design is consistently characterized by an uncompromising and harsh directness. On a poster for a Lou Reed album, lyrics from one of Reed's songs are handwritten across his face like graffiti (Fig. **24–57**).

Werner Jeker (b. 1944) works as a graphic designer in Chatillens and Lausanne, Switzerland, mainly for cultural institutions. In his poster "Saison," a single image is endowed with a double meaning through a simple modification, a change in color (Fig. **24–58**). Jean-Benoît Lévy (b. 1959) divides his time between San Francisco and Basel, where he studied at the Basel School of Design from 1978 until 1983. Lévy is one of the few poster designers from the Basel School of Design who remained in Basel. Combining figurative elements, frequently a face, with typography and natural or geometrical forms, his posters invite reflection and contemplation. His designs witness the rigor of his Swiss training blended with a conceptual vision (Figs. **24–59** and **24–60**).

Before moving to France during the 1960s, Rudi Meyer (b. 1943), a native of Basel, studied with Armin Hofmann and Emil Ruder at the Basel School of Design. He has taught at the École Nationale Supérieure des Arts Décoratifs and as a graphic designer produces visual identity programs, posters, logos, exhibitions, products, and cartography. As a teacher he

24–53. Makoto Saito, "Sunrise Sunset Yusaku Kamekura," poster, 1999. Commissioned by the Toppan Printing Company, Ltd., this poster serves as a monumental homage to the late designer Kamekura.

24–54. Shin Matsunaga, "JAGDA Member's Poster Exhibition," poster, 2003.

24–55. Mitsuo Katsui, "Hommage à Yusaku Kamekura," poster, 1998.

24–56. Jianping He, poster advertising Hesign Studio Berlin, 2004

24–57. Stefan Sagmeister, Lou Reed poster, 1996. "We designed a poster announcing his new album 'Set the Twilight Reeling,'" explains Sagmeister. "The lyrics are extremely personal. We tried to show this by writing those lyrics directly over his face."

24–58. Werner Jeker, "Saison," poster, 2000. With recollections of Man Ray, in Jeker's poster announcing the 2000–2001 season for the Théâtres Vidy-Lausanne, a leaf which becomes lips implies both "season" and "voice."

24–59. Jean-Benoît Lévy, poster for RAR, 2001. In this poster for a small boutique selling hand-crafted objects and flowers, photography and typography are integrated and layers of information are presented in a manner that is characteristic of Lévy's vision. The "street poster" tradition in Switzerland provides smaller companies with low-budget advertising that can be used over a number of years or for periods of two to three weeks.

24–60. Jean-Benoît Lévy, poster for AIGA, 2002. This poster announces the opening of nine design studios in San Francisco to local AIGA members. The word *seam* was suggested as a theme, and Lévy sought imagery that implied mining. Diamonds numbered from 1 to 9 represent the nine design studios and the quality of their work. The black-and-white photograph of a tearful fashion model with running makeup was taken by the Swiss photographer Robert Schlatter, now living in San Francisco. According to Lévy the tears could be caused by the heat of a mine, by sadness, or by anger. The question lingers.

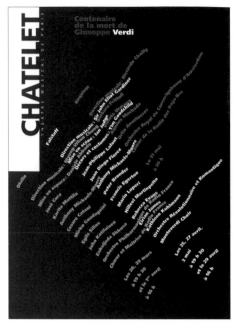

24–61

24–62

24–63

24–61. Rudi Meyer, Verdi poster, 2001. The operas of Verdi are implied by undulating lines of type in the colors of the Italian national flag.

24–62. Rudi Meyer, poster for the opera *Lucie de Lammermoor*, 2002. The melancholy nature of the opera is implied through the overlapping imagery of a ruined abbey and foliage.

24–63. Niklaus Troxler, "Typoplakate," poster, 1996. In this purely typographic design, the subject, an exhibition on the typographic poster, is implied by its very absence.

24–64. Niklaus Troxler, "Solo Vocals," poster, 2004. The subject, Solo Vocals, is represented by a single tube of lipstick.

24–65. Karl Dominic Geissbuhler, poster for *Die schweigsame Frau* (The Silent Woman), 2001. The opera's subject is expressed by having the vertical title cross the lips like a typographic finger.

24–66. Karl Dominic Geissbuhler, poster for *Maria Stuarda*, 2002. The *A* in Stuart's name becomes her decapitated head below the chopping block.

24–67. Uwe Loesch, "Fly By," poster, 2003. A poster for an exhibition of Loesch's own designs curiously mingles flies with the typography.

24–68. Holger Matthies, "Hamburger Sommer 2003," poster. In this poster for Hamburg summer cultural events the season is indicated by tomato sunglasses and the woman's suntan.

24–69. Philippe Apeloig, poster for the exhibition Bateaux sur l'Eau, 2003. This poster was designed for a temporary exhibition, Boats on Water: Rivers and Canals, in Rouen, France. The exhibition displayed models of ancient barges; the typography implies how they traveled on water.

has inspired a generation of graphic designers by stressing the importance of basic design principles, typographic research, and the rich tradition of French poster design. Whether typographical or image-based, Meyer's work consistently displays a graceful elegance (Figs. **24–61** and **24–62**).

Niklaus Troxler (b. 1947) was introduced to graphic design while working as a typographic apprentice. He went on to receive formal training at the Art School of Lucerne from 1967 until 1971. He worked as an art director for Hollenstein Création in Paris before starting his own graphic design studio in Willisau, Switzerland, in 1973. An avid jazz fan, he has created many posters for jazz concerts and festivals. Equally at home with typographic and illustrative interpretations, Troxler is without exception one of the leading forces in poster design today (Figs. **24–63** and **24–64**).

Beginning his graphic design training with Ernst Keller and Johannes Itten at the Kunstgewerbeschule in Zurich, Karl Dominic Geissbuhler (b. 1932) completed his graphic art studies at the Kunsthochule in Berlin. After working as an art director for a German advertising agency, he became a freelance graphic designer. During his long career Geissbuhler has designed over 200 posters for such clients as British Airways and the Zurich Opera House, where he has also created notable stage designs for seasonal festivals of music and theater. As demonstrated by his posters "Die schweigsame Frau" (The Silent Woman) and "Maria Stuarda," Geissbuhler is a master of understatement (Figs. **24–65** and **24–66**). In the same vein, Uwe Loesch (b. 1943), a native of Dresden, Germany, provides the viewer with few clues to the meaning of his minimalist and

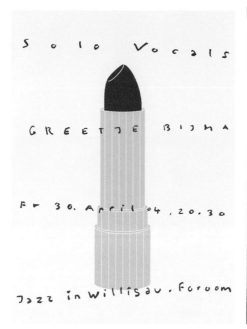

24–64

24–65

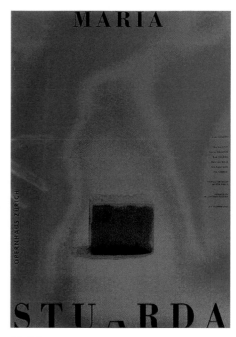

24–66

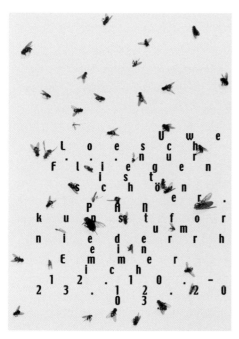

24–67

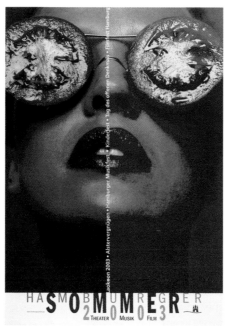

24–68

24–69

arcane messages (Fig. **24–67**). The Berlin/Hamburg graphic designer Holger Matthies (b. 1940) delights in presenting ordinary objects and situations in unusual ways: tomatoes become sunglasses.

The Parisian Philippe Apeloig (1962) was educated at the École Nationale Supérieure des Arts Appliqués and the École Nationale Supérieure des Arts Décoratifs. He then worked as an intern for Total Design in Amsterdam, an experience that greatly enhanced his interest in typography. In 1985 he began working as a designer for the Musée d'Orsay in Paris, and in

1988 he worked and studied in Los Angeles with April Greiman. After returning to Paris, Apeloig began his own studio and became the art director for *Jardins des modes*. In 1997 he became a design consultant for the Louvre Museum, where he is currently the art director. Whether image-based or typographic, Apeloig's designs are dominated by an expressive and decisive use of typography that not only provides information but also functions as a visual pun (Fig. **24–69**).

The Middle East deserves far more attention than space will allow in this volume. The Israeli graphic designer David

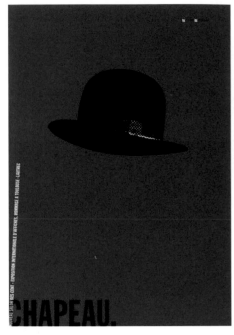

24–70

24–71

24–72

Tartakover (b. 1944) studied at the Bezalel Academy of Art and Design in Jerusalem before graduating from the London College of Printing in 1968. Since 1976 he has served as senior lecturer in the visual communication department at the Bezalel Academy of Art and Design and has been a frequent speaker at professional seminars and art colleges throughout Israel and overseas. Since 1975, he has operated his own studio in Tel Aviv, specializing in visual communications on cultural themes (Fig. **24–70**).

Graphic design in Iran has developed an increasingly idiosyncratic flavor. The typographic expressive posters of the Iranian graphic designer Reza Abedini (b. 1967) reflect both his training in graphic design and his later education as a painter. Often combining Farsi with English or French, his posters radiate a graceful elegance. As with his prize-winning poster for the film *Reves de sable,* his type and image frequently become one and the same (Figs. **24–71** and **24–72**).

The conceptual book cover
The designs of Charles I. (Chip) Kidd (b. 1964) for Alfred A. Knopf have helped to foment a revolution in book jacket design. In a recent monograph on his work, Veronique Vienne focuses on the essence of his appeal: "By distancing the title from the image on the cover, Kidd puts a very specific kind of pressure on readers: he asks them to bridge the gap between what they read and what they see. In the process he empowers them by demanding they take control of the communica-

tion." Like Gitte Kath, Kidd frequently uses vintage images such as old prints and family albums found in flea markets and junk shops. His visual cues are elusive and require the viewer to excavate the message. In his words, "I never really know if the readers get the subtle visual puns of my jackets, but I can't let that inform my design to the point where I will compromise" (Figs. **24–73** and **24–74**).

In the late 1980s Katsumi Asaba (b. 1940), who founded the Katsumi Asaba Design Office in 1975, transformed a surviving pictographic script, Dongba (Tompa), used by the Naxi tribe in China, into a personal design language titled "Katsumi Asaba's Tompa Character Exhibition: The Last Living Pictographic Script on Earth." As demonstrated by the jacket for the book *Spy Sorge,* one of his goals has been to forge a connection between contemporary graphic design and ancient writing systems (Fig. **24–75**).

A voice from Africa
Chaz Maviyane-Davies (b. 1952), called "the guerilla of graphic design," creates posters with richly metaphoric yet hopeful messages. The risks he has taken in his personal life and in his work result in cross-cultural images that communicate with incisive effectiveness.

Born and raised in Rhodesia (Zimbabwe, since independence in 1980), he eventually went to London, where he studied graphic design. Maviyane-Davies has worked in Japan studying three-dimensional design, and in Malaysia for the

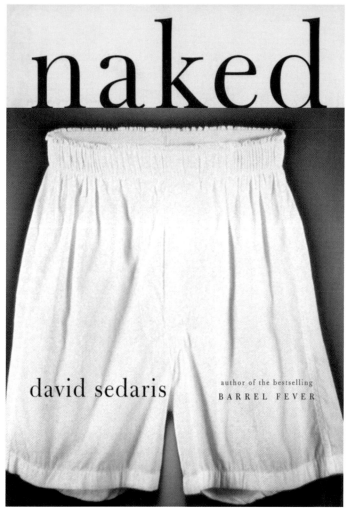

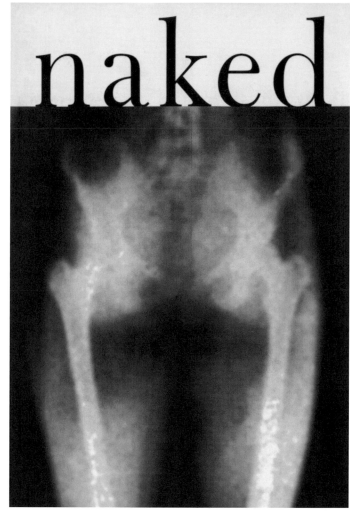

24–73

International Organization of Consumers Unions and the JUST World Trust. His professional experience in London includes time with Fulcrum Design Consultants, Newell and Sorrel Design, Ltd., and the graphic design department of BBC. From 1983 until January 2001, he had his own design studio in Harare, Zimbabwe, creating his Human Rights series, for which he has gained worldwide renown (Fig. **24–76**).

Maviyane-Davies believes that design is a powerful tool for social change. His last fourteen years in Zimbabwe saw a consistent loss of the freedom and economic improvement promised by the government of Robert Mugabe. As a result Maviyane-Davies's political convictions have been the source of many of his own projects. The Human Rights series was originally produced at his own expense, but eventually adopted by the United Nations. By the time he left Zimbabwe, he was Africa's best known graphic designer. In January 2001 he began teaching and working in Boston (Fig. **24–77**).

24–70. David Tartakover, poster celebrating the Henri de Toulouse-Lautrec centennial, 2001. The beauty of this poster comes from its minimalism and from the tension created by the intersection of the horizontal and diagonal text.

24–71. Reza Abedini, "Reves de sable," poster, 2003. The sable cloak is created from a collage of Farsi lettering.

24–72. Reza Abedini (graphic designer) and Mehran Mohajer (photographer), "Photo and Graphic Exhibition in Yazd," poster, 2004. This typographic poster is designed to be read from four directions.

24–73. Chip Kidd, book cover for *Naked*, 1997. Two covers in one, this design reveals an X-ray after the dust jacket is removed. Photography by Peter Zeray/Photonica.

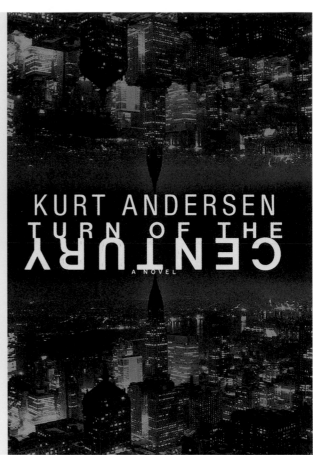

24–74

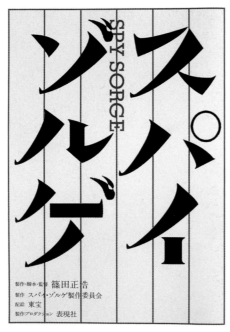

24–75

24–76

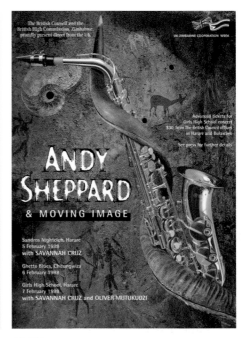

24–77

24–78

24–79

24–74. Chip Kidd, book cover for *Turn of the Century,* 1998. A mirror image is used to depict the subject of this novel about the media-driven world of New York and Los Angeles. Photography © Corbis/UPI.

24–75. Katsumi Asaba, book cover for *Spy Sorge,* 2003

24–76. Chaz Maviyane-Davies, poster on Human Rights Article 4, 1996. In every image Maviyane-Davies makes, especially his United Nations human-rights articles, the images are powerful and positive and exude confidence and dignity.

24–77. Chaz Maviyane-Davies, poster for a concert by U.K. jazz musician Andy Shepard in Zimbabwe, 1998. Maviyane-Davies inter-twines a kudu horn with a saxophone, working images from prehistoric African cave paintings into the background.

24–78. Film title for *Spiderman,* 2002.

24–79. Film title for *Spiderman,* 2002.

A new generation of film titles

Imaginary Forces was launched in 1996 by Kyle Cooper, Chip Houghton, and Peter Frankfurt. It rapidly became the van-guard of film title design, and by integrating graphic design, motion, and interactive media, it has created a new approach to this genre. Its multidisciplinary staff consists of designers, art directors, animators, editors, writers, and producers. In 2000 the founding members of Imaginary Forces were joined by Mikon van Gastel, Karin Fong, Kurt Mattila, Michael Riley, Linda Nakagawa, and Saffron Kenny. All partners have their own style and area of expertise but work in other areas according to the demands of a particular project. Describing his methodology, Cooper stated: "Everything starts with the words. I read the script. If the script is based on a novel, I try to read the book. I like it when main titles tap into some-body's obsession" (Figs. **24–78** and **24–79**).

The digital vanguard

Graphic design in the 1990s often incorporated the digital process in complex visual combinations of information archi-tecture, media, technology, and culture. Two designers who have used the computer to explore the infinite possibilities of the digital process are Erik Adigard (b. 1953) and Patricia McShane (b. 1953) of M.A.D. Design. Their frontispiece designs for *WIRED* magazine built visual essays out of the cover stories. In "Money is Just a Type of Information,"

24–80

24–81

24–80. Erik Adigard, "Money is Just a Type of Information," *WIRED*, July 1994.

24–81. Erik Adigard, HOTBOT logo, 1996.

24–82. John Maeda, calendar, 1996.

24–83. Vaughan Oliver, Central St. Martin's Fashion Show invitation, 2004.

24–84. Michael Johnson, "Design Decisions," poster, 1996. One of a series of posters created for Britain's Design Council. They were intended to be displayed in schools and to spur children's interest in the design process by using beautifully "wrong" images.

24–85. Why Not Associates, book cover, 1998.

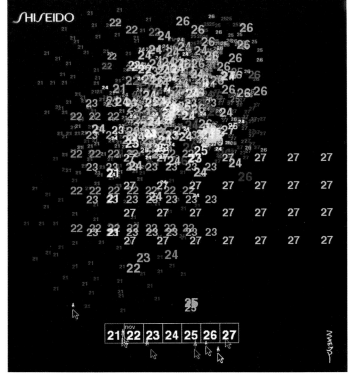

24–82

designed by Adigard for *WIRED*'s July 1994 issue (Fig. **24–80**), he combined a collage of foreign currency designs with the verso design of the U.S. $1 banknote converted to red ink, financial and stock ticker data, vernacular images, and digital patterns and gradations to create densely packed montages commenting on the effects of new technologies. The work of Adigard and McShane exemplifies the development of the designer as illustrator working with what had, in just a few years, become fast paced, powerful, and revolutionary computer applications.

Adigard designed the HOTBOT logo for the first commercial search engine with customized search features, launched by WIRED Digital in 1996 (Fig **24–81**). The concentric *O*s were also navigation links. The typographic forms ironically have more in common with early twentieth-century typographic experiments such as those of Russian constructivist Rodchenko than with the new technologies the mark represents.

John Maeda, a graduate of both the Massachusetts Institute of Technology and Tsukuba University Institute of Art and Design in Japan, heads the MIT Media Lab's Visible

24–83   24–84   24–85

Language Workshop. He is widely acknowledged for his lead-ing role in the transition of graphic design from print to digital media and is constantly seeking new ways to integrate artistic expression with the new digital technology (Fig. **24–82**).

Recent British graphic design

With its constantly changing consumer market and ever-expanding multicultural population, London is often charac-terized as fleeting and enigmatic. Herein lies a visual culture coupling new media and the development of computer tech-nology with a multitude of emerging design studios offering different approaches to visual problem solving.

Many London graphic design studios embrace contempo-rary fine art that is eclectic and connected to ephemeral pop culture. Many also draw inspiration from traditional graphic design.

As a young designer with a passion for independent rock music, Vaughan Oliver (b. 1957) collaborated with Ivo Watts-Russell (b. 1954), founder of the 4AD Records label. Employed by Ivo's South London company, Oliver created a remarkable series of record covers and promotional print collateral for well known musical groups such as the Cocteau Twins, This Mortal Coil, the Pixies, Bush, and Lush. At 4AD, Oliver was given creative independence and a succession of design assignments for independent rock music. Motivated by his intense bond with music, he committed himself to high stan-dards, bold exploration, and the imaginative use of found imagery. Oliver has often worked with the photographer Nigel

Grierson (23 Envelope) and more recently collaborated with Chris Bigg (b. 1962), producing graphic design for such clients as Microsoft, Sony, BBC, JP Morgan Private Bank, the Victoria and Albert Museum, Harrods, Virgin, Warner Bros., and Raygun Publishing (Fig. **24–83**).

Michael Johnson (b. 1964) got his start at Wolf Olins in the 1980s. After a short time working in Australia and Japan as an art director, he returned to London and set up his own graphic design studio. His work is both witty and clever, using wordplay and strong visual puns as a communication strategy (Fig. **24–84**). Why Not Associates was established by Andrew Altmann (b. 1962), David Ellis (b. 1962), and Howard Greenhalgh (b. 1963) in 1987. This multidisciplinary, experi-mental London-based design company has worked on diverse projects, including postage stamps, corporate identity, exhibi-tion design, television titles, and motion graphics. Clients include the typography magazine *U&lc,* the Royal College of Art, the Kobe Fashion Museum in Japan, Armani, Nike, Saab, and First Direct (Fig. **24–85**).

Pentagram's philosophy continues to be based on the con-cept of a mutual interdisciplinary design practice and an intu-itive exchange among partners. The London office hosts pub-lic events such as lectures and exhibitions in its Notting Hill gallery. Pentagram has diversified with the addition of archi-tect Lorenzo Apicella (b. 1957), book designer Angus Hyland (b. 1963) (Fig. **24–86**), and *Colors* magazine creative director Fernando Gutiérrez (b. 1963). Other notable members of the London office include David Hillman (b. 1943) (Fig. **24–87**),

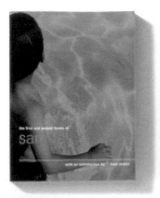

24–86

24–89

24–90

24–88

24–87

who was previously commissioned to design the French daily newspaper *Le Matin de Paris*; John McConnell (b. 1939), whose previous clients include the leading 1960s boutique Biba; the distinguished product and package designer John Rushworth (b. 1958); and the industrial and vehicle designer Daniel Weil (b. 1953), whose work can be found in the collections of the Victoria and Albert Museum and the Museum of Modern Art (MoMA) in New York.

Vince Frost (b. 1964) solves graphic design problems through a close collaboration with photographers, illustrators, and writers. This association is exemplified in the design and editing of the literary magazine *Zembla*. Representing a new era in magazine design, *Zembla*'s fusion of writing, photography, illustration, and expressive typography challenges all previous mores (Fig. **24–88**).

Alan Kitching (b. 1940), the eminent specialist and teacher of letterpress typographic design and printmaking, is internationally renowned for his innovative use of wood and metal letterforms. In typographical compositions, books, packaging, and monoprints, Kitching skillfully adapts type from the past for modern communication.

24–86. Angus Hyland, book jackets from the second Pocket Canons series, published by Canongate, 1999.

24–87. David Hillman, Millennium Stamps series for the Royal Mail, United Kingdom, 1999.

24–88. Vince Frost, page spread for *Zembla Magazine* 10, issue 3, Spring 2004.

24–89. Alan Kitching, *Hamlet I,* letterpress edition print, 2001.

24–90. Alan Kitching, *Blood, Toil, Tears, and Sweat,* letterpress edition print, 2004. This print was created for the exhibition Public Address System in London and Berlin, 2004.

Beginning as an apprentice compositor at the age of 14, he founded the Typographic Workshop in Clerkenwell, London, in 1989, for both students and professionals. In 1999 Kitching formed a partnership with designer and teacher Celia Stothard and moved the Typography Workshop and presses to Lambeth in South London. In 1992, Kitching set up letterpress workshops as a senior tutor of typography at the Royal College of Art and as visiting professor at the University of the Arts in London (Figs. **24–89** and **24–90**).

Wood is breathing. It is the most appropriate materials to the climate of Japan. SHIKI is very proud of their confidential skilled works as a professional wood worker.

24–91

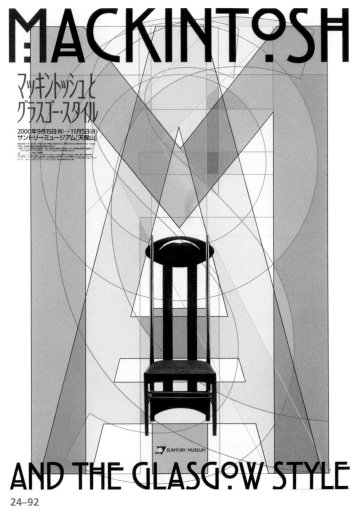

24–92

New typographic expression

Long before the arrival of the computer, artists and designers were liberating type from the page by turning them into expressionist signs. Futurist artist and designer Filippo Marinetti celebrated "words in freedom" in his *Technical Manifesto of Futurist Literature* of 1912. The personal computer has enabled designers to freely stretch the limits of typographic form to create unbounded words or letters on the page. Shuichi Nogami (b. 1954) is a designer who creates posters using expressionist typographic forms. In "Shiki" (Fig. **24–91**), the designer has combined letterforms and stretched their shapes into a wooden sculpture floating in space for a poster to promote the work of an architect working with wood in Japan. Nogami often takes surprising photographic images and letters and combines, overlaps, merges, and stretches them into experimental letterforms that float as three-dimensional objects on the page. The designs of Shinnoske Sugisaki (b. 1953), both elegant and poetic, display a unique blend of Western and Japanese features (Fig. **24–92**).

Among the leading figures in contemporary Swiss graphic design are Ralph Schraivogel (b. 1960) and Melchior Imboden

(b.1956). A graduate of the Zurich School of Design, Schraivogel established his own graphic design studio in 1982. He has developed posters for a wide range of institutions and cultural events, including Zurich's Filmpodium, the Museum of Design Zurich, the Festival of African Films (Cinemafrica), and the Theatre am Neumarkt (Fig. **24–93**). Imboden arranges elements of simple, geometric compositions through minimal and decisive use of color to create bold, visually arresting, and illusionistic typographical abstractions. His expressive work combines a penetrating and rhythmic use of space with abstraction, repetition, flat geometric planes of color, and experimental typography. Imboden has designed many posters, books, and catalogues for Swiss cultural institutions that have earned recognition at numerous international exhibitions (Figs. **24–94** and **24–95**).

Paula Scher continues to be a major force in graphic design, a leader who reinvents herself with apparent ease. She continues to draw upon historical models while transforming them into her own unique form of expression. Reflecting music posters from the 1960s, her poster "Diva Is Dismissed" is an ex-

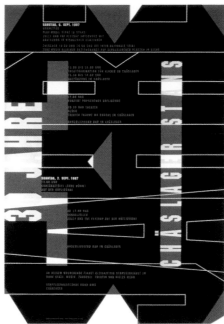

24–93   24–94   24–95

ample of this ability. Her poster for the 1995 New York Shake-speare Festival's productions of *The Tempest* and *Troilus & Cressida* seems like a refined version of the typographic posters of the nineteenth century (Figs. **24–96** and **24–97**).

Nancy Skolos (b. 1955) and Thomas Wedell (b. 1949), a husband and wife team of photographer and graphic designer, "work to diminish the boundaries between graphic design and photography—creating collaged three-dimensional images influenced by modern painting, technology and architecture. This unique collaboration, as well as the dialogue between the makers themselves and the pieces being made, is a process of continuous curiosity and discovery" producing posters, corporate identities, books, exhibits, web sites, and videos for mainly high-technology clients. The intense energy, vibrant color, and textures of their work deftly evoke the spirit of technology itself. In addition to their studio work, they both teach graphic design at the Rhode Island School of Design (Figs. **24–98** and **24–99**).

Hans Dieter Reichert (b. 1959) first studied graphic design and visual communication with Willi Fleckhaus at the Universities of Essen (Folkwang School) and Wuppertal in Germany. Following a brief period of design studies in Switzerland he eventually graduated from the London University of the Arts. He worked at BRS Premsela & Vonk with Guus Ros and at Total Design with Jelle van der Toorn Vrijthoff, then returned to London to work at the London design company Banks & Miles, Ltd., for five years. In 1993 he launched his own company, HDr Visual Communication, in Kent, England, and in 1995 he co-

24–91. Shuichi Nogami, poster for the architectural firm Shiki, which works exclusively in wood on residential buildings in Japan, 2002.

24–92. Shinnoske Sugisaki, poster for the exhibition Mackintosh and the Glasgow Style, 2000. Using symetrical overlapping letterforms Sugisaki deftly suggests the ascending elegance of the Glasgow Style.

24–93. Ralph Schraivogel, "Henry van de Velde," poster, 1993. The spirit of Van de Velde is invoked as his name is placed in one of his chair designs.

24–94. Melchior Imboden, poster for the Swiss exhibition 30 Jahre Chäslager Stans (30 Years of the Gallery Chäslager Stans), 1997.

24–95. Melchior Imboden, Kunst, exhibition poster, 1999.

founded Bradbourne Publishing, Ltd. Here he began the remarkable quarterly international typographic magazine *baseline*, for which he serves as publisher, editor, art director, and designer. Book designs by HDr Visual Communication include *Alexey Brodovitch,* by Kerry William Purcell, Steven Heller's 1999 monograph *Paul Rand,* and *Merz to Emigre and Beyond,* also by Heller (Figs. **24–100** and **24–101**).

The use of text as signs or as visual form began as far back as 33 B.C., when it was referred to as pattern poetry. The cubists, Dadaists, and futurists all explored word-images and shaped text. The cubist work of Guillaume Apollinaire (Figs. 13–15 and 13–16), who shaped text to illustrate ideas in his

24–96

24–97

24–99

24–98

24–96. Paula Scher, "Diva is Dismissed," poster, 1994.

24–97. Paula Scher, "1995 New York Shakespeare Festival: The Tempest/Troilus & Cressida," poster, 1995. Silkscreen on paper.

24–98. Nancy Skolos and Thomas Wedell, page spread, "Purple Prototype," from *Ferrington Guitars Book*, 1992. With this book Skolos and Wedell helped to redefine to definition of a book's form as both type and objects move in and out of space.

24–99. Nancy Skolos and Thomas Wedell, poster for the IDSA IDEA Award call for entries, 1999. In this photomontage one is invited to "enter" the indus-trial design awards competition.

24–100. Hans Dieter Reichert and Paul Arnot, magazine spread for "Hearing Type," by Frank Armstrong, *Baseline International Typographics Journal*, no. 42, 2003.

24–101. Hans Dieter Reichert and Paul Spencer, table-of-contents spread for *Alexey Brodovitch*, by Kerry William Purcell, 2002.

calligrammes and editorial pages, has been an inspiration for others seeking to use text to illustrate a story. These pieces challenge viewers to "see" text as images as well as something to be read.

Bosnia and Herzegovina émigré Mirko Ilic (b. 1956) has exploited the computer to design word-image pieces in book designs and op-ed pieces for the *New York Times*, where he has been a frequent contributor. He began as an editorial illustrator and designer and has worked as an editorial art director for *Time* magazine as well as the *New York Times*. His firm Mirko Ilic, Inc., is based in New York City. In both design and illustration he uses the computer to develop an immediate and detailed style. He is as adept at design as he is at illustration, and he uses both as devices of visual analogy to communicate his

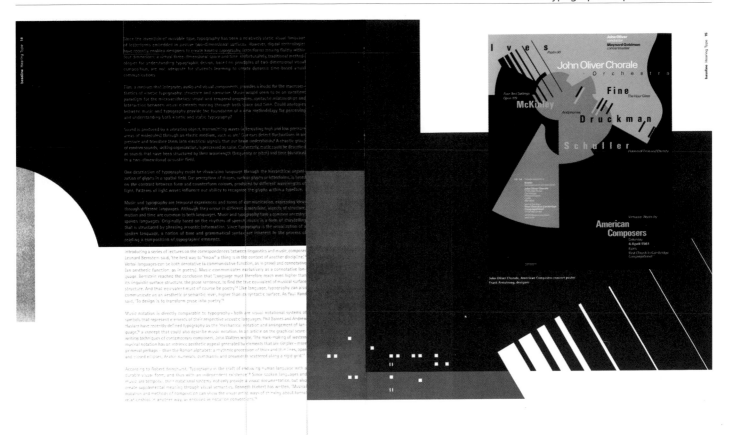

'Could analogies between music and typography provide the foundation
of a new methodology for perceiving and understanding kinetic and static typography?'

24–100

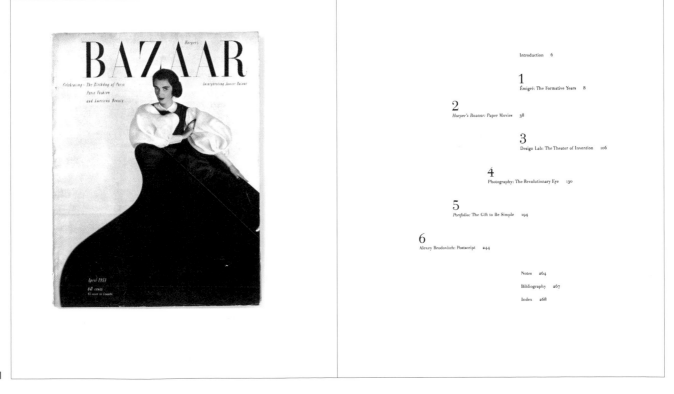

24–101

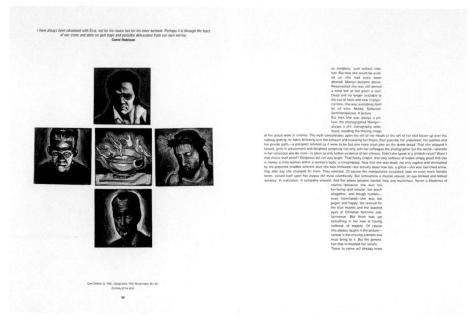

24–102

24–103

24–102. Mirko Ilic, shaped text spread for *Elvis + Marilyn 2X Immortal*, 1994.

24–103. Wladyslaw Pluta, poster for the exhibition Image of Jazz in Polish Posters, 2002.

24–104. Wladyslaw Pluta, poster for the exhibition Pollnische Plakate des 21. Jahrhunderts (Polish Posters of the Twenty-first Century), 2003.

24–105. Ahn Sang-Soo, poster for the Jeonju International Film Festival, 2002.

24–106. Michael Bierut, poster for a Yale University School of Architecture lecture and exhibition series, 2002.

24–107. Helmut Schmid, poster for the exhibition On Typography, Kobu Design University, Japan, 2000.

24–104

24–105

ideas. In his book design for Elvis + Marilyn 2X Immortal, full pages of text are shaped as the iconographic signs, +, 2, and X, also the signs used in the title. This style is directly inspired by early twentieth-century text designs such as Apollinaire's pages for *SIC* magazine in 1917. Apollinaire shaped negative space and text painstakingly, using hand-set type. Ilic's shaped text designs, which challenge the reader both to see text as image to read it, would be impractical or impossible without the computer and the page design applications available in the late twentieth century (Fig. **24–102**).

The Polish graphic designer Wladyslaw Pluta (b. 1949) skillfully uses type to evoke the content of his designs. Humor, expressive color, and the attempt to play "intellectual games with the viewer" are all aspects of Pluta's work. Devoted to graphic design education, Pluta serves as chair of the visual communication department of the Faculty of Industrial Design at the Academy of Fine Arts in Cracow, his alma mater (Figs. **24–103** and **24–104**).

In the early 1980s the Korean graphic designer Ahn Sang-Soo (b. 1952) designed a succession of experimental letters

24–106

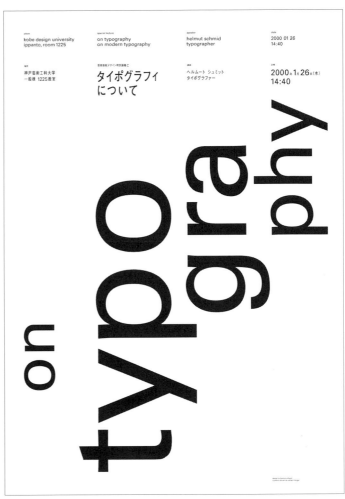

24–107

based on older Korean typefaces. This series was the first to deviate from the rigidity of Hangul typography, a Korean alphabet created in the mid-fifteenth century, and the square frame of Korean writing. In his poster designs Sang-Soo incorporates the letters as free and playful elements (Fig. **24–105**).

It is clear from the work of Michael Bierut (b. 1957) and Helmut Schmid (b. 1942) that the International Typographic Style is not only alive but thriving. Before becoming a partner in Pentagram's New York office in 1990, Beirut worked for ten years at Vignelli Associates, eventually becoming vice president of graphic design (Fig **24–106**). Now a German citizen, the Austrian-born Schmid first apprenticed as a type compositor in Germany and then studied under Emil Ruder, Robert Buechler, and Kurt Hauert at the Basel School of Design in Switzerland. Since 1977 he has worked as a graphic designer in Osaka, Japan, where he produces packaging and brand identities for consumer products. A typographic master, he

has written valuable essays on typography for international magazines, including *TM* (Switzerland), *Idea, Graphic Design* (Japan), *Grafisk Revy* (Sweden), *Graphische Revue* (Austria), and *Baseline* (United Kingdom). His inspiring book *The Road to Basel: Typographic Reflections by Students of the Typographer and Teacher Emil Ruder* was published in German, English, and Japanese in 1997 and reprinted by Robundo Publishers, Tokyo, in 2004. Schmid's design clearly reflects the teaching of Ruder, yet he has given it an additional refinement that is totally his own (Figs. **24–107**).

Graphic designers in the Netherlands remain on the cutting edge of their field. Selecting a few leading designers to profile in this chapter was not only a difficult task—it was virtually an impossible one. The Netherlands has a design culture so rich and diverse that it warrants a separate volume. Many designers cited in chapter 22 are as active today as they were in previous years. Prime examples are Studio Dumbar in Rotterdam and

24–108

24–109

24–110

Anthon Beeke in Amsterdam, whose work remains vibrant, surprising, and increasingly intellectually rich. A new design studio that stands out is Koeweiden-Postma in Amsterdam, begun by Jacques Koeweiden (b. 1957) and Paul Postma (b. 1958). As with the scope of Dutch graphic design as a whole, the graphic design of Koeweiden-Postma is so varied that describing a particular project can only touch upon the wide range of the studio's creations. The Hortus Botanicus, a small but opulent botanical garden, is a unique place in the center of Amsterdam. Signs printed in the new Hortus house style developed by Koeweiden-Postma gently familiarize Amsterdam residents with what lies beyond the gates of their botanical garden (Fig. **24–108**).

Max Kisman (b. 1953) started his own graphic design studio soon after graduating from the Gerrit Rietveld Academy in 1977. During the mid-1980s he applied digital technology to his graphic design for *Vinyl* and *Language Technology* magazines, posters for the Paradiso theater in Amsterdam, and Red Cross stamps for the Dutch postal service. In 1986 he cofounded *TYP/Typografisch Papier*, a magazine devoted to typography and art. From 1989 until 1992 he lived in Barcelona, where he digitized many of his early typefaces for FontShop International in Berlin. From 1992 until 1996 he worked as a graphic designer and animator for VPRO Television in the Netherlands. In 1994 he became involved in graphic design for interactive media for *VPRO-digital,* a Dutch agency specializing in new media, and the online magazine *HotWired* in San Francisco, and in 1997 he began working for Wired Television and then as art director for *Wired Digital,* also in San

Francisco. Kisman maintains his studio MKDSGN in Mill Valley, California, and founded Holland Fonts to market his own typeface designs in 2002. As shown in his poster celebrating the century-old legacy of Henri de Toulouse-Lautrec, Kisman approaches his work with openess and wit (Fig. **24–109**).

Having lived and worked together since 1993, Nikki Gonnissen (b. 1967) and Thomas Widdershoven (b. 1960) founded the Amsterdam design firm Thonik in 2000, the name being derived from a combination of their surnames. From its inception Thonik has been at the vanguard of a new generation of Dutch graphic designers. Working simultaneously as designers, art directors, and conceptual and media artists, the firm has undertaken a steady stream of largely unrelated assignments, and not a single solution has fallen within the realm of the predictable. Gonnissen and Widdershoven are concerned with the world of ideas, and their uncompromising designs are not for easy consumption. As stated in a 2001 monograph on their work, "Thonik's approach is a breath of fresh air. Intellectual but not intellectualized." (Fig. **24–110**)

A Mexican vanguard

Mexico has over 104 million people who speak Spanish, various Mayan, Nahuatl, and other regional indigenous languages. European and Pre-Colombian cultures are major resources for the Mexican design movement. Modern interpretations of ancient traditions help to preserve Mexico's cultural heritage as the country and its people react to the accelerated economic and social developments of today. Mexico's expanding political and economic business environment has provided incentives and

Name   Felix Beltran
Client   Galeria Artis
City   Mexico DF
Year   2001
Purpose   Cover of an invitation for an exhibi-
          tion of graphic design

24–111

24–112

24–113

challenges for the contemporary Mexican graphic designer. With colorful energy and Latin spirit, many Mexican designers successfully express motifs and themes from their culture.

A number of Mexican designers, including Félix Beltrán (b. 1938), were born in other countries. A native of Havana, Cuba, Beltrán went to the United States in 1956 to study painting and graphic design at the School of Visual Arts, the Art Students League, the American School of Art, and Pratt Institute. In 1962 he returned to Cuba, where he designed a series of social and political posters about the Cuban revolution, indigenous art, public safety, and the new economy. For the past fifteen years Beltrán has lived in Mexico, where he works as principle designer for the Beltrán-Asociados Studio (Figs. **24–110**). With its architectural, structural framework, Beltrán's graphic design follows the traditions of the international style.

Although from Mexico, Luis Almeida's (b. 1946) background is international, having studied architecture at the Universidad Nacional Autonoma de Mexico, industrial design at the University of Florence, Italy, and semiotics at the Sorbonne in Paris. His corporate identities include the Mexico City emblem as well as the National Council for Culture and the Arts, Mexico. He works primarily as an editorial designer for the magazines *Saber-Ver* and *Artes de Mexico* and the journals *El nacional* and *La cronica*. As demonstrated by his poster "Cervantes XXXII," honoring the Spanish author Miguel de Cervantes, Almeida's designs are often direct and confrontational (Figs. **24–112** and **24–113**). Like Almeida, German Montalvo (b. 1956) received a European education, studying at the National Institute of the Fine Arts and the Scuola del Libro, Società Umanitaria, both in

24–108. Koeweiden-Postma, poster for Amsterdam's Hortus Botanicus, 2001. Through enlargement the delicacy and intricacy of plant life is revealed.

24–109. Max Kisman, poster celebrating a century of Henri de Toulouse-Lautrec, 2001. Here direct manual digital lettering is created using a drawing tablet.

24–110. Thonik. n8, poster, 2004. This announcement for "museumnacht" (museum night) in Amsterdam advertises the event without emphasizing a particular museum. The title "n8" is a pun derived from the letter *n* and the number *8* which in Dutch is spelled *acht*. Thus combined with *n* it becomes the *nacht* meaning "night".

24–111. Félix Beltrán, cover of an invitation for an architecture exhibition, 2001.

24–112. Luis Almeida Herrera, "Cervantes XXXII," poster for the Thirty-second International Festival of Cervantes, 2004. This poster won the judges award at the poster competition, "Premio Cervantino de Cartel," for its technical qualities and for its fresh and controversial message.

24–113. Luis Almeida Herrera "Quixote," poster, 2004; a variation on the original poster.

Milan, Italy. His designs for the Fondo de Cultura Economico, the National University of Mexico City, the National Institute of the Fine Arts, and the Centro Cultural Arte Contemporaneo have placed him in the mainstream of Mexican graphic design. As indicated by his poster celebrating the poet José Gorostiza, Montalvo is clearly in the Polish poster tradition (Figs. **24–114**).

24–114   24–115

24–116

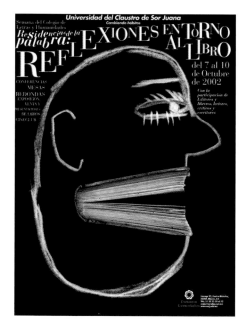

24–117

24–114. German Montalvo, "José Gorostiza," poster, 2002. This poster celebrates 100 years since the birth of Mexican poet José Gorostiza

24–115. Gabriela Rodriguez, "I Don't Need Legs if I Have Wings for Flying," poster, 2001. This poster is an ode to Toulouse-Lautrec from Mexico.

24–116. Alejandro Magallanes, "Las (a)versiones del ojo" (Eyes' (A)versions), poster, 2000. "This poster dwells on a pun: version/aversion," explains Magallanes. "Several of my works reveal the influence of those designers whom I admire—Roman Cieslewicz is one of them."

24–117. Alejandro Magallanes, "Reflexiones en torno al libro" (Reflections on the Book), poster, 2002.

Gabriela Rodriguez (b. 1956) studied graphic design at the Escuela de Diseño del Instituto Nacional de Bellas Artes. As a graphic designer, she works mainly on children's books, magazines, posters, and contemporary art catalogues. Her whimsical designs, like Montalvo's, are inspired by Polish poster designers such as Roman Cieslewicz (Fig. **24–115**). The work of independent graphic designer Alejandro Magallanes (b. 1971) also has roots in the Polish conceptual realm. With overtones of surrealism, he employs collage and freehand drawing with wit and intellectual prowess (Figs. **24–116** and **24–117**).

In the 1980s access to high-end computer equipment and early generations of desktop microprocessors enabled designers to explore the digital realm; quantum leaps forward in digital technology during the 1990s and today continue to transform the communications industry. As the graphic design field expands and evolves, a process of redefining the very nature of communications, work, authorship, display media, and graphic design is underway, taking place at an increasingly rapid pace. Professional designers are now joined by others whose design activities are extensions of their vocational or avocational activities, while graphic designers are extending their medium into self-initiated and fine arts-related experimentation. A dynamic flux, with rapidly expanding technical capabilities and expanding creative possibilities, is underway.

Epilogue

At the time of this writing, human affairs are undergoing a new revolution comparable to the industrial revolution that launched the machine age. Electronic circuitry, microprocessors, and computer-generated imagery threaten to radically alter our culture's images, communications processes, and the very nature of work itself. Graphic design, like many other spheres of activity, is experiencing profound changes. The graphic-design community is responding to this new age of electronic circuitry by an involvement in media graphics, systems design, and computer graphics.

The tools—as has happened so often in the past—are changing with the relentless advance of technology, but the essence of graphic design remains unchanged. That essence is to give order to information, form to ideas, and expression and feeling to artifacts that document human experience.

The need for clear and imaginative visual communications to relate people to their cultural, economic, and social lives has never been greater. As shapers of messages and images, graphic designers have an obligation to contribute meaningfully to a public understanding of environmental and social issues. Graphic designers have a responsibility to adapt new technology and to express their zeitgeist by inventing new forms and new ways of expressing ideas. The poster and the book, vital communications tools of the industrial revolution, will continue in the new age of electronic technology as art forms, and graphic designers will help to define and extend each new generation of electronic media.

Bibliography

The complete bibliography for this book contains over five thousand entries, including books, journal articles, tapes, and notes from interviews, lectures, presentations, and artifacts such as books, posters, and other graphic designs. Of necessity, this bibliography is limited to books selected for further reading on specific topics. Books covering more than one section or chapter are listed at the first area of coverage. Lists of general surveys and periodicals appear at the end of the bibliography.

PART I. THE PROLOGUE TO GRAPHIC DESIGN
The visual message from prehistory through the medieval era

1. The Invention of Writing
Allen, Thomas George. *The Book of the Dead or Going Forth by Day.* Chicago: University of Chicago Press, 1974.

Breasted, James. *Development of Religion and Thought in Ancient Egypt.* Gloucester, MA: Scribner's, 1959.

Budge, E. A. Wallis. *The Book of the Dead.* London, 1909.

———. *The Dwellers on the Nile.* New York: Benjamin Blom, 1972.

———. *The Rosetta Stone in the British Museum.* New York: AMS Press, 1976.

Collon, Dominique. *First Impressions.* London: British Museum, 1987.

Dowson, Thomas A. *Rock Engravings of Southern Africa.* Johannesburg: Witwatersrand University Press, 1992.

Gelb, I. J. *A Study of Writing.* Rev. ed. Chicago: University of Chicago, 1952.

Giedion, S. *The Eternal Present.* Vol. 1, *The Beginning of Art.* New York: Pantheon, 1962.

Grayson, A. Kirk, and Redford, Donald B. *Papyrus and Tablet.* Englewood Cliffs, NJ: Prentice-Hall, 1973.

Graziosi, Paolo. *Paleolithic Art.* New York: McGraw-Hill, 1960.

Huyghe, Rene. *Larousse Encyclopedia of Prehistoric and Ancient Art.* New York: Prometheus Press, 1962.

Jackson, Donald. *The Story of Writing.* New York: Taplinger, 1981.

Leakey, Richard E., and Lewin, Roger. *Origins.* New York: Dutton, 1977.

Lewis-Williams, J. D., and Dowson, T. A. *Images of Power: Understanding Bushman Rock Art.* Johannesburg: Southern Book Publishers, 1989.

Lewis-Williams, J. D. *Discovering Southern African Rock Art.* Cape Town: David Philip Publishers, 1990.

Michalowski, Kazimierz. *Art of Ancient Egypt.* New York: Abrams, 1978.

Petrie, W. M. Flinders. *Buttons and Design Scarabs.* Warminster, England, Aris & Phillips, 1974.

Parrot, Andre. *The Arts of Assyria.* New York: Golden Press, 1961.

Porada, Edith. *Ancient Art in Seals.* Princeton, NJ: Princeton University Press, 1980.

Rossiter, Evelyn. *The Book of the Dead.* Fribourg-Geneva: Productions Liber SA, 1979.

Strommenger, Eva. *5000 Years of the Art of Mesopotamia.* New York: Abrams, 1964.

Teissier, Beatrice. *Ancient Near Eastern Cylinder Seals.* Los Angeles: University of California Press, 1984.

The Trustees of the British Museum. *Introductory Guide to the Egyptian Collection.* Oxford: Oxford University Press, 1971.

Vinnicombe, Patricia. *People of the Eland.* Pietermaritzburg, South Africa: University of Natal Press, 1976.

Wilkinson, Richard H. *The Complete Gods and Goddesses of Ancient Egypt.* New York: Thames & Hudson, 2003.

2. Alphabets
Anderson, Donald M. *The Art of Written Forms.* New York: Holt, Reinhart and Winston, 1969.

Daniels, Peter T., and Bright, William, eds. *The World's Writing Systems.* New York: Oxford University Press, 1996.

Diringer, David. *The Alphabet: A Key to the History of Mankind.* 3rd ed. New York: Funk and Wagnalls, 1968.

———. *The Book Before Printing: Ancient, Medieval, and Oriental.* New York: Dover, 1982.

———. *Writing.* New York: Praeger, 1962.

Doblerhoffer, Ernest. *Voices in Stone.* New York: Viking, 1961.

Drucker, Johanna. *The Alphabetic Labyrinth: The Letters in History and Imagination.* New York: Thames & Hudson, 1995.

Fairbank, Alfred. *A Book of Scripts.* London: Faber, 1977.

Hutchinson, James. *Letters.* New York: Van Nostrand Reinhold, 1983.

Kraus, Theodor. *Pompeii and Herculaneum: The Living Cities of the Dead.* New York: Abrams, 1975.

Logan, Robert K. *The Alphabet Effect: The Impact of the Phonetic Alphabet on the Development of Western Civilization.* New York: Morrow, 1986.

Nesbitt, Alexander. *The History and Technique of Lettering.* New York: Dover, 1950.

Ouaknin, Marc-Alain. *Mysteries of the Alphabet.* New York: Abbeville Press, 1999.

Roberts, Colin H., and Skeat, T. C. *The Birth of the Codex.* London: Oxford University Press, 1983.

Sutton, James, and Bartram, Alan. *An Atlas of Typeforms.* New York: Hastings House, 1968.

Trudgill, Anne. *Traditional Penmanship.* New York: Watson-Guptill, 1989.

Turner, E. G. *Greek Manuscripts of the Ancient World.* London: Institute of Classical Studies, 1986.

Ullman, B. L. *Ancient Writing and Its Influence.* New York: Longmans, Green, 1932.

3. The Asian Contribution

Carter, Thomas F., revised by Goodrich, L. Carrington. *The Invention of Printing in China and Its Spread Westward.* New York: Ronald Press, 1955.

Chang, Leon Long-Yien. *Four Thousand Years of Chinese Calligraphy.* Chicago: University of Chicago Press, 1990.

DeVinne, Theodore L. *The Invention of Printing.* New York: Francis Hart & Co., 1876.

Kapleau, Philip. *The Three Pillars of Zen.* New York: Beacon, 1967.

Tsien, Tsuen-Hsuin. *Written on Bamboo and Silk.* Chicago: University of Chicago Press, 1962.

Twitchett, Denis. *Printing and Publishing in Medieval China.* New York: Beil, 1983.

Williams, C. A. S. *Outlines of Chinese Symbolism and Art Motives.* New York: Dover, 1976.

4. Illuminated Manuscripts

Alexander, J. J. G. *The Decorated Letter.* New York: Braziller, 1978.

———. *Italian Renaissance Illuminations.* London: Chatto & Windus, 1977.

Atiyeh, George N., ed. *The Book in the Islamic World: The Written Word and Communication in the Middle East.* Albany: State University of New York Press; Washington, DC: Library of Congress, 1995.

Backhouse, Janet. *The Illuminated Manuscript.* Oxford: Phaidon Press, 1979.

Banks, Doris H. *Medieval Manuscript Bookmaking.* Metuchen, NJ: Scarecrow Press, 1989.

Brown, Peter. *The Book of Kells.* London: Thames and Hudson, 1980.

Beach, Milo Cleveland. *The Grand Mogul: Imperial Painting in India, 1600–1660.* Williamstown, MA: Sterling and Francine Clark Art Institute, 1978.

———. *The Imperial Image Paintings for the Mughal Court.* Washington, DC: Freer Gallery of Art, Smithsonian Institution, 1981.

Chaitanya, Krishna. *A History of Indian Painting.* New Delhi: Abhinav Publications, 1976.

D'Ancona, P., and Aeschlimann, E. *The Art of Illumination.* London: Phaidon Press, 1969.

Drogin, Marc. *Medieval Calligraphy: Its History and Technique.* Montclair, NJ: Allenheld & Schram, 1980.

Fairbank, Alfred. *The Story of Handwriting.* New York: Watson-Guptill, 1970.

Fremantle, Ann. *Age of Faith.* New York: Time-Life, 1965.

Gutmann, Joseph. *Hebrew Manuscript Painting.* New York: Braziller, 1978.

Hassall, A. G. and W. O. *The Douce Apocalypse.* New York: Thomas Yoseloff, 1961.

Henderson, George. *From Durrow to Kells: The Insular Gospelbooks 650–800.* London: Thames and Hudson, 1987.

Henry, Francoise. *The Book of Kells.* New York: Knopf, 1974.

Karp, Abraham J. *From the Ends of the Earth: Judaic Treasures of the Library of Congress.* New York: Rizzoli, 1991.

Ker, N. R. *Medieval Scribes, Manuscripts, and Libraries.* London: Scholar Press, 1978.

Morison, Stanley. *Selected Essays on the History of Letterforms in Manuscript and Print.* Cambridge: Cambridge University Press, 1983.

Mutherich, Florentine, and Gaehde, Joachim E. *Carolingian Painting.* New York: Braziller, 1976.

Nordenfalk, Carl. *Celtic and Anglo-Saxon Painting.* New York: Braziller, 1977.

O'Neill, Timothy. *The Irish Hand: Scribes and Their Manuscripts from the Earliest Times to the 17th Century, with an Exemplar of Irish Scripts.* Portalaoise, Ireland: Dolmen Press, 1984.

Pognon, Edmond. *Les Trés Riches Heures du Duc de Berry: 15th Century Manuscript.* Fribourg-Geneva: Productions Liber SA, 1979.

Petrosyan, Yuri A. *Pages of Perfection.* Lugano, Italy: ARCH Foundation, 1995.

Robb, David M. *The Art of the Illuminated Manuscript.* London: Yoseloff, 1973.

Robinson, B. W., et al. *Islamic Painting and the Arts of the Book.* London: Faber and Faber, 1976.

Rogers, J. M. *Islamic Art & Design, 1500–1700.* London: British Museum Publications, 1983.

Schmitz, Barbara, et al. *Islamic Manuscripts in the New York Public Library.* New York: Oxford University Press, 1992.

Swietochowski, Marie Lukens, et al. *Illustrated Poetry and Epic Images: Persian Painting of the 1330s and 1340s.* New York: Metropolitan Museum of Art, 1994.

Titley, Norah M. *Persian Miniature Painting.* London: The British Library, 1983.

Weitzmann, Kurt. *Late Antique and Early Christian Book Illumination.* New York: Braziller, 1977.

Welch, Stuart Cary. *Persian Painting: Five Royal Safavid Manuscripts of the Sixteenth Century.* New York: Braziller, 1976.

Williams, John. *Early Spanish Manuscript Illumination.* New York: Braziller, 1977.

———. *The Illustrated Beatus: A Corpus of the Illustrations of the Commentary on the Apocalypse.* London: Harvey Miller, 1994.

PART II. A GRAPHIC RENAISSANCE
The origins of European typography and design for printing

5. Printing Comes to Europe

Anman, Jost, and Sachs, Hans. *The Book of Trades.* Reprint, New York: Dover, 1973.

Beatty, Nancy Lee. *The Craft of Dying: A Study in the Literary Tradition of the* Ars Moriendi *in England.* New Haven: Yale University Press, 1970.

Blades, William. *The Life and Typography of William Caxton.* London: Joseph Lilly, 1861.

Breitkopf, Johann G. I. *Versuch den Ursprung der Spielkarten, Die Einfuhrung des Leinenpapieres, und den Anfang der Holzschneidekunst in Europa.* Leipzig, 1784.

Carter, John, and Muir, Percy H. *Printing and the Mind of Man.* London: Cassell, 1967.

Chatto, William Andrew. *A Treatise on Wood Engraving.* London: Chatto and Windus, Piccadilly, 1861.

Colin, Clair. *A Chronology of Printing.* New York: Cassell, 1969.

Dowding, Geoffrey. *An Introduction to the History of Printing Types.* Clerkenwell, England: Wace and Company, 1961.

Eisenstein, Elizabeth L. *The Printing Revolution in Early Modern Europe.* Cambridge: Cambridge University Press, 1983.

Gress, Edmund. *The Art and Practice of Typography.* New York: Oswald, 1917.

Haebler, Konrad. *Incunabula: Original Leaves Traced by Konrad Haeber.* Munich: Werss and Company, 1927.

Hansard, Thomas. *Typographia: An Historical Sketch of the Origin and Progress of the Art of Printing.* London: Baldwin, Cradock, & Joy, 1825.

Hellinga, Lotte. *Caxton in Focus: The Beginning of Printing in England.* London: British Library, 1982.

Ing, Janet Thompson. *Johann Gutenberg and His Bible: A Historical Study.* New York: Typophiles, 1988.

Kapr, Albert. *Johann Gutenberg: The Man and His Invention.* Trans. Martin Douglas. Brookfield, VT: Scolar Press, 1996.

Lavarie, Norma. *The Art and History of Books.* New York: Heineman, 1968.

Lehmann-Haupt, Hellmut. *Gutenberg and the Master of the Playing Cards.* New Haven: Yale University Press, 1966.

Lockombe, Philip. *The History and Art of Printing.* 1771.

McLuhan, Marshall. *The Gutenberg Galaxy: The Making of Typographic Man.* Toronto: University of Toronto, 1962.

McMurtrie, Douglas C. *The Book: The Story of Printing and Bookmaking.* New York: Oxford University Press, 1943.

Morison, Stanley. *German Incunabula in the British Museum.* New York: Hacker Art Books, 1975.

———, and Day, Kenneth. *The Typographic Book.* London: Ernest Benn; Chicago: University of Chicago, 1963.

Norton, F. J. *Printing in Spain 1501–1520.* Cambridge: Cambridge University Press, 1966.

Steinberg, S. H. Revised by Trevitt, John. *Five Hundred Years of Printing.* New Castle, DE: Oak Knoll, 1996.

6. The German Illustrated Book

Anzewlewsky, Fedja. *Dürer: His Art and Life.* New York: Alpine, 1980.

Bailey, Martin. *Dürer.* London: Phaidon Press, 1995.

Bliss, Douglas Percy. *A History of Wood-Engraving.* London: J. M. Dent and Sons, 1928.

Dodgson, Cambell. *Catalog of Early German and Flemish Woodcuts.* Vols. I and II. London: British Museum, 1903.

Dürer, Albrecht. *Of the Just Shaping of Letters.* Trans. R. T. Nichol. New York: Dover, 1965.

———. *Underweysung der Messung mit dem Zirckel und Richtscheyt.* Nuremburg, 1525.

Gilver, William. *Masterworks in Wood: The Woodcut Print.* Portland, OR: Portland Art Museum, 1976.

Hind, Arthur M. *An Introduction to a History of Woodcut.* Boston and New York: Houghton Mifflin, 1935.

Hoetink, Hans. *Dürer's Universe.* Woodbury, NY: Barron's, 1971.

Hollstein, F. W. H. *German Engravings Etchings and Woodcuts ca. 1400–1700.* Amsterdam: Menno Hertzberger, 1962.

Johnson, A. P. *Selected Essays on Books and Printing.* New York: Van Gendt, 1970.

Kurth, Dr. Willi. *The Complete Woodcuts of Albrecht Dürer.* New York: Crown, 1946.

Muther, Richard. *German Book Illustration of the Gothic Period and the Early Renaissance (1460–1530).* Metuchen, NJ: Scarecrow Press, 1972.

Panofsky, Erwin. *The Life and Art of Albrecht Dürer.* Princeton, NJ: Princeton University Press, 1955.

Rossiter, Henry Preston. *Albrecht Dürer: Master Printmaker.* Boston: Museum of Fine Arts, 1971.

Strauss, Walter L. *The German Single-Leaf Woodcut, 1550–1600.* New York: Abrams, 1975.

Talbot, Charles W., ed. *Dürer in America: His Graphic Work.* New York: Macmillan, 1971.

Wilson, Adrian. *The Making of the Nuremberg Chronicle.* Amsterdam: Nico Israel, 1976.

7. Renaissance Graphic Design

Armstrong, Elizabeth. *Robert Estienne the Royal Printer: An Historical Study of the Elder Stephanus.* Cambridge: Cambridge University Press, 1954.

Arrighi, Ludovico. *The First Writing Book; An English Translation and Facsimile Text of Arrighi's Operina, The First Manual of The Chancery Hand.* New Haven: Yale University Press, 1954.

Barker, Nicolas. *Aldus Manutius and the Development of Greek Script & Type in the Fifteenth Century.* 2nd ed. New York: Fordham University Press, 1992.

Barolini, Helen. *Aldus and His Dream Book: An Illustrated Essay.* New York: Italica Press, 1992.

Benson, John Howard. *The First Writing Book.* New Haven: Yale University Press, 1955.

Bernard, Auguste. *Geofroy Tory.* Trans. George B. Ives. New York: Houghton Mifflin, 1909.

Calzolari, Francesco. Fahy, Conor, ed. *Printing a Book at Verona in 1622, the Account Book of Francesco Calzolari.* New Castle, DE: Oak Knoll, 1993.

DeVinne, Theodore L. *A Treatise on Title-Pages.* 1901. Reprint. New York: Haskell House, 1972.

Fletcher, H. George. *New Aldine Studies: Documentary Essays on the Life and Work of Aldus Manutius.* San Francisco: B. M. Rosenthal, 1988.

Johnson, A. P. *Selected Essays on Books and Printing.* New York: Van Gendt, 1970.

Johnson, Fridolf. *A Treasury of Bookplates from the Renaissance to the Present.* New York: Dover, 1977.

le Bé, Pierre. *Modéles de lettres de Pierre le Bé.* Paris, 1601.

Lowry, Martin. *The World of Aldus Manutius.* Ithaca, NY: Cornell University Press, 1979.

McCrillis, John O. C. *Printer's Abecedarium.* Boston: Godine, 1974.

McKitterick, David, ed. *Stanley Morison and D. B. Updike: Selected Correspondence.* London: Scholar Press, 1972.

Meynell, Sir Francis, and Simon, Herbert, ed. *Fleuron Anthology.* Boston: Godine, 1979.

Morison, Stanley. *First Principles of Typography.* Cambridge: Cambridge University Press, 1936.

Mortimer, Ruth. *Catalogue of Books and Manuscripts.* Part 1, *French 16th Century Books.* Cambridge, MA: The Belknap Press of Harvard University Press, 1964.

Schreiber, Fred. *The Estiennes: An Annotated Catalog.* New York: E. K. Schreiber, 1982.

Standard, Paul. *Arrighi's Running Hand.* New York: Taplinger, 1979.

Tannenbaum, Samuel A. *The Handwriting of the Renaissance.* New York: Ungar, 1930.

Williamson, Hugh. *Methods of Book Design.* New Haven: Yale University Press, 1983.

Woodfield, Denis. *Surreptitious Printing in England 1550–1640.* New York: Bibliographical Society of America, 1973.

8. An Epoch of Typographic Genius

Ball, Johnson. *William Caslon, 1693–1766.* Kineton, England: Roundwood Press, 1973.

Bartram, Alan. *The English Lettering Tradition from 1700 to the Present Day.* London: Lund Humphries, 1986.

Berry, W. Turner, and Johnston, A. F. *Catalog of Specimens of Printing Types by English and Scottish Printers and Founders 1665–1830.* New York: Garland, 1983.

Bodoni, Signora, and Orsi, Luigi, eds. *Manuale tipografico.* Parma, Italy, 1818.

Bultin, Martin. *William Blake 1757–1827.* London: Tate Gallery, 1990.

Carter, Henry, trans. *Fournier on Typefounding.* New York: Lenox Hill, 1972.

Didot, Ambroise Firmin-. *Essai sur la typographie.* Paris, 1851.

Fournier, Pierre Simon. *Manuel typographique.* 2 Vols. Paris, 1764–66.

Franklin V, Benjamin. *Boston Printers, Publishers, and Booksellers: 1640–1800.* Boston: G. K. Hall, 1980.

Holloway, Owen E. *French Rococo Book Illustration.* New York: Transatlantic Arts, 1969.

Holmes, Nigel. *Designer's Guide to Creating Charts and Diagrams.* New York: Watson-Guptill, 1984.

Hutt, Allen. *Fournier, the Compleat Typographer.* London: Frederick Muller, Ltd., 1972.

Lowance, Mason I., Jr., and Bumgardner, Georgia B., eds. *Massachusetts Broadsides of the American Revolution.* Amherst: University of Massachusetts, 1976.

Osborne, Carole Maroot. *Pierre Didot the Elder and French Book Illustration.* New York: Garland, 1985.

Oswald, John Clyde. *Printing in the Americas.* New York, 1937.

Pignatti, Terisio. *The Age of Rococo.* New York: Paul Hamlyn, 1966.

Playfair, William. *The Commercial and Political Atlas.* London: J. Debrett, 1786.

Plomer, Henry R. *English Printer's Ornaments.* New York: Burt Franklin, 1924.

Sewter, A. C. *Baroque and Rococo.* New York: Harcourt Brace Jovanovich, 1972.

Twyman, Michael. *Printing 1770–1970.* London: Eyre & Spottiswoode, 1970.

PART III. THE INDUSTRIAL REVOLUTION
The impact of industrial technology upon visual communications

9. Graphic Design and the Industrial Revolution

Abbot, Charles D. *Howard Pyle, A Chronicle.* New York: Harper's, 1925.

Alistair, Allen, and Hoverstadt, Joan. *The History of Printed Scraps.* London: New Cavendish Books, 1983.

Annenberg, Maurice. *A Typographic Journey through the Inland Printer.* Baltimore: Maran Press, 1977.

Arnold, H. J. P. *William Henry Fox Talbot: Pioneer of Photography and Man of Science.* London: Hutchinson Benham, 1977.

Baker, Elizabeth Faulkner. *Printers and Technology.* Westport, CT: Greenwood Press, 1957.

Bidwell, John, ed. *Specimens of Type . . . American Type Founders Co.* New York: Garland, 1981.

Billington, Elizabeth T. *The Randolph Caldecott Treasury.* New York: F. Warne, 1978.

Black, Mary. *American Advertising Posters of the Nineteenth Century.* New York: Dover, 1976.

Blackburn, Henry W. *Randolph Caldecott; A Personal Memoir of his Early Art Career.* London: S. Low, Marston, Searle, & Rivington, 1886.

Brady, Mathew B. *National Photographic Collection of War Views, and Portraits of Representative Men.* New York: C. A. Alvord, printer, 1869.

Bruce, David, Jr., and Eckman, James, eds. *History of Type-founding in the United States.* New York: The Typophiles, 1981.

Buckland, Gail. *Fox Talbot and the Invention of Photography.* Boston: Godine, 1980.

Crane, Walter. *Walter Crane as a Book Illustrator.* London: Academy Editions, 1975.

Day, Kenneth, ed. *Book Typography 1815–1965 in Europe and the United States of America.* Chicago: University of Chicago Press, 1965.

Dobson, Austin. *Thomas Bewick and His Pupils.* London: Chatto and Windus, Piccadilly, 1884.

Durant, Stuart. *Victorian Ornamental Design.* London: Academy Editions, and New York: St. Martin's Press, 1972.

Eckman, James. *The Heritage of the Printer.* Philadelphia: North American Publishing Company, 1965.

Engen, Rodney K. *Kate Greenaway: A Biography.* London: Macdonald, 1981.

Freeman, Larry. *Louis Prang: Color Lithographer.* Watkins Glen, NY: Century House, 1971.

Gowan, Al. *T. J. Lyons: A Biography and Critical Essay.* Boston: Society of Printers. 1987.

Gray, Nicolete. *Nineteenth Century Ornamented Typefaces.* Berkeley and Los Angeles: University of California Press, 1976.

Greenaway, Kate. *Kate Greenaway.* New York: Rizzoli, 1977.

Hammond, John H. *The Camera Obscura: A Chronicle.* Bristol, England: Adam Hilger, 1981.

Hillier, Bevis. *100 Years of Posters*. New York: Harper and Row, 1972.

Huss, Richard E. *The Development of Printer's Mechanical Typesetting Methods 1822–1925*. Charlottesville: University of Virginia Press, 1973.

Jammes, Andre. *William H. F. Talbot, Inventor of the Positive-Negative Process*. New York: Macmillan, 1973.

Jarvis, Simon. *High Victorian Design*. Woodbridge, Suffolk, England: Boydell, 1983.

Jones, Owen. *The Grammar of Ornament* (folio edition). London: B. Quaritch, 1910.

———. *The Grammar of Ornament*. Reprint, New York: Portland House, 1986.

Kelly, Rob Roy. *American Wood Type: 1828–1900: Notes on the Evolution of Decorative and Large Types*. New York: De Capo, 1969.

Konody, Paul George. *The Art of Walter Crane*. London: G. Bell, 1902.

Lassam, Robert. *Fox Talbot: Photographer*. Wiltshire, England: Compton, 1979.

Lehmann-Haupt, Hellmut. *The Book in America*. New York: Bowker, 1951.

Lewis, John. *Typography/Basic Principles*. New York: Reinhold, 1966.

McClinton, Katharine Morrison. *The Chromolithographs of Louis Prang*. New York: Clarkson N. Potter, 1973.

McLean, Ruari. *Victorian Book Design and Colour Printing*. 2nd ed. Berkeley: University of California Press, 1972.

Maindron, Ernest. *Les affiches illustrées*. Paris: H. Launette, 1886.

Marzio, Peter C. *The Democratic Art*. Boston: Godine, 1979.

Matthews, Oliver. *Early Photographs and Early Photographers: A Survey in Dictionary Form*. New York: Pitman, 1973.

Meredith, Roy. *Mr. Lincoln's Camera Man*. New York: C. Scribner's Sons, 1946.

Morse, Willard Samuel. *Howard Pyle; A Record of His Illustrations and Writings*. Wilmington, DE: Wilmington Society of the Fine Arts, 1921.

Mosley, James. *British Type Specimens before 1831: A Hand List*. Oxford: Bodleian Library, 1984.

Mott, Frank Luther. *A History of American Magazines*. Cambridge, MA: Belknap Press of Harvard University, 1957.

Muir, Percy. *Victorian Illustrated Books*. New York: Praeger, 1971.

Muybridge, Eadweard. *Descriptive Zoopraxography; or, The Science of Animal Locomotion Made Popular*. Philadelphia: University of Pennsylvania, 1893.

Newhall, Beaumont. *The History of Photography*. New York: Museum of Modern Art, 1964.

Paine, Albert Bigelow. *Thomas Nast: His Period and His Pictures*. Princeton, NJ: Payne Press, 1904.

Pardoe, F. E. *John Baskerville of Birmingham: Letter-Founder and Printer*. London: Frederick Muller, 1975.

Parton, James. *Caricature and Other Comic Art*. New York: Harper & Brothers, 1877.

Pierce, Sally, and Slautterback, Catharina. *Boston Lithography: 1825–1880*. Boston: Boston Athenaeum, 1991.

Pitz, Henry C. *Howard Pyle: Writer, Illustrator, Founder of the Brandywine Press*. New York: C. N. Potter, 1975.

Pollack, Peter. *The Picture History of Photography*. New York: Abrams, 1969.

Potenniée, Georges. *The Literature of Photography: The History of the Discovery of Photography*. New York: Arno Press, 1973.

Reed, Talbot Baines. *A History of the Old English Letter Foundries*. Revised by A. F. Johnson. London: Faber and Faber, 1952.

Rosenblum, Naomi, ed. *A World History of Photography*. New York: Abbeville, 1981.

Shove, Raymond H. *Cheap Book Production in the United States, 1870 to 1891*. Urbana: University of Illinois Library, 1937.

Silver, Rollo G. *Typefounding in America: 1787–1825*. Charlottesville: University of Virginia Press, 1965.

Snyder, Joel. *American Frontiers: Timothy O'Sullivan*. Millerton, NY: Aperture, 1981.

Southward, John. *Practical Printing: A Handbook for the Art of Typography*. London: Printer's Register Office, 1882; reprint, New York: Garland, 1980.

Spencer, Isabel. *Walter Crane*. London: Studio Vista, 1975.

Stern, Madeleine B. *Publishers for Mass Entertainment in Nineteenth Century America*. Boston: G. K. Hall, 1980.

Stillman, Jacob Davis Babcock. *The horse in motion as shown by instantaneous photography, with a study on animal mechanics founded on anatomy and the revelations of the camera, in which is demonstrated the theory of quadrupedal locomotion*. Boston: J. R. Osgood and Company, 1882.

Talbot, William Henry Fox. *The Pencil of Nature*. London: Longman, Brown, Green and Longmans, 1844–46.

Thompson, John Smith. *History of Composing Machines*. Chicago: The Inland Printer, 1904.

———. *The Mechanism of the Linotype*. Chicago: The Inland Printer, 1902.

Tracy, Walter. *Letters of Credit: A View of Type Design*. London: Gordon Fraiser, 1986.

Tuckerman, Henry T. *Book of the Artists: American Artist Life*. New York: G. P. Putnam and Sons, 1867.

Upton, Barbara London, and Upton, John. *Photography*. 4th ed. New York: Harper Collins, 1989.

Wade, John. *A Short History of the Camera*. Watford, England: Fountain Press, 1979.

Weinbergen, Norman S. *The Art of the Photogram: Photography Without a Camera*. New York: Taplinger, 1981.

Wolpe, Berthold, ed. *Vincent Figgins Type Specimens: 1801–1815*. London: Printing Historical Society, 1967.

Wornum, Ralph N. *Analysis of Ornament*. London: Chapman and Hall, 1879.

10. The Arts and Crafts Movement

Anscombe, Isabelle, and Gere, Charlotte. *Arts and Crafts in Britain and America*. London: Academy Editions, 1978.

Arts and Crafts Exhibition Society. *Arts and Crafts Essays*. London: Longmans Green and Company, 1893.

Ashbee, Charles R. *Craftsmanship in Competitive Industry*. Campden, England: Essex House, 1908.

———. *An Endeavor Towards the Teaching of John Ruskin and William Morris*. London: Edward Arnold, 1901.

———, ed. *The Manual of the Guild and School of Handicraft*. London: Cassell, 1892. Reprint, New York: Garland, 1977.

Balston, Thomas. *The Cambridge University Press Collection of Private Press Types: Kelmscott, Ashendene, Eragny, Cranach.* Cambridge: B. Crutchley, 1951. .

Bell, Malcolm. *Edward Burne-Jones.* London: Bell, 1892.

Bell, Quintin. *Ruskin.* New York: Braziller, 1963.

Blumenthal, Joseph. *Bruce Rogers: A Life in Letters, 1870–1957.* Austin: W. T. Taylor, 1989.

Bruckner, D. J. R. *Frederic Goudy.* New York: Abrams, 1990.

Carter, Sebastian. *Twentieth Century Type Designers.* London: Trefoil, 1987.

Cave, Roderick. *The Private Press.* New York: Watson-Guptill, 1971.

Cobden-Sanderson, Thomas James. *Ecce Mundus and the Arts and Crafts Movement.* Hammersmith, England: Hammersmith Pub. Society, 1902–1905. Reprint, New York: Garland, 1977.

Colebrook, Frank. *William Morris: Master Printer.* Council Bluffs, Iowa: Yellow Barn Press, 1989.

Crane, Walter. *Of the Decorative Illustration of Books Old and New.* London: Bell, 1896.

———. *William Morris to Whistler.* London: Bell, 1911.

Crawford, Alan. *C. R. Ashbee. Architect, Designer, and Romantic Socialist.* New Haven: Yale University Press, 1985.

Fairclough, Oliver. *Textiles by William Morris and Morris and Co: 1861–1940.* New York: Thames and Hudson, 1981.

Ferebee, Ann. *A History of Design from the Victorian Era to the Present.* New York: Van Nostrand Reinhold, 1970.

Franklin, Colin. *The Ashendene Press.* Dallas: Birdwell, 1986.

———, and Turner, John R. *The Private Presses.* 2nd ed. Brookfield, VT: Gower, 1991.

Gibbs-Smith, C. H. *The Great Exhibition of 1851.* London: Her Majesty's Stationery Office, 1951.

Gillow, Norah. *William Morris: Designs and Patterns.* London: Bracken, 1988.

Goudy, Frederic W. *The Alphabet and Elements of Lettering.* Berkeley: University of California Press, 1942.

———. *Goudy's Type Designs.* 2nd ed. New Rochelle, NY: Myriade Press, 1978.

———. *Typologia.* Berkeley: University of California Press, 1940.

Harvey, Charles. *Art, Enterprise, and Ethics: The Life and Works of William Morris.* London; Portland, OR: Frank Cass, 1996.

Keynes, Geoffrey. *William Pickering: Publisher.* Revised ed. London: Galahad Press, 1969.

Koch, Rudolf. *Das ABS Büchlein.* Leipzig: Insel-Verlag, 1934.

———. *The Book of Signs.* Trans. Vyvyan Holland. New York: Dover Publications, 1955.

———. *The Little ABC Book of Rudolf Koch.* Boston: D. R. Godine, 1976.

Konody, Paul George. *The Art of Walter Crane.* London: Bell, 1902.

Ludwig, Coy L. *The Arts and Crafts Movement in New York State, 1890s–1920s.* Hamilton, NY: Gallery Association of New York State, 1983.

Mackail, J. W. *The Life of William Morris.* New York: Oxford University Press, 1950.

McLean, Ruari. *Modern Book Design from William Morris to the Present Day.* London: Faber and Faber, 1958.

———, ed. *Typographers on Type: An Illustrated Anthology from William Morris to the Present Day.* New York: Norton, 1995.

———. *Victorian Book Design and Colour Printing.* 2nd ed. Berkeley: University of California Press, 1972.

Morris, William. *The Ideal Book: Essays and Lectures on the Art of the Book.* Ed. William S. Peterson. Berkeley: University of California Press, 1983.

———. *Selected Writings.* Ed. William Gaunt. London: Falcon Press, 1948.

———. *William Morris by Himself: Designs and Writings.* Boston: New York Graphic Society, 1988.

Naylor, Gillian. *The Arts and Crafts Movement.* Cambridge, MA: MIT Press, 1971.

Parry, Linda. ed. *William Morris.* New York: Abrams, 1996.

———, *William Morris Textiles.* London: Weidenfeld and Nicol, 1983.

Peterson, William S. *The Kelmscott Press: A History of William Morris's Typographical Adventure.* Oxford: Oxford University Press, and Berkeley: University of California Press, 1991.

Pissarro, Lucien. Thorold, Anne, ed. *The Letters of Lucien to Camille Pissarro, 1883–1903.* Cambridge: Cambridge University Press, 1993.

Ransom, Will. *Kelmscott, Doves and Ashendene: The Private Press Credos.* New York: The Typophiles, 1952.

———. *Private Presses and Their Books.* New York: Bowker, 1929.

Rogers, Bruce. *Paragraphs on Printing.* New York: William E. Rudge's Sons, 1943.

Rosenberg, John D. *The Darkening Glass: A Portrait of Ruskin's Genius.* New York: Columbia University Press, 1961.

Skoblow, Jeffrey. *Paradise Dislocated: Morris, Politics, Art.* Charlottesville: University of Virginia Press, 1993.

Sparling, H. Halliday. *The Kelmscott Press and William Morris, Master Craftsman.* London: Macmillan, 1924.

Smart, William. *John Ruskin: His Life and Work.* New York: Heywood, 1973.

Stansky, Peter. *Redesigning the World; William Morris, the 1880s, and the Arts and Crafts.* Princeton, NJ: Princeton University Press, 1985.

Tidcombe, Marianne. *The Doves Bindery.* London: British Library, 1991.

Thompson, Susan Otis. *American Book Design and William Morris.* New Castle, DE: Oak Knoll Press, 1997.

Thorold, Anne. *A Catalogue of the Oil Paintings of Lucien Pissarro.* London: Athelney, 1983.

———, and Erickson, Kristen. *Camille Pissarro and His Family.* Oxford: Ashmolean Museum, 1993.

Triggs, Oscar Lovell. *Chapters in the History of the Arts and Crafts Movement.* Chicago, 1902. Reprint, New York: Arno Press, 1979.

Updike, D. B., et al. *The Work of Bruce Rogers, Jack of All Trades: Master of One.* New York: Oxford University Press, 1939.

Urbanelli, Lora. *The Wood Engravings of Lucien Pissarro and a Bibliographical List of Eragny Books.* Cambridge: Silent Books; Oxford: Ashmolean Museum, 1994.

Vallance, Aymer. *William Morris: His Art, His Writings, and His Public Life.* London: George Bell and Sons, 1897.

Volpe, Todd, and Cathers, Beth. *Treasures of the American Arts and Crafts Movement.* New York: Abrams, 1988.

Warde, Frederic. *Bruce Rogers, Designer of Books.* Cambridge, MA: Harvard, 1925.

11. Art Nouveau

Abrams, Leslie E. *The History and Practice of Japanese Printmaking: A Selectively Annotated Bibliography of English Language Materials*. Westport, CT: Greenwood Press, 1984.

Amaya, Mario. *Art Nouveau*. New York: Schocken Books, 1985.

Ando, Shin. *The Influence of Hiroshige on Whistler: A Study of Japonisme*, 1983.

Ando, Hiroshige. *Hiroshige: Birds and Flowers*. New York: Braziller, 1988.

———. *One Hundred Famous Views of Edo*. New York: Braziller, Brooklyn Museum, 1986.

———. *Prints by Utagawa Hiroshige in the James A. Michener Collection*. Honolulu, HI: Honolulu Academy of Arts, 1991.

Arsene, Alexandre, et al. *The Modern Poster*. New York: Charles Scribner's Sons, 1895.

Arwas, Victor. *Belle Epoque Posters and Graphics*. New York: Rizzoli, 1978.

———. *Berthon and Grasset*. New York: Rizzoli, 1978.

Aslin, Elizabeth. *The Aesthetic Movement: Prelude to Art Nouveau*. London: Elek Books, 1969.

Bavilli, Renato. *Art Nouveau*. London: Cassell, 1987.

———. *The Later Work of Aubrey Beardsley*. London: Lane, 1901.

Beeh, Wolfgang. *Jugendstil: Kunst um 1900*. Darmstadt, Germany: Roether, 1982.

Botwinick, Michael, et al. *Belgian Art, 1880–1914*. Brooklyn, NY: Brooklyn Museum, 1980.

Bradley, William H. *Will Bradley: His Chap Book*. New York: The Typofiles, 1955.

Brandt, Frederick R., Koch, Robert, and Meggs, Philip B. *Designed to Sell: Turn-of-the-Century American Posters*. Richmond, VA: Virginia Museum of Fine Arts, 1994.

Brinckmann, Justus. *Jugendstil*. Dortmund, Germany: Havenberg, 1983.

Broido, Lucy. *The Posters of Jules Cheret*. New York: Dover, 1980.

Bargiel, Rejane. *Steinlen affichiste: Catalogue raisonne*. Lausanne, France: Editions du Grand-Pont, 1986.

Canning, Susan Marie. *Henry van de Velde (1863–1957): Paintings and Drawings*. Antwerp: Koninklijk Museum voor Schone Kunsten; Otterlo, Belgium: Rijksmuseum Kröller-Müller, 1987.

Castleman, Riva, and Wittrock, Wolfgang. *Henri de Toulouse-Lautrec*. New York: Museum of Modern Art, 1985.

Cate, Philip Dennis, and Hitchings, Sinclair Hamilton. *The Color Revolution*. Santa Barbara, CA, and Salt Lake City, UT: Peregrine Smith, 1978.

Cate, Philip Dennis, Finby, Nancy, and Kiehl, David W. *American Posters of the 1890s*. New York: Abrams, 1987.

Chibbett, David. *The History of Japanese Printing and Book Illustration*. Tokyo: Kodansha, 1977.

Cirker, Hayward and Blanche. *The Golden Age of the Poster*. New York: Dover, 1971.

Constantine, Mildred, and Fern, Alan M. *Word and Image*. New York: Museum of Modern Art, 1968.

Delevoy, Robert L., Culot, Maurice, and Brunhammer, Yvonne. *Guimard, Horta, Van de Velde*. Paris: Musée des Arts Decoratifs, 1971.

Engen, Rodney. *Laurence Housman*. Stroud, England: Catalpa Press, 1983.

Eschmann, Karl. *Jugendstil*. Kastellann, Germany: Aloys Henn Verlag, 1976.

Fields, Armond. *George Auriol*. Layton, UT: Peregrine Smith, 1985.

Forrer, Matthi. *Hokusai*. New York: Rizzoli, 1988.

Frey, Julia Bloch. *Toulouse-Lautrec: A Life*. New York: Viking, 1994.

Gerhardus, Maly and Dietfried. *Symbolism and Art Nouveau*. Oxford: Phaidon Press, 1979.

Gibson, David. *Designed to Persuade: The Graphic Art of Edward Penfield*. Yonkers, NY: Hudson River Museum, 1984.

Gillon, Edmund V., Jr. *Art Nouveau: An Anthology of Design and Illustration from the Studio*. New York: Dover, 1969.

Götz, Adriani. *Toulouse-Lautrec: The Complete Graphic Works*. New York: Thames and Hudson, 1988.

Grasset, Eugéne. *Eugéne Grasset: Lausanne 1841–Sceaux 1917*. Paris: Y. Plantin et F. Blondel, c. 1980.

Green, William. *Japanese Woodblock Prints: A Bibliography of Writings from 1822–1992, Entirely or Partly in English Text*. Leiden, Netherlands: Ukiyo-e Books, c. 1993.

Hermand, Jost. *Jugendstil: Kunst um 1900*. Stuttgart: Metzlersche, 1965.

Hiatt, Charles. *Picture Posters*. London: George Bell and Sons, 1995.

Hiesinger, Kathryn B., ed. *Art Nouveau in Munich: Masters of the Jugendstil*. Munich: Prestel-Verlag, 1988.

Hillier, Jack Ronald. *The Art of Hokusai in Book Illustration*. Berkeley: University of California Press, 1980.

———. *The Japanese Print: A New Approach*. Rutland, VT: C. E. Tuttle, 1975.

———. *Suzuki Harunobu*. Philadelphia: Philadelphia Museum of Art, 1970.

———. *Utamaro: Colour Prints and Paintings*. 2nd ed. Oxford: Phaidon, 1979.

Hofstatter, Hans H. *Art Nouveau: Prints, Illustrations, and Posters*. New York: Greenwich House, 1968.

Horning, Clarence P. *Will Bradley: His Graphic Art*. New York: Dover, 1974.

Houfe, Simon, ed. *The Birth of "The Studio": 1893–1895*. Woodbridge, England: Antique Collectors' Club, 1976.

Huguette Beres (Art Gallery). *Utamaro: Estampes, Livres Illustres*. Paris: Huguette Beres, c. 1977.

Hutchison, Harold F. *The Poster*. New York: Viking, 1968.

Izzard, Sebastian. *Hiroshige: An Exhibition of Selected Prints and Illustrated Books*. New York: Ukiyo-e Society of America, c. 1983.

Julien, Edouard. *The Posters of Toulouse-Lautrec*. Monte Carlo: Andre Sauret, 1966.

Keay, Carolyn. *American Posters of the Turn of the Century*. London: Academy Editions, 1975.

Kempton, Richard. *Art Nouveau: An Annotated Bibliography*. Los Angeles: Hennessey & Ingalls, 1977.

Kitagawa, Utamaro. *A Chorus of Birds / Utamaro*. New York: Metropolitan Museum of Art, Viking Press, 1981.

Kobayashi, Tadashi. *Utamaro*. Trans. Mark A. Harbison. Tokyo and New York: Kodansha International, 1982.

———. *Utamaro: Portaits from the Floating World*. Trans. Mark A. Harbison. Tokyo and London: Kodansha International, 1993.

Lane, Richard. *Hokusai, Life and Work.* New York: Dutton, 1989.

Lemonnier, Camille, and Verneuil, Maurice Pillard. *Eugéne Grasset et son oeuvre.* Paris: Editions de "La Plume," 1900.

Levy, Merwyn. *Liberty Style: The Classic Years 1889–1910.* New York: 1986.

Madsen, Stephan T. *Sources of Art Nouveau.* New York: Da Capo, 1975.

Maindron, Ernest. *Les affiches étrangéres.* Paris: 1897.

———. *Les affiches illustrées.* Paris: H. Launetter, 1886.

Margolin, Victor. *American Poster Renaissance.* New York: Watson-Guptill, 1975.

Meech, Julia, and Weisberg, Gabriel P. *Japonisme Comes to America.* New York: Abrams, 1990.

Morse, Peter. *Hokusai, One Hundred Poets.* New York: G. Braziller, 1989.

Mucha, Juri. *Alphonse Mucha.* New York: St. Martin's Press, 1971.

Murray-Robertson, Anne. *Grasset: Pionnier de l'Art Nouveau.* Lausanne: Editions 24 Heures: Diffusion Payot, 1981.

Nagata, Seiji. *Hokusai: Genius of the Japanese Ukiyo-e.* Trans. John Bester. Tokyo and New York: Kodansha International, 1995.

Nyns, Marcel. *Georges Lemmen.* Antwerp: de Sikkel, 1954.

Oka, Isaburo. *Hiroshige.* Tokyo and New York: Kodansha International, 1982.

Oka, Isaburo. *Hiroshige: Japan's Great Landscape Artist.* Tokyo and New York: Kodansha International, 1992.

Osthaus, Karl Ernst. *Van de Velde.* Hagen, Germany: Folkwang, 1920.

Penfield, Edward. *Posters in Miniature.* New York: R. H. Russell and Son, 1896.

Plasschaert, A. *Jan Toorop.* Amsterdam: Vorst & Tas, 1929.

Price, Charles Matlock. *Poster Design: A Critical Study of the Development of the Poster in Continental Europe, England, and America.* Rev. ed. New York: George W. Bricka, 1913.

Rappard-Boon, Charlotte van, et al. *Hiroshige and the Utagawa School: Japanese Prints, c. 1810–1860.* Amsterdam: Rijksprentenkabinet, Rijksmuseum, 1984.

Rennert, Jack. *Posters of the Belle Epoque.* New York: Wine Spectator Press, 1990.

Richards, Maurice. *Posters at the Turn of the Century.* New York: Walker, 1968.

Ricketts, Charles. *A Defence of the Revival of Printing.* London: Ballantine Press, 1909.

Sainton, Roger. *Art Nouveau Posters and Graphics.* New York: Rizzoli, 1977.

Selz, Peter, and Constantine, Mildred, eds. *Art Nouveau.* New York: Museum of Modern Art, 1959.

Sembach, Klaus-Jürgen, et al. *1910, Halbzeit der Moderne: Van de Velde, Behrens, Hoffmann und die Anderen.* Stuttgart: Hatje, 1992.

———. *Henry van de Velde.* Trans. Michael Robinson. New York: Rizzoli, 1989.

Sharp, Dennis. *Henri van de Velde, Theatres 1904–1914.* London: The Architectural Association, 1974.

Shibui, Kiyoshi. *Utamaro.* New York: Crown Publishers, 1962.

Solo, Dan X. *Art Nouveau Display Alphabets.* New York: Dover, 1976.

Sterner, Gabriele. *Jugendstil Art Deco Malerei and Grafik.* Munich: Wilhelm Heyne Verlag, 1981.

Strange, Edward Fairbrother. *Hiroshige's Woodblock Prints: A Guide.* New York: Dover Publications, 1983.

———. *Hokusai, The Old Man Mad with Painting.* Folcroft, PA: Folcroft Library Editions, 1977.

Sunshine, Linda. *The Posters of Alphonse Mucha.* New York: Harmony Books, 1975.

Read, Brian. *Aubrey Beardsley.* New York: Bonanza, 1968.

Taylor, John Russell. *The Art Nouveau Book in Britain.* Edinburgh: Paul Harris Publishing, 1979.

Terrence, Kathy. *An Art Nouveau Album.* New York: Dutton, 1981.

Troy, Nancy J. *Modernism and the Decorative Arts in France: Art Nouveau to Le Corbusier.* New Haven: Yale University Press, 1991.

Ulmer, Renate. *Mucha.* Cologne: Taschen, 2003.

Velde, Henri Van de. *Deblaiement d'art.* Brussels: Monnom, 1894.

———. *Henri Van de Velde.* Cologne: Wienand, 1992.

———. *Die Renaissance im Modernen Kunstgewerbe.* Berlin: Cassirer, 1903.

Vergez, Robert. *Early Ukiyo-e Master: Okumura Masanobu.* Tokyo: Kodanshu, 1983.

Verneuil, M. M. P., Auriol G., and Mucha, A. *Combinaisons Ornementales.* Paris: Librairie Centrale des Beaux Arts, 1901.

Weisser, Michael. *Im Stil der "Jugend."* Frankfurt: Fricke, 1979.

Wichmann, Siegfried. *Japonisme: The Japanese Influence on Western Art in the 19th and 20th Century.* New York: Harmony Books, 1981.

12. The Genesis of Twentieth-Century Design

Ades, Dawn, et al. *The 20th Century Poster: Design of the Avant Garde.* New York: Abbeville, 1984.

Adlmann, Jan Ernst. *Vienna Moderne: 1898–1918.* Houston: University of Houston, 1979.

Banham, Reyner. *Theory and Design in the First Machine Age.* New York: Praeger, 1967.

Baroni, Daniele, and D'Auria, Antonio. *Kolo Moser: Graphic Artist and Designer.* New York: Rizzoli, 1986.

Behrens, Peter. *Feste des Lebens und der Kunst, eine Betrachtung des Theaters als Höchsten Kultursymbols.* Leipzig: Eugen Diederichs, 1900

Billcliffe, Roger. *Charles Rennie Mackintosh: The Complete Furniture, Furniture Drawings, and Interior Designs.* London: J. Murry, 1986.

Bliss, Douglas Percy. *Charles Rennie Mackintosh and Glasgow School of Art.* Glasgow: Glasgow School of Art, 1979.

Bruckhardt, Lucius. *The Werkbund: History and Ideology, 1907–1933.* New York: Barron's, 1977.

Buddenseig, Tilmann. *Industrialkultur: Peter Behrens and the AEG.* Cambridge, MA: MIT Press, 1984.

———, et al. *Peter Behrens: Umbautes Licht: Das Verwaltungsgebäude der Hoechst AG.* Frankfurt: Prestel-Verlag, 1990.

Campbell, Joan. *The German Werkbund: The Politics of Reform in the Applied Arts.* Princeton, NJ: Princeton University Press, 1978.

Clair, Jean, et al. *Vienne 1880–1938: L'Apocalyspe Joyeuse.* Paris: Editions du Centre Pompidou, 1986.

———. *Line and Form.* London: G. Bell & Sons, Ltd., 1900.

Crawford, Alan. *Charles Rennie Mackintosh.* London and New York: Thames and Hudson, 1995.

Eadie, William. *Movements of Modernity: The Case of Glasgow and Art Nouveau.* London and New York: Routledge, 1990.

Eisler, Max. *Gustav Klimt.* Vienna: Rikola, 1921.

Fenz, Werner. *Koloman Moser.* Salzburg and Vienna: Residenz Verlag, 1904.

Fleischmann, Benno. *Gustav Klimt.* Vienna: Deuticke, 1946.

Garvey, Eleanor M., Smith, Anne B., and Wick, Peter A. *The Turn of a Century 1885–1910: Art Nouveau–Jugendstil Books.* Cambridge, MA: Harvard University Press, 1970.

Green, Oliver. *Art for the London Underground: London Transport Posters 1908 to the Present.* New York: Rizzoli, 1990.

Hanks, David A. *The Decorative Designs of Frank Lloyd Wright.* New York: Dutton, 1979.

Haslam, Malcolm. *In the Nouveau Style.* Boston: Little, Brown, 1989.

Helland, Janice. *The Studios of Frances and Margaret Macdonald.* Manchester, England, and New York: Manchester University Press, 1996.

Hoeber, Fritz. *Peter Behrens.* Munich: Georg Muller and Eugen Rentsch, 1913.

Hoepfner, Wolfram. *Das Haus Wiegand von Peter Behrens in Berlin-Dahlem.* Mainz: Von Zabern, 1979.

Hoffman, Werner. *Gustav Klimt.* Trans. Inge Goodwin. Greenwich, CT: New York Graphic Society, 1974.

Howarth, Thomas. *Charles Rennie Mackintosh and the Modern Movement.* London: Routledge and Kegan Paul, 1952.

Kadatz, Hans-Joachim. *Peter Behrens.* Leipzig: VEB E. A. Seemann Verlag, 1977.

Kallir, Jane. *Viennese Design and the Wiener Werkstätte.* New York: Braziller, 1986.

Koschatzky, Walter, and Kossatz, Horst-Herbert. *Ornamental Posters of the Vienna Secession.* London: Academy Editions, 1974.

Lane, Terence. *Vienna 1913.* Melbourne: National Gallery of Victoria, 1984.

Latham, Ian. *Josef Maria Olbrich.* London: Academy Editions, 1980.

Loos, Adolf. *Spoken into the Void: Collected Essays 1897–1900.* Cambridge, MA: MIT Press, 1982.

Loubier, Hans. *Die Neue Deutsche Buchkunst.* Stuttgart: Felix Krais Verlag, 1921.

MacLeod, Robert. *Charles Rennie Mackintosh: Architect and Artist.* New York: Dutton, 1983.

MacMillan, Andy, and Futagawa, Yukio. *Charles Rennie Mackintosh: The Glasgow School of Art.* Tokyo: A. D. A. Edita, 1979.

Meehan, Patrick J., ed. *Truth Against the World: Frank Lloyd Wright Speaks for an Organic Architecture.* New York: Wiley, 1987.

Messina, Maria Grazia. *Hoffmann: I "mobili semplici" Vienna 1900/1910.* Florence: Galleria dell'Emporio, 1977.

Meyer, Christian. *Josef Hoffmann: Architect and Designer 1870–1956.* Vienna: Galerie Metropol, 1981.

Nebehay, Michael Christian. *Ver Sacrum: 1898–1903.* New York: Rizzoli, 1977.

Neuwirth, Waltraud. *Wiener Werkstätte: Avantgarde, Art Deco, Industrial Design.* Vienna: Neuwirth, 1984.

Noever, Peter, and Oberhuber, Oswald. *Josef Hoffmann: Ornament Zwischen Hoffnung und Verbrechen.* Vienna, 1987.

Oliver, Cordelia. *Jessie M. King, 1875–1949.* Edinburgh, 1971.

Pevsner, Nikolaus. *Charles R. Mackintosh.* Milan: Il Balcone, 1950.

———. *The Sources of Modern Architecture and Design.* London: Thames and Hudson, 1968.

Powell, Nicolas. *The Sacred Spring: The Arts in Vienna 1898–1918.* Greenwich, CT: New York Graphic Society, 1974.

Sarmany-Parsons, Ilona. *Gustav Klimt.* New York: Crown, 1987.

Schuster, Peter-Klaus, ed. *Peter Behrens und Nürnberg.* Munich: Prestel-Verlag, 1980.

Schweiger, Werner J., et al. *Koloman Moser: 1868–1918.* Vienna: Hochschule für Angewandte Kunst in Wien, 1979.

———. *Wiener Werkstaette: Design in Vienna 1903–1932.* New York: Abbeville, 1984.

Tummers, Nic H. M. *J. L. Lauweriks, zijn werk en zigninvloed op architectuuren vormgevingrond 1910: DeHagenerlmpls.* Hilversum, Netherlands: Uitgeverij F. van Saane, 1968.

Varnedoe, Kirk. *Vienna 1900: Art, Architecture, and Design.* New York: Museum of Modern Art, 1986.

Vergo, Peter. *Art in Vienna 1898–1918.* London: Phaidon, 1975.

———. *Vienna 1900: Vienna, Scotland, and the European Avant-Garde.* Edinburgh: Her Majesty's Stationery Office, 1975.

Vienna Secession. *Katalog der Kunst-Ausstellung der Vereinigung Bildenden Künstler Osterreichs, nos. 1–14.* Vienna: 1898–1902.

Weber, Wilhelm. *Peter Behrens.* Berlin: Pfalzgalerie Kaiserslautern, 1966.

Werde, Stuart. *The Modern Poster.* New York: Museum of Modern Art, 1988.

White, Colin. *The Enchanted World of Jessie M. King.* Edinburgh: Canongate, 1989.

Windsor, Alan. *Peter Behrens: Architect and Designer.* New York: Whitney, 1981.

PART IV. THE MODERNIST ERA
Graphic design in the first half of the twentieth century

13. The Influence of Modern Art

Ades, Dawn. *Photomontage.* London: Thames and Hudson, 1976.

Apollinaire, Guillaume. *Calligrammes.* Paris: Editions Gallimard, 1925.

———. *The Cubist Painters, Aesthetic Meditiations, 1913.* New York: Wittenborn, 1962.

Apollonio, Umbro, ed. *Futurist Manifestos.* New York: Viking Press, 1973.

Baldacci, Paolo, and Daverio, Philippe. *Futurism 1911–1918.* Milan: Galleria Daverio, 1988.

Baxandall, Lee. *Radical Perspectives in the Arts.* Middlesex, England: Penguin Books, 1972.

Benson, Timothy O. *Raoul Hausmann and Berlin Dada.* Ann Arbor, MI: UMI Research Press, 1987.

Brown, Jonathan, ed. *Picasso and the Spanish Tradition.* New Haven: Yale University Press, 1996.

Calvocoressi, Richard. *Magritte.* London: Phaidon, 1994.

Cassou, Jean, and Leymarie, Jean. *Fernand Leger Drawings and Gouaches*. Greenwich, CT: New York Graphic Society, 1973.

Cendrars, Blaise. *La fin du monde*. Reprint, Paris: Pierre Seghers, 1949.

Cohen, Arthur A. *The Avant Garde in Print*. Vols. I–V. New York: Ex Libris, 1983.

Cooper, Philip. *Cubism*. London: Phaidon, 1995.

Crane, Arnold W. *Man Ray Photo Graphics*. Milwaukee, WI: Milwaukee Art Center, 1973.

Crone, Rainer. *Paul Klee: Legends of the Sign*. New York: Columbia University Press, 1991.

Damase, Jacques. *Revolution typographique*. Geneva: Galerie Motte, 1966.

De Rache, Andre, ed. *Joan Miro*. Brussels: Gemeentelijke Casino, 1971.

D' Harnoncourt, Anne, et al. *Paintings from Europe and the Americas in the Philadelphia Museum of Art: A Concise Catalogue*. Philadelphia: University of Pennsylvania Press, 1994.

Drucker, Joanna. *The Visible Word: Experimental Typography and Modern Art*. Chicago: University of Chicago Press, 1994.

Duchamp, Marcel. *Duchamp*. New York: Cameo/Abrams, 1996.

Dupin, Jacques. *Miro*. New York: Abrams, 1993.

Elderfield, John. *Kurt Schwitters*. London: Thames and Hudson, 1985.

Enyert, James. *Bruguiere: His Photographs and His Life*. New York: Knopf, 1977.

Ernst, Max. *Une semaine de bonté*. New York: Dover, 1976.

Evans, David. *John Heartfield: AIZ/VI 1930–38*. New York: Kent, 1992.

Fischer Hannelore. *Käthe Kollwitz: Meisterwerke der Zeichnung*. Cologne: DuMont, 1995.

Foresta, Merry; Naumann, Francis; and Foster, Stephen C, et al. *Perpetual Motif: The Art of Man Ray*. New York, 1988.

Foster, Steven B., ed. *Dada/Dimensions*. Ann Arbor, MI: UMI Research Press, 1984.

Fraser, James, and Heller, Steven. *The Malik Verlag 1916–1947, Berlin, Prague, New York*. New York: Goethe House; Madison, NJ: Fairleigh Dickinson University, 1985.

Freeman, Judi. *The Dada and Surrealist Word-Image*. Cambridge, MA: MIT Press, 1989.

Fry, Edward F. *Cubism*. London: Thames and Hudson, 1966; New York: Oxford University Press, 1978.

Gombrich, Lisbeth, trans. *Käthe Kollwitz*. Berlin: Henschelverlag Kunst und Gesellschaft, 1980.

Greenberg, Allen Carl. *Artists and Revolution: Dada and the Bauhaus. 1917–1925*. Ann Arbor, MI: UMI Research Press, 1979.

Habasque, Guy. *Cubism*. Paris: Skira, 1959.

Haenlein, Carl-Albrecht. *Dada Photomontagen*. Hannover, Germany: Kestner-Gesellschaft Hannover, 1979.

Hausmann, Raoul, and Schwitters, Kurt. *PIN*. London: Gaberbocchus Press, 1962.

Heartfield, John. *Photomontages of the Nazi Period*. New York: Universe, 1977.

Hewitt, Andrew. *Fascist Modernism: Aesthetics, Politics, and the Avant-garde*. Stanford, CA: Stanford University Press, 1993.

Hubert, Renee Riese. *Surrealism and the Book*. Berkeley: University of California Press, 1988.

Huelsenbeck, Richard, ed. *The Dada Almanac*. London: Atlas Press, 1993.

Hulten, Pontus, ed. *Futurism and Futurisms*. New York: Abbeville, 1986.

———. *Memoirs of a Dada Drummer*. New York: Viking, 1969.

Kahn, Douglas. *John Heartfield: Art and Mass Media*. New York: Tanam, 1985.

Kinross, Robin. *Modern Typography: An Essay in Critical History*. London: Hyphen Press, 1992.

Klein, Mina C. *Käthe Kollwitz, Life in Art*. New York: Schocken Books, 1975.

Kozloff, Max. *Cubism/Futurism*. New York: Charter House, 1973.

Lippard, Lucy R., ed. *Dadas on Art*. Englewood Cliffs, NJ: Prentice-Hall, 1971.

Lista, Giovanni. *Futurismo e Fotografia*. Milan: Multhipla Edizioni, 1979.

Little, Roger. *Guillaume Apollinaire*. London: Athlone Press, 1976.

Loria, Stefano. *Pablo Picasso*. New York: Peter Bedrick Books, 1995.

Marcus, George H., ed. *Treasures of the Philadelphia Museum of Art and the John G. Johnson Collection*. Philadelphia: Museum of Art, 1973.

Marinetti, Filippo T. Flint, R. W., ed. *Marinetti Selected Writings*. New York: Farrar, Straus and Giroux, 1971.

Martin, Marianne W. *Futurist Art and Theory 1909–1915*. Oxford: Clarendon Press, 1968.

Meyer, Esther da Costa. *The Work of Antonio Sant'Elia: Retreat into the Future*. New Haven: Yale University Press, 1995.

Michaud, Guy. *Mallarmé*. New York: New York University Press, 1965.

Moure, Gloria. *Marcel Duchamp*. New York: Rizzoli, 1988.

Nadeau, Maurice. *The History of Surrealism*. Cambridge, MA: Harvard University Press, 1989.

Nagel, Otto. *Käthe Kollwitz*. Greenwich, CT: New York Graphic Society Ltd., 1971.

———, et al. *Käthe Kollwitz, die Handzeichnungen*. Stuttgart: W. Kohlhammer, 1980.

Newell, Kenneth B. *Pattern Poetry: A Historical Critique from the Alexandrian Greeks to Dylan Thomas*. Boston: Marlborough House, 1976.

Noun, Louise R. *Three Berlin Artists of the Weimar Era: Hannah Höch, Käthe Kollwitz, Jeanne Mammen*. Des Moines, IA: Des Moines Art Center, 1994.

Passamani, Bruno. *Fortunato Depero*. Luglio, Italy: Bassano del Grappa, 1970.

Polizzotti, Mark. *Revolution of the Mind: The Life of André Breton*. New York: Farrar, Straus and Giroux, 1995.

Read, Herbert. *A Concise History of Modern Painting*. New York: Praeger, 1959.

Richardson, Tony, and Stangos, Nikos, eds. *Concepts of Modern Art*. New York: Harper and Row, 1974.

Rosenbaum, Robert. *Cubism and Twentieth-Century Art*. New York: Abrams, 1966.

Rothschild, Nannette F., et al. *Encounters with Modern Art*. Philadelphia: Philadelphia Museum of Art, 1996.

Rye, Jane. *Futurism*. London: Studio Vista, 1972.

Samaltanos, Katia. *Apollinaire: Catalyst for Primitivism, Picabia, and Duchamp*. Ann Arbor, MI: UMI Research Press, 1984.

Schmalenbach, Werner. *Fernand Leger.* New York: Abrams, 1976.

Schwartz, Arturo. *Man Ray: Rigour of Imagination.* New York: Rizzoli, 1972.

Scudiero, Maurizio. *Futurismi postali.* Rovereto, Italy: Longo Editore, 1986.

———, and Leiber, David. *Depero futurista & New York.* Rovereto, Italy: Longo Editore, 1986.

Seigel, Jerrold E. *The Private Worlds of Marcel Duchamp: Desire, Liberation, and the Self in Modern Culture.* Berkeley: University of California Press, 1995.

Siepmann, Eckhard. *Montage: John Heartfield.* Berlin: Elefanten Press Galerie, 1977.

Steegmuller, Francis. *Apollinaire, Poet among the Painters.* Freeport, NY: Books for Libraries Press, 1971.

Steinitz, Kate Trauman. *Kurt Schwitters: A Portrait from Life.* Berkeley and Los Angeles: University of California Press, 1968.

Sylvester, David. *Magritte.* New York: Praeger, 1969.

Tisdall, Caroline, and Bozzola, Angelo. *Futurism.* New York: Oxford University Press, 1978.

Webster, Michael. *Reading Visual Poetry after Futurism: Marinetti, Apollinaire, Schwitters, Cummings.* New York: Lang, 1995.

Weiss, Jeffrey S. *The Popular Culture of Modern Art: Picasso, Duchamp, and Avant-Gardism.* New Haven: Yale University Press, 1994.

Willett, John. *Heartfield versus Hitler.* Paris: Éditions Hazan, 1997.

14. Pictorial Modernism

Binder, Carla (compiler). *Joseph Binder.* Vienna: Anton Schroll & Co., 1976.

Brown, Robert K., and Reinhold, Susan. *The Poster of A. M. Cassandre.* New York: Dutton, 1979.

Cooper, Austin. *Making a Poster.* London: The Studio, Ltd., 1938.

Darrocott, Joseph. *The First World War in Posters.* New York: Dover, 1974.

Delhaye, Jean. *Art Deco Posters and Graphics.* New York: Rizzoli, 1978.

Duncan, Alastair. *The Encyclopedia of Art Deco.* New York: Dutton, 1988.

Encyclopedia des arts decoratifs et industriels modernes au XXeme siecle. Vol. I–VII. Paris: Impr. Nationale, 1925.

Green, Oliver. *Art for the London Underground.* New York: Rizzoli, 1990.

Gluck, Felix. *World Graphic Design: Fifty Years of Advertising Art.* New York: Watson-Guptill, 1969.

Haworth-Booth, Mark E. *McKnight Kauffer: A Designer and His Public.* Madison, CT: Fraser, 1979.

Heller, Steven, and Fili, Louise. *Italian Art Deco: Graphic Design Between the Wars.* San Francisco: Chronicle Books, 1993.

Hillier, Bevis. *Art Deco of the 20s and 30s.* London: Studio Vista; New York: Dutton, 1968.

———. *The World of Art Deco.* New York: Dutton, 1971.

Hitler, Adolf. *Mein Kampf (My Battle).* Trans. E. T. S. Dugdale. Boston: Houghton Mifflin, 1933.

Hohlwein, Ludwig. *Hohlwein Posters.* New York: Dover, 1976.

———. *Ludwig Hohlwein, 1874–1949.* Munich: Klinkhardt & Biermann, 1996.

Kauffer, E. McKnight. *The Art of the Poster.* London: Cecil Palmer, 1924.

Masutani, Yoko, ed. *Every Face of the Great Master Cassandre.* Tokyo: Suntory Museum, 1995.

Menten, Theodore. *Advertising Art in the Art Deco Style.* New York: Dover, 1975.

Metzl, Ervine. *The Poster: Its History and Its Art.* New York: Watson-Guptill, 1963.

Mouron, Henri. *A. M. Cassandre.* New York: Rizzoli, 1985.

Rawls, Walton. *Wake Up America! World War I and the American Poster.* New York: Abbeville, 1988.

Ray, Timothy. *Imponderable Joys: The Work of Austin Cooper.* Brandon, Manitoba: The Art Gallery of Southwestern Manitoba, 1993.

Rennert, Jack, ed. *100 Posters of Paul Colin.* New York: Images Graphiques, 1977.

Schau, Michael. *J. C. Leyendecker.* New York: Watson-Guptill, 1974.

Striner, Richard. *Art Deco.* New York: Abbeville Press, 1994.

Thomson, Oliver. *Mass Persuasion in History.* Edinburgh: Paul Harris, 1977.

Tolmer, A. *Mies en Page. The Theory and Practice of Layout.* London: The Studio, 1930.

Vox, Maximillien. *A. M. Cassandre Plakate.* St. Gallen, Switzerland: Verlag Zollikofer, 1948.

Weill, Alain. *Rétrospective Jean Carlu.* Paris: Musée de l'Affiche, 1980.

15. A New Language of Form

Andel, Jaroslav. *Avant Garde Page Design 1900–1950.* New York: Delano Greenridge Editions, LLC, 2002.

Anikst, Mikhail. *Soviet Commercial Design of the Twenties.* New York: Abbeville, 1987.

———, and Chernevich, Elena. *Russian Graphic Design 1880–1917.* New York: Abbeville, 1990.

Baburina, Nina. *The Soviet Political Poster 1917–1980.* New York: Viking, 1988.

Baljeu, Joost. *Theo van Doesburg.* New York: Macmillan, 1974.

Bann, Stephen, ed. *The Tradition of Constructivism.* New York: Viking, 1974.

Barooshian, Vahan D. *Russian Cubo-Futurism: 1910–1930.* The Hague: Mouton, 1974.

Barron, Stephanie, and Tuchman, Maurice, eds. *The Avant-Garde in Russian, 1910–1930: New Perspectives.* Cambridge, MA: MIT Press, 1980.

Beeren, Wim, et al. *Kazimir Malevich 1878–1935.* Amsterdam: Stedelijk Museum, 1988.

Blake, Patricia, ed. *Vladimir Mayakovsky: The Bedbug and Selected Poetry.* Princeton, NJ: Princeton University Press, 1975.

Bojko, Szymon. *New Graphic Design in Revolutionary Russia.* London: Lund Humphries, 1972.

Bowlt, John E., ed. and trans. *Russian Art of the Avant-Garde: Theory and Criticism 1902–1934.* New York: Viking, 1976.

Broos, Kees, and Hefting, Paul. *Dutch Graphic Design: A Century.* Cambridge, MA: MIT Press, 1993.

Charters, Ann and Samuel. *I Love: The Story of Vladimir Mayakovsky and Lili Brik.* New York: Farrar, Straus and Giroux, 1979.

Chernevich, Elena. *Russian Graphic Design, 1880–1917.* New York: Abbeville, 1990.

Cohen, Arthur A., ed. *ExLibris 6: Constructivism & Futurism: Russian and Other.* New York: ExLibris, 1977.

Compton, Susan P. *Russian Avant-Garde Books: 1917–34.* Cambridge, MA: MIT Press, 1993.

———. *The World Backwards: Russian Futurist Books 1912–16.* London: British Museum Publications, 1978.

Constantine, Mildred, and Fern, Alan. *Revolutionary Soviet Film Posters.* Baltimore, MD: Johns Hopkins University Press, 1974.

Contensou, Bernadette, and Lemoine, Serge. *Domela: 65 ans D'Abstraction.* Paris: Musée d'Art Moderne, 1987.

Dickerman, Leah, ed. *Building the Collective: Soviet Graphic Design 1917–1937: Selections from the Merrill C. Berman Collection.* New York: Princeton Architectural Press, 1996.

Dluhosch, Eric, and Svácha, Rostislav, eds. *Karel Teige, 1900–1951: L'Enfant Terrible of the Czech Modernist Avant-Garde.* Cambridge, MA and London: MIT Press, 1999.

Doig, Allan. *Theo van Doesburg: Painting into Architecture, Theory into Practice.* Cambridge: Cambridge University Press, 1986.

Elliott, David. *Rodchenko and the Arts of Revolutionary Russia.* New York: Pantheon, 1979.

Franciscono, Marcel. *The Modern Dutch Poster: The First Fifty Years 1890–1940.* Cambridge, MA: MIT Press, 1987.

Friedman, Mildred, ed. *De Stijl: 1917–1931. Visions of Utopia.* New York: Abbeville Press, 1982.

Grey, Camilla. *The Great Experiment: Russian Art 1863–1922.* New York: Abrams, 1962.

Jaffe, Hans. *De Stijl.* New York: Abrams, 1971.

———. *Mondrian und De Stijl.* Cologne, Germany: Galerie Gmurzynska, 1979.

Karginov, German. *Rodchenko.* London: Thames and Hudson, 1979.

Khan-Magomedov, S. O. *Rodchenko: The Complete Work.* Cambridge, MA: MIT Press, 1987.

King, David, and Porter, Cathy. *Images of Revolution: Graphic Art from 1905 Russia.* New York: Pantheon, 1983.

Lissitzky-Kuppers, Sophie, ed. *Lissitzky: Life Letters Texts.* London: Thames and Hudson, 1967.

Lissitzky, El. Trans. Christina Van Manen. *About Two Squares.* Cambridge, MA: MIT Press, 1991.

———, and Ehrenburg, Ilya, eds. *Vesc Objet Gegenstand.* Reprint. Baden: Verlage Lars Muller, 1994.

Lodder, Christina. *Russian Constructivism.* New Haven: Yale University Press, 1983.

Margolin, Victor. *The Struggle for Utopia: Rodchenko, Lissitzky, Moholy-Nagy, 1917–1946.* Chicago and London: University of Chicago Press, 1997.

Markov, Vladimir. *Russian Futurism: A History.* London: MacGibbon & Kee, 1969.

Martinet, Jan. *H. N. Werkman "Druksel" Prints and General Printed Matter.* Amsterdam: Stedelijk Museum, 1977.

———. *The Next Call.* Utrecht: Uitgeverij Reflex, 1978.

Milena, Richard and Kalinovska. *Art into Life: Russian Constructivism 1914–1932.* New York: Rizzoli, 1990.

Milner, John. *Vladimir Tatlin and the Russian Avant-Garde.* New Haven: Yale University Press, 1983.

Moholy-Nagy, Laszlo, and Kassák, L. *The Book of New Artists.* Reprint. New York: Princeton Architectural Press, 1996.

Mondrian, Piet. *Plastic Art and Pure Plastic Art.* New York: Wittenborn, 1951.

Neumann, Eckhard. *Functional Graphic Design in the 20's.* New York: Reinhold, 1967.

Nisbet, Peter. *El Lissitzky: 1890–1941.* Cambridge, MA: Harvard University Art Museums, 1987.

Overy, Paul. *De Stijl.* London: Studio Vista, 1969.

Purvis, Alston. *Dutch Graphic Design: 1918–1945.* New York: Van Nostrand Reinhold, 1992.

Railing, Patricia. *More About Two Squares.* Cambridge, MA: MIT Press, 1991.

Rodchenko, Alexsandr M., and Stepanova, Varvara F. *The Future Is Our Only Goal.* Munich: Prestel-Verlag, 1991.

Roman, Gail Harrison, and Hagelstein Marquardt, Virginia, eds. *The Avant-Garde Frontier: Russia Meets the West, 1910–1930.* Gainesville, FL: University of Florida Press, 1992.

Rubinger, Krystyna, Bojko, Szymon, and Bowlt, John E., et al. *Women Artists of the Russian Avantgarde, 1910–1930.* Cologne: Galerie Gmurzysnka, 1980.

Rickey, George. *Constructivism: Origins and Evolution.* New York: Braziller, 1967.

Seuphor, Michel. *Piet Mondrian.* New York: Abrams, 1956.

Spencer, Herbert. *The Liberated Page.* San Francisco: Bedford Press, 1987.

———, ed. *Pioneers of Modern Typography.* London: Lund Humphries, 1969.

Stapanian, Juliette R. *Mayakovsky's Cubo-Futurist Vision.* Houston, TX: Rice University Press, 1986.

Tupitsyn, Margarita. *El Lissitzky: Beyond the Abstract Cabinet.* New Haven and London: Yale University Press, 1999.

Tupitsyn, Margarita. *Gustav Klusis and Valentina Kulagina: Photography and Montage After Constructivism.* New York: International Center of Photography; Göttingen, Germany: Steidl Publishers, 2004.

Van Straaten, Evert. *Theo Van Doesburg: Schilder en Architect.* 'S-Gravenhage, Netherlands: SDU Uitgeverij, 1988.

White, Stephen. *The Bolshevik Poster.* New Haven: Yale University Press, 1988.

Woroszylski, Wiktor. *The Life of Mayakovsky.* New York: Orion Press, 1970.

16. The Bauhaus and the New Typography

Albers, Josef. *Interaction of Color.* New Haven: Yale University Press, 1975.

———. *Search versus Research.* Hartford, CT: Trinity College Press, 1969.

Aynsley, Jeremy. *Graphic Design in Germany: 1890–1945.* London: Thames & Hundson Ltd., 2000.

Barker, Nicolas. *Stanley Morison.* Cambridge, MA: Harvard University Press, 1972.

Bayer, Herbert, Gropius, Walter, and Gropius, Ise, eds. *Bauhaus 1919–1928.* New York: Museum of Modern Art, 1938.

———. *Herbert Bayer: Painter Designer Architect.* New York: Reinhold, 1967; London: Studio Vista, 1967.

Blaser, Werner. *Miès van der Rohe: Less Is More.* Zurich: Wasser Verlag, 1986.

Brady, Elizabeth. *Eric Gill: Twentieth Century Book Designer.* Metuchen, NJ: The Scarecrow Press, 1974.

Brewer, Roy. *Eric Gill: The Man Who Loved Letters.* London: Frederick Muller Ltd., 1973.

Broos, Kees. *Piet Zwart.* The Hague: Gemeentemuseum, 1973.

Chanzit, Gwen F. *The Herbert Bayer Collection and Archive at the Denver Art Museum.* Denver: Denver Art Museum, 1988.

Dearstyne, Howard. *Inside the Bauhaus.* New York: Rizzoli, 1986.

Franciscono, Marcel. *Walter Gropius and the Creation of the Bauhaus at Weimar: The Ideals and Artistic Theories of Its Founding Years.* Urbana, IL: University of Illinois Press, 1971.

Garlan, Ken. *Mr. Beck's Underground Map.* London: Capital Transport, 1994.

Geelhaar, Christian. *Paul Klee and the Bauhaus.* Greenwich, CT: New York Graphic Society, 1973.

Gill, Eric. *An Essay on Typography.* London: Sheed and Ward, 1931.

———. *The Letter Forms and Type Designs of Eric Gill.* Westerham, England: Eva Svensson, 1976.

Gropius, Walter. *The New Architecture and the Bauhaus.* Cambridge, MA: MIT Press, 1965.

———, ed. *The Theatre of the Bauhaus.* Middletown, CT: Wesleyan University, 1961.

Gropius, Walter, et al. *Offset Buch und Werbekunst, Heft 7.* Leipzig: Der Offset-Verlag GMBH, 1926.

Gropius, Walter and Moholy-Nagy, Laszlo, ed. *Staatliches Bauhaus Weimar, 1919–1923.* Munich: Kraus Reprint, 1980.

Hahn, Peter. *Bauhaus Berlin.* Weingarten, Germany: Kunstverlag Weingarten GmbH, 1985.

Haus, Andreas. *Moholy-Nagy: Photographs and Photograms.* New York: Pantheon, 1980.

Hight, Eleanor M. *Moholy-Nagy: Photography and Film in Weimar Germany.* Wellesley, MA: Wellesley College Museum, 1985.

Itten, Johannes. *Design and Form: The Basic Course at the Bauhaus and Later.* New York: Reinhold, 1963.

Kagan, Andrew. *Paul Klee: Art & Music.* Ithaca, NY: Cornell, 1983.

Kandinsky, Wassily. *Complete Writings on Art.* New York: Hall, 1982.

———. *Concerning the Spiritual in Art.* New York: Wittenborn, 1947.

———. *Point and Line to Plane.* New York: Dover, 1979.

Klee, Paul. *Pedagogical Sketchbook.* New York: Praeger, 1953.

Kostelanetz, Richard. *Moholy-Nagy.* London: Allen Lane, 1974.

Kroll, Friedhelm. *Bauhaus 1919–1933.* Dusseldorf: Verlagsgruppe Bertelsmann GmbH, 1974.

Lupton, Elaine, and Miller, J. Abbott, eds. *The ABC's of The Bauhaus and Design Theory.* New York: Princeton Architectural Press, 1995.

Lupton, Elaine and Cohen, Elaine Lustig. *Letters from the Avant Garde: Modern Graphic Design.* New York: Princeton Architectural Press, 1996.

Marzona, E., and Fricke, R., ed. *Bauhaus Photography.* Cambridge, MA: MIT Press, 1969.

McLean, Ruari. *Jan Tschichold: Typographer.* London: Lund Humphries, 1975.

Middendorp, Jan. *Dutch Type.* Rotterdam: 010 Publishers, 2004.

Modley, Rudolf. *Handbook of Pictorial Symbols: 3,250 Examples from International Sources.* New York: Dover Publications, 1976.

———. *How to Use Pictorial Statistics,* 2nd ed. New York: Harper, 1937.

Moholy-Nagy, Laszlo. *The New Vision and Abstract of an Artist.* New York: Wittenborn, 1947.

———. *Vision in Motion.* Chicago: Paul Theobald, 1947.

Moholy-Nagy, Sibyl. *Experiment in Totality.* Cambridge, MA: MIT Press, 1969.

Moran, James. *Stanley Morison: His Typographic Achievement.* London: Lund Humphries; New York: Hastings House, 1971.

Muller, Fridolin, ed. *Piet Zwart.* Teufen, Switzerland: Verlag Arthur Niggli, 1966.

Naylor, Gilliam. *The Bauhaus Reassessed: Sources and Design Theory.* London: Herbert Press, 1985.

Neumann, Eckhard. *Bauhaus and Bauhaus People.* New York: Van Nostrand Reinhold, 1970.

Passuth, Krisztina, and Senter, Terence A. *L. Moholy-Nagy.* London: Arts Council of Great Britain, 1980.

Plant, Margaret. *Paul Klee: Figures and Faces.* London: Thames and Hudson, 1978.

Poling, Clark V. *Kandinsky's Teaching at the Bauhaus: Color Theory and Analytical Drawing.* New York: Rizzoli, 1986.

Purvis, Alston W. *H. N. Werkman.* New Haven: Yale University Press, 2004.

Roh, Franz, and Tschichold, Jan, eds. *foto-auge.* Stuttgart: Akademischer Verlag Dr. Fritz Wedekind, 1929.

Sandberg, Willem. *Now: In the Middle of the XXth Century.* Hilversum, Netherlands: De Jong, 1959.

Schlemmer, Oskar. *Man: Teaching Notes from the Bauhaus.* Cambridge, MA: MIT Press, 1971.

Schmidt, Joost, Entwurf. *Offset Buch und Werbekunst, 1926.* Dessau, Germany: Dünnhaupt, 1926.

Schmoller, Hans. *Two Titans, Mardersteig and Tschichold: A Study in Contrasts.* New York: Typophiles, 1990.

Skelton, Christopher. *Eric Gill: The Engravings.* Boston: David Godine, 1990.

Speaight, Robert. *The Life of Eric Gill.* London: Methuen, 1966.

Thorp, Joseph. *Eric Gill.* London: Jonathan Cape, 1929.

Tower, Beeke Sell. *Klee and Kandinsky at the Bauhaus.* Ann Arbor, MI: UMI Research Press, 1981.

Tschichold, Jan. *Asymmetric Typography.* New York: Reinhold, 1967.

———. *Designing Books.* New York: Wittenborn, Schultz, Inc., 1951.

———. *Die neue typographie.* Berlin: Verlag Des Bildungsverbandes, 1928.

———. *The New Typography: A Handbook for Modern Designers.* Trans. Ruari McLean. Berkeley: University of California Press, 1995.

Whitford, Frank. *Bauhaus.* London: Thames and Hudson, 1984.

Wingler, Hans Maria. *The Bauhaus: Weimar Dessau Berlin Chicago.* Cambridge, MA: MIT Press, 1969.

Zwart, Piet. *Keywords.* The Hague: Staatsdrukkerij den Haag, 1966.

17. The Modern Movement in America

Blum, Stella. *Designs by Erté: Fashion Drawings and Illustrations from "Harper's Bazar."* New York: Dover Publications, 1976.

Chanzit, Gwen Finkel. *Herbert Bayer and Modernist Design in America.* Ann Arbor, MI: UMI Research Press, 1987.

———. *The Herbert Bayer Collection and Archive at the Denver Art Museum.* Seattle: University of Washington Press, 1988.

DeNoon, Christopher. *Posters of the WPA.* Los Angeles: Wheatley, 1987.

Duncan, Alastair. *American Art Deco.* New York: 1986.

Dwiggins, William Addison. "New Kind of Printing Calls for New Kind of Design." *Boston Evening Transcript.* The Graphic Arts Section, Part 3. Boston: Henry W. Dutton, 1922.

Ehrlich, Frederic. *The New Typography and Modern Layouts.* New York: Stokes, 1934.

Goudy, Frederic. *Why Go Modern.* New York: Diamant Typographic Service, 1944.

Grundberg, Andy. *Brodovitch.* New York: Abrams, 1989.

Harris Neil, and Norelli, Martina Roudabush. *Art, Design, and the Modern Corporation: The Collection of Container Corporation of America.* Washington, DC: Smithsonian, 1985.

Hurlburt, Allen. *Publication Design.* New York: Van Nostrand Reinhold, 1976.

Jacobson, Egbert, ed. *Seven Designers Look at Trademark Design.* Chicago: Paul Theobald, 1952.

Johnson, J. Stewart. *The Modern American Poster.* New York: Museum of Modern Art, 1983.

Judd, Denis. *Posters of World War II.* New York: St. Martin's Press, 1973.

Kepes, Gyorgy. *Catalog Design Progress: Advancing Standards in Visual Communications.* New York: Sweet's Catalog Service, 1950.

———. *Language of Vision.* Chicago: Paul Theobald, 1945.

———. *The New Landscape.* Chicago: Paul Theobald, 1956.

Lönberg-Holm, K., and Sutnar, Ladislav. *Catalog Design.* New York: Sweet's Catalog Service, 1944.

Massey, John, ed. *Great Ideas.* Chicago: Container Corporation of America, 1976.

McMurtrie, Douglas C. *Modern Typography and Layout.* Chicago: Eyncourt Press, 1929.

Purcell, Kerry William. *Alexey Brodovitch.* London: Phaidon Press Limited, 2002.

Remington, Roger, and Hodik, Barbara J. *Nine Pioneers of American Graphic Design.* Cambridge, MA: MIT Press, 1989.

Remington, R. Roger. *Lester Beall: Trailblazer of American Graphic Design.* New York: Norton, 1996.

Remington, R. Roger, and Bodenstedt, Lisa. *American Modernism: Graphic Design 1920 to 1960.* London: Laurence King Publishing Ltd., 2003.

Rhodes, Anthony. Victor Margolin, ed. *Propaganda: The Art of Persuasion, World War II.* New York: Chelsea House, 1976.

Sutnar, Ladislav. *Package Design: The Force of Visual Selling.* New York: Arts, 1953.

Tibbel, John. *The American Magazine: A Compact History.* New York: Hawthorne Books, 1969.

Weber, Eva. *Art Deco in America.* New York: Exeter Books, 1985.

Zeman, Zbynek. *Selling the War: Art and Propaganda in World War II.* London: Orbis, 1978.

PART V. THE INFORMATION AGE
Graphic design in the global village

18. The International Typographic Style

Aicher, Otl. *Typographie.* Berlin: Ernst and Sohn, 1988.

Bill, Max. *Modern Swiss Architecture 1925–1945.* Basel: Verlag Karl Werner, 1945.

Diethelm, Walter. *Visual Transformations.* Zurich: ABC Verlag, 1982.

Douroux, Xavier. *Art Concret Suisse, Mémoire et Progrés: Andreas Christen, Camille Graeser, Marguerite Hersberger, Verena Loewensberg, Richard Paul Lohse, Nelly Rudin, Carlo Vivarelli.* Dijon, France: Coin du miroir, 1982.

Frutiger, Adrian. *Der Mensch und Seine Zeichen.* Echzell, Germany: Horst Heiderhoff Verlag, 1978.

———. *Signs and Symbols: Their Design and Meaning.* New York: Van Nostrand Reinhold, 1989.

———. *Type Sign Symbol.* Zurich: ABC Verlag, 1981.

Gasser, Manuel. *Exempla graphica.* Zurich: Hug and Sohne, 1967.

Gerstner, Karl, and Kutler, Marcus. *Die Neue Grafik/The New Graphic Art.* New York: Hastings House, 1959.

Gerstner, Karl. *Compendium for Literates: A System for Writing.* Trans. Dennis Q. Stephenson. Cambridge, MA: MIT Press, 1968.

———. *Designing Programmes.* Teufen, Switzerland: Verlag Arthur Niggli, 1968.

Grieshaber, Judith M. and Kröplien. *Die Philosophie der Neuen Grafik.* Stuttgart: Edition Cantz, 1990.

Henrion, F. H. K. *Top Graphic Design.* Zurich: ABC Verlag, 1983.

Hochuli, Jost, and Kinross, Robin. *Designing Books: Theory and Practice.* London: Hyphen Press.

Hofmann, Armin. *Armin Hofmann: His Work, Quest, and Philosophy.* Basel; Boston: Birkhäuser Verlag, 1989.

———. *Graphic Design Manual.* New York: Van Nostrand Reinhold, 1965.

Hüttinger, Eduard. *Max Bill.* Zurich: ABC Editions, 1978.

Jong, Cees W. de; Purvis, Alston W.; and Friedl, Friedrich. *Creative Type: A Sourcebook of Classic and Contemporary Letterforms.* London: Thames & Hudson, 2005.

Jury, David. *About Face: Reviving the Rules of Typography.* Switzerland: RotoVision SA, 2002.

Kane, John. *A Type Primer.* London: Laurence King Publishing, 2002.

Kappeler, Suzanne. *Carlos Vivarelli.* Zurich: ABC Verlag, 1988.

Lindinger, Herbert, ed. *Ulm Design: The Morality of Objects.* Cambridge, MA: MIT Press, 1990.

Maier, Manfred. *Basic Principles of Design.* New York: Van Nostrand Reinhold, 1980.

Margadant, Bruno. *The Swiss Poster: 1900–1983.* Basel: Birkhäuser Verlag, 1993.

Matter, Herbert. *Herbert Matter Foto-Grafiker: Sehformen der Zeit.* Baden, Switzerland: Verlag Lars Muller, 1995.

Müller, Lars. *Josef Müller-Brockmann: Gestalter.* Baden: Verlag Lars Müller, 1994.

Müller-Brockmann, Josef. *The Graphic Artist and His Design Problems.* Teufen, Switzerland: Verlag Arthur Niggli, 1968.

———. *Grid Systems.* Niederteufen, Switzerland: Verlag Arthur Niggli, 1981.

———. *Josef Müller-Brockmann: Pioneer of Swiss Graphic Design.* Ed. Lars Müller. Baden, Switzerland: Verlag Lars Müller, 1996.

Odermatt, Siegfried, and Tissi, Rosmarie. *Graphic Design.* Zurich: Waser Verlag, 1993.

Papanek, Victor. *Design for the Real World.* New York: Pantheon, 1970.

Pirovano, Carlo. *Max Huber.* Milan: Electra, 1982.

Rotzler, Willy. *Constructive Concepts.* New York: Rizzoli, 1989.

Ruder, Emil. *Typography: A Manual of Design.* New York: Hastings House, 1981.

Ruegg, Ruedi. *Basic Typography: Design with Letters.* New York: Van Nostrand Reinhold, 1989.

Ryan, David. *Letter Perfect: The Art of Modernist Typography, 1896–1953.* Petaluma, CA: Pomegranate, 2001.

Schmid, Helmut. *The Road to Basel: Typographic Reflections.* Tokyo: Robundo Publishing, Inc., 1997.

Schmid, Helmut. *Typography Today.* Tokyo: Seibundo Shinkosha, 1980.

Stankowski, Anton. *Anton Stankowski: Art and Design, Photography.* Stuttgart: Institut für Auslandsbeziehungen, 1991.

———. *Bildpläne.* Stuttgart: Edition Cantz, 1979.

———. *Buchhandelsausg.* Stuttgart: Hatje, 1991.

———. *Visual Presentation of Invisible Processes.* Teufen, Switzerland: Verlag Arthur Niggli, 1966.

———. *Works of Anton Stankowski: Exhibition, Sponsored by the Composing Room, Inc.* New York: The Gallery, 1964.

Winkler, Dietmar, ed. *Jacqueline S. Casey, 30 Years of Design at MIT.* Cambridge, MA: MIT Museum, 1992.

Wichmann, Hans, ed. *Armin Hofmann: His Work, Quest and Philosophy.* Springer-Verlag, 1990.

Wirth, Günther. *Formfinden: Anton Stankowski.* Stuttgart: G. Hatje, 1991.

Zapf, Hermann. *Calligraphic Salutations: Hermann Zapf's Letterheadings to Paul Standard.* Rochester, NY: Rochester Institute of Technology, 1993.

———. *Hermann Zapf: Ein Arbeitsbericht.* Hamburg, Germany: Maxmillian-Gesellschaft, 1984.

———. *Manual Typographicum.* Frankfurt: Z-Press, 1968.

———. *Manuale Typographicum.* Cambridge, MA: MIT Press, 1954.

———. *Typographic Variations: On Themes in Contemporary Book Design.* New Rochelle, NY: Myriade Press, 1978.

19. The New York School

Bass, Saul. *Saul Bass.* Tokyo: Ginza Graphic Gallery, 1993.

Burns, Aaron. *Typography.* New York: Reinhold, 1961.

Carter, Rob. *American Typography Today.* New York: Van Nostrand Reinhold, 1989.

Chermayeff, Ivan. *Ivan Chermayeff.* Tokyo: Ginza Graphic Gallery, 1994.

Dobrow, Larry. *Ivan Chermayeff: Collages, 1982–1995.* Washington, DC: Corcoran Museum of Art, 1995.

———. *When Advertising Tried Harder.* New York: Friendly Press, 1984.

Draper, Robert. *Rolling Stone Magazine: The Uncensored History.* New York: Doubleday, 1990.

Heller, Steven. *Paul Rand.* London: Phaidon Press Limited, 1999.

Higgins, Denis. *The Art of Writing Advertising: Conversations with William Bernbach . . .* Lincolnwood, IL: NTC Business Books, 1990.

Hurlburt, Allen. *Layout: The Design of the Printed Page.* New York: Watson-Guptill, 1977.

Kamakura, Yusaku, ed. *Paul Rand: His Work from 1946–1958.* New York: Knopf, 1959.

Lee, Marshall, ed. *Books for Our Time.* New York: Oxford, 1951.

Levenson, Bob. *Bill Bernbach's Book: A History of the Advertising that Changed the History of Advertising.* New York: Villard Books, 1987.

Lois, George. *$ellebrity: My Angling and Tangling with Famous People.* London: Phaidon Press Limited, 2003.

Lois, George, and Pitts, Bill. *The Art of Advertising: George Lois on Mass Communications.* New York: Abrams, 1977.

McLuhan, Marshall. *Culture is our Business.* New York: McGraw-Hill, 1970.

———. *From Cliche to Archetype.* New York: Viking Press, 1970.

———. *The Mechanical Bride.* New York: Vanguard, 1951.

———. *Understanding Media: The Extensions of Man.* New York: McGraw-Hill, 1964.

———. *Verbo-Voco-Visual Explorations.* New York: Something Else Press, 1967.

McLuhan, Marshall and Fiore, Quentin. *The Medium is the Massage.* New York: Bantam, 1967.

Nunoo-Quarcoo, Franc. *Paul Rand: Modernist Design.* Baltimore: Center for Art and Visual Culture, University of Maryland, 2003.

Rand, Paul. *Design Form and Chaos.* New Haven: Yale University Press, 1993.

———. *From Lascaux to Brooklyn.* New Haven: Yale University Press, 1996.

———. *Paul Rand: A Designer's Art.* New Haven: Yale University Press, 1985.

———. *Thoughts on Design.* New York: Van Nostrand Reinhold, 1970.

Rondthaler, Edward. *Life with Letters—As They Turned Photogenic.* New York: Hastings House, 1981.

Snyder, Gertrude, and Peckolick, Alan. *Herb Lubalin: Art Director, Graphic Designer, and Typographer.* New York: American Showcase, 1985.

Thompson, Bradbury. *The Art of Graphic Design.* New Haven: Yale University Press, 1988.

Wolf, Henry. *Visual Thinking: Methods for Making Images Memorable.* New York: Rizzoli, 1988.

Woods, Gerald, Thompson, Philip, and Williams, John. *Art Without Boundaries.* London: Thames and Hudson, 1972.

20. Corporate Identity and Visual Systems

Aicher, Otl. *World as Design.* Berlin: Ernst + Sohn, 1994.

Bass, Saul, et al. *Saul Bass and Associates.* Tokyo: Seibundo Shinkosha, 1978.

Celant, Germano, et al. *Design—Vignelli.* New York: Rizzoli, 1990.

Consuegra, David, ed. *ABC of World Trademarks.* Bogotá: Primera Editions, 1988.

Golden, Cipe Pineles, Weihs, Kurt, and Strunsky, Robert, eds. *The Visual Craft of William Golden.* New York: Braziller, 1962.

Helms, Janet Conradi. *A Historical Survey of Unimark International and Its Effect on Graphic Design in the United States*. Ames, IA: Iowa State University, 1988.

Herdeg, Walter. *Film & TV Graphics*. Zurich: Graphis Press, 1967.

———. *Film & TV Graphics 2*. Zurich: Graphis Press, 1976.

Hess, Dick, and Muller, Marion. *Dorfsman and CBS*. New York: American Showcase, 1987.

Igarashi, Takenobu, ed. *World Trademarks and Logotypes II*. Tokyo: Graphic-sha, 1987.

Iinkai, Kokomasu. *Corporate Design Systems: Identity through Design*. New York: PBC International, 1985.

Napoles, Veronica. *Corporate Identity Design*. New York: Van Nostrand Reinhold, 1988.

Rosen, Ben. *The Corporate Search for Visual Identification*. New York: Van Nostrand Reinhold, 1970.

Rotzler, Willy. *Constructive Concepts*. New York: Rizzoli, 1977.

Schmittel, Wolfgang. *Corporate Design International*. Zurich: ABC Editions, 1984.

Shapira, Nathan H., et al. *Design Process: Olivetti, 1908–1978*. Milan, Italy: Olivetti, 1979.

Vignelli, Massimo and Lella. *Design: Vignelli*. New York: Rizzoli, 1981.

Yew, Wei. *The Olympic Image: The First Hundred Years*. Edmonton, Alberta: Quon Editions, 1996.

21. The Conceptual Image

Alcorn, John, et al. *The Push Pin Style*. Palo Alto, CA: Communication Arts, 1970.

Centre National d'Art et de Culture Georges Pompidou. *Culture et révolution: L'affiche cubaine contemporaine: Exposition*. Paris: Pompidou Center, 1977.

Cieslewicz, Roman. *Posters: Collages*. Heidelberg, Germany: Braus, 1984.

Chwast, Seymour. *The Left-Handed Designer*. New York: Abrams, 1985.

Czestochowski, Joseph S. *Contemporary Polish Posters*. New York: Dover, 1979.

Davis, Paul. *Faces*. New York: Friendly Press, 1985.

———. *Paul Davis Posters and Paintings*. New York: Dutton, 1977.

Glaser, Milton. *Milton Glaser*. Tokyo: Ginza Graphic Gallery, 1995.

———. *Milton Glaser: Graphic Design*. Woodstock, NY: Overlook Press, 1972.

———. *The Milton Glaser Poster Book*. New York: Harmony Books, 1977.

Goines, David Lance. *David Lance Goines: Posters 1970–1994*. Berkeley: Ten Speed Press, 1994.

Heller, Steven. *Innovators of American Illustration*. New York: Van Nostrand Reinhold, 1986.

Herring, Jerry, et al. *Design in Texas*. Houston: Graphic Design Press, 1986.

Hornig, Norbert. *Leipziger Plakatkunst*. Leipzig: VEB E. A. Seeman, 1985.

Jacobs, Karrie, and Heller, Steven. *Angry Graphics: Protest Posters of the Reagan/Bush Era*. New York: Peregrine Smith, 1992.

Kieser, Gunther. *Kieser, Plakate: Exchange*. Mainz, Germany: H. Schmidt, 1995.

———. *Das zweite Gesicht: Plakate von Günther Kieser*. Mainz, Germany: H. Schmidt, 1989.

Kowalski, Tadeusz. *The Polish Film Poster*. Warsaw: Filmowa Agencja Wydawnicza, 1957.

Martin, Susan, ed. *Decade of Protest: Political Posters from the United States, Viet Nam, Cuba 1965–1975*. Santa Monica, CA: Smart Art Press, 1996.

Massin, Robert. *Letter and Image*. New York: Van Nostrand Reinhold, 1970.

McMullan, James. *Revealing Illustrations*. New York: Watson-Guptill, 1981.

Pierce, Donald L., Jr. *100 Texas Posters*. Houston: Graphic Design Press, 1985.

Rambow, Gunther. *Plakate von Gunther Rambow im Museum Wiesbaden*. Wiesbaden, Germany: Museum Wiesbaden, 1988.

Rouard-Snowman, Margo. *Roman Cieslewicz*. London: Thames and Hudson, 1993.

Stermer, Dugald. *The Art of Revolution, Castro's Cuba: 1959–1970*. New York: McGraw-Hill, 1970.

Testa, Armando. *Armando Testa: 40 Years of Italian Creative Design*. Turin, Italy: Allemandi, 1987.

Tomaszewski, Henryk. *Henryk Tomaszewski*. Tokyo: Ginza Graphic Gallery, 1992.

Wesselius, Jacqueline. *Grapus 85*. Utrecht, Netherlands: Reflex Verlag, 1985.

Wieczorek, Stanislaw. *Henryk Tomaszewski*. Warsaw: Akademia Sztuk Pieknych, 1993.

22. National Visions within a Global Dialogue

Broos, Kees. *Design, Total Design*. Utrecht, Netherlands: Reflex Verlag, 1983.

Bruinsma, Max. *Beeld Tegen Bleed: Wild Plakken*. Utrecht, Netherlands: Centraal Museum Utrecht, 1993.

Fukuda, Shigeo. *Posters of Shigeo Fukuda*. Tokyo: Misumura Tosho Shuppan, 1982.

———. *Visual Illusion*. Tokyo: Rikuyosha, 1982.

Gaetan-Picon, Genevieve, et al. *L'affiche japonaise*. Paris: Musée de l'Affiche, 1979.

Gerken, Hanna. *Studio Dumbar*. Mainz, Germany: Verlag Hermann Schmidt, 1993.

Gibbs, David, ed. *Pentagram: The Compendium; Thoughts, Essays and Work from the Pentagram Partners in London, New York and San Francisco*. London: Phaidon, 1993.

Gorb, Peter, ed. *Living by Design: Pentagram*. London: Lund Humphries, 1978.

Hefting, Paul, and Van Ginkel, Dirk. *Hard Werken Inízio: From Cultural Oasis to Multimedia*. Rotterdam, 1995.

Igarashi, Takenobu. *Igarashi Alphabets*. Zurich: ABC Editions, 1987.

———. *Rock, Scissors, Paper: Design, Influence, Concept, Image*. Tokyo: Graphic-sha, 1991.

———. *Seven Graphic Designers*. Tokyo: Graphic-sha Publishing Company, 1985.

———. *Space Graphics*. Tokyo: Shoten Kenchiku-sha, 1983.

Kamekura, Yusaku, et al. *The Works of Yusaku Kamekura*. Tokyo: Rikuyo-sha, 1983.

Lupton, Ellen, ed. *Graphic Design and Typography in the Netherlands: A View of Recent Work*. New York: Cooper Union and Princeton Architectural Press, 1992.

Myerson, Jeremy. *Beware Wet Paint: Designs by Alan Fletcher.* London: Phaidon, 1996.

Nagai, Kazumasa. *The Works of Kazumasa Nagai.* Tokyo: Kodansha, 1985.

Shibata, Kaori, and Hachiga, Toru, eds. *New Typo Graphics.* Tokyo: P-I-E Books, 1993.

Sparke, Penny. *Modern Japanese Design.* New York: Dutton, 1987.

Staal, Gert, and Wolters, Hester. *Holland in Vorm: Dutch Design 1945–1987.* The Hague: Stichting Holland in Vorm, 1987.

Tadashi, Masuda. *Works of the Masuda Tadashi Design Institute.* Tokyo: Seibundo Shinkosha, 1966.

Tanaka, Ikko. *Ikko Tanaka.* Tokyo: Ginza Graphic Gallery, 1993.

———. *Posters of Ikko Tanaka.* Tokyo: 1981.

———. *The Work of Ikko Tanaka.* Tokyo: 1975.

Tanikawa, Koichi. *100 Posters of Tadenori Yokoo.* Tokyo: Kodansha, 1978.

Thornton, Richard S. *The Graphic Spirit of Japan.* New York: Van Nostrand Reinhold, 1991.

Waldmann, Geneviéve. *The Activities of Pieter Brattinga.* Tokyo: Kodansha, 1989.

Yelavich, Susan, ed. *Profile: Pentagram Design.* London: Phaidon Press Limited, 2004.

Yokoo, Tadanori. *The Complete Tadanori Yokoo.* Tokyo: Kodansha, 1991.

———. *Tadanori Yokoo.* Woodbury, NY: Barron's, 1977.

23. Postmodern Design

Aldersey-Williams, Hugh. *New American Design.* New York: Rizzoli, 1988.

Bertens, Hans. *The Idea of the Postmodern.* London: Routledge, 1995.

Branzi, Andrea. *The Hot House: Italian New Wave Design.* Cambridge, MA: MIT Press, 1984.

Brody, Neville. *The Graphic Language of Neville Brody.* New York: Rizzoli, 1988.

Elam, Kimberly. *Expressive Typography.* New York: Van Nostrand Reinhold, 1990.

Friedman, Dan. *Dan Friedman: Radical Modernism.* New Haven: Yale University Press, 1994.

Hiebert, Kenneth J. *Graphic Design Processes: Universal to Unique.* New York: Van Nostrand Reinhold, 1992.

Horn, Richard. *Memphis.* Philadelphia: Running Press, 1985.

Levin, Kim. *Beyond Modernism.* New York: Harper and Row, 1988.

Lupton, Elaine. *Mixing Message: Graphic Design in Contemporary Culture.* New York: Princeton Architectural Press, 1997.

Lupton, Elaine, and Miller, J. Abbott. *Design Writing Research.* New York: Princeton Architectural Press, 1996.

Poynor, Rick. *No More Rules: Graphic Design and Postmodernism.* London: Laurence King Publishing, 2003.

Radice, Barbara. *Memphis: Research, Experiences, Results, Failures, and Successes of the New Design.* New York: Rizzoli, 1984.

Sottsass, Ettore, et al. *Sottsass Associati.* New York: Rizzoli, 1988.

Sparke, Penny. *As Long as It's Pink: The Sexual Politics of Taste.* London and San Francisco: Pandora, 1995.

———. *Italian Design: 1870 to the Present.* London: Thames and Hudson, 1988.

Stone, Allucquére Rosanne. *The War of Desire and Technology at the Close of the Mechanical Age.* Cambridge, MA: MIT Press, 1995.

Thackara, John, ed. *Design After Modernism.* London: Thames and Hudson, 1988.

Venturi, Robert, Brown, Denise Scott, and Izenour, Steven. *Learning from Las Vegas: The Forgotten Symbolism of Architectural Form.* Cambridge, MA: MIT Press, 1977.

Weingart, Wolfgang. *Weingart: Typography: My Way to Typography.* Switzerland: Lars Muller Publishers, 2000.

Wozencroft, John. *The Graphic Language of Neville Brody.* New York: Rizzoli, 1988.

———. *The Graphic Language of Neville Brody 2.* New York: Rizzoli, 1994.

24. The Digital Revolution and Beyond

Adobe Systems Incorporated. *Adobe Type 1 Font Format.* Mountain View, CA: Adobe Systems, 1990.

Aldersey-Williams, Hugh, et al. *Cranbrook Design: The New Discourse.* New York: Rizzoli, 1990.

Apeloig, Philippe. *Inside the Word.* Baden, Switzerland: Lars Muller Publishers.

Beeke, Anthon. *Dutch Posters 1960–1996: A Selection by Anthon Beeke.* Amsterdam: BIS Publishers, 1997.

Bierut, Michael, Drenttel, William, Heller, Steven, and Holland, D. K, eds. *Looking Closer 2: Critical Writings on Graphic Design.* New York: Allworth Press, 1997.

Blackwell, Lewis, and Carson, David. *The End of Print: The Graphic Design of David Carson.* San Francisco: Chronicle Books, 1995.

Bos, Ben, and van Lier, Frans. *De Appels van Jan Bons: Affices voor Toneelgroep de Appel.* Hoorn, Netherlands: Affichemuseum, 2004.

Codrington, Andrea. *Kyle Cooper.* London: Laurence King Publishing, 2003.

Escher, Gielijn. *Affiches Posters Plakate.* Amsterdam: Stichting Prent & Publiciteit-Nederlands Reclamearchief, 1996.

Fiel, Charlotte and Peter. *Graphic Design for the 21st Century: 100 of the World's Best Graphic Designers.* Cologne: Taschen, 2003.

Gibbs, David, ed. *The Compendium: Pentagram.* London: Phaidon Press Limited, 1993.

Greiman, April. *Hybrid Imagery: The Fusion of Technology and Graphic Design.* New York: Watson-Guptill, 1990.

Hall, Peter. *Sagmeister: Made You Look.* London: Booth-Clibborn Editions, 2001.

Heller, Steven, and Ilic, Mirko. *Genius Moves: 100 Icons of Graphic Design.* Cincinnati: North Light Books, 2001.

van Hinte, Ed, Schwartz, Ineke; and Stall, Gert. *Thonik.* Amsterdam, Netherlands: BIS Publishers, 2001.

Hoffland, H. J. A., et al. *Grafische Verleiders: Affiches Van PTT 1920–Heden.* Zwolle, Netherlands: Uitgeverij Waanders b.v., 1998.

Kath, Gitte. *40 Plakater.* Kolding, Denmark: Jørn Thomsen Offset, 2000.

Licko, Zuzana, Vanderlans, Rudy; and Gray, Mary E. *Emigre: Graphic Design in the Digital Realm.* New York: Van Nostrand Reinhold, 1993.

Matsunaga, Shin. *Shin Matsunaga: Design World.* Japan: Sezon Museum of Art, 1997.

McLuhan, Eric. Introduction to *Trek: David Carson—Recent Works.* Essays by Drew Kampion and Jamie Brisick. Corte Madera, CA: Gingko Press, 2003.

Meggs, Philip B., and Carson, David. *Fotografiks.* London: Laurence King Publishing, 1999.

Miller, J. Abbott. *Dimensional Typography: Word in Space.* New York: Princeton Architectural Press, 1997.

Mok, Clement. *Designing Business: Multiple Media, Multiple Disciplines.* San Jose, CA: Adobe Press, 1996.

———, ed. *Graphis New Media.* New York: Graphis, 1996.

Poyner, Rick, and Booth-Clibborn, Edward. *Typography Now: The Next Wave.* London: Internos Books, 1991.

Poyner, Rick. *The Graphic Edge.* London: Booth-Clibborn Editions, 1993.

Smeijers, Fred. *Counterpunch: Making Type in the 16th Century, Designing Typefaces Now.* London: Hyphen Press, 1996.

Staal, Gert, and Staal and De Rijk Editors, eds. *Dietwee/New Dutch Graphic Design.* Amsterdam: BIS Publishers, 2002.

Stone, Sumner. *On Stone: The Art and Use of Typography on the Personal Computer.* San Francisco: Bedford Arts, 1991.

Trulove, James, ed. *New Design: Berlin: The Edge of Graphic Design.* Gloucester, MA: Rockport Publishers, Inc., 2000.

Vienne, Véronique. *Chip Kidd.* London: Laurence King Publishing, 2003.

Wallis, Lawrence W. *The Modern Encyclopedia of Typefaces: 1960–90.* New York: Van Nostrand Reinhold, 1990.

White, Jan V. *Graphic Design for the Electronic Age.* New York: Watson-Guptill, 1988.

Wurman, Richard Saul. *Information Anxiety.* New York: Doubleday, 1989.

———, et al. *Information Architects.* Ed. Peter Bradford. Zurich: Graphis, 1996.

Zapf, Hermann, and Dreyfus, John. *Classical Typography in the Computer Age.* Los Angeles: University of California Press, 1991.

General Surveys

Barnicoat, John. *A Concise History of the Poster.* London: Thames and Hudson, 1972.

Berry, W. Turner, Johnson, A. F., and Jaspert, W. P. *the Encyclopaedia of Type Faces.* London: Blandford, 1958.

Bettley, James, ed. *The Art of the Book: From Medieval Manuscript to Graphic Novel.* London: V & A Publications, 2001.

Blackwell, Lewis. *20th Century Type.* New York: Rizzoli, 1992.

Booth-Clibborn, Edward, and Baroni, Daniele. *The Language of Graphics.* New York: Abrams, 1980.

Burke, Christopher. *Paul Renner: The Art of Typography.* London: Hyphen Press, 1998.

Gallo, Max. *The Poster in History.* New York: American Heritage, 1974.

Garner, Anne, ed. *The 1325 Greatest Moments in the History of Graphic Design (so far).* Montana State University, 1987.

Glaister, Geoffrey Ashall. *Encyclopedia of the Book.* New Castle, DE: Oak Knoll, 1996.

Gottshall, Edward M. *Typographic Communications Today.* Cambridge, MA: MIT Press, 1989.

Gress, Edmund G. *The Art and Practice of Typography.* New York: Oswald, 1917.

Heller, Steven, and Chwast, Seymour. *Graphic Style from Victorian to Post-Modern.* New York: Abrams, 1988.

Heller, Steven. *Merz to Émigré and Beyond: Avant-Garde Magazine Design of the Twentieth Century.* London: Phaidon Press Limited, 2003.

Heller, Steven, and Meggs, Philip B., eds. *Texts on Type: Critical Writings on Typography.* New York: Allworth Press, 2001.

Hellier, Bevis. *Posters.* New York: Stein and Day, 1969.

Hollis, Richard. *Graphic Design: A Concise History.* New York: Thames and Hudson, 1994.

Kepes, Gyorgy. *Language of Vision.* Chicago: Paul Theobald and Co., 1944.

Lewis, John. *Anatomy of Printing.* London: Faber and Faber, 1970.

Livingston, Alan and Isabella. *The Thames & Hudson Dictionary of Graphic Design and Designers.* London: Thames & Hudson Ltd., 2003.

Malhotra, Ruth, et al. *Das frühe Plakat in Europa un den USA.* Vols. I–III. Berlin: Gebr. Mann Verlag, 1973.

Meggs, Philip B. Foreword to *Six Chapters in Design.* Texts by Louis Dorfsman, Martin Scorsese, Henry Wolf, Milton Glaser, Tadanori Yokoo, Yusaku Kamekura, Takahashi Mutsuo, and Shoji Katagishi. San Francisco: Chronicle Books, 1997.

Miller, R. Craig. Introduction to *U.S. Design: 1975–2000.* Munich, London, and New York: Prestel-Verlag, 2001.

Moran, James, ed. *Printing in the 20th Century.* New York: Hastings House, 1974.

Müller-Brockmann, Josef. *A History of Visual Communications.* New York: Hastings House, 1967.

———, and Müller-Brockmann, Shizuka. *History of the Poster.* Zurich: ABC Editions, 1971.

Olmert, Michael. *The Smithsonian Book of Books.* Washington, DC: The Smithsonian Institution, 1992.

Pitz, Henry C. *Two Hundred Years of American Illustration.* New York: Random House, 1977.

Polano, Sergio. *ABC of 20th-Century Graphics.* Milan: Electra, 2002.

Poynor, Rick. *Typographica.* London: Laurence King Publishing, 2001.

Purvis, Alston W., and Le Coultre, Martijn F. *Graphic Design 20th Century.* New York: Princeton Architectural Press, 2003.

Schippers, Inleiding K. *Marten Jongema.* Amsterdam: SSP, 1994.

Sparke, Penny. *Design Source Book.* Secaucus, NJ: Chartwell, 1986.

———. *An Introduction to Design and Culture in the Twentieth Century.* London and Boston: Allen & Unwin, 1986.

Updike, Daniel Berkeley. *Printing Types: Their History, Forms, and Use.* Cambridge, MA: Harvard University Press, 1937.

Wrede, Stuart. *The Modern Poster.* New York: Museum of Modern Art, 1988.

Weill, Alain. *Graphic Design: A History.* New York: Harry N. Abrams, Incorporated, 2004.

Weill, Alain. *The Poster: A Worldwide Survey and History.* Boston: G. K. Hall & Co., 1985.

Major periodicals

Arts et métiers graphiques. Nos. 1–68. Paris: Arts et métiers graphiques, 1927–1939.

Ars Typographica. Vols. 1–3. Douglas C. McMurtrie, ed. New York: Douglas C. McMurtrie, 1981–1931.

Bauhaus Journal. Nos. 1–15. Dessau, Germany: 1926–1931.

The Century Guild Hobby Horse. Arthur H. Mackmurdo, ed. London: 1884–1888.

Communication Arts. Vol. 1 No. 1, 1959–Vol. 39 No. 3, 1997.

De Stijl. Vols. I–VIII. Theo van Doesburg, ed. 1917–1931. Reprint, Amsterdam: Athenaeum, 1968.

Design Issues. Vol. 1 No. 1, 1984–Vol. 13 No. 2, 1997.

The Dolphin. Vols. I–IV. New York: Limited Editions Club, 1933–1941.

The Fleuron: A Journal of Typography. Nos. 1–7. Stanley Morison, ed. London: The University Press (Cambridge), 1923–1930. Reprint, Westport, CT: Greenwood, 1970.

Graphis. Vol. 1 No. 1, 1944–Vol. 53 No. 303, 1996.

Journal of the Ulm School of Design. Nos. 1–21. Ulm, Germany: 1958–1968.

Jugend. Munich: 1896–1910.

Neue Grafik (New Graphic Design). Richard P. Louse, Josef Müller-Brockmann, Hans Neuberg, and Carlo L. Vivarelli, eds. Nos. 1–16. Zurich: 1959–1963.

Novum Gebrauchgraphik (formerly *Gebrauchgraphik*). Vol. 1 No. 1, 1925–Vol. 68 No. 2, 1998.

Print. Vol. 1 No. 1, 1940–Vol. 52 No. 2, 1998.

The Studio. London: 1893–1900.

Van Nu en Straks. Brussels and Antwerp: 1892–1901.

Ver Sacrum, Organ der Vereinigung Bildender Küenstler Österreichs. Vols. 1–16. Vienna: 1898–1903.

Visible Language (formerly *The Journal of Typographic Research*). Vol. 1 No. 1, 1967–Vol. 31 No. 1, 1997.

Picture Credits

Abedini, Reza: 24-71, 24-72.
Adigard, Erik/MAD, WIRED magazine, January, 1993. Erik Adigard/MAD and John Plunkett (designers), John Plunkett, Barbara Kuhr (art directors): 24-80.
Adobe Systems, Inc: Carol Twombly: 24-23, 24-25; Robert Slimbach: 24-24.
AEG Firmen-archiv, Frankfurt/M., Germany: 12-41, 12-43.
Agora Excavations, American School of Classical Studies, Athens: 2-13, 2-14.
Alma Law Archive, Scarsdale, NY: 15-26, 15-27.
Anderson, Charles S.: 23-46, 23-50, 23-51, 24-45.
Apeloig, Phillpe: 24-69.
Apple Computer, Inc.: 24-1; 24-2 © 1983, Used with permission, All rights reserved.
Armando Testa S.p.A.: 21-1, 21-2.
Artists Rights Society (ARS), New York ©2006:
ARS/ADAGP, Paris: 13-5, 13-6, 13-7, 13-42, 13-47, 14-50, 14-51, 17-24; ARS/

ADAGP, Paris/ Succession Marcel Duchamp: 13-25; ARS/ Beeldrecht, Amsterdam: 15-44, 15-45, 14-56, 15-57, 16-43, 22-34; ARS/ DACS, London: 17-9; ARS/ ProLitteris, Zurich: 18-4, 18-5; ARS/ SABAM, Brussels: 11-58; ARS/ SIAE, Rome: 11-76, 13-8, 13-9, 13-11, 13-12, 13-17, 13-20, 13-21, 13-41; ARS/ VG Bild-Kunst, Bonn: 11-67, 11-69, 12-10, 12-32, 12-33, 12-34, 12-37, 12-38, 12-39, 12-42, 12-43, 12-44, 12-45, 12-46, 12-48, 12-49, 13-26, 13-27, 13-28, 13-29, 13-30, 13-31, 13-32, 13-33, 13-34, 13-36, 13-37, 13-38, 13-39, 13-46, 13-48, 14-6, 14-7, 14-12, 14-20, 14-21, 14-31, 14-32, 14-33, 14-34, 14-35, 14-36, 15-8, 15-9, 15-10, 15-11, 15-12, 15-13, 15-14, 15-15, 15-16, 15-18, 15-21, 15-22, 15-23, 15-24, 15-51, 15-53, 15-60, 16-4, 16-22, 17-29, 21-9.
Asaba, Katsumi: 24-75.
Asia Society, New York: 3-5, From the collection of Dr. Paul Singer.

Athenaeum-Polak & Van Gennep, Amsterdam: 15-47, 15-52, 15-53.
Aufuldish, Bob: 24-43, 24-44.
Baer, Roger (photographer): 16-12.
Bass, Saul: 19-19, 19-21, 19-22, 20-28.
Bauhaus Archiv: 8-18, 8-19.
Baumberger, Otto: 14-18.
Bayer, Estate of Herbert: 16-5, 16-14, 16-15, 16-18, 16-19, 16-20, 16-21, 17-30, 17-31, 17-35, 17-36, 17-51.
Bayerisches National Museum: 9-22.
Beall, Estate of Lester: 17-6, 17-7, 17-8, 17-28, 20-22, 20-23.
Beeke, Anthon: 22-38.
Beltran, Felix: 24-111.
Biblioteca Apostolica Vaticana (Vatican): 2-20, 4-1, 4-3.
Biblioteca Nacional, Madrid: 4-12, 4-13, 4-14.
Biblitheque Nationale de France: 4-2, 8-1, 8-2, 9-35.
Bierut, Michael: 24-106.
Bildarchiv Preussischer Kulturbesitz/ Art Resource, NY: 1-24, 2-10.
Binder, Estate of Joseph: 14-55, 17-18, 17-26.
Birmingham Public Library, Birmingham, England; Reference Library, Local Studies Dept.: 8-11.
Blumenfeld, Erwin/*Vogue* **©1945 Conde Nast Productions, Inc.**: 17-16.
Bodeleian Library, Univeristy of Oxford: 4-15, 4-16.
Brade, Helmut: 24-46.
British Library: 3-13, 4-6, 15-4, by permission.
British Museum: 1-8, 1-16, 1-17, 1-25, 1-26, 2-3, 4-10.
Brody, Neville: 23-52, 23-53, 23-54.
C. Harscovici, Brussels/ Artists Rights Society (ARS), New York ©2006: 13-43.
Carson, David: 24-12, 24-13, 24-14.
Carter, Matthew: 24-27.

CBS: 20-4, 20-5, 20-8, 20-9, 20-10.
CBS Records: 19-14, 21-39, 21-40, 21-32.
Cher, Paula: 24-96, 24-97.
Chermayeff & Geismar Associates: 19-25, 19-27, 20-25, 20-26.
Chermayeff, Ivan/Chermayeff & Geismar: 19-26.
Chwast, Seymour: 21-24, 21-25, 21-26, 21-27.
Cieslewicz, Roman: 21-7, 21-13, 21-14.
Commune di Como, Como, Italy: 13-18.
Cook and Shanosky Associates, Inc: 20-42, 20-43.
Cooper, Kyle, Prologue Films: 24-78, 24-79, with permission of Cloumbia Tristar Motion Picture Group.
Cooper Union, Herb Lubalin Study Center, New York, NY: 19-56, 19-57, 19-58, 19-59, 19-60, 19-61, 19-62, 19-63, 19-64, 19-65, 19-66, 19-67, 19-68.
Cronan, Michael: 23-37.
Crouwel, Wim: 22-32.
D. Stempel AG, Frankfurt/M., Germany: 10-36.
Dali, Salvador, Gala-Salvador Dali Foundation/ Artists Rights Society (ARS), New York ©2006: 13-44.
Davis, Paul: 21-31.
de Harak, Rudolph: 18-40, 18-41, 18-42.
Doyle Dane Bernbach, New York: 19-47, 19-48, 19-49, 19-50, 19-52.
Duffy Design Group: 23-47, 23-48, 23-49.
Egyptian Museum: 1-15.
Eisenman, Alvin: 19-28, 19-29.
Émigré Graphics: 24-6, 24-7, 24-8, 24-26.
Escher, Ghislain (Gielijn) Daphnis: 22-40, 22-41, 22-42.
Ex Libris, New York: 15-31, 19-8, 19-9, 19-10, 19-11, 19-12.
Federico, Gene: 19-53.
Fella, Edward: 24-10, 24-11.

16-38, 16-40, 16-46, 16-57, 16-58, 17-3, 17-4, 17-9, 17-10, 17-11, 17-12, 17-23, 17-27, 17-38, 17-39, 18-6, 18-25, 19-45, 21-3, 21-5, 21-9, 21-52, 21-65, 21-66, 21-67, 22-6.

Metropolitan Museum of Art, New York: 1-7, Purchase, by exchange, 1911 (11.217.29); 7-45, Elisha Whittelsey Collection, The Elisha Whittelsey Fund, 1949 (49.70.64); 2-16, Fletcher Fund, 1924 (24.97.21a,b); 3-17, gift of Paul Pelliot, 1924 (24.114.1-.4); 9-23, Harris Brisbane Dick Fund, 1936 (36.37); 7-44, Rogers Fund, 1922 (22.67.15); 7-39, Rogers Fund, 1918 (18.32.1). Photographs, all rights reserved, The Metropolitan Museum of Art.

Meyer, Rudi and Theatre du Chatelet: 24-61, 24-62.

MIT Press: 20-29, 20-30.

Moguzzi, Bruno: 23-9.

Moholy-Nagy, Estate of Laszloz: 16-7, 16-8, 16-9, 16-10, 16-11, 16-17.

Mok, Clement: 24-42, 24-43.

Moscoso, Victor: 21-45, 21-46.

Montalvo, German: 24-114.

Mosley, James, photographer: 2-17, 2-18, 2-21.

Ms. Magazine: 19-44.

Mucha Trust/ ADAGP, Paris/ ARS, New York ©2006: 11-32, 11-33, 11-34, 11-35.

Muller-Brockmann, Josef: 18-26, 18-28, 18-29, 18-30, 18-32, 18-34, 18-35.

Musee Carnavalet, Paris: 9-53.

Musee de la Publicite, Paris: 11-8.

Musee de la Publicite, Paris: 11-9.

Musee des Antiquites Nationales, St. Germain-en-Laye, France: 1-4.

Museum of Decortative Arts, Prague: 17-47, 17-48, 17-49, 17-50.

Museum of Fine Arts, Boston: 1-12, Acc. 98.706, Hematite handle on cylinder of intaglio gem, H: 0.053 x 0.022m, Henry Lillie Pierce Fund; 1-13, 1-14, Acc. 12.978, 0.034 x 0.031m, Gift of Mr. and Mrs. Donald P. Edgar; 1-18, Acc. 13.3532; 1-20, Acc. 24.593 H: 1.19 x .79m, purchased from Services des Antiquités of Egypt; 1-21, Acc. 23.729, Coffin and lid of King Aspalta with lower parts of a hawl and jackal on top of lid (upper parts missing), Granite, H: 1.58m, W: 0.44m, L: 3.05m, Harvard-MFA Expedition; 1-22, Acc. 72.4295, .216 x .05m, Hay Collection, Gift of C. Granville Way; 1-23, Acc. 60.1472, Linen, 1.110 x 0.635m, Gift of Horace L. Mayer; 1-27, 1-28, Acc. 1973.108, Glazed Stealite, 6 x 4.4 x 3.2 cm, Helen and Alice Colburn Fund; 2-9, Acc. 35.61, Bronze, 0.16m, William Amory Gardiner Fund; 2-11, Acc. 94.14, Relief Marble, 0.72 x 0.43 x 0.06m, Gift of Mrs. Charles Amos Cummings; 2-12, Acc. 72.4358, Wood, 0.216 x 0.06m, Hay Collection, Gift of C. Granville Way; 2-15a, Acc. 27. 690, "Dolphin", Chalcedony mottle with Jasper, L: 0.024m; 2-15b, Acc. 21.1206, "Heron", Chalcedany, scaraboid intaglio, L: 0.02m; 2-15c, Acc. 27.689; 2-15d, Acc. 27.698, "Race Horse", L: 0.02m; 2-15a-d, Francis Bartlett Fund; 3-6, Acc. 1975.1, Ink on paper, Keith McLead Fund; 3-7, Acc. 55.387, Handscroll ink on paper, 0.280 x 2.789m, Keith McLeod Fund; 3-10, Acc. 10.275, Limestone, 42.1 x 24.9cm, Otis Norcross Fund; 3-11, Acc. 12.588, Dark grey limestone, 46.8 x 113.3 cm, Gift of Denman Waldo Ross and G.M. Lane; 3-12, Acc. 17.1266, Wood with gesso, H: 22cm, Denman Waldo Ross Collection.

Nakajima, Hideki: 24-51.

National Gallery of Art: 6-16.

Nogami, Shuichi: 24-91.

Odermatt & Tissi: 18-36, 18-37, 18-38, 18-39,23-3, 23-4, 23-6.

Olden, Estate of Georg: 20-6, 20-7.

Oliver, Vaughan: 24-83.

Oxenaar, R.D.E.:22-36.

Palazzo, Peter: 19-41.

Pelavin, Daniel: 23-45.

Pentagram Design: 22-1, 22-2, 22-4; David Hillman: 24-87; Angus Hyland: 24-86; Paula Scher: 24-96, 24-97.

Philadelphia Museum of Art: 13-3, 13-5, 13-24, 13-47, 13-48.

Photofest: 14-56.

Picasso, Estate of Pablo/ Artists Rights Society (ARS), New York ©2006: 13-1, 13-3.

Pierpont Morgan Library, New York: 6-24, 6-27, PML 812; 7-18, 7-42.

Pineles, Estate of Cipe: 19-31, courtesy of Rochester Institute of Technology, Pineles Archive.

Pintori, Giovanni: 20-1, 20-2, 20-3.

Pioneer Moss Photoengraving, New York, NY: 9-28, 9-67.

Pirtle, Woody: 21-31, 21-41, 21-42.

Pluta, Wladyslaw: 24-103, 24-104.

Private Collection: 9-5, 21-12.

Purvis, Alston W.: 10-28, 10-29, 10-30, 10-31, 10-32, 10-33, 10-34, 13-29, 15-46, 15-57, 15-69, 15-70, 16-52, 16-54, 16-55, 16-60, 16-61, 17-2, 24-108.

PWS Publishing Co., Boston, MA: 24-33, 24-34, 24-35.

Rambow, Gunter: 21-55, 21-56, 21-57, 21-58; Rambow & Michael van de Sand: 21-53, 21-54.

Rand, Estate of Paul: 19-1, 19-2, 19-3, 19-4, 19-5, 19-6, 19-7, 20-14, 20-15, 20-16, 20-17, 20-18, 20-19, 20-20, 20-21 20-24, 21-34.

Reichert, Hans Dieter: 24-100, 24-101.

Reinhold Brown Gallery, New York: 14-42, 14-43, 14-45.

Remington, Roger: 17-40.

Réunion des Musées Nationax/ Art Resourse, NY: 1-5, 1-10, 1-11.

Rietberg Museum: 18-1.

RIT/ Cary Graphic Arts Collection: 10-42; RIT/Hearst Magazine: 17-14; RIT/Lester Bell Collection: 17-5.

Robert Miles Runyan & Associates: 20-56.

Rodriguez, Gabriela: 24-115, photography by Maria Lopez and Mario Jimenez.

Rolling Stone Magazine, Fred Woodward, Art Director: 24-15, 24-16, 24-17, 24-18.

Rotis Buros, Otl Aicher, Leutkirch, Germany: 20-31, 20-31, 20-33, 20-34, 20-50, 20-51, 20-52, 20-53, 20-54, 20-55.

Royal PTT Nederland NV (KPN): 22-30, 22-35, 22-46.

Ruffins, Reynold: 21-17.

Sagmeister, Stefan: 24-57, © 1996, Warner Brothers Music, Inc.

Saito, Makoto: 24-52, 24-53.

Saks, Arnold: 18-47.

Salisbury, Mike: 19-46.

Sang-Soo, Ahn: 24-105.

Sato, Koichi: 22-27, 22-28, 22-29.

Savignac, Raymond: 21-38.

Scher, Paula: 23-38, 23-55.

Schmid, Helmut: 24-107.

Schraivogel, Ralph: 24-93.

Science Museum London: 9-24, 9-25.

Skolos & Wedell: 24-98, 24-99.

Solomon, Barbara Stauffacher: 23-2.

Stadt Nurnberg: 6-10.

Stankowski, Anton: 18-9, 18-11, 18-12.

Stedelijk Museum, Amsterdam: 15-54; from the collection of Mrs. A. M. Daalder-Vos; 15-6.

Stermer, Dugald: 19-42.

Stiftsbibliothek, St. Gallen: 2-19.

Stone, Sumner: 24-3, 24-22.

Storch, Otto: 19-33, 19-34, 19-35, 19-36.

Studio Anton Beeke: 22-37.

Studio Dumbar: 22-43, 22-44.

Successió Miró/ Artists Rights Society (ARS), New York ©2006: 13-45.

Sugisaki, Shinnoske: 24-92.

Sussman/Prejza & Co.: 20-57, 20-58, 20-59, 20-60.

Sutnar, Ladislav: 15-66, by permission of the Ladislav Sutnar family.

Tadashi, Masuda & Mitsu Doki: 22-13.

Tanaka, Ikko: 22-15, 22-16.

Tartakover, David: 24-70.

The Board of Trinity College Dublin: 4-5, 4-7, 4-8, 4-9.

The Times of London: 9-16, 16-41.

The Upjohn Company: 17-20.

Toledo Museum of Art: 6-20, Museum Purchase, 1925.17; 7-37, Museum Purchase, 1957.24.

Tomaszenwski, Henryk: 21-4.

Total Design: 22-31.

Troxler, Niklaus: 24-63, 24-64.

Tscherny, George: 19-24.

Tschichold, Estate of Jan: 16-24, 16-25, 16-26, 16-27, 16-29, 16-30, 16-31, 16-32.

University of Chicago Press: 3-2. 3-3.

Van Abbemuseum, Eindhoven, The Netherlands: 15-12.

Vanderbyl, Michael: 23-31, 23-32, 23-34.

VU Magazine, by Alexander Liberman: 17-15.

Walker Art Center, Minneapolis, Matt Eller, Design Director: 24-28, 24-29.

Weingart, Wolfgang: 18-19, 23-10, 23-11, 23-12, 23-13, 23-14, 23-15, 23-16.

Werner Druck AG: 18-4.

Westvaco, New York: 19-15, 19-16, 19-17, 19-18.

Why Not Associates: 24-85.

Wild Plakken, Amsterdam: 22-48, 22-49, 22-50.

William Morris Gallery, London: 10-5.

Wired **Magazine**, Plunkett & Kuhr: 24-19, 24-20, 24-21.

Wissing, Benno: 22-33.

Wolf, Henry: 19-37, 19-38, 19-39, 19-40.

The Wolfsonian at FIU, The Mitchell Wolfson, Jr. Collection: 11-60, 11-61, 11-63, 11-64.

Wyman, Lance: 20-45, 20-47, 20-48, 20-49.

Yokoo, Tadanori: 22-21, 22-22, 22-23.

Young & Rubicam, New York: 19-54.

Zaid, Barry: 21-28, 21-29.

Zapf, Hermann: 18-16, 18-17, 18-18.

Index